S0-BNH-892

WORLD CINEMA THROUGH GLOBAL GENRES

Additional resources are available at: www.wiley.com/go/costanzo

- Sample Syllabi and Weekly Lesson Schedules
- Questions for Discussion
- Individual Student Projects: Ideas for further exploration and research
- Group Activities: Short, collaborative tasks that focus on key aspects of genre, globalism, and film as a business, art, or technology
- Filmographies from the text
- Teachers' Manual and other aids

WORLD CINEMA THROUGH GLOBAL GENRES

WILLIAM V. COSTANZO

WILEY Blackwell

This edition first published 2014
© 2014 John Wiley & Sons, Inc

Registered Office
John Wiley & Sons Ltd, The Atrium, Southern Gate, Chichester, West Sussex, PO19 8SQ, UK

Editorial Offices
350 Main Street, Malden, MA 02148–5020, USA
9600 Garsington Road, Oxford, OX4 2DQ, UK
The Atrium, Southern Gate, Chichester, West Sussex, PO19 8SQ, UK

For details of our global editorial offices, for customer services, and for information about how to apply for permission to reuse the copyright material in this book please see our website at www.wiley.com/wiley-blackwell.

Library of Congress Cataloging-in-Publication Data
Costanzo, William V.
    World cinema through global genres / William V. Costanzo.
        pages   cm
    Includes bibliographical references and index.
    ISBN 978-1-118-71291-7 (hardback) – ISBN 978-1-118-71292-4 (paper) – ISBN 978-1-118-71304-4
1. Motion pictures–Study and teaching.   2. Film genres.   I. Title.
    PN1993.7.C69 2014
    791.43071–dc23
                                                                        2013030479
A catalogue record for this book is available from the British Library.

Cover image: *Hero / Ying Xiong*. Beijing New Picture / Elite Group / The Kobal Collection.
Cover design by Simon Levy Associates

Set in 11/13pt Dante by SPi Publishers, Pondicherry, India

1   2014

For Diana, my cherished wife and angelic muse, whose love and

support are the foundations of this book and of my life

CONTENTS

PREFACE

As the art of cinema advances well into its second century, filmmakers have been cutting across national boundaries toward a new internationalism. Fueled by an increasingly global economy, fostered by changes in world politics, facilitated by modern technologies, and shaped by a heightened cross-cultural awareness, the character of movies has become global as never before.

World Cinema through Global Genres addresses an important need by making the complex forces of global filmmaking accessible to students of film. Instead of tracing the long histories of cinema country by country or region by region, it uses engaging, recent films like *Crouching Tiger, Hidden Dragon* (China), *Monsoon Wedding* (India), *Ring* (Japan), and *Motorcycle Diaries* (Brazil) as entry points, linking them to comparable American and European films. The book is organized around clusters of films connected by genre and theme. A section on "The Warrior Hero" includes kung-fu movies from Hong Kong, *wuxia* features from Mainland China, samurai films from Japan, and Hollywood Westerns. A section on "The Wedding Film" looks at films like *The Wedding Banquet*, *Monsoon Wedding*, and *My Big Fat Greek Wedding*, which dramatize conflicts of cross-cultural relationships in the context of ethnic wedding rituals. Two more sections on Horror Films and Road Movies explore what people find horrifying in other parts of the world and why they take to the road. In this way, readers learn to look for reasons behind the similarities and differences among movies. They come to understand how today's films are part of a dynamic world phenomenon, drawing on local traditions and foreign influences to meet the needs and desires of an increasingly multicultural, globally conscious audience.

McLuhan's vision of the global village has never been more compelling than it is today. The world in which our students are coming of age – and which they are helping to create – calls for greater international understanding and cooperation. These qualities are important factors in the new globalism of cinema, and they are strong motivating principles behind this book. By studying the cultural flows and cross-currents shaping our most popular global genres, today's students can form a deeper appreciation not only of the films and their stories, but also of the people, societies, and beliefs behind these films – people, societies, and beliefs they will be encountering in one form or another throughout their lives.

All of these pressure points and movements have contributed to the world's expanding storehouse of stories and storytelling styles. By exploring them beyond the familiar borders of local movie screens, students everywhere can enlarge their vision of the world and increase their possibilities for engaging with its rich diversity.

World Cinema through Global Genres provides a wide array of useful tools. Based on the premise that we live in a global culture, it approaches the world's great stock of movies as gateways to other lives and environments. The book uses case studies, visual organizers, filmographies, selective reading lists, and focused questions to get students actively involved in examining their assumptions about the world. It helps them test those assumptions through close readings of films from Africa, Asia, Latin America, Europe, and the Middle East as well as from Hollywood and familiar English language films. It helps them cross the barriers of subtitles and translation to experience the universal drama in these films while appreciating differences in culture and cinematic style. And it guides them through informed explorations of the social, economic, and political contexts of each movie text, with regular references to theory and scholarship.

These are the kinds of questions they will ask:

- Who are the heroes of these films? What are their stories? How do language and location affect the lives they lead?
- What are the underlying beliefs? How do these heroes and their stories function to affirm ideological assumptions, to rationalize certain kinds of action? To what degree do cultural codes and cinematic conventions change when they go global?
- Why do some movies seem to fall into genres? How can their similarities and differences be explained?
- What do movies say about us as individuals, as nations, as members of the groups to which we belong? How do they help to define our cultural identity, our imagined community, our place in a changing world?
- What other purposes do movies serve? To what degree is film a business or an art, an expression of high culture or the popular imagination, a site of politics or pleasure, a tool for reflecting or refashioning modern myths?
- What are the defining myths of national and individual identity? What stories and canonical texts do they rely on? What makes a film Chinese, British, or American? Why does any of this matter?

For a demonstration of how such questions may be answered, please see the extended analysis of *Crouching Tiger, Hidden Dragon* in "Deep Focus on Chinese Cinemas" in Unit I.

Some Personal Connections

Writing this book has been a journey of connections. To be sure, it has connected me to a wider world of movies than I knew existed. It has also helped me forge new bonds with colleagues and with students while strengthening old ties. But what surprised me most were the personal affinities with each genre that I discovered along the way. Take the road movie, for example.

In my younger days, the open road meant freedom. The old Vanderbilt Parkway on Long Island, once revealed, was my escape route from the dreary landscape of suburbia. My good pal Peter, a fellow inmate at the local high school, was my bicycle companion, my buddy on the asphalt road to high adventure. Along the abandoned parkway, we discovered wooded acreage, tiny refuges of green in the vast wasteland of shopping malls and parking lots, which became our private Camelot. We found a secret northwest passage to the Long Island Sound, where we imagined ourselves on board one of Melville's whalers or Conrad's frigates bound for islands far away. A few years later, when my dad was stationed in France, Peter shipped on board an ocean liner bound for Europe – his dad worked for Cunard Lines – and we resumed our bicycling journeys through the countryside of Normandy, the Loire Valley, the southern pasturelands of England. Now, instead of peanut butter sandwiches, our saddle bags were filled with crisp baguettes and bottles of Bordeaux. Here, in the heart of history, real history, the castles and cathedrals were authentic. The lanes and byways that led us from one French or English village to another opened our eyes to a world of vitality and beauty we had only dreamed about before. Both of us were hooked. Forever after, the open road would be our seductive siren, luring us back to the promise of exploration and excitement.

I kept packing my bags to head back across the Atlantic, hitching at first, taking buses or trains when I could afford them. One summer trip took me through Eastern Europe to Russia for a peek behind the mysterious iron curtain. The Russian word for road, *doroga*, became my new cry of freedom. But so did *autostrada*, *Autobahn*, *camino*, *dromos*, and many other words besides. Language had become another pathway to adventure and discovery.

This was the sixties, when a whole generation of youth was on the move. In Europe, people my age dressed in tie-dyed clothes were hitching rides to Munich, Florence, Barcelona, and destinations as distant as Afghanistan or India. I was not a hippie. My wardrobe included only two pairs of jeans and two shirts, one of them white. My bags contained a mess kit, a flashlight, and a Boy Scout knife. But most of my gear was books, paperbacks I picked up in the student section of each town. Strangely, I had not read Kerouac or Kesey. If I was part of the great movement of traveling American romantics stretching from Whitman and the Beats to the hippies and psychedelic trippers of the Magic Bus, it was news to me. All I knew is that I was on a personal quest, inventing the itinerary as I went along.

Whatever I was I looking for – escape, evasion, excitement, or identity – being on the road was liberating. The experience of stepping into unfamiliar streets, tasting new foods, trying out another language was like auditioning for a fresh personality. I could be one person in French, another in German, yet another in Italian. By casting off the burden of a suburban education and a Brooklyn accent, I could invent different versions of myself and test-drive each new model. No wonder Sartre's existential philosophy appealed to me. Every fork in the road was an invitation to choose my very being, moment to moment, lane by lane.

But while escape or self-discovery may have driven me then, what motivates me now? At my age, I know who I am, and I enjoy the place that I call home. What calls me, then, to go on the road again, to travel to China or Africa? And what connects me to the cinematic journeys of films like *Easy Rider* and *The Motorcycle Diaries*? These are questions that I asked myself while writing, and I hope that you, dear reader, will pose questions of your own, that you will look for personal connections to each genre, to each film.

We can watch these cinematic fictions and appreciate them as cultural history, the record of a nation or a people on the move. But we can also see something of ourselves in each: who we were, who we want to be, and who we are becoming.

ACKNOWLEDGMENTS

A textbook, not unlike a film, is a collaborative effort. My co-authors include colleagues, students, librarians, the publishing community, supportive institutions, and others who have all made valued contributions to *World Cinema through Global Genres*.

This book took shape with the help of two important programs that foster scholarship and teaching. I wish to thank the Rockefeller Foundation for a productive month's residency at the Bellagio Study and Conference Center in Italy, where I made momentous progress on the manuscript that has become this book. Much of my ongoing research was facilitated through New York University's Faculty Resource Network, which gave me access to the extensive resources of the Bobst Library and enabled me to audit a new course every semester for six years. For these invaluable opportunities, I am especially grateful to FRN's executive director Debra Szybinski, to her gracious assistant Anne Ward, and to the outstanding faculty who specialize in the cinemas of Africa, Brazil, China, India, Japan, Korea, Europe, and elsewhere.

Throughout the process of writing and revising, I have relied on the expertise of distinguished film scholars. I am especially grateful to Dudley Andrew, Diane Carson, Jung-Bong Choi, Manthia Diawara, Bruce Kawin, Moya Luckett, Ranjani Mazumdar, Robert Stam, and Juana Suárez for their professional judgment and collegial good will. Other colleagues, though not film specialists, assisted me with their cultural knowledge and perceptive comments. For these contributions, I am indebted to Robert DiYanni, Zarina Hock, and Evelyn Lu.

For more than 40 years, Westchester Community College has been my academic home. I am much obliged to Dr. Joseph Hankin, WCC's devoted president, for fostering an environment where excellence in teaching and scholarship can flourish side by side. The library staff at WCC is first rate, and I especially wish to thank Diana Matson, Chris Kern, Una Shih, and Towanda Mathurin for assisting in my many tasks. Thanks, too, to Craig Padawer, chair of WCC's Film Curriculum and Arts Department, who well understands the intricate dynamics of writing while teaching. Finally, I am extremely grateful to the many film students who taught me so much about movies and about learning over the years. I hope they were able to take as much from my classes as I did from their lively participation.

A work like this would never see the light of day without a team of dedicated publishing professionals. I wish to acknowledge Jeanne Zalesky, who invited me to undertake the project in the first place, and Ziki Dekel, who guided my progress through most of its development with wisdom and consummate skill. It was Jayne Fargnoli, Wiley-Blackwell's Executive Editor extraordinaire, who best understood my vision and found a way to bring it to fruition. I am deeply grateful to Jayne, to her able assistant Allison Kostka, to Joanna Pyke, an exceptionally gracious and meticulous project manager, and to Julia Kirk, Wiley-Blackwell's hard-working and congenial Project Editor, for their collective talents, patience, and enthusiasm.

Many film teachers across the country have reviewed portions of this text and helped to shape its current form. For their generous attention and insightful feedback, I acknowledge them most gratefully.

HOW TO USE THIS BOOK

A unique feature of this text is its organization. In contrast to traditional approaches, which follow the cinematic history of nations or regions, *World Cinema through Global Genres* arranges films in units, or clusters, each cluster positioned around a central genre with formal and thematic links. This arrangement allows instructors and their students to compare films within a common framework, noting how a genre's characters, plots, settings, and visual styles reflect the history and culture of their place of origin while addressing fundamental human needs. This also makes it easier to trace the complex webs of intertextuality by which films and filmmakers influence each other.

One of the great challenges of any film survey course is coverage. A common problem with pushing through world cinema one nation or era at a time is that some cinemas are inevitably left out. In the rush to cover more territory, some of the most important objectives may also be short-changed. The cluster-based approach reduces the anxiety of coverage. It works more like a hologram than the linear progression of a scroll. With each cluster, students may acquire a progressively sharper understanding of key concepts. They build a critical vocabulary for analyzing film texts, learn how technology and business practices contribute to film art, see how films represent cultural values and traditions, gain a working knowledge of world history, and investigate significant topics through focused projects and substantive research. Since every cluster addresses these goals, reinforced through repetition and variation, instructors can choose those modules that meet their criteria for interest, diversity, and importance. Finally, this book gives deliberate attention to the role of commercial film industries that are often slighted by art-film oriented texts. It seeks to restore some of the pleasure in watching entertaining films.

World Cinema through Global Genres includes an introduction, four main units or modules, background material on individual films, in-depth explorations of selected regional cinemas, and generous supplementary material.

A substantial **Introduction** identifies tools and perspectives for studying individual film texts and their broader contexts. It will help you, as a student of film, to understand both how and why movies are studied as an art form, a technology, a business, an index of culture, a social barometer, and a political instrument. This section introduces some of the key terms and concepts (nation, globalism, postcolonialism, diaspora, Orientalism, co-productions, point of view editing, myth of the hero) that you will be encountering throughout the book. It will make it easier to sort through issues like subtitles, dubbing, and global genre study. And it will show you how to read a scene with close attention to film technology and cinematic style.

The four **Units** cover each genre cluster and are introduced by a core **Chapter** with a general discussion of its themes and history as well as the cultural and artistic traditions from which it springs. This core chapter is where you'll learn about the elements that characterize horror movies, for example: why they arise at specific moments in a country's evolution, how they reflect the particularities of a nation and its film industry (Britain's gothic monsters, Italy's *giallo* aesthetics, Spanish Civil War ghosts, Japan's avenging *yurei* spirits, Hong Kong's hopping vampires) while borrowing elements of style and content across geographical boundaries. Each of the four core chapters integrates relevant issues of theory, technology, history, marketing, and film aesthetics into the narrative.

The **Deep Focus** section in each unit probes more deeply into one national or regional film tradition that is particularly strong in the selected genre. Each of these sections centers on a body of films (Chinese, Indian, Japanese, Latin American) that tends to be underrepresented in many texts on world cinema. Here is where you'll learn about the local history, geography, people, cultural life, and economic forces that shape the films from this part of the world.

The **Close-ups** in each unit (four per unit) present individual films that exemplify important traditions and trends explored more generally in the unit's core chapter. These short takes will give you background information about the film's production, financing, reception, cast, director, and crew. Use them as opportunities to focus closely on engaging cinematic texts, considering the various ways that individual movies develop along national or linguistic lines, grow locally around well-defined communities, or cross boundaries. You will be encouraged to view these films not as isolated texts from different places but as participants in a dynamic world phenomenon. Notice how they conform to, expand, or challenge the world's vast repertoire of visual storytelling. Although these films have been carefully selected for their quality, diversity, and accessibility, they represent only a few among many choices. Your instructor may decide to focus on other examples that reflect more directly the scope and objectives of your course.

Throughout the text, you will find frame enlargements, questions for discussion and research, filmographies (film lists), suggested readings, maps, and timelines to help you understand key concepts and guide your further study. The book concludes with a full glossary and index. A quick glance at the illustrations will give you some idea of the kinds of films and issues explored within these pages.

Each photograph is a **frame enlargement** taken from an actual film. Some of these photos are paired for comparison. A shot from *The Magnificent Seven* is displayed alongside a comparable scene from *Seven Samurai*, highlighting similarities and differences between American Westerns and Japanese samurai films. Shots from the 1950 and 1991 version of *Father of the Bride* are shown together, inviting a comparison of wedding movies then and now. Some shots are grouped for a particular purpose. For example, a series of frames from *Citizen Kane* demonstrates how careful film analysis can reveal the artistry behind good camera work and editing. A sequence from *Potemkin* illustrates the principles of Soviet montage. A "Gallery of Movie Vampires" shows how a single movie monster can cross borders, spreading horror or delight across the globe.

The **genre maps** in each core chapter illustrate the point that some genres are truly transnational, showing when and where selected genre films appear around the world. The **timelines** in the Deep Focus sections offer side by side comparisons of a region's film production with historical events. Use these maps and timelines as visual aids to help you navigate your way through the geography and history of global genre films. The **filmographies** at the end of each unit's core chapter can also assist with global positioning. These lists are arranged chronologically within each genre for easy reference to a film's date, country of origin, original title, and director. A quick look down one column or another will help you make connections across eras, regions, and filmmakers. Remember, though, that dates, titles, and genre labels can present problems for anyone studying world cinema, particularly in an age of global co-productions. A movie may be released at different times in different regions. It may be known by several titles. It may have been financed and produced by an assortment of companies and individuals, all with different nationalities. And with so many hybrid movies being released, it is trickier than ever to classify films by genre. How would you classify Quentin Tarantino's *Kill Bill* films, for example, when they deliberately mix elements of Westerns, samurai movies, kung fu, comedy, and horror? As you become more knowledgeable about genres, you will be encouraged to question the way certain films are linked to certain genres in the filmographies, in the media, and throughout this book.

For the sake of consistency, I have chosen to use the original **release dates** specified in the online International Movie Database (imdb.com), which has become a standard reference point for students, scholars, and film professionals alike. I have also relied on this source for authoritative **titles**. In most cases, I give the English language title first, with the original language title and release date in parentheses. However, some films are better known to English-speaking audiences by their Spanish or Italian titles. For movies like Alejandro González Iñárritu's *Amores Perros* (2000) and Federico Fellini's *La Strada* (*The Road*, 1954), I give the original title first.

Any field of study has its own specialized vocabulary, and film study is no exception. Some terms are strictly technical, like crane shot or aspect ratio. Other terms, like globalism and postcolonialism, have taken on particular meanings and nuances among film scholars and historians. You'll find many of these terms explained in the Introduction, where their first appearance is marked in boldface type. Elsewhere in the book, new terms are generally introduced and explained in context. If you come across an unfamiliar term in your reading, check the **Glossary** or **Index** at the end of the book.

If some topic draws your special interest, you may want to explore it in more depth. Each section of *World Cinema through Global Genres* ends with a list for **Further Reading**. Whether you are skeptical about some questionable claim, curious about a new idea, or eager for more information, these readings will lead you to some of the best books and articles available. I hope what I have put together here will help to speed you on your journey.

INTRODUCTION

To study film is to engage with some of the world's greatest stories. Movies plunge us into the midst of different lives, transport us to other times and places, and explore far reaches of the human heart. What do movies tell us about others and ourselves: as nations, as members of communities, as individuals? How do they reflect our cultural identity, our stage and status in life, our place in a changing world?

Whatever view you have of movies, a good map is indispensable. *World Cinema through Global Genres* provides a starter atlas of world cinema on which to place the films you already know and the films you will encounter. The purpose of this introduction is to offer some coordinates and tools to help you get your bearings. Film scholars have charted various courses through the terrain of global cinema, studying movies as a business, an art, and a social institution; tracing the politics behind production and the history of audience response; subjecting individual films to close analysis and taking a wide-angle view of movies as the myth-makers of our age.

To understand a movie calls for close attention to three main factors: its production (or authorship), its content, form, and cinematic style (the film text), and its reception (audience), all of which are intricately related to each other and to issues of history and culture. To understand the history of cinema itself, how movies have evolved over time since their first appearance in the 1880s, it helps to keep in mind that cinema is an industry as well as an art form, an invention of technology, and a social institution. These four strands – economic, aesthetic, technological, and societal – are woven through the tapestry of film history. While it isn't necessary to be an economist, art critic, mechanic, or sociologist to follow the whole story, it will be useful to know something about each strand.

World Cinema through Global Genres, First Edition. William V. Costanzo.
© 2014 John Wiley & Sons, Inc. Published 2014 by John Wiley & Sons, Inc.

The Business of Cinema

Movies are big business and have been for a long time. Thomas Edison understood this back in 1893 when he patented the first **Kinetoscope** machine, a box that let viewers watch short films by peering through a peep hole and cranking a handle. Edison's idea was to maximize sales by charging each customer a nickel a movie. But as Louis and Auguste Lumière soon discovered, it was more profitable to project films on a large screen for a large audience. The Lumière brothers opened their first movie theatre in Paris in 1895. Their invention, the *Cinématographe*, was both a camera and a projector, setting worldwide standards for motion pictures as a projected medium. In 1902, the Lumières sold their patents to the French Pathé company, which improved on the technology, set up production studios, and opened a chain of theatres stretching to Russia, Australia, and Japan. Undaunted by the success of his French rivals, Edison produced hundreds of short films in his New Jersey studio, the "Black Maria," and even built a new camera for outdoor shooting. In those early days, the film business was a vigorous, disorderly affair, with practitioners in Europe and the United States borrowing and stealing freely from each other. In 1907, Edison helped to organize the chaos by founding the Motion Picture Patents Company. The MPPC, also known as the Edison Trust, united the major American film companies and controlled the three main links of the film chain: **production** (making movies), **distribution** (arranging for their circulation), and **exhibition** (showing them in theatres). This three-tiered system, called **vertical integration**, ensured a smooth, cost-effective flow of cinematic goods from producer to consumer. For a select number of producers, the MPPC transformed the nature of commercial cinema, setting precedents that would influence the industry for decades. Although Edison may not have invented movies, he left his mark as film's first major businessman.

The Edison Trust itself did not survive World War I. When a trust is abused, when it makes insiders rich by stifling all competition, it can be busted in court as an illegal monopoly, just as the MPPC was in 1915. This left the field open to independent companies. These **Independents** brought fresh ideas and talent, revitalizing the movie business. Many innovators were Jewish immigrants from Europe or children of these immigrants who saw the young industry as a chance to make their mark in the New World. They left the crowded streets of New York City and headed westward, where they set up operations under the sunny skies of Southern California. While Europe was preoccupied with war, the new Americans created Hollywood, what Neal Gabler calls "an empire of their own."[1] One by one, between 1912 and 1928, the **major studios** – Paramount, MGM, Warner Bros., Twentieth-Century Fox, and RKO – established their power, followed by the three "minors": Columbia Pictures, Universal, and United Artists. Part of their success was due to the **studio system**, an efficient method of mass producing motion pictures modeled on Henry Ford's automobile factories. All the elements required to make movies were concentrated on the studio lot. There were pools of writers, carpenters, and set designers; warehouses filled with reusable props and costumes; special departments for handling budgets, editing, and sound recording; elaborate indoor and outdoor sets. This high degree of specialization and standardization was the equivalent of Ford's assembly line, enabling the studios to construct movies piece by piece. Part of the "genius of the system," as one film historian called it,[2] was Hollywood's emphasis on stars and genres. Since any new film is in a sense an unknown product, unlike the relatively predictable ingredients of, say, a bar of soap or a box of cereal, studio strategists sought to minimize consumer risk by offering familiar ingredients. The **star system** ensured success at the box office by cashing in on the popularity of individual actors. The image of each star performer was carefully crafted and promoted by the studio that owned the actor's contract. The **genre system** promised well-known story lines. Viewers could expect a certain kind of film experience from a new Western, musical, or romance. As the studios grew, they became involved in distribution and exhibition, reaping the economic benefits of vertical integration once enjoyed by the Edison Trust.

The system worked for decades. During the golden age of Hollywood, from 1929 to 1948, nearly everyone in the country from six to 60 years of age – roughly 80 to 90 million Americans – attended neighborhood theatres or the grand movie palaces of that era every week.[3] At the same time, Hollywood aggressively courted foreign markets. After World War I, it competed with the most developed European film industries in France, Italy, Britain, Germany, and Scandinavia. During World War II, with Europe once again embroiled in military conflict, the American film industry looked southward, leveraging the Good Neighbor policy to sell US movies throughout Latin America. But after that war, Hollywood's grip began to fail. New anti-trust legislation attacked the studio structure. Television was replacing motion pictures as the preferred medium of entertainment. Americans were also spending more time on the highways and taking part in more outdoor activities like gardening and fishing. The Hollywood empire fought back with a succession of new ways to watch films, including drive-in theatres, Cinerama, CinemaScope, and 3-D. But rising movie costs and falling box office revenues took their toll. By 1950, attendance had dropped to 60 million per week, slipping to 46 million by 1953 and plummeting below 20 million by the late 1960s.[4]

As we'll see throughout this book, the film industry reinvented itself through various means in the following decades. In the United States, during the 1960s and 1970s, a fresh crop of independent-minded **auteurs** – directors who saw themselves as the creative authors of their films – appealed to a younger audience with different values from their parents, planting the seeds of a Hollywood renaissance. Elsewhere in the world, where government funding and legislation favored the growth of national cinemas, new waves rose up in France and Germany, Brazil and Czechoslovakia, Iran and Korea, cresting and spreading to other shores. Even regions without much state support, like India, Japan, and Hong Kong, managed to sustain vigorous commercial industries. More recently, as the term globalization has entered our everyday vocabulary, business practices have assumed a more obviously global character. If Hollywood studios of the 1930s and 1940s were run like Henry Ford's assembly-line factories, Hollywood these days functions more like the modern auto industry, **outsourcing** part of the production process internationally (shooting in Budapest, editing in Britain) and sometimes **offshoring** the entire process to another country. Today's Hollywood has become a system of integrated packaging, more fit for making deals than making movies.

Making movies, especially big movies with high production values, is expensive. The cost of an average Hollywood feature has risen steadily, from $11 million in the early 1980s to $50 million in the 1990s, to $64 million in 2005. And this figure represents only the **negative cost** – the expenses leading up to the first negative film print from which multiple copies will be made. For many productions, comparable sums are needed for advertising and distribution. This means that a studio must make three times its production cost just to break even.[5] Although non-Hollywood films are typically cheaper to make, the budget for a French or Japanese art film may run to $10 or $15 million. With expenses like these, financing often is a filmmaker's greatest challenge.

One important funding strategy in the global economy has been co-productions. **Co-productions** combine the resources of two or more film companies, often from different countries, which increases the opportunities for funding, talent, and audience appeal. Sometimes the partnership is chiefly monetary. Sylvain Chomet's animated masterpiece, *The Triplets of Belleville* (*Les Triplettes de Belleville*, 2003), was jointly financed by French, Belgian, British, and Canadian investors, but Chomet remained in complete creative control of the film. By the mid-1990s, France was regularly releasing more co-productions than strictly national productions.[6] Increasingly, more movies resemble *The Russia House* (1990). Made with European co-financing and produced by MGM-Pathé in cooperation with Star Partners III, *The Russia House* was based on a British novel by John Le Carré, scripted by Czech-born writer Tom Stoppard, and directed by Fred Schepisi, an Australian. Its stellar cast included actors from England (James Fox, James Mahoney), the United States (Michelle Pfeiffer, Roy Scheider), Scotland (Sean Connery), and Germany (Klaus Maria Brandauer). Its theatrical, video, and DVD distributors spanned the United States, Germany, Argentina, and Brazil. Since 1995, such cross-national affiliations have been assisted by the World Trade Organization, which has reduced trade barriers, strengthened copyright laws, and generally facilitated the flow of capital.

New trends in distribution have shifted the flow of the films themselves. Historically, the world's largest film exporter has been the United States. Before 1914, France and Italy were the big distributors. After World War I, US studios boosted their exports to regions beyond the sphere of combat – South America, Asia, Australia, and New Zealand – gaining a competitive advantage that has rarely lost its edge. After World War II, just when anti-trust laws and the rise of television were weakening the big studios and American audiences were declining, Europe fought Hollywood's hegemony with government subsidies, quota systems, and protectionist legislation. In the 1980s, the European Economic Community (EEC) encouraged European co-productions, enabling director, writer, cast, and crew to come from any member country. Yet, few countries were able to outgross American imports. The US industry's economic leverage, combined with the wide appeal of the Hollywood style, continue to keep American movies on the world's screens. The size of Hollywood's domestic market is a key factor. Although Americans have never returned to the theatres in such large numbers as they did between 1930 and 1945, their movie-going habits have supported the enormous budgets that keep Hollywood's production values (if not aesthetic values) high. Statistics released by the Motion Picture Association of America for 2011 gave the total box office revenue for US films as $32.6 billion. Less than a third, $10.2 billion, was collected in the United States and Canada, which means that most of the revenue derived from foreign sales. And these figures do not include income earned from DVDs, cable, streaming video, or other means of distribution.

Movie festivals have long been a prominent feature of global film economics. The festivals at Cannes, Venice, or Berlin offer a revolving showcase of the latest movies, especially art films that have limited audiences at home and small budgets for publicity. In 1932, Venice became the first city to host an exhibition of new films from other countries. When Venice became politically contentious (*Grand Illusion*, Renoir's great anti-war film, was passed over for the top prize, then called the Mussolini Cup), an alternative venue opened at Cannes in 1939. Since then the number of host cities has grown, slowly at first but quite rapidly in recent years. By 2012, filmfestivals.com was listing more than 4000 festivals around the world. The number of festival films is growing too. Cannes alone shows some 1,500 films each year. The festivals provide a moveable shopping mall for distributors and convenient meeting grounds for making international deals. Festivals still offer alternatives to censorship at home. When Iranian and Chinese films were banned by local governments during the 1990s, directors like Jafar Panahi and Zhang Yimou brought or sent them to the festivals, where they received international acclaim. Iranian filmmakers won more than 100 awards in 1997 and 1998 alone, providing them with political leverage at home as well as funds to make more films. This approach, however, may have different consequences in different situations. The Chinese government approved Zhang's later epic films and let him direct the opening ceremony at the 2008 Olympics in Beijing. In contrast, Panahi was arrested in 2010, charged with producing anti-Iranian propaganda, banned from making movies for 20 years, and sentenced to six years in prison.

Yet another aspect of global economics is the **runaway production**, an American movie filmed on foreign soil. Originally intended to circumvent domestic labor costs and taxes, such productions also serve aesthetic purposes. A location in Bulgaria or in the Czech Republic may look more like a nineteenth-century American town than the town itself today, or a mountain in New Zealand may provide the perfect setting for a Tolkien fantasy. Often, however, filmmakers choose another country because it's cheaper. *My Big Fat Greek Wedding* (2003), though set in Chicago, was shot in Toronto and produced no revenue for the state of Illinois.

Perhaps the most striking development in the film industry worldwide has been the rise of global conglomerates. The big studios of old Hollywood, once the apex of a vertically integrated industry, became themselves pieces of larger media conglomerates. Of the major studios, only MGM remained independent by 2010, owned by a group of private investors after difficult bankruptcy proceedings. Columbia became part of Sony, Fox was part of News Corporation, Paramount belonged to Viacom, Universal was owned by Vivendi Universal, and Warner Bros. was a division of Time Warner. By 2012, Disney owned motion picture studios, television networks, radio stations, cable channels, publishers, retail stores, toy makers, resorts, and theme parks all over the world. The big fish keep eating little fish, a practice that continues up the economic food chain in an ever widening ocean.

Nobody knows the precise number of movies produced per year. According to one estimate, over 100 countries contribute to an average annual total of some 4,000 films, with Asia providing about half, Europe a third, and the combined nations of Africa, Latin America, and the Middle East accounting for about 10%.[7] Surprisingly, the United States produces only 6% of the world's total output in this calculation. Such statistics say relatively little, though, about costs and revenues. They tell us even less about the artistic merits of the films or their cultural influence. For these important perspectives, we need to look more closely at the global history of film technology, aesthetics, and reception.

The Technology of Cinema

Without technology there can be no movies. Think of all the equipment and machinery required to tell a story cinematically. There are lights and cameras on the set, devices for recording sound, machines to help with editing, computers to add digital imagery, and mechanical projectors or electronic services to bring the final movie to your screen, whether you watch it in a multiplex theatre or in the palm of your hand.

While film technology keeps changing with the times, the basic process of making a movie still can be described in four stages. The **development** stage starts with an idea and ends with a proposal. This is when the film concept gets worked out in enough detail to convince someone to fund it. A writer may sketch out the main idea in a brief **synopsis** or story outline, which may be expanded later into a **treatment**, a fuller version of the narrative that may contain scenes, character development, and some dialogue, much like a short story. Further along, a scenario or **screenplay** fleshes out the action, adding dialogue and perhaps some directions for the camera. The most complete version before production is the **shooting script**, which typically provides a shot-by-shot blueprint of the film. Any of these versions may be modified by other writers, who may or may not be credited in the tricky business of collaborative authorship. In addition to script development, a number of key decisions are made before a proposal gets the green light. In large studios, specialists estimate expenses, investigate the market, and consider legal risks. With so many considerations and barriers to funding, relatively few ideas make it past development to the pre-production stage. **Pre-production** takes the scripted concept from approval to production, getting everything in place before the actual shooting starts. Actors are cast in the leading roles. Locations are scouted. For large productions, there may be screen tests of the actors, props to make, elaborate sets to design and construct. Eventually, the **producer**, who bears responsibility for the final film, agrees on a budget and a **shooting schedule**, which sets the dates, locations, and personnel for each shot in the script.

For many, the most exciting stage of any movie is **production**. The set is lighted, microphones are ready, the actors are poised for action, and the camera is ready to roll. Everyone is waiting for the director's signal to begin shooting. For the **director** is in charge. He or she directs the actors and supervises the technicians who manage all operation on the set. An **assistant director** may handle lower-level tasks, like planning the day's shoot, managing the extras, and keeping intruders out of the way. The **script supervisor** keeps track of changes in dialogue during shooting, while the person in charge of **continuity** notes details like accidental changes in an actor's clothing or a corpse that shifts its position unaccountably from shot to shot. Directly responsible for the camerawork and related functions is the **cinematographer**, or director of photography (**DP**). In large crews, a camera operator will run the camera itself while an assistant or two may **follow focus**, adjusting the lens when the actors or the camera moves. Other crew members take care of sound (a **production sound mixer** may be in charge of all sound recorded live on the set), lighting (the **gaffer** is the chief electrician; the **best boy** is the gaffer's chief assistant), and miscellaneous tasks (**grips** take care of equipment, sets, and props; **gofers** run errands when they're told "go for this and go for that"). Everything must be in place for each **setup**, the position of the camera (angle, location) before shooting begins. The length of film produced from a single running of the camera is called a **shot**. Since a director may not be pleased with the first results, a shot may require several **takes**, or repeats. An actor may have flubbed his lines or missed his **marks** (markings on the floor to guide his movements). The camera angle or the lighting might not be satisfactory. These shots and takes are numbered, often on a **clapboard** ("Shot 12, Take 3") for future reference. The best takes for each shot will be chosen later from the day's shooting, known as **dailies** or **rushes**.

A film goes into **post-production** after the director calls it "a wrap": the shooting ends and the film is safely stored, ready for editing. An **editor**, often in consultation with the director, selects the good takes, trims each shot, and assembles the shots into **scenes** (shots related by time and space) and **sequences** (segments of film composed of scenes from different times or locations but unified by a common idea). A special kind of sequence, sometimes referred to as a **montage sequence** (or simply **montage**), combines brief shots from related scenes in quick succession to show the passage of time or to illustrate an idea, such as the process of falling in love. In *Citizen Kane* (1941), this montage technique is used to show the deterioration of Kane's first marriage. As the years pass, Mr. and Mrs. Kane grow apart, separated by an increasingly larger table, expensive tableware, and antagonistic words that culminate in hostile silence. In the first scene of this sequence (Figure 0.1 and Figure 0.2), they regard one other lovingly at a close distance. In the next scene (Figures 0.3 and 0.4), a hint of suspicion arises among the flowers set between them. Their discord is more visible in scene three (Figure 0.5 and Figure 0.6), and by the last scene, they sit silently at far ends of a long table reading rival newspapers (Figure 0.7 and Figure 0.8).

The editor's task was once a demandingly physical process of synchronizing magnetic sound tape with celluloid film stock and aligning the results into a rough **assembly cut**, a tighter **director's cut**, and the final **fine cut**. Today, the job is expedited by computers. Sound tracks composed of dialogue, music, sound effects (**SFX**), or voice-over narration can all be added digitally. So can **special effects** (**SPFX**), like simulated explosions and flying superheroes, and **transitions** between shots, like **dissolves** (one image blending into another) or **fades** (an image disappearing into black or emerging from the darkness). Big productions may involve original music performed by orchestras, **dubbing** (dialogue added in the post-production studio), or **Foley editing** (replacing live sound effects with synchronized substitutes, like the sound of a smashed pumpkin to simulate the thud of a boxer's punch). For some films, the most creative work occurs during this post-production stage.

All this activity behind the scene and before or after shooting relies on the remarkable inventions that make motion pictures possible. These tools of the trade represent the ingenuity of individuals working in different fields and different countries, all contributing something important to the inventions of global cinema. Let's take a quick look at the machinery behind the movies and the minds behind the machines.

Consider the motion picture camera. Before anyone could take moving pictures of live action, they needed a way to record images clearly on some kind of medium

FIGURES 0.1–0.8   "A marriage just like any other marriage." The deterioration of Kane's first marriage is shown in a succession of dinner table scenes. Each scene in the sequence consists of one or more shots, demonstrating the couple's gradual estrangement. *Citizen Kane* (Dir. Orson Welles, 1941).

FIGURE 0.1   [Romantic music.]   FIGURE 0.2   "I absolutely adore you."

FIGURE 0.3 "Do you know how long you kept me waiting last night?"

FIGURE 0.4 "My dear, your only correspondent is the *Inquirer.*"

FIGURE 0.5 "Sometimes I think I'd prefer a rival of flesh and blood."

FIGURE 0.6 "I don't spend that much time on the newspaper."

FIGURE 0.7 [Silence.]

FIGURE 0.8 [Silence.]

so that the recorded images could be played back in a smooth, continuous sequence. In other words, they needed to solve the problems of photography and projection. The principle of the camera has been known since the Renaissance, when artists like Leonardo da Vinci admitted outside light into a darkened room through a tiny hole in a window shade. Our word **camera** comes from *camera obscura*, a Latin term meaning dark room. What these artists saw (and anyone today can see) is an inverted image from the street projected on the opposite wall. It took several centuries before a Frenchman, Louis Daguerre, was able to capture that image clearly on a silvered copper plate in the 1830s. Instead of a dark room, he used a box with a hole in one end and a plate on the other. About the same time, an Englishman named William Henry Fox Talbot discovered how to capture images on chemically treated paper so they could be reproduced from a negative imprint. Within a few years, a moveable shutter was added to the **aperture** (hole), and faster plates allowed photographers to catch an athlete in mid-action. But how could the unbroken action itself be caught and released as photographed motion? During the early nineteenth century, a number of simple toys with complicated names, like Phenakistoscope and Zoetrope, demonstrated that a sequence of individual drawings could be spun on a wheel or rotated in a drum to create the illusion of motion. They worked much like a flip chart, the separate images blending into one continuous action thanks to a trick of the human brain. In 1877, it was Eadweard Muybridge, an Englishman living in California, who took the next big step. Muybridge wanted to settle a bet about a horse. To prove that all four hooves left the ground at some point in the horse's gallop, he set up 24 cameras spaced along the track. When the horse strode past, it tripped a series of wires attached to the cameras. Muybridge won the bet and spent another 20 years perfecting his multiple-camera technique, mounting his pictures on a rotating cylinder for display. Soon a swarm of inventors – Englishmen, Frenchmen, and Americans – were devising their own instruments, experimenting with coated-paper rolls of film, sprocket holes, and timed shutters to synchronize their mechanisms. Although the first inventors of the motion picture camera and projector are still a matter of dispute, it was Edison and the Lumière brothers who emerged as financial winners, as we've seen.

Other innovations followed. Although *The Jazz Singer* (1927) is often credited with launching the sound era in the United States, efforts to add synchronous sound to movies date back much earlier, with varying degrees of success. Edison originally conceived of moving pictures as an adjunct to his phonograph machine, a principle later embodied in the Vitaphone (1925), which coupled a turntable with a projector. Soon after World War I, German inventors developed the Tri-Ergon Process in Europe, converting sound into light so that an optical sound track could be recorded directly on the film itself. A similar method was refined in America by Lee De Forest, who called his invention the Phonofilm. Whereas the earliest films were shot in monochrome (black and white), often colored by hand or machine, from the 1920s Hollywood made major advances in color photography, using Eastmancolor, Technicolor, and increasingly richer, more stable motion picture processes to compete with television, which was still broadcasting in black and white. To emphasize the big screen advantage of movies, exhibitors experimented with the stereoscopic effect of 3-D, the curved screens of Cinerama, and the super-widescreen optics of CinemaScope. These novelties were short-lived, but today's widescreen formats, IMAX, and polarized 3-D are their descendants.

More recently, technology has changed not only how movies are projected, but also where they are screened. Hollywood made peace with television by merging forces, using the technology of broadcasting and later cable to turn TVs into exhibition hubs for movies. By the 1990s, most American homes had VCRs as well as television sets, enabling families to watch films on video cassettes, and by 2002, DVDs were outselling prerecorded videos. The difference between **VHS** (Video Home System) and **DVD** (Digital Video Disc or Digital Versatile Disc) is essentially the difference between analog and digital technology. **Analog** information is fluctuating and continuous, much like a wave. The pictures and sounds on a VHS tape are recorded as patterns of magnetic signals varying in intensity. **Digital** information is discrete and discontinuous, like the on/off positions of a light switch. The movies on a DVD are encoded as tiny bits of information representing sounds and images that can be read by laser light and translated into the binary language of computers as 1s or 0s, on or off. Since digital information is independent of the storage medium, a digitized movie can be transferred to a computer's hard disc or streamed through the Internet without much loss in quality. This flexibility and durability overcome many limitations of celluloid film and magnetic tape, which erode over time and can be clumsy to manipulate. Movies in digital form can be edited electronically on computers without the need for heavy machinery. They can be copied quickly and compactly, without the need to make expensive, bulky prints of 35mm film from negatives, and each digital copy is as clear as the first.

The digital revolution has transformed the entire movie process from start to finish and the industry itself from top to bottom. Computers are involved in screenwriting, shooting, and editing as well as in producing, distributing, and exhibiting the films. Advances in **CGI**, Computer-Generated Imagery, have altered the craft of movie animation and allowed digital characters to engage with live performers, blurring distinctions between real and simulated actors, between authentic actions and virtual acts. Much of the magic in the Harry Potter movies springs from this fusion of technologies. And it is only part of a larger trend of digital convergence, a trend that merges previously separate kinds of texts (written, spoken, visual), genres (sitcoms, documentaries, novels, feature films, video games), and delivery systems (television, movie theatres, computer screens, tablets). The digital revolution has helped to drive another trend as well, the move to an increasingly global economy. Think of those international media conglomerates that control cable companies, film studios, publishers, and theme parks around the planet – a global reach facilitated by technology.

The Art of Cinema

If cinema is a business and a technology, it is also a kind of language. That is, it communicates meanings through a system of codes and conventions that must be learned. Although watching a movie may seem effortless, like watching life roll by, it involves a certain amount of interpretation. How do we recognize that the huge mouth on the screen in *Citizen Kane* represents a close-up of Kane's lips as he breathes his final word, and not the lips of some colossal giant? How do we know that Kane's story is moving back in time when the white page of a diary dissolves into a snowy scene in Colorado? Flashbacks, close-ups, and dissolves are **conventions**, pieces of the code by which we make sense of the movie. Most of us learn such codes over time by watching lots of movies, focusing most of our attention on the characters, their relationships, and the emotions of each scene. We might be so involved in the stories, what movies are about, that we lose sight of the **discourse**, the means by which they're told. We might not notice the position of the camera, how a scene is lit, or where one shot ends and another shot begins. But when we're puzzled by an unconventional story, when the unusual technique of an experimental film or the unfamiliar style of a film from China distracts us, we may begin to focus on the cinematic discourse, remembering that movies are constructions.

To help us understand the discourse, to appreciate how the language of film works as a system of images and sounds, it is useful to know terms like "key light," "dolly shot," and "jump cut." This technical vocabulary enables us to recognize the choices made behind scenes, to see more clearly how the technology and art of cinema go hand in hand.

The filmmaker's toolbox includes cameras, lights, sound equipment, and editing machines. The camera's **lens** acts as a glass eye to focus rays of incoming light onto some kind of storage medium (typically a strip of film, videotape, or electronic sensor). Lenses are classified by **focal length**, which determines the size of the image and other visual effects. The focal length of a normal lens (35–55 mm) gives the least distortion. A **wide-angle lens** (or short-focus lens) takes in a wider field of view and makes objects seem farther away, creating an illusion of greater depth. A **telephoto lens** (long-focus lens) has a narrower field of view and a shallower **depth of field** (the area in sharp focus), making objects appear closer. If the camera operator wants to magnify and isolate a window in the distance, she might use a telephoto lens. If she wants to get the entire building in focus, she might choose a wide-angle lens. And if she wants to shift attention between the window and the whole building, she could use a **zoom lens**, which combines the features of different focal lengths into a single lens. Twisting the lens one way (toward the wide angle position) zooms out from the window; twisting the other way (toward the telephoto position) zooms in.

Alternately, the cinematographer might decide to move the camera. Vertical movements up or down through space are called **boom shots**, or **crane shots**, because the older, heavy cameras were originally mounted on mobile booms or cranes. Horizontal movements on the ground are called **dolly** shots, or **tracking**

shots, because the camera originally traveled on wheels or tracks. Strictly speaking, a **panning shot** (or **pan**), which might scan the horizon from a fixed position, is not really a camera movement since the camera only pivots on its axis horizontally. The same is true of a **tilt shot**, for which the camera pivots up or down, as it might to shift our attention from a lower window to a higher one. In all these shots, the camera is essentially grounded by dollies or cranes, in contrast to **aerial shots** in which it may fly above the subject with the aid of a helicopter or an airplane. Of course, lighter cameras can and do move more freely in multiple ways, combining boom shots, tilts, and tracking shots in a single fluid motion. The **Steadicam** mount, invented in 1975, keeps the camera level during any movement, allowing for extremely smooth and varied handheld traveling shots.

Directors and cinematographers give close attention to **framing** their subjects, carefully composing the elements of each shot within the rectangle of the camera's viewfinder. A **close-up** fills most of the frame with a single object, like an actor's face or the villain's gun. A **medium shot** reveals more of the subject; it might show the actor from the ankle, knees, or waist up. A **long shot** takes in more of the background and can range from a **full shot**, which shows an entire human figure, to a longer shot of several figures in a room or an **extreme long shot** of an entire city skyline. *Citizen Kane* uses an extreme close-up when Kane speaks his dying word, "Rosebud" (Figure 0.9) and an extreme long shot of all the useless things he leaves behind (Figure 0.10). Angles are important too. A **high-angle shot** that captures a child from above might make the child seem small and powerless, as it does in Figure 0.11 when young Charlie Kane celebrates his first Christmas away from home. A **low-angle shot** might cause a figure to seem menacing or aloof, as it does in Figure 0.12 when Charlie looks up at a haughty butler. In most instances, though, actors are photographed straight-on using an **eye-level shot**, which is how most of us face each other in everyday life.

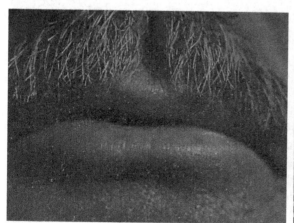

FIGURE 0.9   The magnitude of Kane's final words is shown in an **extreme close-up** of his lips. *Citizen Kane.*

FIGURE 0.10   The insignificance of Kane's material possessions is emphasized in an **extreme long shot**. The camera hovers above his collection in an extended **aerial view**, **boom**ing down to zero in on the one thing he really cared about. *Citizen Kane.*

FIGURE 0.11   A **high-angle shot** of young Charlie surrounded by his new "family" (together with the spoken words "Merry Christmas. Merry Christmas") accentuates the boy's sense of helplessness and alienation on his first Christmas away from home. *Citizen Kane.*

FIGURE 0.12   A **low-angle shot** of Charlie's new guardian makes the man seem intimidating and aloof, a cold figure looming over the child. *Citizen Kane.*

FIGURE 0.13   The party scene in *Citizen Kane* uses **high-key lighting** to create a lighthearted atmosphere.

FIGURE 0.14   **Low-key lighting** adds mystery and menace to a gloomy moment in *Citizen Kane.*

In addition to these aspects of the camera work – movement, distance, angle – a good deal more goes into the design of any scene. Critics, scholars, and directors use a French term, *mise-en-scène*, to describe the way a scene is staged. The choice of location; the furniture and props on a set; the actors' facial expressions, gestures, and movements; their makeup and costumes: all these contribute to the scene's atmosphere, its texture, and its tone. So does lighting. When a scene is flooded with bright illumination and the main source of light (**key light**) is high (in position and intensity), the overall effect (known as **high-key lighting**) can be cheerful and buoyant, as it is in the party scene from *Citizen Kane* (Figure 0.13). When the scene is dimly lit and soaked in shadows (**low-key lighting**), the mood may seem melancholy or mysterious as it is in Figure 0.14.

The sound track plays a major role in creating atmosphere in addition to its many other functions. Try turning off the sound and ask what's missing from the movie. You'll notice that what we call sound is composed of many layers. There is the ordinary background noise, called **ambient sound**, without which a film feels eerily unreal. That's why filmmakers routinely add the rustling leaves, the whoosh of passing cars, or voices in the distance. Even though we may not be aware of them, we miss these environmental buzzes when they're absent. To emphasize certain sounds that are important to the story, like a gunshot or stealthy footsteps in the snow, sound technicians add **sound effects**, which may be recorded live, taken from a prerecorded sound library, or created during post-production by a Foley artist. A distinction is sometimes made between **diegetic sound** (emanating from within the world of the story, like a song playing on a car radio) and non-diegetic sound (like orchestral music added to intensify a scene's emotional effect). Another distinction is made between **dialogue** (words spoken aloud by the actors) and **voice-over** (words spoken by an off-screen narrator or by a character whose lips aren't moving, to convey the character's inner thoughts). The soundscape created by these noises, voices, and melodies gives depth to what we see. As French director Robert Bresson liked to say, "The eye is superficial, the ear profound."[8]

The earliest movies were simply shot and shown. Edison had his cameraman capture *Fred Ott's Sneeze* (1894) in a single take, and customers in his Kinetoscope parlors could watch the whole sneeze as a single, uninterrupted action by turning the crank. The Lumière brothers filmed and projected *Arrival of a Train* (*L'arrivée d'un train en gare de La Ciotat*, 1896) in much the same way. But pioneers like the French magician Georges Méliès and the American Edwin S. Porter soon learned to break scenes into shots, rearranging them for dramatic effects. In *A Trip to the Moon* (*Le voyage dans la lune*, 1902), Méliès divided the action into some 30 separate shots, one shot per scene, shifting the story from one location to another and occasionally stopping the camera in mid-take to make his actors disappear like magic. Porter used even more sophisticated transitions between scenes in *The Great Train Robbery* (1903), sometimes changing the position of his camera within a single scene and creating an impression of simultaneous actions (the bandits escaping in one shot while the heroine unties her father in another). Méliès and Porter had discovered the advantages of **editing**, the practice of selecting, trimming, and reassembling filmed material into a continuous sequence.

In the United States, D. W. Griffith (1875–1948) probably did more than any other filmmaker to formulate and refine the art of editing during his long career in silent cinema. Griffith perfected the technique of **cross-cutting**, or **parallel editing**, which alternates between simultaneous actions in separate locations. In *The Lonedale Operator* (1911), when he cuts back and forth between a speeding train and the heroine in distress, the dynamic rhythm between the two scenes heightens the dramatic tension. Later, when the girl holds off the bandits with a concealed weapon, we learn that her "pistol' is really an ordinary wrench. Her deception is revealed with a close-up of the wrench. Elsewhere, Griffith uses such **cut-ins** (shots inserted into a scene revealing details of the scene) as well as **cutaways** (shifts to objects off screen, like a bird flying overhead) and **reaction shots** (showing the emotional response of onlookers) to help tell the story. His smooth use of **match cuts** (continuing the action from one shot to the next) moves the story forward seamlessly. This mastery of **continuity editing** (a technique that creates a sense of uninterrupted flow, disguising its own methods) became a hallmark of American movies. Over time, such practices evolved into a kind of grammar with its own rules and conventions. It became standard practice to open with an **establishing shot** to orient viewers, as when we see the skyline of Manhattan before zooming into the life of an individual New Yorker. When a character looks at something off screen, typically what follows is an **eyeline match**, a cutaway showing what he sees. Eyeline matches are part of a more general principle of **point-of-view editing**, designed to engage us in the world of the characters by showing things from their perspective. Another convention is the **180 degree rule**. This "rule," observed more frequently in earlier days than it is today, keeps the camera on one side of an imaginary line drawn through the action so that the actors remain in consistent relation to each other. The standard **shot/ reverse angle shot sequence**, which alternates between the perspectives of two speaking characters, is an example of point-of-view editing. If we don't notice these editing techniques, it is because they were designed to keep us in the movie, not looking at the way it is made. The **classical Hollywood style** of invisible editing keeps us engaged in the story, focusing our interest on the characters so that we're eager to find out what happens next. The classical style favors clarity, unity, and progression. The action moves forward in a chain of clearly linked causes and effects toward some resolution of a driving conflict.

While the Hollywood style is a powerful model, aggressively marketed and frequently copied throughout the world,[9] it is far from the only way to make movies. Throughout this book, we will be encountering other cinematic styles and film movements. At the same time that Griffith was experimenting with continuity editing, filmmakers in Russia were taking a very different approach to postproduction. In the wake of the Russian Revolution of 1917, young directors like Vsevolod Pudovkin and Sergei Eisenstein were more interested in changing the way people thought than in perpetuating old stories. They wanted to use editing as a conceptual tool. Adapting the French word *montage* (which can mean mounting, assembling, or editing), Eisenstein developed his theories of **dialectic montage**, splicing shots together as a violent collision of ideas. This technique is sometimes called **intellectual montage** or **Soviet montage** in contrast with Hollywood's practice of continuity editing. In *Strike* (*Stachka*, 1925), when he cuts between a shot of workers fleeing from the Tsar's soldiers to a slaughterhouse scene, we are asked to make an intellectual and emotional connection between the men and slaughtered animals. Watching the Odessa steps sequence from *Battleship Potemkin* (*Bronenosets Potyomkin*, 1925) is an even more wrenching experience. The camera cuts aggressively between soldiers and civilians, oblique angles and horizontal planes, close-ups and long shots, deliberately violating the 180 degree rule and the principles of matching action (see Figure 0.15, Figure 0.16, Figure 0.17, Figure 0.18, Figure 0.19, Figure 0.20). Instead of offering entertaining stories by way of comfortably seamless editing, Soviet montage compels audiences to think,

FIGURES 0.15–0.20   Montage editing (also known as constructive editing) accentuates conflict through a collision of images in the Odessa Steps scene from *Battleship Potemkin* (*Bronenosets Potyomkin*, Dir. Sergei Eisenstein, 1925).

FIGURE 0.15

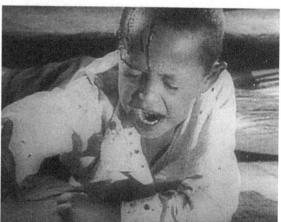

FIGURE 0.16

FIGURE 0.17

FIGURE 0.18

FIGURE 0.19

FIGURE 0.20

to question the status quo, to recognize that movies, like the ideological systems they embody, are constructions and thus can be reconstructed another way.

The 1920s was an era of artistic experimentation throughout Europe. In Germany, filmmakers continued the efforts of Robert Wiene in *The Cabinet of Dr. Caligari* (*Das Cabinet des Dr. Caligari*, 1920) to depict the extreme mental states of characters through *mise-en-scène*. Their use of eerie, low-key lighting, oddly shaped sets, and disorienting camera work to represent subjective (inner) truths rather than objective reality became known as **Expressionism**. In France, the leading edge of artistic innovation (the avant-garde) experimented with **Impressionism** (intensifying psychological experience through techniques like superimposition, slow motion, and out-of-focus photography) as well as **Surrealism** (reproducing the weird logic of dreams on screen). In the 1930s, on the eve of World War II, French directors turned to a more realistic style, known as **Poetic Realism**, focusing on working-class heroes beset by relentless social forces. These three French movements are exemplified respectively in Luis Buñuel and Salvador Dalí's *An Andalusian Dog* (*Un chien andalou*, 1929), Jean Epstein's *The Fall of the House of Usher* (*La chute de la maison Usher*, 1928), and Jean Vigo's *L'Atalante* (1934).

After World War II, during the late 1940s and early 1950s, Italian filmmakers took a further step toward realistic depictions of social issues. Faced with the diminished material resources of a postwar economy, directors like Roberto Rossellini (*Rome: Open City*/*Roma: città aperta*, 1945) and Vittorio De Sica (*Bicycle Thieves*/*Ladri di biciclette*, 1948) took their cameras to the streets, using available lighting and non-professional actors to focus on the lives of ordinary people. This nearly documentary approach became widely known as **Neorealism**, one of cinema's most influential styles because it is so easily adapted to places in the world where funds are scarce and the incentive to tell local stories is strong. Italian Neorealism proved to be an inspiration for Brazil's ***Cinema Novo*** (new cinema), Argentina's **Third Cinema**, and other film movements, from Iran to sub-Saharan Black Africa. Features of Italian Neorealism also turn up in the French ***nouvelle vague*** (new wave) of the 1960s, when young filmmakers with small budgets and big ideas like François Truffaut and Jean-Luc Godard set out to reinvigorate their country's cinematic heritage with films like *The 400 Blows* (*Les quatre cents coups*, 1959) and *Breathless* (*À bout de souffle*, 1960). Every so often, a "new wave" swells up somewhere in the world in the form of a New German Cinema (late 1960s through 1980s), a Japanese new wave (*nuberu bagu*, 1950s through early 1970s), or a New Korea Cinema (1980s through 2000s), each with its own distinctive accent.

The Social Side of Cinema

All the artistic creativity, commercial ingenuity, and technological advances of cinema have little value if a movie doesn't find an audience. It is the viewers who give the film its final significance, interpreting its meanings and assessing its worth. Scholars have proposed various theories to explain how viewers respond to films.

Marxist theorists like Walter Benjamin (a German) and Louis Althusser (a Frenchman) regarded movies as instruments of political propaganda or social change, emphasizing the power of mass media like motion pictures to reproduce ideological messages for mass consumption. According to their thinking, a society's network of values (its **ideology**) is stitched into every cinematic **text** (the whole fabric of a film's story, characters, *mise-en-scène*, and editing codes), helping to shape a spectator's view of the world and of himself. So a movie like *Sex and the City* (2008) might encourage certain attitudes about women and consumerism even though it presents itself as a love story. **Cultural theorists** like Stuart Hall (an Englishman) questioned the idea that spectators passively consume what movies dish out. Hall argued that individuals interpret what they see on screen through their particular cultural background and life experiences, "negotiating" meanings and value judgments in a kind of dialogue with the movie and the dominant ideology behind it.

In the language of film studies, a distinction is sometimes made between **spectators** (a term that refers to viewers as "typical" individuals) and **audiences** (actual viewers seen within cultural and historical contexts). A branch of **psychoanalytic spectatorship theory**, based on the works of Sigmund Freud and Jacques Lacan, sought to connect the spectator's film experience with key moments in the development of the human psyche, identifying the source of visual pleasure with terms like scopophilia, narcissism, and voyeurism. Taking a cue from these ideas, **feminist theorists** like Laura Mulvey and Mary Anne Doane argued that women are presented in cinema from a male perspective. Mulvey's groundbreaking essay on "Visual Pleasure and Narrative Cinema" argued that the visual pleasure of watching classical Hollywood films is essentially a male prerogative. She maintained that these films are constructed for a voyeuristic "male gaze," which turns the screen images of women into overvalued fetishes (women as saints) or undervalued erotic objects (women as whores).[10] Either way, Mulvey might argue, these images of women are controlled by a masculine point of view; they become the property of a **patriarchal** (male dominated) system. Mary Anne Doane and others focused their attention on female genres, especially "The Woman's Film," concluding that the textual system of these movies posits a female spectator who identifies with the female body on screen as spectacle, an identification that is narcissistic in Freudian terms.

More recently, feminist critics and their descendants have turned away from psychoanalysis, which they find inadequate to explain the great variety of cinematic engagement experienced by different viewers at different times. Whereas psychologists (who study people as individuals) tend to generalize, or "**essentialize**" these experiences, sociologists and ethnographers (who study people in groups) account for variations between groups. Not all women watch movies the same way. African American women, Koreans, and lesbians, for example, may relate differently to the same female character or movie star. To understand how different viewers respond differently to the same film, some contemporary film scholars look to sociology and ethnography for models of research. Academics like Charlotte Brundson, Moya Luckett, Diane Negra, Hilary Radner, Jackie Stacey, and Shelley Stamp are interested in historical and cultural contexts. So while Doane originally took a theoretical, largely psychoanalytical view of spectatorship, Stacey brings a research-based, historically minded focus on actual audiences. In contrast to the previous generation of feminists, these third-wave feminists, or **post-feminists** as they are sometimes called, make more allowances for the pleasures of marriage and family. They see no need to renounce motherhood, femininity, or even consumerism. Women can be powerful, have babies, and still wear high heels.

The feminists, Marxists, and other theorists who have turned to more fact-based ethnographic research about audiences, take historical and cultural variations into account. They seek to tell the story of cinema as a social institution, a force that both reflects and molds communities at particular times in particular regions. During the first ten years of motion pictures in the United States, from 1895 to 1905, movies attracted the same middle-class audience that regularly attended live vaudeville shows. Then small movie theatres, accommodating roughly 200 people, started to spring up throughout the country. Known as **nickelodeons** because admission was only five cents, these new theatres drew working-class and lower-middle-class crowds, who could now afford the price. Movies became a means for integrating new immigrants into American culture, helping to create a homogenized society. By the 1910s and 1920s, when more Americans moved from the country to big cities, exhibitors were building larger theatres. These grand **movie palaces**, furnished with exotic Roman and Egyptian decor, could accommodate thousands, allowing ordinary individuals to live like emperors and pharaohs, at least for the duration of two silent features, an orchestral overture, and the live entertainment that typically accompanied each show. Exhibitors made special efforts to appeal to women, providing child care services, comfortable spaces to socialize, and elaborate displays of tie-ins in the lobby, from printed versions of the story to fan magazines. Elsewhere in the world, the way motion pictures were shown and watched adapted to local social customs, traditions reflected in the bustling movie halls of India and the traveling theatres of rural Latin America. In time, with changes like the advent of multiplex theatres, home video, and Internet technologies, the paradigms of reception would also change. Some theorists would say that local differences were giving way to more standardized viewing practices, reflecting the broad trend toward globalism.

Redrawing the Political Map

Many of the recent changes in filmmaking around the world stem from changes in world politics. To understand the new economic and cultural alliances that shape the films we watch, it will help to review some broad political forces that have shaped those alliances. Within the last 50 years, old boundary lines have been erased as new borders were drawn and new lines marked in the sand.

Chief among these changes is the collapse of Soviet Communism. During the **Cold War** (roughly 1945–1990), much of the world was allied politically with one of the two great superpowers (see Figure 0.21). In Europe, an imaginary Iron

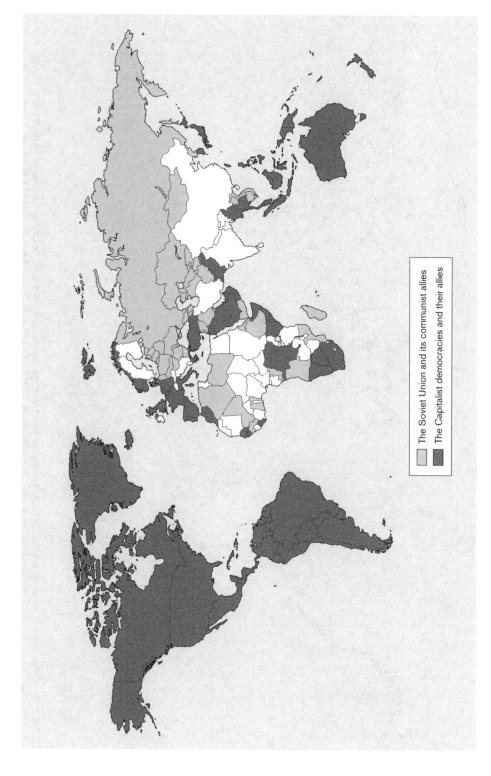

The Soviet Union and its communist allies

The Capitalist democracies and their allies

FIGURE 0.21 The Cold War (1945–1990) divided the world map into two competing power blocs: the Soviet Union and its communist allies vs. the capitalist democracies and their allies.

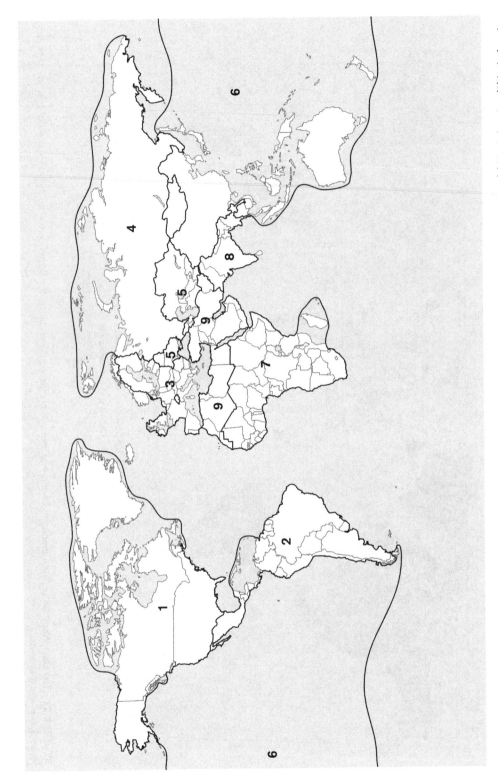

FIGURE 0.22 A view of the "new world order," c. 2013. After the Cold War, the world map assumed new configurations, including (1) North America, (2) Latin America, (3) the European Union, (4) Russia, (5) former Soviet States, (6) the Pacific Rim, (7) Sub-Saharan Africa, (8) South Asia, and (9) North Africa and the Middle East.

Curtain divided West from East. The Western democracies allied themselves with the United States; the Eastern countries of the Soviet Bloc were tied to the Soviet Union. Germany, divided by treaties after World War II and by a real wall after 1961, was split into two states, each with its own film industry and ideology. These divisions and alliances were reflected elsewhere in the world. The Soviets extended their influence into Africa, Asia, and Latin America, often using motion pictures to spread their ideological messages. Filmmakers like Senegal's Ousmane Sembene and Mali's Souleymane Cissé were trained in Moscow, returning to their native lands in Africa equipped with a working knowledge of Eisenstein and Pudovkin. Under Fidel Castro, Cuba assumed an active role in championing the cause of class struggle, encouraging solidarity among Third World filmmakers in the 1970s and 1980s.

But the greatest purveyor of cinematic messages within the former Soviet Union and among developing countries around the world has been India. India has boasted a robust movie industry since the days of silent films, an industry that blossomed during the 1940s into a Golden Age of Indian cinema. During the Cold War, assisted by its alliance with the Soviet Union, India gained access to large audiences within the Soviet sphere of influence, including Eastern Europe, the vast Soviet Union itself, and developing countries seeking alternatives to Western values. From Romania to Malaysia, from Haiti to Iraq, Indian stars and stories still dominate local movie screens. Children in Nigeria, Ghana, and Morocco sing songs in Hindi with their friends, lyrics they have learned by heart from the latest Bollywood feature. Although most Hindi films are meant to be more entertaining than polemic, they have provided a politically and culturally acceptable alternative for millions of people who prefer to bring their emotional needs to the Indian temple of desire rather than to the Hollywood dream factory.

Meanwhile, Hollywood continues to be the mightiest purveyor of Western values, aggressively seeking to dominate the world's screens. The end of Moscow's reign as a central unifying power left much of the Soviet empire in fragments (see Figure 0.22). This meant that newly independent states like Ukraine and Kazakhstan were free to develop their own cinemas. In the former Yugoslavia, filmmakers identified themselves as Bosnian, Serbian, Croatian, or Macedonian. The people of Czechoslovakia voted to separate the Czech Republic from the Slovak Republic. But elsewhere in the world, global forces were uniting people rather than dividing them. When the Berlin Wall came down in 1989, East and West Germans celebrated their reunification by turning the old state-owned DEFA facilities of East Germany into Studio Babelsberg, a new center for European film and television production bankrolled by the global conglomerate Vivendi. More broadly, the European Union brought together the nations of Eastern and Western Europe as they had never been before, paving the way for cross-national cooperation and co-productions.

Developments in the Pacific Rim have also brought previously separated states and film industries together. In contrast to Communist Russia, Communist China maintained its political power while pursuing a vigorous policy of economic growth, converting the People's Republic of China (PRC) to a market economy through careful central planning rather than by default. The historical and political forces that divide the PRC from Hong Kong and Taiwan have so far proved less consequential than the economic motives that are driving the three Chinas to a cinematic grand alliance. As a British colony, Hong Kong flourished financially during the twentieth century and provided a safe haven for Chinese capitalists during China's civil war in the 1920s and the Japanese invasion of the mainland in the 1930s. In this fiscally sound environment, Hong Kong prospered, creating in its boom years (the 1970s and 1980s) the third largest film industry in the world, after the United States and India. There was a similar migration of talent and money to Taiwan, where millions sought refuge from the Communists in the 1940s. Much of the Shanghai film industry moved to Taiwan after 1949, providing the infrastructure for a robust Taiwanese cinema. Although Hong Kong remained largely autonomous financially after its official return to China in 1997 ("one country, two systems"), and Taiwan fiercely continued to guard its political independence, film companies in both Hong Kong and Taiwan were investing heavily in the PRC by the early 2000s, turning increasingly to the mainland for its stars, its settings, and its audience.

Africa began emerging from colonial rule during the 1960s, with 17 countries gaining independence in 1960 alone. Tired of movies that used their land as an exotic backdrop for Western romance and adventure tales, black Africans like Sembene took cameras into their own hands. "The development of Africa," he declared, "implies among other things the production of its own images."[11] Sembene, whose work now ranks with the top directors in the world, released his first film, *Borom Sarret*, in 1963, winning first prize at the International Film Festival in Tours, France. By 1969, Africa had its own festival, the Pan-African Film Festival (FESPACO in French) in Burkina Faso. More than 40 years later, FESPACO regularly draws some 4,000 people to watch and discuss the latest creative efforts of the continent. Yet few countries in sub-Saharan Africa can support their own motion picture industry. In **Francophone** (French-speaking) Africa, when subsidies from the French government disappeared, local filmmakers had to seek funding elsewhere. Some fear that the pressure to appeal to broader markets will cancel out Sembene's vision of producing images of Africa for Africans. The dream of independence, they worry, will be swallowed up by globalism, leaving Africa to be colonized not by richer nations but by wealthy international conglomerates.

Similar concerns are voiced in Latin America. While vigorous new waves of committed and original filmmaking emerge from time to time – *cinema novo* in Brazil, Solanas and Getino in Argentina, Solás and Gutiérrez Alea in Cuba – a current trend appears to favor themes and genres that will cross the border to more affluent theatres and festivals in Europe and the United States. Films like *City of God* (*Cidade de Deos*, 2002) and *The Motorcycle Diaries* (*Diarios de motocicleta*, 2004) from Brazil, *Nine Queens* (*Nueve Reinas*, 2000) from Argentina, and *Amores Perros* (2001) from Mexico, have all been funded and distributed through global partnerships. Sometimes it is the filmmakers themselves who cross the borders. A recent case in point is Mexico's Alfonso Cuarón, whose success with *Y tu mamá también* (2001) led to a big-budget contract with Warner Bros. to direct films like *Harry Potter and the Prisoner of Azkaban* (2004). Meirelles and Salles have also crossed the language line, with films like *The Constant Gardener* (Meirelles, 2005) and *Dark Water* (Salles, 2005), both in English.

Among the few regions of the world that still seem relatively untouched by these global film deals, the most notable is Iran. After the Islamic revolution of 1979, the Shah's liberal policies gave way to a surge of anti-Western sentiment. Movie theatres were attacked and destroyed. In one notorious case, the Rex Theatre in Abadan was locked and set on fire with the audience still inside. Some 400 people burned to death. Soon, however, the new government under Ayatollah Khomeini declared that it was not against movies *per se*, but against moral corruption. Khomeini proposed an "Islamized cinema," supported by the state and reflecting the traditional values of the state religion. By the late 1990s, a revitalized film industry was thriving in Iran, despite – or perhaps because of – tight censorship. Women in the movies, like women in Iranian society, had to wear body-concealing chadors in public. Unmarried male and female actors could have no physical contact on screen. Sex, violence, and political criticism were off limits. But the censor's watchful eye sometimes provokes the committed artist's best creative efforts. Directors like Abbas Kiarostami, Jafar Panahi, and Moshen Makhmalbaf learned to circumscribe these restrictions. They devised allegorical scripts, often using child actors and deceptively simple plots to convey their messages indirectly. They sent their films abroad to foreign film festivals, where they won an unprecedented number of awards. Critics around the world hailed their work as the most exciting development in cinema since the French New Wave of the 1960s. In a world where Islamic fundamentalism dominates the headlines, the Islamized cinema of Iran is an important phenomenon to watch.

Globalization, Globalism, and Global Cinema

So far in this chapter, we have been following the story of world cinema as if it were composed of several threads: economic, artistic, technological, and sociological. Along the way, we've added a political strand. Each strand of the story is entangled with the others and, as the historical narrative progresses, becomes increasingly intertwined with terms like hybridity, cosmopolitanism, globalism, and globalization. This is a good place to sort out some of these terms and the thinking behind them.

We'll begin with a basic distinction between globalism and globalization. **Globalism** can be understood as a view of the whole world as a complex network of interconnected elements – economies, information, peoples, cultures – that transcends national barriers and spans entire continents. **Globalization** refers to the process by which this worldwide integration accelerates over time. In film studies, the word global has come to be used more often than terms like **international** (which typically refers to transactions between two nations), **multinational** (involving several nations), or even **transnational** (extending beyond national boundaries), as the world is seen increasingly as a network of interdependent entities rather than a collection of individual nations. In the 1950s, Hollywood's Universal Studios and London's Hammer Studios agreed to share monster movie icons for mutual benefit, an example of *international* cooperation between the United States and Britain. In the 1980s and 1990s, when Japan's Sony Pictures began buying studios abroad to make movies in Hollywood, India, Russia, and elsewhere, it became a *multinational* production company spanning many nations. The concept of transnational cinema is more complex and still much debated among scholars. Sometimes used to refute the idea of **national cinemas** (focusing on movies country by country) or to correct a perceived **Eurocentric** bias (viewing the world from a limited European perspective), the term *transnational* more generally applies to film practices (funding, production, distribution) that are not bound by national borders.

In a progressively global culture, the boundaries between villages, cities, and nations grow less and less significant. As the world becomes more globalized, our everyday lives depend more on what we learn and experience through travel and the media than where we happen to live. Arjun Appadurai, an Indian-born anthropologist interested in the cultural implications of globalism, stresses the fluidity of transnational connections by describing them as pathways along which culture flows. He uses the terms ethnoscapes (mobile people), mediascapes (mobile images), technoscapes (mobile technology), financescapes (mobile global capital), and ideoscapes (mobile ideologies) to describe five dimensions of a new global landscape unbound by oceans, mountains, or political borders.[12] Drawing on Benedict Anderson's concept of **imagined communities**, the manner in which people perceive their reality in relation to a group, Appadurai argues that globalism has altered people's perception of group identity. Anderson reasons that since members of a nation, religion, or other community will never meet everyone in their community face to face, their sense of belonging is imaginary, constructed of images from speeches, newspapers, television, and the like. Appadurai points out that in an age of escalating global flows, with large numbers of immigrants in transition, money circulating internationally, and more messages coming to us through worldwide media, our sense of belonging stretches to include a wider share of the planet. Since movies are important sources of community identity, the globalization of cinema helps us feel more connected to an imagined global community.

Globalization is not a new phenomenon. The ancient Persians, the classical Greeks and Romans, the Asante Union in West Africa, Aztecs in Mesoamerica, Incas in South America, Vikings from northern Europe, and Ottomans from central Asia all extended the reach of local peoples through trade and military conquest, creating overlapping economies, political spheres, religious doctrines, and other cross-cultural influences. Many of these entities were known as **empires**, territorial extensions of a central power that took in other states and populations, typically united by force and ruled by a single monarch. Beginning in the 1500s, European powers like Spain, Portugal, Britain, and France enlarged their sphere of authority and influence by establishing **colonies** in Asia, Africa, and the Americas. The era of colonialism enabled certain groups to exercise control over indigenous populations, creating unequal relationships between a dominant center and a subjugated periphery. According to **postcolonial** theorists like Edward Said, who focus on the after-effects of colonialism, the inequalities of colonial thinking continued well into the twentieth century and beyond. Said, a Palestinian scholar, used the term **Orientalism** to describe the false assumptions that people in the West perpetuate about people in the Middle East, assumptions he considered to spring from deeply rooted biases and superior attitudes. Terms like **colonialism** (defined by Said as "the implanting of settlements on a distant territory") and **imperialism** ("the practice, the theory and the attitudes of a dominating metropolitan centre ruling a distant territory")[13] are highly charged and heatedly disputed, but since they crop up in many fields of film study, these terms are important to any understanding of how cinema is viewed throughout the world.

Also crucial to this understanding is the concept of nationhood. In common speech, a **nation** is a country whose population shares a common territory and government, but the word may also refer more broadly to a community of people with a common language, history, and culture independently of physical borders. Precisely what constitutes national identity is, like other political questions, a matter of debate. Can countries with two languages, like Canada and Belgium, be said to constitute a single nation like single-language states? What about Chinese people who share a common language and ethnicity but live in different lands under different governments? And why is any of this relevant to the study of world cinema?

From the viewpoint of world history, nation states are newcomers. The people of France did not consider themselves members of a sovereign nation until after the French revolution of 1789 displaced the kingdom of France. Germany and Italy did not become nations until the nineteenth century. Since motion pictures were invented in an age of nation states, much of cinematic history is a history of national cinemas. Our names for movements like German Expressionism, Italian Neorealism, and the French New Wave reflect this perspective. State-funded film industries and national media policies have reinforced filmmaking practices within national boundaries as a way of doing business. Additionally, powerful commonalities of language, history, and culture all contribute to national film styles and narrative traditions. But if nations are imagined communities, as Anderson suggested, if they are constructs of consciousness, what images of cultural identity will be constructed in an age of globalism? Some theorists make the case that we are witnessing a major shift in consciousness, that the speed and quantity of money, people, media, and ideas flowing across national boundaries has tipped the balance in favor of a uniquely globalized shared identity. To the extent that our collective cultural imagination is fed by countless images from television, magazines, and movies produced and marketed by international conglomerates, are we becoming what we consume? Are the rich, distinctive traits of national identities and folk traditions being replaced by some form of homogenized mass culture, as some fear?

Some critics of Hollywood complain that American mainstream movies take over the world's screens like invasive plants, choking out local competition. They see Hollywood's **media hegemony**, its dominance in the mass communications market, as a form of cultural imperialism. Antonio Gramsci, for example, the influential Italian Marxist critic, taught that Hollywood exported American values along with its products. But others regard Hollywood's success not so much as a matter of brute force as an ability to give audiences the kind of entertainment they want. Ed Buscombe, for example, reasons that Hollywood films are popular around the world not because they reproduce capitalist ideology but because they give audiences, American or otherwise, "a vivid knowledge of the dynamism and force of its social life, represented in a style at once concrete and multi-faceted."[14] Moreover, Hollywood regularly employs a range of multinational talent and borrows ideas freely from abroad.

Nor is Hollywood the only game in town. Other film industries, like Bollywood (based in India) and Nollywood (based in Nigeria) produce quite different kinds of popular movies for large markets. Some nation-based producers have specialized in local niche genres, like Hong Kong's kung fu films of the 1970s or Japan's J-horror in the 2000s. Still others deliberately critique Hollywood, as the Third Cinema movement did in Latin America during the 1960s and 1970s. In contrast to **mainstream** cinema, intended for popular audiences, the tradition of **art cinema** appeals to a smaller range of viewers who profess to be more interested in originality and depth than in an evening's entertainment. Typically made by independent auteurs (directors regarded as the creative authors of their work), art films usually find limited release at festivals or in special art house theatres. But in a time when more and more films are circulated as videos, DVDs, or electronic artifacts on hand-held mobile devices, it makes less and less difference where a movie is screened. This technological mobility, too, is part of the decentering of contemporary cinema, a gradual removal of industry, aesthetic style, and audience from the particularities of place. While terms like globalism and imperialism may make the trend seem negative to some, a few theorists prefer the word **cosmopolitanism**, with its more positive implications. Diogenes, the Greek philosopher, is said to have coined the word around 413 BCE when asked where he was from. His answer yoked together the Greek words for world and citizen: "I am cosmo-politan, a citizen of the world." Another philosopher, Kwame Anthony Appiah, who was born in Ghana and now divides his time between Britain and the United States, proposes cosmopolitanism as a suitable outlook for today. His humanistic philosophy starts by taking "individuals – not nations, tribes or 'peoples' – as the proper object of moral concern."[15] When Appiah visits colleges around the country, he invites students to expand their world with foreign language films. He tells his audience, no matter where they're from or what groups claim their utmost loyalty, "See one movie with subtitles a month."[16]

Analyzing a Film

The act of reading books and other printed texts is often regarded as a three-part conversation between the author, the text, and the reader (Figure 0.23). In simple terms, the author creates the text and the reader interprets it. Of course, this is rarely a straightforward process of transferring information from a writer to a reader through a stream of written words. Authors put all sorts of things into a text, some intentional, others unintended. The texts themselves may vary from one version to another. And readers filter what they read through a web of personal and cultural experience. For students of film, the process of "reading" movies is even more complex (see Figure 0.24). For one thing, the author of a movie is not just an individual writer but a team. Directors, producers, script writers, cinematographers, editors, sound technicians, set designers, actors, and a host of other specialists all contribute to a film's production. This notion of **collaborative authorship** can be expanded even further to include those aspects of the film industry that influence what goes into any film, aspects such as budget and marketing, which may determine what kind of film is made, which actors are selected, where the film is shot, and even what gets left out of the script. If the text of a literary work is made primarily of words, the **film text** is a multimodal fabric of words, images, and sounds. Film study expands the notion of text to include elements of cinematic **style** like camerawork, lighting, dialogue, music, and editing as well as narrative **content** (what's in the story) and **form** (the kind of story being told). As for the audience, those who watch and make sense of the movie, film students learn to take a multitude of psychological and social factors into account. Where do individual spectators fit themselves into the film? With whom do they identify? How do they judge the characters and groups as they are represented on the screen? What difference does it make to watch the movie in a theatre, on a television screen, or on a hand-held device? Such questions of identity, representation, and technology are even more interesting to ask from the perspectives of history and culture. How is the same film viewed during different eras, in different countries, and by different ethnic groups? Is it possible to step into the same movie twice?

To understand a movie, then, requires close attention to three main factors: its authorship (production), its content, form, and cinematic style (the film text), and

FIGURE 0.23 Reading as a three-sided exchange.

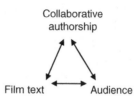

FIGURE 0.24 The dynamics of reading a movie.

its reception (audience), all of which are intricately related to each other and to matters of history and culture. One approach begins with a close reading of the film text, focusing on elements of the *mise-en-scène* and editing scene by scene. This **formal analysis** then becomes the basis for making broader observations about production, reception, history, and culture.

Let's take that flashback from *Citizen Kane* when young Charlie Kane is playing in the snow near a wooden lodge. Inside the lodge, three adults are discussing his future. A quick shot of a sign above the door identifies the building as Mrs. Kane's Boarding House (Figure 0.25). The next shot begins with a long view of the boy throwing snowballs at a snowman, shouting "Come on boys, the Union forever." Suddenly, a figure enters the frame from the left, calling out with a mother's concern, "Be careful, Charles; pull your muffler around your neck." Mrs. Kane is leaning out a window looking at her son at play (Figure 0.26). We know this because, as the camera pulls back in a prolonged tracking shot, we see the window from *inside*, framing Mrs. Kane on the left and a well-dressed gentleman on the right (Figure 0.27). The dialogue between these two figures tells us that the man is Mr. Thatcher, a banker from New York who has come to take the boy away. The camera keeps moving back as Charlie's mother walks toward us, obscuring Mr. Thatcher, but another figure now appears behind her to the left. This is Charlie's father (Figure 0.28). As Mrs. Kane sits down at a table, Mr. Thatcher seats himself beside her and begins reading aloud a legal contract granting his bank financial control of the Kane mine in exchange for Charlie's care and education. The **composition** at this point in the shot captures the power relationships of the drama within the frame: The dominant figures, the ones signing the contract, are closest to us. Mr. Thatcher stands apart, looking smaller and pointedly ignored. Charlie, whose fate is being decided at this moment, is a tiny speck outside in the cold. Since he is about to be separated from his family, his earlier words about the Union, probably a reference to the American Civil War, take on an ironic significance (Figure 0.29). When Mrs. Kane rises, having signed the documents, the camera rises with her and follows her brisk stride past the two men to the window (Figure 0.30), which she opens (her husband, significantly, had closed it moments earlier) just before the camera cuts to another position just outside the window so we can see her face as she calls out to him in a heartbreaking voice (Figure 0.31). Behind her we see the two men, but also the wooden ceiling, an oil lamp, a pot-bellied stove, the meager but carefully tended furnishings that Charles will be trading for a life of privilege in the city. All these objects and actors are clearly visible thanks to Welles's use of **deep focus photography** (skillfully deployed by cinematographer Greg Tolland), which keeps the background and foreground in sharp focus. Figure 0.32 is another good example of deep focus photography.

The whole shot (Figure 0.26, Figure 0.27, Figure 0.28, Figure 0.29, Figure 0.30), moving rearward from the window into the room, pausing for the signature, and moving forward to the window again with Mrs. Kane, lasts for two full minutes, a lengthy duration for any film. This gives us time to take in the rich *mise-en-scène*,

FIGURES 0.25–0.31   Screen shots from the boarding house scene in *Citizen Kane*.

FIGURE 0.25

FIGURE 0.26

FIGURE 0.27

FIGURE 0.28

FIGURE 0.29

FIGURE 0.30

FIGURE 0.31

FIGURE 0.32   Kane tends to his wife in the middle ground while someone runs for help in the background. Meanwhile, we see the instruments of her suicide attempt in the foreground. Cinematographer Greg Tolland pioneered this use of **deep-focus photography** in *Citizen Kane* to capture multiple planes of action clearly in a single shot.

everything carefully arranged within the shot. In addition to the camera work, we may notice details of performance, clothing, lighting, set design, and sound. We take note of Mrs. Kane's prim high collar and tightly coiled hair, the lighting that sculpts her stony face, Thatcher's fur-lined coat and condescending looks at Mr. Kane. We take in the wooden ceiling and the hand-made floor rug, details that characterize Charlie's life in Colorado and lend a sense of authenticity to the scene. Looking beyond this dynamic single shot at the whole Colorado scene, we might see that the scene is composed of five or six shots. There is another long take during which the camera moves out of the cabin towards Charlie when all three adults try to break the news to him. As the confused boy shoves Thatcher away with his sled, the camera pans left with his thrust. Then, when his mother gives the striking reason for her decision, there is an abrupt match cut to a close-up of her face and his. The scene ends with a slow dissolve from the snow-covered sled to a white sheet of wrapping paper. The paper is ripped away, revealing a shiny new sled that is clearly poor compensation for the immensity of Charlie's loss. With more time, we might notice other directorial decisions, like Welles's use of editing to present the story like a jig-saw puzzle from different points of view, or his use of musical **motifs** (short melodies associated with particular characters, events, or ideas) to link pieces of the whole.

If we leave the cinematic text itself and do some research on the film's production, we might learn about Welles's notorious struggles with studio producers or his technical and artistic innovations on the set. Reading about the director's early life might provide some parallels to Charlie Kane's childhood. Following the film's reception – the efforts to suppress its release, the first critical reviews, and later reassessments – throws further light on how a controversial film can become a celebrated classic. Each line of investigation "behind the scene" may lead us to new clues, information that may expand our understanding of the scene and deepen our appreciation of its artistic merits.

Watching Foreign Films

Analyzing a movie like *Citizen Kane* reminds us how precise and powerful the tools of cinema can be in the hands of a master. Even if we speak English and are familiar with the society that shaped Kane's life, any scene can be quite subtle and complex to read. But what if the movie is in a foreign language and depicts an unfamiliar culture? What can help us get past the immediate problems of translation to understand the story and appreciate what is happening on screen? The Canadian director Atom Egoyan points out that "every film is a foreign film, foreign to some audience somewhere."[17] Egoyan's comment helps to put the notion of "foreignness" in perspective.

The early silent films required little or no translation. Most of the action was intelligible even without the **intertitle cards** that rendered dialogue in phrases like "We're being watched" or "Kiss me, my fool!" Since these cards were spliced between shots, they could be written and read in any language without competing with the picture for attention. The coming of sound film in the late 1920s posed special problems for the international market. If the new "talkies" talked in English, how could audiences follow the dialogue in France or South America? One solution was to create multiple versions of a movie, each version filmed in a different language. *Dracula* (1931) was filmed in English, then in Spanish, scene by scene with different actors. *The Blue Angel* (*Der blaue Engel*, 1930) was filmed in German, then in English, with actors who could speak both languages. These **multilanguage films** were tricky to make, however, and were at best limited to a few languages. Another strategy was to dub a finished film during post-production. In **dubbing**, the original voices are replaced by voices delivered in another language. John Wayne's lines are repeated by a Spanish speaker who tries to emulate Wayne's intonation and synchronize his words to the movement of Wayne's lips. While this method allows a foreign audience to watch the picture without having to read translations at the bottom of the screen, it comes with its own distractions. Actors are chosen partly for their voices. It's a rare dubbing performer who can capture the vocal nuances of the original actor or get the synching just right. More often, the dubbed version seems hollow, artificial, detached from those faces on the screen. That's why many viewers prefer **subtitles**. Even though part of their attention is focused on those white or yellow titles just below the action, they get more of the flavor of an actor's speech, those pauses and inflections that cannot be translated simply into words. Reading subtitled films may seem uncomfortable at first, but most viewers get used to them with a little practice. By comparing the dubbed and subtitled versions of a film like Ang Lee's *Crouching Tiger, Hidden Dragon* (*Wo hu cang long*, 2000) or Zhang Yimou's *Hero* (*Ying xiong*, 2002), they quickly see the advantages of preserving the original Chinese soundtrack in the background.

The foreignness of foreign films is not only a question of language. Things like courtship customs, gender roles, and dress codes are far from universal, which is why some Americans have trouble following *The Syrian Bride* (2004) while the humor in *Wedding Crashers* eludes some audiences in the Middle East. Wedding films are particularly good test cases of cultural convergence and misunderstanding, as we can see by looking closely at the banquet scene from Ang Lee's *The Wedding Banquet* (*Xiyan*, 1993).

The scene opens with a stream of guests arriving at the banquet hall. Asians and Caucasians, all are dressed for the big event, men in Western suits, women in colorful outfits. Lee films them from the right and from the left, creating an impression of tumultuous excitement. Some of them are signing florid guest lists. One woman sets her child on the wedding bed, saying, "Come, Little Rock, jump on the bed to make a boy like you." Everyone applauds this ritual forecast of fertility (Figure 0.33). Soon the camera finds the wedding couple, moving with them through the approving crowd to the table of honor. A long shot shows the vast room brimming with people and festive decorations (Figure 0.34). Red is the ruling color, dominating the curtains, paper lamps, and tablecloths. There seem to be more than a dozen tables, all round, each elaborately set for ten. This shape and this number, we assume, must be part of the ritual. Now the focus shifts to the father of the groom, dressed in a traditional, plum-colored Chinese robe. He steps up to the podium, which is festooned with red ribbons, backed by two gold dragons and a pair of Chinese ideograms that spell out "double happiness" (Figure 0.35). Even if we don't know Chinese or the symbolic meaning of dragons and all that red, we can guess that all these cultural details are signs of joyful celebration and good fortune. We know that lengthy speeches are another time-honored tradition because as soon as the groom's father begins his speech, the scene cuts to a chef carving ornamental birds in the kitchen. When the waiter tells him who is speaking, the chef says, "I got forty minutes" (Figure 0.36). Back in the banquet hall, dinner is being served. The Western guests are struggling with chopsticks. Someone uses her sticks to tap a glass, and soon the room is filled with tapping. The groom, who has lived long enough in the United States to know the drill, whispers something to his bride and kisses her lightly on the cheek. But the crowd wants more, a real kiss. "Put some passion into it," someone shouts. What they don't know is that the groom is gay and the whole wedding is a show to please his parents. When he embraces her again, this time with exaggerated energy, her reaction is caught in one close-up (Figure 0.37) and the reaction of the groom's gay partner is captured in another (Figure 0.38). What follows next is a mixture of Western and Asian wedding practices. Some rituals, like the ringing glasses, are well known to American audiences: the groom is roasted by his old college room-mate, the bride tosses her bouquet to a group of hopeful maidens, and the couple cuts a tiered white wedding cake. Other customs may seem more puzzling to non-Chinese viewers. What is that bizarre, winged creature dangling between the bride and groom for them to eat as "punishment" (Figure 0.39)? Why does the bride appear in a different dress in the middle of the banquet? What are all those Chinese dishes? Why is there so

FIGURES 0.33–0.40   The big celebration in *The Wedding Banquet* (Dir. Ang Lee, 1993) is a global concoction of Asian and Western traditions.

FIGURE 0.33

FIGURE 0.34

FIGURE 0.35

FIGURE 0.36

FIGURE 0.37

FIGURE 0.38

FIGURE 0.39

FIGURE 0.40

much noise and boisterous drinking? As if to acknowledge such questions, one of the Western guests says aloud, "I thought the Chinese were meek, quiet, math whizzes." A Chinese man behind him leans over to explain, "You're witnessing the results of 5,000 years of sexual repression." That man is Ang Lee (Figure 0.40).

Lee knows that viewers on both sides of the Pacific won't understand every detail, but he wants his film to appeal to Asians and Westerners alike. The dialogue is in both English and Chinese Mandarin, and the banquet itself is a hybrid celebration. As one guest observes, "This is a cross-cultural event. Anything goes." We don't need to know every ritual or recognize each food to appreciate the mood of jubilation and those occasional moments of discomfort. Lee provides plenty of long shots to give us the big picture, alternating between medium shots and close-ups so we can see reactions of the groom, the bride, the boyfriend, parents, and individual guests. However, if we take time to do some research, we might discover layers of illuminating cultural information underlying the scene. We might learn, for example, that round tables symbolize reunion and community. Since Chinese people eat with chopsticks and reach for food from the center of the table, the round shape makes it easier for everyone to share the common meal. Chinese also attach special meaning to homophones, words that sound alike. They avoid the number four because it sounds similar to the word for death in Mandarin, but they prize the number eight, which sounds like the word for prosperity. In Chinese belief, good things come in pairs, which explains the poster for "double happiness" on the wall and the ten place settings (for five couples) at each table. After the banquet, when the couple goes off to the bridal chamber, it is the custom for their friends to play practical jokes (*nao dong fang*) that warm things up for their first night together. Making toasts at every table helps them lose their inhibitions. As for the bride's dress, while the bride in a traditional wedding wears only one gown, the practice in some hybrid ceremonies is to wear traditional attire for the wedding itself but exchange it for a Western-style gown for the banquet.

For viewers unfamiliar with international films, this kind of background information can help to clarify what they are watching. *World Cinema through Global Genres* will provide a good measure of explanatory cultural and historical details. It also helps to realize that the broader outlines of character and story, particularly for the films selected in this book, are recognizable to audiences no matter where they live. As for the barrier of subtitles, it should come as comforting news that the universal language of screen images usually has more to say than those words at the bottom of the screen. Besides, reading subtitles, like reading images, is an acquired skill, and the following units, are designed to develop your skill in both.

Studying Genres

To speak of wedding films or horror movies raises the issue of **genre**, a topic of central concern in this book. In simple terms, genre refers to a way of classifying movies, grouping them in categories that share similar traits. Horror films constitute a genre that aims to horrify its audience with stories about monsters and images of terror or disgust. Wedding films usually center on a wedding ceremony, with its nuptial rituals, family conflicts, romantic promises, and disappointments. But like most objects of study, genre can be a complex and elusive concept when placed under the microscope of close analysis. For example, *Abbot and Costello Meet Frankenstein* (1948) shares much of its monster imagery with Universal Studio's *Frankenstein* of 1931, but can it be called a horror film if it seeks to evoke laughter rather than fear? Should *Syrian Wedding* be classified as a wedding movie with *The Wedding Banquet* or *Wedding Crashers* if the former is more about Middle Eastern politics than marriage rites or romance? Before beginning the four units of this book, we should be prepared to ask some basic questions about film genres: how are they defined, how do they work, what purposes do they serve, when and where do they appear, and why are they worth studying?

Writing about Hollywood genres in 1981, Thomas Schatz observed that genre films "involve familiar, essentially one-dimensional characters acting out a predictable story pattern within a familiar setting."[18] The sheriffs and outlaws of the typical Western, the mobsters and the G-men of the classical gangster film, with their six-guns and machine guns, their horses and their motorcars, inhabit worlds that are easily recognized and enjoyed on any screen.

Eighteen years later, in *Film/Genre*, Rick Altman pointed out that the term genre has different meanings for different parties. It can provide a structure for scriptwriters (who fit their scenes, dialogue, and themes within an established framework), a blueprint for producers (who choose stories, stars, and settings according to a convenient formula), a label for distributors and exhibitors (who may market their products as action films, dramas, or comedies), and a contract with audiences (who expect a certain kind of movie-going experience).[19] For students and scholars of film, genre also provides "an historically grounded method of establishing 'family resemblances' between films produced and released under widely differencing circumstances," as Barry Langford wrote in 2005.[20]

These family relationships are an important feature of watching genre films. To constitute a genre, a large number of similar films must be made, shown, and understood in a consistent manner. Fans of the genre learn to assimilate and anticipate the rules. So every new Western or horror film is experienced not only as an individual film text but also **intertextually**, in relation to other Westerns or horror films. Part of the viewing pleasure is in recognizing the familiar iconography and moments of the genre: the showdown in the saloon or the monster hiding in the basement. Part of the pleasure is in being surprised by variations in the recipe: the gunslinger who turns out to be a woman or the monster who pops out from behind the couch. This combination of formula and novelty is what keeps audiences coming back for more, and it is what drives the industry to keep the genre going.

Drawing on the work of other scholars, Schatz suggests that genres may undergo a kind of evolution over time. They begin in an *experimental* stage, when the genre's codes and conventions are tentatively formulated, then pass through a *classic* stage, when they become established and widely understood, continue through a period of *refinement*, when new films add formal details and stylistic flourishes, and finally enter a period of *baroque* embellishment, when self-conscious preoccupation with the genre's codes shifts attention from the substance of the genre to its style.[21] This developmental notion of genre has been both accepted and refuted by other scholars, as we'll see, but it can serve as a useful introduction to the history of the genres we'll be studying. It can also serve as an example of how a promising hypothesis can be put to the test.

Altman is one of those who question the idea that genres go through such predictable life cycles. After asking when a genre becomes a genre, he examines the historical record of advertisements, press books, and posters in search of evidence. What he discovers is that terms like musical and Western were used as descriptive adjectives ("a musical version of *The Three Musketeers,*" "Western Romance and Adventure at its Best") before they were used as nouns denoting categories (a musical, a Western).[22] In other words, promoters considered music and Western trappings to be add-ons before they recognized that music and the Wild West could be the generic substance of a new kind of film. Altman finds a certain pattern in this process of **genrification**: when an individual studio's **cycle** of films (a succession of releases with similar subjects, themes, or tone) become successful, other studios try to cash in by copying the features of that cycle. The adjectival labels are substantiated as a genre, as the musical was during the 1930s. Since the major studios work to differentiate their work from competitors, it is usually the smaller studios that exploit the ready-made categories of genre films. Meanwhile, the majors establish new cycles, adding fresh features and labels to existing genres, starting yet another round of genrification. The process continues, constantly in flux.

A distinction is often made between the commercial aims of genre films and the artistic aspirations of auteur directors. Genre films tend to be mass produced for mass markets while art films are individually crafted for the "serious viewer." But while this division has sometimes been used to belittle the merits of "low brow" movies in contrast to "art cinema," some scholars have found value in the very fact that genres are made collectively, that they arise and succeed because of their popular appeal. "If genre is society speaking collectively to itself," as Schatz proposes,[23] then genres can be studied as reflections of public interests. Or, as Langford puts it, genres give us access to an "ongoing national conversation" about relevant issues.[24] Studying the history of genre films thus becomes a way to trace the public's changing beliefs and concerns over time.

If genres have a history, theories of genre have their own history. Although studios in Europe and Asia have turned out genre films, most theories of film genre have been based on studies of the Hollywood studio system, the world's most influential producer. Langford traces genre theory through three main phases.[25] The earliest examples were concerned with categories, classifying and defining individual genres in terms of their iconography, character types, and story lines, like Robert Warshow's studies of the Western and the gangster film. The focus later shifted to broader meanings and social function in a second phase, when theorists looked for the ideological messages embodied in particular genres. They began to see genres as ritual reenactments of cultural conflicts: between law and order (crime films), civilization and the wilderness (Westerns), self fulfillment and maternal sacrifice (the woman's film). More recently, genre theorists have given more attention to historical contexts and institutional practices, asking how studios market genres and how they are consumed at different times.

This book takes Hollywood genres as starting points but looks beyond the borders of American filmmaking to include martial arts films from China, wedding films from India, horror films from Japan, road films from Latin America, and a good deal more. We'll be asking how these genres are defined in different parts of the world, how they resemble and depart from their overseas cousins, and what the differences tell us about the cultures behind them.

We will notice how genres mutate and intermingle as they circulate around the world. We will ask how recent trends toward hybrid genres and self-conscious reflexivity relate to the phenomenon of globalization in a postmodern age.

Mythical Dimensions

If you want to understand a people, listen to the stories that they tell and retell. In the actions of their heroes, in the twists and turns of character and plot, are clues to what the storytellers value and believe. When the Greek poet Homer began narrating *The Iliad*, he was offering more than a history of the Trojan War. Within the fabric of his epic poem he wove the fears and aspirations, the rituals and daily practices, the world view of a whole society. When the *Beowulf* poet recounted his hero's battles with Grendel, Grendel's mother, and the dragon, he stitched the ideology of Anglo-Saxon England into every scene. A nation's folklore, literature, and enduring myths can be viewed as mirrors, reflecting who its people are and what they stand for.

Today, we're more likely to learn about the Trojan War and Grendel's mother from Wolfgang Petersen's *Troy* (2004) and Robert Zemeckis's *Beowulf* (2007), movies that reveal as much about our own times as they do about ancient Greece or ninth-century England. Contemporary heroes and their milieus, from Batman and Princess Leia to Harry Potter and Elle Woods, come to us mainly through the medium of motion pictures, which perform much of the storytelling role once played by poets, dramatists, and novelists. Arguably, genre films are particularly well suited to this purpose because they represent stories validated by the interest of countless viewers over time and honed by repeated telling.

In *The Hero with a Thousand Faces*, Joseph Campbell compared the culture heroes in myths from around the world. He found common elements in their stories that form the basis of a foundational narrative, which he called, the **monomyth**.

Campbell described this mythic story as a journey through distinct stages. The hero receives a call to adventure from his ordinary life, crosses a threshold, and enters a strange world where he (or sometimes she) faces trials and enemies that test the hero's worthiness. After surviving these ordeals, perhaps with the help of a guide or mentor, he achieves a major goal or boon, finally returning to his world with his reward, an elixir for his later life and for his people. Like other comparative mythologists, Campbell believed that the hero's journey represents fundamental truths deeply rooted in the human psyche. Some version of the same basic story is told and repeated in hundreds of languages, even in communities that have no connection with each other, because people throughout the world share its underlying assumptions about life.

Carl Jung shared this interest in universal myths. Like his colleague Sigmund Freud, Jung believed that much of humanity's mental and emotional activity occurs below the threshold of awareness, in the realm of the **unconscious**. But whereas Freud limited his analysis to individuals and their personal unconscious experience, Jung posited the existence of a collective unconscious, a shared system of impersonal and universal forms, which he called **archetypes**. These archetypes include some of the stages and characters in Campbell's journey of the hero as well as a wide range of other moments (initiation, courtship, marriage, death), figures (the great mother, father, devil), and motifs (the creation, the deluge).

In the *Star Wars* series (1977–2005), for example, Luke Skywalker can be regarded as an archetypal hero whose quest for the Force takes him through familiar rites of passage: the Call to Adventure (Princess Leia's message), Crossing the Threshold (on the desert planet Tatooine), Training (with the lightsaber), enumerable Trials, Temptation (by the Dark Side), Initiation (into the Jedi knighthood), the Boon (destruction of the Death Star and victory over the Evil Empire), and the Triumphal Return (in the Millennium Falcon as a full-fledged Jedi). Along the way, he encounters Shapeshifters and Tricksters (Hans Solo, CP30), an Oracle (Yoda), the Wise Old Man (a fatherly Obi-Wan Kenobi), the Shadow (Darth Vader, a darker version of the father figure), and the feminine principle of Anima (Princess Leia, who combines the attributes of a sister, mother, partner, and goddess). In this reading, Luke's battle with the Dark Force is everyman's struggle with his inner demons, the impulses that Jung calls our shadow side.

The literary critic Northrop Frye regarded archetypes as complex variables with multiple meanings, linking them to myth and ritual. For Frye, myth in literature is analogous to abstract art, like painting stories with archetypal symbols, in contrast to literary realism, which aspires to copy nature much as does representational art. Frye regarded rituals as recurrent acts expressing a society's persistent desires and fears. Harvest rituals embody a desire for abundance and fertility; expulsion rituals embody fears of contamination by scapegoats. Like recurring dreams, rituals allow a culture to work out the conflicts of daily life in symbolic form, conflicts that are given voice in mythic stories.

Filmmakers have been particularly interested in the work of Jung and Campbell. We have seen how George Lucas drew on the monomyth's characters and plot devices for *Star Wars*. Christopher Vogler wrote a popular handbook, *The Writer's Journey*, now widely used by screenwriters as a guidebook for their scripts. In *Myth and the Movies* Stuart Voytilla, a student of Vogler, showed how Campbell's archetypal characters and plots appear in dozens of movies, from *The Searchers* (1956) and *The Godfather* (1972) to *Raiders of the Lost Ark* (1981) and *Boyz n the Hood* (1991). These books suggest how genre films can be a fruitful source of stories for studying universal themes. By noting points of similarity and difference in the way a genre is treated within various national cinemas, we can learn much about local cultures and overlapping global values, what makes the world's diverse communities distinctive and what we have in common with each other.

We see, then, that movies can be studied as an industry, an art, a technology, and a social force. They have a history rooted in world politics and ideologies. Movies can be analyzed individually, scene by scene, or collectively as genres, even as a storehouse of contemporary mythology. As modern life becomes more globalized, as the dynamics of filmmaking converge, cross-pollinate, and play against each other, it is more important than ever to understand our position in the larger picture. With these perspectives and conceptual tools at hand, we're ready to spread out the map and begin our exploration of global movie genres.

Notes

1. Neal Gabler, *An Empire of Their Own: How the Jews Invented Hollywood* (Doubleday, 1988).

2. Thomas Schatz, *The Genius of the System: Hollywood Filmmaking in the Studio Era* (Pantheon, 1988).

3. John Belton, *American Cinema/American Culture*, 2nd edition (McGraw-Hill, 2005), 4.

4. Belton, 304.

5. Bruce Kawin and Gerald Mast, *A Short History of the Movies*, 10th edition (Pearson, 2008), 672.

6. Peter Lev, *The Euro-American Cinema* (University of Texas Press, 1993), 20.

7. James Chapman, *Cinemas of the World: Film and Society from 1895 to the Present* (Reaktion Books, 2003), 33.

8. Quoted in Jean-Pierre Gueuns, *Film Production Theory* (State University of New York Press, 2000), 198.

9. See Andrew Horton, *Screenwriting for a Global Market* (University of California Press, 2004), for a screenwriter's perspective of the role of the Hollywood model in global filmmaking today.

10. Laura Mulvey, "Visual Pleasure and Narrative Cinema," *Screen* 16(3) (1975): 6–18.

11. Quoted in Françoise Pfaff, *The Cinema of Ousmane Sembene: A Pioneer of African Film* (Greenwood Press, 1984), 2.

12. Arjun Appadurai, "Disjuncture and Difference in the Global Cultural Economy," *Public Culture* 2(2) (1990): 1–23.

13. Quoted in Carolyn Gallaher, Carl T. Dahlman, Mary Gilmartin, et al., *Key Concepts in Political Geography* (Sage Publications, 2008), 116.

14. Edward Buscombe, "Film History and the Idea of a National Cinema," *Australian Journal of Screen Theory* 9/10 (1981): 150.

15. Kwame Anthony Appiah, "Toward a New Cosmopolitanism," *New York Times Magazine*, January 1, 2006: 33.

16. Sissi Aguila, "Kwame Appiah Discusses 'World Citizenship' at FIU," *FIU News*, Florida International University, March 23, 2010. Available at: http://news.fiu.edu/2010/04/kwame-appiah-discusses-%E2%80%98world-citizenship%E2%80%99-at-fiu/13443 (accessed May 13, 2013).

17. Atom Egoyan and Ian Balfour, *Subtitles: On the Foreignness of Film* (MIT Press, 2004), 1.

18. Thomas Schatz, *Hollywood Genres: Formulas, Filmmaking, and the Studio System* (Random House, 1981), 6.

19. Rick Altman, *Film/Genre* (Palgrave Macmillan, 1999), 14.

20. Barry Langford, *Film Genre: Hollywood and Beyond* (Edinburgh University Press, 2005), 1.

21. Schatz, 37–38.

22. Altman, 50–62.

23. Schatz, 38.

24. Langford, 20.

25. Langford, 10–11.

UNIT I
THE WARRIOR HERO

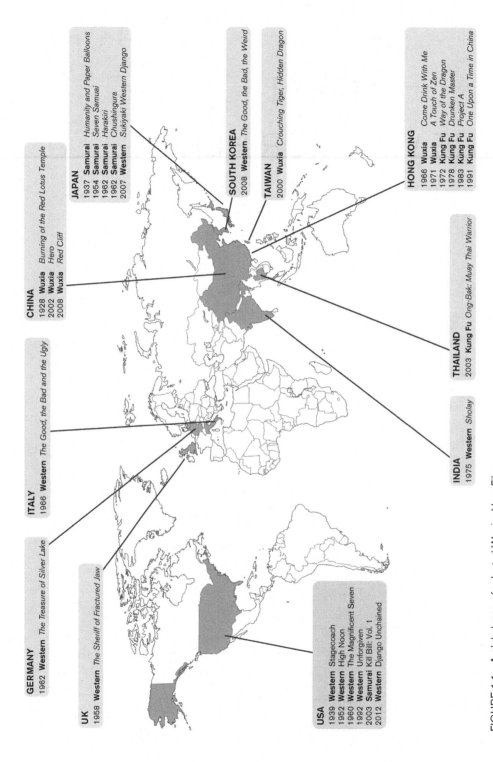

GERMANY
1962 **Western** *The Treasure of Silver Lake*

ITALY
1966 **Western** *The Good, the Bad and the Ugly*

UK
1958 **Western** *The Sheriff of Fractured Jaw*

USA
1939 **Western** Stagecoach
1952 **Western** High Noon
1960 **Western** The Magnificent Seven
1992 **Western** Unforgiven
2003 **Samurai** Kill Bill: Vol. 1
2012 **Western** Django Unchained

CHINA
1928 **Wuxia** *Burning of the Red Lotus Temple*
2002 **Wuxia** *Hero*
2008 **Wuxia** *Red Cliff*

JAPAN
1937 **Samurai** *Humanity and Paper Balloons*
1954 **Samurai** *Seven Samurai*
1962 **Samurai** *Harakiri*
1962 **Samurai** *Chushingura*
2007 **Western** *Sukiyaki Western Django*

SOUTH KOREA
2008 **Western** *The Good, the Bad, the Weird*

TAIWAN
2000 **Wuxia** *Crouching Tiger, Hidden Dragon*

HONG KONG
1966 **Wuxia** *Come Drink With Me*
1971 **Wuxia** *A Touch of Zen*
1972 **Kung Fu** *Way of the Dragon*
1978 **Kung Fu** *Drunken Master*
1983 **Kung Fu** *Project A*
1991 **Kung Fu** *One Upon a Time in China*

THAILAND
2003 **Kung Fu** *Ong-Bak: Muay Thai Warrior*

INDIA
1975 **Western** *Sholay*

FIGURE 1.1   A global map of selected Warrior Hero Films.

CHAPTER 1
THE WARRIOR HERO

The Western Hero and the Samurai

In the early 1960s, when gun-toting cowboys dominated movie screens across America, audiences got to watch three Westerns with a curious connection. It was not the films' directors, stars, or stories that linked them to each other. *The Magnificent Seven* (1960), directed by John Sturges, is about an ill-assorted group of gunmen who defend a Mexican village from a band of brutal bandits (see Close-up: *The Magnificent Seven*). *The Outrage* (1964), directed by Martin Ritt, centers on an incident involving a robbery, a rape, and a corpse. In *A Fistful of Dollars* (*Per un pugno di dollari*, 1964), a Man with No Name arrives in a Mexican border town and sees a chance to make some money by playing two feuding families against each other. The movie was filmed in Spain by Sergio Leone, an Italian, featuring Clint Eastwood and a cast of European actors using phony American names. What these three movies had in common was their source. Sturges's film was based on *Seven Samurai* (1954), Ritt's film on *Rashomon* (1950), and Leone's on *Yojimbo* (*Bodyguard*, 1961). All three films were from Japan and directed by Akira Kurosawa.

Kurosawa set his movies during the long feudal period of his nation's history when samurai swordsmen roamed the countryside much as men with six-guns once wandered through the American West. Relics of a warrior society, masterless samurai called *ronin*, having lost their social status but not their skill, offered themselves as hired swords for money or adventure. The samurai hero, with his personal code of honor and swift sword, has fascinated Japanese audiences since the early days of cinema much as the Western film hero has captured and sustained popular interest both in the United States and abroad. Like other Japanese directors, Kurosawa freely acknowledged his interest in Westerns, just as American directors have acknowledged their debt to samurai films. Comparing these two genres is a good way to explore the dynamics of mutual cultural influence. In this

World Cinema through Global Genres, First Edition. William V. Costanzo.
© 2014 John Wiley & Sons, Inc. Published 2014 by John Wiley & Sons, Inc.

FIGURES 1.2 and 1.3   Two ways to settle a dispute: showdowns in the West and in the East.

FIGURE 1.2   Knife vs. gun in *The Magnificent Seven* (Dir. John Sturges, 1960).

FIGURE 1.3   Sword vs. sword in *Seven Samurai* (*Shichinin no samurai*, Dir. Akira Kurosawa, 1954).

chapter, we'll be using the term **warrior hero** to include samurai warriors, Western gunfighters, and a few other cinematic action figures. Although this broad term may not define an established genre as such, it will serve as a convenient starting point for comparing cultures and understanding how genres work.

Let's begin with a close look at two comparable scenes, one from *The Magnificent Seven* (Figure 1.2) and one from *Seven Samurai* (Figure 1.3).

Westerns are filled with violent face-offs, tense moments when two men fight each other to the death with weapons drawn. One of these moments takes place in *The Magnificent Seven* when an unnamed braggart boasts that he can shoot faster than Britt can throw a knife. Britt (played by James Coburn) is lying against a fencepost, his hat covering his eyes, minding his own business. The braggart tries to provoke him, kicking Britt's boot and calling him a coward. Britt rises slowly, saunters to one corner of the fence, and takes his position without saying a word. The other man takes a few paces, faces Britt, and calls for the starting signal. With astonishing speed, Britt's knife flies through the air, striking a post near the gunman before he can even draw. But this braggart will not concede defeat. He wants another round, this time for real. Watch how the scene is staged. The cowboy gear, cattle cars, and corral fence immediately place us in the world of the Wild West. We note how the characters are defined through dialogue and gesture, how the camera builds suspense by cutting back and forth between them. We pay attention to the reaction shots of other cowboys, particularly the close-ups of Chris (Yul Brynner), who we know is scouting talent for his squad of mercenaries. Reading these cues, we make decisions about who will win the duel, whose side we take, and why we care.

In *Seven Samurai*, the duelists fight with swords. When we arrive on the scene, they are already squaring off with bamboo sticks. The challenger makes a big show of it, charging at his quiet opponent with a mighty cry. When the braggart claims a tie, the master swordsman Kyuzo (Seiji Miyaguchi) simply says "No" and walks away, declining to kill this foolish stranger with a real sword. But the challenger, defending his bruised sense of honor, pushes for a battle to the death. We recognize the dramatic situation – two men fighting over a matter of pride – but a quick look at the setting tells us we are in feudal Japan, not on the American frontier. The architecture, weaponry, and clothing are among the many clues to place, character, and genre. Cinematically, Kurosawa uses some of the principles of camerawork and editing employed by Hollywood directors, but his pacing is much slower. He give more attention to the bystanders, especially to Takashi Shimura, Yul Brynner's counterpart, who mutters "What a waste." The social status of the warriors and peasants is clearly marked by their hats and swords, in contrast to the American West, where every cowboy wears a holster and a wide-brimmed hat. In fact, the social context of Kurosawa's action scenes is emphasized throughout *Seven Samurai*, reflecting a broad cultural difference between American individualism and the hierarchical, communal values of Japan. Who are the real heroes? What values do they live by? How are their actions shaped by local circumstances, generic conventions, and the changing trends of filmmaking? These kinds of questions about character and theme, cinematography and culture, are the motivating issues of this chapter.

Men with Guns: The Western Hero

Of all the film forms emanating from Hollywood, none seems as distinctively American as the Western. With its majestic stone mesas and cactus-dotted landscapes, its rowdy saloon brawls and high-noon showdowns, its slow-talking, fast-shooting cowboys in ten-gallon hats, the Western is arguably the American genre *par excellence*. Thomas Schatz calls it "the richest and most enduring genre of Hollywood's repertoire."[1] Historically, it has also been the most popular. As John Belton points out, in a period of more than 40 years, from 1926 to 1967, Hollywood produced more Westerns than any other kind of film.[2] Yet the taste for these films seems to waver. More than 800 Westerns were made during the 1950s, only about 200 in the 1960s, and a mere handful in the 1970s and 1980s, followed by a renewed interest in more recent times. What are the hallmarks of this genre? What accounts for its immense popularity, its rise, fall, and apparent revival? How did it begin, how did it evolve, and how do its shifting forms reflect changes in American culture?

Historians trace the Western to literary sources like *The Leatherstocking Tales*, a series of fictional adventures penned by James Fenimore Cooper in the early 1800s and loosely based on the real-life exploits of frontiersman Daniel Boone. Cooper's romanticized hero, called Natty Bumpo, inspired hundreds of dime novels later in the century, pulp fiction that fed the popular imagination for years to come. With the invention of motion pictures, Bumpo's offspring and their many tales made the leap from page to screen. In *Cripple Creek Bar-Room* (1899), early viewers got to spend one minute in a Wild West saloon. In *The Great Train Robbery* (1903), they witnessed a railroad holdup, and they were jolted in their seats when a mean-looking outlaw with a mustache and black hat pointed a pistol directly at the audience. Both movies were filmed in New Jersey, well before the industry itself headed west to Hollywood.

Anyone who has sat through several Westerns will recognize the genre's classical traits. Its setting is the vast, open western frontier that lured Americans in search of freedom, adventure, and economic opportunity from about 1840 to 1900. They came as pioneers, cattle ranchers, and fugitives, as men and women evading the social and legal restrictions of the East. The Western's cast of characters includes variations of the tough cowboy, the lonely sheriff, the loyal or deceitful Indian, the lady of easy virtue with a heart of gold. Their attire and accessories – a wide-brimmed hat, leather boots with spurs, holsters slung low over the hips, maybe a rifle and a marshal's badge – are distinctive icons. Familiar, too, are the stock scenes of cattle drives, saloon card games, stagecoach holdups, and the cowboy's silhouette riding off into the sunset.

These building blocks, the genre's basic lexicon, have been recombined and recycled at different moments in the nation's history to reflect particular historical concerns. During the Korean War, when American troops were halted at the 38th parallel separating Korea into north and south, Hollywood sent a contingent of cavalry across the Mexican border to victory in *Rio Grande* (1950). When news of the My Lai massacre troubled the conscience of Americans during the conflict in Vietnam, Arthur Penn dramatized a similar massacre of Indian women and children at Washita River, Oklahoma in *Little Big Man* (1970). During the 1990s, well after John Wayne and Gary Cooper had tied their horses to the hitching post for the last time, a number of "revisionist Westerns" breathed new life into old stories by giving fresh interpretations to stereotyped roles. Kevin Costner's *Dances with Wolves* (1990) pitted cowboys against Indians, but this time Native Americans held center stage and got to speak in their own tongues, rendered in English subtitles for audiences ignorant of the Pawnee and Sioux languages. Clint Eastwood's *Unforgiven* (1992) paired an aging gunfighter (Eastwood) with an African American sidekick (Morgan Freeman) hired to avenge a houseful of women. Far from glorifying its fast-drawing protagonists, *Unforgiven* presented an unattractive picture of the violence, misogyny, and problematic flows of capital in the Old West. A few years later, in Sam Raimi's *The Quick and the Dead* (1995), Sharon Stone showed that women can exact vengeance on their own. Dressed from hat to spurs in the outfit of a cowboy, Stone kicked open the swinging doors of the town saloon and confronted her enemies with six-guns drawn. By following the evolution of this distinctively American genre and its protagonists, it is possible to trace a partial trajectory of American cultural ideals.

In his early, influential essay on the Western hero, Robert Warshow[3] stresses the inner conflict of the gunfighter who lives by a strict code of honor, yet survives by killing other men. Typically, he is a man of action and few words, a rugged individual living on the border of civilized society. In *The Virginian* (1929), Gary Cooper sacrifices his friend to the higher demands of the code. He does what he must and lives with the guilt. In *High Noon* (1952), Cooper has married a pacifist and turned in his marshal's badge, but he is drawn into a violent showdown by the Hadley gang. Unable to recruit townspeople as deputies, he chooses to face the gang alone. In *The Searchers* (1956), John Wayne embarks on a long quest to find the

Comanche Indians who raped and killed members of his brother's family, a quest that he pursues with single-minded, some might say pathological ferocity. In *The Shootist* (1976), Wayne's last film, he plays a retired gunfighter dying of cancer, a legendary figure forced to fight old enemies and young would-be legends who want to kill him. The film is partly biographical (Wayne died of cancer three years later), signaling an end to the kind of ultra-masculine hero epitomized by Wayne.

No doubt, the Western's enormous popularity during the 1950s and 1960s had much to do with the appeal of this hero to American males at the time. A generation of men who had fought in World War II and were now raising families in the suburbs would understand the conflict between civilized society and the violence of the Wild West. Some see the classic Western as a clash of cultures, with women serving as ambassadors of social order and Indians representing the wilderness. In *Stagecoach* (1939), for example, the moralistic "Law and Order League" is run by women from the East while the Indians are faceless savages. Curly, the film's young hero (John Wayne in his breakthrough role), has little sympathy for the League's high-minded ways. In *The Searchers*, Wayne's character is closer to the Indians. He admires their tracking skills, follows their customs, and clearly belongs to their world of open spaces, in contrast to the domesticated interiors of his sister-in-law's homestead. Jim Kitses analyzes this contrast in broad thematic terms. For Kitses, the Western dramatizes a deep and persistent division in American life between the individual and the community, integrity and compromise, pragmatism and idealism, nature and culture, west and east.[4] For Kitses, the Western is a national myth that defines important features of American identity.

Yet, despite its distinctively American character, the genre appealed and continues to appeal to people well beyond the boundaries of the United States. In *The Sheriff of Fractured Jaw* (1958), an English gentleman becomes a sheriff after unintentionally stopping an Indian attack during his travels through the American West. An international co-production featuring stars from two countries (Britain's Kenneth More and America's Jayne Mansfield) and shot in Spain, it ushered in a flood of European Westerns. West Germans made them in Yugoslavia, building on the immense popularity of Karl Mai's adventure books for boys about Indian chief Winnetou and his white blood brother, known as Shatterhand. The actors in these Winnetou films (*The Treasure of Silver Lake/Der Schatz im Silbersee*, 1962, was the first in a long series) might be Germans, Austrians, Englishmen, Frenchmen, Hungarians, or Americans seeking work abroad. Soon Spanish and Italian production companies joined the wagon train, setting their stories in the back lots of Cinecittà Studios near Rome or in the arid desert region between Barcelona and Madrid.

The most famous of these "spaghetti Westerns" were directed by Italy's Sergio Leone. Unlike many of his European peers, Leone was not content to follow a prescribed Western formula. In his "Man with No Name" trilogy (*A Fistful of Dollars*; *For a Few Dollars More/Per qualche dollaro in più*, 1965; *The Good, the Bad and the Ugly/Il buono, il brutto, il cattivo*, 1966) and *Once Upon a Time in the West* (*C'era una volta il West*, 1968). Leone bought his own unique vision to the genre. His heroes and villains look uncannily alike. Dirty, sweaty, and unshaven in his poncho and black hat, the Man With No Name (played by Clint Eastwood in all three films) is a moral cipher, ambiguous in his motives, a man capable of brutal violence and random acts of decency, a loner who might save a poor family in distress for a few dollars, not for the cause of justice. Or he might clean up a town just because the bad guys annoy him. Perhaps because his films were dubbed, Leone paid more attention to their visual qualities and the music track than to their dialogue. Dramatic camera movements, extreme close-ups alternating with lengthy long shots, and Ennio Morricone's emotional scores are features of his signature style.

From Asia to Africa, non-Western filmmakers have also tried their hand at making Westerns. Some of them, like *Sukiyaki Western Django* (*Sukiyaki: Uesutan Jango*, 2007), by Japanese director Takashi Miike, and *The Good, the Bad, the Weird* (*Joheunnom nabbeunnom isanghannom*, 2008), by Korea's Kim Jee-woon, are homages to cult classics. Others, like *The Return of an Adventurer*, shot in Niger, bear more complex connections to the genre. *The Return of an Adventurer* (*Le retour d'un aventurier*, 1966) was made by Alassane Moustapha, one of black Africa's first film directors. It begins in a traditional African village when a character called Jimmy steps off an airplane carrying a suitcase filled with blue jeans, wide-brimmed hats, six-guns, and other souvenirs of the Old West. He distributes these outfits to his friends, who take on American names and immediately start to act like cliché cowboys. They drink whiskey, play cards, start a saloon brawl, and ride on horseback down to the local gulf, terrorizing the villagers. The film's imagery is riddled with incongruity: an airplane landing among thatched roofs, cowboys stampeding a herd of giraffes, a council of elders taking on the Kelly Gang. Moustapha exploits the conventions of comedy and Westerns to court African audiences that were raised on those genres. At the same time, he uses parody to poke fun at Hollywood, offering a sly critique of cultural imperialism. In India, Ramesh Sippy put the Western to yet another use. His *Sholay* (*Embers*, 1975) has become a classic in its own right. Set in a region of eastern India that resembles the American badlands, *Sholay* follows two petty criminals who are hired to save a town from marauding bandits. Although it makes frequent, self-conscious references to Leone, Sturges, and Peckinpah, this "curry Western" is also distinctively Indian, reflecting the native themes and aesthetics of Hindi cinema. *Sholay* offers a good opportunity for understanding how one culture appropriates another's native genre and adapts it for a home audience (see Close-up: *Sholay*). It's also an instructive example of how local warrior heroes can become part of a global mythology.

Men with Swords: The Samurai Tradition

When Akira Kurosawa began making *Seven Samurai* and *Yojimbo* in the 1950s and early 1960s, he was, like many other Japanese directors, well acquainted with American films. As a boy, he had laughed at Charlie Chaplin's acrobatic comedies and thrilled to the gritty cowboy adventures of William S. Hart. Kurosawa openly acknowledged his particular debt to the Westerns of John Ford. But whatever he owed to Hollywood, he was also drawing on a robust native tradition of samurai movies. Like the Western in the United States, the samurai genre was particularly popular for a 50-year period, from the 1920s through the 1960s. Japanese audiences flocked to these pictures to watch men with swords take on their enemies, and sometimes each other, in dazzling displays of courage and skill from a bygone age.

Comparisons between the historical settings of the Western and the samurai film can be tempting, but misleading. While the American frontier sprawled westward into the vast prairie heartland and more rugged regions of the Rockies and south-western deserts from roughly 1800 to 1890, civilization in Japan spread from west to east into the untamed land of the Kanto Plain, a rich agricultural area inhabited by the Ainu people. Samurai swordsmen were instrumental in fighting and displacing the indigenous Ainu, much as American pioneers, cavalry, and cowboys drove Cherokees and Navajos off their land. In fact, samurai have been called "pioneers with swords."[5] But the samurai belonged to a feudal order that had dominated Japan well before Europeans landed on the shores of North America. Highly trained and fiercely loyal to their lords, they followed a strict code of *Bushido*, "the way of the warrior." A typical samurai carried two swords, a two-foot long *daito* and the shorter *shaku*, but he could also wield the bow and arrow or fight unarmed, either on horse-back or on foot. As members of the warrior class, the samurai enjoyed a special sta-tus, but during the relatively peaceful Edo era, when all Japan was ruled by the Tokugawa family, many became bureaucrats and landowners. Still others lost their masters and their privileges, joining the ranks of unemployed *ronin* looking for work or adventure. These *ronin* held a particular fascination for Japanese audiences.

As with the storied heroes of the American frontier, tales of famous samurai circulated widely in oral narratives and popular printed fiction before the arrival of motion pictures. Samurai legends like Miyamoto Musashi, the fastest sword in Japan, appealed to Japanese children just as Wyatt Earp and Daniel Boone excited youngsters in the United States. Their exploits were also celebrated in the classical Kabuki theatre, which staged elaborate ritualistic swordfights called *tachimawari*, and later, less gracefully, in the *Shinkokugeki* (New National Drama), which appealed to spectators looking for more thrills than elegance. The bloodier, more realistic form of fighting came to be known as *chanbara*, an onomatopoeic word that imitates the clashing sound of swords: chan-chan, bara-bara.

The distinction between ritual and realism is crucial to any understanding of Japanese art forms, including motion pictures. Donald Richie, one of the West's most influential interpreters of Japanese aesthetics, points out that Japan has no tradition of what we call realism.[6] What passes for realistic in Japan seems highly stylized to most Westerners. Drama in Japan, like gardens and floral arrangements, is considered more lifelike when its elements are carefully trimmed and displayed for viewing. This emphasis on presentation rather than representation applies to movies too. According to Richie, the Japanese regarded film as a new form of theatre, not of photography as it was in France and the United States. To early Japanese directors, the film frame cor-responded to the stage, a site where action is composed, not simply captured.

Japanese movies are classified into two broad categories: *jidai-geki*, a generic term for historical dramas chiefly set during the Edo period (1603–1867), and *gendai-geki*, films about contemporary life. In the mid 1950s, *jidai-geki* accounted for nearly 40% of the country's total film production. By 1969, the figure had fallen to 8%.[7] What accounts for the extraordinary appeal of these period films and their most popular variety, the samurai film, at a moment in Japan's history when Westerns were reaching their height in the United States? To find an answer, we might look at the evolution of the samurai genre and its various subgenres.

Before World War II, the most notable samurai pictures tended to be deliberately unrealistic and ironic. Mansaku Itami's classic *Akanishi Kakita* (*Capricious Young Man*, 1936) pitted two swordsmen against each other. One, a superb warrior who follows the *Bushido* code, fights for glory and maintains an unquestionable loyalty to his corrupt master. The other, a comic figure who first seems spineless and inept, turns out to be the better samurai. Both roles are played by the same actor, underscoring the film's moral ambiguities. Sadao Yamanaka's *Humanity and Paper Balloons* (*Ninjo kami-fusen*, 1937) is set in the lower depths of eighteenth-century Tokyo, where a penniless *ronin* tries, but fails, to become a good samurai again. Unemployed and desperately poor, the protagonist becomes involved in a hare-brained kidnapping scheme that ends tragically. Such films, far from glorifying combat, tend to be critical of the militaristic fervor sweeping through Japan in the 1930s. It seems ironic, then, as film historian Michitaro Tada points out, that films like Itami's and Yamanaka's were banned during the Allied Occupation of Japan from 1945 to 1952. Among other things, the Supreme Command for the Allied Powers (SCAP), which controlled Japan after the war, prohibited films "favoring or approving feudal loyalty [and] direct or indirect approval of suicide," effectively making samurai films illegal.[8]

By the mid 1950s, though, the genre was making a huge comeback, led by the success of Kurosawa's *Seven Samurai* (see Close-up: *Seven Samurai*). David Desser identifies four subgenres that flourished in the postwar era.[9] The first of these he calls Nostalgic Samurai Dramas, which include films like Hiroshi Inagaki's *Chushingura*, (1962). Based on a Kabuki classic that was itself based on a true incident, *Chushingura* is an epic story of conflicting obligations and revenge (Figure 1.4). When their master is tricked and unfairly sentenced to death, his 47 vassals are commanded by the Shogun to break up his estate and disperse. They must decide whether to follow orders or obey their individual sense of justice. This conflict between duty (*giri*) and personal inclination (*ninjo* in Japanese) is a recurring theme in Japanese cinema and culture. But what makes Inagaki's film nostalgic is its elegiac tone, the way it savors a vanishing past. Desser links this sensibility to a Japanese predilection for "*mono no aware*," a "feeling of sweet sadness, or an almost inexpressible sensation of life's mortality which is pleasantly painful."[10] This poignant awareness that nothing lasts forever can be traced throughout Japanese art from *The Tale of Genji*, Lady Murasaki's classic novel, to landscape painting and haiku poetry. In *Chushingura*, we do not expect the heroes to outlive

FIGURE 1.4   A band of loyal warriors attack the stronghold of their master's wrongdoers in *Chushingura* (Dir. Hiroshi Inagaki, 1962). To some viewers, their black figures seem to advance across the snow like Japanese writing on rice paper.

the story, but we may take a deep, bittersweet satisfaction in acknowledging the transience of life.

Desser's second subgenre, the Anti-Feudal Drama, is exemplified by Masaki Koboyashi's *Harakiri* (*Seppuku*, 1962), in which the samurai hero loses his position through no fault of his own and avenges the death of his cherished son-in-law. Koboyashi's film, like others of its kind, is critical of the feudal order that placed individuals at odds with their better instincts. Desser finds a possible political message in the Anti-Feudal subgenre. By questioning the moral status of an outmoded system of military alliances, such films could be seen as protests against the Mutual Defense Pact of 1960 that made Japan a Cold War ally of the United States.

Desser calls his third category "Zen Fighters," a subgenre that allows the samurai hero to transcend the social contracts of his times by leaping into the spiritual realm. In Hiroshi Inagaki's *Samurai* (*Musashi Miyamoto*, aka *Samurai Trilogy*, 1954–1956), the hero learns the art of fencing from a Zen Buddhist monk. For years, he practices the martial arts, becoming a perfect samurai ready to face his lifelong enemy. In the paradoxical philosophy of Zen, the best swordsman never uses his sword. What enables him to triumph in battle is not caring if he wins or dies. Through such contradictory feats of logic and swordplay, Zen-based films like *Samurai* opened the way to yet another form of swordfight films. Desser calls this subgenre "The Sword Film," noting that its detractors use the term *chanbara* while its admirers connect the films to *jidai-geki*. Taken as a group, the Sword Film is characterized by generous bloodletting and towering body counts. The more limbs hacked off the better. In films like Kenji Misumi's *The Tale of Zatoichi* (*Zatoichi monogatari*, 1962) and the *Lone Wolf and Cub* (*Kozure Okami*) series (1972–1974), the heroes, far from being samurai or even *ronin*, might be humble peasants or even blind men who happen to be handy with a sword. Typically, the protagonist's main motives are money and spectacular displays of martial dexterity, though he may have a good heart and harbor a sense of justice. Ultimately, though, his efforts are empty and meaningless. A relentless strain of nihilism runs through this most popular of movie entertainments.

The rough progression of samurai films from celebrations of a vanished past to ahistorical slaughterfests seems much like the evolution of Westerns from Ford to Tarantino, part of a global trend toward more explicit violence. But we should not lose sight of the differences between the pasts being celebrated or the sources of these violent impulses. Japanese society during the Edo period was strictly hierarchical, a system of castes and loyalties fixed by birth. If you were born into the samurai class, you enjoyed the rights of your rank but you were also bound by certain prescribed duties. Your identity, your meaning as an individual, was dependent on your place within the social order. The rules by which you conducted your life were not personal, but part of the *Bushido* code. The central conflict for a samurai, then, is usually a choice between competing social commitments (*giri*) or between *giri* and his individual humanity (*ninjo*), but always in a social context.

The Western hero, by contrast, lives on the frontier of civilization and the wilderness, continually drawn to the call of the wild beyond and within. Whereas the samurai is usually tied to a distinct social role, the cowboy is more likely a loner, answerable only to his conscience and his personal code. While the samurai follows a centuries-old tradition of stringently defined conduct, the cowboy adheres to a vaguely articulated sense of honor. As Lee J. Cobb puts it to Clint Eastwood in Don Siegel's *Coogan's Bluff* (1968), "a man's got to do what a man's got to do." But the behavior of both figures is very much alike. They both do a lot of heavy drinking, engage in occasional womanizing at the saloon or the local public house, and continually practice their fighting skills, the swordsman even more than the gunslinger. Rarely seen without their weapons, they strike iconic poses when confronted with a duel. The images of John Wayne, palms poised above his holsters, or Toshiro Mifune set to unsheathe his deadly *daito* were irresistible models for millions of young males.

While the samurai film is traditionally a male-dominated genre, women often appear as prostitutes or innocent girls about to be turned into courtesans. Like the samurai himself, they are indentured to the system; they are owned. Their main weapon is their sexuality. But they may also be fighters. The Kabuki theatre had its *onnabudo* (samurai women), and some cinematic female fighters, like the heroine of Tokuzo Tanaka's *Wet Haired Beauty* (*Nuregami Botan*, 1961), could cross swords with the best male fighters. By the beginning of the new millennium, women warriors were soundly beating their male and female opponents with swords, guns, and bare hands. Watch how Uma Thurman takes on Lucy Liu (Figure 1.5), Vivica A. Fox, and David Carradine in Quentin Tarantino's *Kill Bill* series (2003–2004), reshuffling the weaponry of Hollywood Westerns and the samurai tradition in a multicultural, trans-Pacific bloodfest.

The term warrior fits the samurai better than the Western gunslinger. Samurai were professional combatants, born into a military class and trained to live or die by the sword. The Western hero assumed his role by choice. He became a sheriff

FIGURE 1.5   West meets East. Uma Thurman crosses swords with Lucy Liu in *Kill Bill: Vol. 2* (Dir. Quentin Tarantino, 2004).

or a hired gun because he was a better shot or possessed more courage than other men. Yet both inhabited a world where violence ruled the day. If the American frontier was not officially a combat zone, it still required a soldier's skills and outlook to survive. This may help to explain why the samurai film, like the Western, enjoyed such popularity soon after World War II. For American and European males, the historical West resembled the lawless, violent no man's land of combat. The Western became a stage for acting out aggressive impulses unleashed beyond the pale of ordinary civilized society. For Japanese audiences, the Edo period may have served a similar purpose, but with a gloomier perspective. The sun seemed to be rising on America's future and setting on Japan's celebrated past. At the end of the movie, while the cowboy rides off into the sunset to live another day, the samurai knows his day is done.

Enchanted Swords and Flying Fists: Wuxia and Kung Fu

Meanwhile, somewhere in China, another kind of warrior hero was preparing to enter the fray. Armed with magic swords, deadly potions, and feats of gravity defying acrobatics, this sword-wielding warrior with supernatural powers burst forth on the global screen at the beginning of the new millennium in Ang Lee's *Crouching Tiger, Hidden Dragon* (2000). To most Western audiences, the sight of a beautiful young woman (Zhang Ziyi) exchanging sword thrusts with her male antagonist (Chow Yun Fat) high in the canopy of a bamboo forest appeared as something fresh and alluringly strange. Leaping and parrying from branch to branch, swaying with the motions of the wind, the couple seemed to be caught in a medley of erotic dance and mortal combat.

For Chinese viewers, though, the movie's characters and props were nothing new. They belonged to an ancient narrative tradition dating back well before the advent of American cowboys or Japanese samurai, a form of storytelling known as *wuxia*. *Wuxia* is a kind of chivalrous combat. The word *wu*, connoting valor, refers to the Chinese word for martial arts, *wushu*. The word *xia* has been variously translated as hero, swordsman, adventurer, soldier of fortune, warrior, or roving knight. The *wuxia* protagonist is often an independent mercenary swordsman who follows a strict moral code, not unlike the Japanese *ronin*, the European knight errant, or the hired gun of the American West. Historically, *xia* warriors dominated the Warring States period in China before the first Qin emperor suppressed them around 220 BC and replaced the old feudal system with a legalistic monarchy. The *xia* class gravitated to the lower levels of society, tarnishing their reputation, but emerged again at different times as Shaolin monks, secret societies, and various disenfranchised groups, which sometimes included women and minorities. During the Ming dynasty (1368–1644), stories were told of a secret Underground – *jianghu* in Mandarin, literally "rivers and lakes" – composed of vagrants, priests, cultists, beggars, outlaws, impoverished scholars, and other refugees from the social mainstream. In the legendary *jianghu*, a high value is placed on extraordinary martial skills, honor, loyalty, and the sacred duty of revenge. There are also strong strains of fantasy and romance in *wuxia* literature. The young lovers are often masters of the martial arts with superhuman skills fighting side by side.

The Chinese films from which Ang Lee drew much of his inspiration grew out of this *wuxia* literature much as the American Western sprang from the pages of pulp fiction. The visual elements of the genre – exciting action, exotic settings, larger-than-life heroes, ingenious props – and its appeal to mass audiences made it a natural for the mass medium of motion pictures. Like Hollywood Westerns, wuxia movies date back to the early days of silent films. *Burning of the Red Lotus Temple* (*Huo shao hong lian si*, 1928), based on a book by Xian Kairen, spawned a generation of violent fighters who delivered lethal blows and flew across the screen. The escalating violence and political subtexts in these films led the government to ban their production in the 1930s. In the 1950s, they reappeared in a more traditional form, linked stylistically to Chinese opera and conventional moral themes. It was in the 1960s, however, that the genre really took off. Energized by feats of graceful choreography, ingenious wirework, and increasingly complex characters and plots, the "new style" wuxia movies of this period gained widespread popularity.

After the Communist Revolution, when the People's Republic of China stopped making martial arts films, the genre's creative center shifted to the island of Taiwan and to Hong Kong, the British Colony on the mainland's southern coast to which much of the Shanghai film industry had fled during the 1930s. The largest producer in Hong Kong was the Shaw Brothers Studio, led by Sir Run Run Shaw and his brother Runme Shaw. Efficiently run, with a large stable of stars, the Shaw Brothers Studio made Hong Kong the "Hollywood of the East." In the mid-1960s, many of these films were made in Mandarin Chinese for a population in exile, nostalgic stories set in the old homeland like King Hu's *Come Drink With Me* (*Da zui xia*, 1966). Meanwhile, a new generation was coming of age in Hong Kong, less rooted in the mainland. When this generation started making movies in the mid-1970s, they adopted the local Cantonese language and breathed new life into a film form known as *kung fu*. Kung fu featured fighting without weapons. It favored masculine heroes like Bruce Lee, who popularized the form with *Way of the Dragon (Meng long guo jiang*, 1972) and *Enter the Dragon (Long zheng hu dou*, 1973). Like their wuxia predecessors, kung fu movies were mostly high testosterone ritual combats between men. It is this masculine subgenre, with its male bonding and secret brotherhoods, that made the strongest impact on American audiences. It also left an imprint on American films, from *First Blood* (1982) and *Lethal Weapon* (1987) to *The Matrix* (1999) and *Kill Bill: Vol. 1* and *Vol. 2*.

The gradual merger of these two traditions, as with the cross-fertilization of Westerns and samurai films, is part of the larger story of globalization. Today's action movies, with or without subtitles, are likely to blend elements of kung fu hand chops, wuxia wirework, samurai swordsmanship, and a Western saloon brawl in a single fight scene.

Evolution of the Wuxia Hero

When Zhang Shichuan showed *Burning of the Red Lotus Temple* in 1928, he hardly realized that his silent film would start a cinematic conflagration. Released serially in 18 installments over three years, it offered thrilling action scenes that kept local audiences coming back for more. Its extravagant displays of the martial arts, androgynous women warriors, and elaborate special effects set standards for the industry and inspired a flock of imitators. During the four-year period from 1928 to 1932, some 50 studios turned out an estimated 241 wuxia films, about 60% of the city's total motion picture output.[11] Many of these films were loosely based on classical texts, like *The Cave of the Spider-Spirit (Pansi dong*, 1927), adapted from the popular sixteenth-century novel *Journey to the West (Xi you ji)*. Others took their plots from contemporary newspapers, magazines, or comics, which catered to the craze with serialized stories of dark magic and flying assassins.

In contrast to the early Westerns and samurai films, the women in these pictures were often fierce and valiant fighters, as their titles announced: *The Female Knight-Errant (Nuxia li feifei*, 1925), *Five Vengeful Girls (Wunu fuchou*, 1928), *The Great Woman (Wu dalishi*, 1929), *The Female Pirate (Wu haidao*, 1929), *Girl Bandit (Lan guniang*, 1930), *Woman Bodyguard (Nu biaoshi*, 1931).[12] Actresses like Wu Lizhu (1910–1978), Hu Die (1908–1989), Wu Suxin (1905–?), and Fan Xuepeng (1908–1974) were stars on a par with their male counterparts. Audiences cheered when the heroine in *Swordswoman of Yellow River* series (*Huangjiang nuxia*, 1929–1932) leapt across chasms and over courtyard walls. They roared as Cloud Maiden, the orphan girl in *Red Heroine (Hong xia*, 1929), learned the martial arts from her old Daoist mentor, the White Monkey, defeated an evil band of scantily dressed females, and vanished into the sky in a cloud of smoke.

If the wuxia fad excited the masses, it did not go down well with the new Nationalist government and intellectuals from the left or right, who wanted to modernize the country. Concerned that superstitious tales and images of China's feudal past might impede the march of progress, or perhaps worried by the low production values and competitive chaos of the movie market, officials soon banned the genre on the mainland.

When it reappeared again in Hong Kong in the 1960s, wuxia took on new directions. Chang Cheh, who directed more than 100 films for the Shaw Brothers studio in his long career, introduced the hero with a handicap. In *One-Armed Swordsman* (*Dubei dao*, 1967), Fang Gang, the top student at a martial arts school, is scorned by his high-born classmates for his lowly origins. When the master's jealous daughter challenges him to a fight without weapons, he easily defeats her, but in a moment of impetuous rage she cuts off his arm with a sword. Despite this disability, he masters the art of one-armed swordplay with the help of a secret manual and a beautiful orphan. Like Gary Cooper's Quaker wife in *High Noon*, the orphan implores Fang to give up his violent career for the peaceful life of farming, and he agrees, but an insistent sense of duty to his master and his comrades keeps calling him back. In the film's bloody conclusion, Fang hacks his way triumphantly through a throng of foes before returning to his woman and walking with her hand in hand into a landscape that looks a little like the American prairie. Chang gleaned some of his ideas from samurai films, especially the Zatoichi Blind Swordsman series. His protagonists typically spring from the lower classes and achieve their skills through diligent practice, forming strong bonds with other young men. Like Robin Hood and his merry followers, these robust bands of brothers in arms protect the weak and innocent from harm, but they wreak more bloodshed and destruction than their English counterparts. In time, they learned to mix their swordplay with the flying fists and rapid legwork of kung fu. Chang (also known as Zhang) has come to be revered as "the godfather of Hong Kong martial arts cinema," leaving a legacy for filmmakers like Zhang Yimou and Quentin Tarantino, who dedicated *Kill Bill: Vol. 2* to him.

Another master of wuxia films was King Hu (aka Hu Jinquan), who brought a new level of technical artistry and a touch of Buddhist philosophy to the genre. Hu also drew on his knowledge of samurai movies, integrating their camera techniques with Western editing conventions and adding elements from Chinese opera to usher in a new style of swordplay cinema. In *Come Drink With Me*, Cheng Pei-Pei plays Golden Swallow, sent to rescue her brother from a gang of bandits who hold him hostage at a local inn. She quickly dispatches the brigands (Figure 1.6) and befriends a drunken beggar who turns out to be a master of the martial arts and head of a secret society. In contrast to the rough and tumble male vs. male fighting in Chang Cheh's films, King Hu staged his fight scenes like ballets, emulating the ritualized action of Peking Opera. It's no accident that Cheng Pei-Pei had been a professional dancer. When Ang Lee made *Crouching Tiger, Hidden Dragon* in 2000, he cast Cheng Pei-Pei as the evil mentor to his young wuxia heroine, played by Zhang Ziyi, who dispatches her foes in balletic leaps (Figure 1.7), much as her predecessor did in the 1960s.

King Hu, originally a northerner from Beijing transplanted to Hong Kong, left the Shaw Brothers in 1966 and moved to Taiwan, where he made cult classics such

FIGURES 1.6 and 1.7   The wuxia woman warrior then and now.

FIGURE 1.6   Golden Swallow (played by Cheng Pei-Pei) routs a gang of armed thugs at the inn in *Come Drink With Me* (*Da zui xia*, Dir. King Hu, 1966).

FIGURE 1.7   King Hu's wuxia heroine inspired a similar scene in Ang Lee's *Crouching Tiger, Hidden Dragon* (*Wo hu cang long*, 2000), in which Zhang Ziyi is the heroine and Cheng Pei-Pei plays a villain.

as *Dragon Gate Inn* (*Long men ke zhan*, 1966) and *A Touch of Zen* (*Xia nu*, 1971). His heroines occupy a superior position in these films. Morally and physically, they stand above the rabble, tough yet graceful, energetic yet disciplined, never losing their femininity. One of Hu's favorite settings is the inn, which becomes a mythical space where the principles of physics are suspended and the confinements of architecture are transcended. In *The Fate of Lee Khan* (*Ying chun ge zhi Fengbo*, 1973), the waitresses at the Spring Inn are all skilled martial artists who defy the rules of gravity, leaping among the tables and gliding over rafters, propelling the bodies of their foes through space like weightless dolls. Their actions, though, are not gratuitous roughhousing. They are motivated by a patriotic cause: to rid the country of foreign rulers, the Mongol invaders. The fact that these women come from the margins of society is typical of wuxia heroes. One is a pickpocket, another a street performer, a third is a con artist, while a fourth specializes in highway robbery. Together, they form an underground sorority of extraordinary fighters, much like the Tang Dynasty rebels in Zhang Yimou's *House of Flying Daggers* (*Shi mian mai fu*, 2004). These women, like drunken masters and one-armed swordsmen, can be seen as symbolic figures in a national narrative. Their seemingly weak and afflicted bodies represent the body of the beleaguered Chinese people waiting for the right moment to emerge strong, resilient, and victorious.

Zhang Yimou's "Hero" and Chinese Aesthetics

Zhang Yimou went further still, refining the genre and redefining its notions of the hero. In *Hero* (*Ying xiong*, 2002), he invented a new kind of action scene, lyrical in its rhythms and more deeply dyed with emotions. Conventional wuxia action scenes are first and foremost fights: bone-jarring contests between martial artists out to prove their prowess. Zhang's scenes are more like dances of color, highly choreographed moments that interrupt the story like lyrics in a musical. Yet they also continue the narrative, using movement instead of words to drive the story forward. His actors convey a wide range of feelings in balletic lunges, swoops, and glides. Their actions come from the heart, not just from the hip. Sometimes, the emotional tenor of a scene is underscored with music, often in striking counterpoint to the action, as when a flight of melancholy female voices soars above the pointed thrusts of Moon and Flying Snow fencing in the oak grove. Sometimes a scene's emotional textures are reflected and magnified in the landscape, in the serene surface of a lake or the steady pulse of rain dripping from the eaves of a pavilion. There is something uniquely personal in Zhang's style, and something distinctly Chinese, an aesthetic sensibility rooted in the graceful rigors of classical Chinese music, poetry, and painting.

One of the film's most striking features is its use of color. Each segment of the story is associated with a different hue. The first section saturates the screen in a vivid red, the color of love and death. The walls of the calligraphy school and the students' robes are bathed in a deep scarlet. When Moon challenges Flying Snow in the autumn grove, the falling leaves turn crimson. The setting that ends section two, when Nameless confronts Broken Sword on the lake, sets the tone for another episode: a span of blues echoed in the sky, the water, and the warriors' robes. In the third segment, when Flying Snow rides to save her lover in the desert, the camera picks up the sandy whites of Kazakhstan, a tint repeated in the costumes and in the décor of the bamboo library. Later on, a pale green tinges the flashback in which Broken Sword and Flying Snow attack the palace in flowing lime-colored robes, a hue reflected in the still, jade waters of the Li River and which prefigures the fight between Nameless and the king among cascades of floating emerald curtains.

A prism of perceptions and perspectives, *Hero* is also a beautifully painted work of art. Zhang has always been an extraordinary colorist, a fact that shines through the glowing reds of *Raise the Red Lantern* (*Da hong deng long gao gao gua*, 1991) and *Red Sorghum* (*Hong gao liang*, 1987) or the brilliant yellow swaths of cloth hanging in the dye factory of *Ju Dou* (1990). Such rich colors are atypical of traditional Chinese painting, which favors the subtle shades of pen and ink. They are more characteristic of Chinese folk art, the brightly colored "peasant paintings" produced in the northern province of Shaanxi where Zhang worked on his first films. The style is said to have developed in the late 1950s when peasants working on a new reservoir began documenting their progress in pictures. Without ready-made materials, they created their own paints from soot, lime, and the local red soil. Later, during the Cultural Revolution, professional artists sent into the hinterlands were fascinated by this work and publicized it abroad. Zhang's cinematic palette may owe something to this vivid local color drawn from the natural surroundings. But Zhang makes movies, not paintings. If the primary ingredient of motion pictures is motion, his movies are pure cinema. In *Hero*, the entire screen is filled with things in movement: countless raindrops pouring from the sky, hosts of arrows soaring through the air, a cyclone of red and yellow leaves whirling round the characters as they carry on their deadly duel. At times, the actors and their actions seem to blur into a work of abstract art, like a Jackson Pollock canvas in motion.

Some critics found *Hero* too abstract, too kinetic, too "arty." Asian viewers accused Zhang of selling out to Western audiences with a big-budget action epic. Others, mostly non-Asian, found him guilty of distorting history, of emphasizing visual effects at the expense of character development, and of muddling the story with a convoluted structure. Zhang justified his choices in transcultural terms. "I tried to get across themes that would be understood by a Western audience," he said. "There are elements that are purely Chinese, but I made an effort to keep a balance between the two."[13] *Hero*, he emphasized, is not so much an art house film as a commercial action movie.

On the Chinese side, *Hero* connects swordplay to other forms of traditional culture like chess, music, and calligraphy. When Sky faces Nameless at the chess pavilion, the location itself is telling. The ancient Chinese board game of Go (*weiqi* in Mandarin), often likened to chess, is a cerebral game of martial strategy. Each player tries to eliminate the other player's army, represented by smooth black or white stones, by encircling the opponent's stones. Simple in appearance, the game is actually highly complex and analytic. Among good players, every move is first carefully planned and executed in the mind. These parallels between Go and the martial arts are underscored by the black and white scene in which Sky and Nameless do battle with lance and sword. The entire sequence of lunges, parries, and elaborate evasions takes place in their heads, indicated by the colorless photography, while both men stand motionless confronting each other. When the fight begins, a blind musician starts to play an ancient song. "Martial arts and music share the same principles," says Nameless. "Both wrestle with complex chords and rare melodies." As the clash of weapons mingles with the old man's strident voice, raindrops land on blades and chess board like individual notes of music. A string breaks and the fight resumes in color. Nameless's sword smashes through ribbons of rain, turning them one by one into spray as we hear his weapon slashing toward Sky, catching him just under his lance, and he falls. Nameless sheathes his sword before Sky's weapon falls to the stone floor, yielding to stillness and the sound of dripping rain.

Zhang explores another set of analogies between traditional Chinese arts and the martial arts in the calligraphy school sequence. Nameless has come to the school, he says, to get a scroll for his dying father. He asks Broken Sword to write the word for sword (*jian*), alluding to the rumor that Sword's skills with the blade (*jianfa*) are rooted in his calligraphy, or writing skills (*shufa*). Holding a stick above a sandbox like a pen over paper, Broken Sword begins to write in the sand but decides that red ink is required for the job. Later, with the arrows of Qin's attacking army whizzing past him, Broken Sword plucks an arrow from the air and holds it like a pen. In the act of writing, his whole body moves as if he were wielding a sword (Figure 1.8). His movements are not so much external actions as emanations from within. Calligraphy and combat, we understand, require coordinated motions of the wrist and heart.

The journey to this insight calls for more than physical agility and skill, as King Qin explains: "In the first stage, man and sword become one and each other. Here even a blade of grass can be used as a lethal weapon. In the next stage, the sword resides not in the hand but in the heart. Even without a weapon, the warrior can

FIGURE 1.8   Zhang Yimou explores affinities between the traditional Chinese arts of calligraphy and sword fighting in *Hero* (*Ying xiong*, Dir. Zhang Yimou, 2002).

slay his enemy from a hundred paces. But the ultimate ideal is when the sword disappears altogether. … only peace remains." This description of the hero's progress evokes ancient principles of Daoism that precede the Qin Dynasty. Laozi, the supposed founder of Daoism, sought an alternative to the feudal warfare of his times in the balance and harmony of nature. The path to universal peace requires a willingness to embrace nothingness, a total renunciation of the self – a path trodden by countless Chinese individuals throughout their history.

Male or female, nameless or renowned, the wuxia hero shares a mythic dimension with other wandering warriors. Like the medieval knight errant, the Western gunman, and the masterless samurai, he or she appears during times of anarchy. These people are usually underdogs, drawn from the flotsam and jetsam of a world in disarray, subversive figures who do battle with the unworthy powers in charge, aiding the poor and oppressed, following strict codes of justice and integrity. Historically, they evoke the lawless eras of the American West, Tokugawa Japan, or the Warring States period of China, reappearing on the screen in our own times of distress when people seek icons of personal empowerment. Psychologically, as followers of Carl Jung might say, their magical abilities and supernatural powers spring from the realm of the collective unconscious, a reservoir of archetypal images that represent deep-seated spiritual and emotional needs. Watching these movies together in the dark, we share a kind of universal dream. The breathless, heart-pounding action on the movie screen, a projection of our innermost fears and desires, engages us in a visceral experience, enabling us to work out the psychic tangles of our inner lives by proxy, leaving us elated, cleansed, and satisfied.

The Kung Fu Craze Begins

Tough and irrepressible, ever shifting with the times, the warrior hero with a thousand faces underwent yet another transformation in 1970s Hong Kong. Although its precise origin is obscure, the term *kung fu* (local dialect for Mandarin *gong fu*) means something like "skill master." The kung fu practitioner fights expertly with bare hands and feet. In contrast to the wuxia swordsman and swordswoman, who rely on polished blades and supernatural stunts, kung fu artists depend on their bodies alone, achieving mastery through rigorous training and practice. While the wuxia hero belongs to the chivalrous fantasy world of ancient China, kung fu is more straightforward and pragmatic, an achievable skill for those who live in a modern urban environment like Hong Kong, Singapore, or Los Angeles.

How does a transnational genre like kung fu emerge in a particular place at a particular time? Hong Kong, remember, is a city, not a nation, a multicultural community with strong connections to mainland China, yet increasingly cosmopolitan in attitude and outlook. As a former British colony, a harbor town, a settlement of immigrants, it has absorbed influences from the greater Southeast Asian region and the West. In this atmosphere of receptivity and open competition, with easy access to international resources, and relatively free from the government restrictions imposed in Shanghai, Beijing, or Taiwan, filmmakers in Hong Kong were able to follow their creative impulses, producing new subgenres and fresh styles. By the 1960s, Shaw Brothers and their rival studio Cathay had established a vertically integrated infrastructure for producing, distributing, and exhibiting movies not only in local theaters but throughout the Chinese diaspora and into non-Chinese-speaking communities abroad. The popular genres of earlier years – historical costume dramas, musicals, romantic melodramas, and wuxia films – had run their course. Something new was needed, something to appeal to a young generation of urbanized filmgoers, better educated, comparatively more affluent, less tied to the traditional values of their rural parents and ready for a new kind of hero. The time was ripe for Bruce Lee and Jackie Chan.

Enter the little dragon: Bruce Lee

In his short lifetime (1940–1973), Lee achieved the status of a global kung fu icon. A Chinese American actor, director, screenwriter, and founder of the Jeet Kune Do fighting philosophy of "Intercepting Fists," no other figure accomplished so much to promote the martial arts throughout the world. He was born in San Francisco's Chinatown (his Cantonese name was Lee Jun Fan, and he later adopted the stage name of Li Xiao Long, or "little dragon") and moved to Hong Kong with his father, a leading film and Cantonese opera performer, just months before the Japanese invasion of the city. The crowded neighborhood where he grew up teemed with refugees. The streets were ruled by rival gangs. Young Lee was forced to defend himself, learning the Wu style of *t'ai chi* fighting from his father and eventually enrolling in the Wing Chun School of close combat, but ultimately developing his own hybrid form of self-defense.

Like many martial arts forms, Wing Chun evolved in Southern China during the resistance movement against the foreign Qing dynasty. Its philosophy stresses body structure and balance. The Wing Chun stance is like bamboo, flexible yet firm. Rooted in the ground and positioned along a vertical axis, the practitioner recovers swiftly from attack or strikes out with straight punches and short kicks. The Wu family style of *t'ai chi* training involves a lot of jumping, tumbling, and grappling. It stresses the philosophy of "pushing hands," enabling the fighter to redirect an opponent's force instead of resisting it. The Wu practitioner learns to sense her foe's intentions, using her opponent's energy and strength against himself. David Bordwell, an astute observer of the action in martial arts films, contrasts this "soft" approach of southern *t'ai chi* (fist fighting) styles to the "hard" style favored in northern China. The soft style relies on upper-body strength, perhaps because so many people in southern China developed their hands and arms through centuries of carrying heavy burdens or pushing boats with poles. The hard approach, where force meets force directly in explosive bursts of energy, depends more on fancy legwork, akin to the graceful acrobatics of Peking Opera, perhaps because northerners were used to walking long distances and controlling horses with their legs.[14] Bruce Lee assimilated elements from all these styles, as well as Western boxing and European fencing, in his Jeet Kun Do philosophy. Lee did not consider this a system or a school but a pragmatic compilation of methods and ideas, a set of tools that should be practiced and applied to different situations.

In his first major movie, *The Big Boss* (*Tang shan da xiong*, 1971), Lee plays Chen Zhen, an immigrant from southern China working with his cousins in an ice factory in Thailand. When he learns that the boss is behind the mysterious disappearance of his cousins, he vows to take revenge. Released in several versions for different markets, *The Big Boss* made Lee a star throughout Asia. Lee plays the same character in his next film, *Fist of Fury* (*Jing wu men*, 1972), set in an international compound in Shanghai, where the native population is harassed by Japanese racists. Once again, he assumes the role of protecting his people against ill treatment by foreigners. Neither of these two films was initially popular with American audiences, a fact reflected in the confusing array of titles they were given in the United States.[15] Lee's international career really took off with his next two movies, the first of which he wrote and directed himself. *Way of the Dragon* (1972) is set in Rome. Lee's character, Tang Lung, has come from Hong Kong to help out with a restaurant owned by friends of the family but which is under threat by the local crime syndicate. The film's big showdown, a one-on-one match between Tang and the famous karate fighter Colt (played by Chuck Norris), takes place in the Colosseum, a battle to the death. Despite its fierce combat scenes, *Way of the Dragon* is more playful than the earlier films. Tang's naivety and ignorance of European ways is the target of much humor, though he always has the last laugh (see Close-up: *Way of the Dragon*).

Lee's last completed work was *Enter the Dragon* (1973), a Hong Kong/Hollywood coproduction, the first Chinese martial arts film to be produced by a major American studio (Warner Brothers) in conjunction with Hong Kong studios (Golden Harvest and Lee's Concord Production Company). As directed by Robert Clouse, *Enter the Dragon* is an action film. Its focus is on spectacle and physical sensation rather than the coherence of its plot or the psychology of its characters. It is also another chance to see Lee's body in performance, stripped to the waist and ready for a fight. This time he is a member of a Shaolin Temple, recruited to investigate an alumnus of the Temple, the mysterious Han, who is suspected of using a tournament on his private island to front an opium operation. Lee teams up with two Americans, a white gambler hiding from the mafia and a black activist on the run from the law, to infiltrate the competition.

Lee never made another movie. He died under mysterious circumstances six days before the film's scheduled release. He was hailed by some as a nationalist hero, a fierce foe of foreign intervention. For Asians and many urban minorities, particularly African American and Hispanic youths, he stood as a model of non-white masculinity, a positive force for power and dignity in the face of racial prejudice. For others, he appeared xenophobic and narcissistic, inciting ill will against outsiders and indulging in excessive admiration for his own body. Perhaps the most important lesson of his screen persona and his private life can be summed up by the ironic wisdom of his Shaolin master: the enemy is only an illusion; the real enemy is oneself.

Jackie Chan: Master of kung fu comedy

If the 1970s was the decade of Bruce Lee, the 1980s belonged to Jackie Chan. Born in Hong Kong in 1954 (his given name, Chan Kong Sang, means "born in Hong Kong"), he shaped his personal life into a successful screen persona that catapulted him to the top of the Southeast Asian movie charts, where he dominated the box office for more than 20 years. With over 100 movies to his credit, his impressive resume spans the occupations of actor, action choreographer, comedian, entrepreneur, director, martial artist, producer, screenwriter, stuntman, singer, and producer. In contrast to Lee's screen character, who is sternly confident of his ability from the beginning, Chan's character starts out as a cocky, often bungling novice who comes by his fighting skills the hard way, through painstaking training and determination, with plenty of beatings along the way. If Lee is an emblem of cultural pride, a rock-solid model of ethnic identity, Chan offers a self-ironic hero, a comic figure who undercuts his obvious talent with playful acts of buffoonery. His character is basically decent and upstanding, but lazy and mischievous, a mediocre student of the martial arts until something or someone changes his attitude. Then he undergoes a lengthy preparation and an escalating series of fight sequences that inevitably lead to the main villain. He emerges victorious but often bruised and bandaged.

When he was six years old, Chan's family moved to Australia, but he was sent back after a year to a special Peking Opera school. This is where he learned the skills of music, dance, tumbling, acrobatics, and kung fu. For ten years, young Chan endured the strenuous instruction and frequent beatings that figure so notably in his films. It is also where he began performing, both on stage and on screen, getting small roles in films by Han Hsiang Li (*The Love Eterne/Liang Shan Bo yu Zhu*

FIGURE 1.9 Jackie Chan, doing his own stunts, hangs from a clock face in *Project A* (*"A" gai wak*, Dir. Jackie Chan, 1983).

Ying Tai, 1963), King Hu (*Come Drink with Me*), and Bruce Lee (*Fist of Fury, Enter the Dragon*).

Chan came into his own in 1978 with *Snake in the Eagle's Shadow* (*Se ying diu sau*) and *Drunken Master* (*Zui chan*), which set the bar for kung fu comedy. In these films, Chan befriends disheveled old beggars who turn out to be kung fu masters in disguise and teach him a style of fighting that enables him to trounce his adversaries. Both films were directed by Yuen Woo-ping, who later choreographed the action for *The Matrix* (1999), *Crouching Tiger, Hidden Dragon*, and the *Kill Bill* films. After several pictures for Lo Wei Studio and Golden Harvest in Hong Kong, Chan appeared in a few Hollywood films (*Battle Creek Brawl*, 1980; *The Cannonball Run*, 1981) before returning home to make *Project A* (*"A" gai wak*, 1983), *Wheels on Meals* (*Kuai can che*, 1984), and *Police Story* (*Ging chat goo si*, 1985). In all these films, Chan performed his own stunts, much as did American comedians of the silent period. In a scene in *Project A* reminiscent of Harold Lloyd in *Safety Last!* (1923), he falls 60 feet from the hands of a clock tower through two flimsy awnings to the hard ground, head first (Figure 1.9). In *Wheels on Meals*, he zooms around a square in Barcelona on a skateboard (think of Chaplin on roller skates in *Modern Times*, 1936), serving food to tourists and whipping a gang of surly bikers. *Police Story* ends in a shopping mall, where Chan leaps from a ledge and slides down a pole wrapped in light bulbs, popping the bulbs and crashing through a glass ceiling on the way down. Buster Keaton couldn't have made a better exit.

With their overseas settings, multiethnic casts, and sly allusions to world cinema, Chan's movies catered increasingly to an international market. Audiences around the globe warmed to his everyman character, enjoyed his humor and grace, and appreciated the fact that he did his own acrobatics with a minimum of gimmicks or special effects. When you watch Jackie Chan, you feel his energy. The constant motion of his body propels the movie forward, carrying you with it from the first staccato punches through all the tumbling, stumbling, and rumbling to the end of the dance.

Hong Kong's Movie Industry Comes of Age

While Lee and Chan were carrying their audiences through the progressive stages of kung fu, the Hong Kong film industry moved forward through its own evolutionary process. In 1970, two executives from Shaw Brothers formed their own studio, Golden Harvest. Raymond Chow and Leonard Ho followed a more flexible approach to film production and distribution than the old centralized model. By offering higher salaries and more creative freedom to their talent, they attracted stars like Lee and Chan. They also entered into pioneering co-productions with Hollywood. By the end of the decade, they were running the top movie studio in Hong Kong.

Meanwhile, smaller independent producers began to spring up, flooding the market with martial arts films and other popular genres in Cantonese. In 1980, three comic actors – Raymond Wong, Karl Maka, and Dean Shek – founded Cinema City. Their first movie, *Aces Go Places* (*Zuijia paidang*, 1982), was a spoof on James Bond spy films. Directed by Eric Tsang, it features Sam Hui as a debonair ex-burglar named King Kong who teams up with a bungling American detective (played by Maka) to fight criminals in Hong Kong. In one zany scene reminiscent of the Marx Brothers, the odd duo stumbles onto a stage production of Swan Lake and brings the house down. With each sequel, their stunts become wilder and increasingly high tech. In *Aces Go Places 3* (*Zuijia paidang zhi nuhuang miling*, 1984) they ride motorcycles off a roof and fly a motorized hang glider through the Hong Kong subway system with Maka hanging from the tail. Local audiences enjoyed seeing the familiar landmarks of their own city on the screen, encouraging more directors to follow suit. Tsui Hark, who had set his earlier films in traditional landscapes, made Hong Kong the setting in his postmodern parody, *All the Wrong Clues* (*Gui ma zhi duo xing*, 1981), adding his own brand of visual polish and rhythmic control to the comic scenes. Sammo Hung continued the trend with kung fu comedies like *Winners and Sinners* (*Qi mou miao ji: Wu fu xing*, 1983) and *Twinkle, Twinkle Lucky Stars* (*Xia ri fu xing*, 1985), both with Jackie Chan. These films, with their improved production values, modern special effects, and easy-to-get, non-stop, slapstick humor, appealed more and more to the international market.

Much has been made of Hong Kong's reputation as "Hollywood of the East." As the dominant force in today's commercial movie world, Hollywood is the yardstick against which other global film industries are measured. So we hear frequent references to Bollywood (centered in the Indian city of Mumbai, once known as Bombay) or Nollywood (in Nigeria). As David Bordwell points out, most countries are too small to support a vibrant film industry on the basis of local audiences alone. To pay for production costs, they must export their cinematic products to other lands or receive hefty government subsidies, as in the case of Europe. Since only one in five European films is screened outside the country where it was made, Bordwell does not consider any European nation to have a truly global cinema.[16] And except for Hollywood and India, with its immense, self-sustaining home markets, neither does any other film center, including Hong Kong. Yet as we have seen, this tiny region on the southern tip of China has enjoyed a vigorous cinematic history for more than 60 years. During the 1980s and early 1990s, when Hollywood controlled so many markets around the world, less than 30% of the theatres in Hong Kong screened American films. Studios like Shaw Brothers, Golden Harvest, and Cinema City not only catered to the local taste for action genres, but they also whet and fed a growing appetite for martial arts films in places like Thailand, Singapore, Malaysia, Indonesia, South Korea, and Taiwan as well as in the Chinatowns of North America and cult audiences throughout the West.

But in the mid-1990s, even before Hong Kong's 1997 handover to the People's Republic of China, this boom suffered a drastic decline.[17] Hollywood blockbusters began to encroach on local markets. Overproduction, reliance on tired formulas, and lower standards took a toll on audience demand. The Asian fiscal crisis and video piracy contributed to the problem. By the end of the decade, the industry's production and revenue were reduced by half. Yet Hong Kong directors continued to explore new directions. Tsui Hark revived the legend of China's kung fu hero Wong Fei-hung in his *Once Upon a Time in China* series (*Wong Fei Hung*, 1991–1997) with Jet Li in the leading role for four of the six films. John Woo experimented with police films, adding guns to the traditional arsenal of fists, feet, knives, and nunchucks in *A Better Tomorrow* (*Yin hung boon sik*, 1986) and *The Killer* (*Dip huet seung hung*, 1989) before going off to Hollywood. When he returned to Asia, it was to direct *Red Cliff* (*Chi bi*, 2008), a lavish, four-hour epic set during the Han Dynasty. On a lighter note, Stephen Chow combined new digital effects and surrealistic parody in *Shaolin Soccer* (*Siu lang juk kau*, 2001) and *Kung Fu Hustle* (*Gong fu*, 2004), two of Hong Kong's most commercially successful movies ever. *Red Cliff* was another success, breaking the box office record previously held in mainland China by *Titanic* (1997). Following in the wake of Zhang Yimou's blockbusters – *Hero*, *House of Flying Daggers*, and *Curse of the Golden Flower* (*Man cheng jin dai huang jin jia*, 2006) – Woo's co-production marked a new spirit of collaboration between the former Crown Colony and the People's Republic, a pooling of impressive talent, financial resources, and cinematic styles.

Kung Fu, Wuxia, and the Aesthetics of Action

Although popular genre films are often criticized for lacking the originality, subtlety, and depth of art house oriented cinema, there are good reasons for attending to their aesthetic qualities, their look and sound and feel. There is a kind of genius in the genres, a stylistic brilliance that reflects the way they have evolved over time in response to audiences' tastes and the demands of the marketplace. Whether or not specific names and dates can be assigned to particular breakthroughs in sound effects, camerawork or editing, an impressive body of technical achievements and stylistic trends has emerged from so many filmmakers trying to capture the martial arts in action.

What makes Hong Kong action films so distinctive? One outstanding trait is their sheer speed. The kinetic performances, brusque movements, clipped dialogue, rapid cutting, split-second shot length, and energetic sound tracks all keep the story moving forward at a breathless pace. Esther Yau relates this rapidity to the frantic pace of production in a competitive market, which ranged from seven days in the 1960s to an average of three to five months in the 1980s and 1990s.[18] Speed also reflects the rhythms of the city itself and the schedules of spectators who consume films like fast food. Another trait that viewers often notice is a drive to excess. Movies made in Hong Kong have more blood, more violence, more dismemberment, more pains per minute than the average Hollywood film. They are also louder and often more sensual and visually flamboyant. So much so that export versions often are toned down for Western markets. This audacity can be read as vulgarity or vitality, a lack of subtlety that David Bordwell calls "expressive amplification."[19] The deliberate use of exaggerated violence and sound effects magnifies the emotional experience.

Bordwell believes that the fight scenes in Hollywood action films are comparatively clumsy and ineffective. While *Lethal Weapon* (1987) and *The Fugitive* (1993) go for "massive carnage and incessant hustle," Hong Kong films offer "well-calibrated views of precise, staccato movement."[20] This precision is achieved partly through constructive editing, the Soviet approach to building a scene inductively from partial views of the action as opposed to analytic editing, the classical style of showing a broad establishing shot before the details. Hong Kong editors alternate long pauses with bursts of energy, a technique that may owe something to the explosive movements and frozen poses in Peking opera. This method renders the quick attacks and sudden stops of kung fu fighting as clean, well delineated motions, while Hollywood cutting tends to create a general sense of commotion and confusion. Bordwell sees differences in the camerawork as well. While Hollywood tends to focus on the face, Hong Kong shows the dynamics of the entire body as it leaps, tumbles, and detonates with energy. As a result, the action scenes in Hollywood films are visual experiences, but the Hong Kong scenes are visceral. We feel their "delicious kinetic exhilaration."[21]

In many ways, the art of kung fu is a triumph of imagination both in combat tactics and in film aesthetics. The human body has only two arms and two legs. How many ways can these four limbs be deployed to attack an army or defend against an onslaught of modern weaponry? How many variations of arm and leg motions can be invented to keep a movie moving or a genre going without losing its audience?

Watch Jackie Chan's feats of kinetic engineering in *Drunken Master* when he practices the technique of "drunkard with inner strength." The camera cuts from an open manual to Jackie's face, then pulls back as he sucks in his breath, his rock-hard body taut with determination. He stirs, wavers, leans as if to fall, then regains his balance and leaps into a series of staccato stances. With fingers hooked, elbows cocked, and one leg lifted at an angle, he bounds from one position to another. Now he's in the air, now he's spinning on his back, whipping both legs to propel him in a graceful arc. Later we see these moves in action as a bully attacks him with a formidable stick and Jackie fends him off like child's play, pretending to sip wine from a cup or a jug the whole time. An hour and a half into the film, he has finally become a drunken master. The camerawork and editing in *Drunken Master* are generally unobtrusive and straightforward (see Figure 1.10, Figure 1.11, and Figure 1.12). Most of the action is photographed at eye level from one side, as in a training video. There are occasional shots from above, below, and even the opponent's point of view, as if the audience is being attacked, but the main focus is the body in motion. There is little attention here to framing, color, lighting, or other elements of cinematic style.

Now look closely at the climactic battle scene in *Once Upon a Time in China*. The setting is an American ship harbored in the southern port of Foshan in the 1800s. A powerful martial artist named "Iron Vest" Yim (Yee Kwan Yan) is out to prove that he can beat the hero, Wong Fei-hung (Jet Li), using a new kung fu technique. Yim has allied himself with the evil Shaho gang and an American profiteer named Jackson. The big match takes place in the cargo hold of Jackson's ship, where Yim and Wong square off one on one. Yim's skills are formidable. He attacks Wong with boundless energy, strength, and ingenuity. Both men draw from large repertoires of martial moves, but they also grab props from the surroundings. Yim reaches for a ladder with this foot and sends it flying toward Wong with a well-aimed kick. A broken rafter or a bale of hay becomes a weapon in his hands. Both men are as spontaneously inventive as Gene Kelly recruiting an umbrella or a lamp post for his dance number in *Singin' in the Rain* (1952). The cinematography is equally inventive. Many of the shots show the fighters from oblique angles, accentuating the dynamic forces at work. (Spike Lee calls these "Chinese angles" and uses them liberally in *Do the Right Thing*, 1989.) The camera's wide-angle lens captures the precarious moment when Wong and Yim face each other on a bridge of crisscrossed ladders, then cuts to a high angle to show how the ladders are arranged like pickup sticks. At one point, the action stops abruptly as the men catch their balance and square off. As the camera swoops in on each figure from below, we feel the tension, expectation, an ominous pause before the next round. Smoke fills the air, and tongues of fire flicker in the background. When the action resumes, it happens in a rapid burst of images, some 52 shots within the next minute. During that time, the camera is in constant motion. We watch from high above as Yim grabs a ladder with both hands. We cut to a close-up as he plants one end on his wooden perch, look through his legs in a low angle shot as he kicks it forward toward his opponent (Figure 1.13), and move slightly with the ladder as it falls in a long slant toward Wong, still waiting calmly on the other side, a blue wisp of smoke behind him. A long shot from the side shows both men squaring off again (Figure 1.14), another catches them from high above (Figure 1.15). When Yim rushes toward Wong from rung to rung, we're right below him (Figure 1.16). When Wong leaps up with legs apart and crashes down to snap the ladder in two, we're with him high and low (Figure 1.17). Although the fighters' bodies hold center stage, we're also aware of their surroundings: the earth tones of the wood, the stacks of bags, the entire *mise-en-scène*. We're also aware of the editor at work. Close-ups show the edges of the ladder planted in the dirt, striking a wooden beam, or ripping through a bag of grain. Cross cuts take us back and forth between the main fight and nearby sites of action where a woman is about to be raped and American sailors prepare to fire on a Chinese delegation.

FIGURES 1.10–1.17 Hong Kong kung fu film aesthetics. Yuen Wo-ping's camerawork and editing are relatively unobtrusive in *Drunken Master* (*Zui chan*, 1978), where Jackie Chan does all the work (Figures 1.10–1.12). Compare this cinematic style to Tsui Hark's dynamic use of camera, editing, and wire work (Figures 1.13–1.17) in *Once Upon a Time in China* (*Wong Fei Hung*, 1991).

FIGURE 1.10

FIGURE 1.13

FIGURE 1.11

FIGURE 1.14

FIGURE 1.12

FIGURE 1.15

FIGURE 1.16

FIGURE 1.17

All these strands of the story come together in a final showdown between the foreign villains and the Chinese heroes. Wong and his loyal band of kung fu students win the day, of course, but they learn a hard lesson about Western technology. You can't fight guns with fists.

Once Upon a Time in China gives the kung fu craze a local habitation and a cause. Historically, it refers to the Boxer Rebellion of 1900 when a group calling itself "the Society of Righteous and Harmonious Fists" gathered a large following to oppose the dragon of Western imperialism with bare hands. Though some were lightly armed, they believed that China's real strength lay in its people, a mantra repeated often in the film. In contemporary terms, the story captures the exuberance of a people who had come into their own by the 1990s as Hong Kong reached new heights of success and prepared to shed the symbolic mantle of British rule. The choice of Wong Fei-hung as central character is no accident. Wong was a local culture hero, the subject of a long-lived Cantonese-language kung fu cycle that ran from the 1940s through the 1970s and spanning more than 90 films. His role may be an expression of Cantonese pride in the face of Hong Kong's return to the Mandarin bias of mainland China. But why are the villains American? Is this a reference to the big guns of Hollywood who send their global fleet of movies to dominate the world? The independent Hong Kong filmmakers may ultimately be no match for American technology and marketing firepower, but with their resourcefulness, resilience, and the home grown techniques of kung fu, they put up a vigorous and immensely entertaining fight.

Filmography

The entries in this table have been simplified for convenience. Few films fit neatly into a single genre. *Once Upon a Time in China*, for example, combines elements of wuxia swordplay and barehanded kungfu combat as well as a touch of Western gun fighting. The *Kill Bill* movies add features from the samurai tradition to the mix. Students should learn to question these categories as a way of exploring the collaborative, transnational, multi-genre nature of filmmaking today. Many films, although listed as the product of one country, are really multinational co-productions (Sergio Leone's "spaghetti Westerns," for example, typically were made with funding and talent from Italy, Spain, and Germany). Titles vary too. A Bruce Lee movie might have four or five English names, and even the Chinese names of Hong Kong films might differ depending on whether they are given in Mandarin or Cantonese. In most cases, I have used the Mandarin forms, syllable by syllable, except for proper names. Asian names can be confusing to Western readers since the established custom in countries like China, Korea, and Japan is to give the family name first and the given name last. For example, Zhang Yimou's family name is Zhang and his given name is Yimou. For the sake of consistency and clarity, I have followed IMDb's practice of using the Western word order (given name first, family name last) for all names in the filmographies, whether Asian or Western. For example, Zhang Yimou is listed here as Yimou Zhang although he is referred to as Zhang Yimou in the chapter itself. For the dates, I have consulted the International Movie Data Base (imdb.com), which usually gives the original release date.

Filmography

Main Genre	Country	English Language Title	Original Title	Director	Date
Kung Fu	Hong Kong	The Big Boss (aka Fists of Fury)	Tang shan da xiong	Wei Lo	1971
Kung Fu	Hong Kong	Fist of Fury (aka The Chinese Connection)	Jing wu men	Wei Lo	1972
Kung Fu	Hong Kong	Way of the Dragon (aka Return of the Dragon)	Meng long guo jiang	Bruce Lee	1972
Kung Fu	Hong Kong, USA	Enter the Dragon (aka The Deadly Three)	Long zheng hu dou	Robert Clouse	1973
Kung Fu	Hong Kong	Drunken Master	Zui chan	Woo-ping Yuen	1978
Kung Fu	Hong Kong, USA	Battle-Creek Brawl (aka The Big Brawl)	Shashou hao	Robert Clouse	1980
Kung Fu	Hong Kong	All the Wrong Clues	Gui ma zhi duo xing	Hark Tsui	1981
Kung Fu	Hong Kong	Aces Go Places (aka Mad Mission)	Zuijia paidang	Eric Tsang	1982
Kung Fu	Hong Kong	Project A	"A" gai wak	Jackie Chan	1983
Kung Fu	Hong Kong	Winners and Sinners	Qi mou miao ji: Wu fu xing	Sammo Kam-bo Hung	1983
Kung Fu	Hong Kong	Wheels on Meals	Kuai can che	Sammo Kambo Hung	1984
Kung Fu	Hong Kong	Police Story	Ging chat goo si	Jackie Chan	1985
Kung Fu	Hong Kong	Twinkle, Twinkle Lucky Stars	Xia ri fu xing	Sammo Kambo Hung	1985
Kung Fu	Hong Kong	Once Upon a Time in China	Wong Fei Hung	Hark Tsui	1991
Kung Fu	Thailand	Ong-Bak: Muay Thai Warrior	Ong-Bak	Prachya Pinkaew	2003
Samurai	Japan	Capricious Young Man	Akanishi Kakita	Mansaku Itami	1936
Samurai	Japan	Humanity and Paper Balloons	Ninjo kami fusen	Sadao Yamanaka	1937

(Continued)

Filmography (*Continued*)

Main Genre	Country	English Language Title	Original Title	Director	Date
Samurai	Japan	*Rashomon*	*Rashomon*	Akira Kurosawa	1950
Samurai	Japan	*Seven Samurai*	*Shichinin no samurai*	Akira Kurosawa	1954
Samurai	Japan	*Samurai I: Musashi Miyamoto*	*Miyamoto Musashi*	Hiroshi Inagaki	1954
Samurai	Japan	*Bodyguard*	*Yojimbo*	Akira Kurosawa	1961
Samurai	Japan	*The Loyal Forty-Seven Ronin*	*Chushingura*	Hiroshi Inagaki	1962
Samurai	Japan	*Harakiri*	*Seppuku*	Masaki Koboyashi	1962
Samurai	Japan	*The Tale of Zatoichi*	*Zatoichi monogatari*	Kenji Misumi	1962
Samurai	USA	*The Last Samurai*		Edward Zwick	2003
Samurai	USA	*Kill Bill: Vol. 1*		Quentin Tarantino	2003
Western	USA	*The Great Train Robbery*		Edwin Porter	1903
Western	USA	*The Virginian*		Victor Fleming	1929
Western	USA	*Stagecoach*		John Ford	1939
Western	USA	*Rio Grande*		John Ford	1950
Western	USA	*High Noon*		Fred Zinnemann	1952
Western	USA	*Shane*		George Stevens	1953
Western	USA	*The Searchers*		John Ford	1956
Western	UK	*The Sheriff of Fractured Jaw*		Raoul Walsh	1958
Western	USA	*The Magnificent Seven**		John Sturges	1960
Western	Germany	*The Treasure of Silver Lake*	*Der Schatz im Silbersee*	Harald Reini	1962
Western	Italy	*A Fistful of Dollars**	*Per un pugno di dollari*	Sergio Leone	1964

Main Genre	Country	English Language Title	Original Title	Director	Date
Western	USA	The Outrage*		Martin Ritt	1964
Western	Italy	The Good, the Bad and the Ugly*	Il buono, il brutto, il cattivo	Sergio Leone	1966
Western	Niger	The Return of an Adventurer	Le retour d'un aventurier	Alassane Moustapha	1966
Western	Italy	Once Upon a Time in the West	C'era una volta il West	Sergio Leone	1968
Western	USA	Coogan's Bluff		Don Siegel	1968
Western	USA	Little Big Man		Arthur Penn	1970
Western	USA	Buck and the Preacher		Sidney Poitier	1972
Western	India	Sholay (aka Embers)	Sholay	Ramesh Sippy	1975
Western	USA	The Shootist		Don Siegel	1976
Western	USA	Dances with Wolves		Kevin Costner	1990
Western	USA	Unforgiven		Clint Eastwood	1992
Western	USA	The Quick and the Dead		Sam Raimi	1995
Western	Japan	Sukiyaki Western Django	Sukiyaki: Uesutan Jango	Takashi Miike	2007
Western	USA	3:10 to Yuma		James Mangold	2007
Western	Korea	The Good, the Bad, the Weird*	Joheunnom nabbeunnom isanghannom	Jee-woon Kim	2008
Western	USA	Django Unchained		Quentin Tarantino	2012
Wuxia	China	Burning of the Red Lotus Temple	Huo shao hong lian si	Shichuan Zhang	1928
Wuxia	Hong Kong	Come Drink With Me	Da zui xia	King Hu	1966
Wuxia	Hong Kong	Dragon Gate Inn (aka The Dragon Inn)	Long men kezhan	King Hu	1967
Wuxia	Hong Kong	The One-Armed Swordsman	Dubei dao	Cheh Chang (Che Zhang)	1967

(Continued)

Filmography (*Continued*)

Main Genre	Country	English Language Title	Original Title	Director	Date
Wuxia	Hong Kong	A Touch of Zen	Xia nu	King Hu	1971
Wuxia	Hong Kong	The Fate of Lee Khan	Ying chun ge zhi Fengbo	King Hu	1973
Wuxia	Taiwan	Crouching Tiger, Hidden Dragon	Wo hu cang long	Ang Lee	2000
Wuxia	China	Hero	Ying xiong	Yimou Zhang	2002
Wuxia	China	House of Flying Daggers	Shi mian mai fu	Yimou Zhang	2004
Wuxia	China	Curse of the Golden Flower	Man cheng jin dai huang jin jia	Yimou Zhang	2006
Wuxia	China	Red Cliff	Chi bi	John Woo	2008
Samurai	Japan	Hara Kiri: Death of a Samurai	Ichimei	Takashi Miike	2011
Samurai, Kung Fu, Wuxia	China	The Sword Identity	Wo kou de zong ji	Haofeng Xu	2011
Kung Fu	Taiwan/China	The Grandmaster	Yi dai zong shi	Wong Kar-wai	2013

*Remakes

Notes

1. Thomas Schatz, *Hollywood Genres: Formulas, Filmmaking, and the Studio System* (Random House, 1981), 45.

2. John Belton, *American Cinema / American Culture*, 2nd edition (McGraw-Hill, 2005), 248.

3. Robert Warshow, "Movie Chronicle: The Westerner" (1954), in Leo Braudy and Marshall Cohen, eds., *Film Theory and Criticism*, 5th edition (Oxford, 1999), 654–667.

4. Jim Kitses, *Horizons West: Directing the Western from John Ford to Clint Eastwood* (Indiana University Press, 1998).

5. Michitaro Tada, "The Destiny of Samurai Films," *East-West Film Journal* 1(1) (December 1986): 48.

6. Donald Richie, *A Hundred Years of Japanese Film* (Kodansha International, 2001), 22–27.

7. J.L. Anderson, "Japanese Swordfighters and American Gunfighters," *Cinema Journal* 12(2) (Spring 1973): 1–21.

8. David Desser, "Toward a Structural Analysis of the Postwar Samurai Film," *Quarterly Review of Film Studies* 8(1) (Winter 1983): 145.

9. Desser, 25–41.

10. Desser, 27.

11. Zhang Zhen, "Bodies in the Air: The Magic of Science and the Fate of the Early 'Martial Arts' Film in China," in Sheldon Hsiao-peng Lu and Emilie Yeh, eds., *Chinese-Language Film: Historiography, Poetics, Politics* (University of Hawai'i Press, 2005), 54.

12. Zhang Zhen, 65.

13. Quoted in Craig Smith, "'Hero' Soars, and Its Director Thanks 'Crouching Tiger,'" *The New York Times*, September 2, 2004.

14. David Bordwell, *Planet Hong Kong: Popular Cinema and the Art of Entertainment* (Harvard University Press, 2000), 201.

15. Since *The Big Boss* was also given the American name *Fists of Fury*, the 1972 film (*Fist of Fury* in

Hong Kong) went by other names in the United States, including *The Iron Hand* and *The Chinese Connection*. *Way of the Dragon* (literally "The Fierce Dragon Crosses the River" in Chinese) is also known as *Return of the Dragon* in the United States. *Enter the Dragon*, originally titled *Blood and Steel* in the United States, is also known in English as *The Deadly Three*.

16. Bordwell, 82.

17. Stephen Teo, *Hong Kong Cinema: The Extra Dimensions* (British Film Institute, 1997).

18. Esther Yau, ed., *At Full Speed: Hong Kong Cinema in a Borderless World* (University of Minnesota Press, 2001), 3.

19. See David Bordwell, "Aesthetics in Action: Kungfu, Gunplay, and Cinematic Expressivity," in Esther Yau, ed., *At Full Speed: Hong Kong Cinema in a Borderless World* (University of Minnesota Press, 2001), 73–93.

20. Bordwell, *Planet Hong Kong*, 228.

21. Bordwell, "Aesthetics in Action," 91.

Further Reading

1. The Western in Hollywood and Abroad

Altman, Rick. "A Semantic/Syntactic Approach to Film Genre." In Leo Braudy and Marshall Cohen, eds., *Film Theory and Criticism*, 5th edition, 630–653. Oxford University Press, 1999.

Anderson, J.L. "Japanese Swordfighters and American Gunfighters." *Cinema Journal* 12(2) (Spring 1973): 1–21.

Belton, John. "The Making of the West." In *American Cinema / American Culture*, 2nd edition, 248–276. McGraw-Hill, 2005.

Berg, Chuck. "Fade-Out in the West: The Western's Last Stand?" In Wheeler Winston Dixon, ed., *Film Genre 2000: New Critical Essays*, 211–226. State University of New York Press, 2000.

Chopra, Anupama. *Sholay: The Making of a Classic*. Penguin, 2000.

Hughes, Howard. *Once Upon a Time in the Italian West: The Filmgoers' Guide to Spaghetti Westerns*. I.B. Tauris, 2004.

Kaminsky, Stuart. "The Samurai Film and the Western." *Journal of Popular Film* 1(4) (1972): 312–324.

Kitses, Jim. *Horizons West: Directing the Western from John Ford to Clint Eastwood*. Indiana University Press, 1998.

McGee, Patrick. *From Shane to Kill Bill: Rethinking the Western*. Blackwell, 2007.

Schatz, Thomas. "The Western." In *Hollywood Genres: Formulas, Filmmaking, and the Studio System*, 45–80. Random House, 1981.

Slotkin, Richard. "Gunfighters and Green Berets; *The Magnificent Seven* and the Myth of Counter-Insurgency." *Radical History Review* 44 (Spring 1989): 64–90.

Warshow, Robert. "Movie Chronicle: the Westerner" (1954). In Leo Braudy and Marshall Cohen, eds., *Film Theory and Criticism*, 5th edition, 654–667. Oxford University Press, 1999.

Weisser, Thomas. *Spaghetti Westerns: The Good, The Bad, and the Violent*. McFarland, 1992.

2. Japanese Cinema and the Samurai Tradition

Anderson, J.L. "Japanese Swordfighters and American Gunfighters." *Cinema Journal* 12(2) (Spring 1973): 1–21.

Desser, David and Arthur Nolletti, Jr. *Reframing Japanese Cinema*. Indiana University Press, 1992.

Desser, David. "Toward a Structural Analysis of the Postwar Samurai Film." *Quarterly Review of Film Studies* 8(1) (Winter 1983): 25–41.

Kaminsky, Stuart. "The Samurai Film and the Western." *Journal of Popular Film* 1(4) (1972): 312–324.

Richie, Donald. *A Hundred Years of Japanese Film*. Kodansha International, 2001.

Richie, Donald. *The Films of Akira Kurosawa*. University of California Press, 1970.

Silver, Alain. *The Samurai Film*. Overlook Press, 2005.

Standish, Isolde. *Myth and Masculinity in the Japanese Cinema: Toward a Political Reading of the "Tragic Hero."* Curzon, 2000.

Tada, Michitaro. "The Destiny of Samurai Films." *East-West Film Journal* 1(1) (December 1986): 48–58.

3. *Chinese Cinema, Wuxia, and King Fu*

Berry, Michael. *Speaking in Images: Interviews with Contemporary Chinese Filmmakers.* Columbia University Press, 2005.

Bordwell, David. *Planet Hong Kong: Popular Cinema and the Art of Entertainment.* Harvard University Press, 2000.

Browne, Nick, Paul Pickowicz, Vivian Sobchack, and Esther Yau, eds. *New Chinese Cinemas: Forms, Identities, Politics.* Cambridge University Press, 1994.

Desser, David. "The Martial Arts Film in the 1990s." In Wheeler Winston Dixon, ed., *Film Genre 2000: New Critical Essays*, 77–109. State University of New York Press, 2000.

Ehrlich, Linda and David Desser, eds. *Cinematic Landscapes: Observations on the Visual Arts in China and Japan.* University of Texas Press, 1994.

Fu, Poshek and David Desser, eds. *The Cinema of Hong Kong: History, Arts, Identity.* Cambridge University Press, 2000.

Marchetti, Gina and Tan See Kam, eds. *Hong Kong Film, Hollywood and the New Global Cinema: No Film Is an Island.* Routledge, 2007.

Lu, Sheldon Hsiao-peng and Emilie Yeh, eds. *Chinese-Language Film: Historiography, Poetics, Politics.* University of Hawai'i Press, 2005.

Lu, Sheldon Hsiao-peng, ed. *Transnational Chinese Cinemas: Identity, Nationhood, Gender.* University of Hawai'i Press, 1997.

Lu, Sheldon H. and Anne Ciecko, eds. *China, Transnational Visuality, Global Postmodernity.* Stanford University Press, 2001.

Stokes, Lisa Odham and Michael Hoover. *City on Fire: Hong Kong Cinema.* Verso, 1999.

Teo, Stephen. *Hong Kong Cinema: The Extra Dimensions.* British Film Institute, 1997.

Yau, Esther, ed. *At Full Speed: Hong Kong Cinema in a Borderless World.* University of Minnesota Press, 2001.

Zhang, Yingjin. *Screening China: Critical Interventions, Cinematic Reconfigurations, and the Transnational Imaginary in Contemporary Chinese Cinema.* University of Michigan Center for Chinese Studies, 2002.

DEEP FOCUS ON CHINESE CINEMAS

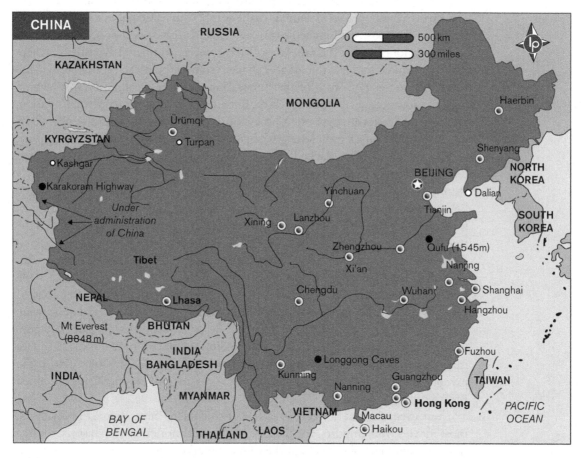

FIGURE 1.18   The three regions of China: Hong Kong, Taiwan, and the People's Republic of China (mainland).

World Cinema through Global Genres, First Edition. William V. Costanzo.
© 2014 John Wiley & Sons, Inc. Published 2014 by John Wiley & Sons, Inc.

In this Unit on the Warrior Hero, we have been looking at Chinese martial arts movies alongside the American Western and the Japanese samurai film. This is a good opportunity to step back and consider how developments in the wuxia and kung fu genres fit into the larger story of Chinese cinema. A brief overview of the geography, history, and cultural identities of Hong Kong, Taiwan, and the People's Republic of China will help to place Asian martial arts films into a broader context.

The Three Chinas

China is a land of impressive proportions. With a population exceeding 1.3 billion, it embraces a fifth of the world's people within its boundaries, which stretch more than 3,000 miles across East Asia from India and Kazakhstan in the west to the Pacific Ocean and Korea in the east, bordering Russia and Mongolia to the north and Vietnam and Burma (Myanmar) to the south. China also has one of the planet's oldest civilizations, with archeological evidence dating back over 5,000 years. For most of its long history, this area was ruled by powerful imperial dynasties that kept its people united within a remarkably stable system of political, economic, and cultural institutions. For much of that time, China was the wealthiest, most technologically advanced civilization on earth. But after centuries of prosperous isolation, attacked by Western powers seeking lucrative trade advantages and weakened by internal strife, China's great strength began to erode during the nineteenth century.

The system finally cracked in 1912, when a new Republic of China was declared, replacing the lengthy line of Qing emperors with the Nationalist Party (Kuomintang). Soon the country was in the grip of a brutal civil war waged between the Kuomintang, led by General Chiang Kai-shek, and Communist forces led by Mao Zedong, a grip loosened only by the uneasy truce between the two groups when Japanese troops attacked the mainland. The Second Sino-Japanese War, China's piece of World War II, lasted from 1937 to 1945, after which Mao and Chiang resumed their fighting. When the struggle ended in 1949, Mao's Communist Party emerged victorious, founding the People's Republic of China (PRC) on the mainland. Chiang Kai-shek retreated to the island of Taiwan, founding the Republic of China (ROC) in exile. Meanwhile, the tiny, densely populated territory of Hong Kong (about 7 million people squeezed into 426 square miles) was enjoying relative peace and prosperity as a British Colony, with the exception of its occupation by Japan from 1941 to 1945. Hong Kong remained British until sovereignty was handed over to the PRC in 1997.

These events helped to steer the course of cinema in China. Before the Civil War, most movies were imports. For the first 50 years of motion picture history, foreign films accounted for about 90% of the Chinese market. Nevertheless, local talent on the mainland, roused to action by a progressive "left-wing" movement, helped to launch a golden age of Chinese cinema in the 1930s. Many of their films championed the struggles of common people. Sun Yu's *The Big Road* (*Dalu*, 1934) is about workers trying to build a highway in the war against the Japanese. Wu Yonggang's *The Goddess* (*Shennu*, 1934) tells the story of a young woman (played by the era's biggest star, Ruan Lingyu, in one of her last roles) forced into prostitution to support her young son. During this period, the Kuomintang took steps to bring movies into line with its nationalist agenda. Chiang Kai-shek banned movies it considered frivolous and reclaimed the studios from foreign ownership. This dual policy of censorship and protectionism became cornerstones of government policy under the Communists as well. When Mao established the PRC in 1949, he regarded movies as a powerful tool for unifying the country. The private film studios were consolidated under state control. Familiar entertainment genres – melodrama, martial arts, and costume dramas – gave way to political films glorifying revolution, class struggle, and defeat of the imperialists. Under Mao, the Chinese people got to watch movies like *Woman Basketball Player No. 5* (*Nu lan 5 hao*, 1957), in which the title character falls in love with an athlete and joins the national team to seek victory in international competition. More artistic films like Fei Mu's *Spring in a Small Town* (*Xiaocheng zhi chun*, 1948), a strong romantic drama made just before the Communist revolution, were left to languish because they lacked the required political zeal. During the Cultural Revolution (1966–1976), the Beijing Film Academy was closed entirely, and film production nearly came to a standstill.

The extraordinary talent and energy that revitalized Chinese mainland cinema in the 1980s has been called the Fifth Generation movement, named after the first students to graduate from the Film Academy after it reopened. Young men like Chen Kaige and Zhang Yimou, who had been yanked out of school during the Cultural Revolution and sent out to remote farms and factories for "reeducation," now had cameras in their hands and something meaningful to say. Their program of "cultural reflection" (*wenhua fansi*) and historical reflection (*lishi fansi*) involved both a questioning of tradition and a return to Chinese roots.[1] The earliest Fifth Generation films experimented with the medium, creating stylized images of communal China (*One and Eight / Yi ge he ba ge*, 1983; *Yellow Earth / Huang tu di*, 1984; *Horse Thief / Dao ma zei*, 1986). As the movement evolved, it grew more diverse, encompassing a wide range of subjects and styles from Huang Jianxin's *The Black Cannon Incident* (*Hei pao shi jian*, 1986) to Chen Kaige's *Life on a String* (*Bian zou bian chang*, 1991), but pointedly rejecting the socialist realism favored by Mao and his followers. The events of Tiananmen Square in 1989, combined with China's transition to a market economy, contributed to yet another shift as state funding declined while state censorship continued. Amid the consumerism, pop culture, and postmodernism of the post-New Era (*hou xin shiqi*) there emerged a new generation of independent filmmakers, all in their mid- to late 20s in 1989.

In contrast to the historical melodramas of their predecessors, these "Sixth Generation" directors made gritty, realistic films about laid-off workers, prostitutes, artists, homosexuals, petty criminals, and other disenfranchised groups living on the margins of China's cities. Using underground production tactics, they turned out edgy films like Zhang Yuan's *Beijing Bastards* (*Beijing za zhong*, 1993), Wang Xiaoshuai's *Beijing Bicycles* (*Siqi sui de dan che*, 2001), and Jia Zhangke's *Unknown Pleasures* (*Ren xiao yao*, 2002). Though made with small budgets and often banned on the mainland, these movies circulated widely at festivals, on the Internet, and through word of mouth on video and DVD. It was largely their facility with new technologies for producing and distributing their work that enabled bright, ambitious, young filmmakers to circumvent the system and offer creative alternatives to costly or officially sanctioned films.

While cinema was going through these stages on the mainland, there were parallel developments in Hong Kong and Taiwan. In its heyday, Hong Kong boasted the third largest film industry in the world, after the United States and India. It became the East Asian hub for film production and distribution, exporting its hybrid commercial products throughout the Chinese diaspora and creating new markets in Africa, Latin America, Europe, and the United States. Meanwhile, across the Taiwan Strait, the island of Taiwan emerged from decades of insularity and Japanese control to become a creative and financial force in Chinese-language cinema.

Chinese filmmakers were directing movies in Hong Kong as early as 1909 with Western assistance. The first native feature film, dating from 1913, was based on Chinese opera, which continued to have a strong influence on Hong Kong movies for years to come. After sound arrived in the 1930s, regional dialects became an issue. Hong Kong became the center for films in Cantonese, the dialect spoken in southern China, especially after the Kuomintang government began enforcing a policy that made Mandarin, spoken mostly in the North, the official state language. During the Second Sino-Japanese War, patriotic war films became popular, boosted by an influx of refugees from Shanghai. When the British returned in 1945, and as civil war heated up on the mainland, the ranks of immigrants swelled, especially from the South. Cantonese made a strong comeback, and the Hong Kong film industry mushroomed into big business, exporting Cantonese opera movies, low-budget martial arts films, swordplay fantasies, and family melodramas throughout the world. These genre films were now made in both Cantonese and Mandarin, with English subtitles mandated by British law. During the 1970s, the enormously successful Shaw Brothers studio and its rival, Golden Harvest, presided over the kung fu boom. Bruce Lee and Jackie Chan became world figures. The next two decades were boom years for Hong Kong. Its local industry raised production values, perfected distinctive forms of stunt work and visual effects, and learned to market an exportable trio of action, comedy, and sex. By 1997, however, when Hong Kong was handed over to the PRC, the film industry appeared to lose much of its vitality.

On the island of Taiwan, cinema also developed in stages. From 1901 to 1937, under a prolonged Japanese occupation, the industry was heavily influenced by Japanese practices such as live *benzi* narrators for silent films. When the Kuomintang took over in 1945, it encouraged the production of films in Mandarin with a nationalist perspective. Rapid modernization during the 1960s yielded a steady output of commercial entertainment and investments in Hong Kong films. The economic boom also created conditions for a New Cinema in the 1980s. Auteur directors like Hou Hsiao-Hsien and Edward Yang became internationally known for their realistic portraits of native Taiwanese life. Hou's award-winning trilogy (*City of Sadness/Bei qing cheng shi*, 1989; *The Puppetmaster/Xi meng ren sheng*, 1993; *Good Men, Good Women/Hao nan hao nu*, 1995) spans a century of Taiwan history (from Japanese colonial times through Nationalist rule to modern Taipei) as well as the history of visual technologies (photography, shadow play, theatre).

During the 1990s, the film industries of the "three regions" (*san di*) of Taiwan, Hong Kong, and the PRC became increasingly intertwined. As production costs rose, Hong Kong turned to the mainland for cheap labor and expansive settings. As output dropped on the island of Taiwan (from 215 to 33 films in 1992 alone), investment capital began to flow more freely across the Taiwan Straits. By 1993, about a quarter of all films made in the PRC received foreign funding. The mainland government discovered that dropping barriers could raise revenues. In 1994, it initiated a policy of importing ten "mega films" a year, sharing box-office receipts with producers. These imports included Hollywood blockbusters like *The Fugitive* (1993) and *Forest Gump* (1994), but also Hong Kong kung-fu films like *Drunken Master II* (*Jue ken II*, 1994) with Jackie Chan.

Significantly, some of China's best-known filmmakers have migrated to the West. Ang Lee moved from Taiwan to New York in the 1980s. John Woo left Hong Kong for Hollywood in the 1990s. Their work straddles the split world of the Chinese diaspora, one foot set in the traditional culture of the mainland while the other steps out into Western territory. Other directors, like Wayne Wang, grew up outside of China. Wang was named after John Wayne by his American father. Many of his films, like *Dim Sum: A Little Bit of Heart* (1984) and *The Joy Luck Club* (1993), dramatize the generational conflicts of culture among Chinese Americans. These overseas Chinese filmmakers have added new dimensions to the issue of Chineseness in a global age.

Timeline (Figure 1.19)

Dates	Chinese History	Mainland Cinema	Hong Kong Cinema	Taiwan Cinema
1644–1911	Qing Dynasty			
1842			Hong Kong becomes a British Crown Colony	
1894–1895	First Sino-Japanese War			
1900	Boxer Rebellion opposes foreign influence in China			
1895–1945				Japanese occupation of Taiwan influences local productions
1912	Republic of China founded		Hong Kong begins producing local films	

(Continued)

Timeline (*Continued*)

Dates	Chinese History	Mainland Cinema	Hong Kong Cinema	Taiwan Cinema
1919	Students lead "May Fourth Movement," stirring Chinese nationalism			
1925	Chiang Kai-shek assumes leadership of right-wing Nationalist army			
1927–1950	Chinese civil war between Kuomintang Nationalists and Communists			
1928		Zhang Sichuan's *Burning of the Red Lotus Temple* (*Huo shao hong lian si*)		
1931	Japan invades Manchuria		Hong Kong becomes center for Cantonese language films	
1934		Sun Yu's *The Big Road* (*Dalu*)		
1937	Nanjing massacre			
1937–1945	Second Sino-Japanese War			
1941–1945			Japan occupies Hong Kong	
1943–1976	Mao Zedong, Chairman of Communist Party			
1948		Fei Mu's *Spring in a Small Town* (*Xiaocheng zhi chun*)		
1949	People's Republic of China founded on mainland, Republic of China on Taiwan		Influx of filmmakers from Shanghai boosts local production	Filmmakers sympathetic to Nationalist government begin arriving from mainland

Dates	Chinese History	Mainland Cinema	Hong Kong Cinema	Taiwan Cinema
1950		Beijing Film Academy founded		
1958–1961	Great Leap Forward	Communist government promotes "socialist realism"		
1966			King Hu's *Come Drink With Me* (*Da zui xia*)	
1966–1976	Cultural Revolution	Feature film production stops on mainland		
1970			Golden Harvest studio opens	
1972			Bruce Lee's *Way of the Dragon* (*Meng long guo jiang*)	
1976	Mao Zedong dies	"Exploratory films" move away from revolutionary models		
1978–1992	Economic reforms under Deng Xiaoping's leadership opens PRC to "market socialism"			
1982		Fifth Generation directors graduate from Beijing Film Academy		
1983			Jackie Chan's *Project A* ("*A*" *gai wak*)	Edward Yang's *That Day on the Beach* (*Hai tan de yi tian*)
1984		Chen Kaige's *Yellow Earth* (*Huang tu di*)		
1988		Shift to market-driven cinema	New rating system spawns adults only "Category III films"	
1989	Tiananmen Square incident			Hou Hsiao-Hsien's *City of Sadness* (*Bei qing cheng shi*)

(Continued)

Timeline (*Continued*)

Dates	Chinese History	Mainland Cinema	Hong Kong Cinema	Taiwan Cinema
1991		Zhang Yimou's *Raise the Red Lantern (Da hong deng long gao gao gua)*	Tsui Hark's *Once Upon a Time in China (Wong Fei hung)*	
1993		Zhang Yuan's *Beijing Bastards (Beijing za zhong)*		Hou Hsiao-Hsien's *The Puppetmaster (Xi meng ren sheng)*
1994				Ang Lee's *Eat Drink Man Woman (Yin shi nan nu)*
1997	British give Hong Kong to PRC			
2000				Ang Lee's *Crouching Tiger, Hidden Dragon (Wo hu cang long)*
2002		Jia Zhangke's *Unknown Pleasures (Ren xiao yao)*		
2004			Stephen Chow's *Kung Fu Hustle*	
2008		John Woo's *Red Cliff (Chi bi)*		Wei Te-sheng's *Cape No. 7 (Haijiao qi hao)*
2011	PRC joins World Trade Organization		Wong Kar-wai's *The Grandmaster (Yi dai zong shi)*	

Chinese Language and Identity in a Global Culture

What makes a film Chinese? Is it a matter of where the film is made, or who makes it, or what it is about? Is it a question of culture or language? To what extent is Ang Lee's *Crouching Tiger, Hidden Dragon* a Chinese film if its director has lived half his life in North America and imbues its story with Western elements? Even *Hero (Ying xiong,* 2002), made in China and directed by Fifth Generation filmmaker Zhang Yimou, has been accused of being non-Chinese because of its international financing, global crew, and special appeal to foreign audiences. In an industry increasingly characterized by co-productions, border-crossing film directors, and global marketing, how can one speak of a national Chinese cinema?

In an anthology of studies on Chinese history, politics, and filmmaking, Sheldon Lu and Emilie Yueh-yu Yeh suggest replacing the notion of "Chinese cinema" with the term "Chinese-language cinema." By redrawing the cinematic map along linguistic rather than geographical lines, Lu and Yeh broaden the idea of national consciousness and culture. Their definition covers "all the local, national, regional, transnational, diasporic, and global cinemas related to the Chinese language."[2] This wider category accommodates the complex flows of Chinese talent, funding, imagery, and themes across boundaries of the PRC, Hong Kong, Taiwan, Macau, Singapore, France, the United States, and everywhere else that Chinese-speaking filmmakers practice their craft. The China in many of these films, if pictured at all, is a projection of the imagination, highlighting Benedict Anderson's contention that nationhood itself is an imagined community. What constitutes Chinese culture is particularly abstract in genre films. What gets projected on the screens of wuxia and kung fu movies is not so much a reflection of what one might find on Chinese soil, wherever that might be, but a mythical dimension of airborne bodies, rapid reflexes, and enchanted weapons. It's a China of extraordinary power, energy, and skill, especially appealing to a people who have suffered humiliation at the hands of foreign nations and endured decades of civil warfare, political division, poverty, famine, and natural disasters all within the last century.

Crouching Tiger, Hidden Dragon: The Making of a Transnational Chinese-Language Film

Directed by Ang Lee, a Chinese émigré working with an international production team and a transnational cast, *Crouching Tiger, Hidden Dragon* is a truly global creation. The way it came to be, from funding to scripting, shooting, and distribution, is a prime example of how contemporary filmmaking can cross national and cultural borders with remarkable success. In this section, we'll focus in depth on the global aspects of Lee's film. First, we'll review its production history. Next, we'll consider the story and its heroes: who they are and where they come from. Then we'll look more closely at the film's style and themes: how it's told and what it means. We'll see how *Crouching Tiger, Hidden Dragon* builds on a long tradition of warrior heroes and gives them new life on the world's movie screens.

Lee was born in 1954 on the island of Taiwan, where his parents had taken refuge from the Communists on the mainland. Like many other conservative Chinese families, they escaped with their lives during the 1940s civil war and helped to transplant their cultural values in a new land, which was itself emerging from 50 years of Japanese colonialism. Lee left Taiwan for the United States in 1978, where he earned a bachelor's degree in theatre from the University of Illinois and a master's degree in film production from New York University, settling near Manhattan.

FIGURE 1.20   The closing credits from *Crouching Tiger, Hidden Dragon* (*Wo hu cang long*, Dir. Ang Lee, 2000) acknowledge its cross-regional cast, multinational financing, and transnational crew.

By now, he has spent more time in the United States than in his home country, although he still retains his Taiwanese citizenship.

Lee's prolific career spans an impressive array of genres and styles. His first three features, affectionately known among some fans as the "Father Knows Best Trilogy," focused on families caught between traditional Chinese culture and the disruptive forces of modern life. *Pushing Hands* (*Tui shou*, 1992), *The Wedding Banquet* (*Xiyan*, 1993), and *Eat Drink Man Woman* (*Yin shi nan nu*, 1994) were all made with Taiwanese actors and financing, although their scripts were partly in Mandarin and English. His other films have taken him as far from China as eighteenth-century England (*Sense and Sensibility*, 1995), 1970s suburban Connecticut (*The Ice Storm*, 1997), the American Civil War (*Ride with the Devil*, 1999), Marvel comics (*Hulk*, 2003), a Wyoming ranch (*Brokeback Mountain*, 2005), and a lifeboat on the Pacific Ocean (*Life of Pi*, 2012). *Crouching Tiger* was a kind of homecoming. As a member of the Chinese diaspora – the 30 million ethnic Chinese who have spread out over every continent since the fifteenth century – Lee sought to recreate a collective image of the homeland on film. "In some ways," he has said, "we're all looking for that old cultural, historical, abstract China – the big dream of China that probably never existed."[3]

For *Crouching Tiger, Hidden Dragon*, Lee selected his actors from different parts of the Chinese-speaking world (see Figure 1.20). Zhang Ziyi is from the mainland, Chang Chen from Taiwan, Chow Yun-Fat from Hong Kong, and Michelle Yeoh originally from Malaysia. The casting choices link Lee's characters with a global catalog of genres and roles. Cheng Pei Pei, who plays the cunningly venomous Jade Fox, was born in Shanghai and became a popular figure in Hong Kong martial arts films during the 1960s. Michelle Yeoh, another veteran of martial arts and widely known as Jackie Chan's co-star, had an active part in the James Bond picture *Tomorrow Never Dies* (1997). Chow Yun-Fat appeared in several Hollywood films after a long, successful career in Hong Kong. These casting choices provide rich intertextual connections for Chinese movie fans.

The film's production crew was even more international in perspective and work experience. Yuen Woping (sometimes spelled Yuen Woo-ping or Yuan Heping) served as martial arts choreographer. Born in southern China in 1945, Yuen studied the martial arts with his father as a child and came to Hong Kong in the 1960s, directing Jackie Chan's first big kung fu film, *Snake in the Eagle's Shadow/Se ying diu sau*, in 1978 and becoming one of the most influential masters of the genre. His work on *The Matrix* in 1999 brought him international acclaim. Cinematographer Peter Pau, born in Hong Kong and educated in Guangzhou, China, and San Francisco, has worked on both sides of the Pacific. His contributions to *Crouching Tiger* won an Academy Award. Hong Kong born Tim Yup, who also earned an Oscar for his production designs, has worked on co-productions involving Hong Kong, Japan, and France. The film's inclusive reach is echoed in its musical score, which combines the talents of composer Tan Dun (who studied in Beijing and New York), cellist Yo-Yo Ma (born in Paris and a resident of New York since the age of four), pop singer Coco Lee (born in Hong Kong, raised in San Francisco, and well known throughout Asia), and Ma Xiao Hui (a native of the mainland). Perhaps the most interesting aspect of this multicultural collaboration is the script itself. Based on a 70-year-old novel by a Manchurian Chinese writer, Wang Dulu, the story passed through many hands, including story editor Jean Castelli and three principal writers, Tsai Kuo Jung, Wang Hui-lin (both Tawianese), and James Schamus (an American), who developed the script in English and Chinese as it evolved.

The production itself involved five companies in five different countries: Taiwan, Britain, the PRC, Hong Kong, and the United States. The principal shooting lasted five months and took Lee to places on the mainland like the bamboo forests of Anji in the south, the imperial city of Chengde in the north, the city of Urumqi in the far west, the Gobi Desert, and the Taklamakan Plateau north of Tibet. This was his first lengthy visit to the PRC, the first opportunity to compare the actual countryside to the China in his mind.

With all these international arrangements, Lee and his collaborators were clearly courting a worldwide audience. Not only was the film aimed at two sides of the Pacific, but it targeted two kinds of viewers: the commercial market in China and art house audiences in the United States. By all measures, *Crouching Tiger, Hidden Dragon* was both a critical and financial success. It garnered festival awards in Hong Kong, Taiwan, New York, and Hollywood, where it was nominated for a record ten Academy Awards. It won Oscars for the best foreign-language film, cinematography, art direction, and original score. Critics at the Cannes Film Festival gave it a standing ovation. Made for only $15 million, the film earned well over $200 million, becoming the highest-grossing Chinese-language film in Asian history. In the United States, it earned $128 million at the box office and another $112 million in video and DVD rentals and sales by 2004, proving that a Chinese-language art film could appeal to a mainstream audience.[4] Yet, despite this unprecedented reception, *Crouching Tiger* was not uniformly appreciated by Chinese speakers and English speakers alike. The reasons, though still in dispute, reveal some important facts about global filmmaking today.

One of the common complaints among Chinese viewers is the film's dialogue. The actors speak chiefly in Mandarin, in keeping with the story's source and setting. But of the principal actors, only Zhang Ziyi speaks flawless Mandarin. The others use dialects or accents reflective of their origins. This proved to be distracting to native speakers and gave the dialogue an inauthentic ring. Another complaint is that the script itself does not seem authentically Chinese. This is not surprising given the way it was composed. As Schamus describes the process, he took the plot summary made by Lee and Jean Castelli from Wang's sprawling novel and turned it into "an action-packed, tightly plotted, swashbuckling, rousingly romantic adventure." By his own admission, though, Schamus's version was "culturally tone-deaf." He had "failed to absorb any of the nuance and inflection that not only inform the style of the great *wuxia* masterpieces, but that embody its very essence."[5] What followed were six months of bilingual composition, writing a scene in English, translating it into Chinese, revising the Chinese, and translating it back into English. The result is a hybrid script merging the strands of two languages and two cultural traditions. Many native Chinese viewers disliked what they saw as foreign elements. Die-hard wuxia fans bemoaned the story's deviations from the genre. From a transnational perspective, however, what is interesting is the common denominator, what transcends the barriers of language and culture and speaks to all audiences alike. To understand this, to appreciate what *Crouching Tiger* contributes to the evolution of global cinema and how it works as cinema, we need a close look at the film text. We'll see how a detailed analysis of this or any film can answer basic questions about the film's heroes, stories, visual styles, and themes.

Characters and relationships: Who are the heroes?

At the center of the story are three women and two men. Jen Yu (Zhang Ziyi) is the daughter of a wealthy provincial governor who has arranged for her marriage to a man she does not love. Strong-willed and independent-minded, Jen dreams of being powerful and free, attributes not normally accorded to women in eighteenth-century China. Her parents are unaware that she has been secretly learning the martial arts from a notorious female criminal known as Jade Fox. Jade Fox (Cheng Pei-Pei) honed her ferocious fighting skills with the aid of a secret manual that she stole from her former master after murdering him. Meanwhile Li Mu Bai (Chow Yun-Fat), the master's ablest student, is nearing the end of his career. He is ready to retire his signature weapon, the Green Destiny Sword, with only one mission to complete: avenging his master's death. He gives the sword to Yu Shu Lien (Michelle Yeoh), an accomplished fighter and a woman he can trust, asking her to bring it to an old friend, Sir Te (Lung Sihung), for safekeeping. It is clear that Li and

FIGURE 1.21   "Calligraphy is so similar to fencing." Jen and Shu Lien compare the writing brush to a sword in *Crouching Tiger, Hidden Dragon*.

Shu Lien have been in love for many years, but they have not married out of respect for Yu's former fiancé, now deceased. Midway through the film, we learn that Jen has a secret lover, Lo (Chang Chen), a highwayman who once attacked the Yu family's caravan when it was crossing through the western desert. Early in the film, Jen meets Shu Lien and is enraptured by her lifestyle. Here is a woman who seems to have the freedom and respect that she desires for herself. She wants Shu Lien to be her older sister. Thus, the five main characters are linked by four bonds: two couples romantically (Li and Shu Lien, Jen and Lo), two by strong female affinities (Jen and Jade Fox, Jen and Shu Lien). Later on, Li and Jen are linked by the expectations of a master and his (would be) disciple.

The female relationships are developed dramatically in two intimate scenes. In one of these, we learn about Jen's upcoming marriage to a man she does not love. Jen is sitting in her room practicing calligraphy when Shu Lien pays a visit. Jen offers to write Shu Lien's name "just for fun," wielding the brush with a graceful hand. Shu Lien is impressed. "I never realized that my name looks like 'sword,'" she says, adding, "Calligraphy is so similar to fencing" (Figure 1.21). The connection between writing and swordplay is an important one in Chinese culture, a link that Zhang Yimou explores more elaborately in *Hero*, as we noted in Chapter 1. Here, it serves to underscore the privileged nature of two arts traditionally reserved for men: the art of calligraphy and the martial arts. Jen has been practicing the martial arts clandestinely, and Shu Lien is hinting that she knows this. The maid arrives with tea, and the topic turns to Jen's arranged wedding. It is a good career move for Jen's father, but not for Jen. "I wish I were like the heroes in the books I read," she says. "Like you and Li Mu Bai. ... to be free to live my own life, to choose whom I love. That is true happiness." This is when Shu Lien reveals the secret of her previous engagement. She is not as free as she appears. In the exchange of secrets and desires, the two women agree to be like sisters.

This moment contrasts sharply with a later scene when Jade Fox, disguised as the Yu family governess, confronts Jen in her room at night. In contrast with the

FIGURE 1.22 "Kill or be killed. Exciting, isn't it?" Jen weighs the dangerous allure of Jade Fox's dark powers in *Crouching Tiger, Hidden Dragon*. Low-key lighting underscores their shady business.

lightness and refinement of the day, it is now a dark place of chiaroscuro shadows (Figure 1.22). The relationship here is of a demanding master and her defiant disciple. Jen is upset that Fox has killed a policeman earlier that night. "You'll bring ruin on my whole family," Jen cries. Jade retorts that Jen herself is partly responsible for the death because she stole the Green Destiny Sword. "Like a little girl, you thought stealing would be fun?" asks the old woman, pointing out that actions have consequences. "It's the Giang Hu fighter lifestyle … kill or be killed. Exciting, isn't it?" When the two women break into a fight, Jen has the upper hand. Her upper-class education has enabled her to read the stolen manual, learning techniques unknown to her illiterate teacher. But Fox has the final words: "Believe me, I still have a lesson or two to teach you!"

In her search for power and freedom, Jen has turned to two older women as her heroes. Jade Fox is a creature of dark forces. What power she has comes from treachery and anger. She stole the Wudan manual when the male teacher she had trusted showed more interest in seducing his female students than in teaching them. Although this provides a motive for her murderous revenge, the murder of her master brands her as an outlaw, a permanent outsider in need of a companion. Shu Lien is a wiser, nobler mentor. She has learned the martial arts through honest effort and a life of dedicated practice. Yet she has more to offer Jen than fencing technique; there are lessons to be learned about discipline, trust, integrity, and love.

Narrative traditions: Where does the story come from?

If Jade Fox and Shu Lien sometimes seem like figures in a fable, the two main male characters also play roles commonly found in the *wuxia* literature and wuxia movies described earlier in Chapter 1. More specifically, Lee's film is loosely based on Part IV of Wang Dulu's epic *wuxia* romance series *Crane-Iron Pentalogy* (1938–1942), a set of five related novels that have never been translated into English. Viewed broadly, the characters perform many of the mythic functions explored by Joseph

FIGURE 1.23 Lo swoops down on Jen's caravan, a trickster figure of freedom and romance in *Crouching Tiger, Hidden Dragon*.

Campbell in *The Hero with a Thousand Faces*.[6] Lo, the young desert bandit known as Dark Cloud, swoops down on Jen's caravan and steals her comb (Figure 1.23). Jen leaps from her coach to pursue him, and the two ride off in a rollicking chase scene reminiscent of a dozen Hollywood romantic films. Like a Turkish Johnny Depp, Lo teases her with a rough game of "come and get it," alternately cocky and crude or tender and passionate. He plays the part of trickster, an elusive agent of change, a figure of comic relief. Shifting shapes from alien provocateur to exotic lover, he shifts the narrative from high adventure to comedy and romance. Like other archetypal shapeshifters described by Joseph Campbell, Lo represents unconscious drives within the hero. He releases the sexual energy, the *animus*, within Jen, reminding her that such forces can have dire consequences. Later, pointing to a cliff, Lo tells her an old legend: "Anyone who jumps from that mountain, God will grant his wish. If you believe, it will happen," adding, "a faithful heart makes wishes come true."

In contrast to Lo, Li Mu Bai is an older, serious man, a respected master of the Wudan fighting code. His inflexible adherence to the code has also made him obdurate, insensitive to his deepest feelings for Shu Lien. Recalling his master's teaching, he tells her "The things we touch have no permanence. Nothing we can hold onto in this world lasts." Her response is to touch his hand. "Isn't my hand real?" she asks. Later, Li wants to take on Jen as his disciple. He explains to a skeptical Shu Lien that his motive is to help the young woman find a righteous path for her talents: "She needs direction ... and training." Jen herself resists this offer (Figure 1.24), perhaps remembering Jade Fox's experience with male teachers, perhaps thinking of Lo or of her freedom. If Li is a mentor figure, the superego's envoy, representing an ideal standard of morality, the hero's conscience, he is an ambiguous one.

There is nothing ambiguous about the Green Destiny Sword. Dating back before the Qin era, it could easily have sprung from the pages of a Western chivalric romance. In *Crouching Tiger*, the sword becomes a fetish, a symbol of male

FIGURE 1.24   Li is a mentor figure, the superego's envoy, representing an ideal standard of morality in *Crouching Tiger, Hidden Dragon*.

power. Li, its owner, relinquishes the sword together with his life of fighting. Throughout the story, it keeps changing hands. When Shu Lien presents it to Sir Te, the good man is reluctant to accept the gift: "It is a great hero's weapon! He is the only one in the world worthy of carrying it," says Te. Later Jen steals the weapon, fondling the gleaming blade and dreaming of the power it will give her. Shu Lien tries to take it back, calling out to Jen: "Without the Green Destiny, you are nothing." At one point, Shu Lien comes across Li dancing with the sword alone, like a boy with his toy. Near the film's conclusion, in a sexually charged duel among the swaying tops of bamboo trees, Li wrenches the sword from Jen and throws it into the rushing waters below. It is only after Li dies in her arms that the sword returns to Shu Lien, who sends it back to Sir Te for safekeeping.

Aesthetics: How is the story told?

Phallic swords and magic manuals are the standard props of many narrative traditions, Eastern and Western alike. With *Crouching Tiger*, Ang Lee returns to the mainland aesthetics of earlier wuxia fiction and operatic melodrama. His decision to use the Mandarin language and to center his story on women is both a step back and a step forward, blending elements of ancient Chinese tradition with elements of modern globalism. We can trace some of his intentions by comparing the film script to Wang Dulu's original novel. Lee and his writers simplified a long and intricate series of adventures, romances, intrigues, and escapes, focusing the narrative on Jen and her relationships to two women and two men. By relegating Bo (the novel's chief male hero) to a minor role, removing a vengeful monk, eliminating Jade Fox's husband, and killing off Li (in the novel, he lives and Shu Lien dies), the script of *Crouching Tiger* becomes the story of a young woman's fight for freedom, pleasure, and power in a man's world, a story for a modern audience. The film's ambiguous ending (it is not clear whether Jen survives her leap) and Jen's ambivalence throughout the story (she makes an alliance with a criminal but doesn't want to see her family disgraced; she seeks the story-book excitement of a *jianghu* life but cherishes her class privileges) transform the wuxia plot into something richer both thematically and emotionally.

More than most martial arts films, *Crouching Tiger* draws on skillful acting and understated cinematography to tell its story. Ang Lee creates richly textured theatrical moments like the two scenes described earlier involving Len, Shu Lien, and Jade Fox. The relationships between these women are conveyed less through what they say than by how they look and act. The women's embroidered garments and elaborate coiffures speak subtly of their traditional roles in Qing dynasty China. The décor of Jen's room, with its elaborate writing desk, ornamental vases, scroll hangings, latticed garden window, and bonsai tree, speak of rank and privilege (Figure 1.21). Jen's handwriting, elegant and sure, bespeaks her youthful confidence, but when Shu Lien makes the analogy to swordplay, the younger woman's smile betrays the slightest hesitancy. Later, as they sit down to tea, close-ups reveal traces of Shu Lien's life-long disappointment when Jen talks naively of true happiness, and they share secrets. The duel taking place beneath their polite conversation gives way to intimacy and trust. In contrast, as we've noticed (Figure 1.22), the scene with Jade Fox takes place during the dark of night. The women's faces, lit by a single candle, reflect the progress of a deadly contest of wills. A raised eyebrow, a curled lip, a glint in the eye, or a raised thumb communicates a daughter's anger and defiance, a mother's pain and power.

Peter Pau's cinematography contributes to the film's restrained aesthetics by favoring a middle-tone, low-contrast palette. He mimics the negative space and desaturated colors of Chinese paintings. Lee and Pau choose red for the desert scenes, associated with the tiger, and green for the forest, representing the hidden dragon. The Green Destiny sword and Jade Fox are linked by color to this scheme.

Yet the film's most cinematic and creative features are arguably the fight scenes. While typical wuxia and kung fu moments offer lots of stylized aggression, Yuen Woping's martial choreography in *Crouching Tiger* breaks the mold. More than one critic has compared martial arts movies to musicals, and *Crouching Tiger* explicitly invites the comparison. The *qingqong* (literally "light skill") fighting technique gives practitioners the ability to defy gravity. Yuen's brilliant wirework, so striking in *The Matrix*, lifts the actors off their feet into dazzling displays of aerial acrobatics when Shu Lien chases Jen over the rooftops of Beijing or when Li Mu Bai spars with Jen above the bamboo forest (Figure 1.24). Pau's camera catches the action at revealing angles, sometimes from below, sometimes in an overhead shot recalling the aerial camerawork of Busby Berkeley. Yuen Woping's fluid imagination, aided by Tim Squyres's editing, stitches the shots into the seamless flow of dance.

When Jen steals the Green Destiny Sword, Shu Lien chases her from roof to roof. They go bounding from wall to wall, hurdling over red tiles, soaring high above the neighborhood. At one point, they confront each other in a frenetic kung fu ballet, a whirl of flying feet and fists, two matched dancers spinning, springing, and leaping in sync. But the two women have different movements, different fighting styles. Younger and lighter, Jen is ever striving toward the sky. Shu Lien's motions are aligned with gravity. She throws a bundle at the thief, then a piece of masonry to bring her down. "Get down here," she cries, striving to pin her opponent to the pavement with her feet. Compare this interaction to the scene in Jen's room, where the younger woman shows off her deft calligraphy and expresses her desire to be free. The gravity in Shu Lien's face, the face of experience, shows how little about freedom or desire Jen really knows. Here, with no need for subtitles, the fight on the rooftops enacts Jen's flightiness and Shu Lien's efforts to ground her in the discipline of life.

Later, in a tavern, Jen is seated alone with her sword and a cup of tea. A mean-looking group of men arrives with weapons on display as the regular clientele scramble to make room. They all have impressively bad names: Iron Arm, Flying Saber, Shining Phoenix Mountain Gou. It is the *jianghu* gang (Giang Hu in the script), the underground brotherhood of misfits who practice martial arts in the mountains. They provoke Jen to battle and she rises to the task, dispatching Iron Arm with a few casual strokes, smashing others through the railings to the ground floor below. She leaps over her opponents, fighting four at once with one hand behind her back. Her body is a blur, somersaulting down a staircase full of armed men, then twirling upward to the second floor again. When Monk Jing demands to know her identity, she proclaims in measured lines, "I am the Invincible Sword Goddess. Armed with the Incredible ... Green Destiny. Be you Li or Southern Crane, lower your head and ask for mercy. I am the desert dragon. I leave no trace. Today I fly over Eu-Mei. Tomorrow ... I'll kick over Wudan Mountain!" (Figure 1.7). Her boasts sound like something out of Marvel comics. The brawl itself, played as comedy, could have taken place in a Western saloon or a Jedi bar. We might recognize the tavern as a staple of Hong Kong action films like *Come Drink with Me* (*Da zui xia*, 1966), a place where the laws of physics and male physical superiority are suspended (Figure 1.6). The scene winks at these kindred genres and tells us something about Jen's internal world, the fantasy of the self-styled superhero.

Near the film's conclusion, Jen meets her match in Mu Bai when the Green Destiny's thief and owner confront each other in the bamboo forest. Visually, this is Ang Lee's most inspired scene, a lofty homage to King Hu's *A Touch of Zen* (*Xia nu*, 1971). The two duelists float and glide among the treetops in an ecstasy of green, the color of the hidden dragon. Mu Bai is superbly in control. Cool and centered, he manages to stay slightly above her as the branches bend or snap, catapulting them to different heights. Their swords clash lightly as they pass in long, slow-motion arcs. They glide above the canopy in graceful long shots. Only when Mu Bai looks into Jen's beautiful face, framed in close-up by the bamboo stalks, does he falter and fall. Jen takes flight, skipping over the surface of a jade-like pool until they land together on a rock and speak face to face. Again there is no need for dialogue. Even before he tells her that he wants to be her teacher, her master, we know his feelings and intentions. We see them in his haughty posture, one hand behind him as they fence. We feel them in the sensual play of bodies swaying in the wind. His story is narrated in the universal language of action films.

Thematics: What is the story telling us?

Lee uses many of the conventions of the wuxia genre: the secret handbook, the magic sword, the relationship of master and student. He also develops some of the genre's traditional themes: the motivation of revenge, the need for discipline, the perilous distractions of romance, and the centrality of physically powerful women. We've already seen how this last feature is quite common in Chinese martial arts genres in contrast to traditional Westerns or samurai films. In this respect, the women warriors in *Crouching Tiger* and their female ancestors anticipate more recent trends in the global representation of women. Think of *Bend It Like Beckham* (2002), *Whale Rider* (2002), or *Kill Bill: Vol. 1* (2003) and *Vol. 2* (2004).

Lee's film also reflects a current worldwide focus on ethnicity. The desert episodes take place in the west of China, where ethnic minorities have lived on the fringes of Han society for centuries. Lo belongs to one of these minorities. The tribal song he sings to Jen while she is bathing sounds like Turkish. She calls him a barbarian, and he is surprised to learn that she is Manchurian, not a member of the Han majority. These references to disenfranchised groups make a political statement, however veiled, about the marginalized people of China including, perhaps, the Taiwanese. The *jianghu* underworld, with its ragtag assortment of social outcasts, may suggest another fact of modern China, the growing gap between wealthy capitalists and an impoverished underclass. Seen from this perspective, *Crouching Tiger* offers a challenge to China's patriarchal and ethnocentric traditions.

Where does the film fit into ongoing debates over global and national cinemas? Executive producer and screenwriter James Schamus acknowledged the desire to make "an Eastern movie for Western audiences and in some ways a more Western movie for Eastern audiences."[7] Lee himself has responded to the accusation that his films are "too Hollywood." In the preface to the illustrated book of the film, Lee describes *Crouching Tiger, Hidden Dragon* as "a kind of dream of China, a China that probably never existed, except in my boyhood fantasies in Taiwan. ... fired by the martial arts movies I grew up with and by the novels of romance and derring-do I read instead of doing my homework."[8]

It might be accurate to say that *Crouching Tiger* is located somewhere between history and myth, embedding certain cultural particularities of China in an eclectic matrix of world culture, arising from personal motives and aspiring to universal truths. *New York Times* film critic Elvis Mitchell wrote that the film combined "girl-power cool and the soap-opera bloodshed of 'Buffy, the Vampire Slayer.'" He found elements of *The Scarlet Pimpernel, Zorro, The Bostonians,* screwball comedy ("Hit Me Kate"), and comedy of manners ("'Sense and Sensibility' with a body count"). Ultimately, he commended Lee for bringing a "new perspective" to the genre, introducing "spirituality not normally found in these pictures."[9]

Jen's struggle for freedom within traditional Qing society can be read in many ways. Historically, it dramatizes an age-old conflict between individual happiness and social responsibility, between the Daoist pursuit of one's nature ("the way") and the communal obligations of Confucianism. The Confucian concepts of propriety and filial piety, honoring one's parents, have been pillars of Chinese life for more than two millennia. Daoism, which teaches harmony with nature and oneself, may be even older. More recently, Jen's inner conflict echoes a younger generation's aspirations to break free from conventional constraints, a conflict dramatized in Ang Lee's first three films, in which Chinese-American children resist the old-fashioned ways of their Chinese parents but suffer the guilt of betrayal. *Crouching Tiger* reminds us that this struggle is not a simple conflict between East and West; it has deep roots in Chinese ethical and religious history. And, as Campbell and Vogler might point out, it has been a staple of myths throughout the world. The journey of the hero is an inner journey, a narrative of passage from childhood to adulthood. The mentors and monsters met along the way represent aspects of the self as it matures. In fashioning his film from elements of worldwide genres, in accommodating his characters and story to the eyes of Eastern and Western audiences, Ang Lee has advanced the art of global cinema along the road of universal humanism.

Notes

1. Sheldon Hsiao-peng Lu, ed., *Transnational Chinese Cinemas: Identity, Nationhood, Gender* (University of Hawai'i Press, 1997), 7–8.

2. Sheldon Hsiao-peng Lu and Emilie Yeh, eds., *Chinese-Language Film: Historiography, Poetics, Politics* (University of Hawai'i Press, 2005), 2.

3. Christina Klein, "*Crouching Tiger, Hidden Dragon*: A Diasporic Reading," *Cinema Journal* 43(4) (Summer 2004): 18–42.

4. Klein.

5. James Schamus, "The Polyglot Task of Writing the Global Film," *The New York Times*, November 5, 2005: 2A25.

6. Joseph Campbell, *The Hero with a Thousand Faces*, 3rd edition (New World Library, 2008). See also Christopher Vogler, *The Writer's Journey* (Michael Wiese Productions, 1998) and Stuart

Voytilla, *Myth and the Movies* (Michael Wiese Productions, 1999).

7. The Guardian/BFI Interview, Ang Lee and James Schamus, November 7, 2000. Available at: http://www.guardian.co.uk/film/2000/nov/07/guardian interviewsatbfisouthbank (accessed June 8, 2013).

8. Ang Lee, James Schamus, Huiling Wang, *et al.*, *Crouching Tiger, Hidden Dragon: A Portrait of the Ang Lee Film* (Newmarket Press, 2000), 7.

9. Elvis Mitchell, "Action Fans, Be Prepared For Heart And Feminism," *The New York Times*, October 9, 2000. Available at: http://www.nytimes.com/2000/10/09/movies/film-festival-review-action-fans-be-prepared-for-heart-and-feminism.html?n=Top%2fReference%2fTimes%20Topics%2fPeople%2fL%2fLee%2c%20Ang (accessed June 8, 2013).

Further Reading

Berry, Chris and Mary Anne Farquhar. *China on Screen: Cinema and Nation*. Columbia University Press, 2006.

Cornelius, Sheila. *New Chinese Cinema*. Wallflower, 2000.

Cui, Shuqin. *Women through the Lens: Gender and Nation in a Century of Chinese Cinema*. University of Hawai'i Press, 2003.

Curtin, Michael. *Playing to the World's Biggest Audience: The Globalization of Chinese Film and TV*. University of California Press, 2007.

Ehrlich, Linda and David Desser, eds. *Cinematic Landscapes: Observations on the Visual Arts in China and Japan*. University of Texas Press, 1994.

Fu, Poshek. *Between Shanghai and Hong Kong: The Politics of Chinese Cinemas*. Stanford University Press, 2003.

Lu, Sheldon. *China, Transnational Visuality, Global Postmodernity*. Stanford University Press, 2001.

Lu, Sheldon, ed. *Transnational Chinese Cinemas: Identity, Nationhood, Gender*. University of Hawai'i Press, 1997.

Lu, Sheldon and Emilie Yeh, eds. *Chinese-Language Film: Historiography, Poetics, Politics*. University of Hawai'i Press, 2005.

Zhang, Yingjin. *Screening China: Critical Interventions, Cinematic Reconfigurations, and the Transnational Imaginary in Contemporary Chinese Cinema*. University of Michigan Center for Chinese Studies, 2002.

Zhen, Ni. *Memories from the Beijing Film Academy: The Genesis of China's Fifth Generation*. Translated by Chris Berry. Duke University Press, 2002.

Zhu, Ying. *Chinese Cinema during the Era of Reform: The Ingenuity of the System*. Praeger, 2003.

CLOSE-UP
THE MAGNIFICENT SEVEN

FIGURE 1.25   *The Magnificent Seven* (Dir. John Sturges, 1960).

Directed by John Sturges.
Written by William Roberts (uncredited: Walter Bernstein, Walter Newman, Akira Kurosawa, Shinobu Hashimoto, and Hideo Oguni).
Cinematography by Charles Lang.
Editing by Ferris Webster.
Music by Elmer Bernstein.
Art Direction by Edward Fitzgerald.
Produced by Walter Mirisch, Lou Morheim, and John Sturges.
Distributed by United Artists in 1960.
Running Time: 128 minutes.

Chris Larabee Adams	Yul Brynner
Vin Tanner	Steve McQueen
Calvera	Eli Wallach
Bernardo O'Reilly	Charles Bronson
Lee	Robert Vaughn
Harry Luck	Brad Dexter
Britt	James Coburn
Chico	Horst Buchholz
Old Man	Vladimir Sokoloff

World Cinema through Global Genres, First Edition. William V. Costanzo.
© 2014 John Wiley & Sons, Inc. Published 2014 by John Wiley & Sons, Inc.

Aside from the sheer pleasure of watching a well-made action film, *The Magnificent Seven* merits special attention for its contributions to the genre and its relationship to global cinema. Based on Akira Kurosawa's *Seven Samurai* (1954) and directed by John Sturges in 1960, *The Magnificent Seven* is credited with introducing Hollywood to a new type of Western hero, the hard-bitten professional killer, and a new type of Western, a postmodern genre in which villains can be likeable and the good guys wear black hats. It also popularized the idea of misfits on a mission, a plot device that crosses genres and includes *The Dirty Dozen* (1967), *The Wild Bunch* (1969), *Stand by Me* (1986), and *The A-Team* (2010).

Sturges shifts the location of Kurosawa's film from feudal Japan to the American Wild West, where a Mexican village of defenceless farmers is prey to periodic raids by bandits. Poor, hungry, and tired of watching the fruits of their hard labor stolen every season by Calvera and his well-armed band, the farmers decide to fight back. They send an envoy to buy guns at an American border town, where they are persuaded that gunfighters are cheaper than guns. The seven gunmen whom they hire sign up for the job for different reasons, but they become a fighting unit and train the villagers to fight with them. After several skirmishes and a major battle, the Calvera gang is defeated and all but one of the surviving gunmen ride off into the hills.

Like *Seven Samurai*, *The Magnificent Seven* can be roughly divided into three sections: recruiting the Seven, preparing for battle, and fighting the bandits. Like Kurosawa, Sturges varies the pacing of his film, alternating lengthy lulls with moments of explosive action. The opening credits appear over a widescreen view of the Mexican town, with its brick church and tepees of stacked corn drying in the sun: a vision of peace. Suddenly, a cloud of dust appears, announcing Calvera and his gang. He has come to charm and bully the village to get what he wants, food and money for his hungry men. When we cut to the border town, it looks like a typical one-street Western set, but this town is run by racists; they won't let Old Sam be buried in Boot Hill because he was an Indian. A stranger in a black hat volunteers to drive the hearse. This is Chris Adams (Yul Brynner), who is joined by another stranger, Vin (Steve McQueen). Together they take on snipers and the bigoted "reception committee" to finish the job. Watching this show of bravery, skill, adventure, and principle, the Mexican envoys enlist Chris's help.

It's clear that Chris is motivated largely by a personal code of honor. He steps onto the driver's seat of Old Sam's hearse because it is the right thing to do. But the others join his team for different reasons. Bernardo (Charles Bronson) is an Irish-Mexican American who happens to be broke. Lee (Robert Vaughn) is a gunman on the run from the law and from his enemies. Vin, a gambler down on his luck, also needs the money. Harry Luck (Brad Dexter) believes there is a secret stash of gold. Chico (Horst Buchholz), the youngest, wants to prove he is a man. The prime interest of Britt (James Coburn) is in sharpening his knife-throwing skills. Like a Zen master, he's competing with himself.

Surprisingly, what motivates Calvera is more complex than what drives most Western villains. Like the renegade *ronin* in *Seven Samurai*, his men are hungry, and their best means of employment are their weapons. But that does not explain why Calvera sets the Seven free once he has captured them. For the farmers, he has nothing but contempt. "If God didn't want them sheared, He wouldn't have made them sheep," he scoffs. But he admires the Americans, not only for their shooting skills but because he sees himself in them. "We're in the same business," he tells them, and later asks Chris uncomprehendingly, "Why did you come back, a man like you?"

Why, indeed? Feeling frustrated and betrayed after their capture, the gunfighters are ready to leave the village to its own devices. But they are not the same men they used to be. Bernardo, who has Mexican blood in him, has made friends with the farmers' children, who see him as a hero. Chico has found a pretty village girl who loves him. Harry still thinks there is hidden treasure, but he now believes in something else as well. What's more, the seven men have formed a special bond. They have become a team. When Chris makes his decision to head south again, he is not alone.

The first confrontation between Chris and Calvera reveals much about each man as well as Sturges's directing style. Calvera rides in from one side of the frame, followed by his 40 men on horseback. Chris walks out from the other side, backed by Vin, also on foot. For more than three minutes of screen time, Sturges observes the 180 degree rule, keeping Calvera on the left and Chris on the right. The bandit is filmed against the sky from a low angle, with two men at his rear. His mood swings from ironic pleasantries to haughty anger as his tactics shift from bribes to threats. Chris appears mostly in close-ups, his face immobile and determined. For much of this time, the two sides test each other with words. "New wall?" Calvera asks, surveying the town. "There are lots of new walls," Chris answers, "... all around." Calvera's retort is cocky, self-assured: "They won't keep me out." "They were meant to keep you in," is Chris's reply. The progress of this verbal banter is echoed in the music soundtrack, which alternates between an ominous bandit motif and the heroic melody of the title theme. "How many of you did they hire?" probes Calvera. "Enough," comes the curt response. One by one, the magnificent seven appear, stepping out from doorways, perched on roofs. When the shooting starts, the words give way to gunfire. Sturges's camera picks up the pace with shorter takes and more varied shots. Pistols blaze, horses rear, men fall or duck for cover. The air is filled with dust and smoke. Calvera and the remaining members of his gang escape, but we know that they'll be back.

The final battle takes place in broad daylight, another melee of leaping men, galloping horses, gun smoke, swung shovels, and death on all sides. Only three of the Seven survive. The Old Man sums up the score for them. "Only the farmers have won. They remain forever. They are like the land itself. You helped rid them of Calvera, the way a strong wind helps rid them of locusts. You're like the wind – blowing over the land and passing on." Only one, Chico, decides to stay, removing his gun belt, rolling up his sleeve to join his girl. As the music rises, Chris and Vin ride off with the wind.

In this broad outline, *The Magnificent Seven* recycles many of the scenes and themes of Kurosawa's film. What makes the Seven so magnificent is not only their fighting skills, but also, and primarily, their allegiance to the group effort. Rugged individualists to start with, they learn to subordinate their personal interests to the greater good. There are, of course, important cultural differences between the American frontier and feudal Japan. Samurai did not define themselves as individuals. Their pride came from membership in an elite social class. They were professional warriors attached to a warlord or *daimyo*. Nor did they fight with guns. There is a big difference between firing a pistol or a shotgun at a distance and confronting the enemy in close combat. Kurosawa's samurai fight by the sword but die by gunfire, marking them as both valiant and obsolete. It seems clear from the ending of Sturges's film that the days of men like Chris and Vin are numbered. The future belongs to the farmers and their way of life. But the class conflicts explored in *Seven Samurai* are cast in *The Magnificent Seven* as racial issues, reflecting tension within American society in 1960. Film historians point to the bigotry against Indians at Boot Hill and the superiority of the American gunfighters over the Mexican farmers, who are incapable of fighting their own battles. In fact, the DVD commentary explains how the script was changed in deference to Mexican sensibilities. Instead of coming to the border town in search of Americans to solve their problems, as they did in an earlier version of the script, the Mexicans are only looking to buy guns for self-defense. Hiring seven gunfighters seems more like an afterthought. All through the shooting of the film, local censors were on the scene making sure that the Mexican actors did not succumb to stereotyping. This may explain why their white clothing never seems to get dirty or unkempt.

Richard Slotkin explores another topical connection to the 1960s.[1] During the American involvement in Vietnam, filmmakers sometimes used Westerns to comment on the war. Movies like *The Wild Bunch*, *Little Big Man* (1970), and *Ulzana's Raid* (1972) thus indirectly reenacted the Tet Offensive or the My Lai massacre of 1968, drawing on incidents and imagery from television coverage of these conflicts. Slotkin considers *The Magnificent Seven* to be the first "Vietnam Western." When American gunfighters cross the border into Mexico, they get to make commando raids on a predatory enemy and save the local inhabitants.

When comparing *Seven Samurai* to *The Magnificent Seven*, we should bear in mind important differences between an auteurist filmmaker like Kurosawa, who has nearly complete control of his production from script to final cut, and a Hollywood genre director like John Sturges, whose work is more collaborative. Sturges (1910–1992) began his career in the art and editing departments of RKO Studio, working his way up. He made documentaries for the Air Force during World War II, and worked with major talents like David O. Selznick and William Wyler. At the peak of his career, Sturges specialized in male-oriented action films like *Bad Day at Black Rock* (1955), *Gunfight at the O.K. Corral* (1957), *The Great Escape* (1963), and *Ice Station Zebra* (1968), all successful box office hits. He was a master of the multiple story film and knew how to make the best of CinemaScope's widescreen format. His mantra was to focus on the "gut" of the picture, not the head.

According to the documentary film *Guns for Hire*, the idea of remaking *Seven Samurai* as a Western came from associate producer Lou Morheim, who optioned the rights and interested Anthony Quinn in the project.[2] Through a succession of exchanges, not entirely friendly, the rights ended up with Walter Mirisch, who became executive producer, assembled a team of freelance writers, and hired Sturges, who had just made the successful Western *Gunfight at the O.K. Corral*, to direct. They watched Kurosawa's film together many times and began casting the main parts. Yul Brynner, who had played the title role in *The King and I* (1956), brought a regal bearing to the part of Chris Adams. Steve McQueen and Charles Bronson had worked with Sturges before, and James Coburn learned about the film from his college roommate, Robert Vaughn. Horst Buchholz became Chico, a German playing a Mexican. Recruiting the seven actors was almost like building the gunfighter team; making them work like a team posed other challenges. Throughout the shooting, Brynner and McQueen kept trying to upstage each other, a rivalry that Sturges reportedly encouraged because he liked the effect on their performance. Meanwhile, the Mexican actors in Eli Wallach's bandit gang adopted him, a Jewish actor from New York, teaching him how to ride a horse and wield a gun. All this contributed to the spirit of the film.

United Artists did not expect much from the movie's general release, but it was a hit in Europe and box office sales climbed after its return to the United States. *The Magnificent Seven* became a classic, inspiring a television series and three sequels: *Return of the Seven* (1966), *Guns of the Magnificent Seven* (1969), and *The Magnificent Seven Ride Again* (1972). The unforgettable score by Elmer Bernstein took on a life of its own. Even those who never saw the film can recognize it in the theme for Marlboro cigarette commercials, Euro Disneyland, rock groups, and other popular media. Meanwhile, many of the young actors went on to successful screen careers. But perhaps the best tribute came from Kurosawa himself, who said he loved the film and presented Sturges with a ceremonial sword.[3]

Questions

1. Which groups or characters do you find most interesting or sympathetic? Explain what draws you to them and whether your view changes in the course of the film.

2. Violence is a staple of frontier life and its representation on film. In Westerns, the hero is often a gunfighter who faces the wilderness outside and the savagery within. What role do violent actions play in *The Magnificent Seven*?

3. Explore the motives of the film's main characters. What are they seeking and what do they find? Does *The Magnificent Seven* promote individualism or collaboration as an ideology?

4. After negative reactions to the way Mexicans were portrayed in another film, *Vera Cruz* (1954), United Artists employed local censors to monitor shooting on location. What do you think of the way Mexicans, their village, and their way of life are represented in *The Magnificent Seven*?

5. John Sturges is noted for his direction of male actors, his use of widescreen photography, and the pacing of his action films. Assess the director's cinematic accomplishments in this film.

6. Aficionados of the genre are fond of quoting lines from the script. When the Mexicans go scouting for hired guns, one says, "There's one – look at the

scars on his face!" but another replies, "The man for us is the one who gave him that face." When Calvera boasts "those walls won't keep me out," Chris tells him, "They were meant to keep you in." Then there is the story Vin tells about the man who fell from a ten-story building. The people on each floor kept hearing him say, "So far, so good. So far, so good." What lines in the script do you find most memorable? What do they tell you about the film's characters and their attitudes toward life?

7. Make your own comparison between *Seven Samurai* and *The Magnificent Seven*. Where does the American film follow Kurosawa's film and where does it differ? What reasons can you give for these changes?

8. The Western is sometimes said to embody America's most cherished myths. What foundational beliefs do you find in *The Magnificent Seven*? Consult Christopher Vogler's book on mythic structures, *The Writer's Journey*, and see how many archetypes and of the journey narrative you can identify in Sturges's film.

Notes

1. Richard Slotkin, "Gunfighters and Green Berets: *The Magnificent Seven* and the Myth of Counter-Insurgency," *Radical History Review* (Spring 1989): 64–90.
2. Documentary directed by Louis Heaton, *Guns for Hire: The Making of "The Magnificent Seven."* 2000.

See also Glen Lovell, *Escape Artist: The Life and Films of John Sturges* (University of Wisconsin Press, 2008), 192–193.

3. Jay Robert Nash and Stanley Ralph Ross, eds., *The Motion Picture Guide* (Cinemabooks, 1988), 1809.

Further Reading and Other Media

Anderson, J.L. "Japanese Swordfighters and American Gunfighters." *Cinema Journal* 12(2) (Spring 1973): 1–21.

Donovan, Barna William. *The Asian Influence on Hollywood Action Films.* McFarland & Company, 2008.

Guns for Hire: The Making of "The Magnificent Seven." Documentary TV film, directed by Louis Heaton. 2000.

Kaminsky, Stuart. "The Samurai Film and the Western." *Journal of Popular Film* 1(4) (1972): 312–324.

Lovell, Glen. *Escape Artist: The Life and Films of John Sturges.* University of Wisconsin Press, 2008.

McGee, Patrick. *From "Shane" to "Kill Bill": Rethinking the Western.* Blackwell, 2007.

Slotkin, Richard. "Gunfighters and Green Berets: *The Magnificent Seven* and the Myth of Counter-Insurgency." *Radical History Review* (Spring 1989): 64–90.

The Magnificent Seven. DVD Special Edition. Commentary by James Coburn, Eli Wallach, producer Walter Mirisch, and assistant director Robert Relyea. MGM Home Entertainment, 2001.

CLOSE-UP
SEVEN SAMURAI

FIGURE 1.26 *Seven Samurai* (*Shichinin no samurai*, Dir. Akira Kurosawa, 1954).

Directed by Akira Kurosawa.
Written by Akira Kurosawa, Shinobu Hashimoto, and Hideo Oguni.
Cinematography by Asakazu Nakai.
Editing by Akira Kurosawa.
Music by Fumio Hayasaka.
Art Direction by So Matsuyama.
Produced by Sojiro Motoki.
Distributed by Toho (Japan) and Columbia Pictures (United States) in 1954.
In Japanese with English subtitles.
Running Time: 207 minutes.

Kikuchiyo	Toshiro Mifune
Kambei	Takashi Shimura
Shino	Keiko Tsushima
Shichiroji	Daisuke Kato
Katsushiro	Isao Kimura
Heihachi	Minonu Chiaki
Kyuzo	Seiji Miyaguchi
Gorobei	Yoshio Inaba
Wife	Yukiko Shimazaki
Farmer Manzo	Kamatari Fujiwara
Farmer Rikichi	Yoshio Tsuchiya

World Cinema through Global Genres, First Edition. William V. Costanzo.
© 2014 John Wiley & Sons, Inc. Published 2014 by John Wiley & Sons, Inc.

Anyone interested in Japanese cinema and its contribution to global action films, particularly to the samurai genre, will find no better place to begin than with Akira Kurosawa (1910–1998) and his ground-breaking picture, *Seven Samurai* (1954). Internationally acclaimed as the *sensei* – the acknowledged master and mentor – Kurosawa is widely known as a director's director. In the United States, his influence is acknowledged by such filmmakers as Robert Altman, Francis Ford Coppola, Steven Spielberg, Martin Scorsese, and Sam Peckinpah. A quick inventory of remakes demonstrates how readily the world of samurai warriors depicted in his films can merge with the Wild West. Martin Ritt based *The Outrage* (1964) on Kurosawa's *Rashomon* (1950); Sergio Leone remade *Yojimbo* (1961) as *A Fistful of Dollars* (1964), and John Sturges recast *Seven Samurai* as *The Magnificent Seven* (1960). George Lucas cited *The Hidden Fortress* (1958) as an important source for *Star Wars*, that science fiction series in which the Western frontier is transported to the New Frontier of outer space. Kurosawa, in turn, expressed a lively interest in American films, particularly Westerns, listing John Ford and John Huston among his inspirations. Yet in his own country, he was criticized during his lifetime by an older generation for being insufficiently Japanese and by younger filmmakers for being reactionary and irrelevant.

Akira Kurosawa was born in Tokyo to a family that traced its lineage back to a famous samurai warrior of the Genji period. His father, fiercely proud of this military heritage, taught physical education in an army school. A strict disciplinarian, the older Kurosawa instilled a strong sense of self-control in his son, who studied Kendo sword fighting while young but gravitated naturally toward the arts. Akira loved literature, especially Dostoevsky, and studied painting before applying for a job to Photo Chemical Laboratories, the movie studio that would later become Toho, one of Japan's leading film producers. As a hard-working studio apprentice, he developed a great admiration for his mentor, Kajiro Yamomoto, who recognized the young man's talent and encouraged him to make movies his life work. It was Yamomoto who taught him the importance of script writing, a skill he was to practice throughout his life. After assisting on more than two dozen films, Kurosawa began directing his first feature *Sanshiro Sugata* (*Sugata Sanshiro*), a samurai film, in 1942. It was released in the following year to popular and critical acclaim.

The years during which Kurosawa launched his 50-year career posed challenges for any young filmmaker. Japanese cinema had been slow to evolve. Early directors made little use of creative editing or camera work, preferring to focus on presentation and performance. Tied to dramatic traditions of the stage, the industry employed male actors (*oyama*) in female roles as late as 1922 and used *benshi* narrators to give off-screen commentaries until the mid-1930s. Kurosawa's older brother was a *benshi*, a job that got Akira free admission as a child. During World War II, Japan's military leadership censored all productions to keep them in line with its nationalist agenda. After the war, the Allied Occupation enforced its own form of censorship, prohibiting films that it considered to be undemocratic, anti-foreign, or militaristic. Samurai films were banned until the mid-1950s.

Over the years, Kurosawa developed film techniques and production methods that served him well. Typically, his scripts were collaborations, written with another writer or a team in order to bring different perspectives to his vision. Often, the scripts were crafted with particular performers in mind, especially Toshiro Mifune and Takashi Shimura, his favorite actors. The cast would do readings, followed by walk-through rehearsals and dress rehearsals, with lights and cameras in position. Then the filming began. Unlike many directors, Kurosawa preferred to shoot chronologically, following the script, and editing the footage every night. This approach, he believed, maintained momentum and allowed him to "capture the flow." On the set and in post-production, he had a reputation for keeping strict control. Nothing in the final cut was accidental. Every gesture, every angle, every shadow, every breeze was a deliberate decision by "the emperor," or *tenno*, as he came to be known among his inner circle.

We see this firm command in *Seven Samurai*. Yet Kurosawa's hand is never gratuitously artful. Stop the film at nearly any point and you're likely to see a carefully composed shot. Look again, observe the shot in context, and you'll realize that Kurosawa's composition serves a larger purpose. The placement of each human form, the texture of a wall, the driving rain, the play of shadows on water is always motivated by the story. And while much of the film's genius lies in the details, it never loses sight of the broad design. Epic in length (more than 200 minutes in the original director's cut) and cultural sweep (revealing elements of feudal Japan that still resonate in contemporary life), *Seven Samurai* is a brooding commentary on loyalty and violence, on individuals and groups, on human nature under pressure, a story that is also comic, thrilling, and vastly entertaining.

Kurosawa made his film soon after the American Occupation, when he was free to revisit Japan's feudal past. The story is set during the Sengoku "Warring States" period, a time of brutal conflict and social chaos also known as the Onin War (1467–1477). Feuding warlords razed each other's forts and plundered villages, hiring samurai to fight for them. When a warlord was defeated, his samurai were left to wander through the countryside as *ronin*, "wave men," sometimes pillaging farms for food. Some samurai became teachers and doctors, like Kurosawa's ancestors, but many more became bandits, relying on their martial skills to prey on unarmed peasants. It was a time of lawlessness and sporadic violence, much like the Wild West. But it was also a time of opportunity. Without a strong, central authority, the old social order had broken down, and it was possible for a poor peasant with courage and ambition, or with foolhardy pretense, to take up a sword and rise above his class.

In *Seven Samurai*, the farmers in a mountain village hire seven samurai to help protect them from a band of marauding *ronin*. The plot unfolds in three parts, reflecting the director's interest in process, how things are done. Part One introduces the film's main characters: the villagers debate the idea of hiring mercenaries and the samurai join the band of warriors one by one. In Part Two, the samurai prepare their plan of defence and train the villagers for battle. In Part Three, the plan is put into action, culminating in a fierce battle scene and a solemn moment at the burial ground. Kurosawa takes great pains to give this fictional world an authentic feel. His use of deep focus photography, for example, enables us to watch several planes of action at once. While men confront each other in the foreground, the villagers go about their daily chores in the background. His use of three cameras during shooting, a new practice for Kurosawa, enables us to experience the ferocious energy of a cavalry charge in detail and in full almost simultaneously. The screen may be filled with the complexities of village life or the chaos of warfare, but we never lose our bearings. At one point, Kambei, first of the seven samurai, takes his men to the four corners of the village to explain his plan, incidentally giving us the lay of the land. At another point, he paints symbols for the samurai and bandits on a flag, allowing us to keep score throughout the battle. We always know precisely where we are.

The movie opens with a shot of the horizon, dark clouds looming low, as a group of horsemen in silhouette rides from right to left, then towards us in the narrow band of morning light. The soundtrack amplifies the sound of galloping hooves and adds a drumbeat that becomes the bandits' *leitmotif*, a musical phrase announcing their presence. In this film, each group has its musical accompaniment. The villagers are associated with a folk tune played by flutes and percussion. The samurai are announced by a brooding male chorus and brassy horns. A lap dissolve signals a shift in our perspective, one shot melting into the next. Now we're on the hilltop with the riders, fully armed and armored, overlooking a village far below. The bandits decide to postpone their attack. They will return later, when the barley has ripened. Word reaches the villagers, and now the camera shifts to their huddled bodies, heads bowed in clusters of despair and self-pity. A telephoto lens flattens the perspective, accentuating their closeness and conformity. One man moans, "Farmers are born to suffer." Another stands and calls for action. It is Rikichi, a young firebrand who will figure prominently later in the picture. Gradually, several villagers emerge as individuals. There is Mosuke, whose home lies outside the village, exposed to a first attack. There is Manzo, endlessly obsessing about his daughter's virtue. There is Yohei, whose droll face and nervous temperament make him a comic foil. And there is Gisaku, the wizened village patriarch, respectfully called "Grandad" by all. When Manzo objects to the idea of hiring samurai, fearing they may rape his daughter, Gisaku tells him, "What's the use of worrying about your beard when your head's about to be taken?"

The seven samurai make their entrances one at a time. Kambei (played by Takashi Shimura) is first seen shaving his topknot, an act unthinkable for a samurai until we learn that his motive is to save a child being held hostage by a desperate *ronin*. Kambei, embodying the Bushido code of integrity and selflessness, becomes the leader of the samurai team and a kind of spokesman for Kurosawa himself. A young warrior named Katsushiro admires Kambei's courage and begs to be his disciple. Later, they are joined by Kambei's old friend, Shichiroji, and by Gorobei, a skilled archer whom Kambei recruits as his second in command. Gorobei in turn recruits Heihachi, a wood cutter who makes up for weak fighting skills with a strong fighting spirit. The sixth samurai to join, though at first reluctant, is Kyuzo, the most skillful swordsman of the lot. In the film's only instance of one-on-one combat, we watch him dispatch a hot-headed bully with the stony-faced precision that becomes his trademark. Finally, there is Kikuchiyo (Toshiro Mifune), the most energetic and complex of them all. He first appears as a buffoon claiming noble birth. His actions are apish, his sword much too big, his dress ludicrously inapt. Kikuchiyo is the wild card, the trickster, the clown – always a risk in any fighting unit – but he brings the important ingredients of comedy, vitality, and surprise to the story. With his swagger and mocking humor, he can marshal the farmers into troops, and he can show fearless, if imprudent, courage under fire. Kikuchiyo reveals an even deeper, serious side when a stash of hidden armor is discovered in Manzo's hut. The samurai are angered by this exposure of the farmers' treachery. Kikuchiyo knows better. Farmers are cowardly and sneaky, he says, but who made them this way? Perhaps the most revealing moment for Kikuchiyo is when he runs into the burning mill and rescues a baby from its dying mother's arms. "The same thing happened to me," he cries. "I was just like this baby." Cradling the bundle in his arms, he breaks down in tears.

Kurosawa's focus is on character throughout. Some figures, like the bandits, are never fully realized, and only one woman, Manzo's daughter Shino, has a name. But in the course of the film, we learn revealing secrets about Rikichi and Manzo. We watch Katsushiro grow into a man. We come to admire Kambei's wisdom and the noble heart behind Kyuzo's stone face. Most of all, we come to understand something of Kikuchiyo's inner self, the reasons for his outlandish behaviour and his drive to be a samurai. When he is finally accepted by the other six, it is the culmination of his life.

Only three of the seven samurai are left alive. Turning to Gorobei, Kambei says simply, "Again we've survived" and the camera fixes on the fluttering flag, a mute reminder of the toll of battle. At daylight, the farmers are in the field again, moving in synch to the age-old cadence of flute and drum as they plant a new crop of rice. The rhythms of nature, of life itself go on. Across the river, the three surviving warriors turn to leave, pausing at the burial mounds of their fallen comrades. Katsushiro stands apart; he will stay with Shino and become a villager. Kambei speaks once more: "Again we're defeated. The winners are those farmers, not us." The camera tilts up to the graves as the sound of the wind and the lugubrious samurai theme grow louder.

As Joan Mellen puts it in the British Film Institute's book about the film, "the samurai have won the battle, but lost the war."[1] Kambei's days are numbered; the heroic ideals he represents are giving way to a new world of common, practical necessity. Kurosawa mourns the loss of old Japan, figured here in the noble spirit of the samurai, just as he acknowledges the superior survival value figured in the dogged persistence of the villagers. What makes the film more interesting than a simple either/or dichotomy, however, is the way it complicates the matter. Historically, as feudal Japan moves toward peace (not unlike modern Japan in 1954), the superior morality and skills of the warrior class are less important than the economic utility of farmers. Not that Kurosawa's images of battle look especially heroic. There is little of the valiant swordplay typical of the genre. The samurai are unceremoniously killed by gunfire, not in grandly staged, face-to-face duels. Bandits are torn from their horses and savagely stabbed with sharpened bamboo poles. Combatants and horses grovel in the mud. Homes are set on fire with people in them. These are grim, realistic views of man's inhumanity to man. To be sure, we see individual acts of courage, like Heihachi's selfless effort to pull Rikichi from a burning hut or Kyuzo's wordless raid on a bandit gun post. We witness admirable examples of male friendship, like the strong, unspoken bond between Kambei and Gorobei. But we also see how reckless individuality, like Kikuchiyo's copycat mission to steal another gun, can endanger the lives of others. "In war, it is teamwork that counts," Kambei reminds the group. "He who thinks only about himself will destroy himself, too." His admonition underscores the age-old Japanese distinction between duty (*giri*) and humane personal inclination (*ninjo*).

Seven Samurai took some 18 months to make. Kurosawa wrote the script with his collaborators, Shinobu Hashimoto and Hideo Oguni, in 45 days. The role of Kikuchiyo, not part of the original conception, was added for comic relief, though in Mifune's hands it became much more. The production team strove for unusual authenticity and depth. Kurosawa created detailed descriptions and personal histories for each of the samurai, and he invented an entire registry for all the farmers, specifying their family connections so that the actors could live together as a real village during shooting. These relationships are underscored by Kurosawa's careful blocking and composition. At first, farmers and samurai appear as separate groups. The camera and editing stress their divided loyalties. As they move closer in a common cause, their interdependence is affirmed cinematically. A long tracking shot around Kambei during his speech before the final battle shows how the samurai and farmers are all behind him. During the melee, rapid cutting captures their confusion and their unity. All class distinctions vanish in the driving rain.

While *Seven Samurai* was a big success at the box office, it was not much appreciated by the critics at first. Purists found it too "Western." Pacifists thought it promoted militarism, and Marxists disliked the way it represented the lower class. But the film revived fresh interest in the genre, starting a new wave of samurai films that reached some 40 titles a year by the early 1960s. Eventually, it took its place in the pantheon of world cinema, one of the finest films by one of Japan's greatest filmmakers.

Questions

1. The film represents different groups and subgroups: bandits, samurai, villagers; men and women; those who take action and those who resist. To what extent does Kurosawa seem to favor any of these groups over the others? With which group do you identify most closely? Is it possible to read against the grain and appreciate any of these groups even if the film seems to demean them or give them little serious attention?

2. David Desser calls Kurosawa a "dialectical filmmaker," noting the humanist and formalist

tendencies at play in his work and pointing out how the opposing social classes, villagers and samurai, converge in *Seven Samurai*. Kurosawa also alternates scenes of immobility with moments of intense action. What evidence can you find in the film for Desser's dialectical reading?

3. Select a scene that illustrates Kurosawa's aesthetic rigor at its most effective. Notice how he uses composition, camera movement, sound, editing, and other film tools to construct the scene. What larger purpose do these cinematic choices serve?

4. Kurosawa borrows elements from high-toned *jidai-geki* and the coarser *chanbara* films, mixing the heroic with the comic. Find examples of both in *Seven Samurai*. What are the targets of his humor? How seriously do we take characters like Shino, Yohei, and Kikuchiyo?

5. Watch the film again, but this time pay special attention to the sound track. What musical instruments does Kurosawa choose to represent various characters and groups, and how does he use these identifying *leitmotifs*? What do the film's sound effects contribute? Sometimes the sound track seems completely unexpected, as when we hear birds chirping during a scene of conflict. What other examples of this deliberate counterpoint can you find?

Note

1. Joan Mellen, *Seven Samurai* (British Film Institute, 2002), 77.

Further Reading

Desser, David. *The Samurai Films of Akira Kurosawa*. UMI Research Press, 1983.

Desser, David and Arthur Nolletti, Jr. *Reframing Japanese Cinema*. Indiana University Press, 1992.

Donovan, Barna William. *The Asian Influence on Hollywood Action Films*. McFarland & Company, 2008.

Galbraith, Stuart. *The Emperor and the Wolf: The Lives and Films of Akira Kurosawa and Toshiro Mifune*. Faber and Faber, 2002.

Goodman, James. *Akira Kurosawa and Intertextual Cinema*. Johns Hopkins University Press, 1994.

Mellen, Joan. *Seven Samurai*. British Film Institute, 2002.

Prince, Stephen. *The Warrior's Cinema: The Cinema of Akira Kurosawa*. Princeton University Press, 1991.

Richie, Donald. *The Films of Akira Kurosawa*. University of California Press, 1970.

CLOSE-UP
SHOLAY

FIGURE 1.27   *Sholay* (Dir. Ramesh Sippy, 1975).

Directed by Ramesh Sippy.
Produced by G.P. Sippy.
Script by Salim-Javed.
Cinematography by Dwarka Divecha.
Edited by M.S. Shinde.
Music by R.D. Burman.
Released by United Producers and Sippy Films in 1975.
In Hindi, with English subtitles.
Running Time: 188 minutes.

Veeru	Dharmendra Deol
Jai Dev	Amitabh Bachchan
Thakur Baldev Singh	Sanjeev Kumar
Basanti	Hema Malini
Radha	Jaya Bhaduri
Gabbar Singh	Amjad Khan
Ramlaal	Satyen Kappu
Imam	A.K. Hangal
Ahmed	Sachin
Sambha	Mac Mohan
Jailor	Asrani

World Cinema through Global Genres, First Edition. William V. Costanzo.
© 2014 John Wiley & Sons, Inc. Published 2014 by John Wiley & Sons, Inc.

Twenty-one years after *Seven Samurai* (1954) and 15 years after *The Magnificent Seven* (1960), Indian filmmakers G.P. Sippy and his son Ramesh released a movie that some refer to as the first "curry Western." Loosely based on the earlier two films, *Sholay* ("embers" in Hindi) became a massive hit in South Asia and a global classic. It also propelled its male leads Amitabh Bachchan, Dharmendra Deol, Amjad Khan, and Sanjeev Kumar into Bollywood stardom. The film broke all box office records, running for five consecutive years, and continues to be celebrated by millions of devoted fans. Its song and dance numbers and much of the dialogue are household memorabilia in many parts of the world. Anupama Chopra, who wrote a book about the making of *Sholay*, calls the film a textbook of Indian cinema, arguing that it "transformed action into high art" and set new standards for "the way a nation speaks to itself."[1]

Just as the release of *Seven Samurai* and *The Magnificent Seven* can be linked to local events in Japan and the United States, there are historical reasons why a film like *Sholay* would be made in India in 1975. After an era of optimistic nation-building following India's Independence in 1947, the country had fallen into a troubling malaise by the 1970s. Religious conflict, government corruption, criminal violence, and a general breakdown of law and order had taken a toll on the national spirit. The plot and overall tone of *Sholay* reflect these grim conditions at the same time that it offers comic relief.

Gabbar Singh, a cruel and charismatic bandit (played by Amjad Khan), has been terrorizing the village of Ramgarh, a remote settlement in southern India. The village patriarch, a retired policeman known as Thakur Baldev Singh (Sanjeev Kumar), wants to bring Gabbar to justice, but he is powerless to do the job himself. He decides to hire two young men, Veeru and Jai Dev, who both had demonstrated skill and courage when he arrested them as petty thieves five years before. Veeru (Dharmendra) and Jai (Bachchan) are hardly the Magnificent Seven. In one scene, they take to the open road on a motorcycle wearing jeans and denim jackets over muscle shirts. Since this is a Bollywood film, they sing exuberantly while riding, performing goofy stunts along the way and hugging each other in open displays of male friendship. But they can also be tough or valiant, amorous or tragic when the situation demands. As in most Bollywood movies, the emotions in this film run the gamut. To identify it with a single style or genre would be to miss the way that Bollywood typically blends dramatic narrative and musical spectacle, action and melodrama into a lively, near three-hour entertainment of song, dance, adventure, laughter, and tears.

Sholay opens with a train pulling into a desolate station. A single man in uniform steps out and asks for the Thakur (a title of respect for a member of the landed gentry, who trace their lineage to a feudal class of warrior-aristocrats). He rides through an arid landscape of rock formations that could be in Wyoming or New Mexico, accompanied by a busy soundtrack of whistling, strumming, and Indian percussion instruments. The Thakur, a brooding figure wrapped in a gray shawl, greets him and explains he needs two men for a mission: Veeru and Jai. When the visitor, a jailor, identifies the pair as worthless crooks, the Thakur says that they have virtues as well as vices, relating how they once saved his life when a band of *dacoits*, Indian bandits, attacked the train. The attack is dramatized in a stirring flashback reminiscent of a dozen Westerns. The dacoits attack on horseback and from cliffs. Taking a chance, the Thakur sets his young captives free by shooting off their handcuffs. Jai and Veeru prove their mettle, fighting with fists, guns, and wits. When the Thakur is shot, they must decide whether to save him or escape. So they toss a coin, a gesture that becomes one of the film's recurring motifs.

Part of the fun of watching *Sholay* is in recognizing its allusions to other films. The "Song of the Road" on motorbike recalls Raj Kapoor's enthusiasm as a vagabond in *Awaara* (1951). The prison warden's spastic antics and Hitler mustache evoke Chaplin's performance in *The Great Dictator* (1940), though Asrani turns the role into a hilarious lampoon of British colonialism. The dacoit bandit Gabbar Singh may remind us of Calvera in *The Magnificent Seven*, but Amjad Khan's performance, despite his blatant outbursts of laughter, is chillingly humorless. He punishes his own followers with a sadistic game of Russian roulette, three bullets for six men, and he treats the Thakur's family, as Henry Fonda's Frank treats McBain's family in *Once Upon a Time in the West* (1968), with monstrous cruelty.

Watch the way this scene of dark revenge is shot and edited. The family's peaceful homestead is shown in a sequence of carefully composed shots. We see the grandson's uncle through the spokes of a wagon wheel, his mother preparing food on a swing, his house behind. His pretty young aunt is hanging out the wash. As they talk of this and that, we hear a round of rifle shots. At first, they think the shots are being fired by Radha's husband, who has been target shooting in the hills. But as they look up from behind the wagon wheel, they see him fall. The uncle runs, the mother runs, the aunt runs, and each one is shot dead in a freeze frame, falling in slow motion like victims in a Sam Peckinpah film, as the clothesline collapses in a heap and the rusty swing continues to creak. The guns are silent now. High on a boulder, a lone man on horseback seems to be applauding, but he is only cracking nuts in his palms. It is Gabbar, escaped from jail, a rifle hanging on his shoulder. As he surveys the fallen bodies, the swing still swaying slowly with its eerie sound, an 8-year-old boy runs out of the house. Gabbar nudges his horse slowly down the rocky slope to where the boy stands trembling. The camera frames him, then the boy, both eying each other across the swing. A harmonica whines mournfully as Gabbar reaches for his rifle and takes aim.

Some of *Sholay*'s embers are romantic. A chatty *tonga* (horsecart) driver named Basanti captures Veeru's heart. When she goes to the temple to ask the god Shiva for a good husband (as unmarried women are wont to do in India), Veeru tries to impersonate the deity, gets caught, and teases her with a song, "Anger makes a pretty girl even prettier." While their early courtship is played for laughs, their romance runs into serious trouble. Basanti is captured by the dacoits and forced to dance in the hot sun or else Veeru will die. While her lover watches helplessly, bound to two large stakes, the bandits break glass beneath her feet, but she continues dancing, singing "I will dance as long as there is breath left in my body." By contrast, the object of Jai's affection is more distant and sedate. Radha, the Thakur's daughter-in-law, wears the white sari of a widow. Since Indian widows are expected to remain unmarried, their smoldering relationship is limited to glances from afar.

The theme of bloody vengeance had special resonance for Indian audiences in the 1970s. Following India's partition into separate countries in 1947, millions of Muslims migrated north to Pakistan while millions of Hindus journeyed south to India. The two groups often clashed along the way, erupting in fierce fighting that left half a million dead and a legacy of animosity that continues to this day. Families were butchered in the streets. Survivors cried out for revenge.

For more than two decades, Indian movies generally avoided the topic of religious retribution. But in 1975, amid a growing crisis of economic instability and accusations of corruption, Prime Minister Indira Gandhi declared a state of national emergency, suspending civil rights for an unprecedented 18 months. It was in this climate of crisis that the Sippys decided to make *Sholay*. G.P. Sippy (1914–2007) had experienced the disruptive violence of partition first hand. Forced to flee with his family from Karachi (now in Pakistan) to Bombay (now Mumbai, in India), he left the family property and savings behind. Though once wealthy, he had to take on odd jobs, selling carpets and working in construction. It was while building a house for the famous Indian actress Nargis Dutt that G.P. became interested in films. After trying his hand as an actor and director, the father persuaded his son to join him. Working together as producer and director, they made some of India's greatest hits, including *Andaaz* (1971) and *Seeta aur Geeta* (*Seeta and Geeta*, 1972). *Sholay* would be an even bigger film, the first Indian feature shot in 70 mm with stereophonic sound. They enlisted their favorite scriptwriting team, Salim Khan and Javed Akhtar, to develop the story from a four-line plot summary. Art director Ram Yedekar and cinematographer Dwarka Divecha constructed a whole town among the boulders and flatlands of Ramanagaram, an hour's drive from Bangalore. Amitabh Bachchan, at a low point in his early career, was cast as Jai and his fiancée, Jaya Bhaduri, was cast as the widow Radha. They were married four months before production began, and she became pregnant during the shoot. Meanwhile, Dharmendra became amorously involved with Hema Malini (cast as Basanti). They were married five years after the film's release.

Production was slow. It took 21 days to shoot the motorcycle number and 24 days to film the massacre of Thakur's family. The lyrics were prerecorded by professional singers called playback artists, as most songs are in Bollywood, and later lip-synched by the actors for the cameras. These playback singers are often as famous in India as movie stars. During post-production, the first cut was edited to four hours, then further cut to 200 minutes by the censorship board, empowered by Indira Gandhi's State of Emergency. Among other things, the censors did not approve the ending in which the Thakur gets revenge by stomping on his enemy with studded boots. Instead, they had police arrive in time to stop him.

Sholay was not a quick success. Its initial release on August 15 (Indian Independence Day) was greeted with unfavorable reviews and a lukewarm reception at the box office. Gradually its reputation improved by word of mouth. It broke all earning records for commercial cinema in India. Gabbar Singh became a national phenomenon. Amitabh Bachchan became a superstar. The music by R.D. Burnam, released on audiocassette, took on a life of its own. And the film took its place in the pantheon of global genres, a distinctly Indian contribution to the myth of the warrior hero.

Questions

1. What seems distinctly Indian about this film? Make a note of words, images, or events that require translation or appear to have meanings unfamiliar to most American audiences. Do some research to discover their significance in Indian culture and relate them to the larger meanings of the film.

2. *Sholay* is filled with references to other films, including American Westerns and Hindi classics. Find examples of this cinematic citation. Is this largely a matter of homage, a failure of imagination, or something else?

3. The film's original ending was changed by the Indian Censor Board, which did not like the idea of people taking the law into their own hands. Why would this be a problem in 1975? Find out more about the alternate ending and give reasons why you think it should or should not have been changed.

4. Select a scene, like the Holi festival of colors (when Gabbar's gang raids the village) or Gabbar's camp (when the belly dancer sings "Mehbooba Mehboob"), and analyze it in cinematic terms. Pay close attention to the use of color, sound, camerawork, and editing. What aesthetic principles do you see at work, and how effective are they?

5. Bollywood is famous for inserting song and dance routines into every film. The best known musical numbers in *Sholay* are "Yeh dosti" (during the motorcycle ride), "Holi ke din dil" (during the festival of colors), "Mehbooba" (in Gabbar's camp), "Koi hasina" (during the *tonga* ride), and "Jab tak hai" (when Basanti dances for her lover's life). Revisit one or two of these numbers and explain their function in the film. For example, do they contribute to the ongoing story or subordinate narrative movement to spectacle?

6. Compare *Sholay*'s setting, characters, and themes to those in *Seven Samurai* or *The Magnificent Seven*. What similarities and differences do you notice between the town in southern India, a rural village in feudal Japan, and a Mexican community after the American Civil War? Are the common people presented more or less sympathetically? What motivates the violence? How is heroism represented in each case?

7. Indian film scholar Wimal Dissanayake in *Melodrama and Asian Cinema* (Cambridge University Press, 1993) points out several cultural issues that may be relevant to *Sholay*. He writes that "Most Asian cultures valorize human suffering as a pervasive fact of life" (4) and that Hindi culture in particular regards evil as "inescapable and important to the social order," acting as a kind of foil, created by the gods to better define the nature of goodness by contrast (190). How do these ideas help us understand Sippy's film, especially in relation to *Seven Samurai* or *The Magnificent Seven?*

Note

1. Anupama Chopra, *Sholay: The Making of a Classic* (Penguin, 2000), 4–6.

Further Reading

Chopra, Anupama. *Sholay: The Making of a Classic.* Penguin, 2000.

Dissanayake, Wimal, ed. *Melodrama and Asian Cinema.* Cambridge University Press, 1993.

Dissanayake, Wimal and Malti Sahai. *Sholay, A Cultural Reading.* Wiley Eastern, 1992.

Ganti, Tejaswini. *Bollywood: A Guidebook to Popular Hindi Cinema.* Routledge, 2004.

CLOSE-UP
WAY OF THE DRAGON

FIGURE 1.28 *Way of the Dragon* (*Meng long guo jiang*, Dir. Bruce Lee, 1972).

Directed by Bruce Lee.
Written by Bruce Lee.
Cinematography by Tadashi Nishimoto.
Editing by Yao Chung Chang.
Music by Joseph Koo.
Art Direction by Hsin Chien.
Produced by Raymond Chow and Bruce Lee.
Distributed by Golden Harvest and Asia Media in 1972. In Mandarin with English dubbing.
Running Time: 99 minutes (Hong Kong), 88 minutes (United States).

Tang Lung (aka Dragon)	Bruce Lee
Chen Ching Hua	Nora Miao
Colt	Chuck Norris
Ho	Ping-Ao Wei
"Uncle" Wang	Chung-Hsin Huang
Fred	Robert Wall
Japanese Fighter	Ing-Sik Whang
Ah Quen	Di Chin
Tony	Tony Liu
Jimmy	Unicom Chan
Tommy	Fu Ching Chen
Boss	Jon T. Benn

World Cinema through Global Genres, First Edition. William V. Costanzo.
© 2014 John Wiley & Sons, Inc. Published 2014 by John Wiley & Sons, Inc.

By most accounts, Bruce Lee is the undisputed champion of Hong Kong kung fu cinema. In the span of his short lifetime (1940–1973) and only a handful of major films, he boosted the genre to international status, created his own style of martial arts, and left a lasting legacy. His screen persona inspired countless sequels, remakes, and look-alike imitations. Books about his life, philosophy, movies, and fighting methods keep coming out. He has been a role model for generations of devoted fans. But Lee's impact is more than personal. As film historian Stephen Teo concludes, "No other figure in Hong Kong cinemas has done as much to bring East and West together in a common sharing of culture as Bruce Lee."[1]

Born in San Francisco to Li Hoi Cheun and his Eurasian wife, Grace, he was given the Cantonese name of Jun-fan ("return again") because his parents, who took their son to their native Hong Kong soon after his birth, believed he would return to the United States as an adult. Later he acquired the Chinese stage name Li Xiaolong ("little dragon") and his English name, Bruce Lee.

Although Grace came from a wealthy family and Hoi Cheun was a successful actor in films and Cantonese opera, life was difficult in Hong Kong. Japan invaded the city in 1941 and occupied it until 1945, closing schools, rationing food, and deporting unemployed families to the mainland. After the war, Lee's neighborhood was choked by masses of Chinese fleeing the other way, from communist China to Hong Kong. Rival street gangs roamed the city, and he was often forced to defend himself. Lee took on the challenge with a passion, engaging in so many fights that his father, a practitioner of Chinese boxing, *tai qi chuan*, taught him what he knew of the martial arts. Hoi Cheun also tried to guide his son's attention toward a more productive outlet: child acting. From age 6 to 18, Bruce appeared in some 20 Hong Kong films. But he kept getting into fights. After one big street brawl, he was introduced to Master Yip Man, a master of the Wing Chun style of kung fu. This was a streamlined approach to the art of self-defense, more practical than the stylized movements of *tai qi*. Bruce absorbed this new style with astonishing energy and skill, devoting a year to rigorous practice. But his street fighting continued. When his father learned from the police that one of his rivals was the son of a Triad mobster, it was time to send Bruce away.

In 1959, the young man returned to San Francisco, then moved to Seattle, where he finished high school and entered the University of Washington. There he majored in philosophy, giving lessons in the martial arts to pay his way. He learned to combine these two interests, philosophy and combat training, by developing his own eclectic version of the martial arts, which he called Jeet Kune Do, "way of the intercepting fist." This personal approach stressed power, flexibility, spontaneity, and practicality. It was designed for the conditions of real street fighting.

In 1964, after building a reputation in tournaments, Bruce moved to Los Angeles with his new wife, Linda. His early efforts to enter Hollywood were not entirely successful. In 1966, ABC hired him for its television show, *The Green Hornet*, but he was assigned to the role of Kato, the hero's valet, while the title character was played by Van Williams. In 1971, after a number of minor appearances, he tried to interest Warner Bros. in a martial arts television series. But the part he wanted was given to David Carradine, who knew little about kung fu but spoke good English and was white. There did not seem to be much of a future at the time for non-Caucasian action heroes on American screens. In Hong Kong, however, where ABC's series was popularly known as "The Kato Show," he was a big hit. Deeply disappointed in his treatment by the American entertainment industry and eager for a better role in movies, he returned to the city of his youth.

At that time, the Hong Kong film industry was dominated by the Shaw Brothers, but they considered Lee's demands for salary and creative freedom too high. Instead, he went to Raymond Chow of the rival studio, Golden Harvest. His first film for Chow was *The Big Boss* (*Tang shan da xiong*, 1971; also released in the United States as *Fists of Fury*). Set and shot in Thailand, *The Big Boss* bears the stamp of Lee's own life and vision. Cheng Chao-on, a country boy from southern China, arrives in Bangkok to work with his cousins in an ice factory. When Cheng's kin discover that the factory is a front for smuggling drugs, they begin to disappear mysteriously. Cheng becomes suspicious and dislikes the way his family is treated, but he has promised his mother not to get into trouble, a promise betokened by her amulet. For the first half hour of the film, he remains on the sidelines itching to take on the hired brutes and bullies who mistreat his family. But when the amulet is ripped from his neck during a melee, he jumps into the fray, whipping the boss's thugs with astonishing skill and unconcealed delight. This is not the ritual combat of a Shaw Brothers film. Cheng is no noble swordsman playing by venerable rules. He is a common man with family loyalties and a good heart facing the kind of violence, crime, and corruption that ordinary people encounter every day. Like ordinary men, he can be temporarily distracted by women and wine, but when he's focused, he can take on every petty hoodlum and gang leader all the way up to the big boss.

Lee's second film for Golden Harvest was *Fist of Fury* (*Jing wu men*, 1972; released in the United States as *The Chinese Connection*). Set in Shanghai during the early 1900s when Japan occupied much of the city, the film strikes a fiercely nationalistic tone. Lee plays Chen Zhen, a student of *Jing Wu* (a Cantonese kung fu style), who goes berserk when he learns that his teacher is dead. Chen suspects foul play, but cautioned by his fiancée and fellow students, he tries to temper his seething rage. To add fuel to the fire, a delegation of Japanese karate experts from a rival school arrive with humiliating taunts. They present Chen's class with a sign that reads "Sick Men of East Asia," implying that Chinese are weaklings. Later, at a public park, he is prevented from entering by an Indian guard who points to a sign, "No dogs or Chinese allowed." Chen is not one to let these slights pass. He challenges the insufferable foreigners, forcing them to eat their words, though it is clear they hold the ultimate power.

Fist of Fury was a big success. The theme of ethnic pride appealed to local audiences, many of whom shared Lee's abhorrence of foreign occupation and identified with his rebellious spirit. Lee's supple body and fierce fighting style were becoming iconic. Meanwhile, the Hong Kong film industry was moving from swords to fists. At the top of his game, Bruce Lee was ready to write, direct, co-produce, and star in a kung fu movie of his own.

That film is *Way of the Dragon* (*Meng long guo jiang*, 1972; retitled *Return of the Dragon* in the United States. A co-production of Golden Harvest and Lee's new company, Concord Productions, *Way of the Dragon* was filmed on location in Italy. Its plot traces a familiar formula. Tang Lung, a farm boy from the Hong Kong countryside, arrives in Rome to help with the family restaurant run by Uncle Wang. Tang Lung (his name means fierce dragon) is greeted coolly by a pretty cousin Chen, who scorns his unsophisticated habits, and he is treated skeptically by the other waiters, who regard him as an inexperienced weakling. But when a gang of ruffians terrorizes the restaurant, Lung springs into action, proving that skillful Chinese boxing can outperform all forms of foreign martial arts or weapons. Squads of thugs and hit men are sent by the mobster who wants the restaurant for his own dark purposes, but Tang rises to the occasion with each attack. He teaches the waiters how to fight, becomes their champion, and earns Chen's romantic admiration. The big showdown is a one-on-one match to the finish against America's champion Karate expert, a blond bruiser named Colt. Lung and Colt (Chuck Norris) fight to the finish in the Colosseum, evoking the gladiatorial combat of ancient Rome, but with only a stray cat as their audience.

When Lee enters the Colosseum, the camera assumes his point of view with a wide panning shot of the interior, then quickly zooms in to a closer shot of Norris standing in one of the stone openings. Norris wears a black belt and white kimono. Lee is dressed entirely in black. The camera shifts back and forth between the two rivals as Norris thrusts out his right fist in a voiceless challenge, giving a thumb down as the ancient Romans used to do. Lee accepts the challenge with a brisk wave of his left hand. In the next sequence of shots, we watch them slowly prepare for battle. A belt is loosened, a shirt unbuttoned, knuckles crack, muscles flex, until both men stand naked to the waist. At this point, the camera alternates between them, catching their warm-up jabs and kicks in medium shots against the blue-grey masonry. The only voice comes from the kitten watching them. When the opponents approach each other, the camera grows more active. It jumps to a high angle shot, framing them between two stone pillars, moves with them as they circle one another, then stops abruptly as Norris takes the first tentative steps, accompanied by drum beats. A sharp meow from the cat signals Lee's attack, angry and aggressive as an animal. We hear each cry and thrust as the camera quickens the pace with rapid cuts, now focusing on Lee, now on Norris, now on both. Lee is the first to go down, but he rises for more punishment: a series of blows to the head and chest, each blow accentuated by the sound track. The fight continues for nearly six more minutes before the tables turn and Norris staggers to the ground, the film rendering his shock with wavering music and a blurred point of view shot. When it's finally over, Lee covers his opponent with the white kimono and black belt, a solemn tribute to the only foe he truly respects.

In some ways, *Way of the Dragon* leads Lee into new territory. Its European setting is emphasized by postcard images of Rome's architectural treasures. Its tone is lighter than Lee's previous two films. Tang, whose stomach growls with hunger at the airport, can't read the menu and has trouble with the food. He keeps asking for the toilet. Later, when Chen tells him to act friendly towards Italians on the street, he ends up going home with a prostitute. These scenes are played for easy laughs, but when Tang takes off his shirt, the clownish mannerisms disappear, replaced by Bruce Lee's taut body and combative ferocity. Lee may look ordinary, even skinny in his street clothes, but stripped for action he's a fierce fighting machine. His supple muscles ripple and expand with every breath. He moves forward and back with astonishing agility, delivering blows that startle his enemy with unexpected power and speed. This is the spectacle his fans wait for, the visual pleasure of Lee's body in motion. It is this universal language of physical prowess that transcends cultural boundaries and global markets.

Lee has been both taken to task and appreciated by critics who link his body to narcissism, nationalism, and racial politics. All that self-conscious posturing in front of mirrors, some say, is not just vanity but the mark of an undeveloped psyche, a personality stuck in an early stage of emotional development. If self-regard is a form of self-defense, Lee's physical self-assertion may look like compensation for a sense of being ignored or pushed aside. But there is a positive side to this self-absorption and aggression. Lee embodied a new form of Chinese masculinity, an image of vigor and strength that challenged notions of the passive Asian "soft body" in Western culture. In Hong Kong, Lee's hard body came to represent a certain spirit of national pride, mirroring the territory's economic competitiveness and creative self-assurance. In countries with an ethnic Chinese population, Lee's muscular figure reminded fans of their connection to a "mother culture," as Stephen Teo calls it: not the state-based nationalism of political maps but a broad cultural concept of greatness that united them as an extended family.[2] The appeal was even broader. Fighting alone or alongside his brothers, using only his bare fists, feet, or a stick snatched from the street, Lee became a singular hero for the disenfranchised, especially among American inner-city youth. The scenes in which he tears down signs of bigotry – "No Dogs or Chinese Allowed," "Sick Men of East Asia" – brought the house down in Hong Kong, Singapore, and Los Angeles. His unarmed struggles against the big bosses and their foreign lackeys – Japanese Karate experts who look down on Chinese boxing, Italian mobsters who think guns are better than fists, intimidating Russian bodyguards – resonated with young people of his day who strove to "fight the power." They continue to be read as bids for dignity, decency, and voice.

Lee began working on his fourth film for Golden Harvest, *Game of Death*, in 1972, but production was interrupted by a better offer. Warner Bros. wanted him to star in *Enter the Dragon* (*Long zheng hu dou*, 1973; also released as *The Deadly Three*). It would be his first and final movie with a major Hollywood studio, a co-production directed by Robert Clouse. The story takes place on an island where the mysterious Han has organized a boxing tournament. Lee, a Shaolin martial artist, is recruited by British intelligence to spy on Han, who is suspected of running a drug and prostitution ring. Lee's partners in this adventure include two Americans: a gambler and an activist, one white and one black, both on the run.

The three men infiltrate Han's stronghold and try to stop his operation, but only one gets out alive. Critics variously received the film as another exercise in narcissism (many mirrors reflect Lee's physique), glorified violence (more blood and higher body counts), or nationalist allegory (the island representing Hong Kong) with racial overtones (white, black, and yellow fighters competing for supremacy). Fans flocked to the theatres, making it one of the year's top grossing hits both in Hong Kong and abroad. Today, *Enter the Dragon* is widely considered to be Lee's most significant work. But he never got to enjoy its success. That summer, just weeks before the film's release, he reportedly complained of a headache, took some medicine, and fell asleep. He never recovered. The medical reports, speculations, and countless conspiracy theories have all added to his legend.

Questions

1. Whether you're a loyal Bruce Lee fan or a newcomer to his work, trace your personal responses to *Way of the Dragon*. What keeps you watching or turns you away? Consider the film's pacing, setting, characters, sound track, and the figure of Lee himself. Relate your level of engagement to specific moments in the film.

2. Analyze the evolving structure and themes of Bruce Lee's films. What are the key features of their plots? What central conflicts motivate the action? What issues are resolved? Who are the villains? What makes Lee a hero in these films?

3. In Bruce Lee's movies and the early films of Jackie Chan, the body is a central focus of the action. Real performers engage in physical feats, executing their own stunts. Compare this kind of kung fu to more recent martial arts films that use wire work (Jet Li's "wire-fu" films, for example) or Computer Generated Imagery (as in Jackie Chan's *The Myth*, 2005). What is gained or lost when the action is manipulated by technology?

4. Compare Lee's kung fu style to other screen practitioners like Chuck Norris, Jackie Chan, Jet Li, and Tony Jaa. What makes Lee's fighting so distinctive? Why do you think his image continues to appeal to fans around the world? What do other actors offer that is missing in Lee's films?

5. Compare Bruce Lee more broadly to other cinematic warrior heroes. What does he share with the Western gunslinger, samurai, or wuxia sword fighter? What makes him stand apart? Consider what actors like Toshiro Mifune, John Wayne, Clint Eastwood, Sylvester Stallone, Jet Li, or Tony Jaa bring to their roles. How do these performers represent local cultures while contributing to a global myth?

6. The circumstances under which Lee died on July 20, 1973 have spawned innumerable theories. Investigate the controversies surrounding his death and report on your findings. What do these debates and speculations say about his life and legacy?

7. Select one scene from *Way of the Dragon* for closer study, like the famous showdown between Lee and Norris in the Colosseum. Analyze the scene shot by shot, noting how each cinematic decision (what the actors wear, where to place the camera, how long to hold the shot, music and sound effects) contributes to the overall effect.

Notes

1. Stephen Teo, *Hong Kong Cinema: The Extra Dimensions* (British Film Institute, 1997), 110.
2. Teo, 111.

Further Reading

Bordwell, David. *Planet Hong Kong: Popular Cinema and the Art of Entertainment*. Harvard University Press, 2000.

Bowman, Paul. *Theorizing Bruce Lee: Film – Fantasy – Fighting – Philosophy*. Rodopi, 2010.

Donovan, Barna William. *The Asian Influence on Hollywood Action Films*. McFarland & Company, 2008.

Fu, Poshek and David Desser. *The Cinema of Hong Kong: History, Arts, Identity*. Cambridge University Press, 2000.

Hunt, Leon. *Kung Fu Cult Masters: From Bruce Lee to Crouching Tiger*. Wallflower Press, 2003.

Kaminsky, Stuart. "Kung Fu Film as Ghetto Myth." *Journal of Popular Film* 3 (1974): 129–138.

Lee, Bruce. *The Tao of Jeet Kune Do*. Black Belt Communications, 1975.

Lee, Linda. *The Bruce Lee Story*. Ohara Publications, 1989.

Rayns, Tony. "Bruce Lee: Narcissism and Nationalism." In Lan Shing-hon, ed., *A Study of Hong Kong Martial Arts Film*, 110–112. Hong Kong Urban Council, 1980.

Shu, Yuan. "Reading the Kung Fu Film in an American Context: From Bruce Lee to Jackie Chan." *Journal of Popular Film & Television* 31(2) (Summer 2003): 50–59.

Teo, Stephen. *Hong Kong Cinema: The Extra Dimensions*. British Film Institute, 1997.

UNIT II
THE WEDDING FILM

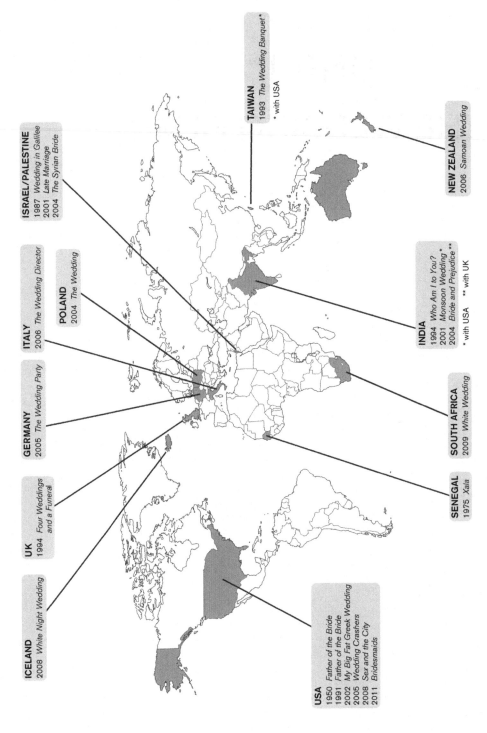

TAIWAN
1993 *The Wedding Banquet* *
* with USA

NEW ZEALAND
2006 *Samoan Wedding*

ISRAEL/PALESTINE
1987 *Wedding in Galilee*
2001 *Late Marriage*
2004 *The Syrian Bride*

ITALY
2006 *The Wedding Director*

POLAND
2004 *The Wedding*

GERMANY
2005 *The Wedding Party*

INDIA
1994 *Who Am I to You?*
2001 *Monsoon Wedding* *
2004 *Bride and Prejudice* **
* with USA   ** with UK

SOUTH AFRICA
2009 *White Wedding*

ICELAND
2008 *White Night Wedding*

UK
1994 *Four Weddings and a Funeral*

SENEGAL
1975 *Xala*

USA
1950 *Father of the Bride*
1991 *Father of the Bride*
2002 *My Big Fat Greek Wedding*
2005 *Wedding Crashers*
2008 *Sex and the City*
2011 *Bridesmaids*

FIGURE 2.1   A global map of selected Wedding Films.

CHAPTER 2
THE WEDDING FILM

In 2002, Nia Vardalos, a Canadian American with Greek roots, wrote and starred in a low-budget movie that became an overnight sensation. Produced for the reported cost of only $5 million, *My Big Fat Greek Wedding* went on to gross over $350 million worldwide, making it one of the most profitable movies of all time. Although reviews were generally positive, what really propelled the film to such unprecedented prominence was word of mouth publicity by enthusiastic audiences. Clearly, something about Vardalos's film touched people both at home and around the globe. Spectators emerged from theatres comparing what they had just seen to the Jewish, Polish, or Italian weddings they knew. They enjoyed reliving the familiar rituals of matrimony while indulging their curiosity about another culture. They delighted in the shared experience of public spectacle and universal storytelling.

Predictably, other wedding movies followed. Films with the word bride or wedding in their titles popped up everywhere and continue to appear. But as a quick search of Netflix or imdb.com reveals, these films have been around for a long time, spanning a wide range of emotional tones, cinematic styles, and cultural terrain. They give us glimpses of nuptial rites in England (*Four Weddings and a Funeral*, 1994), Australia (*Muriel's Wedding*, 1994), Poland (*The Wedding/Wesele*, 2004), Iceland (*White Night Wedding/Brúðguminn*, 2008), India (*Monsoon Wedding*, 2001), Taiwan (*The Wedding Banquet/Xiyan*, 1993), and disputed regions in the Middle East (*Rana's Wedding/Al qods fee yom akhar*, 2002; *The Syrian Bride/Urus suriyya*, 2004) as well as changing practices in the United States (*Father of the Bride*, 1950 and 1991; *A Wedding*, 1978; *The Wedding Planner*, 2001; *Our Family Wedding*, 2010). While some of these films may first appear to be simple entertainment, hardly worth a second look, others raise serious questions about the role of marriage and the place of women in society. Even the lighter romantic comedies can reveal a great deal about the individual assumptions and community values that we often take for granted.

World Cinema through Global Genres, First Edition. William V. Costanzo.
© 2014 John Wiley & Sons, Inc. Published 2014 by John Wiley & Sons, Inc.

In contrast to some established genres like the Western and horror film, which have generated countless books and scholarly studies, relatively little has been written about wedding movies as a group. This gives us a chance to explore new ground while asking basic questions about genres and how they work. What do wedding movies have in common? Who are their heroes? What kinds of stories do they tell? What threats are represented in these stories? What social issues are enacted? How do the history and customs of a particular place inform the local rituals of matrimony and how they are perceived? First, though, we need to ask whether wedding movies constitute a genre in the same way that war movies or gangster films do.

Questions of Genre and Myth

While some genres are named in terms of setting (Westerns, road movies), actions (musicals, kung fu films), or emotional effect (horror, thriller), the word wedding refers to a specific event: the public ceremony that confirms a marriage. But does any movie with a wedding count as a wedding film? *The Godfather* (1972), for example, features two memorable wedding scenes, but it doesn't center on the rituals of marriage as do *Father of the Bride* or *Monsoon Wedding*. So as we work through any list of wedding films, we should consider how essential weddings are to the films' characters, stories, and themes. At the same time, we need to think about each film's place within other generic schemes. Just as warrior hero movies may be seen as a subset of action films, wedding films may be studied as part of some broader grouping, as a subgenre of melodrama, romance, or the woman's film. Furthermore, just as there are war comedies and war musicals, there may be hybrid forms of wedding films, some more farcical than others, some darker, some more overtly political. Instead of trying to force these films into strictly defined categories, it may be more helpful to think in terms of family resemblances: each member sharing a few traits with others in the family, but with no cookie cutter stencil for all of them.

A useful strategy for spotting common traits is to look closely at the films themselves as texts, just as we might analyze a set of similar novels in order to compare them. This means identifying character types, key scenes, themes, icons, narrative structures, and styles that recur in various forms from film to film. Is the hero a naïve bride, a homely bride, a reluctant bride, or the father of the bride? How is the marriage ceremony handled? Does it take place in a church, on a beach, in a van, or does it not take place at all? Is the wedding itself the centerpiece of a romantic story, an opportunity for slapstick humor, or a metaphor for cultural dysfunction? Such questions can be useful guides for a comparative analysis. They can also serve to highlight the intertextuality of wedding films, the way they refer to one another as well as to literary fiction, painting, and even television shows like *Say Yes to the Dress* and *Bridezillas*.

Theories of genre extend well beyond the texts themselves to take other aspects of filmmaking into account, like authorship, audience, history, and ideology.

Authorship refers not only to script writers, directors, and those immediately responsible for creating a film text. It includes the entire film industry and its decisions about production, distribution, and exhibition. Questions of authorship might consider how wedding films are made and marketed. Who decides to put the word bride or wedding in the title? When do wedding films become profitable products? Why does a studio or independent producer choose to advertise its film as part of the genre or as something unique? Audiences, too, contribute to the process. They validate a genre at the box office, as they did with *My Big Fat Greek Wedding*. They form fan clubs and cult followings. So questions about audience are important too. What groups enjoy films about weddings? What pleasures do they seek?

If a genre has a history, it's worth asking how the genre has evolved over time. In the warrior hero chapter, we saw how some theorists believe that certain genres go through stages, developing from an experimental period (in which basic conventions are established), to a classical period (in which conventions become stabilized), a refinement period (in which stylistic flourishes enhance and embellish the conventional form), and a self-conscious period (in which style takes over form).[1] Have wedding films followed a similar trajectory? We have also noted that since no film is value-free, there are questions of ideology and culture to ask. What do wedding movies reveal about the society that produces them? What messages do they send about a culture's deepest beliefs? Like water to fish and air to most humans, ideological assumptions are often invisible to those who take them for granted. It is when we dive into the sea or visit a new country that we become most aware of our original surroundings, including the value-laden atmosphere in which we live and breathe. What once seemed unquestionably natural turns out to be only one set of options among many. By watching wedding films from India or Lebanon, we get to compare our customs and attitudes to others. We get to see how certain rituals of daily life are shaped by religious doctrine, consumerism, patriarchy, romanticism, and other systems of belief. At the same time, we can look for the common denominators underlying wedding customs around the world. By finding points of resemblance in this diversity, we begin to understand how certain deep structures of experience, the most enduring human concerns, are expressed in the world's movies.

Our approach in this chapter begins with wedding films from the United States. We'll look first at familiar stories of romantic longing and family anxieties from the various perspectives of the bride, the father, the groom, and all those men and ladies in waiting, noting how the plots, imagery, and themes of these films shape generic subsets of romance, black comedy, or social satire. Next we'll expand our view to other parts of the world, where wedding movies take on different forms with distinctive cultural implications. We'll consider the mythology of weddings: what the local rituals of a global institution might tell us about humanity's efforts to circumscribe individual impulses of love and desire within the framework of a social order. Finally, we'll see how some theorists, particularly feminists, can help to place the genre within ideological and historical contexts. By the time we arrive at our tentative conclusion, we should have a stronger sense how genres like the wedding movie work and why it's worth studying them from a global perspective.

Every Girl's Dream, Every Father's Nightmare

At the start of *The Wedding Planner*, a young girl is playing with her dolls. As the credits begin rolling, an action figure descends on a string with a tiny wedding cake. A blonde Barbie doll checks her veil in a miniature mirror. There is a toy preacher, a toy photographer, the best man with a ring, a cardboard cathedral, and a winding staircase for the bride's descent. The Ken doll is wearing a white tux. With Ken in one hand and Barbie in the other, the girl (now wearing a communion veil) pronounces those familiar words, "You may now kiss the bride." An organ on the soundtrack breaks into the wedding march as the young officiate offers her marital advice. "From now on he'll take care of you, and you'll take care of him. He'll make you big baloney sandwiches, and you'll buy him new socks, a white brief case, and you'll live happily ever after." Here in one brief scene, enhanced with dreamy lighting and amply furnished with consumer tie-ins, is one young girl's idea of paradise (Figure 2.2). As we soon learn, she will grow up to become a professional wedding planner, adept at organizing everybody's perfect wedding but her own.

A similar scene opens *27 Dresses* (2008). This time the girl is a member of the wedding party who sees the bride accidentally rip her gown before the ceremony. Alert and fashion conscious, the young heroine improvises a quick fix that mends the dress and saves the day. She's hooked for life on weddings, serving as a bridesmaid for 27 of them, each time in a different dress. Some bridesmaids give away their dresses, but she saves hers, dreaming of her own big day when she hopes all 27 brides will attend her wedding in those 27 dresses. In *Bride Wars* (2009), the primal wedding scene takes place in Manhattan's Plaza Hotel. The film's two six-year old protagonists are so moved by the occasion that they vow to hold their own weddings in the same lavish location. An off-screen adult voice describes the scene as if it were a fairy tale: "There was something blue, something borrowed, and something completely magical. And two little girls from New Jersey held in their hands a new dream, that one day they

FIGURE 2.2   A young girl with her dolls and dreams in *The Wedding Planner* (Dir. Adam Shankman, 2001).

would find that one person who would stand by them no matter what. And when they did, they too would have June weddings at the Plaza." We see these childhood playmates acting out their fantasy by dressing up as bride and groom. Their little fingers fill an ornamental box with cutout dolls, toy jewelry, and other bridal paraphernalia, fueling an obsession that will dominate their friendship and their lives until some 20 years later. In *Muriel's Wedding*, the title character is also fixated on the idea of a wedding. Her bedroom walls are papered with photographs from bridal magazines, and she sleeps with a slice of wedding cake under her pillow. What matters most to her, however, is not so much the setting or the cake as the social status that a wedding will confer. The big, public spectacle of her marriage to a highly desirable man signifies the culmination of her wildest dreams.

A more skeptical viewer might ask what lies behind these childhood fantasies. Where do they come from? Who gains or loses from such attitudes toward weddings? We might look more closely at key scenes and notice how the script and visual codes are designed to evoke nostalgia (the soft, rosy glow illuminating a little girl's toys in *The Wedding Planner*) or amused indulgence (the narrative voice in *Bride Wars*). We might count the number of purchasable props (costume jewelry, bridal gowns, wedding magazines) or investigate the multi-million dollar Barbie industry, as Susan Stern does in her documentary film *Barbie Nation: An Unauthorized Tour* (1998).[2] In this way, we might arrive at some conclusions about the romance of weddings and consumerism.

In contrast to the bride's romantic vision, the bride's father tends to sees things from a more practical perspective. In the 1991 remake of *Father of the Bride*, Steve Martin's main concern is how much the spectacle will cost. His image of the ideal wedding banquet is a backyard barbecue where he's dispensing brideburgers and groomburgers in a chef's hat. In the original 1950 version of this movie, Spencer Tracy tries to contain costs by fitting into his old tux and trimming the guest list. Before he knows it, the "small wedding" has mushroomed into a matrimonial extravaganza, with a formal church service, an expensive dress, a multi-layered cake, an orchestra, a moving van, and some 250 guests crammed into their home. Martin and Tracy survive their ordeals, perhaps because they are good fathers and good husbands. Tracy gets the message when his wife explains that she always wanted a gorgeous white gown and a church wedding. "It's what every girl dreams of," she says, "something to remember the rest of her life." When he understands this, he finally relents, wryly acknowledging, "from then on, I was a dead duck."

Much can be learned about acting styles, directors' choices, and historical eras by comparing similar scenes from the two movies. Watch how each actor tries to fit into his old tux. Tracy squeezes his middle-age girth into a tiny vest with grim determination (Figure 2.3), while Martin dances into a suit that is several sizes too small (Figure 2.4). Or compare the opening credit scenes. The 1950 version opens with a slow traveling shot, tilting down from a sprig of hanging mistletoe to a set of lopsided tables strewn with the ruins of a wedding feast. Wilted flowers, broken plates, and empty bottles lie scattered everywhere. The soundtrack plays an

FIGURES 2.3 and 2.4   For the reluctant Father of the Bride, then or now, a daughter's wedding calls for some adjustments. Spencer Tracy (Figure 2.3) and Steve Martin (Figure 2.4) try to fit into their wedding clothes.

FIGURE 2.3   *Father of the Bride* (Dir. Vincente Minnelli, 1950).   FIGURE 2.4   *Father of the Bride* (Dir. Charles Shyer, 1991).

off-tune version of "The Wedding March." It's the morning after, and Spencer Tracy sits alone in his armchair contemplating his daughter's recent rite of passage. The camera continues to move toward him in one uninterrupted take, gliding over the tables and along the littered floor to his shiny black shoes, one on and one off. With a weary hand, he reaches down to massage the stockinged foot, and the camera rises with it, showing his full figure and weary face. "I'd like to say a few words about weddings," he begins. "I've just been through one." During the long monologue that follows (more than 100 seconds), Tracy speaks casually to the audience about weddings from a father's point of view, fiddling with his shoe and occasionally glancing up at or looking pointedly into the lens. The camera frames him in a medium shot as he rambles on, until he harkens back to that moment three months ago "when the storm broke," and the scene dissolves into a flashback. The 1991 version follows much the same trajectory but adds a quicker tempo and a more engaging style. Bright colors replace the older movie's glossy black and white photography. Instead of an off-kilter version of the wedding music, we hear a brisk rendition of the tune as the camera swiftly sweeps across the floor toward Steve Martin seated, it would seem, in the same floral pattern armchair. Martin wears glossy black shoes, a tux, and a carnation (some things never change), although he has exchanged the broad striped tie for a bowtie. The camera's framing here is wider, including a nearby table still tastefully decorated and a darkened window behind. Some of his monologue has been updated ("then comes the day she wants to get her ear pierced"), but the biggest difference is in Martin's performance. He still fiddles with his shoe, but his rapport with the audience is more open and direct. He sits forward in the chair, casually addressing the camera, gesturing expressively and taking a quick swig of champagne before revealing deeper feelings about his little girl. This is not the dispassionate, slightly cynical father of the postwar years but a father of the 1990s who plays basketball with his daughter and doesn't try to hold back his emotions.

Aside from their concern about money, Martin and Tracy are reluctant FOBs (Fathers of the Bride) for another reason. Martin realizes that his daughter is no longer the little girl who used to shoot hoops with him on the driveway basketball court. Tracy faces the same fact when he glimpses Elizabeth Taylor posing "like a princess in a fairytale" before the bedroom mirrors in her stunning wedding dress. In *Rachel Getting Married* (2008), Rachel's dad competes with her new husband in an impromptu dishwasher contest. With the guests cheering them on, each man boasts of his ability to fill the machine with the most tableware in the fastest time, but their playful macho bragging is really a smokescreen for another contest. One man is passing the mantle to another. The father's loss is the groom's gain.

Other film FOBs don't fare as well as Spencer Tracy or Steve Martin. Muriel's father ends up losing his business and his place in the community. The father in Wojciech Smarzoski's *The Wedding*, an emotionally darker Polish film, loses his life's savings, his wife, his daughter, and his dog. But that's because these men are fundamentally abusive and corrupt. In contrast to the lighthearted comedy of *Father of the Bride*, *Muriel's Wedding* and *The Wedding* are caustic social satires that use weddings to critique the evils of patriarchy. In *Wedding in Galilee* (*Urs al-Jalil*, 1987) and *Rana's Wedding*, both set in Palestinian communities, marriage is primarily a negotiation between men. As public displays of patriarchal power and authority, the weddings in these movies serve as focal points for examining local politics and gender issues.

The ceremony in a romantic comedy like *My Big Fat Greek Wedding* means something quite different from the Polish rituals in *The Wedding*, not just because they take place within different cultural milieus but also because these films draw on diverse generic traditions. A wide spectrum of styles and purposes runs between the cheerful comedy of one and the biting satire of the other. These variations can reveal a lot about the way genre can shape our views of rituals that seem as natural as love and marriage.

Wedding Movies as Romantic Comedy

As a popular song has it, "love and marriage go together like a horse and carriage." But why? Why does love so often lead to marriage in the archetypal romantic story? Why do our lyricists and storytellers yoke these two ideas together? In a review of the sociological literature on love and marriage, Raelene Wilding makes a key distinction between the natural, spontaneous emotions of love and the pragmatic character of weddings. While real-life couples speak of their romantic feelings as "uncontrolled, irrational forces," they regard weddings as "social and cultural events," deliberately planned and staged "in relation to a range of practical considerations."[3]

In this view, marriages and weddings are institutions, devised by organized communities to channel instinctive drives and formalize their place within the sphere of civilized society. Put another way, love is a sensation, but marriage is a decision.

FIGURE 2.5   "How are we going to get to Cape Town for the wedding?" In romantic comedies around the world, it's usually a rocky road to the altar. *White Wedding* (Dir. Jann Turner, 2009) is set in Africa.

When a couple says "I do," both parties agree to a social contract. But this distinction between personal and public spaces is frequently obscured in romanticized stories, which trade on popular myths about love at first sight, destiny, the perfect partner, or the most important day in a woman's life.

The romance narrative can be regarded as a kind of quest, not unlike the stories about chivalrous knights and courtly ladies that were popular during the Middle Ages. In a romantic wedding film, the Holy Grail might be the happily-ever-after union of true soul mates symbolized by the wedding ring. Or, in the consumerist version of this story, it might be the perfect dress or a honeymoon suite at the Plaza Hotel. Whatever these wedding icons represent, there must be trials and obstacles along the way. "The course of true love never did run smooth," as Lysander explains to Hermia in Shakespeare's comedy, *A Midsummer Night's Dream*. What was true for medieval romance and Elizabethan comedies still seems true today. From Shakespeare's fairyland forest to the tangled plots of Hollywood, brides and grooms must prove their love to earn their prize.

Sometimes the path to the altar is literally a rocky road. In *White Wedding*, the groom must travel 1,800 kilometers to his wedding in Cape Town at the southern tip of Africa. Along the way, he misses a train, his car breaks down, he confronts a series of temptations and delays. The obstacles include a skeptical best man, a jilted white hitchhiker, and grandma's goat (Figure 2.5). Meanwhile, like Penelope waiting for Odysseus, the bride must fend off rival interests in the form of a wealthy ex-boyfriend. Although set in South Africa, *White Wedding* follows formulas familiar to Western audiences: the road movie and romantic comedy.

More often, the impediments to true love are closer to home. In *My Big Fat Greek Wedding*, *Meet the Fockers* (2004), and *Our Family Wedding*, these obstacles are the in-laws, the modern dragons that the bride's champion must face and overcome.

In the first film, the bride's huge Greek family swarms into the restaurant where she is having a quiet dinner with her fiancé. They descend on Ian like locusts, crushing him in a heap of hugs while Toula is pushed aside. Within seconds, the uninvited guests have set up trays of ethnic food and are dancing wildly to the music of a mandolin. Ian, an Anglo-American from a small family, doesn't know what to make of this. When the bride's brother tells him, "If you hurt her, I'll kill you and make it look like an accident," he's not sure whether to take this as a threat or a joke. When Toula explains to her Aunt Voula that Ian is a vegetarian, that he doesn't eat meat, the woman is incredulous. Voula shouts, "What do you mean he don't eat no meat?" Her voice is so loud that the music stops and everyone stares, until she resolves the problem with a simple declaration: "That's okay; I make lamb."

The gulf between families is hard enough to bridge when the couple is determined to be wed, but it becomes trickier when one of the parties has doubts. In *Sex and the City* (2008), Carrie's ideal boyfriend does the unforgivable when he falters at the steps of their location wedding site, the New York Public Library. It takes Carrie nearly half the film to decide whether or not to pardon him. The protagonist in *White Night Wedding* is another reluctant groom, a philosophy professor who can't make up his mind whether to marry the young would-be bride. Loosely based on Chekhov's play *Ivanov*, this Icelandic comedy explores the themes of doubt and isolation in a remote island community, suggesting parallels between nineteenth-century Russia and twenty-first-century Flatey. In *Four Weddings and a Funeral*, Hugh Grant is the best man for three consecutive weddings. Although many eligible women have their eyes on him, he wonders if he'll ever be a groom. Each wedding is presented as a hotbed of smoldering sexuality, the ideal setting to be scouting for a mate. Grant's evasive tactics and his search for Mrs. Right lead up to the film's fourth wedding and that moment of truth when, like a connubial Everyman, he too must say, "I do."

Sometimes, it's not the man but the woman who has misgivings. In *Runaway Bride* (1999), Julia Roberts has gained a reputation for leaving three disappointed men empty-handed at the altar. Richard Gere, a journalist, travels south to check on her story, at the risk of becoming her fourth jilted groom. In *The Wedding Planner*, Jennifer Lopez evades marriage for herself by organizing other women's dreams. When her father pressures her to wed a childhood friend, she too must listen to her inner voice in the face of those momentous words, "speak now or forever hold your peace." In some of these variations on the theme of weddings, it's not always clear whether the story will end in marriage or whether marriage is always the best ending.

In her book *What a Girl Wants?*, film scholar Diane Negra links these movies to what she calls "postfeminist fantasies," a resurgence in the 1990s of traditional family values like motherhood and matrimony among women who also desire power, glamor, and sexual pleasure. Negra traces the plot of *Runaway Bride* to a tabloid news story about a would-be bride's "failure to pay homage to the notion that a large and costly wedding is the inevitable high point of a woman's life." She finds evidence of this notion in *The Wedding Planner* when Jennifer Lopez tries to pull her new designer shoe from a manhole cover in the face of oncoming traffic. For Negra, this Cinderella rescue scene exemplifies an "adherence to the norms of luxury consumerism" that "brings a reward in intimacy." She sees Nia Vardalos's makeover in *My Big Fat Greek Wedding* as further confirmation that the road to personal empowerment is lined with consumer goods. Negra concludes that the historical shift from prefeminism to postfeminism is also a "shift from enforced domesticity to an excessively celebrated elective domesticity in the lives of many women." Her book is a good example of critical analysis that probes beneath the entertaining surfaces of movies to reveal contradictions in contemporary culture.[4]

Best Friends, Buddies, and Other Wedding Saboteurs

Not every movie with the word *bride* or *wedding* in the title is primarily about romantic love. In *Bride Wars* and *Wedding Crashers* (2005), for example, the opposite sex seems less important than friendship between women or men. These comic offshoots of the genre often veer away from the formulas of romance toward the conventions of buddy movies, sex comedies, and Animal House humor. The two protagonists in *Bride Wars* (Kate Hudson as Olivia and Anne Hathaway as Emma) are best friends who share the same dream. Their childhood pact to hold June weddings at the Plaza Hotel turns into a vigorous rivalry when a clerk mistakenly books both weddings on the same date. Their secret efforts to sabotage each other's plans escalate as Olivia slips bright orange dye into Emma's tanning cream and Emma mixes blue dye into Liv's hair coloring. Emma raises the ante by sending candy that she knows will make Liv too fat for her dress. Liv responds by substituting an embarrassing Spring Break video for Emma's wedding DVD. Throughout this sisterly combat, as the women turn wedding icons into ammunition, the men are relegated to secondary roles. Even at the altar, it is female friendship that holds center stage.

In *Wedding Crashers*, the primary relationship is between two men, long-time pals and business partners in a firm that specializes in divorce mediation. John Beckwith (played by Owen Wilson) and Jeremy Grey (Vince Vaughn) have seen enough embittered couples to be skeptical of matrimony. "The real enemy here is the institution of marriage," says Beckwith after one particularly hostile mediation session. But both men have also witnessed enough weddings to know that wedding banquets are a great place to pick up dates. Moved by the lavish ambiance of romance, lured by the prospect of catching the bouquet, women are at their most vulnerable after the vows are done. John and Jeremy are masters in the art of crashing weddings in search of female prey. They have learned to dance with the girl's mother first to win the daughter's heart. They know how to appeal to her maternal instincts by entertaining the kids with toy balloons. They have invented a dozen stories that hint at their hidden sensitivity. They have also memorized the repertoire of every kind of ethnic wedding. A sequence early in the movie shows them singing "*Hava Nagila*" at a Jewish wedding, lifting glasses at an Irish reception, and mastering the nuptial customs of Indians and Chinese alike, followed by a montage of half-naked women falling into bed. At one of these events, Jeremy finds himself falling in love, threatening to break the iron-clad rules against marriage that bind him to his buddy. From that point on, the film shifts into combat mode, John and Jeremy doing battle with each other and their own emotional entanglements. As in *Bride Wars*, the film's tone swerves back and forth between romantic moments and broad comedy, frequently crude and sophomoric, suggesting that *Wedding Crashers* aims to take in audiences that would otherwise shun a wedding film. In this respect, it may be classified with teen comedies like *American Pie* (1999) and its nuptial-minded sequel, *American Wedding* (2003).

Rivalry between girlfriends or guy friends is not the only kind of jealousy that can wreck a wedding. In *Monster-in-Law* (2005), the saboteur is the groom's mother. Viola (Jane Fonda) tries to destroy her son's marriage to Charlotte (Jennifer Lopez) because she doesn't want to lose him the way she's just lost her career. Lopez fights back, but Fonda really meets her match in her own mother-in-law, played by Elaine Stritch. The film's title makes the analogy of family as adversary all too plain, reminding us perhaps that many of the monsters in our earliest forms of storytelling, from folk tales to epic romance, were demonized embodiments of threatening kith and kin. In *My Best Friend's Wedding* (1997), Julianne (Julia Roberts) tries to sabotage the wedding of her old childhood friend Michael (Dermot Mulroney). In college, Michael once told her, "If you're not married at 28, marry me." Now, a few days before her twenty-eighth birthday, Michael announces his upcoming marriage to Kimberly (Cameron Diaz), who is smart, young, beautiful, and rich. Julianne decides that Kim is all wrong for her old flame and launches a campaign to separate them. Part of the fun is watching her rig each step of the traditional wedding preparations.

The showdown takes place in the women's room of Wrigley Field Stadium, a scene that says a lot about genre, gender, and supportive camera work. As Kim and Julianne confront each other, an audience of curious women gathers round, responding to each turn of the dialogue as if they were watching a sitcom or a melodrama (Figure 2.6). The camera keeps the two antagonists centered in the foreground but lets us see the onlookers behind them. When Kim accuses Julianne of kissing her fiancé "at my parents' house … on my wedding day," the crowd cries out in alarm and indignation. When she announces she will never give up the man she loves to some "two-faced, big-haired food critic," the women break into applause. Kim and Julianne square off, circle each other, and cross over the imaginary 180 degree line that runs between them, exchanging sides as their battle changes course. Julianne admits her error, accepts her loss, and the mood turns sympathetic. By the time the two rivals make up and embrace, there isn't a dry eye in the place. The camera reflects each emotional nuance with reaction shots, close-ups, a slow zoom, and reverse angle shots, adding music at the climax. The scene could be a summary of the movie's plot, of any number of romantic plots, with the women bystanders acting as a kind of mirror for a typical audience's reactions. This inclusion of stand-in spectators within the *mise-en-scène* reminds us that

FIGURE 2.6   Showdown in the women's room. *My Best Friend's Wedding* (Dir. P.J. Hogan, 1997).

My Best Friend's Wedding, like many romantically focused wedding movies, is aimed primarily at women and their emotional engagement in the would-be-bride's dilemmas.

Black Comedy and Dysfunctional Families: Wedding Films as Social Satire

If the road to the altar is a matter of trial and error, romantic comedy typically involves more errors than trials. The other variations we've been considering so far – sex comedy, teen comedy, buddy movies – also handle the trials and tribulations of relationships with a generally light touch. A much darker view pervades a set of wedding films that are more about troubled families, and the families in these films often stand for society at large.

Director Robert Altman brings a psychological realism to *A Wedding*, his 1978 study of two families with secrets to hide. The film takes place in a single day, starting with a high-toned Episcopal Church wedding and ending after a lavish banquet when nearly everyone has left the family mansion of the groom. He comes from new money, the bride from established northern stock, but these differences only hint at deeper fractures and divisions. Small cracks begin opening at the start. The elderly bishop presiding at the ceremony flubs his lines. The bride has a spot on her dress. And as the day wears on, the skeletons come marching out of closets. Altman juggles a complex web of subplots and relationships. For him, the wedding is a crucible for human drama at its most extreme, a pressure cooker of emotions, when repressed feelings run rampant and the stakes are high. Nearly every one of some 50 characters, including the wedding staff, reveals some personal peculiarity or hidden flaw. Old rivalries and new lusts emerge as guests turn out to be drunks and perverts, communists and gangsters. Altman keeps shifting the tone, swerving from stinging satire to melodrama to outlandish farce. In a film that involves a tornado, a corpse, and a nude painting of the bride, there is no telling what the next scene will bring.

Thirty years later, Jonathan Demme used the wedding setting for a similar project in *Rachel Getting Married*. The wedding here is multicultural and unortho- dox, a New Age affair involving Indian saris, gospel-style responsive chants, and jazz. The band plays a rendition of "Here Comes the Bride" arranged for trumpet, violin, drums, and electric guitar. But it all works because of the evident good will between Rachel's Jewish American family and the groom's African American kin. The expressions of love from both sides seem harmonious and genuine. That is, until Rachel's sister Kym arrives, straight from rehab. Anne Hathaway plays Rachel as a sharp-tongued fury: neurotic, narcissistic, and intense. At the pre-rehearsal dinner, she grabs a glass and gives a tipsy toast that is more about her 12-step pro- gram and her guilt than about the bride and groom. Hathaway's performance is a tour de force, a blend of volatility and vulnerability that manages to make an unlikable character almost sympathetic. It also embodies a challenge to a certain kind of New Age family wedding. Meanwhile, Demme uses the stylistic devices of *cinéma vérité* – jumpy cutting, edgy close-ups, handheld camera work, overlapping dialogue – to highlight the psychological dimensions of each scene. Like Altman, he is less interested in the wedding as a subject than as a metaphor, or as a site for exploring family dynamics. Noah Baumbach's *Margot at the Wedding* (2007) contin- ues this trend with a dark film about two sisters who are alternately tender and mean to each other. Their push and pull relationship and the film's nervous cam- erawork are often painful to watch. Baumbach focuses on character, mood, and a symbolic tree, dispensing with the wedding altogether.

The distinction between mainstream wedding films, produced primarily for entertainment, and independent films that use weddings for more pointed pur- poses may be clarified with another look at P.J. Hogan's *Muriel's Wedding*, the breakthrough film he made in Australia a few years before going on to Hollywood to make *My Best Friend's Wedding*. Muriel's father has a nasty streak that seems too malevolent for light comedy, too realistic to be dismissed as mere caricature. As council president, he enjoys a certain social status and profitable privileges that belie an underlying malice and dishonesty. He belittles his wife as a mindless accessory and berates his daughter as a useless "deadweight." As the film progresses, it becomes clear that they both have lived down to his expectations. Their failures as human beings are due, in large part, to the way he constantly erodes their self-esteem while engaging in shady deals, underhanded politics, and an extramarital affair. For Muriel, a high school dropout who can't hold on to a job or the respect of her school mates, marriage seems like an escape, and the idea of an ostentatious wedding offers the promise of self-vindication. Her wedding is a weapon in a story of revenge. But although she is finally wed in style to a wealthy, handsome young athlete from South Africa, the marriage is a sham (Figure 2.7). It is a loveless marriage of convenience arranged so that her husband can compete in the Olympics as an Australian citizen.

It is also the starting point in Muriel's search for self. Gradually, she comes to realize that a false image of success (not unlike her father's) is no substitute for a genuine relationship based on honesty and love. The film ends with Muriel leaving her husband and moving in with Rhonda, the first person to appreciate

FIGURE 2.7   "She's all yours, Mate!" Dad passes the bride to a reluctant groom in *Muriel's Wedding* (Dir. P.J. Hogan, 1994).

her as herself. *Muriel's Wedding*, then, like Altman's *A Wedding*, can be read as a study in identity and a critique of the romantic wedding film. Some scholars, like Jill Mackey, find a subversive subtext in the story. Mackey sees an erotic element in the relationship between Muriel and Rhonda signaled in the "tantalizing, charged moment" when they exchange glances in the cab at the film's end.[5] This is just one of the reasons why *Muriel's Wedding* has become a gay and lesbian cult classic.

Weddings take on a particularly sinister cast in European films, where they are often occasions for emblematically bad behavior. The way families conduct themselves at these public events is symptomatic of defects in the national character. In Dominique Deruddere's German film, *The Wedding Party* (*Die Bluthochzeit*, 2005), the father of the groom, Hermann Walzer, is violent and domineering (Figure 2.8). When his wedding party is served a plate of spoiled shrimp at a local restaurant, Hermann picks a fight with the owner, Franz Berger. It turns out there is a history behind this fight. Berger, a proud man, has refused to sell his establishment to Hermann, despite the latter's bullying threats. Hermann refuses to pay the bill and leaves, not realizing that his wife and the bride are still upstairs in the ladies' room. Berger locks the door, holding the women as prisoners. The quarrel escalates. Guns are brandished, a grenade is thrown, a Mercedes explodes. The two men find themselves waging a private war that threatens the lives of their families and innocent bystanders. Clearly, the wedding motif in this film (its German title, *Bluthochzeit*, means "Blood Wedding") is ironic. The bride, groom, and most of the wedding party are hostage to the arrogance and hot tempers of two stubborn men entrenched in their longstanding feud. It's no accident that Hermann's father appears early on in a Nazi helmet and that the grenade is a live relic from World War II.

FIGURES 2.8 and 2.9   Dysfunctional weddings in these European films put the national character on comic display.

FIGURE 2.8 *The Wedding Party* (*Die Bluthochzeit*, Dir. Dominique Deruddere, 2005).

FIGURE 2.9 *The Wedding* (*Wesele*, Dir. Wojciech Smarzowski, 2004).

No less cynical or unpredictable, though in different ways, is Marco Bellocchio's Italian film, *The Wedding Director* (*Il regista di matrimoni*, 2006). Franco, the protagonist, is a celebrated film director who has arrived in Sicily to evade a scandal at home. His chance encounter with a man who makes his living by filming weddings leads to a powerful, menacing Sicilian prince. This prince, an admirer of Franco's work, wants the famed director to film his daughter's wedding. The ceremony is staged as a grand affair with a distinctly local flavor. The chorus sings "Hosanna" with ferocious intensity; the priest smiles benignly before a curtain of stained glass windows; the bride steps up to the altar wearing a white veil. No-one is prepared for the startling ending of the ceremony and the film. Ultimately, the splendor of the wedding stands in ironic contrast to the film's real targets: the director's artistic affectations, the moribund society represented by the prince, and much else in modern Italy.

The history of Poland supplies ample material for black comedy. Invaded and partitioned by Russia, Prussia, and the Habsburg Monarchy during the nineteenth century, crushed by the Nazi blitz early in World War II, and subsequently dominated by the Soviet Union until the 1980s, the Polish people have good reason to be skeptical of history and human nature. Their cynicism has found comic relief in three related works about a wedding. The first was Stanislaw Wyspianski's classic play, *The Wedding* (*Wesele* in Polish), written in 1901. Set during a village wedding celebration at a time when Poland was controlled by foreign powers, the play makes fun of the people's indifference to their own fate. The wedding guests pay more attention to their carousing and petty arguments than to the married couple: a young poet and his peasant bride. Later, they are joined by ghosts from Poland's glorious past, one of whom presents the host with a symbolic golden horn, urging him to rouse the people to revolt against their oppressors. But the guests go on dancing like puppets, missing their big opportunity for freedom. In 1959, Poland's great director Andrzej Wajda adapted Wyspianski's play for the screen, shifting the time to Germany's invasion of 1939. The wedding in his film (it bears the same title as the play, *Wesele*) is a surrealistic event that features a stunning white horse, representing the spirit of Polish resistance and the inevitable death of that spirit in the face of overwhelming odds.

More recently, the wedding metaphor has been revived in Wojciech Smarzowski's debut film, *The Wedding* (*Wesele*, 2004). Smarzowski sets his version of the story in post-Communist Poland, where Soviet dictatorship has been supplanted by the tyranny of cash. Wieslaw Wojnar, the bride's father, has thrown an ostentatious banquet at his home, presenting the groom with an expensive Audi sports car as a gift. It turns out, however, that the lavish wedding is a cover-up for his daughter's pregnancy and that the Audi is a bribe. In fact, nearly everything at the festivities is tainted by deception, corruption, and hypocrisy. Wojnar bribes his accountant to falsify the signature on the deed he used to buy the car. When he learns that the Audi was stolen, he pays off the police. By the end of the day, he has run out of cash and credibility, not unlike the corrupt governments of post-Communist Poland. Meanwhile, the wedding guests continue drinking, dancing, and carousing, oblivious to the spoiled cabbage stew and an overflowing toilet. The banquet becomes a cesspool of gluttony, greed, lust, sloth, envy, wrath, and pride. In the course of a single evening, the film evokes all seven deadly sins – and more. At one point, someone sings the beginning words of "Rota" (The Oath), a poem once proposed to be the Polish national anthem. Everyone joins in the rousing chorus: "We will not abandon the land whence come our folk … We will not allow our foe to hold us down … We are the Polish nation, the Polish people." But the tune dies down, Wojnar turns to his next dishonest deal, and the guests resume their drinking (Figure 2.9). The spirit of "Rota" proves to be as ephemeral as the golden horn or the white horse, demonstrating that in 2004, Poland's national wedding satire has not lost the sting it had in 1901 or 1959.

Arab Brides on the Border

While the European wedding films we have examined offer national critiques, a group of recent films from the Middle East uses weddings as starting points for exploring local political and cultural conflicts. *Wedding in Galilee*, *Rana's Wedding*, and *The Syrian Bride* all take place within the contested space of Israel, where Arabs and Israelis live uneasily side by side. *Wedding in Galilee* was directed by Michel Kleifi, an Arab Palestinian who lives in Belgium. Set mostly in a Palestinian village within Israeli-governed Galilee, the story follows Abu Adel, the patriarch of an Arab family and father of the bride, as he tries to host his daughter's wedding amid rising tensions. The Israeli governor is reluctant to allow the celebration to take place because of recent, bloody Arab demonstrations. He will agree only if his staff can attend the ceremony. Local Arab leaders warn Abu Adel not to fraternize with the enemy. Under such conditions, something as intimate and private as a wedding becomes a political event.

The Syrian Bride was directed by Eran Riklis, an Israeli filmmaker whose works include *Cup Final* (1992) and *Lemon Tree* (2008), both noted for their sympathetic portraits of Palestinians. The Syrian bride in the film is Druze, not Palestinian. Mona belongs to a community that, while Arabic in language and culture, has followed its own distinct religious practices for more than a thousand years and chooses not to identify with mainstream Arab nationalism. Mona lives in the Israeli-occupied Golan Heights, separated from the rest of Syria by a demilitarized zone that is patrolled by the United Nations. Her problem is that the man she is to marry, a man she has never met, lives across the border. It has taken six months to secure permission for the trip, and she will never be able to return home. Her predicament thus involves two kinds of issues, the political pressures arising from years of Arab-Israeli antagonism and the cultural challenges of negotiating an arranged marriage in a patriarchal society. Mona's father, Hammed, is respected in the village for his pro-Syrian activities. He has just been released on parole from an Israeli prison. But he faces dissension within his own family. His eldest son has violated Druze tradition by marrying a foreigner, a Russian doctor. The village elders threaten to ostracize Hammed if he admits this son to the wedding, although they have no problem with his younger son, a womanizer and shady businessman. Furthermore, Hammed's married daughter is growing restless. Unhappy with her marriage and her options as a woman, she rebels by wearing trousers and secretly applying to college. Meanwhile, the bride goes through the preparatory rituals, some familiar to Western audiences, some not. She communes with her female relatives, gets her hair fixed like a movie star, and chooses a white gown. Sheep are slaughtered; the guests are seated for a bountiful outdoor feast, men and women at separate tables. But the groom and his family can only wait across the border. To communicate with the bride's father, they must shout through megaphones. At the moment of truth, dressed in bridal white, Mona faces her uncertain future through the iron bars of the border gate. A last minute dispute over her visa between Israeli and Syrian bureaucrats leaves her momentarily in limbo. The bride and groom can only stare at one another across no man's land with their families behind them (Figure 2.10). That's when Mona decides to act, taking tradition and affairs of state in her own hands to pursue her nuptial dream.

In *Rana's Wedding*, the quest to find a husband is complicated by the fact that the bride is a Palestinian woman living in Jerusalem. The winding streets bristle with ominous signs of danger. A dog growls at her, people throw things from roofs, a discarded handbag might contain a bomb. Sand bags and concrete barriers rise to bar her way while armed Israeli soldiers watch her every move. Rana's plight is further complicated by an ultimatum from her father. She must get married by 4 p.m. or leave with him for Egypt. Her father, a widower, has given Rana a list of eligible bachelors, mostly older men with respectable positions. But she would rather marry the young theatre director she loves – if she can find him first. Palestinian director Hany Abu-Assad brings a gritty documentary realism to the film, using Rana's wedding to highlight the claustrophobic quality of her life under political occupation on the one hand and traditional Arab patriarchy on the other. Somehow, she manages to get her hair done and find a wedding dress. But there is no mosque wedding. The Muslim official who should preside over the ceremony is stuck at a roadblock. He ends up conducting the formalities in a yellow minibus (Figure 2.11). Only the men are actively involved, making it clear that this wedding

FIGURES 2.10 and 2.11 Some films from the Middle East use the wedding motif to explore local political and cultural conflicts.

FIGURE 2.10 "Barrier Ahead." *The Syrian Bride* (*Urus suriyya*, Dir. Eran Riklis, 2004).

FIGURE 2.11 "I marry you, Rana, according to the law of Islam." *Rana's Wedding* (*Al gods fee yom akhar*, Dir. Hany Abu-Assad, 2002).

is essentially an agreement between the bride's father and her husband. As they fix the price of her dowry and the alimony, she is a silent witness to her fate.

These images of Middle Eastern women in marriage veils guide our critical attention in two directions, inviting us to analyze the films in terms of colonial history and feminist discourse. They point an accusing finger outward at the consequences of territorial expansion and control. The lives of Mona, Rana, and Abu Adel's daughters would be much improved if they were free to travel back and forth across the boundary lines of international politics. Another finger points inward at the social pressures and restrictions that confine them. For Mona's sister, marriage precludes certain personal liberties and the opportunities of a formal education. Rana, too, has little to gain; her wedding is an exchange of legal property from one man to another. For the Druze bride in Galilee, the traditional expectations of her culture strain her wedding night, her husband, and their relationship to the breaking point.

Rites of Passage, Icons of Success: The Mythology of Wedding Films

With so many variations on the theme of weddings, what ties these films together? We have seen how each film reflects the time and culture that produced it. But are there also common threads that run through Hollywood romantic comedies, national satires from Europe, and political/cultural critiques from the Middle East? One place to look for answers to such questions is at the crossroads of mythology. In Unit I on "The Warrior Hero," following the lead of Joseph Campbell and Christopher Vogler, we sought to identify certain archetypal figures in Westerns, samurai films, kung fu movies, and swordplay fantasies. These characters include the Warrior Hero (Campbell's "Hero with a Thousand Faces"), the Monster, the Mentor, and the Trickster, each of whom plays a familiar role in the hero's quest (what Campbell calls "The Journey of the Hero"). The journey itself follows a predictable path as the protagonist ventures from comfortable surroundings into dangerous territory, where he or she may be trained and tutored by the mentor, tempted by the trickster, and challenged by any number of monsters before gaining the treasured prize. This journey, then, proceeds in stages, to which Vogler gives archetypal names: the Call to Adventure, Crossing the Threshold, Meeting the Mentor, Tests, Ordeals, and Rewards.

The point here is to see how cinematic genres, like other forms of storytelling, may reflect deep concerns shared by people everywhere. The details of these stories may be as varied as the cultures of the world, but they spring from a common source, the human mind in search of images for basic emotional and spiritual needs. Arguably, they contribute to a global mythology of wedding practices, not in the sense of myth as false belief but as a reflection of universal truths.

In the warrior hero films, we've seen how the hero, usually male, needs to prove himself worthy to others and himself. His journey is partly a matter of testing skills, forging character, and living up to the standards of a moral code. The prize, whether it is victory over the enemy, peace for the community, or some symbolic treasure, must always be earned. So what about wedding films? Do they have their own archetypal characters? Does the wedding hero, the bride more often than the groom, follow a familiar trajectory of trials and ordeals on her way to the altar? Does she get to be a kind of knight in shining armor, the warrior in a wedding dress?

In the wedding films that we've been studying, the parallels to martial arts films are striking. Think of what is implied by the titles of *Bride Wars*, *Monster-in-Law*, or *Die Bluthochzeit* (*Blood Wedding*). In film after film, the wedding ceremony or the banquet becomes a kind of battle ground. Preparations for the big day can seem like basic military training. In *License to Wed* (2007), the analogy to boot camp is explicit in the film's marketing publicity and in the premise of its plot. Robin Williams plays Pastor Frank, the unconventional leader of the local church in which the bride wants to get married. But before the couple can wed, he requires them to undergo a grueling, unorthodox, frequently bizarre prenuptial training course. The trials include mechanical babies that cry and wet their diapers, encounter groups that test how couples fight, and no sex before the wedding. Is Reverend Frank a wise eccentric or a dangerous hypocrite? We see him leading Sunday School children in a game of Commandment Challenge, an off-beat biblical version of Jeopardy. The game board summarizes all Ten Commandments in whacky, pop religious babble. "Covet? Don't Love It." "It Ain't Fly to Lie." "Be Chill. Don't Kill." "Show me adultery," Frank shouts out to the kids. Later, he puts the bride behind the wheel of a car, blindfolds her, and makes the groom give her driving directions from the back seat. Frank seems to shift from amusing minister to meddling mentor to maniacal monster, as if mocking each archetypal figure along the hero's journey.

Bride Wars and *License to Wed* are light comedies that may hit or miss their mark, but there is a serious side to wedding myths. Ethnologists who study rituals around the world find special meaning in wedding customs. Because the wedding is a rite of passage, marking a key transition in an individual's journey through life and in that person's place within the community, the details surrounding the wedding ceremony can reveal significant facts about a people's values and beliefs. Among the most important traditions in Europe and the United States is the formal "white wedding," credited to Britain's Queen Victoria, who wore a white dress at her wedding to Prince Albert in 1840. Originally a status symbol of the upper class, the dress and its surrounding rituals trickled down to the middle class and crossed the Atlantic, where they set standards for early twentieth-century brides. Hollywood helped to popularize the white wedding in movies like Frank Capra's *It Happened One Night* (1934), George Cukor's *The Philadelphia Story* (1940), and especially Vincente Minnelli's *Father of the Bride* (1950). The scene in which Spencer Tracy walks young Elizabeth Taylor down the aisle, he in a new tux and top hat, she in a modest but resplendent white gown, could serve as a how-to guide for the classic American wedding. The church pulsates with excitement and solemnity. Both sides of the aisle, festooned with flowers and candles, are filled with family and friends. First comes the groom, escorting the bride's mother to her place in the front pew and taking his position on the right side of the altar. Next come the groomsmen, all in step, followed by the bridesmaids in coordinated gowns. Then all heads turn to watch the bride, leaning on her father's arm and stepping slowly down the aisle to Wagner's well-known Bridal Chorus. The priest repeats words that, in one form or another, have become familiar through dozens of movies and live events. "Dearly beloved, we are gathered here together in the sight of God and in the face of this company to join together this man and this woman in holy matrimony." Tracy's role, his "only line in the show," is to give his daughter to the new man in her life. There is the exchange of vows, the token rings, the kiss, the audience's sighs, and then the organ breaks into Mendelssohn's recessional "Wedding March" as bride and groom now step back up the aisle as husband and wife.

In her book *Wedding as Text*, Wendy Leeds-Hurwitz observes how such American weddings combine elements of performance and entertainment, social significance and consumerism.[6] Diane Meier Delaney explores these elements one by one in *The New American Wedding*, noting how the relatively simple forms of courtship and ceremony in the 1950s have blossomed into big business, with proposals written in the sky, elaborate diamond rings, and expensive locations.[7] The chapters of Delaney's book describe stages of the couple's journey, from the proposal and commitment jewelry to the reception and honeymoon getaway. Each stage might be illustrated with scenes from the movies in this Unit.

We have already seen how Charles Shyer's version of *Father of the Bride* updates the rituals to 1991. The ceremony is shorter, less formal, with Pachelbel's Canon replacing Mendelssohn's "Wedding March." The big proposal scenes in both *Sex and the City* and *Runaway Bride* are performed on bended knee. But in *Bride Wars*, courtship is more of a joke. Emma's boyfriend hides her engagement ring in a fortune cookie. Emma uses email to dispatch her save-the-date announcements. Much more time and effort in all these films is invested in the planning of the wedding itself. The date and venue must be chosen. Someone must select the music, flowers, and décor. There is a menu for the banquet, outfits for the wedding party, and a hundred other details to arrange. It's no wonder that novices seek professional help.

Nor is this advice always a pleasant experience. Spencer Tracy's condescending caterer makes him feel cheap and unsophisticated, Steve Martin's effete wedding planner snubs him at every opportunity, and the hired staff in Altman's *A Wedding* thrashes the groom's uncle as if he were a thief. But Jennifer Lopez in *The Wedding Planner* is a marvel of improvisation and efficiency. In one continuous tracking shot, we watch her fix the bridesmaid's bodice with a clothespin, usher the priest toward the altar, adjust a floral arrangement, stop the staff from flirting, relocate a guest with an unwieldy hairdo (Figure 2.12), cue in the lights and music, and sprint to find the bride's missing father (Figure 2.13), stopping along the way to the alert the groomsmen (Figure 2.14) before rousing the FOB from a drunken stupor with assorted pharmaceuticals hidden in a toolkit under the jacket of her tidy suit (Figure 2.15).

As Leeds-Hurwitz points out, the wedding ceremony underwent changes in the late 1960s, when young people, rejecting the traditions of their parents, starting writing their own vows, experimenting with new forms of dress and music, a shift illustrated in the casual eclecticism of films like *Rachel Getting Married*. Leeds-Hurwitz also notes a trend in pre-wedding parties. The standard bachelor's night out was superseded by extravagant parties, spiced with exotic dancers and inflatable sheep, or with getaway weekends in Las Vegas. We see this trend in male-oriented wedding films like *American Wedding* and even in *Bride Wars*, when Emma crashes Liv's bachelorette party at a male strip joint. While such crude goings on may seem to some like evidence of modern decay, ethnologist Claudia De Lys links them to a long history. In early times, the best man and his groomsmen, known then as "bride knights," once served to help the groom capture a reluctant bride, carrying her away from her home.[8] De Lys traces the coordinated outfits of today's bridesmaids to another ancient custom, based on the belief that evil spirits intent on harming the bride could be fooled if they all wore similar costumes.[9]

The bride's dress, of course, has come to be the most iconic, most emotionally charged, and often most expensive part of modern wedding pageantry. An elaborate montage is devoted to this icon in *Sex and the City* as Carrie Bradshaw glides through a succession of designer labels from Vera Wang and Christian Dior to Oscar de la Renta and Vivienne Westwood, each more stunning than the previous gown. The scene is pure spectacle, with the gowns stealing center stage. As someone says in *Bride Wars*, "You don't alter Vera Wang to fit you; you alter yourself to fit Vera." It's not surprising that a film like *The Wedding Dress* (2001) should cast the dress itself as the central character in a love story spanning seven decades, multiple locations, and a variety of life styles. Much of the pleasure in such films is focused on the female body and its adornments. This partly explains why the narrative in so many wedding films is interrupted by shopping sprees and fashion shows. The fashion show in *Sex and the City*, like similar sequences in *Roberta* (1935) and *The Women* (1939), stops the story while a group of female characters get to enjoy the spectacle of other women in fancy, often fanciful clothes. If there are men in the scene, or in the audience for that matter, their views count less than the women's. Even when Katherine Heigl puts on an impromptu fashion

FIGURES 2.12–2.15 Jennifer Lopez supervises the perfect ceremony in a single tracking shot, from *The Wedding Planner* (Dir. Adam Shankman, 2001).

FIGURE 2.12 "Penny, go to M-12. We have a Dark Tower choking the AV."

FIGURE 2.13 "Cover me up North. The FOB is MIA."

FIGURE 2.14 "Hey guys, put on your jackets."

FIGURE 2.15 "I have a 20 on the FOB."

show for her male visitor in *27 Dresses*, it's clear that she enjoys the spectacle more than he does. In *Sex and the City*, Carrie Bradshaw dances through her old wardrobe, performing for the pleasure of her three best friends. The "male gaze" seems to be beside the point.

The connection between shopping and romance is made early on in *Sex and the City* when Carrie Bradshaw's voice-over explains that "young girls come to the city for labels and love." There are plenty of product placements in this film, but none is more memorable than the blue Manolo Blahnik shoes placed in Carrie's penthouse closet. The closet itself, disappointingly small when her boyfriend Big buys the apartment for her, is enlarged and upgraded into the closet of her dreams, an apt signifier for pleasurable purchases to come. She calls it "love at first sight." That closet and those blue shoes within it are what bring her and Big back together again after a lengthy separation. She returns to retrieve the shoes only to find him there – he was just going to bring the shoes to her – and they embrace in the empty closet. When he gets down on his knee to place one on her foot, it is the proposal scene she always wanted. It is also a nod to Cinderella and those other romantic stories in which shoes bring the princess together with her prince charming. The lesson Carrie learns, the one she makes explicit at the film's end, is that "love is the one label that never goes out of style." It's the man, not the gown or the wedding hall, that counts. As if to emphasize this point, she gets married at City Hall in a dress without a name. But if this anti-consumer moral of the story seems a little hollow, it's because what we remember most are those gorgeous designer dresses and those blue Manolo Blahnik shoes.

With so much attention focused on display, the spectacle of weddings seems to trump the meaning of marriage. It's more about saying yes to the dress than "I do" to the groom. But consider the other extreme, as Ang Lee does in *The Wedding Banquet* when Gao and Wei-Wei go to City Hall. Their civil wedding comes after the official has just wed a couple in shorts and jeans. He repeats the required words unceremoniously, then shuffles over to a cluttered desk where the marriage certificate is stamped. Gao and his bride are better dressed, but the bored bureaucrat mispronounces their names, Wei-Wei flubs the vows, and Gao's parents leave deeply disappointed. For them, a Chinese wedding should a big public event, a celebration of community hosted by proud parents for family and friends.

That's why there are banquets, the part of the wedding when guests get to participate. At the reception banquet, marriage becomes a party, with music, dancing, speeches, good food, and much drinking in attractive surroundings. Some of these events are strictly governed by tradition. In Altman's film (*A Wedding*), the master of ceremonies explains precisely how the first dance will proceed once the bride and groom are on the floor: "Then the FOG will cut in and dance with the bride while the groom dances with the MOB. Then the FOB will cut in and dance with his daughter while the FOG will cut in on his son and dance with the MOB." The MC's acronyms and overblown exactitude are all part of the satire.

The traditional toast to the couple, more often a roast than a toast, plays a particularly big part in many banquet scenes. In *Four Weddings and a Funeral*, the speech that Charles makes early in the film – affable, witty, and heartfelt – immediately mark him as an appealing character. When someone else tries to imitate his humor at another wedding, the speech falls flat because it lacks Charles's charm. In *Wedding Crashers*, the maid of honor also falters when she tries to roast the bride, until she's rescued by one of the crashers, who is more practiced in such matters. In *Rachel Getting Married*, after a round of warm, affectionate toasts around the table, Rachel's sister raises her glass and breaks the mood with a painfully self-centered speech. One of the most devastating toasts, really a narrated slide-show, comes near the end of *27 Dresses*. Jane is furious with her sister Tess for betrothing the man she loves under false pretense, but she is even angrier that Tess has altered their mother's wedding dress. As revenge, she projects a series of photos that expose Tess as a liar to her husband to be. In each case, the ritual of toasting is a kind of test.

For some films, as we have seen, the entire reception becomes an ordeal that tests the compatibility of families and the couple's resolve. Will Betsy's marriage hold up after her liberal-minded Jewish parents spend the evening with her husband's conservative Italian clan under an increasingly leaky tent? Will Dino and his bride survive as a couple in *A Wedding* after the Corellis and the Brenners sit out a tornado in the wine cellar and their family skeletons run amok? What will happen to Wieslaw Wojnar, his daughter, their guests, and the Polish nation that they represent in Smarzowski's The *Wedding* when the wedding party's over? Such questions drive our interest in the narrative as we wonder how the bride, groom, or hopeful couple will negotiate the rites of passage, following or deviating from the well-worn path taken by so many wedding heroes before them.

Comparative Weddings 101

At times, watching a film about a culture much unlike our own may leave us feeling like outsiders, like ethnographers observing the behavior of a strange society, trying to understand how people in different environments organize their daily lives. Wedding movies can serve an ethnographic function, but as fiction films – as stories about people whom we come to care about – they can also break through the barriers of scientific objectivity. When we identify with the characters, we enter their world, share their emotions, join the celebration. This ability of motion pictures to transport us into new cultural contexts is one of the most compelling features of world cinema. We get to understand other people, other peoples, with our hearts as well as with our heads. And movies do more than give us access. They give us new ideas, new options for organizing our own lives. So movies may become a way to transport cultural practices from one place to another. They become agents of change in an age of global exchange.

At the same time, we should remember that films are rarely if ever neutral. The views they afford of other peoples and their practices may be tinted by agendas or limited by particular perspectives. In *Rite Out of Place*, ritual theorist Ronald Grimes

FIGURE 2.16   Staging local wedding practices for a global audience in *Fiddler on the Roof* (Dir. Norman Jewison, 1971).

analyzes *Fiddler on the Roof* (1971) as an example. Grimes compares the wedding at the movie's center to a typical twentieth-century eastern European Jewish ceremony. In the film, we see the bride and groom share the traditional glass of wine, surrounded by candles and their families dressed in the customary black Orthodox attire (Figure 2.16). But in place of their vows and the rabbi's speech, what we hear is a song expressing the sentimental reflections of the parents. "Is this the little girl I carried? Is this the little boy at play?" Missing is the ritual reading of the marriage contract (identifying the bride as a transferable asset passed from father to husband) and the groom's words of patriarchal authority ("You are sanctified unto me"). Instead of such cultural particularities, we get an appeal to universal experience, naturalized by references to the seasonal cycle ("Sunrise, sunset, swiftly fly the years"). The ceremony itself, about 20 minutes of screen time, is continually interrupted by local squabbles, signs of poverty, and more ominous references to Russian anti-Semitism. The whole wedding, Grimes notes, is "transformed by the cinematic process."[10] For the purpose of understanding wedding movies as a genre, it is important to recognize how genres impose their own conventions on local customs.

It is also worth pausing here to explain a few nuptial practices that we might not understand just by watching the film. What are Toula and Ian wearing on their heads during the service in *My Big Fat Greek Wedding*, and why does her aunt spit as the bride walks down the aisle? Why do the women paint their hands red in *Monsoon Wedding*? Why do the guests break into the couple's bedroom in *The Wedding Banquet*? What's all the fuss about hidden shoes in *Who Am I to You*? Without some explanations, we might be reduced to saying, like Ian's father, "It's all Greek to me."

When the Greek Orthodox priest crowns Toula and Ian, he is repeating a venerable religious ritual. The flower crowns, called *stefana*, symbolize God's glory and honor, and the white ribbon that joins them represents their unity in marriage. The priest then leads the crowned couple around the altar three times, three for the Holy Trinity, taking their first steps together as a married couple. Aunt Voula spits toward the bride to ward off evil spirits, a folk custom that is neither venerable nor religious.

In parts of the world where marriages are arranged, dating is forbidden or frowned upon without formal approval by the couple's families. The arrangement may be brokered by a matchmaker, typically a woman in the community, like Yente in *Fiddler on the Roof*, who specializes in finding the right pair. There is little time for romance before the wedding, hence few romantic wedding movies in the Western sense. In Arab films like *Wedding in Galilee* and *Rana's Wedding*, the focus, as we've seen, is on getting to the ceremony, a matter of overcoming cultural confinements and crossing borders. In *The Syrian Bride*, the bride hasn't even met the man she's marrying. *Late Marriage* (*Hatuna Meuheret*, 2001), an Israeli film, dramatizes the anguish that can arise when a man loves a woman deemed unsuitable by his family. For years, Zaza's parents have been trying to find a fitting match for their 31-year-old son, but he is secretly dating an older divorcée with a child. When his family discovers this, they resort to humiliation and intimidation to force him into line.

When marriages are arranged, the couple usually meets for the first time under the watchful eyes of relatives. The chaperones may sit separately, but within reach, as the prospective bride and groom become acquainted. We can observe one of these meetings in *Late Wedding* when Zaza is introduced to an eligible 17-year-old. While the parents discuss their children's qualifications in the living room, Zaza and the girl get to share a few minutes alone in the bedroom. Both sides engage in complex negotiations about income, education, fertility, and sexual experience, reflecting centuries of sharply honed tradition. This conception of marriage as a form of bartering is illustrated in many movie scenes, some deeply disturbing, some comic, some tenderly touching. In *Tulpan* (2008), two nomadic Mongolian families discuss marriage prospects in a *yurt* (a portable nomad dwelling) while the girl remains out of sight. The young man, accompanied by his father and a few odd gifts, sends all the wrong messages while the girl's mother impatiently whisks flies from her tea. In *The Namesake* (2003), a film about Indian-born Americans directed by Mira Nair, the bride-to-be listens from behind a curtain while her fate is being sealed. When nobody is looking, she steps into her future husband's shoes and takes the first steps of a journey with the stranger who will be her companion for life.

In parts of Africa, where the ratio of marriageable women to men is about 2 to 1, polygamy is a common fact of life. According to some estimates, about 30% of the men in West Africa have more than one wife. Both Muslims and animists defend the practice, explaining that it can double or triple a family's household resources and help prevent adultery. But polygamy can lead to problems, as Ousmane Sembene slyly illustrates in his Senegalese satire, *Xala* (1975). In most cases, it is men who make the marital decisions, but among the Fulani people of Niger, it is the women who traditionally decide. A man's physical appeal is measured partly by the whiteness of his eyes and teeth. During the Gerewol festival, the eligible village men dress like women, roll their eyes, and flash their teeth while the women choose their partner for the night or for the rest of their lives. In Dakar, the capital of Senegal, the Miss Djongama contest celebrates the traditional ideal of feminine beauty, favoring women with full figures and a measured gait, in contrast to the more contemporary attributes of Miss Senegal: slim, sassy, and fast-paced.[11]

Throughout the world, time-honored wedding rituals are giving way to modern practices. In China, for example, where tradition requires that the bride leave her household to live with the groom's family, she might be isolated with her closest friends before the wedding to mourn the loss of her early relationships. On her wedding day, she might take a cleansing bath, a special moment beautifully evoked in Zhang Yang's *Shower* (1999). The groom's family might send a procession of musicians and porters to carry her to the wedding in a red sedan chair, a ritual that is celebrated with boisterous humor in Zhang Yimou's *Red Sorghum* (1987). The color red, signifying love, luck, prosperity, and happiness, still dominates Chinese weddings. We can see this and a number of enduring traditions in Ang Lee's *The Wedding Banquet* (see Close-up: *The Wedding Banquet*).

Wedding scenes have long been a staple of Indian movies. Mehboob Khan's *Mother India* (*Bharat Mata*, 1957), for example, begins with an elaborate village wedding, alternating between long shots of the cattle-driven chariots and frequent close-ups of the bride richly bejeweled and painted with red henna. The festivities of henna, when the bride's female friends and relatives sing, dance, and eat while decorating her palms and feet with the rich red dye of the henna plant, are famously staged in *Monsoon Wedding*, an affectionate homage to the cultural traditions of Punjab in northwestern India (see Close-up: *Monsoon Wedding*). Many of these rituals and more appear in *Who Am I to You?* (*Hum Aapke Hain Koun...!*, 1994), so prominently, in fact, that the film has been ridiculed by some critics as a glorified wedding video. This is one reason for its popularity, especially among overseas Indians who flocked to see what "a real Indian wedding" is like. The wedding sequences are sometimes lifted from these films, repackaged, and sold separately for the diaspora market. Mixed in with the traditional imagery are images of the modern world. Some of the men wear Western business suits. Bottles of name brand beverages are prominently placed with their labels facing out. The message is that Hindi conventions and consumerism can enjoy a peaceful coexistence.

Towards a Definition of the Genre

Let's return now to some of the questions that we posed about genre early in this chapter. Although the movies we've considered span a wide range of characters, cultures, and cinematic styles, they do appear to share a critical mass of common traits. The hero is usually a bride-to-be, sometimes a would-be groom, occasionally a close relation to the married couple, but always someone on a journey through the matrimonial landscape. The bride, groom, father of the bride, or jealous ex-lover may follow different cultural traditions in each film, but the protagonists must always face and try to overcome a set of obstacles before gaining the prize. Typically, the pathway to the altar is beset with the familiar iconography of wedding rituals: the rings, veils, gowns, and banquet food that signify the couple's union, the community's blessing, or the bride's most memorable day. Along the way, there may be mentors to learn from, foes to fight, supportive allies, and deceptive tricksters. The stages of the journey may include a proposal scene, introductions to the family, shopping for the dress, the banquet, toasts, a bachelor party, and the ceremony itself, although these rites and rituals may vary depending on the country and its practices. Or the journey's twists and turns may depend largely on generic choices, whether the film is written as a romantic comedy, a melodrama, an irreverent lampoon, or a cultural critique. The journey's goal may differ, too, depending on what the wedding represents: true love, personal fulfillment, social status, ethnic unity, the tyrannies or treasures of tradition.

As we've seen, sometimes wedding movies can look more like a subgenre than a distinct genre of its own. The four volumes of the *Shirmer Encyclopedia of Film* contain entries for romantic comedy, melodrama, and the woman's film, but none for wedding films. David Shumway notes that the term romantic comedy (sometimes referred to as rom-coms) generally includes "all films that treat love, courtship, and marriage comically."[12] He classifies *My Best Friend's Wedding* as a conservative treatment of screwball comedy, which would make it an example of a subgenre of a subgenre. In another entry on melodrama, John Mercer concludes that "Melodrama cannot be defined simply as a genre," noting that the term's meaning and status are hotly debated topics.[13] Annette Kuhns, in her entry on "woman's pictures" observes that this term overlaps in setting and theme with Hollywood melodrama.[14] Both melodrama and the woman's picture commonly are set in middle-class environments and focus on individuals beset by conflicts involving sexuality, family, and home. What distinguishes the woman's picture, she points out, is its identification with a central female character, often to the point of tears. Although Kuhns doesn't discuss wedding films per se, we might observe that whereas films like *Bride Wars* and *Sex and the City* may cater to female audiences, others like *Wedding Crashers* do not.

Nor do wedding films appear to follow a clear evolutionary pattern, advancing, say, from an experimental phase to classical or baroque periods, a claim made for other genres by historians like Thomas Schatz. It might be more accurate to speak of cycles, as Rick Altman does: successive releases of films with similar subjects, themes, and tones that are motivated by audience interests and commercial success, like the round of rom-com wedding films that followed *My Big Fat Greek Wedding* in the United States or the wave of conservative family-centered Hindi wedding movies in the 1990s. Some of these trends involve hybridity, which might blend the momentary popularity of teen pics or buddy movies with brides and grooms. Such cyclical variations of the wedding film highlight the role of commercial interests and audience interests in creating and sustaining genres.

What also shapes these journeys and their outcomes are strong historical or cultural forces. These may be explicit, like the Israeli roadblocks in *Rana's Wedding* and the tradition of arranged nuptials in *Late Marriage*. Or they may be unspoken forces operating beneath the surface, like the specter of Nazi Germany in *The Wedding Party* or the toxic generations of class inbreeding and corruption in *The Wedding Director*. A successful film like *Sex and the City* may reflect or revive a nation-wide interest in weddings, adding themes of sexual freedom and fulfillment to traditional romance, linking them to an elaborate franchise of products and consumer-oriented television shows. Understanding these forces through the lenses of theory, industry analysis, and film aesthetics is one of the rewards of studying the wedding film, whether we consider it a genre, a subgenre, or a cyclical trend. Whatever their generic status may be, wedding movies tell us volumes about the ideologies, the economic structures, and the artists that produced them. They also reveal much about the audiences who watch them. Tracking their course over time and across national boundaries gives us glimpses into our past and future in an increasingly globalized cultural environment. In all this tracking and analysis, however, we should not forget to enjoy the genre's many pleasures. For those of us who like our weddings big and Greek or Jewish or Punjabi, there are plenty of wedding movies inviting us to join in the celebration.

Filmography

Country	English Language Title	Original Title	Director	Date
USA	Father of the Bride		Vincente Minnelli	1950
USA	Fiddler on the Roof		Norman Jewison	1971
Poland	The Wedding	Wesele	Andrzej Wajda	1973
Senegal	Xala		Ousmane Sembene	1975
USA	A Wedding		Robert Altman	1978
Ghana	Love Brewed in the African Pot		Kwaw Ansah	1981
Israel/Palestine	Wedding in Galilee	Urs al-Jalil	Michel Khleifi	1987
USA	Betsy's Wedding		Alan Alda	1990
USA	Father of the Bride		Charles Shyer	1991
Taiwan/USA	The Wedding Banquet	Xiyan	Ang Lee	1993
India	Who Am I to You?	Hum Aapke Hain Koun...!	Sooraj R. Barjatya	1994
Australia	Muriel's Wedding		P.J. Hogan	1994
UK	Four Weddings and a Funeral		Mike Newell	1994
USA	My Best Friend's Wedding		P.J. Hogan	1997
India	Sometimes Things Do Happen	Kuch Kuch Hota Hai	Karan Johar	1998

(Continued)

Filmography (*Continued*)

Country	English Language Title	Original Title	Director	Date
USA	Runaway Bride		Garry Marshall	1999
USA	The Wedding Planner		Adam Shankman	2001
India/USA	Monsoon Wedding		Mira Nair	2001
Israel	Late Marriage	Hatuna Meuheret	Dover Koshashvili	2001
USA	My Big Fat Greek Wedding		Joel Zwick	2002
Israel/Palestine	Rana's Wedding	Al qods fee yom akhar	Hany Abu-Assad	2002
India/UK	Bride and Prejudice		Gurinder Chadha	2004
Israel	The Syrian Bride	Urus suriyya	Eran Riklis	2004
Poland	The Wedding	Wesele	Wojciech Smarzowski	2004
Germany	The Wedding Party	Die Bluthochzeit	Dominique Deruddere	2005
USA	Wedding Crashers		David Dobkin	2005
New Zealand	Samoan Wedding (aka Sione's Wedding)		Chris Graham	2006
Italy	The Wedding Director	Il regista di matrimoni	Marco Bellocchio	2006
USA	Margot at the Wedding		Noah Baumbach	2007
USA	License to Wed		Ken Kwapis	2007
Iceland	White Night Wedding	Brúðguminn	Baltasar Kormákur	2008
Iceland	Country Wedding	Sveitabrúðkaup	Valdís Óskarsdóttir	2008
USA	27 Dresses		Anne Fletcher	2008
USA	Rachel Getting Married		Jonathan Demme	2008
USA	Sex and the City		Michael Patrick King	2008
South Africa	White Wedding		Jann Turner	2009
USA	Bride Wars		Gary Winick	2009
USA	Our Family Wedding		Rick Famuyiwa	2010
Zimbabwe	Playing Warriors		Rumbi Katedza	2011
USA	Bridesmaids		Paul Feig	2011
Denmark	Melancholia		Lars Von Trier	2011
Israel	Fill the Void	Lemale et ha'halal	Rama Burshtein	2012

Notes

1. Thomas Schatz, *Hollywood Genres: Formulas, Filmmaking, and the Studio System* (Random House, 1981), 37–38. See the Introduction, Chapter 1, and Chapter 3 in the present book for more discussion of evolutionary theories of genre.

2. Susan Stern with Wendy Kolmar, "Remembering *Barbie Nation*: An Interview with Susan Stern," *Women's Studies Quarterly* 30(1/2) (Spring/Summer 2002): 189–195.

3. Raelene Wilding, "Romantic Love and 'Getting Married': Narratives of the Wedding in and out of Cinematic Texts," *Journal of Sociology* 29(5) (2003): 373–389.

4. Diane Negra, *What a Girl Wants? Fantasizing the Reclamation of Self in Postfeminism* (Routledge, 2009). Quotations are from pp. 44, 125, 123, and 152 respectively.

5. Jill Mackey, "Subtext and Countertext in *Muriel's Wedding*," *National Women's Studies Association Journal* 13(1) (Spring 2001): 86–104.

6. Wendy Leeds-Hurwitz, *Wedding as Text: Communicating Cultural Identities through Ritual* (Erlbaum, 2002).

7. Diane Meier Delaney, *The New American Wedding: Ritual and Style in a Changing Culture* (Penguin, 2005).

8. Claudia De Lys, *How the World Weds: The Story of Marriage, Adultery & Divorce* (Martin Press, 1929), 67.

9. De Lys, 68.

10. Ronald Grimes, *Rite Out of Place: Ritual, Media, and the Arts* (Oxford University Press, 2007), 41–47.

11. *"Will You Marry Me?" Marriage Customs in Ethiopia, Mali, Niger, and Senegal*. DVD, directed by Chema Rodriguez (Film Media Group, Films for the Humanities and Sciences, 2008).

12. David Shumway, "Romantic Comedy," in *Schirmer Encyclopedia of Film*, Vol. 4 (Thomson Gale, 2007), 1.

13. John Mercer, "Melodrama," in *Schirmer Encyclopedia of Film*, Vol. 3 (Thomson Gale, 2007), 133.

14. Annette Kuhns, "The Woman's Picture," in *Schirmer Encyclopedia of Film*, Vol. 4 (Thomson Gale, 2007), 367–373.

Further Reading

Curtis, Richard. *Four Weddings and a Funeral: The Screenplay*. St. Martin's Press, 1994.

De Lys, Claudia. *How the World Weds: The Story of Marriage, Adultery & Divorce*. Martin Press, 1929.

Delaney, Diane Meier. *The New American Wedding: Ritual and Style in a Changing Culture*. Penguin, 2005.

Doane, Mary Anne. *The Desire to Desire: The Woman's Film of the 1940s*. Indiana University Press, 1987.

Doane, Mary Anne. "The Economy of Desire: The Commodity Form in/of the Cinema." *Quarterly Review of Film and Video* 11 (1989): 22–33.

Elsaesser, Thomas. "Tales of Sound and Fury: Observations on the Family Melodrama." *Monogram* 4 (1972): 2–15.

Kuhn, Annette. "Women's Genres." *Screen* 25(1) (1984): 18–28.

Leeds-Hurwitz, Wendy. *Wedding as Text: Communicating Cultural Identities through Ritual*. Erlbaum, 2002.

Luckett, Moya. "A Moral Crisis in Prime Time: *Peyton Place* and the Rise of the Single Girl." In Mary Beth Haralovich and Lauren Rabinovitz, eds., *Television, History, and American Culture*, 75–97. Duke University Press, 1999.

Mackey, Jill. "Subtext and Countertext in *Muriel's Wedding*." *National Women's Studies Association Journal* 13(1) (Spring 2001): 86–104.

Mulvey, Laura. "Visual Pleasure and Narrative Cinema." *Screen* 16(3) (Autumn 1975): 6–18.

Otnes, Cele and Elizabeth Pleck. *Cinderella Dreams: The Allure of the Lavish Wedding*. University of California Press, 2003.

Pauwels, Heidi R.A. *The Goddess as Role Model: Sita and Radha in Scripture and on Screen*. Oxford University Press, 2008.

Radner, Hilary. *Neo-Feminist Cinema: Girly Films, Chick Flicks and Consumer Culture*. Routledge, 2011.

Stamp, Shelley. *Movie Struck Girls: Women and Motion Picture Culture after the Nickelodeon.* Princeton University Press, 2000.

Wilding, Raelene. "Romantic Love and 'Getting Married': Narratives of the Wedding in and out of Cinema Texts." *Journal of Sociology* 39(4) (2003): 373–389.

Yaqub, Nadia. "Weddings in Motion Pictures." *Journal of Middle East Women's Studies* 3(2) (Spring 2007): 56–85.

DEEP FOCUS ON INDIAN CINEMAS

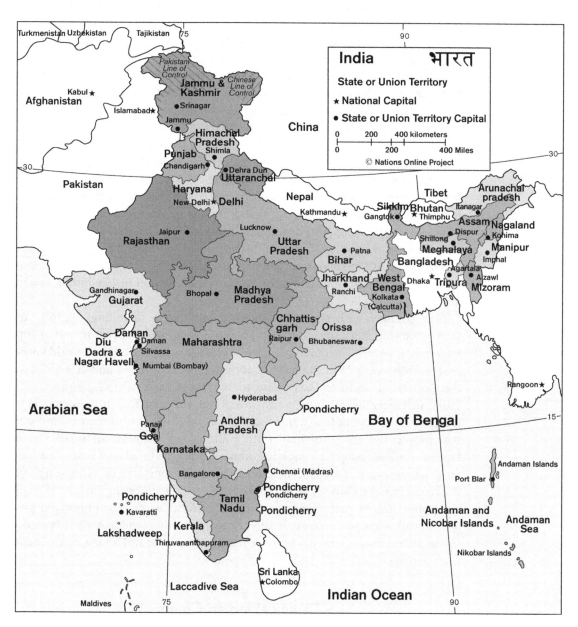

FIGURE 2.17 Map of India and neighboring countries.

World Cinema through Global Genres, First Edition. William V. Costanzo.
© 2014 John Wiley & Sons, Inc. Published 2014 by John Wiley & Sons, Inc.

The vast subcontinent of India, home to one of the world's oldest civilizations and the second largest national population on earth, after China, is also the world's leading film producer. By the 1970s, India had surpassed all other countries in production quantity, releasing an average of two films a day, one fifth of all features produced worldwide.[1] India's film industries maintain a steady output of between 800 and 1,000 films a year, feeding some 13,000 local theatres and 11 million viewers daily.[2] It also holds the record for foreign distribution in emerging markets, exporting more films than it imports, and often outperforming the United States in regions like North Africa, the Middle East, and the Far East.[3] By 2002, Indian movies had sold an estimated 3.6 billion tickets worldwide, about a billion more than Hollywood, although India's sales figures continue to be substantially lower.[4]

While film industries have thrived throughout the subcontinent in major hubs like Calcutta and Madras, each producing movies in its native languages and dialects, the cinematic center of India has always been Mumbai (called Bombay before 1995). Mumbai's distinctive style of commercial filmmaking, popularly known as Bollywood, is a unique blend of melodrama, superstars, colorful sets and costumes, energetic songs and dance. The movies from this part of the world are sometimes known as "Hindi cinema" because most are made in Hindi, the Sanskrit-based version of the Hindustani language used in northwest India, although some expressions creep in from Urdu, the Persian-based version of Hindustani favored in Pakistan.

In a country with some 22 "official" languages, including English, and widely varying cultural traditions, it is more accurate to speak of Indian cinemas rather than Indian cinema, but by and large what the outside world knows best is Bollywood. With its frankly commercial aspirations and eclectic style, the Bollywood industry has come to represent India to mass audiences in India, in emerging markets, and throughout the vast Indian diaspora. In an increasingly global industry, it is the Bollywood producers, directors, and stars who project the images of India onto millions of screens for all to see. On the face of it, these images are mostly fantasies, a magical realm of story and spectacle where every story is a melodrama and the spectacle of saris, song, and dance overwhelms history with ecstasy. Beneath the glittering surface, though, are potent forces performing important cultural work. As Bollywood goes global, this work has taken new directions. To understand just what is changing and what those changes mean we need to step back and review some Indian film history.

Classical Indian Cinema

As in China, movies were imported to India from the West quite early. The first Lumière shorts were shown in Bombay on July 7, 1896 at the elite Watson's Hotel. Soon the magic of motion pictures was being exhibited in tent theatres

Timeline (Figure 2.18)

Date	National History	Film History
c.563–483 BC	Life of Buddha	
268–232 BC	Ashoka the Great rules the Maurya Empire	
320–550	Gupta Empire reunites the subcontinent, India's "Golden Age"	
700s	Islamic sultanates introduce Muslim rule	
1600s	Mughal Empire reaches height of power and wealth	
1700s	British rule begins	
1896		Lumière projectionists screen first film in India at Watson's hotel, Bombay
1913		Dadasaheb Phalke directs *Raja Harishchandra*, India's first feature film
1918		Indian Cinematograph Act establishes system for censorship and theatre licensing
1920	Mahatma Gandhi leads non-cooperation movement against British rule	
1929		Prabhat studio founded
1931		Silent film companies give way to sound film studios
1934		Bombay Talkies studio established
1947	India wins independence from Britain but is partitioned into India and Pakistan Jawaharlal Nehru becomes India's first Prime Minister	
1947–1948	India and Pakistan go to war over Kashmir	
1948	Mahatma Gandhi is assassinated	
1951		Raj Kapoor's *Awaara* (*The Vagabond*)
1953		Prabhat studio closes
1955		Satyajit Ray's *Pather Panchali* (*Song of the Little Road*)
1957		Mehboob Khan's *Bharat Mata* (*Mother India*)

(*Continued*)

Timeline (*Continued*)

Date	National History	Film History
1959		Guru Dutt's *Kaagaz Ke Phool* (*Paper Flowers*)
1964	Nehru dies	
1965	Second border war between India and Pakistan	
1966	Nehru's daughter, Indira Gandhi, becomes Prime Minister	
1973		Ritwik Ghatak's *Titas Ekti Nadir Naam* (*A River Called Titas*)
1975	Indira Gandhi declares state of emergency	Ramesh Sippy's *Sholay* (*Embers*)
1977		Manmohan Desai's *Amar Akbar Anthony*
1984	Indira Gandhi is assassinated	
1994		Sooraj R. Barjatya's *Hum Aapke Hain Koun…!* becomes biggest Indian hit of all time
1995		Aditya Chopra's *Dilwale Dulhania Le Jayeng* (*Brave Heart Will Take the Bride*)
1998		Karan Johar's *Kuch Kuch Hota Hai* (*Sometimes Things Do Happen*) Government grants official industry status to filmmaking
2001	US lifts sanctions after India supports War on Terror following September 11 attack	Ashutosh Gowariker's *Lagaan: Once Upon a Time in India* nominated for Academy Award
2002		Ram Gopal Varma's *Company*, a crime thriller hit in India and abroad
2004	Indian Ocean tsunami kills 230,000 people in 14 countries, 18,000 in India	
2008	Pakistan-based militants blamed for attacks in Mumbai	
2009		Paresh Mokashi's *Harishchandrachi Factory*, a Marathi film about the birth of Indian cinema British director Danny Boyle and Indian co-director Loveleen Tandan's *Slumdog Millionaire*, inspired by Indian cinema and one-third scripted in Hindi, wins 8 Oscars

and playhouses like the Novelty Theatre, where both middle-class and lower-class audiences could enjoy it under one roof. By 1910, films were being shown in cinema halls and theatre palaces in all major cities. India's first native director, Hiralal Sen, filmed plays in Calcutta. But the real founder of Indian cinema was Dhundiraj Govind Phalke, the son of a Sanskrit scholar. As the story goes, while watching a picture called *The Life of Christ* (1910), he wondered if he could replace Christ with Lord Krishna, a popular Hindu deity. He sold his life insurance policy, traveled to London, and returned with a camera to make India's first feature film, *Raja Harishchandra*, in 1913. Others followed his example in the 1920s, turning out "mythologicals," historical movies, and stunt films. The coming of sound in the 1930s created problems for a country with so many languages, but it also opened film to sound and music, widening its appeal to the middle classes. This era saw the rise of great studios like Prabhat (founded in 1929), New Theatres (1931), and Bombay Talkies (1934), which thrived on the star system. When Hindi became the national language, Bombay came to be seen as the national hub of the industry, featuring northern stars with fair Punjabi features.

The 1940s and 1950s have been dubbed the Golden Age of Indian cinema. Some of the country's greatest directors did their best work during this time, including Mehboob Khan, Raj Kapoor, Guru Dutt, and Bimal Roy. Mehboob Khan's *Mother India* (*Bharat Mata*, 1957) featured the celebrated actress Nargis as a poor peasant woman whose life of hardship represents the new nation's struggle toward independence and modernization. Mehboob portrayed her and the villagers with a deeply sympathetic realism, but he was also capable of making movies in the classical Hollywood style, like *Andaz* (*Style*, 1949), a film about two men who love the same rich, modern heiress (also played by Nargis). Raj Kapoor borrowed Chaplin's little tramp and turned him into an urban Indian hero in *Awaara* (*The Vagabond*, 1951) and *Shree 420* (1955). He plays Raju, the male lead, in both films opposite Nargis. The elaborate dream sequence in *Awaara*, with its temple architecture, spiral staircase, Hindu statues, Busby Berkeley camerawork, and blend of classical and tribal dance, typifies the eclectic ingenuity with which Kapoor drew from many sources to tell his story. Like Mehboob, Kapoor showed real feeling for the downtrodden, although his portrait of the homeless pavement dwellers in *Shree 420* as a close-knit community is more lively and upbeat. Guru Dutt's films are anything but upbeat. If Kapoor was the ever the showman, Guru Dutt was the eternally melancholic artist. His *Pyasaa* (*The Thirsty One*, 1957) is the sad story of a spurned poet-lover. *Kaagaz Ke Phool* (*Paper Flowers*, 1959) is another downbeat film, this time about a film director thirsting for love and recognition who falls hopelessly in love with his star. Lyrical, sensitive, and profoundly pessimistic, *Kaagaz Ke Phool* now seems autobiographical, especially after its director was found dead from an overdose of sleeping pills in 1964.

Of these three directors, only Raj Kapoor lived beyond the 1960s, when two younger talents from another part of India, Bengal, brought a distinctly different vision to the medium. The films of Satyajit Ray and Ritwik Ghatak are associated

FIGURE 2.19   Satyajit Ray's *Pather Panchali* (*Song of the Little Road*, 1955) was a big hit at international film festivals.

with the New Cinema movement of the 1960s and 1970s, sometimes referred to as Parallel Cinema, a wave of low-budget films by socially conscious directors who worked parallel to India's commercial film industry. Ray is by far the better known of these Indian auteurs. He began making movies in the 1950s with his Apu trilogy, including *Pather Panchali* (*Song of the Little Road*, 1955), *Aparajito* (*The Unvanquished*, 1956), and *Apur Sansar* (*The World of Apu*, 1959). These were filmed in his native region of Bengal, featuring Bengali-speaking actors and non-actors in realistic settings (Figure 2.19). Ray was an auteur, an independent artist who developed styles to suit the serious messages he wanted to convey, but while his name was well known at international festivals and art houses around the world, his audience within India has always been small, even though he took native people, places, and events for his subjects. After the celebrated Apu trilogy, Ray continued to make a string of outstanding films, experimenting with new styles to suit new themes. As he grew more disenchanted with the state of nationhood, he abandoned realism for expressionism and other cinematic forms that might better communicate the extreme conditions of his times, conditions like rampant urban unemployment (*Mahanagar/The Big City*, 1963) and the devastating Bengali famine of 1943 (*Asani Sanket/Distant Thunder*, 1973).

Ritwik Ghatak, born in East Bengal, was acutely troubled when the political Partition of India from Pakistan separated him from his homeland. The personal pain of this cultural schism and uprooting became the driving force behind his work. His radically political films are often brilliant but uneven, achieving moments of raw power through idiosyncratic film techniques. He was always seeking fresh ways to capture the inner life of his characters with unusual framing, ominous shadows, or distorted soundtracks as they struggled with the breakup of their family (*Meghe Dhaka Tara/Cloud Capped Star*, 1961) or the loss of their village (*Titas Ekti Nadir Naam/A River Called Titas*, 1973). In his final film, *Jukti Takko Aar Gappo* (*Arguments and a Story*, 1974), Ghatak himself played the leading role of an alcoholic intellectual, prefiguring his untimely death in 1976.

In general, the lines between Parallel Cinema and India's commercial film industry were never crossed. The movies issuing from Bollywood in the 1960s grew more flamboyant, more Western, more detached from native roots. In the campy *Teesri Manzil* (*The Third Floor*, 1966), Raj Kapoor's younger brother Shammi plays Rocky, a James Dean/Elvis look-alike. In the convoluted plot of Dev Anand's *Hare Rama Hare Krishna* (1971), siblings are separated at birth. The brother discovers that his sister has become a hippie hooked on drugs. The most popular movie of the 1970s, Ramesh Sippy's *Sholay* (*Embers*, 1975), borrowed elements from John Ford's *Stagecoach* and Sergio Leone's spaghetti Westerns (some called *Sholay* a "curry Western") and introduced audiences to the great actor Amitabh Bachchan. *Sholay* ushered in a surge of violent vendetta movies, and Bachchan became a new kind of anti-hero, the Indian angry young man. In *Deewaar* (*The Wall*, 1975) and *Amar Akbar Anthony* (1977), he played characters that turn to lives of crime in response to parental abandonment. Significantly, both films are about siblings who choose different paths. In *Deewaar*, Bachchan joins the underworld while his brother becomes a policeman. In *Amar Akbar Anthony*, he and his siblings are separated in childhood. One is adopted by a Muslim, another by a Hindu, and Bachchan by a Christian priest. Looking back at this period, film scholars recognize a pattern in these stories of separated siblings, driving vengeance, and troubled outlaws, seeing them as a delayed response to historical events. Before examining such connections between Indian cinema and Indian history, it will be helpful to sketch out a bare outline of India's recent past.

History, Politics, and the Indian Film

For the first few thousands years, the land we know as India, Pakistan, and Bangladesh was conquered by a succession of invaders – Aryans, Persians, Greeks, and Muslims – or unified by native rulers like Chandragupta and Ashoka, who established powerful empires. In more recent times, Britain achieved dominance by controlling trade through the East India Company during the 1700s and then consolidating political power through the Raj system of governance in the 1800s. After World War II, Mohandas "Mahatma" Gandhi's non-violent campaign for self-rule gained momentum, eventually driving out the British in 1947, and Jawaharlal Nehru, leader of the India National Congress, became India's first Prime Minister. But India's independence was marred by long-standing conflicts between Hindus and Muslims, which erupted in appalling violence. While Gandhi preached tolerance for all religions, Mohammed Ali Jinnah, leader of the Muslim League, called for India's division into two religiously segregated states. The Partition that created

Pakistan in 1947 left millions of Hindu and Muslim minorities stranded in hostile territory. As these huge groups fled in opposite directions, Hindus to India, Muslims to Pakistan, they clashed fiercely, leaving half a million people dead. Gandhi's assassination in 1948 added fuel to the fire. On Nehru's death in 1964, he was succeeded briefly by Lal Bahadur Shastri, who engaged in a war with Pakistan over disputed Kashmir, then by Nehru's daughter, Indira Gandhi, who took office in 1966. After a series of economic crises, and amid accusations of corruption, she declared a state of national emergency in 1975, suspending civil rights for an unprecedented 18 months. She was killed by a Sikh assassin in 1984 after her soldiers launched a bloody attack against Sikh extremists in their holiest shrine, the Golden Temple. The next 25 years were marked by continued hostilities with Pakistan (largely over Kashmir), more ethnic conflicts (involving the Tamil Tigers in Sri Lanka), another assassination (Indira's son, Rajiv, by Tamil sympathizers), natural disasters (a tsunami in 2004, an earthquake in 2005), and terrorist attacks on Mumbai (by Pakistani-based militants) in 2008. But at the same time, while negative news tended to dominate the headlines, India had begun to enjoy a trend of steady economic growth by 1990, fueled in part by foreign capital, the outsourcing of high tech services from other countries, and an impressive increase in India's middle class.

By and large, India's main film industry has developed independently from government control. Bollywood, like Hollywood, is an essentially commercial enterprise, a hugely profitable vessel run by entrepreneurs riding the waves of supply and demand. At times, however, the government has sought to steer a prescribed course, and many film directors have tried to follow their own political agendas. In India, where nationalism was such a major issue during the years in which cinema evolved, the question underlying so many movies is "What does it mean to be Indian?" Gandhi turned to tradition for his answer, "India lives in its villages." He envisioned the nation as a community writ large. His *swadeshi* movement encouraged consumers to boycott foreign goods, to buy instead home-grown products made in village industries. He regarded big cities and technology with suspicion, as dangerous purveyors of a modernity that robbed people of their humanity. Phalke, the "father of Indian cinema," recognized that film technology could be a powerful instrument for nurturing nationhood. "My films are Swadeshi," he said, "in the sense that the capital, ownership, employees, and stories are all home grown."[5] The British recognized this power too. As Gandhi's anti-colonial efforts began to take hold, the government started censoring movies that carried his image, name, or message. This censorship continued until Independence.

Meanwhile, a number of talented poets, theatre activists, and filmmakers, all committed to the creation of a popular cinema, joined forces under the banner of the Indian People's Theatre Association (IPTA), loosely affiliated with the Indian Communist party. K.A. Abbas, who wrote the scripts for *Awaara* and *Shree 420*, was a member. Raj Kapoor, Bimal Roy, Ritwik Ghatak, and Mehboob Khan (who took the hammer and sickle for his logo) were sympathetic to its cause. After Independence, Nehru took steps to make cinema an active agent of change. As leader of the new nation, and in contrast to Gandhi, he believed that movies were more important than newspapers and books combined. In keeping with this belief, he took steps to support a national cinema of quality.

The face of Indian politics has been variously mirrored on the movie screens. Sometimes it has been conspicuously absent. During the years before Independence, the lexicon of images defining "Indianness" shifted from myth and legend to more realistic views of villagers and workers. Images of women, especially the patiently suffering figure of Mother India, came to represent the nation as a whole. The three most popular genres – mythologicals, historicals, and stunt films – merged into one, the "social," with the Indian family at its center. During the Nehru years, the nation's high hopes for independence eventually burst and turned to bitter ashes. Nehru's belief that modern science and urban planning would build a strong economy for the new nation was reflected initially in a new subgenre of city films like *Taxi Driver* (1954) and *Black Market* (1956). Raj Kapoor, a personal friend of Nehru, set *Shree 420* in Bombay. The film's hero, Raj, arrives in the bustling big city from traditional Allahabad (Nehru's birthplace) with great expectations for a decent job. Raj's optimism soon collides with the pervasive cynicism of Bombay's citizens. A stranger advises him that the honest people are all unemployed and the petty cheats are all in jail. Only the big-time swindlers are doing well. They run the city. Unable to find work, Raj tries to join a group of homeless people sleeping on the pavement, but even they want to charge him rent. Eventually, Raj follows the stranger's advice, trading his rags for ill-gotten riches and, in the process, abandoning an honest girl named Vidya ("wisdom") for a vamp named Maya ("illusion"). What he eventually learns, however, is that the communal spirit of the poor is preferable to the backstabbing egoism of Bombay's high society. He finally returns to Vidya, and the film ends with a Nehruvian vision of affordable "people's housing." Not surprisingly, *Shree 420* was a big hit in the Soviet Union, and Kapoor's *Awara* was reputed to be a favorite of China's Chairman Mao.

For the most part, though, commercial films of the time were apolitical. There was practically no mention of Partition and the ensuing Hindu-Muslim violence for nearly 20 years. Some considered this to be "a conspiracy of silence." Nor did Bollywood give much attention to Indira Gandhi's crackdown on the radical Naxalite movement in the 1960s or her imposition of Emergency in the 1970s. The emotional scars of these events began to surface, if only indirectly, during the late 1970s and 1980s. In the pervasive, wanton violence of *Sholay* (see Close-up: *Sholay*), and in the "lost and found" stories of *Deewaar* and *Amar Akbar Anthony*, critics see symbolic narratives of a lost India, a country torn by religious strife and political dismemberment. The anger in Amitabh Bachchan's angry young man is fueled by memories that cannot be ignored.

Native Aesthetics

The sheer exuberance of Bollywood cinema, the vitality of its larger-than-life stars, its indulgence in the pleasure of emotions, the driving energy of its music, dancing, and spectacle – these are the hallmarks of popular Indian film aesthetics.

To criticize Bollywood for being superficial, unrealistic, or commercial is, some would say, to apply the wrong aesthetic criteria. It should be judged on its own terms, on native grounds.

We have already noted the industry's favorite genres: the mythologicals, historicals, stunt films, devotionals, and romantic dramas that dominated the silent era and the "socials" of the Golden Age. These were supplemented by refinements and subgenres unique to Indian films. A flourishing of "Muslim socials" in the 1960s drew on Islamic poetry and imagery (veils, courtesans, wealthy Nabobs, and architecture reminiscent of the glory days of Mughal rule).[6] The bloody vengeance movies of the 1980s, for all their similarities to Hollywood action films, gained special cultural resonance through stories of divided families and lost siblings. But the most important form of Indian cinema, the mother of all genres, is melodrama. In fact, it could be argued that all Indian commercial films are melodramas. Since India lacks an aesthetic tradition of realism like the European novel, it makes sense to apply the standards of melodrama rather than of realism to India's popular cinema. This means evaluating its stories in terms of emotional power, symbolic significance, universality, and closure rather than verisimilitude, historical accuracy, or complexity of character.

To do this, we might, with many native scholars, turn to Rasa theory. The term *Rasa* has been traced back two millennia to the writings of Sage Bharat. While Aristotle was formulating his thoughts on the emotional catharsis of Greek drama, Bharat was exploring the role of emotions in Indian theatre. In his writings, Bharat described Rasa as a phenomenon of mind, the spectator's delight in witnessing emotions acted out on stage. The term is associated in early Hindu texts with the juice of the Soma vine, suggesting fluidity, something that moves the mind.[7] Rasa is a highly sensory experience. All arts, including drama, painting, and sculpture, appeal to the emotions through the senses. Bharat identified and classified the essential emotions, including humor, pathos, anger, valor, fear, loathing, amazement, and love. The greatest of these is *Shringara* – love. The actor's role is to embody these emotions, through his or her performance, pulling the spectator (*rasika*) into a sphere of sentiment.

Another useful concept when judging Indian cinema is *darshan*, a term borrowed from Hindu worship. When the image of a deity, person, or object is beheld, the gaze is experienced as reciprocal, imparting a blessing to the viewer. This "two-way look" constitutes *darshan*, a form of mutual adoration, something given by the image and taken by the beholder.[8] In Indian films, it occurs at certain standard moments, often during a song or a dramatic pause in the narrative momentum when a star or a statue of some god seems to look at us looking at him. This moment of consensual pleasure is quite different from the voyeuristic gaze in Western films where the spectator identifies with a character, usually male, peeking at someone, usually female, who does not know she is being watched. The pleasure of *darshan* is not the voyeur's guilty pleasure but the worshipper's joy at being blessed by a reciprocated message through the eyes.

Song, Saris, Dance, and Stars

Bollywood's special brand of song and dance provides the melody in melodrama. It would be hard to imagine a Bollywood film without a song and dance number. Very few, if any, of the estimated 28,000 popular movies made in India during the last 70 years have not had some form of singing or dancing. A good chunk of Indian film revenues today comes from their music (film music accounts for well over half of the market's audio cassette and CD sales), and music performers now command large salaries. Some of these "playback singers," the unseen vocalists whose voices are prerecorded and later lip-synched on camera by the actors, are as famous in India as the stars themselves. Lata Mangeshkar and her younger sister Asha Bohsie are each said to have recorded songs for more than a thousand Hindi films.

Music has always been an essential ingredient of Indian culture, not confined to formal performances but found everywhere in the rhythms of daily life. From time out of mind, the air has pulsated with *Bhajans* (Hindu religious songs), *Qawwalis* (Sufi devotional songs), and boatman songs, and as well as the music for *Annaprasan* (first ceremonial feeding of the grain), *Mundan* (head shaving ceremony), or *Holi* (festival of colors), to name a few. The great foundational texts themselves, the *Ramayana* and *Mahabharata*, were memorized, and possibly performed, by singing.

Hindi films are famously long, and a good part of their length is due to the song and dance routines. These interludes continually interrupt the story. Sometimes the characters break into song and start to dance in unison. Sometimes the musical number is inserted as a dream sequence or a lover's fantasy montage. A song may begin in India, continue in Germany or Switzerland, and end in India again. In earlier days, these interludes were often about longing, intimacy, and love, appealing to the audience's erotic desires in ways that the narrative could never satisfy. More recently, the singing and dancing have been threaded more closely into the text. They continue the narrative, advancing the action while revealing character and setting tone.

Bollywood took its star system from Hollywood and then surpassed it. As late as the 1940s, middle-class Indian viewers knew more about actors like Charlie Chaplin and Douglas Fairbanks, Sr. than their own screen performers. After Independence, these American figures were replaced by native talent like Nargis, Dilip Kumar, and Dev Anand. Directors like Raj Kapoor and Guru Dutt regularly starred in their own films. Their celebrity as directors boosted their star status. In the 1970s, Amitabh Bachchan introduced his new image of the common man, the tough anti-hero with sad eyes, becoming India's greatest megastar of all time. Female stardom also underwent a transformation in the 1970s and early 1980s, when Rekha took the lead, marking a shift from Nargis's patient, sacrificial Mother to a demonic anti-heroine in a black sari bent on revenge. Today's stars, both male and female, are slimmer and more athletic than their predecessors. For women, the current road to stardom is not so much the actor's studio as the fashion school and beauty pageant. They tend to be younger, hipper, mixing English phrases with their Hindi dialogue, but they must always appear as stars first, not actors playing realistic roles. These superstars seem to be forever winking at us from their firmament.

Questions of Influence

For all the emphasis on nationalism and native roots, Indian cinema has always been a hybrid creature, freely assimilating genres, images, and techniques from the banquet of world cinema. The technology of motion pictures was itself, of course, imported from Europe and the United States. As in most non-Western countries, the earliest films enjoyed by Indian audiences were largely imports, and Indians continued to show a marked preference for Hollywood until the 1950s. Many of India's best directors were influenced by foreign art films. Bimal Roy began introducing neorealist aesthetics into his films after seeing De Sica's *Bicycle Thieves* (1949). Raj Kapoor borrowed elements from Chaplin, Welles, Renoir, and German expressionism. This debt was famously acknowledged in the opening song of Kapoor's *Shree 420*:

> *Mere juta hai Japoni,*
> *Ye patloon Englistani,*
> *Sar pe lal topi russi,*
> *Phir bhi dil hai Hindustani*

> My shoes are Japanese,
> my pants were made in England,
> on my head's a red Russian cap,
> but still my heart is Indian!

Kapoor sings these words in the role of Raju, the migrant tramp, as he leaves the countryside of gypsies, cobras, and elephants for the modern city of Bombay (see Figure 2.20). Here on the busy streets, the ubiquity of foreign cars and Coca-Cola signs bears witness to the global nature of modernity. Like Raju's wardrobe, Bollywood may be a composite of borrowed elements, but it has remained Indian at heart.

The Indian heart, its teeming emotions openly expressed through dramatic sentiment and spectacle, has always been the pulsating core of Indian cinema. Bollywood's distinctive character is not just a matter of economic independence. Those who work in the industry are proud that their films have thrived for decades on the strength of native audiences and have found loyal followers throughout the non-Western world. If Egyptians, Nigerians, Russians, and even Americans are drawn to these films, is it because they speak to universal needs?

Lately, popular Indian cinema has begun to create waves and inspire imitators in the West. *Lagaan* was nominated for an Oscar in 2001, more than four decades after *Mother India*. In the same year, Baz Luhrmann paid homage to Bollywood in *Moulin Rouge* (2001) with its lush visual style, emotional exuberance, and over-the-top dance numbers. The next year, Andrew Lloyd Webber brought Bollywood to London's West End (and later Broadway) with *Bombay Dreams*. By 2008, Danny Boyle's international hit, *Slumdog Millionaire*, was sweeping the Academy Awards, winning a total of eight Oscars.

FIGURE 2.20 "My hat is Russian, but my heart is Indian." Raj Kapoor opens *Shree 420* (*Mr. 420*, 1955) with a comic song about global identity.

Bollywood in the 1990s: *Hum Aapke Hain Koun...!* and Family Wedding Films

Who Am I to You?, better known by its Hindi title *Hum Aapke Hain Koun...!* (and commonly abbreviated as *HAHK*), broke all box office records in India. After years of flagging ticket sales, *HAHK* drew millions of television viewers back into the theatres and reaped a hefty $20.8 million profit. One reason for its unprecedented popularity is the film's focus on domestic drama. In contrast to the violence-oriented plots of earlier years, *HAHK* is about family relationships. Even when it leaves the insular environments of home and school, where it moves to is a fictitious summer camp hermetically sealed from reality. There is no real antagonist in the film, no evil criminal or indifferent bureaucracy, only a bad accident. The main question is not "Who will triumph, the good or evil ones?" but "What is my relationship with you?" as the Hindi title may be translated.

HAHK is remarkable for the thinness of its plot. There is an arranged marriage between Rajesh (Mohnish Bahl) and Pooja (Renuka Shahane), both from wealthy families. Rajesh's father, a successful businessman, and Pooja's father, a professor, are old college friends, and the two families spend much time planning the ceremonies, enjoying a big wedding, and adoring the first child. Meanwhile, Rajesh's younger brother Prem (Salman Khan) falls in love with Pooja's younger sister, Nisha (Madhuri Dixit), and the two secretly pledge themselves to one another. The main conflict does not begin until well into the film, after some two hours, when

Pooja suddenly dies and the families decide that Rajesh should get remarried for the child's sake – to Nisha. An interlude of discord interrupts the domestic harmony as parental will and family duty clash with the passion of true love. The conflict over Nisha's marriage must be sorted out in terms of family relationships. Will Prem remain Nisha's brother-in-law or become her husband? This is an epic question in India, where nearly all stories are about the family and the family is a microcosm for the nation at large.

Critics of *HAHK* and the family films that it inspired dismiss them as "frilly," "simplistic," or "designer films." At first sight, they might seem so to Western eyes or to Indians partial to the classics. For our purpose, though, it will be worth looking beyond these curt assessments to understand the reasons for their enormous success and their place in the evolution of global cinema toward more transnational films like *Monsoon Wedding* and *Bride and Prejudice*. Again, we'll be asking basic questions about character, plot, genre, aesthetics, and theme in the context of globalism. Who are the heroes of these movies, and what are their stories? Where do the stories come from, how are they told, what are they telling us, and why do they matter? Finally, what do they contribute to the storehouse of world cinema?

The heroes of the film seem like ordinary people. They are privileged, to be sure, enjoying the benefits of education, successful jobs, and an endless array of consumer goods. They live in large, lavishly decorated homes, drive expensive cars, and play cricket on the lawn. But they genuinely care about each other and have decent hearts. Rajesh and Pooja are the responsible first-born children of professionals. He is opening a factory, and she has passed her Bachelor's exam. Prem and Nisha are the playful, younger siblings. While Prem leads an easygoing life at home, Nisha zips around her living room on roller skates. Much of the time, they act as an ordinary upwardly mobile middle-class family might behave under ideal conditions. The boys ogle the girls; the girls sneak peeks at the boys. Dad enjoys cooking with his daughter in the kitchen while Auntie exuberantly meddles in everyone's affairs. There is a good deal of good-natured silliness about whoopee cushions, broken jars, and stolen shoes. But mixed in with all these contemporary high jinks are icons of traditional India. Pooja's father has a statue of the goddess in his study, and when his wife asks who broke the jar he quotes a mythical story about Siv's broken bow. Significantly, the arranged meeting between Rajesh and Pooja takes place in Ramtek, site of an ancient holy temple. Ramtek is associated with the story of Lord Rama, his consort Sita, and his brother Lakshman, celebrated in the *Ramayana*. Further parallels can be drawn between family relationships in the great Sanskrit epic and the relationships of brother/husband, wife/sister-in-law, and brother/brother-in-law in *HAHK*. The film's 20-something protagonists can thus be seen as modern embodiments of India's ancient heroes. *HAHK* affirms the old social norms. Pooja may have a B.A., but at her wedding she sings, "My husband is my god now" (Figure 2.21). And mixed among the wedding gifts – the diamonds, the imported car, and the VCR – is a copy of the *Ramayana*. While the film's parental figures are often presented as benignly comic figures, Prem and Nisha are ready

FIGURE 2.21 "My husband is my god now." Hindi cinema returns to traditional family values in *Hum Aapke Hain Koun...!* (*Who Am I to You*? Dir. Sooraj Barjatya, 1994).

to defer to the judgment of their elders even when this judgment thwarts their secret love. In the end, the script reconciles the competing claims of arranged marriage and true love by letting the elders see into their children's hearts, finally granting their blessing to a marriage of true love. For an Indian audience struggling between tradition and modernity, *HAHK* offers a satisfying compromise.

Much of the film's appeal may be ascribed to the filmmakers' ingenuity in fusing fundamental Indian values with the changing mores of the modern world. This synthesis of local and global elements is mirrored in the film's aesthetics. The opulent domestic sets are reminiscent of Douglas Sirk's melodramas of the 1950s. Their ornate tea tables, grand staircases, and pink and white interiors, all seem like Indian versions of Sirk's enclosed middle-class world. The background chorus of the credit sequence sounds like the opening of *Written in the Wind* (1956). And there are other, more self-consciously ironic allusions to American movies. Before the wedding, Prem crashes a traditional females-only function disguised as a woman, leaping to the balcony and onto a chandelier like Douglas Fairbanks, singing "Oh Lord, it's the age of girls!"

The wedding itself is ostentatiously traditional. Wedding scenes have long been a staple of Indian movies. *Mother India*, for example, begins with an elaborate village wedding, alternating between long shots of the cattle-driven chariots and frequent close-ups of the bride richly bejeweled and painted with red henna. Most of the traditional wedding rituals appear in *HAHK*, so prominently that the film has been mocked as a consumer's guide to Hindi weddings.

A typical Punjabi wedding begins with a meeting at the future bride's house (*rota*) where she exchanges commitments with her future groom, after which they are free to court each other. Later, both families celebrate the engagement with gifts (*chunni chadana*), and rings are exchanged (*sagan*). Close friends and family members are invited to a special session (*sangeet*) when they sing traditional wedding songs and dance. The groom's mother sends henna body dye (*mehndi*) to be applied to the bride. On the morning of the wedding, the bride is given a set of red and ivory bangles for her wrist by her maternal uncle (the *chuda* ceremony) and the groom is offered a floral crown for his turban by his father (*sehrabandi*). The groom and his family march in procession (*baraat*) from their house to the wedding, where they are formally greeted with flowers and hugs (*milni*). The wedding itself may be officiated by a Hindu priest, or *pundit*, in a holy space (*mandap*) created by a raised platform and canopy. Traditionally, the couple never speaks. Their vow is signified through an exchange of garlands (*varmala*), the non-verbal equivalent of "I do." After the wedding, the families enjoy a big meal. There may also be a few mantras, a formal prayer (*puja*), some circling around the sacred fire (traditionally, there are seven steps, *sapta-padi*, each step symbolizing the couple's pledge to each other for the future) and more playful activities, such as binding the couples together with a cloth (*chunni*) or stealing the groom's shoes so that he must buy them back from the bride's family. This game with shoes, which takes up a lengthy scene in *HAHK*, reflects a preoccupation with footwear in many wedding films around the world.

HAHK also invites comparison and contrast to other romance films in terms of "the look." Earlier, we identified two kinds of cinematic looking: the voyeuristic gaze associated with Western films (the audience catches someone sneaking a peek at someone else, usually a woman) and the Indian concept of *darshan* (the reciprocal gaze between god and devotee, imparting blessings on the viewer). *HAHK* has moments when both looks come into play. Near the start of the movie, the two sisters peer at the two brothers from behind a kitchen wall. Minutes later, Prem and Nisha spy on Rajesh and Pooja from their shuttered windows. Contrast these one-sided stares with a moment near the movie's end when Doctor Laloo is praying to the statue of Lord Krishna for a miracle. The doctor wants to stop the ill-planned marriage between Nisha and Rajesh. The camera zooms in to Krishna's face, then zooms in to the face of Tuffy, the family dog. It cuts back and forth between god and dog, closer and closer, as if their eyes were fixed in a mutual understanding. Then Tuffy runs upstairs, finds Pooja's necklace, and delivers it so that Nisha and Prem are free to wed each other. It is a case of divine intervention through Tuffy, *canis ex machina*.

HAHK was followed by more family-centered wedding films with even greater success. *Dilwale Dulhania Le Jayenge* (*DDLJ/Brave Heart Will Take the Bride*), a feel-good movie about young globe-trotting Indians, begins in Britain and concludes in India, demonstrating how it is possible to enjoy the fruits of global capitalism while remaining Indian at heart. *DDLJ* was the big hit of 1995 and became the longest-running Bollywood movie of its time. In 1998, the top grossing film was *Kuch Kuch Hota Hai* (*KKHH/Sometimes Things Do Happen*), which takes up the question of second marriages. A young man whose first wife dies soon after childbirth is presented with the chance to marry the woman who was his best friend in college. Meanwhile, the actors get to wear Western clothes, joke around in English, and drive white jeeps while remaining true to Indian traditions like temple worship and the extravagances of a big Punjabi wedding. Once more, the story is an affirmation of the *desi dil*, the Indian heart.

The directors of these films (Sooraj Barjatya (*HAHK*), Aditya Chopra (*DDLJ*), and Karan Johar (*KKHH*) respectively) were all under 30 when they reached national prominence. Their work was more technically sophisticated than earlier films and more unreservedly eclectic. Their dance numbers mixed classical *mujra* choreography with MTV and spandex pants along with the traditional fashion of *salwar-khamees*. In contrast to the common man figure popularized by Amitabh Bachchan in the 1970s, the new stars tended to be wealthy, cosmopolitan, and upper caste. Shahrukh Khan became the superstar of the 1990s, personifying the new yuppie hero, equally comfortable with consumer culture and American idioms. Shahrukh, once dubbed "the consumable hero of globalized India," has been quoted as saying, "The yuppie believes in capitalism, not communism. Actually, he believes in a new 'ism' every day."[9] This ideological flexibility does not extend to certain values, though. In his films, and in his public life, Shahrukh Khan is always seen adhering strictly to the centrality of family and its age-old rituals.

Despite their insular plots and airbrushed views of India, it is possible to see indirect allusions in these films to the grimmer realities of Indian life. Just as the stylized violence and "lost and found" genres of the 1970s can be regarded as responses to Partition and its bloody aftermath, the family dramas of the 1990s can be read as metaphors or metonyms (one thing representing another) for national politics. In the recurring theme of forbidden love, for example, we might see an image of the troubled relationship between India and Pakistan, noting that the star-crossed lovers can only express their feelings freely in someone else's house, as in England or the United States. The trend of shooting scenes in Switzerland is another telling example. The ideal setting for an Indian honeymoon has always been Kashmir, but since the mountains between India and Pakistan are now off limits, film crews have taken their cameras to the Alps. Every Swiss idyll in a Hindi film becomes an oblique reminder of paradises lost at home.

Bride and Prejudice: The Indian Diaspora and Beyond

Meanwhile, large groups of Indian viewers have wandered far from home. The number of Indians living abroad is now conservatively estimated at around 11 million, with some 1.3 million in Great Britain and 2 million in North America.[10] The diaspora radiated out from the South Asian subcontinent in two waves, first as indentured labor to the British colonies (South Africa, Fiji, Trinidad, Guyana, Singapore, Malaysia, Sri Lanka) and later as emigrants seeking economic opportunities after the 1960s. The second group, variously called NRIs (Non Resident Indians) or ABCDs (American Born Confused *Desis*) tends to be well educated, socially mobile, and financially secure. They have established successful lives in the new land, and their children often blend into the native culture, but they miss the music, colors, scents, and rituals of their homeland. For these transplanted Hindustanis, Bollywood is the umbilical chord to Mother India.

Technology has strengthened the umbilical cord. In addition to the neighborhood cinemas specializing in Indian films, diaspora audiences can now be connected to India by cable, satellite TV, video, DVD, and the Internet. Online websites mail thousands of movies throughout the world to families that gather around the home screen on movie night for a taste of the old country. What they see, of course, is an idealized version, what filmmakers in Mumbai think these families want to see. The industry takes its cues from consumers like the Patels and Mukherjees in Jackson Heights, New York, who want their children to know what a Hindu wedding looks like, how good Indians behave, and why family is so important. In countries where the local culture may seem alien and threatening, this focus on the family is fundamental.

Gurinder Chadha belongs to the growing ranks of transnational Indian film-makers who aim beyond the Hindi-speaking community. Her *Bride and Prejudice* (2004) widens the field of reference to include an English literary classic. Although Chadha's film is frankly commercial, the parallels it draws between Bollywood conventions and Jane Austen's 1813 novel are remarkably apt. In the wake of films like *KKHH*, *HAHK*, and *DDLJ*, it makes perfect sense to set the story of the Bennet family, with its five eligible daughters and a mother's obsession with upward mobility through marriage, in middle-class Indian society. The famous opening of *Pride and Prejudice* translates all too easily into colloquial Hinglish, blending Hindi sentiments with English values: "All mothers say that any single guy with big bucks must be shopping for a wife." For all its flaws and unpretentious fun, *Bride and Prejudice* is an instructive case of transnational filmmaking that both celebrates and gently mocks the phenomenon of global consumerism.

Like Mira Nair, Chadha is well qualified to make movies for and about expatriate Indians. Born in Kenya in 1951 and raised in Southall, London, she married a Japanese American and moved to Los Angeles, where she manages a successful film career. A former BBC news reporter and documentary director, she has used the medium of film to investigate topics like multicultural weddings and global views of women's roles. Chadha's second feature, *What's Cooking?* (2000), focuses on four families – Vietnamese, Mexican American, Jewish, and African American – as they celebrate Thanksgiving in the same Los Angeles neighborhood. Like her other films, it explores issues of tradition and assimilation with a light touch and won several awards. *What's Cooking?* was intended for a mainstream audience, but it was not until *Bend It Like Beckham* (2003) that Chadha achieved her first popular success. *Beckham* has all the ingredients of a modern NRI story. Jess, the youngest daughter of a middle-class Punjabi family living in Southall, is expected to follow the example of her older sister, who is engaged to a nice Indian boy. But Jess loves soccer, "footie" as her British friends call it, and has secretly joined a women's team. Comic contrasts are continually made between Jess's conventional family and the eccentric Anglo-Saxon parents of her best friend Jules. The film plays with issues of homophobia, teenage rebellion, assimilation and identity, and women in sports. Jess sneaks off to play for her team's big game, and the movie ends in a big wedding. It broke box office records in Britain, and in the United States became the biggest hit of any movie with an Indian theme.

Like other transnational films, *Bride and Prejudice* is global in its financing, cast, crew, setting, style, and theme. "Everything about it is a combination of Bollywood and Hollywood tied together in a British sensibility," as its director has observed.[11] The film's opening credits give some idea of the business arrangements that take place behind the screen of a modern co-production: "Miramax and Pathé Pictures present / In association with the UK Film Council / In association with Kintop Pictures and Bend It Films / A Nayar Chadha production / Produced in association with Inside Track / A Gurinder Chadha Film." Chadha wrote the script with her husband, Paul Mayeda Berges. The cinematographer was Santosh Sivan, director of *Asoka* (2001) and other Hindi hits.

For a multinational movie, Chadha wanted a multicultural cast. In addition to the native Indians, there was Martin Henderson from New Zealand, Daniel Gillies from Canada, Nitin Chandra Ganatra (born in Kenya), Naveen Andrews (born in London), and several Americans (including Alexis Bledel and Marsha Mason). Ashanti, born Ashanti Shequoiya Douglas in Long Island, New York, is of African, American, Hispanic, and Chinese descent. Each shoot was like a gathering at the United Nations.

Bride and Prejudice is set in India, London, and Los Angeles. The Bennet household is transported from Longbourn to the holy city of Amritsar and the Bennets transformed into the Bakshis, an upwardly aspiring middle-class Indian family. The distracted Mrs. Bennet becomes the ditzy Mrs. Bakshi, obsessed with the idea of finding wealthy bachelors for her four daughters (reduced by one from the original story): Jaya, Lalita, Maya, and Lakhi. Lalita is the heroine (Elizabeth in the novel), played by Aishwarya Rai (formerly Miss World). Darcy, the proud owner of a large English estate in the novel, is updated as William Darcy (Martin Henderson), an American workaholic whose family owns an international fleet of luxury hotels. When Darcy visits Amritsar with his friend Balraj, an expatriate Indian living in London, he is instantly disliked by Lalita. While Balraj is charming and polite, the perfect Indian suitor, Darcy's comments about India ("It's bedlam. Where the hell have you taken me?") and Indians ("Their practice of arranged marriage is a little backward, don't you think") sound condescending. Worse yet, he can't dance.

A good deal is made about American ignorance of Hindi life. Chadha's script turns the class conflict of Austen's England into cultural misunderstanding. Darcy's mother, overbearing and manipulative, is a classic ugly American. When she muses, "What with Yoga and spices and Deepak Chopra and the wonderful Eastern things here, I don't suppose there's any point in traveling to India anymore," Lalita retorts, "People haven't stopped going to Italy because Pizza Hut's opened around the corner." But Lalita's judgment of Darcy proves hasty. She fails to understand his motives or see his generous heart. Besides, Darcy's early prejudice against the Bennet family is not entirely ill founded. Mrs. Darcy's blatant materialism is one of the film's targets, although she and the consumerist mentality of her class are handled with good humor. The crudest comedy is reserved for Kholi, an Indian transplanted to L.A., who is more vulgarly Californian than any native-born American. His incessant chatter about hot tubs and super jets is

FIGURE 2.22 Gurinder Chadha's *Bride and Prejudice* (2004) transports Jane Austen's 1813 novel from England to modern India for an international audience.

interspersed with annoying, braying laughs. Kholi represents the unfaithful émigré, ashamed of his roots, of "all those uneducated, mini-cab 7-Eleven store types." Then why did you come back?" asks Mr. Bakshi. To get an Indian wife is his casual reply, "No life without wife."

In keeping with the subgenre, *Bride and Prejudice* takes its characters on a journey, this time to Los Angeles with a stopover in London. London is the postcard capital of England – land of The Tower Bridge and the Queen – but it is also home to the diasporic community (the same Southall Street from *Bend It Like Beckham*) and the setting for a chase through a riverside amusement park. L.A. is a romantic backdrop for Darcy and Lalita, pictured in a falling-in-love montage of glass skylines, illuminated fountains, dancing surfers, and gospel singers on the beach. There is even a fantasy sequence of Switzerland, when Lalita's pastoral dream of wedding Wickham in a mountain chapel turns into a nightmare of Darcy's face.

Most of the big dance numbers are party scenes. Jane Austen's gentry ball is converted into a colorful Bollywood spectacle, the girls watching from the balcony while the boys strut their stuff below. Belraj's sister translates their lyrics as the girls quiver down the grand staircase. "O these pretty girls fluttering temptingly like kites without strings." But many of the dances are more Western in style. Ashanti's sultry performance on the beach is punctuated with rock concert pyrotechnics. When the Bakshi sisters sing "No Life without Wife" in their pajamas, their gestures are deliberate allusions to the American movie *Grease* (1978). But the movie's grand finale is a big Punjabi wedding. Back home in India, a marching band is blaring through the streets, the groom's family arrives in a silver car, and Darcy is drumming in an Indian folk band. Lalita and Darcy embrace as the camera rises skyward for an aerial shot of the street, a kaleidoscope of teeming celebrants singing "Life is great, let's celebrate the sacred union two souls have found." It's bedlam, Bollywood style (Figure 2.22). But it is also true to the conventions of English literary comedy, which almost always ends in friendship, fun, and the cosmic denouement of marriage.

Global Bollywood and the Wedding Myth

Family wedding films of the 1990s like *Hum Aapke Hain Koun...!* and hybrid versions of the genre like *Bride and Prejudice* are important contributions to the global flow of cinematic stories, styles, and themes. They illustrate how a topic of universal interest, in this case the enduring conflicts between love and marriage, between individual aspirations and social institutions, may find expression in local terms. Hindi cinema binds the wedding tale to the Ramayana epic, dressing its archetypal characters in the Punjabi garb of turbans and saris, adding henna parties and pilfered shoes to its repertoire of rituals. It grounds the wedding imagery in the native aesthetics of *rasa* and *darshan* as well as the vibrant song and dance of Bollywood. And it self-consciously mixes these indigenous ingredients with elements from abroad, courting international markets while trying to remain true to the Indian heart. We have watched a similar process at work in the genre of the warrior hero, as Chinese directors incorporated features of America's Western and Japan's samurai tradition into their kung fu and wuxia films while maintaining a distinctive cultural independence. To be sure, the cinemas of India and China reach far beyond the province of these genre films. The Hindi language films of Bollywood are only part of the Indian film industry, which produces as many as a thousand features a year in India's many languages for its diverse populations. The cities of Madras and Hyderabad, for example, home to the Tamil and Telegu language film industries in southern India, turn out more movies annually than Bombay. Meanwhile, as we saw in Unit I, the three main producers of Chinese language films (Hong Kong, Taiwan, and the mainland) continue to release movies in Mandarin and Cantonese for a growing audience. Taken as a whole, China ranked among the world's top three movie makers by 2010.[12] We will continue to explore the intricate connections between genres and regions when we take up the topic of horror films in Japan and road movies in Latin America.

Notes

1. Bruce Kawin and Gerald Mast, *A Short History of the Movies*, 9th edition (Pearson Longman, 2006), 489.

2. Vijay Mishra, *Bollywood Cinema: Temple of Desire* (Routledge, 2002), 1.

3. Ashish Rajadhyaksha and Paul Willemen, eds., *Encyclopedia of Indian Cinema* (British Film Institute, 1995), 678.

4. According to statistics compiled by the Motion Picture Association of Association, see Shombit Sengupta, "Carried Away by Bollywood," *The Indian Express*, June 24, 2012. Available at: http://m.indianexpress.com/news/carried-away-by-bollywood/965966/ (accessed June 9, 2013).

5. Quoted in Mishra, 13.

6. Ira Bhaskar and Richard Allen, *Islamicate Cultures of Bombay Cinema* (Tulika Press, 2009).

7. P.C. Jain and Dr. Daljeet, "The Indian Way of Seeing It: A Discourse on Indian Theory of Rasa in Relation to Visual Arts," ExoticIndiaArt Pvt Ltd, 2005. Available at: shivarea.com/LiteratureRetrieve.aspx?ID=41690 (accessed June 9, 2013).

8. Mishra, 100.

9. Quoted in Raminder Kaur and Ajay Sinha, eds., *Bollywood: Popular Indian Cinema through a Transnational Lens* (Sage Publications India, 2005), 186.

10. Mishra, 235.

11. "Bringing Bollywood to L.A.: The Making of *Bride and Prejudice*," DVD documentary (Buena Vista Home Entertainment, 2005).

12. Hillary Brenhouse, "As Its Box Office Booms, Chinese Cinema Makes a 3-D Push," *Time World*, January 31, 2011. Available at: http://www.time.com/time/world/article/0,8599,2044888,00.html (accessed June 9, 2013).

Further Reading

Barnouw, Erik and Subrahmanyam Krishnaswamy. *Indian Film*. Oxford University Press, 1980.

Bhaskar, Ira and Richard Allen. *Islamicate Cultures of Bombay Cinema*. Tulika Press, 2009.

Desai, Jigna. *Beyond Bollywood: The Cultural Politics of South Asian Diasporic Film*. Routledge, 2004.

Dwyer, Rachel and Divia Patel. *Cinema India: The Visual Culture of Hindi Film*. Rutgers University Press, 2002.

Ganti, Tejaswini. *Bollywood: A Guidebook to Popular Hindi Cinema*. Routledge, 2004.

Gopalan, Lalitha. *Cinema of Interruptions: Action Genres in Contemporary Indian Cinema*. British Film Institute, 2002.

Jolly, Gurbir, Zenia Wadhwani, and Deborah Barretto, eds. *Once Upon a Time in Bollywood: The Global Swing in Hindi Cinema*. Tsar, 2007.

Kaur, Raminder and Ajay Sinha, eds. *Bollywood: Popular Indian Cinema through a Transnational Lens*. Sage Publications India, 2005.

Kumar, Dudrah Rajinder. *Bollywood: Sociology Goes to the Movies*. Sage, 2006.

Lai, Vinjay and Ashis Nandy. *Fingerprinting Popular Culture: The Mythic and the Iconic in Indian Cinema*. Oxford University Press, 2006.

Mishra, Vijay. *Bollywood Cinema: Temple of Desire*. Routledge, 2002.

Pendakur, Manjunath. *Indian Popular Cinema: Industry, Ideology and Consciousness*. Hampton Press, 2003.

Rajadhyaksha, Ashish and Paul Willemen, eds. *Encyclopedia of Indian Cinema*. British Film Institute, 1995.

Ramdya, Kavita. *Bollywood Weddings: Dating, Engagement, and Marriage in Hindu America*. Rowman & Littlefield, 2010.

Thoraval, Yves. *The Cinemas of India*. Macmillan India, 2000.

Vasudevan, R., ed. *Making Meaning in Indian Cinema*. Oxford University Press, 2000.

CLOSE-UP

MY BIG FAT GREEK WEDDING

FIGURE 2.23 "What do you mean, he don't eat no meat?" Groom meets the family in *My Big Fat Greek Wedding* (Dir. Joel Zwick, 2002).

Directed by Joel Zwick.
Produced by Gary Goetzman, Tom Hanks, and Rita Wilson.
Script by Nia Vardalos.
Cinematography by Jeff Jur.
Edited by Mia Goldman.
Music by Alexander Janko and Chris Wilson.
Production Design by Gregory P. Keen.
Art Direction by Kei Ng.
Set Decoration by Enrico Campana.
Costume Design by Michael Clancy.
Released by IFC Films in 2002.
Running Time: 95 minutes.

Toula Portokalos	Nia Vardalos
Ian Miller	John Corbett
Gus Portokalos	Michael Constantine
Toula (age 12)	Marita Zouravlioff
Maria Portokalos	Lainie Kazan
Aunt Voula	Andrea Martin
Nick Portokalos	Louis Mandylor
Athena	Stavroula Logothettis
Cousin Nikki	Gia Carides
Rodney Miller	Bruce Gray
Harriet Miller	Fiona Reid
Mike	Ian Gomez

World Cinema through Global Genres, First Edition. William V. Costanzo.
© 2014 John Wiley & Sons, Inc. Published 2014 by John Wiley & Sons, Inc.

In contrast to its extravagant title, *My Big Fat Greek Wedding* is a small film with a slim plot and relatively little time devoted to the nuptial ceremony. It was made on a modest budget, featuring little-known actors, with a TV director at the helm, so that it often feels more like a routine television sit-com than a break-through movie. Some critics found the storyline to be predictable and trite, a retelling of the Cinderella fairy tale in a thick Greek accent. Less than a quarter of its 95-minute length is about the wedding itself. Yet there are good reasons for studying this movie in relation to other wedding films. First, it combines many of the genre's recurring elements (romance, comedy, family drama, cultural issues, consumerism, and wedding iconography) in instructive ways. Second, the story of its production offers insights into contemporary moviemaking, demonstrating how a movie can be produced and marketed beyond the citadel of Hollywood, yet within the system. Finally, the film's enormous popularity and financial success (by some reckonings, the most profitable movie of all time) raise important issues about reception and spectatorship: why do people watch wedding movies, what makes these films enjoyable, and how do viewers identify with the characters and issues on screen?

The movie offers many easy access points. Women who enjoy the story often point to the sympathetic character of Toula (played by the film's writer, Nia Vardalos). Despite her ethnically specific name ("Toula" is short for Fotoula, meaning "bright"), many viewers identify with her lot in life. The first time we see her as an adult, she looks tired and depressed. It's raining. Behind the monotonous windshield wipers of the family car, her conservative Greek father is reminding her that at 30, she is getting old. She should be married, like her sister, to a nice Greek boy. Once inside the family restaurant, as she prepares for yet another day of routine work, we read her body language like a book: the drab mustard yellow sweater, her wilted hair, the glasses that she hides behind, a blank face staring out through the window blinds as if they were prison bars. Her future looks anything but bright. A brief flashback of Toula's childhood shows that she has always felt like an outsider. While the pretty blonde girls went to Brownie meetings, she had to go to Greek school. While they sat together laughing in the school dining room eating Wonder Bread sandwiches, she sat alone eating her *moussaka*, which they ridiculed as "Moose ka-ka." These early images of silent suffering and the explanatory flashback, familiar conventions of the woman's picture, enlist our sympathy, our personal connection to Toula. But it's her voice-over commentary – witty, self-ironic, and confessional – that really draws us in. While her father Gus drones on about her life clock running out, she quips about her "expiration date." While he talks about her model sister, she sums up his view of women: "Nice Greek girls are supposed to do three things in life: marry Greek boys, make Greek babies, and feed everyone, until the day we die."

If fans readily relate to Toula's struggle for identity, they also feel included in the family drama. The Portokalos clan is big and loud, energetic and self expressed. The household pulsates with non-stop motion and emotion, like the Greek music playing in the background. This can be alternately appealing, amusing, and overbearing.

There is always a place at the table and plenty of food for everyone. But everyone's nose is in everybody else's plate. There is nowhere to hide, no way to harbor a secret dream or carry on a private romance.

The film accentuates the family's ethnicity and plays it for laughs. The Portokalos house has Corinthian columns and a stately portico, like a Greek temple. Toula's father is particularly proud of his heritage. He can find the Greek root in any word, even *kimono*. But the flip side of this pride is *xenophobia*, a disdain for foreigners, whom he calls *xenos* (outsiders) even though he is an immigrant himself. So when Toula falls in love with Ian Miller, the idea is intolerable to him. Ian, an only child, comes from a very different kind of family. His parents are caricatures of the White Anglo-Saxon Protestant, as stiff and reserved as Toula's parents are impulsive and outgoing. The Millers are equally clueless about foreigners. "Didn't you have a Greek receptionist?" asks Mrs. Miller. Then after considering she might have been Armenian, they conclude that she was Guatemalan. Meanwhile, Gus muses to himself in Greek, "When my people were writing philosophy, your people were still swinging from trees." Watching the collision of cultures is part of the fun when the two families meet. Rodney and Harriet Miller don't know quite what to make of the effusive hugs, the gaudy décor, heavy jewelry, and mounds of strange food. Their idea of a tasteful gift is a *bundt* cake. Toula's mother is mystified. "There's a hole in the cake!" she exclaims. Whether audiences relate more closely to the Portokalos family or to the Millers, such cultural conflicts between generations and ethnicities are familiar staples of modern wedding movies and the multicultural societies that they reflect.

As for the central love story, *My Big Fat Greek Wedding* follows most of the stages of film romance from the lightning bolt to the altar. Toula is smitten when Ian walks into the restaurant, a tall, athletic, handsome stranger with the head of an Adonis. Her first reactions are to gawk, make awkward small talk, then hide behind the counter. But he finds her intriguing, appealingly different from the other girls. His attention gives her confidence. She gets a new job, curls her hair, and goes shopping. When they meet again at the travel agency, they literally fall for each other. While watching her through the window, he trips over an old lady on the street. Inside, she's yanked down by the telephone cord when she moves to get him a brochure. This romantic comedy is full of slapsticks and pratfalls. But there are serious moments, too: the first kiss, a dreamy evening on the bridge, the cautious pulling back from intimacy, those risky little steps that lovers take toward one another as they emerge from their shells. The breakthrough scene comes when Ian agrees to be baptized in the Greek Orthodox Church. He will do what it takes to be with the woman he loves.

Thus begin the wedding preparations. Here, too, the film meets conventional expectations. Toula's family dives headlong into the arrangements, selecting the invitations (there's a Greek flag on the front) and changing the color of the bridesmaids' dresses without the bride's knowledge. On the big day, the men struggle with their tuxes in one room while the women fuss with stockings, gowns, and facial hair in another. Toula has a big zit on her chin. But the ceremony itself is majestic and reverential. Gus proudly walks his daughter down the aisle, lifts her veil, and presents her to the groom, who kisses his hand before the priest leads the couple thrice around the altar, their floral crowns tied together as they take their first steps as man and wife. At the reception, Gus gives his speech half in English, half in Greek. Stretching both languages a bit, he identifies the root of Miller as *milo*, the Greek word for apple. Then he points out that the word *portokalos* means orange. This marriage may be mixing apples and oranges, "but in the end we're all fruit."

So in its partly dramatic, partly comic way, the film ties together the loose threads. Toula has asserted her true identity without giving up her family. She and Ian have found true love. Her father gets to watch his daughter raise her family in the house next door. And thanks to the magic of Windex, Toula's zit disappears. The last scene, balancing the earlier flashback of Toula's childhood, flashes forward to her daughter. The girl wants to go to Brownies, but her mother wants her to attend Greek school. Off she goes to school, but with Toula's promise that she can marry anyone she wants.

In her DVD commentary and elsewhere, Vardalos says that she based much of the script on her own experience growing up in Winnipeg, Canada. "I took every crazy incident in my life and reduced it to ninety minutes of film."[1] Many of the characters are based on members of her family. She really did have 27 first cousins, and her grandmother used to wander through the neighborhood muttering about the Turks. Her father, a fervent Greek traditionalist, liked to demonstrate that any word – even *kimono* – was really Greek at heart. And the Portokalos house, with its overdressed interiors and Parthenon façade, looks much like the real houses of her people. Even the running Windex gag is part of her family history.

Vardalos set the story in Chicago, the place where she met her real husband, Ian Gomez, and the home of Second City, the comedy group in which she honed her acting skills. Perhaps this change in setting also brings the story closer to American audiences. How Vardalos brought *My Big Fat Greek Wedding* to those audiences has, like the script itself, been described as a Cinderella story.[2] The tale of her script, its overnight rise from humble origins to fame and fortune in the palace of cinema, has been repeated in the media many times and affirmed by her own testimony. It begins with the one-woman show that Vardalos wrote and performed on stage in Los Angeles in 1993. Another actress happened to see the show's only newspaper ad and went to see it. Rita Wilson, who shares Vardalos's Greek heritage, had also married outside the clan. She and her husband, Tom Hanks, were impressed with the performance. Hanks bought the screenplay rights for his production company, Playtone, and tried pitching it around Hollywood, eventually convincing his professional associates at HBO to split the costs with Gold Circle Films, a production/financing company. Hanks and his partners, acting as producers, assembled a cast that included veteran television actor Michael Constantine as Gus and John Corbett, from *Sex and the City*, as Ian. Despite pressure to sign a well-known star for the female lead, Vardalos got the part. The project was originally conceived as a direct-to-cable comedy, but some saw potential for a theatrical release. HBO approved this new direction, and IFC (Independent Film Channel) Films, a film production/distribution company, was commissioned to distribute the film.

Film scholar Alisa Perren challenges the widespread notion that *My Big Fat Greek Wedding* represents the triumph of small-time independent filmmaking over Hollywood. Perren points out that IFC, as a subsidiary of Cablevision, is hardly independent despite its name. HBO, in turn, is owned by Time Warner, the huge media conglomerate whose holdings include Warner Bros., New Line Cinema, Castle Rock Entertainment, and Time Inc. Hollywood today is no longer a massive film factory, a place where picture studios turn out hundreds of movies for mass consumption. Perren describes the new Hollywood as "a complex network of media industries in which major entertainment conglomerates exist at the center, financing products intended for distribution via a number of 'pipelines' around the world."[3] The network includes film and television products that are "packaged" with tie-ins and marketed in a variety of media forms to niche audiences. In the case of *My Big Fat Greek Wedding*, even the "grass-roots" spread of interest was part of a deliberate marketing ploy, which targeted Greek communities, church groups, and ethnic festivals. In other words, the film's success is not so much a challenge to the Hollywood system as a confirmation that the system works, although it works differently than many people realize.

Still, the film's reception history is impressive. Although it never reached first place on the box office charts, it went on to gross over $369 million, a 6150% return on the original $6 million investment, making it arguably the most profitable movie of all time.[4] No less important, in an era of niche movies, it continues to entertain and inspire a wide variety of audiences, spanning generations and cultures around the world. For many, it remains a model of the wedding film genre, bringing exuberance and compassion to a story many love to hear: the transformation of an ugly duckling daughter into a liberated woman in love and a triumphant bridal swan.

Questions

1. List some elements of the wedding film that you find in *My Big Fat Greek Wedding*. How are these elements handled compared to other movies that you know?

2. The multicultural wedding movie has become a familiar subgenre in the United States and abroad. How are the differences between the Millers and the Portokalos family dramatized in *My Big Fat Greek Wedding*? How seriously are we supposed to take their adherences to heritage? What messages about family and tradition come through the comedy?

3. Much depends on how we relate to the central character of Toula. What judgments about her do you make at the film's beginning? Trace her development from child to bride, identifying the conflicts that she faces as a daughter, lover, wife, and mother. How does she finally negotiate the pull of her family, the man she loves, and her own needs?

4. Select a scene from the film that you find particularly memorable. Describe the scene's dominant emotion, and analyze the cinematic choices (lighting, sound, camerawork, acting style, color, location, set design) that contribute to this emotional tone.

5. Conduct a survey of people who have seen *My Big Fat Greek Wedding*. Prepare questions that will help you understand what makes the film so popular across a range of niche audiences. What tentative conclusions can you draw about the appeal of wedding films in general and this film in particular?

6. A year after the film's success in 2002, CBS ran a sitcom with many of the same actors called *My Big Fat Greek Life*. Watch a few episodes and compare them to the original movie. What reasons can you give for the differences you find? How can you account for the short life span of the sitcom?

7. *My Big Fat Greek Wedding* is often cited as evidence that a small, independent film can become a major success outside the Hollywood system. Investigate the film's production history and trace its course from Vardalos's one-woman stage show to the theatrical release. Explain why you agree or disagree with Alisa Perren's claim that "Hollywood's hands are all over this film."

Notes

1. Audio commentary, *My Big Fat Greek Wedding*, DVD (Gold Circle Films in association with Home Box Office and MPH Entertainment, 2002).

2. Rick Lyman, "A Big Fat (and Profitable) Cinderella Story: 'Greek Wedding' Courts a Prince Named Oscar," *The New York Times*, November 28, 2002. Available at: http://www.nytimes.com/2002/11/28/movies/big-fat-profitable-cinderella-story-greek-wedding-courts-prince-named-oscar.html?pagewanted=all&src=pm (accessed June 10, 2013).

3. Alisa Perren, "A Big Fat Indie Success Story? Press Discourses Surrounding the Making and Marketing of a 'Hollywood' Movie," *Journal of Film & Video* 56(2) (Summer 2004): 18–31.

4. "The 15 Most Profitable Movies of All Time," CNBC, September 15, 2010. Available at: http://www.cnbc.com/id/39083257?slide=16 (accessed June 10, 2013).

CLOSE-UP
MONSOON WEDDING

FIGURE 2.24 "No men allowed" at the henna party in *Monsoon Wedding* (Dir. Mira Nair, 2001).

Directed by Mira Nair.
Screenplay by Sabrina Dhawan.
Cinematography by Declan Quinn.
Editing by Allyson C. Johnson.
Music by Mychael Danna.
Art Direction by Sunil Chabra.
Produced by IFC Productions and Mirabai Films.
Released in the United States in 2001 by Focus Features.
In Hindi, Punjabi, Urdu, and English, with English subtitles.
Running Time: 114 minutes.

Lalit Verma	Naseeruddin Shah
Pimmi Verma	Lillete Dubey
Ria Verma	Shefali Shetty
P.K. Dubey	Vijay Raaz
Alice	Tillotama Shome
Aditi Verma	Vasundhara Das
Hemant Rai	Parvin Dabas
Vikram Metha (talk show host)	Sameer Arya
Tej Puri	Rajat Kapoor
C.L. Chadha	Kulbhushan Kharbanda
Shashi Chadha	Kamini Khanna

World Cinema through Global Genres, First Edition. William V. Costanzo.
© 2014 John Wiley & Sons, Inc. Published 2014 by John Wiley & Sons, Inc.

Mira Nair was born in 1959 in Bhubaneswar, the capital city of Orissa (now Odisha), in eastern India. As the daughter of a high-ranking government official, she had a comfortable childhood, but she was disappointed with her education at the local school. Nair managed to get transferred to Miranda House, an exclusive boarding school in New Delhi, where she developed a lively interest in theatre, going on to study drama briefly at Delhi University and experimenting with radical street theatre in Calcutta. At 18, she left India on a scholarship to Harvard. She was a good student, but Harvard's theatre program was too conventional for her. After taking roles in plays by Shakespeare, Chekhov, Sophocles, and contemporary dramatists, she decided to become a filmmaker, the person in control of the whole story rather than the actor who is confined to a single role.

Nair's first films were documentaries about people on the margins of society. *So Far From India* (1983) follows a New York City immigrant whose family remained in India. *Children of Desired Sex* (1987) interviews pregnant Indian women contemplating the abortion of their female fetuses. *India Cabaret* (1985) is about strippers in a Bombay nightclub. These films illustrate Nair's commitment to neglected subjects. Gradually, she shifted to feature films. Her first major movie was *Salaam Bombay* (1988), which dramatized the stories of homeless city children. Made on a $900,000 budget, it became a commercial success and was nominated for an Academy Award. Western critics praised its documentary realism, but native Indians found it sentimental and exploitative, a Hollywood-style effort to romanticize poverty through the universal appeal of real street kids.

Nair has never been afraid to take risks and accept the consequences. She made *Mississippi Masala* (1991) in English, ignoring Hollywood's warnings to include a white protagonist. In *The Perez Family* (1995), a film about the cultural dislocations of Cuban Americans, she cast Brooklyn-born Marisa Tomei in a sexually charged role that was regarded as insulting by many Latinos. *Kama Sutra: A Tale of Love* (1996), a sumptuous story of medieval court life, was made in Hindi. It outraged Indian critics for perpetuating Western stereotypes of the exotic Indian woman, and Indian censors banned the film for its frank depiction of female eroticism. The charge of pandering to the West, of orientalizing and universalizing native culture, has continued to dog her work as it has the films of Zhang Yimou, Ang Lee, and other diaspora directors.

With *Monsoon Wedding* (2001), Nair achieved her most popular success. Her plan was to make a simple movie about a Punjabi wedding based on her own family experience. It was to be a low-budget production, shot in 30 days using a hand-held camera, with her Punjabi relatives and friends among the cast. "It was going back to the essence of drama," she explained in an interview with the *New York Times*, "good acting, urgency and seeing what you could make out of that self-imposed leanness. But of course it was a circus when we were doing it. I mean, a Punjab wedding – who was I kidding?"[1] This casual, home-made quality linked her project to films like *Who Am I to You?* (*Hum Aapke Haim Koun…!*, 1994) and *My Big Fat Greek Wedding* (2002) in many viewers' minds, doubtlessly contributing to its popularity. What could be more universal than a big, chaotic wedding, with its familiar emotional highs and lows, its recognizable family types, and the gaudy jumble of traditional foods and modern fashions?

At the 1999 Cannes Film Festival, Nair was able to reach her $1.5 million funding goal without a script, piecing together funds from India, Italy, Germany, France, and the United States. She chose the steamy summer monsoon season for the shooting, which took place during May and June of 2001. Two-thirds of the film was shot in a big house on the outskirts of Delhi. As with most wedding films, the domestic setting proves to be a fitting site for family-centered drama, and its ostentatious interiors also serve to comment on the materialism of the upwardly mobile middle class. *Monsoon Wedding* is both a high-spirited celebration of Punjabi excess and an affectionate critique. Unlike resident Bollywood directors of the 1990s, however, Nair chose to leave the house often, taking her camera to the city streets, showing us the trendy sari shops of Delhi, the local cafés, street kids, and sidewalk vendors reminiscent of her documentary work. "I wanted to make a portrait of modern contemporary India," she says. It is a "love song to my home city."[2]

If *Monsoon Wedding* is a kind of homecoming for Nair, she has invited along a global crew. The film's credits include Declan Quinn, the American cinematographer of *Leaving Las Vegas* (1995), Mychael Danna, the Canadian composer for *The Sweet Hereafter* (1997), and Caroline Baron, the American producer of *Capote* (2005), all of whom had worked on *Kama Sutra*. The script is by Sabrina Dhawan, a graduate of Columbia University's film program in New York, where the director teaches. This international mixture is reflected on the screen as well. Although all the characters are Indians by birth, a number of them have come to the wedding from overseas. There is a nephew from Sydney, a successful brother from America, a couple from the Middle East, and the groom himself, who lives in Houston, Texas. Amid the visual turmoil of the celebration, people speak a cosmopolitan jumble of Hindi, English, Punjabi, and Urdu.

The film is populated with a spectrum of character types drawn from modern Hindi cinema and the diaspora. Lalit (veteran actor Naseeruddin Shah) is the solid patriarch anchored in tradition, asserting his authority and social status with ostentatious spending while struggling to understand the Western notions of his two marriageable daughters. Aditi, his oldest (played by pop singer Vasundhara Das), is a Cosmo princess. On the eve of her arranged marriage to a man she's never met, she sneaks off to her married lover, a television talk show host (Sameer Arya, a director of photography). On the same night, her pretty cousin Ayesha (Neha Dubey) makes advances toward Rahul (Randeep Hooda), a handsome guest from Australia. An impromptu romance between P.K. Dubey, the man hired to set up reception tents in the yard, and Alice, the family's maid, adds an upstairs/downstairs subplot to the story. Dubey (Vijay Raaz in his first film performance) represents the ambitious upstarts in India's new economy. In public, dressed in an ill-fitting ascot and white suit, he is always barking orders on his cell phone or estimating costs on his calculator watch, but at home we see him sitting in his underwear attending to his aged mother in their squalid apartment. Alice (Tilotama Shome, a literature student), lovely though shy and withdrawn, confines herself to the kitchen, a reminder of her lower caste. There is also the bureaucratic uncle who speaks English with a stiffer accent than the English, a pudgy, couch-potato younger brother who watches cooking shows on television, and a computer software engineer.

Quinn did most of the shooting with a hand-held camera in 16 mm, later blown up to 35 mm. He uses frequent close-ups, jerky camera movements, rapid cuts, and rack focus shots (shifting the focus of the lens between near and distant objects) in the documentary style of *cinéma vérité*. These techniques together with a number of unrehearsed moments and the presence of so many non-actors – a 68-member cast leavened by Nair's extended family, Delhi socialites, and members of the crew – gives the film its homey feel. A special feature of Nair's approach is her attention to female views of Indian life. Some 90% of the crew and most of the cast were women. There are many intimate moments between women, and one of the most memorable scenes is a raucous gathering when women of all ages sing bawdy songs on *mendhi* night, no men allowed (Figure 2.24). Aditi's father is a sympathetic man. As the family patriarch, he tries to do the right thing within the confines of his culture, stretching his budget for the big wedding and confronting his beloved brother-in-law when this means protecting his family. On the eve of the wedding, he kneels quietly besides the sleeping forms of his two daughters, then turns to his wife asking, "How did they grow up so quickly? When did we grow old?" Some of the best scenes are not of the wedding celebrants but of the workers. The male workers sit outside, cracking jokes about their pretentious employers and teasing each other with old Bollywood songs. At one point, Dubey catches a glimpse of Alice through the window. She is trying on her mistress's jewelry, while the other men gather behind Dubey to gawk at the spectacle. It's a classic instance of the male gaze: three men peering through the windowpanes while a vulnerable beauty, thinking she's alone, eyes herself in the mirror.

Monsoon Wedding focuses on the theme and variations of modern love. Increasingly, arranged marriages in India today require the couple's consent, and they are often complicated by pre-marital sexual activity. The bride's family is expected to demonstrate its social status with an escalating display of conspicuous consumption. These facts of contemporary romance are reflected in Aditi's affair with the talk show host and her father's "cash flow problem," obliging him to borrow money from his golf friends to pay for a waterproof tent. By contrast, the romance between Dubey and Alice is a simple, more intimate event. Comic and endearing by turns, Dubey is transformed from a sardonic street-smart con artist into a sweet and gentle lover. In one memorable moment, he woos her adoringly with a bouquet of plastic flowers in hand, his ears moving to the sound of sitar music. It is, in Nair's words, "a magical story," a story of "pure love." Nair introduces a more sinister element in the figure of Tej Puri. At first, he seems to be a charming and beloved member of the family. Only gradually, through a succession of close-ups and exchanged glances, is his dark secret progressively revealed. These three narrative subplots are resolved in the final scene, where Puri is expelled, Alice and Dubey exchange authentic sentiments under a marigold umbrella, and the big Punjabi wedding, gyrating to a sound track of *bhangra* and disco music, culminates in a torrent of artificial monsoon rain.

Ultimately, the film is a valentine to Bollywood, filled with visual and musical allusions. In her DVD commentary, Nair singles out the scene when Alice emerges from the house with windblown hair and sees Dubey offering a heart of flowers, identifying it as a reference to Guru Dutt's classic, *The Cursed* (*Pyaasa*, 1957). The scene when Dubey protects her with his marigold umbrella recalls a similar moment from Raj Kapoor's *The Vagabond* (*Awaara*, 1951). When Alice drops a tray of glasses near Dubey's feet, the sound track plays "Aaj Mausam Bada Beimaan Hai" ("Today the Weather Plays Tricks on Me"), a Bollywood song from *Loafer* (1973). At the big *sanjeet* party before the wedding, cousin Ayesha dances to the tune of "Chunari Chunari," a mix of Jamaican reggae and Punjabi *bhangra* folk music. Several other songs in *Monsoon Wedding* recycle earlier pop hits. This self-conscious intertextuality has become a standard feature of postmodern Bollywood style, the evolving genre quoting its own earlier incarnations.

Questions

1. Mira Nair offers several variations on the themes of love and sexuality. Describe the relationships that Aditi, Ayesha, Alice, and Ria have with men. If you have access to other films by Nair, explore this theme in her *Kama Sutra, Mississippi Masala, The Perez Family,* or "Children of Desired Sex."

2. Compare the representation of marriage in *Monsoon Wedding* to films like *Moonstruck* (1987) and *My Big Fat Greek Wedding* (2002). Pay particular attention to the role of gender, class, and ethnicity in these films.

3. How is music used in the film? Compare Nair's choice of songs (their cultural roots, emotional range, and placement in the story) to American musicals or Bollywood movies that you've seen.

4. Some critics accuse *Monsoon Wedding* of "exoticism": deliberately playing to Western expectations of an imaginary India of colorful dress, spicy foods, and curious rituals. Explain why you agree or disagree with this charge.

5. Nair sets her film near the Indian city of Delhi, alternating documentary location shots with the story's main setting in a modern home. What is the overall effect of these contrasting sets of images?

6. *Monsoon Wedding* is especially popular with the Indian diaspora community. What features of the film would have special appeal for Indians living abroad? How do the film's character types, themes, cast, and crew, as well as its mixture of languages and accents, reflect recent trends in global filmmaking?

Notes

1. Mira Nair, quoted in Elisabeth Bumiller, "Of a Big Punjabi Family, By a Big Punjabi Family," *The New York Times*, February 17, 2002. Available at: http://www.nytimes.com/2002/02/17/movies/ film-of-a-big-punjabi-family-by-a-big-punjabi-family. html?pagewanted=all&src=pm (accessed June 10, 2013).

2. Nair, quoted in Bumiller.

CLOSE-UP
THE WEDDING BANQUET

FIGURE 2.25   Best man removes lipstick from the groom in *The Wedding Banquet* (*Xiyan*, Dir. Ang Lee, 1993).

Directed by Ang Lee.
Produced by Ang Lee, Ted Hope, and James Schamus.
Script by Ang Lee, Neil Peng, and James Schamus.
Cinematography by Lin Jong.
Edited by Tim Squyres.
Music by Mader.
Released in the United States by The Samuel Goldwyn Company in 1993.
In English and Mandarin, with English subtitles.
Running Time: 106 minutes.

Mrs. Gao	Ya-lei Kuei
Mr. Gao	Sihuang Lung
Wei-Wei	May Chin
Wai-Tung Gao	Winston Chao
Simon	Mitchell Lichtenstein
Andrew	Dion Birney
Mao Mei	Vanessa Yang
Bob Law	Yung-Teh Hsu
Wedding Guest	Ang Lee

World Cinema through Global Genres, First Edition. William V. Costanzo.
© 2014 John Wiley & Sons, Inc. Published 2014 by John Wiley & Sons, Inc.

The Wedding Banquet (1993) belongs to a trilogy of films by Ang Lee about the place of traditional Chinese culture in modern times. Although it was the second film in the series to be made, after *Pushing Hands* (1992) and before *Eat Drink Man Woman* (1994), Lee began the script six years before production. Following the first film's modest success in Taiwan, he had enough money and confidence to make a bigger film for a wider audience. He also felt adventurous enough to take mainstream Chinese cinema in a challenging new direction. Not only does the film explore multicultural issues, it places a gay couple at the center.

The Wedding Banquet is set in New York. Its characters speak both English and Mandarin. Wai-Tung Gao, a good-looking, educated young Chinese American, is on the verge of a big real estate deal. He lives with his partner, a non-Chinese American named Simon, a secret that he keeps from his parents back in China. Wai-Tung's mother and father want to see him married. As their only child, only he can carry on the Gao line. Mother Gao sends audio cassettes describing the eligible women they have found for him. Wai-Tung keeps them at bay with a list of impossible standards. He wants a woman who is at least 5 ft 9ins tall, has two doctorates, sings opera, and speaks five languages. When they match him with someone who fits most of these criteria, he realizes that he needs a new strategy. So he persuades one his female tenants, a poor artist of Chinese origin named Wei-Wei, to marry him. In return for this deception, she will get the green card that she needs to stay in the United States.

The problem is that Mr. and Mrs. Gao decide to fly in from Taiwan to meet the girl, bringing a large sum of money for an elaborate wedding. They are delighted by Wei-Wei's traditional charms and her knowledge of Chinese art, though they're a little mystified by Simon's presence in the household. Wai-Tung explains that Simon is his landlord, sneaking off whenever he can for furtive moments with his lover. Much of this subterfuge is played for laughs. When Wei-Wei moves in, down go the photos of male bonding; up go the pictures of Wai-Tung and his "fiancée." The walls are papered with Chinese art. Since Simon is a better Chinese cook than Wei-Wei, they keep exchanging places in the kitchen to make it seem that she has all the expected domestic skills. There are serious moments, too. Wei-Wei is genuinely moved by Mrs. Gao's gifts of family heirlooms. A true bond begins to form between them. Meanwhile, Mr. Gao confides to his son that he really joined the army to avoid an arranged marriage, only later facing his responsibility to carry on the family name. His last wish on earth is to hold his grandson in his arms.

The turning point comes midway through the film when Wai-Tung casually announces at the breakfast table that he and Wei-Wei will be getting married in the afternoon. Their rushed civil ceremony at the courthouse is a family disaster. Mrs. Gao leaves humiliated and depressed. Chinese marriages should be grand events, a spectacle of social status and achievement, more of a celebration for the parents than for the couple. When the chance arises for a big banquet, Wai-Tung's parents embrace the opportunity. It's too late for a traditional wedding ceremony, but the banquet is a model of conspicuous display. Ang Lee devotes some ten minutes to the banquet and another eight to the bridal chamber pranks that follow. The evening is a raucous carnival of good-humored bad behavior, traditional solemnity turned on its head. Ang Lee himself, appearing as one of the wedding guests, comments slyly on this bacchanalia: "We're witnessing the result of five thousand years of sexual repression." The banquet is a hybrid affair, a concoction of rituals and icons from both sides of the Pacific. Like the film itself, it is a blend of Western and Asian elements, of comedy and drama, designed to appeal to a wide, multicultural audience.

Clinking glasses for a kiss is not particularly Chinese, nor is the practice of throwing the bouquet or tossing the bride's garter. But some things at the banquet may be unfamiliar to Western audiences. There is a new bed to insure fertility and a young nephew to jump on it so that the first child will be a boy. The twin Chinese characters hanging from the red curtains mean "double happiness" (*shuang xi*), a common expression of good fortune. Those packets wrapped in red paper (*hong bao*) are gifts of money for the couple. Before the guests enjoy a lavish meal, the groom's father makes a lengthy speech, the new couple cross wine cups (*jiao bei jiu*), and taste a bit of fish, because the Chinese word for fish (*yu*) sounds like the word for plenty. Later, they make the rounds, honoring the guests at each table with a toast. With so many tables to visit, a lot of drinking gets done. Following the reception, after the exhausted couple stumbles to their room, there is a knock on the door. A voice announces, "Room service." Gao tries to warn his bride, but it's too late to stop the flood of rowdy guests who stream into the bedroom. Thus begins the *nao dong fang*, or bridal chamber pranks, a series of stunts and games designed to tease the couple long into the night.

In the bonus interview with Ang Lee on the DVD release, the director explains that much of the film's story is biographical, even autobiographical.[1] He based it loosely on the experience of a friend who lived with his male American lover in Washington, DC. Whenever the friend's parents appeared, they rearranged the house, pretending that the boyfriend was his landlord. Lee claims other personal connections to the plot and its family relationships. Although he doesn't lead a gay life, he did get married at City Hall, much to his mother's chagrin. The figure of Mr. Gao is also modeled on Lee's father, a respected high school principal in Taiwan who disapproved of his first son's ambition to become a filmmaker.

Here lies one of the movie's deep-seated themes. Ang Lee's father had escaped the Civil War in mainland China, replanting his family roots in the island soil of Taiwan. It was his son's duty to nurture and perpetuate those roots. Making *The Wedding Banquet* helped Ang Lee to acknowledge his father's admonition to "honor where we come from," that there are bigger, more important things in life than personal desires. Another theme, one taken up by several critics, is the topic of gay relationships. When Lee's film was shown in China, local audiences had never seen two men kiss on screen. The closeness between Simon and Wai-Tung is expressed in many scenes, some comic, some bordering on erotic. Lee shows us the intimacy of their daily routines. We listen to their playful banter at breakfast. We see them in bed together, bare from the waist up. One day, when they think the house is empty, they run up the steps together flinging clothing on the fly. But as William Leung notes in his 2005 essay, Lee is more interested in telling a character-centered, plot-driven story than in proselytizing against homophobia. Physical intimacy is necessary for the story, but the story is not primarily about gay love. "At its core," Leung concludes, *The Wedding Banquet* "is an old-fashioned comedy of errors made queer – a comic study of the interaction between queer love and parental-filial love – not a satirical essay 'for' or 'against.'"[2]

Sheng-mei Ma, another film scholar, sees the gay theme as an exotic detour, a temporary departure from the Confucian code of conduct akin to the "Carnivalesque transgression" of the banquet scene. For Ma, the movie's relatively happy ending restores the status quo, making the film's deviations from the norm palatable to world markets.[3]

Ang Lee went on to break other barriers. He showed that a director born in China and educated in the West could make award-winning films based on British classics (*Sense and Sensibility*, 1995), contemporary American novels (*The Ice Storm*, 1997), and even comic books (*Hulk*, 2003). Yet he keeps returning to Chinese subjects with films like *Crouching Tiger, Hidden Dragon* (1999) and *Lust, Caution* (2007), pulling the two spheres of his life into closer proximity for himself and for millions of spectators around the globe.

Questions

1. Among other things, *The Wedding Banquet* is a film about relationships. Describe the filial feelings between Wai-Tung and his father, the romantic love between Wai-Tung and Simon, the interactions between Mrs. Gao and her daughter-in-law, and the "marriage of convenience" between Wai-Tung and Wei-Wei. How does each of these relationships change over time?

2. Pay close attention to the banquet scene. Notice the sequence of events, the décor, cuisine, modes of dress, and codes of behavior. To what extent does this seem to be a traditional Chinese event, a hodge-podge of international practices, or a Carnivalesque moment when conventional decorum is suspended?

3. Compare *The Wedding Banquet* to other movies that depict Chinese weddings? What rituals, both modern and traditional, are represented in each film, and what do these depictions say about the changing role of weddings in society today?

4. *The Wedding Banquet*, like *Crouching Tiger, Hidden Dragon*, was aimed at an international audience. Compare the production process of these films. Who wrote the script, who provided financing, who are the main stars, and where did they come from? What can Ang Lee's films teach us about the way global genres are made today?

5. Read what William Leung, Sheng-mei Ma, and other film scholars have to say about the gay relationship in *The Wedding Banquet*. How does Lee's treatment of Simon and Wai-Tung compare to those in other films about gay characters, including Lee's own *Brokeback Mountain* (2005) and *Taking Woodstock* (2009)?

Notes

1. *The Wedding Banquet: A Forbidden Passion*, directed by Greg Carson, bonus interview with Ang Lee accompanying DVD of *The Wedding Banquet* (Central Motion Pictures in association with Good Machine, 2007).

2. William Leung, "So Queer Yet So Straight: Ang Lee's *The Wedding Banquet* and *Brokeback Mountain*," *Journal of Film & Video* 60(1) (Spring 2008): 23–42.

3. Sheng-mei Ma, "Ang Lee's Domestic Tragicomedy: Immigrant Nostalgia, Exotic/Ethnic Tour, Global Market," *Journal of Popular Culture* 30(1) (Summer 1996): 191–201.

CLOSE-UP
WEDDING IN GALILEE

FIGURE 2.26   A scimitar to bless the Arab bride in *Wedding in Galilee* (*Urs al-Jalil*, Dir. Michel Khleifi, 1987).

Directed and Written by Michel Khleifi.
Produced by Michel Kleifi, Jacqueline Louis, and Bernard Lorain.
Cinematography by Walther van der Ende.
Edited by Marie Castro Vasquez.
Music by Jean-Marie Sénia.
Costume Design by Anne Verhoeven.
Released in 1987 by Marisa Films.
Distributed in the United States by Kino International.
In Hebrew and Arabic with English subtitles.
Running Time: 113 minutes.

Father, the Mukhtar (Abu Adel)	Mohamed Ali El Akili
Mother	Bushra Karaman
Military General	Makram Khoury
Groom (Adel)	Nazih Akleh
Bride (Samia)	Anna Condo
Bride's sister (Soumaya)	Sonia Amar
Bride's young brother (Hassan)	Eyad Anis
Bacem	Yussuf Abou-Warda
Ziad	Waël Bargkouti
First Officer	Juliano Mer-Khamis
Second Officer	Ilan Chemi
Female Soldier (Tali)	Tali Dorat

World Cinema through Global Genres, First Edition. William V. Costanzo.
© 2014 John Wiley & Sons, Inc. Published 2014 by John Wiley & Sons, Inc.

Wedding in Galilee was praised when it came out in 1987 as the first Palestinian feature film made by an insider. Michel Khleifi, an Arab Palestinian living in Belgium, directed the film in five different villages in Israel: three in Galilee near Nazareth (Khleifi's birthplace) and two in the West Bank. Although fictional, the film dramatizes the cultural conflicts between Israelis and Palestinians that continue to fuel tensions in that territory and erupt in the recurrent violence that we see today.

When the story begins, Abu Adel is asking permission from the Israeli military governor to lift a curfew so that his son's wedding can be celebrated in proper style. As the Mukhtar (village headman), Abu Adel holds patriarchal power over his community, but the Israeli governor wields political power. The governor is reluctant to agree because Arab protests led to bloodshed just four months earlier. He is finally persuaded to allow the wedding to take place on the condition that he and his staff attend the ceremony. Meanwhile, Arab extremists are planning a terrorist plot. Hatred, fear, distrust, and misunderstanding – counteracted by idealism, jubilation, and gestures of goodwill – sustain the ebb and flow of tensions until the surprising ending of the film.

The idea for Khleifi's movie originated in an incident related to him by his brother-in-law about his uncle's wedding night. But much of the story was invented by the filmmaker for reasons of symbolic economy, "to synthesize forty years of Palestinian experience and history into a single situation."[1] Strictly speaking, the situation is historically inaccurate. The Galilee area in northern Israel, unlike the West Bank and Gaza, was no longer under military rule. Palestinians in Galilee were ruled by emergency laws inherited from the British until 1965, but it was demilitarized after the Six Day War of 1967. Khleifi is interested in another kind of truth. His film is not so much a political tract or a lesson in ethnography, although it embraces political and cultural realities; it is "a kind of modern folklore." As Khleifi explains, "I wanted to give my wedding a mythical connotation, to create a mythical situation out of day-to-day life." Viewers may find allegorical statements in certain scenes: an Arabian steed trapped in a minefield, a female soldier who exchanges her fatigues for Arab dress, a sexually disabled groom.

A striking feature of this film is the centrality of the landscape, with its gentle contours and golden light. In this land that has been occupied by Romans, Turks, British, and Israelis, the Arabs seem to blend naturally into the environment. The Jews by contrast, with their uniforms, armaments, and military vehicles, seem like aliens. Yet, Khleifi doesn't caricature the enemy. The Israelis are not presented as faceless oppressors. Although he is less concerned with their perspective, he recognizes them as human beings.

In this film, unlike *Rana's Wedding* (*Al qods fee yom akhar*, 2002) or *The Syrian Bride* (*Urus suriyya*, 2004), the Israelis are invited to the celebration. Potentially, this opens a door to better understanding, perhaps to mutual respect. If weddings are affirmations of community, Arabs and Israelis have the chance to appreciate each other's customs and share in the emotions of an important event. In fact, several incidents seem to move the story forward along these lines. When the horse from the groom's wedding procession wanders into a minefield, the Israeli soldiers try to help. When a female soldier named Tali faints from the heat, the Palestinian women take her into their midst, a feminized space of flowers, jewelry, dance, and food. They revive her, peeling off her uniform and massaging her with oil before dressing her in Palestinian robes. But these moments of rapprochement are cut short by misunderstanding and mutual suspicion. A fellow soldier tries to pull Tali from the women's house, thinking she's at risk. Meanwhile, at the banquet, a covered basket is passed from guest to guest towards the Israeli soldiers, who fear it might contain a bomb. In each case, it is the regional legacy of mistrust that interrupts the spirit of the wedding.

This wedding in Galilee carries other symbolic freight. Film scholar Anna Ball gives a close reading of the film's rituals to show how they reflect the relationship between men and women in Palestinian society. She emphasizes how Arab masculinity (*rujulah*) traditionally depends on a strict code of honor (*sharaf*), saving face (*wajh*), kinship, and community.[2] This code, which gives men both power and responsibility, is passed down from fathers to sons. For Abu Adel (*Abu* means father), the wedding is a chance to display his wealth and patriarchal authority, but his cultural capital is undermined by the political power of the Israelis. What's more, it has been challenged by his brother Khamis, who refuses to attend the celebration, and by his youngest daughter Soumaya, who wears jeans and flirts with the men. Meanwhile, the bride and groom have problems of their own. After the bride is properly bathed by the women to cleanse her for the wedding night and Adel, in turn, is washed by the men, they enter the bridal chamber together joined by emblematic threads. In silence, each undresses separately before donning the traditional white gowns. She dutifully washes his feet according to the custom, but he cannot perform his proper role as husband. Frustrated and angry, he strikes out at her, then blames his father for giving in to the Israelis. Meanwhile, the families wait outside to see the bloody nuptial sheets that signify a successful union. It is up to the bride to find a solution.

In an insightful essay on the film, Nadia Yaqub interprets this wedding as a failure on several levels.[3] Meant to celebrate the couple's role within the family and society as they rejuvenate the line through fruitful marriage, it ends instead in impotence, disruption, and deception. It is not only the intrusion of Israelis that is problematic. Their presence serves to reveal weaknesses that lie within Palestinian society itself. At a time when sons chafe under rigid paternal authority, when daughters feel hemmed in by their fixed roles and individuals of both genders yearn for freedom, wedding rituals originally intended to cement society, to connect each to each, have the opposite effect. Far from being the happy ending of a romance or a family drama, this wedding in Galilee is rife with fissures that are just beginning to crack.

Michel Khleifi was born in 1950 to a Christian family of Arab Palestinians in Nazareth, where he lived for 20 years before his voluntary exile in Europe. At that time, he was a school dropout working as a car mechanic. "I decided I had three options: to become militant, to become part of the silent majority, or to leave.

I chose exile." En route to Germany to work in a Volkswagen factory, he was persuaded instead to study theater and film at the Institut National Supérieur des Arts du Spectacle in Belgium. In the 1970s, INSAS was a meeting place for Arabs from around the world, many of whom would figure prominently in Third World cinema. In their company, Khleifi found a home for his talents and cultural identity. His first film, *Fertile Memory* (*Al Dhakira al Qasba*, 1980), was a documentary about two Palestinian women, an elderly factory worker and a young novelist. His second documentary, *Ma'loul Celebrates Its Destruction* (1984), focused on a group of Palestinians who are allowed to visit their demolished village each year on the anniversary of Israel's independence. Since making *Wedding in Galilee*, he continues to direct films like *L'ordre du jour* (1993), the story of a dreamer trapped by modern bureaucracy, *Tale of the Three Lost Jewels* (1995), a romantic adventure filmed in the Gaza Strip, and *Zindeeq* (2009), a surrealistic exploration of the tumultuous events of 1948 (*Nakba*) and its survivors.

Khleifi drew his cast from many quarters. The Israeli governor and Bacem, the nephew, are played by Palestinians actors well known in the Hebrew theater. The mother is a Palestinian actress living in Detroit. The only Israeli actors are the female soldier (Tali) and the blond officer with glasses who helps to rescue the horse. Most of the actors are non-professionals. The grandfather is played by Khleifi's 84-year-old uncle, who lived through the Turkish occupation. Hassan, the child, was found in a Jerusalem orphanage. The young officer is half Palestinian (his father is a Palestinian communist) and half Israeli (his mother an Israeli from Hungary). The groom's sister is a Berber from Tunisia. The Mukhtar is an illiterate Bedouin who never saw a film before he acted in this one.

Wedding in Galilee won the international critics award at Cannes and went on to earn worldwide acclaim. It did not play commercially in Israel, where the only offer came from a distributor who wanted to delete 20 minutes and shorten the title to *The Wedding*. While the film enjoyed a successful run in Egypt, it has been banned in much of the Arab world, which was shocked by the female nudity and unflattering depiction of Arab masculinity. In this day of video and digital media, however, it has been secretly screened in cine clubs and private homes. A few months after the film's release, the first Intifada began: a Palestinian uprising against Israeli occupation that spread throughout Gaza, the West Bank, and East Jerusalem, continuing from 1987 to 1993.

Questions

1. Director Michel Khleifi has observed, "Only everyday life is real. Politics, religion are myths; Palestine is a mythic country par excellence." To what extent does *Wedding in Galilee* resemble a documentary of daily life? To what degree is the story mythic or symbolic? How well has Khleifi combined the lives of ordinary people with religion and politics in his film?

2. Trace the film's major conflicts: the clash of authorities, the divergences of male and female points of view. How are these conflicts revealed and played out? Which conflicts, if any, are resolved by the end of the movie?

3. Do you find the film one-sided, or does it give a fair view of both Palestinians and Israelis? Khleifi

has said, "It is not easy for Palestinians to learn that their Israeli oppressors are themselves victims of history: that they are both oppressors and victims. And when you look at Arab society, you discover that this same oppressed society also oppresses others: men oppress women, the rich the poor, mothers their daughters, the strong the weak." Where can you find support for this statement in his film?

4. Review the scene in which Abu Adel speaks to his sleeping youngest son, articulating his dreams for the Palestinian people. "Are your dreams like mine?" he asks. "Why do I want you to learn my dreams by heart?" Nadia Yaqub sees this moment as a comment on national identity: the figment of a patriarch's imagination.[4] Do you agree or disagree with this view of "imagined nationhood"?

5. Explore the imagery and customs surrounding the wedding ceremony. What practice to you? Which ones seem strange explained? Do some research into th this region. What tentative conclu draw about Palestinian society and beliefs from these rituals?

6. *Wedding in Galilee* has been variously called lyrical, neo-realist, meditative, exotic, and erotic. Find examples of the film's aesthetic style and explain what cinematic choices (lighting, camerawork, sound, color, editing, acting) contribute to the overall effect.

7. In the final scene, Abu Adel's youngest son runs up a hill and lies down in peaceful solitude while the troubled village lies enshrouded in mist below. How do you interpret this scene? What do you suppose the boy is thinking? Is this ending hopeful, ironic, conflicted, or something else?

Notes

1. All quotes by Khleifi are taken from the film's press book, released by Kino International Corp, 1985.

2. Anna Ball, "Between a Postcolonial Nation and Fantasies of the Feminine: The Contested Visions of Palestinian Cinema," *Camera Obscura* 23(3) (69) (2008): 1–33.

3. Nadia Yaqub, "The Palestinian Cinematic Wedding," *Journal of Middle East Women's Studies* 3(2) (Spring 2007): 56–85.

4. Yaqub, 5.

UNIT III
THE HORROR FILM

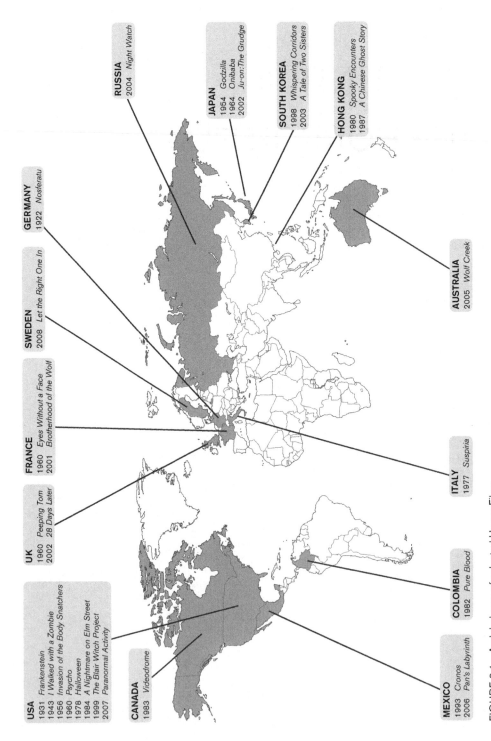

RUSSIA
2004 *Night Watch*

JAPAN
1954 *Godzilla*
1964 *Onibaba*
2002 *Ju-on:The Grudge*

SOUTH KOREA
1998 *Whispering Corridors*
2003 *A Tale of Two Sisters*

HONG KONG
1980 *Spooky Encounters*
1987 *A Chinese Ghost Story*

GERMANY
1922 *Nosferatu*

SWEDEN
2008 *Let the Right One In*

FRANCE
1960 *Eyes Without a Face*
2001 *Brotherhood of the Wolf*

AUSTRALIA
2005 *Wolf Creek*

UK
1960 *Peeping Tom*
2002 *28 Days Later*

ITALY
1977 *Suspiria*

USA
1931 *Frankenstein*
1943 *I Walked with a Zombie*
1956 *Invasion of the Body Snatchers*
1960 *Psycho*
1978 *Halloween*
1984 *A Nightmare on Elm Street*
1999 *The Blair Witch Project*
2007 *Paranormal Activity*

CANADA
1983 *Videodrome*

COLOMBIA
1982 *Pure Blood*

MEXICO
1993 *Cronos*
2006 *Pan's Labyrinth*

FIGURE 3.1 A global map of selected Horror Films.

CHAPTER 3
THE HORROR FILM

The setting is a research lab in England. A team of pro-animal activists in black hoods has just infiltrated the facilities, where they find row after row of primates imprisoned in glass cages. In one room, a chimpanzee has been shackled to a table, forced to watch a set of television screens displaying videos of violent demonstrations. Horrified by the treatment of these animals, the team prepares to set them free, but a scientist appears suddenly and tries to call security. When the intruders disconnect the phone, he protests. "You don't understand," he cries. "The chimps are infected!" When they push him for an explanation, he stammers that the chimps have been infected, infected with rage. The first one they release leaps at the woman activist, ripping at her neck with its bare teeth (Figure 3.2). Blood gushes from her throat. The room erupts in screams of fear and fury. Within seconds, the woman has become a raging animal, spitting blood into her companion's face, infecting *him* with rage. In the chaos of the moment, it's hard to tell the humans from the beasts. The opening scene of *28 Days Later*, directed by Danny Boyle in 2002, plunges the audience into a moment of cinematic horror. The effect is meant to be visceral, a physical sensation of alarm, perhaps of terror, an involuntary tightening in the gut. This raw, emotional response is one of the hallmarks of cinematic horror.

The horror film is one of cinema's earliest and most persistent genres. Like Count Dracula or Freddy Krueger, horror movies keep coming back in one form or another to haunt our screens and agitate our dreams. Boris Karloff's Frankenstein monster stalking the English moors with outstretched arms, Janet Leigh screaming in the shower as a knife stabs her relentlessly, a ragged column of the Living Dead advancing toward the camera: these images and other icons of the genre pervade our cultural landscape, not only in the United States, but throughout the world. More recently, the pale-faced, long-haired, technologically resourceful ghost of Japanese horror (known by fans as J-horror), the revenge-seeking Spanish

World Cinema through Global Genres, First Edition. William V. Costanzo.
© 2014 John Wiley & Sons, Inc. Published 2014 by John Wiley & Sons, Inc.

FIGURE 3.2   The opening scene of *28 Days Later* (Dir. Danny Boyle, 2002) plunges the audience into a moment of cinematic horror.

orphan, and the ruthless tracker of the Australian outback – among other fiendish figures from national cinemas – have added to the global store of scary imagery. Although monsters like the Wolf Man and Nosferatu have always defied national borders, the scale of transnational filmmaking today makes it ever more important to gain an international perspective, to ask what horrifies people in Mexico or South Korea, to understand what fears spring from specific historical and cultural conditions and what fears belong to a broader set of collective anxieties.

Four sets of questions will help to chart our course through a subject that has such vast appeal and has been so thoroughly investigated by critics, scholars, and historians. First, why do we watch horror films? How do they affect us as individuals, and what larger, social purpose do they serve? Second, what defines horror movies as a genre? What kinds of stories do they tell? What do their monsters and heroes have in common? Third, what is the history of horror films? Where do they come from, and how have they evolved over time? Finally, how does a good horror film differ from a bad one? Who gets to decide and on what grounds?

Our approach in this chapter will be mostly chronological, beginning with the sources of horror in Gothic literature and the theatrical tradition of Grand Guignol, proceeding decade by decade to the present. A major part of this chronology will be American, reflecting the historical dominance of Hollywood, but it includes films from Germany, Italy, Spain, Japan, China, and other cinemas that borrow from and contribute to the genre. Instead of treating national cultures separately or taking up questions of theory, film style, industry, and audience as disconnected topics, these factors will be integrated into the narrative, a story of how horror films have evolved from native roots into the global phenomenon they are today.

Why We Watch Horror Films: The Thrill of Fear

There is something primal about horror. H.P. Lovecraft, the American master of "weird fiction," once wrote, "The oldest and strongest emotion of mankind is fear, and the oldest and strongest kind of fear is fear of the unknown."[1] The figure of a primate leaping with rage in *28 Days Later* is frightening in itself, but what makes it even more alarming is the wrath that it awakens within us. The most terrifying monsters are the ones that live inside. Stephen King likened the experience of watching horror films to the act of "lifting a trap door in the civilized forebrain and throwing a basket of raw meat to the hungry alligators swimming around in that subterranean river beneath."[2] His imagery highlights the genre's reputation as a primitive, unsavory corner in the house of cinema, once considered to be far beneath the attention of serious viewers and critics. As King goes on to say, "The mythic horror movie, like the sick joke, has a dirty job to do. It deliberately appeals to all that is worst in us. It is morbidity unchained, our most base instincts let free, our nastiest fantasies realized ... and it all happens, fittingly enough, in the dark."

Freud's work on dreams goes a long way toward explaining what happens in this darkness. His psychoanalytic theories, especially on the dynamics of repression, have given film scholars powerful tools for analyzing horror films, lifting the genre out of the gutter of pop culture into the light of academic respectability. According to Freud, all healthy people learn to repress certain impulses and desires. It's part of being civilized. Society requires us to bottle up those natural drives that would violate its laws and taboos, but these urges manifest themselves, find symbolic expression in jokes, dreams, and fiction. The manifest content of our dreams, their characters and stories, are disguises. They represent a subterranean world of repressed impulses and memories that trouble our unconscious, a world hidden from our everyday awareness. These are the alligators beneath King's trapdoor, the demons in our nightmares and our horror films. Viewed in this way, the horror movie serves an important psychological purpose, the cathartic function of purging our system of toxic emotions. It acts as a cinematic safety valve. Returning to King's metaphor, we might say that it feeds the monsters, keeping the gators down there and us up here.

Carl Jung, Freud's student, delved even deeper. Jung believed there is another layer below the personal unconscious, which he called the collective unconscious, "a collective, universal, and impersonal nature which is identical in all individuals."[3] He likened this realm to a vast reservoir beneath the surface of everyday experience, a pool of pre-existing "archetypes" that all human beings inherit. According to this view, horror films derive much of their power by tapping into the pool. They connect us to our "shadow side," the dark, demonic forces that rage in everyone and which we project as archetypal monsters on screen.

If ghosts and demons represent the return of repressed psychic energies to Freudians, if they symbolize the dark side of a mythic, universal underworld to Jungians, followers of Karl Marx and Fredric Jameson see them as creatures from a kind of political unconscious. Repressed social problems that threaten the status quo – class conflicts, racial tensions, gender inequities – return symbolically in horror films to haunt us in the form of zombies, hillbilly stalkers, and vengeful female ghosts. Their power to disturb us, these theories imply, comes from unresolved issues skulking deep within our psyche, our culture, and shared myths.

But films are only films, not life. Horror movies offer us a second-hand experience. The thrill of rage or fear may feel immediate and real, but it's the characters in the movie that are in danger, not us. Here lies the safety in the safety valve. We get to release the pent up emotions associated with assault, mutilation, guilt, and death knowing that we won't face the physical penalties. At the end of the roller coaster ride, we get to walk away alive and in one piece.

Of course, not everyone enjoys the ride. The sight of Linda Blair's rotating head in *The Exorcist* (1973) or the bloody victims in *Wolf Creek* (2005) may be too scary, too gory, or too realistic for some tastes. Horror is by nature a transgressive genre; it deliberately crosses the boundaries of good taste and acceptable behavior set by society. Its monsters and its narratives pose threats to the established order, unleashing sexual energies and sowing moral chaos, disrupting the harmony of comfortable lives. Historically, as audiences grow accustomed to one generation's horrors, as movies lose their power to shock, another generation of filmmakers finds new limits to transgress. The thrill of breaking taboos is part of the genre's appeal for many viewers, which may help to explain why certain kinds of horror films engage us at different times of our lives. A film that once was truly frightening or exciting may later seem repulsive, silly, or irrelevant, and vice versa. A number of studies by psychologists indicate that children between the ages of three and eight are chiefly frightened by the dark, by animals, by strange creatures and supernatural beings. From nine to twelve, our fears are more likely to be related to personal injury and the death of relatives. These fears continue into adolescence, but then social fears and school-related worries come into play. As we mature, the circle of anxieties widens to include political, economic, and global issues.[4] Our relationship to horror can therefore be a yardstick of personal growth. Yet all of these fears are reflected in the range of monster movies, body horror, teen fright pictures, and films about historical trauma that span the genre.

Bruce Kawin, one of the most insightful scholars of the genre, points out that our comfort level with horror is both a measure of a filmmaker's skill and a sign of our humanity. "The effect of a good horror film," he notes, "is to show us what we are not comfortable seeing but may need to look at anyway."[5] The push-pull experience of watching horror on the screen, the reason we are both drawn and repelled, peering at its painful images through splayed fingers, may come from a recognition deep down that the experience is ultimately good for us because it shakes us out of numbing complacencies, putting us in touch with vital parts of ourselves that might otherwise consume us from within.

What Is a Horror Film? Defining the Genre

Unlike some other genres, like the Western (named for its settings), the gangster film (named for its characters), or the kung fu movie (named for its most distinctive form of action), the horror film derives its name from the intended audience reaction. The term horror can be traced back to its Latin origin, *horrere*, meaning "to bristle with fear." At the word's source is the bodily sensation of *horripilation*, that moment of fear when one's hair stand on end.

According to film historian Rick Worland, the term "horror movie" first appeared in print when film critics and industry representatives began discussing *Dracula* and *Frankenstein*, both released by Universal Studios in 1931.[6] What we now call horror films were made before then, but they were regularly described in other terms: as mysteries, for example, or as Gothic tales. Since the 1930s, so many different kinds of movies have been assigned to the category of horror that it can be tricky to define the genre. We hear of hillbilly horror, body horror, demonic horror, techno-horror, psycho-horror, slasher films, and stalker movies, to name just a few groupings. To make sense of this diversity, spanning more than 100 years of filmmaking and thousands of films, we will follow a broad, far-ranging, historical path, but at this point it is helpful to take a quick inventory of the genre's most typical features – the kinds of characters, settings, scenes, and themes commonly associated with horror films – and consider some reasons why they have persisted so long, producing a veritable horror industry.

Although horror films can seem formulaic, as they often are, there is no single blueprint that accounts for every scene or plot. Rather, as with most genres, it's more useful to think in terms of loosely shared traits, what the Austrian philosopher Ludwig Wittgenstein called "family resemblances." Wittgenstein abandoned the rigidity of formal definition in favor of a more flexible method to classify things. Instead of trying to isolate precise defining features – one description fits all – he focused on relationships, "a complicated network of similarities overlapping and crisscrossing: sometimes overall similarities, sometimes similarities of detail,"[7] much like the mix of hair colors, facial structures, and musical talents that cycle through a family from generation to generation.

Typically, in the family of horror films, there is some kind of monster that disturbs the status quo. It may be partly human, like Dracula, the Wolf Man, or the vampire girl in *Let the Right One In* (*Låt den rätte komma in*, 2008); it may be a deranged killer, like the psychopath in *Psycho* (1960) or *Peeping Tom* (1960); it may be supernatural, like the invisible force in *The Blair Witch Project* (1999) or *Paranormal Activity* (2007). The monster may be a ghost from the unsettled past, like the avenging spirit in *Ring* (*Ringu*, 1998) or the murdered boy in *The Devil's Backbone* (*El espinazo del diablo*, 2001). It might lurk in the threat of contagion, as in *Night of the Living Dead* (1968) or *28 Days Later*. The site of horror also shifts from film to film. The monster once confined its dirty work to remote castles or haunted houses, stalking its victims in the dead of night, which is why we cringe whenever our hero, most likely a woman, ventures into the cellar or the forbidden room. These predictable settings and scenes still haunt the horror screen, but today's fiends are just as likely to attack in broad daylight from the surrounding countryside (*The Hills Have Eyes*, 1977) or from within (*The Shining*, 1980).

The iconography of horror also varies, within broad limits, from film to film. From the early deaths in silent films, discretely executed off screen, to the increasingly graphic images of tortured torsos, severed heads, and other mutilated body parts that litter the landscapes of more recent movies, filmmakers have resorted to ever more inventive and aggressive images to shock audiences. Their weaponry, too, has grown more ingeniously violent. Think of the many ways a modern victim can be pierced, sliced, crushed, and garroted before the final credits. The emotions evoked by these attacks on the spectator's eye and ear can range from terror, panic, and anxiety to dread, loathing, and disgust. The spectrum of responses calls for close attention film by film. So do the themes that underlie the genre. The clear-cut battle lines between good and evil in *Frankenstein* or *The Phantom of the Opera* (1925, revised 1929), or between science and the supernatural in *Dr. Jekyll and Mr. Hyde* (1931) become murky and problematic in later films like *Carrie* (1976) or *Videodrome* (1983).

Describing the features of a genre is one task; understanding its functions in the film industry is another. Why do horror movies continue to be bankrolled and produced? In *Film/Genre*, Rick Altman shows how genre conventions serve as formulas for industry decisions.[8] They provide familiar labels for marketing and a ready framework for structuring individual films. Think of genre as a kind of contract between manufacturers and consumers, a promise to deliver an experience more or less expected by the audience. As long as filmmakers keep turning out the sort of horror people want, horror movies will continue to be made. And since horror films can be relatively cheap to make, producers can expect a reasonable return on their investment even if the box office receipts are small.

Vampires: The Evolution of a Monster

As we noted earlier in this book, some scholars believe that genres follow predictable patterns of development as they evolve over time. Summarizing the work of French art historian Henri Focillon, Thomas Schatz distinguished four stages:[9]

1. *Experimental*: the conventions of the genre are isolated and established.
2. *Classical*: conventions are stabilized so that artists and audiences understand how they work.
3. *Refinement*: filmmakers enrich and embellish the form with certain formal and stylistic details.
4. *Baroque* (or "self-reflexive"): the form and its embellishments become the work's main focus.

Other scholars disagree with such schematic accounts, arguing that genres don't develop linearly but grow, retreat, take detours, and get reworked in a more haphazard fashion. The chronological account of horror cinema in this chapter offers another chance to test these views, but before looking at the whole cloth, it will be instructive to follow the brief history of a single thread, the vampire film.

When John Polidori published his short story, *The Vampyre*, in 1819, there was already a long tradition of blood-sucking demons in European myth and folklore. Polidori's monster appeared in the guise of a sophisticated gentleman who seduces women and drinks their blood to prolong his life. Some 80 years later, Bram Stoker published *Dracula*, adding a touch of Transylvanian nobility to his title character and associating his darker side with bats, rats, and plague. It is Stoker's version that inspired most movie versions, more than 170 to date. Beginning as early as 1896, dozens of screen vampires moved stealthily through the silent days of cinema, crossing borders from France, Sweden, Russia, England, or the United States. Many of these figures were not bats but "vamps," sexy *femmes fatales* who drained men of their money instead of blood, a sign that women could be active agents as well as passive prey.

One the best vampire movies of the period was German, F.W. Murnau's *Nosferatu* (*Nosferatu, eine Symphonie des Grauens*, 1922). Murnau based his story on Stoker's tale, changing the monster's name to Count Orlok because he couldn't obtain rights to the book. Orlok, played by Max Schreck, is a sinister creature with a rodent's face and long, clawed fingers (Figure 3.3). The ship transporting him to Germany arrives with every crew member dead. Once in the city of Wisborg, he carries his own coffin and casts a lean shadow strangely detached from his body. Like the parade of counts before and after him, Orlok has a preference for female victims. In the film's climactic scene, his shadow creeps suggestively over Ellen's body as he approaches her bed. But she is not just Orlok's prey. She is a hunter too, for she has read the book on vampires and knows that he will die if he lingers at her bedside long enough to be pierced by the rays of the rising sun.

In 1932, Danish director Carl Theodor Dreyer made *Vampyr* (*Der Traum des Allan Grey*), based on a different source of vampire tales, so its antagonist lacks the cape and noble pedigree of Stoker's Dracula. As an artist, Dreyer was more interested in originality than in clarity. Instead of avoiding wordless scenes and fuzzy photography, he turned them to advantage, producing more of an avant-garde art film than a work for popular entertainment (Figure 3.4).

Most of these silent films, including *Vampyr*, might be classified as "experimental" in Focillon's scheme. They worked out the basic settings, scenes, and iconography – the moldy castles, shipboard rats, and death by sunlight – that soon became standards of the genre. These conventions were not fully fixed or stabilized until the 1930s, when the horror film arrived at something like a classical stage. Tod Browning's *Dracula* (1931) set many of the industry standards (Figure 3.5). Produced in Hollywood by Universal Studios, this time with legal film rights to the novel, *Dracula* was conceived as a lavish production with big box office potential. In contrast to Schreck's Orlok, Bela Lugosi's Count Dracula is charismatic and

FIGURES 3.3–3.10   A global gallery of movie vampires.

FIGURE 3.3   F.W. Murnau's *Nosferatu* (*Nosferatu, eine Symphonie des Grauens*, 1922), Germany.

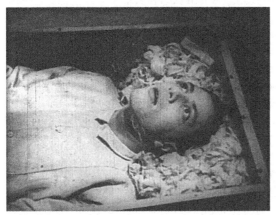

FIGURE 3.4   Carl Theodor Dreyer's *Vampyr* (*Der Traum des Allan Grey*, 1932), Denmark.

FIGURE 3.5   Tod Browning's *Dracula* (1931), USA.

FIGURE 3.6   *Dracula Has Risen From the Grave* (Dir. Freddie Francis, 1968), UK.

FIGURE 3.7   *Blacula* (Dir. William Crain, 1972), USA.

FIGURE 3.8   *Spooky Encounters* (*Gui da gui*, Dir. Sammo Hung Kam-Bo, 1980), Hong Kong.

FIGURE 3.9   Thomas Alfredson's *Let the Right One In* (*Låt den rätte komma in*, 2008), Sweden.

FIGURE 3.10   Catherine Hardwicke's *Twilight* (2008), USA.

refined. With his black cape and slicked back hair, he presides over his castle like a matinee idol. No wonder the ladies fall for him. With an eye on the overseas market, Universal produced a Spanish version simultaneously, employing a new director and cast. The American crew filmed by day, the Spanish crew by night, sharing the same sets, even the same cue marks, but with costumes and dialogue that reflected differences in culture. When the Spanish John Harker knocks at the castle door, Lugosi's counterpart greets him in perfect Spanish: "*Soy Dracula. Esta usted en su casa,*" which translates roughly as "I am Dracula. My house is your house."[10]

Flushed with success, Universal delivered a full line of offspring, including *Dracula's Daughter* (1936) and *Son of Dracula* (1943). Other countries followed suit, adding to the vampire's repertoire. Italy gave him a lurid, sexual appetite in *Lust of a Vampire* (1956); Mexico elongated his fangs in *El Vampiro* (1957). In England, Hammer Film Productions turned out its first Dracula film in 1958, released in the United States as *Horror of Dracula* and starring Christopher Lee as a sophisticated Count. This was followed by *The Brides of Dracula* (1960), *Dracula: Prince of Darkness* (1966), and *Dracula Has Risen from the Grave* (1968, see Figure 3.6). Germany, Sweden, and other countries, mostly European, each contributed its own cultural touches to the legend.

While it may be problematic to label any of these developments as an age of *refinement*, as Focillon might use the term, many of the films did offer formal variations and embellishments of style. As Dracula matured through the 1960s into the 1970s, he adapted his appearance to each new generation. There were vampire Westerns (*Billy the Kid vs. Dracula*, 1966), black vampires (*Blacula*, 1972, see Figure 3.7), lesbian vamps (*La vampire nue*, 1970; *Vampyros lesbos*, 1970), even X-rated vampires (*Lust at First Bite*, 1978). Some of these were playful reworkings of the classical material, self-consciously reflexive in the manner of Focillon's *baroque* stage. Roman Polanski spoofed the Hammer films in *The Fearless Vampire Killers* (1967). In *Love at First Bite* (1979), the Count is expelled from his castle by the communists and flies to New York, where a snafu at the airport sends his coffin to the wrong address, in Harlem. John Badham's sexy *Dracula* (1979) starred Frank Langella, who brought the charismatic count to life yet again in an award-winning Broadway stage production. Mel Brooks added his own zany brand of parody in *Dracula: Dead and Loving It* (1995), with Brooks himself in the role of Van Helsing. More recently, blood-sucking monsters have appeared as young girls – for example, in *Let the Right One In* (*Låt den rätte komma in*, 2008), a Swedish film directed by Thomas Alfredson, see Figure 3.9 – or as handsome high school heart throbs, most notably in the popular Twilight Saga (2008–2012), see Figure 3.10.

These trends have not necessarily been chronological. Universal began poking fun at its own monsters in 1948, with *Bud Abbot and Lou Costello Meet Frankenstein*. There were hints of lesbian attraction in *Dracula's Daughter* (1936) and even earlier. In other words, there has been no strictly linear progression through predicable stages of development. Instead, the figure of the vampire appears and reappears in different guises and in various hybrid forms, horror mixed with comedy, science fiction, or romance.

Nor are vampires confined to the Western hemisphere. Stoker's Dracula and his descendants have been traced to the historical figure of Prince Vlad III of Romania, better known as "Vlad the Impaler," so named for the practice of impaling his enemies on wooden posts. Vlad's legend is associated with the name Dracula (his father was a *Dracul*, a member of the chivalric Order of the Dragon), the devil (referred to as a dragon in the bible), and local folklore about vampires (*vampir* or *upir* in Slavic languages). The diabolic qualities of Dracula the vampire in American and European horror films thus are coded as mysterious, foreign, and evil. Vampire-like creatures that refuse to die and feed off the living appear in other cultures too. In China, for example, a tradition of the "hungry ghost" or "stiff corpse" (called *jiangshi* in Mandarin and *geong si* in Cantonese) dates back to seventeenth-century Chinese literature and even earlier. In the movies, these creatures dress in old-fashioned Mandarin robes instead of capes, have long, blue, fang-like fingernails, and suck their victim's breath (*qi*) instead of blood. Whereas Dracula's pagan powers are subject to the forces of Christianity, the Chinese ghost thrives and fails within the belief systems of Buddhism and Taoism, China's two great religions. For Buddhists, death and damnation are not permanent states but transitory phases on the path to reincarnation and enlightenment. For Taoists, the troubled human soul is not caught in a battle between good and evil, but is on a journey to find internal and external harmony. Ghosts wander the earth and haunt the living because of some imbalance: an unpunished wrong, an unrequited love. Once balance is restored, the ghost is free to rejoin the cycle of rebirth. So while *jiangshi* and *geong si* can appear threatening and scary, they can also be sympathetic characters for a Chinese audience since what happens to the hungry ghosts can happen to anyone.

The Hong Kong film industry revived the *geong si* figure in the 1970s and 1980s. In an effort to fill the vacuum left by Bruce Lee's death in 1973, the local Shaw Brothers Studio collaborated with British Hammer Studios to make *The Legend of the 7 Golden Vampires*. Peter Cushing was cast in the role of Van Helsing, who sets out to fight a band of vampires in rural China with his student (Hong Kong actor David Chiang) and seven siblings, all trained in the martial arts. The film combines elements of British horror (Dracula is disguised as a Taoist monk), kung fu boxing, and *wuxia* swordplay, with nods to Kurosawa's *Seven Samurai*. It also adds a few stylistic innovations; the undead move at the pace of over-cranked silent motion pictures and their bodies slowly disintegrate to nothing when pierced through the heart. *The Legend of the 7 Golden Vampires* was not much of a hit in either hemisphere, but it set a precedent for future films. Martial arts performer and producer Sammo Hung made the *geong si* the central figure in a successful cycle of horror-comedies, beginning with *Spooky Encounters* (*Gui da gui*, 1980) and continuing through a series of Mr. Vampire films. The monster in these movies, stiffened by *rigor mortis*, attacks its victims in a series of standing jumps with outstretched arms, until it is vanquished, usually by a Taoist priest with the help of spells and charms (Figure 3.8). Marketed in the West as the "Chinese hopping vampire," the *geong si* soon became a transnational phenomenon, one that might be seen as a form of global vampirism, Hong Kong rejuvenating local traditions and its own film industry with infusions of foreign iconography. Or it might be regarded as a way of representing national anxieties of identity, the former colony of Hong King precariously poised between administrative autonomy and control by mainland China.

In this respect, it is worth remembering that the vampire has always been a metaphor for perceived threats. To the Victorians of Stoker's England, Dracula personified the fear of foreign invasion, of the predatory beast that prowls beneath the gentleman's civility. Some may see the vampire as the devil incarnate, a treacherous force in the struggle of evil against good. Freudians may regard it as an image of repressed sexuality. Jungians may find an archetype of the shadow self, a devious shape shifter, or the voraciously possessive personality that drains the vitality from other human beings. Marx himself made an analogy to the consuming greed of a capitalist economy in *Das Kapital*, writing that "capital is dead labor which, vampire-like, lives by sucking living labor, and lives more, the more labor it sucks."[11]

In this thumbnail account of vampire films, it is possible to see many of the forces at work in the horror genre at large. A monster taken from the realm of literature, folklore, history, or myth becomes the central figure in a movie. As more filmmakers appropriate this figure, embellishing its appearance, adding new scenes and plot twists to the story, there emerges a cycle of films bearing certain family resemblances to each other. If the cycle coalesces, stabilized by established conventions of content and style, it may be recognized as a series, a genre, or a subgenre. This serves certain practical purposes of the movie industry. Filmmakers have an outline within which to practice their creativity, producers get a hook for marketing their products, and fans get to count on a familiar experience at the theatre. At the same time, students and scholars find a convenient category for studying a corner of film history, for exploring the monster's symbolic dimensions, for uncovering the themes that underlie its stories. As directors seek new directions, breaking the mold, creating new ones, the form is tested, enlarged, hybridized, self-consciously imitated, and spoofed. Meanwhile, all along the way, films from different eras and cultures influence each other through a process of trans-historical, transnational cross-pollination. With this abbreviated, necessarily simplified account in mind, we turn to a wider look at horror and its history.

Gothic Ghosts and Grand Guignol Gore

Before there were scary movies, there were scary tales and scary spectacles. The tales most pertinent to the history of horror in the West are known as Gothic, a term associated with the medieval castles and ruined abbeys in which these stories are often set. Bram Stoker's *Dracula* is part of this tradition, which includes Horace Walpole's *Castle of Otranto* (1764), Ann Radcliffe's *The Mysteries of Udolpho* (1794), and Matthew Lewis's *The Monk* (1796). These late eighteenth-century English novels evoked a supernatural world of ghosts and spirits, a world haunted by past sins and enduring evils. Gothic literature was an outgrowth of Romanticism, a protest against the confining scientific rationalism of eighteenth-century Enlightenment. Romantic writers appealed to the emotions rather than the mind. They found truth and beauty in raw nature, a sublime greatness beyond rational understanding. In the face of nature's power and sheer immensity, they were inspired by a sense of awe. Radcliffe refers to this awesome power when she distinguishes between terror and horror: "the first expands the soul, and awakens the faculties to a high degree of life; the other contracts, freezes, and nearly annihilates them."[12] Gothic is more about terror than horror.

A new generation of writers swept this movement into the nineteenth century. It is their work – chiefly Mary Wollstonecraft Shelley's *Frankenstein; or, The Modern Prometheus* (1818), Robert Louis Stevenson's *Strange Case of Dr. Jekyll and Mr. Hyde* (1886), and Stoker's *Dracula* (1897) – that provided the monsters, narratives, eerie locations, and creepy iconography for Universal's horror movies of the 1930s.

Meanwhile, on the Continent, a new form of popular entertainment was attracting crowds in Paris. They gathered in a tiny former chapel to watch second-rank actors stage graphic scenes of violent murder, torture, and mayhem. Their roles were taken from the city's low life: vagrants, street kids, street-walkers, criminals, and the terminally insane, who performed an endless cycle of stabbings, hangings, garrotings, electrocutions, mutilations, rapes, and other violations of the body on each other for the shocked amusement of the audience. This was the Théâtre du Grand Guignol, founded in 1897 by Oscar Méténier, playwright and former police clerk. Through two world wars, until its doors were closed in 1962, the Grand Guignol continued to push the envelope of narrative coherence and good taste. Placing gruesome spectacle above the niceties of story, its blatant horrors contrasted with the elevated terror of Gothic literature. The aim was shock rather than awe. As cinema began to take on the narrative functions of novels and the performance role of plays, these two tendencies – the supernatural terrors of Gothic ghosts and the realistic horror of Grand Guignol gore – would take various shapes in the horror film.

Soundless Screams on Silent Screens

In *The Horror Genre*, Paul Wells reminds us that "the history of the horror film is essentially a history of anxiety in the twentieth century."[13] Tracing the genre's trajectory through the course of American cinema decade by decade can offer insights into the foremost anxieties of each generation. By extending the investigation further to horror films from other lands, we can learn what has historically troubled people in Spain, Japan, or India. Adam Lowenstein sees history in terms of cultural shocks, or traumas: "To speak of history's horrors, or historical trauma, is to recognize events as wounds."[14] A traumatic incident like the Spanish Civil War or the atom bomb dropped on Hiroshima leaves scars on the national consciousness,

FIGURE 3.11   The distorted aesthetics of German expressionism reflect inner states of mind in *The Cabinet of Dr. Caligari* (*Das Cabinet des Dr. Caligari*, Dir. Robert Wiene, 1920).

scars that show up as moments of cinematic horror. It is significant that the word trauma means wound in Greek and that the German word *Traum* means dream. Horror films project history as a nightmare endlessly repeated on our movie screens.

Probably the most significant historical trauma to haunt movies during the silent era was World War I. Although the battle in Europe lasted only four years, from 1914 to 1918, it left a long-term legacy of ruined landscapes, mutilated veterans, and traumatized populations. In Germany, where the human toll was greatest (more than 2 million military deaths, some 3.8% of the country's population), the war's devastating aftershocks are visible in films like *The Cabinet of Dr. Caligari* (*Das Cabinet des Dr. Caligari*, 1920), *The Golem* (*Der Golem, wie er in die Welt kam*, 1920), and *Nosferatu* (1922). Dr. Caligari appears as an enigmatic hypnotist whose carnival attraction features a sleepwalker named Cesare. Under Caligari's command, Cesare stalks the town in his sleep at night, performing acts of murder. The film's narrator traces the murders back to Caligari, revealed to be the mad director of an insane asylum (Figure 3.11). Or is he? An epilogue informs us that the real madman is the narrator, an inmate in Dr. Caligari's state-run institution. This explains the film's distorted cinematography and set design. The village streets meet at jagged angles, flanked by lopsided houses with irregular windows and doors. The interiors are structurally off kilter, with elongated furniture and trapezoidal walls. What's more, there seems to be no natural source of light; the shadows are painted on. The effect of this strange imagery is heightened by slanted camera angles and exaggerated gestures by the actors. *Caligari's* departure from photographic realism belongs to the aesthetics of Expressionism, an experimental art movement that sought to represent inner states of mind on canvas or a movie screen instead of trying to copy reality objectively.

The movie's surprising plot twist generated much debate among viewers and German film historians. Writing soon after World War II, Siegfried Kracauer argued that the added ending was a form of censorship designed to disguise the film's original critique of tyrannical authority, a malevolent state that sent a generation of Cesares to do its dirty work as soldiers on the battlefields of Europe.[15] In this view, German Expressionism is a fitting style to signify a world gone mad. More recently, however, Thomas Elsaesser has offered an alternative interpretation, asserting that the film's Expressionist style was more of a production strategy, a way to distinguish German films from their more realistic American counterparts.[16] In any event, many of the artists who worked on these films in Germany brought their skills, styles, and memories with them when they emigrated to Hollywood in the 1930s and 1940s. The distortions of Expressionism, so well suited to the psychology of horror, continued to influence directors like Alfred Hitchcock and Tim Burton as the genre moved on.

Meanwhile, another artistic trend was gaining momentum in France. Surrealism, like Expressionism, has strong connections to World War I. Writers and painters who experienced the war first hand came to blame its horrors on a repressive rationalism and oppressive institutions. In their eyes, modern science was not a benign, progressive force but a pernicious tool for fashioning new weapons to injure and enslave humanity. Their "Surrealist Manifesto," published in 1924, launched a revolutionary movement to liberate imagination from what they regarded as the shackles of rationality. This meant, among other things, delving into the realm of dreams described by Freud. Surrealist stories follow the tangled illogic of free association, jumping from one event to another with no clear sense of narrative continuity. Surrealist imagery depicts impossible landscapes and fantastic creatures, reflecting inner visions free from fidelity to "the real world." While potentially liberating, these visions could also be quite scary. Luis Buñuel and Salvador Dalí's short avant-garde film, *Un chien andalou* (1929), contains one of the most horrifying images ever caught on celluloid, involving a razor blade and a woman's eye. Although the Surrealist movement, like Expressionism, was relatively short lived, it too would play an important part in the history of horror movies, reappearing in such nightmarish fantasies as Georges Franju's *Eyes Without a Face* (*Les yeux sans visage*, 1960), David Cronenberg's *Videodrome*, and Guillermo del Toro's *Pan's Labyrinth* (*El laberinto del fauno*, 2006).

Across the Atlantic, far from the battlefields of Germany and France, monsters began stalking the silent screen well before the war. In 1908, Chicago's Selig Polyscope Company made the first Dr. Jekyll and Mr. Hyde picture. In 1910, J. Searle Dawley directed the industry's first Frankenstein in the Bronx, New York for the Edison Company. Fearing a negative reception, Edison played up the story's moral message, toning down the more sensational attributes of Mary Shelley's creation. D.W. Griffith followed a similar strategy in 1914, when he directed *The Avenging Conscience* for Mutual, based on a story by Edgar Allan Poe. But as the industry migrated westward to Hollywood, studio heads at Paramount, MGM, and Universal took bolder steps to shock their audiences with explicitly gruesome images of horror. The master of this new phase was Lon Chaney, "the Man of a Thousand Faces," who specialized in characters afflicted by hideous deformities. The child of deaf parents, Chaney became adept at pantomime, a useful skill for silent film acting. His elaborate experiments with makeup set new standards of grotesqueness. As Quasimodo in *The Hunchback of Notre Dame* (1924) and the masked organist in *The Phantom of the Opera*, elaborate spectacles produced by Universal, Chaney managed to evoke both pity and disgust. In his perceptive and engrossing book, *The Monster Show*, David Skal links these films to battle wounds. Although there are no direct references to the Great War in either story, Skal points out that the settings (Paris) and the physical deformities (the disfigured face, the limp) could be read as allusions to the trauma of combat.[17]

The 1930s: Universal's Classic Monsters

With the coming of sound technology in the 1930s, the monsters found a voice, although more often they spoke with foreign accents or in incoherent grunts and growls. Bela Lugosi's performance in *Dracula* and Boris Karloff's in *Frankenstein* and *The Mummy* (1932) set iconic standards for their characters within the first few years of the decade, and all for Universal Studios. Emboldened by the earlier success of Lon Chaney's Hunchback and Phantom, Universal's studio head Carl Laemmle, Jr. bet that a parade of horrifying figures would draw big audiences and bigger box office revenues. Chaney had died in 1930, but Laemmle found new talent and invested in expensive spectacles, launching what is now widely called the golden age of classic horror films. Its titles include *Bride of Frankenstein* (1935), *Dracula's Daughter* (1936), *Son of Frankenstein* (1939), and *The Wolf Man* (1941).

The Universal monsters and their enemies act out archetypal battles between evil and good, embodying enduring anxieties about human nature. *Dracula* casts Van Helsing as the wise old man, a figure of reason and knowledge up against the vampire's supernatural powers. Dracula's threat lies in his great strength, his uncanny shape-shifting skills, and the potential to turn humans into his own likeness. So when Van Helsing drives the wooden stake into the demon's heart, it is a triumph of the moral order over anarchy and darkness. In *Frankenstein*, by contrast, the man of knowledge is neither fully good nor wise. As a scientist, Dr. Frankenstein takes excessive pride in his profession and its potential powers. In a laboratory animated with chemical reactions and electrical energy, he has patched together pieces of inert matter into a living construct. When his creation begins to stir, Frankenstein boasts, "Now I know what it feels like to be God." By the film's end, we are more likely to sympathize with the monster than with the doctor. *The Wolf Man* explores another archetypal figure from folklore and myth, the shape-shifting werewolf that can transform itself from man into beast. If the Frankenstein monster plays out the human fear of becoming robotized, the werewolf is about the animal in us. A variation of this story was told earlier in Paramount's *Dr. Jekyll and Mr. Hyde* (1931) and later in MGM's film of the same title (1941). In the case of Jekyll and Hyde, however, it seems that science, not nature, is to blame for the alteration in identity.

Stylistically as well as thematically, Universal's monster movies owe something to trends imported from abroad. *Frankenstein's* director, James Whale, is said to have prepared himself by screening several Expressionist films from Germany, including *Caligari*. We see a German influence in the film's high contrast lighting, in the monster's stylized gestures, the tilted camera angles, and the castle's exaggerated architecture. The debt is even more pronounced in *Bride of Frankenstein*, also directed by Whale. David Skal sees another European influence on Universal horror in the form of surrealist imagery and themes. For Skal, these horror films serve as a kind of "populist surrealism, rearranging the human body and its processes, blurring the boundaries between Homo sapiens and other species, responding uneasily to new and almost incomprehensible developments in science."[18] When we add the fact that all these stories come from British literary sources and that many of the studio personnel were immigrants, it becomes clear that Hollywood was then, as it always has been, something of a global phenomenon.

This may be one reason why Hollywood horror appealed not only to Americans but to audiences the world over. The big studios had big budgets to make and distribute films with high production values, but the stories that they chose to tell resonated widely. During the Great Depression of the 1930s, monster movies offered a welcome escape from the daily struggle to survive. In his first inaugural address in 1933, Franklin D. Roosevelt spoke famously of fear: "the only thing we have to fear is fear itself – nameless, unreasoning, unjustified terror which paralyzes needed efforts to convert retreat into advance." Horror movies gave fear a local habitation and a name. After looking into the face of Karloff or Lugosi and releasing a therapeutic scream, filmgoers might be free to catch their breath and move on.

The 1940s: World War II and Horror Noir

Within a few years of FDR's speech, the world would face new traumas in the form of another world war. Hollywood's studios turned much of their attention to the war effort, producing propaganda films and combat features. Only two A-budget horror films were made during the 1940s – the 1941 version of *Dr. Jekyll and Mr. Hyde* and Universal's remake of *The Phantom of the Opera* (1943), with Claude Rains – but B-grade genre films continued to find an audience. The Wolf Man figure was particularly popular, appearing three times during the war, perhaps because the brutality of battle brought out the beast in man. In retrospect, however, the most important horror movies of the time were produced by RKO. Between 1942 and 1946, the studio turned out nine low-budget genre films, all made under the supervision of producer/screenwriter Val Lewton.

FIGURE 3.12 *Cat People* (Dir. Jacques Tourneur, 1942) reflects producer Val Lewton's fascination with Freudian psychology and film noir aesthetics.

The first of these was *Cat People* (1942), directed by French-born Jacques Tourneur. Intended to compete with Universal's *Wolf Man*, *Cat People* was just a title before it was a script. The first treatment for the story was set in the Balkans, where a Nazi Panzer division invades a village. At night, the villagers turn into giant cats and attack the Nazis, while one girl runs away to New York, still haunted by the cat-people curse. In the final treatment, set entirely in New York, this girl becomes Irena, the story's troubled protagonist (Figure 3.12). Irena meets a man, falls in love, and marries him, but believing she will turn into a panther if she sleeps with him, she keeps putting him off. The plot reflects Lewton's fascination with Freudian psychology and a certain cynicism about its practitioners. When Irena seeks the help of a psychiatrist, the doctor advises her to face her fears by submitting to her feelings, offering himself as a willing object. At that point, she becomes a feline beast and rips him apart. Under Tourneur's artful direction, the film is subtler than its storyline. He gives more attention to creating a suspenseful atmosphere than to showing graphic images. Most of the horror is left to the viewer's imagination. Is the curse real or only in her mind? Does Irena actually change her shape, or is she a victim of social pressure, becoming what people expect her to be? An eerie night scene in which a panther's tracks seem to turn into a woman's shoe prints leaves us wondering.

Tourneur's next film for Val Lewton was *I Walked with a Zombie* (1943). The story is narrated in flashback by a nurse, who has come to a Caribbean island to care for the sick wife of a plantation owner. One night, she hears a woman crying in a dark tower and encounters the wife walking in a kind of trance. Further investigations reveal dark secrets. The plantation workers, descendants of African slaves, practice voodoo in the hills. There are hints of jealousies, manipulation, betrayals, perhaps madness in the owner's family. As the nurse probes deeper, she is caught up in passionate attachments that she hardly recognizes. These Gothic elements – an intricate plot, voice-over narration, supernatural forces, a house haunted by family ghosts, intimations of repressed sexuality – give the film a literary quality and open it to intricate interpretations. Is the voodoo magic real or a clever cover for more mundane motives and methods? Is the wife's illness a physical condition, a curse, or part of a sinister plot? Can the story be explained through Freudian psychology as an expression of deferred desires and unconscious drives? Is it a critique of an economic system that makes slaves of human workers to benefit a privileged few? And what does the film say about the roles of women as caretakers, wives, mothers, and lovers?[19]

The Lewton/Tourneur films make more sense if we see them in the context of a larger trend, commonly known as *film noir*. The term was first applied to certain Hollywood productions of the 1940s and 1950s by French critics, who noticed patterns linking them together. These movies, mostly crime films, have a dark look (stark, black and white photography; low-key lighting that casts long shadows; dimly illuminated night scenes, often in the rain) to match a cynical outlook on life. The events in these films are typically presented in flashback, accompanied by the voice-over narration of one character, unfolding in a maze of convoluted subplots. Odd camera angles and startling point-of-view shots, borrowed from German Expressionism, contribute to a sense of unsettling disorientation. The central female figure in *film noir* is usually seductive and untrustworthy, a vamp, adding an erotic subtext to the story.

Viewed historically, the stylistic and thematic attributes of *film noir* can be regarded as expressions of the war. American servicemen who set out for battle under a flag of idealism, returned from Europe scarred by their experience. They brought back with them a darker view of life, a moral skepticism; life no longer looked as simple as it once seemed. Women, too, appeared in a different light. American women had taken jobs previously occupied by men, a threat to male dominance in the workplace and to male egos. And what, exactly, were the wives and sweethearts doing on the home front when their men were off at war? These suspicions and anxieties are written into the texts of films like *Cat People* and *I Walked with a Zombie*, another instance of how horror movies reflect the fears of the times. By the end of the decade, a new kind of war would generate new worries and new monsters.

The 1950s: Creature Features and the Cold War

If Americans entered the 1950s with renewed hopes for lasting peace, their illusions were soon shattered. The decade began with a bitter conflict in Korea and ended with another one in Vietnam. Fueling the hostilities was a worldwide contest between two superpowers and two ideologies. What made the Cold War different from other forms of warfare – and there were plenty of hot spots around the globe – was the chilling threat of nuclear annihilation. Both the United States and the Union of Soviet Socialist Republics (USSR) had enough atomic weapons to destroy the planet several times over.

While few people might want to face their fears of the Bomb directly, they came in droves to watch a giant dinosaur destroy Manhattan in *The Beast from 20,000 Fathoms* (1953) and an oversized octopus attack San Francisco in *It Came from Beneath the Sea* (1955). The subliminal messages in such films were never far beneath the surface. Both creatures are the byproducts of atomic testing, and both are finally vanquished with nuclear weapons. All through the 1950s, audiences never seemed to tire of these mutant monsters, and Hollywood kept them coming. American cities were assaulted by a steady stream of colossal ants (*Them!*,,1954), enormous spiders (*Tarantula*, 1955), and overgrown crustaceans (*Attack of the Crab Monsters*, 1957). These immense, unthinking beings replaced the classic monsters of the 1930s, which now seemed quaint and puny by comparison. They pushed the reach of horror into the realm of science fiction, where not just individuals but entire cities are at risk.

The planet itself was also threatened by a series of invasion narratives, stories in which the monsters are alien aggressors from the red planet Mars and other extra-terrestrial launching pads. One of the most important of these films is *Invasion of the Body Snatchers* (1956), generally seen as an allegory of Cold War conflicts. What makes this film so frightening is that the aliens look just like normal people. By replacing friends and neighbors one by one with perfect replicas of their own species, the Pod People plan to take over the world. One of the most memorable scenes is when one of the main characters turns into one of them in her companion's arms. He runs into the street, yelling at the motorists, and at the audience: "They're after you. They're after all of us. … They're here already! You're next!" Some viewers interpret the film as a cautionary tale about communism, warning how Soviet-style conformity turns humans into unthinking automatons. Others see it as a condemnation of McCarthyism, casting the Senator's followers as mindless clones who have lost their individuality in pods of political compliance. Either way, Don Siegel's ideologically ambiguous direction illustrates how genre pictures fed the paranoia of the age.

The Cold War and its terrors were hardly limited to Hollywood. In 1954, a year after Warner Bros. released its beast from 20,000 fathoms and RKO re-released *King Kong*, Japan's Toho Studios unleashed *Godzilla* (*Gojira*, 1954). The 400-foot dinosaur, awakened from its prehistoric slumber in the ocean by atomic radiation, was a clear reference to past and present dangers (Figure 3.13). For Japanese audiences, fears of nuclear-generated monsters were especially tangible and immediate. Not only did they experience the trauma of Hiroshima and Nagasaki first hand in 1945, but they also watched in helpless horror when the United States exploded its first H-bomb on an island near Japan in 1953. The bomb proved much more powerful than expected, spreading fallout and sickness throughout the area, catching a Japanese fishing boat within its deadly circle. Strictly speaking, this subgenre of non-human monster movies, known as *kaiju eiga* in Japan, is closer to

FIGURE 3.13 *Godzilla* (*Gojira*, Dir. Ishiro Honda, 1954): Japan's monster from the deep evokes the global threat of nuclear annihilation during the Cold War.

science fiction than to horror. There is another Japanese tradition of ghost stories (*kaidan*), more akin to British Gothic and the Universal classics of the 1930s. Originally based on Buddhist cautionary tales and set in Japan's feudal past, these stories tell of restless spirits, or *yurei*, usually women, who return from the dead to avenge a wrong or fulfill some unsatisfied need before they can pass on to another life. In *Ugetsu* (*Ugetsu monogatari*, 1953), a potter who deserts his wife to follow his self-centered dreams is seduced by a beautiful lady who turns out to be a deadly ghost. In *The Ghost Story of Yotsuya* (*Tokaido Yotsuya kaidan*, 1959), based on a Kabuki play, an ambitious, wicked samurai is haunted by the spirit of his murdered wife. Such movies play to the anxieties of overreaching and unfaithful men, but they also dramatize the dangers of armed violence. Both are set during times of war when women suffer from the military ambitions of their husbands. This theme is even more pronounced in *Onibaba* (1964), with symbolic references to Hiroshima. The two women in this film are the wife and the mother of a man missing in battle. In order to survive in their war-torn land, they resort to hunting wounded warriors and selling their armor for food. One day, the mother is captured by a samurai wearing a demon mask. Frightened but resourceful, she leads him to the brink of a huge hole filled with the skeletons of her victims, where he falls to his death. Later, when she uses the mask to frighten her daughter-in-law, it fuses to her skin so that when finally removed, it reveals a face hideously scarred. Her disfigurement evokes the traumas of 1945 (director Kaneto Shindo based the scars on photographs of radiation victims) just as the bone-strewn hole recalls the bomb crater of Hiroshima. In this way, *Onibaba* resurrects the ghosts of World War II and Japan's long military history.

China, as we've seen in the section on vampires, has its own tradition of restless ghosts. Supernatural spirits haunted Chinese films as far back as the 1930s. When they were banished from the mainland, first by Chiang Kai-shek's rightist regime, then by Mao Zedong's leftist government, filmmakers transported them to Hong Kong, where they spoke both Mandarin and Cantonese for regional audiences. Hong Kong, ever a culture on the crossroads, mixed strains of Chinese ghost lore with Gothic elements and other genres to produce hybrid horror films for local consumption and export. *A Maid's Bitter Story* (*Qiong lou hen*, 1949), in Mandarin, and *Ghost Woman of the Old Mansion* (*Guyuan yaoji*, 1949), in Cantonese, were favorites, showing that the most popular avenging spirits were often women.

In England, Hammer Studios reached its stride in the mid-1950s. William Hinds, a comedian and businessman, had started the company as Hammer Productions in 1934, using his stage name, Will Hammer. After banging out a few pictures, Hammer Studios went bankrupt but was resurrected by Hinds's son Anthony and the young man's partner James Carreras, supplying a stream of inexpensive "quota-quickies" to fill the need for local films after the war. Hinds and Carreras first ventured into horror and science fiction with a television serial, *The Quatermass Experiment* (1953), which they soon adapted for the big screen, renaming it *The Quatermass Xperiment* (1955) to capitalize on Britain's new X-rating for horror. The *Xperiment* was a success. Within the next few years, Hammer rolled out three big monster movies in quick succession: *The Curse of Frankenstein* (1957), *Horror of Dracula* (1958), and *The Mummy* (1959). In one sense, they seemed like rip-offs of Universal's 1930s classics; in another sense, this was Britain reclaiming its literary heritage. To widen the distinction between their films and Universal's, the producers at Hammer raised the level of screen violence, adding lurid color and unprecedented quantities of gore. They also introduced the directorial talents of Terence Fischer and two new actors, Peter Cushing and Christopher Lee, whose polished performances added a creepy sophistication to familiar roles.

Hammer had clearly struck a chord, sending shock waves back across the Atlantic, inspiring American filmmakers like Roger Corman, William Castle, and Herman Cohen to make low-budget, high-profit genre flicks. Corman, the "King of the Bs," began producing mischievously gruesome self-parodies like *A Bucket of Blood* (1959) and *The Little Shop of Horrors* (1960). His hectic sets served as boot camp for a long line of A-level directors, including Francis Ford Coppola, Martin Scorsese, Ron Howard, Peter Bogdanovich, Jonathan Demme, John Sayles, and James Cameron. William Castle, a consummate showman with a knack for gimmickry, focused more attention on the audience than on the picture itself. During showings of *House on Haunted Hill* (1959), the screen went black and a glowing skeleton sailed over the audience on a wire. For *The Tingler* (1959), selected seats were wired to vibrate during the film's spine-tingling finale. As the decade drew on, the market for these cheap scares kept growing, especially among young moviegoers. By 1958, nearly three-quarters of the audience were between the ages of 12 and 25.[20] Sensing this, producer Herman Cohen made up titles even before his films had stories. His *I Was a Teenage Werewolf* (1957) and *I Was a Teenage Frankenstein*

(1957) were released by American International Pictures (AIP), the same studio that sponsored Roger Corman.

Horror subgenres could make money by targeting niche markets, especially when they cultivated a cult following. One of the most peculiar variations came from south of the border: the Mexican wrestling horror film. Mexico had been making scary movies since the 1930s, although Westerns and melodramas usually were more popular. Then, in the 1950s, television broadcasts of professional wrestling, *lucha libre*, took the country by storm. In this free-style form of fighting, wrestlers assumed colorful personas, wore masks, and devised elaborate storylines about the good, the bad, and the ugly, much as they do now in the United States. It was a small step from the ring to the movie screen. In 1957, the same year that Fernando Méndez made *El vampiro*, he directed *The Body Snatcher* (*Ladrón de cadáveres*), in which a mad doctor implants a gorilla's brain in the head of a masked grappler. Within six years, Méndez made eight more successful horror films, and the *lucha libre* format became an industry staple. Here is yet another example of global hybridity, a deliberate blending of national culture (masked wrestlers, Mayan pyramids, Aztec mummies) with foreign ingredients (mad scientists, vampires, werewolves) for the international marketplace. Together with fantasy films, these "mexploitation" subgenres accounted for some 20% of the country's output, constituting the lion's share of commercial Latin American cinema imported by the United States.[21] An American entrepreneur named K. Gordon Murray made a small fortune redubbing and recutting them for AIP. To make these films more palatable to American fans, he added rock 'n' roll music to the fight scenes and erased bits of Mexican heritage. As with Japanese monster movies, a lot can be learned about cultural assumptions and identity by comparing Murray's cuts with the originals.

The 1960s: Psychos and Zombies, Civil Rights and Vietnam

In the first year of the next decade, three important films appeared at the other end of the lowbrow/highbrow movie spectrum: Georges Franju's *Eyes Without a Face* in France, Michael Powell's *Peeping Tom* in England, and Alfred Hitchcock's *Psycho* in the United States. Each film is a portrait of a psychopathic killer, more chillingly realistic in style and more deliberately artful than previous forms of recreational horror. Together, they raised the status and intensity of horror to new heights and set precedents for a new subgenre, the slasher film.

Born in 1912, Franju grew up on silent movies and lived through two world wars. Although steeped in the fantastic imagery of French surrealism, his early work in film was documentary. *The Blood of the Beasts* (*Le sang des bêtes*, 1948) explored the workday world of a Parisian slaughterhouse with unflinching shots of butchered animals. *Eyes Without a Face* was fiction, a horror thriller about a surgeon who removes the faces of his victims to replace his daughter's face, disfigured in an accident. In one of the film's most graphic scenes, he carves a mask of

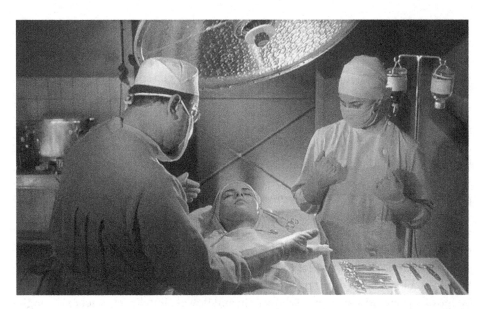

FIGURE 3.14 Georges Franju's *Eyes Without a Face* (*Les yeux sans visage*, 1960) is a French contribution to documentary realism and the psychopathic killer film.

flesh from a young girl while she is still alive, leaving only holes for her mouth and eyes (Figure 3.14). What makes the scene and the entire film so alarming is Franju's methodic, documentary approach to such a gruesome subject. His relentless focus on eyes is both an attack on modern science and a reproach to the audience. The doctor's passionate pursuit of medical experiments and his kennel of ferocious dogs make him all the more repugnant by linking him to Nazi Germany. A commercial craftsman as well as a gifted artist, Franju was highly conscious of a new demand for Euro-horror. One comment by him highlights the challenges of pleasing several national audiences at once: "When I shot *Eyes Without a Face*, I was told, 'No sacrilege because of the Spanish market, no nudes because of the Italian market, no blood because of the French market, and no martyrized animals because of the English market.' And I was supposed to be making a horror film!"[22]

Michael Powell's *Peeping Tom* also implicates the audience's voyeuristic guilty pleasures. This time, the eyes belong to both the victims and the murderer, a deeply disturbed young cinematographer who films his female prey before attacking them. Many of the scenes are presented through the lens of his camera, so that we are watching with the killer as his horrified victims witness their own demise. As in *Eyes Without a Face*, it is Powell's documentary style coupled with the protagonist's flawed humanity that makes the film so terrifying. The film was denounced in the press, and Powell's brilliant career was effectively ended. Hammer's Gothic films could be tolerated as harmless entertainment, but British society was not yet ready to accept Powell's searing realism and sympathetic portrait of a psychopathic monster.

It remained for Hitchcock, the acknowledged "Master of Suspense," to succeed with highbrow critics and popular audiences alike. *Psycho* was released as a thriller, not a horror film. One of its unexpected thrills is the departure of its female star, Janet Leigh, less than midway through the movie. To keep spectators from arriving late, Hitchcock instructed theatres to admit no-one after the film began. Moviegoers formed long lines to get in before the doors were closed. In retrospect, *Psycho* is regarded as a pivotal point between classic and modern horror, the prototype for American slasher movies with their contemporary domestic settings, psychoanalytic views of madness, and moral subtexts linking sexuality with death. Norman Bates seems to be an ordinary guy, a timid loner perhaps, until we realize he is possessed by his mother, by suppressed drives and murderous guilt if not by a supernatural spirit. The famous shower scene set new standards for editing, sound, and realistic violence. Nobody who sits through those three minutes of knife thrusts and bare flesh can forget the bewildering momentum of close-ups and shifting camera angles (some 50 cuts in all), the shrieking sound track, and the vortex of blood-stained water circling the drain, then dissolving into a rotating image of the victim's open eye. Like Franju and Powell, Hitchcock reaches through the screen, attacking the spectator's most vulnerable spot, the optic nerve.

The sixties witnessed the appearance of another menacing creature: the demon child. In 1961, British director Jack Clayton made *The Innocents*, based on Henry James's novella, *The Turn of the Screw*. The literary pedigree of Clayton's source material together with his choice of black and white photography signaled a departure from the garish Hammer films. While it is possible to read the movie as a supernatural tale of innocents possessed by angry ghosts, an alternate psychological interpretation makes perfect sense, and is no less frightening. Ordinary emotional forces that spin out of control and unhinge the mind can be as threatening – and as deadly – as mystical ghosts. Creepy children and sinister infants began showing up in films like *Rosemary's Baby* (1968) and *The Exorcist* (1973), leading some film historians to link the trend to anxieties about abortion and the oral contraceptive pill, first introduced in 1960.

Horror film directors kept inventing new monsters or resurrecting old ones to embody contemporary fears. In 1968, George Romero revolutionized the field with *Night of the Living Dead*. Romero's zombies attack en masse, not as individuals. They are not motivated by madness or revenge, but by a mindless urge to consume human flesh. In contrast to the charismatic monsters of old, these are ordinary people wearing housedresses and work clothes, sometimes no clothes at all, but driven forward like a force of nature. Since one bite from a zombie turns man, woman, or child into one of them, the zombie film feeds on the paranoia of contagion, not unlike the invasion narratives of the fifties. But in 1968, the nation was in the grip of more burning issues than the Cold War. The Vietcong had launched their Tet Offensive in January, and Americans could watch the enemy advance relentlessly on their television sets. Closer to home, racial conflicts flared as the Civil Rights Act went before Congress. It was a year of urban riots and political assassinations, including Robert Kennedy and Martin Luther King, Jr.

These events form the historical backdrop of Romero's film. By presenting the zombies as an unstoppable horde, making his characters fight among themselves, and staging a vigilante attack on a black man, Romero encouraged his audience to make connections to current events. His next zombie film (*Dawn of the Dead*, 1978) would suggest additional links to consumerism when the main characters take refuge in a shopping mall.

Meanwhile, the film industry itself felt threatened. Between 1948 and 1968, Hollywood had lost three-quarters of its audience, thanks to studio-busting legislation, the spread of television, and competing forms of outdoor entertainment. William Castle's gimmickry, AIP's teen horror pics, and fan magazines like *Famous Monsters of Filmland* were all part of an effort to attract crowds back to the theatres. As the public split into niche markets, the Motion Picture Association of America (MPAA) adopted a new rating system, classifying films for different age groups instead of censoring them outright. Castle, Cohen, and Corman continued to make sensational genre pictures. K. Gordon Murray carried on his profitable mexploitation campaign. In Britain, Hammer knocked off more sequels of *Frankenstein* and *Dracula*, spinning out mummy movies and psychological thrillers as well. Japan produced follow-ups to *Mothra* and *Onibaba*. Poland, Russia, West Germany, Sweden, and Brazil added their own spins to the genre.

One of the decade's most original developments in horror began in Italy, the home of Dante's *Inferno*, Michelangelo's *Last Judgment*, and other elaborate visions of hell. In 1961, Mario Bava scored an international hit with *Black Sunday* (*La maschera del demonio*), a vampire film loosely based on Nikolai Gogol's Russian short story, "Viy." Stylish and shocking, alternating between expressionist lyricism and Grand Guignol gore, *Black Sunday* was followed by *Black Sabbath* (*I tre volti della paura*, 1963), taken from a tale by Leo Tolstoy, with Boris Karloff appearing as the vampire. Bava made dozens of movies in a variety of genres and styles, but he is best remembered for his contributions to *giallo* (Italian for yellow), a genre of literature and film named after the cover of cheap paperback thrillers popular in postwar Italy. Bava's operatic excesses, his interest in spectacle over story, and the morbid sexuality running through his work were strong influences on other Italian filmmakers like Lucio Fulci and Dario Argento (see Close-up: *Suspiria*) as well as American directors like Joe Dante, John Carpenter, and Tim Burton in the following decades.

The 1970s: Stalking the American Family

In many ways, the sixties persisted well into the next decade. The war in Vietnam dragged on until 1975, inciting further protests from young people alienated from the values of their parents. Feminists and environmentalists raised their voices louder, championing the cause of women's liberation, marching to protect the planet's natural resources from corporate greed. The hippie movement expanded its experiments with free love and hallucinatory drugs. But by the middle of the decade, things began to change. The economies of the United States and other industrialized nations took a turn for the worse, except for Japan, which grew more prosperous. The Cold War was showing signs of thawing with new moderating leadership in China and the Soviet Union. Throughout the world, a new spirit of conservatism was taking hold, reflected in the Margaret Thatcher government in England and Augusto Pinochet's regime in Chile. In America, the media were now speaking of the "Me decade," signaling a break with the previous generation's emphasis on community and commitment.

In the movies, the American family became a focal point for deep concerns about traditional values and the basic social unit that was supposed to harbor them. Wes Craven's *The Hills Have Eyes* (1977) begins as a family road movie. Its middle-class family, the Carters, is traveling through the Nevada desert on vacation. Parents Bob and Ethel are in the family station wagon that pulls the trailer with their two teenage children. With them are the Carters' eldest daughter, her husband, and the young couple's baby girl. What they don't know is that another family is watching from the hills. Brutish and uneducated, these denizens of the desert survive by scavenging equipment from the nearby military base and killing travelers for food. Papa Jupiter, the patriarch, was born a mutant, apparently the victim of nuclear testing. Violent as a child, he set fire to his own house with his little sister in it. His male children, all named after planets, were raised in the beastly likeness of their father. At first, this family of subhuman monsters appears to be the Carters' mirror opposite, but as the two groups battle for survival, the differences begin to disappear. Big Bob Carter is a retired police officer, a hyper-masculine father figure who rules the roost with an iron hand. He has armed the men in his family with guns and two Alsatian dogs, but they are strangers in a hostile land. The men in Jupiter's tribe employ guerilla tactics reminiscent of Vietnam. They stalk their prey at night through the familiar countryside, regarding the Carters as invaders, using binoculars and walkie-talkies stolen from the Air Force to communicate with one another. If horror films are about survival, Craven's movie questions what it takes to stay alive. The scariest violence is not committed against the Carters but used by them in self-defense. The cold-blooded trickery and fierce aggression to which they resort turn the American family inside out.

Papa Jupiter and his clan of cannibals recall another family, the antagonists in Tobe Hooper's *The Texas Chain Saw Massacre*. Released three years before *The Hills Have Eyes*, Hooper's breakthrough film set the bar for what has been variously called the slasher movie, urbanoia, and hillbilly horror. To be sure, psychotic killers already had been practicing their dirty work with scalpels, knives, and pointed camera tripods in films by Franju, Powell, and Hitchcock, but Hooper moved the violence to rural America, adding an extra layer of cynicism and repugnant imagery. His film begins with a somber voice over a scrolling text in black and white, suggesting that we are about to witness a true story, "one of the most bizarre crimes in the annals of American history." Before any image appears on the black screen, we hear the sounds of someone shoveling dirt. Then a series of strange objects flashes on the screen, sporadically at first, too quickly to make out, then uncomfortably identifiable: a mutilated hand, a damaged foot, two sets of gnarled elongated fingers, an empty eye socket, a human head badly decomposed. The camera fixes on the head, slowly zooming out to show the body propped up against a neighboring corpse. Another voice, a radio announcement, explains that this "grisly work of art" has just been found in a rural Texas cemetery. After this disturbing news, the story begins. A group of youngsters on a road trip – Sally and Franklin Hardesty with three friends – stop to pick up a hitchhiker, their first mistake. Hitchhiker belongs to a family that lives near an abandoned slaughterhouse. Like Jupiter's clan, they are degenerates subsisting on the margins of civilized society. When their workplace closed, they took to slaughtering humans and selling their meat as barbecue. The baby of the family is Leatherface, a demonic figure who seems to come from nowhere and everywhere at once, hunting the travelers one by one. Hooper's film drips with gruesome, adolescent comedy. In one scene, Leatherface invites Sally to their supper table as both a guest and the main entrée, escorting her to an "arm chair" made of severed limbs. But viewers have also found serious messages in the story. For Tony Williams, the Leatherface family is a nihilistic mirror of the Hardestys, "the dark embodiment of the American dream, losers within American ideology."[23]

If *The Texas Chain Saw Massacre* and *The Hills Have Eyes* dramatized America's uneasiness about mistreating marginalized groups, the nation's apprehensions about abusing nature and the human body found expression through two other subgenres: Eco-Horror and Body Horror. In the sixties, flying creatures had taken vengeance on humanity in Hitchcock's *The Birds* (1963) and in the British horror film, *The Deadly Bees* (1966). In the seventies, animals with fins (*Jaws*, 1975) and fur (*The Pack*, 1977) got their turn. Fears about mutation, contagion, deformity, and parasites took dreadful shapes in films like Larry Cohen's *It's Alive* (1974), David Cronenberg's *Shivers* (1975), David Lynch's *Eraserhead* (1977), and Ridley Scott's *Alien* (1979). In one of the more extravagant instances of body horror, Vincent Price played an eccentric madman in two British productions: *The Abominable Dr. Phibes* (1971) and *Dr. Phibes Rises Again* (1972). Dr. Phibes is a disfigured organist, like the phantom of the opera, but he blames the medical profession for his misfortunes and his daughter's death. In a series of elaborate stunts, he sets out to punish the ten physicians he holds responsible by assailing their bodies in improbably ingenious ways.

As horror films grew more insatiable and self-conscious, absorbing contemporary themes and styles into the genre, it became harder to distinguish between the screaming and the laughing. In Hammer's *Dr. Jekyll and Sister Hyde* (1972), the Victorian gentleman transformed into a she-wolf. AIP's *Blacula* (1972) was a blaxploitation comedy. *The Rocky Horror Picture Show* (1975) was a campy musical. But one film was deadly serious in intent. *Halloween* (1978), directed by John Carpenter, set out to scare the wits out of its teenage viewers, and it succeeded beyond even Carpenter's imagining, becoming one of the most profitable low-budget films in movie history. He did this by combining strands from earlier slasher films and adding a few twists of his own.

Halloween opens with the sound of children chanting a familiar rhyme about goblins and ghosts. It is Halloween, 1963, a night for tricks or treats. In a shaky, hand-held tracking shot, we approach the front of an ordinary suburban house, then sneak around the side window to watch a teenage couple making out on the couch. The soundtrack is unsettlingly quiet now except for the ambient chirping of crickets, but a high-strung whine breaks the silence as the camera moves into the house, where a hand grabs a large knife from the kitchen and we continue through each room to the stairway. Upstairs, the hand grabs a toy mask from the children's room, and we watch the next few moments through its eyeholes. The teenage girl is sitting at the bedroom vanity, nearly naked. After a quick glance at the bed, we see her turn toward the camera in horror as the knife slashes at her again and again. The scene is chilling, but the most unnerving shot is when we see the killer out on the front lawn: a cute blond boy in a clown suit with a bloody knife in one hand and a mask in the other. *Halloween* borrows the subjective camera from *Peeping Tom*, putting us as viewers in the stalker's shoes. Its eerie soundtrack echoes the dissonant instrumentation and disconcerting syncopation of *Suspiria*. The figure of young Michael Myers with his kitchen knife recalls the demonic children in movies like *The Exorcist* and *The Innocents*. When Michael grows up and breaks out of the mental hospital, he shows the strength and death-defying powers of Universal's supernatural monsters. One of the film's most troubling aspects is the irrelevance of reason. Michael seems to have no clear-cut motive. Even Dr. Loomis, Michael's psychiatrist, has no rational explanation, referring to his patient as inhumanly evil. He is "the Shape," a relentless, unintelligible force behind a mask (see Close-up: *Halloween*).

The 1980s: Hauntings and Howlings in the Age of Reagan

After two decades of indecisive struggles between political forces of the left and right, the 1980s ushered in a new spirit of conservatism through much of the English-speaking world. In Britain, Margaret Thatcher's and then John Major's Conservative Party reigned from 1979 to 1997. In the United States, Ronald Reagan served two consecutive terms, from 1981 to 1989. Reagan ran on a platform of traditional values, pledging to restore the patriotism and prosperity of the 1950s. In Eastern Europe and the Soviet Union, opposition to communist control led to the fall of the Berlin Wall in 1989 and the eventual demise of the USSR, effectively ending the Cold War. Meanwhile, the People's Republic of China was experimenting with economic reform, introducing elements of capitalism and opening its doors to the West. Japan was undergoing an "economic miracle" throughout the decade, and South Korea was following suit, electing its first democratic leader in 1987, while North Korea became more isolated under its hereditary communist dictatorship.

These trends and other signal events left their mark on the motion pictures of the 1980s. Hollywood, sensing a market for nostalgia, produced a series of successful *Rambo*, *Rocky*, and *Back to the Future* films. Blockbuster escapist franchises like *Star Wars* (Episode V in 1980, Episode VI in 1983) and *Indiana Jones* (*Lost Ark* in 1981, *Temple of Doom* in 1984, *Last Crusade* in 1989) were among the best performers at the box office. In Russia, the collapse of state financing meant that filmmakers would have to take their orders from a new source, the dictatorship of the marketplace. In mainland China, the shift from government-run studios to independent companies was somewhat slower, but Japan and South Korea were already making big new waves.

In the American pantheon of horror, Sean Cunningham's *Friday the 13th* (1980) and Wes Craven's *A Nightmare on Elm Street* (1984) reigned supreme, leading a succession of teenage slasher films popularized by *Halloween*. Now the sinister figures of Jason Voorhees and Freddy Krueger joined Michael Myers to stalk the impressionable imaginations of America's youth. Jason rises from the depths of Camp Crystal Lake, where he drowned as a boy while his counselors were sexually preoccupied. When the camp reopens five years later, he attacks the new crop of counselors one by one. Freddy's motives differ, but his victims are similar. Burned to death by a mob of enraged parents who accused him of molesting their children, he seeks revenge on the parents by murdering their teenage kids. What makes Freddy so daunting is that he attacks his victims through their dreams.

As in earlier stalker films, as in horror movies generally, sex and violence are never very far apart. Michael kills his sister soon after her boyfriend leaves the bedroom, and his next few targets are promiscuous teens. The counselors slaughtered by Jason are also sexually active or smoke marijuana. It's as if they're being punished by a substitute parental force. Freddy's victims, too, are beset by sexual anxieties. Were they abused as children? Were their parents wrong in killing Freddy and keeping his fiery death a secret? In this sense, these narratives of transgression and guilt reflect the conservative values of the times. But their ethical stance isn't always clear. The camera itself contributes to a certain moral ambiguity. In *Halloween*, point of view shots alternate between Michael's perspective and the position of his victims. In *Friday the 13th* and *Nightmare*, the spectator is likewise invited to identify with both the hunter and the hunted. At the same time, the killer's identity is often masked or otherwise obscured, and the camera's placement is mysterious. This creates a moral distance and heightens tension. We don't know who the killer is or when and how he will attack.

A good deal of attention has been given to gender relations in these films, especially by feminist critics. While a quick body count reveals a fairly balanced ratio of male and female victims, more screen time is given to the stalking of women than of men. The last person to be hunted, invariably female, has been dubbed Final Girl. Alice in *Friday the 13th* and Nancy in *A Nightmare on Elm Street*, like Laurie in *Halloween* and Sally in *The Texas Chain Saw Massacre*, are left to face the monster on their own, raising interesting questions about their final role. Does Laurie survive because she is a better baby sitter and less sexually active than her friends? Her household weaponry – a knitting needle, a coat hanger – suggests a certain domestic ingenuity on her part, but ultimately she is no match for a relentlessly reviving

Michael. Are she and the other Final Girls the stereotyped products of male fantasies, or do they represent a new breed of heroines, more resourceful and more capable than their predecessors of turning the table on their male assailants? Are they simply sexual objects in a long line of female victims, as Barbara Creed believes, or women warriors who offer female spectators the same pleasures of vicarious violence previously reserved for men, as Isabel Pinedo argues?[24] It is doubtless no coincidence that Jamie Lee Curtis, the star in *Halloween*, is the real-life daughter of Janet Leigh, who played the helpless Marion in *Psycho*, and that her character is a more resilient figure than her mother's. But it is also true that her Final Girl is finally rescued by a man.

By 1989, *Friday the 13th* had generated seven sequels and *A Nightmare on Elm Street* had slashed its way through four, riding a tidal wave of teen-oriented horror films that swept through American theatres and on to foreign shores. Variously called "stalker," "slasher," or "splatter" movies, these films share certain family resemblances.[25] Typically, they are low-budget, independent productions aimed at a youthful audience that relishes graphic spectacles of violence. The antagonists are psychotic killers who stalk a succession of attractive young people until one, usually a woman, rises to confront her attacker. For much of the story, the aggressor's face is hidden, although the camera repeatedly shifts between his voyeuristic gaze and the perspective of his victims. While we may think him vanquished or subdued at the film's conclusion, he always seems to reemerge with supernatural determination for another sequel. And, as we'll see, the mad slasher's many relatives, male and female, have carried on his bloody work abroad in films from Japan (*Audition/Odishon*, 1999) and France (*High Tension*, 2003) to Australia (*Wolf Creek*) and Hong Kong (*Dream House/Wai dor lei ah yut ho*, 2009).

The slasher stories continue the trend of bringing horror home. In contrast to the remote castles of earlier Gothic films, they take place in familiar or familial settings: in a Midwestern town, on Elm Street, near a children's summer camp. The monsters are neither vampires nor medical experiments but neighbors transformed into angry phantoms by unresolved trauma. The victims on the screen are ordinary people, much like those seated in the theatre. Three films released in quick succession are about American families, seemingly normal, who move into haunted lodgings. In *The Amityville Horror* (1979), the dwelling is a home on Long Island that turns out to be haunted by its history. The previous owner murdered his whole family there. Although the new occupants know this, they can't resist the low price of their dream home, saying "houses don't have memories." But soon after the Lutz family moves in, a series of dreadful paranormal events begins to take a toll on them. In *Poltergeist* (1982), the new house is dominated by a supernatural force, "the Beast," which terrorizes the Freeling family until they discover that it was built on the grave site of mistreated Native Americans. These families learn what every reader of Gothic ghost stories knows, that houses do have memories. They also learn about a dark side of the American dream, that home ownership can be a nightmare rather than a pleasure, that the quest for upward mobility can bring a family down.

In Stanley Kubrick's film, *The Shining* (1980), the family is away from home. Set in a magnificent mountain hotel isolated in mid-winter, the story centers on a family of three. Jack, the father (played by Jack Nicholson), wants the hotel's quiet isolation so he can work on his novel. Wendy, his timid wife (Shelley Duvall), spends the hours wandering through its many rooms, caring for their young son Danny, who talks to an imaginary friend. In contrast to *The Texas Chain Saw Massacre* and *Hills Have Eyes*, where the nuclear family is threatened from outside, the biggest danger in this movie comes from within. Wendy discovers this one day when she finds hundreds of pages of Jack's manuscript with a single sentence typed over and over on every page. He comes after her with everything he's got, including a fire axe, while all she can find is her son's child-size baseball bat. To some extent, Jack's ferocity can be accounted for in psychological terms, as the consequence of cabin fever, alcohol, or a long brewing madness. But these do not explain Danny's prophetic dreams, his telepathic talents, or the appearance of ghosts from the hotel's troubled past. Kubrick breaks many of the rules for horror and invents new ones, staging some attacks in the hotel's airy, well-lit rooms; tracking his mobile camera through winding corridors inches from the floor; making use of mirrors, symmetry, and labyrinthine spaces to create an ambiance of obsession and deception. Like the house in *Poltergeist*, the Overlook Hotel sits on a Native American burial ground. Interpreters of the film have found subtexts about genocide, slavery, imperialism, and other repressed chapters of American history, adding to the cumulative power of its tense forward drive and chilling imagery.

The arsenal of scary imagery was rearmed in the eighties by advances in makeup and special effects, whose craftsmen became well-known artists in their own right. Kevin Yagher designed Chucky, the demonic doll in *Child's Play* (1988), and made Jason and Freddy look even nastier in several sequels. Rick Baker injected new life into the werewolf genre with extraordinary transformation scenes in *An American Werewolf in London* (1981) and *The Howling* (1981). Baker also worked on the cult classic *Videodrome*. Directed by the Canadian filmmaker David Cronenberg, *Videodrome* follows an ambitious cable TV programmer who seeks to boost his ratings with kinky sex and violence. His descent into a nightmarish world of media deals and torture porn leads to his physical and mental unraveling. Cronenberg's paranoiac vision of body horror, a surrealistic fusion of technology and human anatomy, is both viscerally and cerebrally charged.

These cinematic monstrosities and the anxieties that feed them – supernatural slashers that stalk promiscuous teens, haunted homes that threaten families, deformations of the human body into beastly or mechanical shapes – boosted movie production in the United States. The number of horror films rose from 35 in 1979 to 70 in 1980 and to 93 in 1981. By 1987, the annual output reached 105.[26] With the advent of video cassettes, these films were seen in homes as well as theatres, both locally and around the globe. How did these American horror pictures compare to their counterparts elsewhere in the world? What was scaring audiences in Italy, India, or China in the 1980s? To what extent were the monster in those countries

FIGURE 3.15   The traditional settings of Hindi horror are haunted by India's irrational past. A scene from *The Old Mansion* (*Purani Haveli*, Dir. Tylsi and Shyam Ramsay, 1989).

imported or home grown? A small sampling will serve to illustrate the indigenous sources and transnational flows of horror cinema.

In India, the genre was dominated by five brothers who produced, directed, scripted, and edited the nation's most popular horror films through the 1970s and 1980s. The Ramsay brothers injected horror into the Bollywood formula (singing, dancing, comedy, and melodrama), appropriating stylistic flourishes from Bava's *giallo* films (colored gels, macabre deaths, atmospheric sets) and props from Hollywood's stock icons (mansions, fangs, bats) but adding a distinctly Indian ingredient: Tantric magic. Tantrism is a spiritual practice related to Hinduism and Buddhism and associated with the worship of Shakti, the divine embodiment of freedom and feminine creative power. When the British colonized India, they regarded Tantrism as a dangerous force, the enemy of rationalism, a mystical web of polytheism, sexuality, and anarchy. They were alarmed by a creed that advocated magic and liberated its followers from traditional taboos. Many Indians who adopted Western ways assumed the British biases and fears. In *The Old Temple* (*Purana Mandir*, 1984), the Tantric threats take the form of Samri, a monstrous demon who has terrorized the heroine's family for generations with a curse on all its women. The only way to subdue him is with the divine trident of Shiva, a Hindu equivalent of the Christian cross. Five years later, the Ramsay brothers revived this monster and gave it a new setting to haunt (Figure 3.15) in *The Old Mansion* (*Purani Haveli*, 1989). In *Veerana: Vengeance of the Vampire* (*Veerana*, 1988), the ghost of an evil witch in the form of a beautiful woman seduces men and sucks their blood, aided by the dark magic of a Tantric priest and his followers. In *The Closed Door* (*Bandh Darwaza*, 1990), a vampire teams up with a wizard, a witch, a priest, and other Tantric thugs to lure innocent women into their dark cave as prey.

The underlying struggle in these films is between India's modernity and its repressed pre-rational past.

In Chinese cinema, a host of horrors was revived to resuscitate the fading film industry. The kung fu boom had run its course in the 1970s, a victim of formulaic overkill and diminishing standards. Hong Kong's studios restored some of its energy with an infusion of humor, replacing Bruce Lee's earnest intensity with the more playful fighting styles of Jackie Chan and Sammo Hung. In the 1980s, they gave the martial arts genre another boost by adding elements of horror, borrowing a few monsters from Hollywood and Hammer, but reaching into China's own deep tradition of supernatural fears. The *jiangshi*, for example, the "hopping vampire" of Chinese folklore, is associated with the ancient practice of driving corpses to their homeland from remote locations. According to some accounts, Taoist priests were often hired to transport the cadavers, in carts or on foot, tying their bodies to flexible bamboo rods so that they appeared to hop when seen from afar. In *Mr. Vampire* (1985), a whole column of subdued *jiangshi* goes hopping through the streets led by a bell-ringing priest, until someone breaks the spell and unleashes pandemonium. In contrast to these *jiangshi*, which have a spark of life in them, the *sishi*, or ordinary corpses, are merely dead and must wait to be resuscitated, as are dozens of hideous *sishi* in *The Legend of the 7 Golden Vampires*.

Higher on the scale of spiritual beings are Chinese ghosts (*guai*). In Pu Songling's *Strange Stories from a Chinese Studio*, the literary source for many horror movie plots, the ghosts are usually sensuous young women (sometimes in the form of *huli*, fox spirits) who seduce men in order to take possession of their bodies. Their motives are related to the Buddhist belief in reincarnation. After death, the human spirit needs a corporeal form to be born again. These hungry ghosts of Chinese lore may wander the earth and haunt the living because of some impediment – an unpunished wrong, an unrequited love – that has interrupted their progress toward enlightenment. For Taoists, the troubled soul is not caught in a battle between good and evil, as in Christianity; it is on a journey to find internal and external harmony. The Taoist ghost seeks to restore balance between the living and the dead. So while restless ghosts can appear threatening and scary, they can also be sympathetic characters for a Chinese audience since what happens to the ghosts can happen to anyone.

Pu Songling (1640–1717) affected a moralistic tone in his stories, which expose human weakness, particularly the foolishness of men, who will court a female ghost even when they know they're flirting with death. His characters include naive young scholars, easy prey for any temptress, and powerful priests (*fashi*) who battle ghosts and hellish demons with magic spells. Most of these characters appear in *A Chinese Ghost Story (Sien nui yau wan)*, directed by Ching Siu-tung and produced by Tsui Hark in 1987. The young scholar Ning Caichen (played by Leslie Cheung) meets his female nemesis, Xiaoqian, in a deserted temple, not knowing she's a ghost. His protector is Master Yan, an eccentric Taoist hermit who would rather battle demons than socialize with humans. It turns out that Xiaoqian is being used by a terrible Tree Monster named Lao Lao ("grandma"), who thrives on the life force of her male victims. In the film's last big fight scene, Ning and Yan invade the underworld to rescue Xiaoqian, only to be entangled and impaled by Lao Lao's giant, snake-like tongue. While *A Chinese Ghost Story* succeeds on the level of a romantic martial arts horror comedy, it has also been interpreted allegorically. In psychological terms, Lao Lao may represent the monstrous feminine, the figure of maternal engulfment from which every child must break away during the symbolic stage of development in order to acquire language and a separate identity. In political terms, Lao Lao may embody Hong Kong's fears of being devoured by the motherland after the tiny colony's anxiously anticipated return to the People's Republic of China in 1997. Perhaps that's why we hear strains of The Internationale, the left-wing anthem, on the soundtrack during the film's apocalyptic finale.

The metaphor of engulfment becomes even more explicit in *We're Going to Eat You* (*Di yu wu men*), directed by Tsui Hark in 1980, which features a whole village of cannibals. Cannibalism had been a popular motif in American hillbilly horror films of the 1970s, including *The Texas Chain Saw Massacre* and *The Hills Have Eyes*, but China has its own traditions of cannibalistic practices, some reportedly as recent as Mao's Great Leap Forward. So does Latin America. In Brazil, an important cycle of political black comedies used cannibalism as an ironic trope for revolutionary activism, beginning with *How Tasty Was My Little Frenchman* (*Como era gostoso o meu francês*, 1971). Instead of being consumed by imperialist Europe, the indigenous people of Brazil devour their would-be captors. The consumer motif in Tsui Hark's film is sometimes read as a comment on rampant capitalism, sometimes as a comment on Mao's Red Guards, who ran amok in the 1960s. In any case, human pork buns and meat patties became a staple of Category III films (a label for explicit sex and graphic violence introduced in Hong Kong in 1989) well into the next few decades, feeding the public's appetite for grim food jokes in films like *Dr. Lamb* (*Gouyeung yi sang*, 1992), *The Untold Story* (*Bat sin fan dim ji yan yuk cha siu bau*, 1993), and *Dumplings* (*Jiaozi*, 2004). These films ramped up the intensity of gruesome Grand Guignol horror that became known in the following decades as Asia Extreme.

The 1990s: Postmodern Horror and Supernatural Realism at the End of the Millennium

In some ways, the final decade of the twentieth century seemed quieter and more promising than its predecessors. The Cold War, with its intermittent global flareups and the hovering threat of nuclear extermination, drew to a close with the Soviet Union's collapse. The United States emerged as the world's acknowledged superpower. For many nations, the prospects for prosperity were improving. The European Union agreed on a common currency, opening new roads for expansion and free trade. India was making progress toward a free market economy, and China was enjoying unprecedented growth. In 1997, however, a financial crisis reversed the fortunes of Korea and Japan, where signs of social stress began to show in incidents like the 1995 Sarin gas attack on the Tokyo subway. Here and there, alarms both big and small were going off around the world: a deadly siege at Waco, Texas in 1993; the Rwandan genocide of 1994; the Oklahoma City bombing in 1995; the massacre at Columbine High School in 1999. The world's population of six billion plus anticipated the new millennium with a mixture of buoyancy and panic.

In this climate, horror cinema suffered something of a decline. Michael, Jason, and Freddy went on stalking victims with increasing fury, but the teenage slasher genre was losing ground; its adolescent audience was turning to other forms, to fantasy and science fiction films with spectacular digital effects. Hollywood tried several strategies to win them back. It mounted expensive productions with top stars. Jonathan Demme recharged the psychopathic killer theme with *The Silence of the Lambs* (1991), turning it into a chilling game of cat and mouse between an ambitious FBI trainee (Jody Foster) and Hannibal Lecter (Anthony Hopkins), a madman with a brilliant intellect and a taste for human tongue. Demme's film was an immediate hit with spectators and critics, winning an Oscar for Best Picture, the first such award for a horror film. Efforts to revive the Gothic monsters of the 1930s were less successful. Francis Ford Coppola's version of *Bram Stoker's Dracula* (1992) and Kenneth Branagh's *Mary Shelley's Frankenstein* could not stir up much enthusiasm despite their celebrity power and stylistic sparks. Recognizing that audiences were laughing at the old formulas, directors drifted toward more self-conscious parody, filling their films with ironic references to other movies. The characters in Peter Jackson's *Braindead*, released in the United States as *Dead Alive* (1992), Wes Craven's *Scream* (1996), and Ronny Yu's *Bride of Chucky* (1998) seem to know that they are in a horror film. In retrospect, this trend can be seen as part of the broad postmodern movement in cinema that acknowledges a film's artificiality, pays homage to its sources, and lets audiences in on the joke.

Two films did bring fresh ideas to the genre at the decade's end. One was *The Blair Witch Project* (1999). The other was M. Night Shyamalan's *The Sixth Sense* (1999). In The *Blair Witch Project*, three student filmmakers set out to document a local legend. Their search for the seventeenth-century sorceress takes them and their camera deep into the woods, where fatigue, disorientation, and mutual distrust begin to gnaw at their lighthearted confidence. When one member disappears, panic takes hold, but the camera keeps rolling. The project was a sensational success. Filmed in eight days on a reported $20,000 budget, relying on "found footage," novice actors, and an improvisatory style that made the action appear to be caught in real time, the movie grossed over $200 million worldwide. Part of this success was due to a clever use of the Internet to promote the film's story as documentary truth. Partly, though, it appealed to audiences by offering a new kind of experience: a form of supernatural realism that relies on a skillful build-up of mood and suspense instead of violence, bloodshed, or erotic thrills; a formula followed eight years later in another low-budget hit, *Paranormal Activity*. *The Sixth Sense* also focused on supernatural phenomena, though it was backed by high production values and the box office magnetism of Bruce Willis. Willis plays a child psychologist trying to help a troubled boy who tells him, "I see dead people." Shyamalan's subtle mastery of tone, a remarkable performance by young Haley Joel Osment as the boy, and the film's surprise ending helped to make it one of the decade's finest and an inspiration for future horror films.

The New Millennium: Horror to the Extreme

Contrary to some expectations and much media hype, the world did not end on January 1, 2000. But there were plenty of disasters in the ensuing years. On September 11, 2001, Islamic terrorists hijacked four American airliners and crashed three of them into US targets, killing thousands and ending any doubts about the nation's invulnerability. By the end of the year, American troops were fighting in Afghanistan; by 2002 they were in Iraq. A new form of combat had replaced the Cold War, a War on Terrorism, bringing with it new images of horror. There were terrorist attacks in London, Barcelona, and Mumbai. Civil wars in Africa took millions of lives. Natural disasters claimed millions more throughout the world: earthquakes in China, Haiti, El Salvador, Italy, and India; hurricanes in Louisiana and Mississippi; a cyclone in Burma; tornadoes in the American Midwest and South; tsunamis in Southeast Asia and Japan. Maybe the world was coming to an end.

With so much real terror and misery in the world, the future of horror films appeared uncertain. Relatively few were made, or deemed successful, during the earliest years of the millennium. In the United States, teen stalkers of the 1980s tried to stage a comeback by fighting each other in *Freddy vs. Jason* (2003). Robert Zemeckis added a supernatural touch to the Hitchcockian thriller in *What Lies Beneath* (2000). *Resident Evil* (2003) sought to build on the popular video game franchise. George Romero brought his zombies back to life with *Land of the Dead* (2005). But while these efforts met with some measure of approval by filmgoers and reviewers, the genre's major innovations took place abroad. By the end of the 2000s, Hollywood was busy remaking films from Asia, Europe, and Australia.

It is always a challenge to sort out contemporary movies into broad patterns while they are still under construction. Trends are easier to distinguish and to name in retrospect. Still, it may help to view horror films of the past 20 years or so against a spectrum of variants running between two poles, with body gore at one end and spooky ghosts at the other. *Freddy vs. Jason*, *Resident Evil*, and *Land of the Dead* are closer to the former category, along with *giallo*, werewolf movies, zombies, vampires, vengeful hillbillies, and the cannibals of Chinese cinema. Their fascination with raw violence, bloody deaths, and corporeal disfigurement can be traced back to the Théâtre du Grand Guignol. On the other hand, *What Lies Beneath*, with its gentler imagery of restless spirits, haunted homes, and other hauntings from the past, has much in common with the spiritual preoccupations of Gothic literature. As we'll see, these two strands continue to run through the cinemas of France and Spain, Korea and Japan, the United States and Britain, often crisscrossing at critical nodes of terror and dread. And, as we keep noting, although they draw on an ever deepening reservoir of global film culture, they are also linked to local histories and traditions.

Take Spanish language movies, for example. Many of the horror films made in Spain during the sixties and seventies, like *Mark of the Werewolf* (*La marca del hombre lobo*, 1967) and *The Cannibal Man* (*La semana del assesino*, 1974), mirrored the recycled monsters and eroticized violence found in low-budget British, Italian, and American films. More recently, such conventional genre films were made by The Fantastic Factory, a production unit based in Barcelona, which turned out titles like *Faust: Love of the Damned* (*Faust*, 2001) and *Beyond Re-Animator* (2003) for international distribution. At the other end of the spectrum was *The Others* (*Los otros*, 2001), a Spanish/US co-production directed by Alejandro Amenábar. Shot in Spain by a largely Spanish crew, but set on a secluded island off the coast of Britain during World War II, *The Others* features an English-speaking cast led by Nicole Kidman. As Grace, the wife of a soldier missing in action, Kidman has brought her two children to a dark, old mansion because they have a rare, deadly sensitivity to sunlight. When her daughter starts seeing phantom intruders, doors open by themselves, the curtains part mysteriously, and the story veers toward the supernatural. The mansion, ghosts, and morally ambiguous children are all part of English Gothic, but many elements – the isolated setting, Catholicism, motherhood, and hints of wartime atrocities – link this film to a long tradition of Spanish art cinema dealing indirectly with Spain's brutal Civil War.

The Spirit of the Beehive (*El espiritu de la colmena*), for example, was filmed by Victor Erice in 1973, when General Franco was still in power, making any direct criticism of his government dangerous. Erice set his film in 1940 just after the Civil War, when Republican fighters were being hunted down by Franco's Fascist forces. In the film, a traveling movie theatre comes to a remote village and screens *Frankenstein* in the village hall. One young girl in the audience, Ana, is fascinated by the monster and imagines she can speak with him. The adult world around her offers little love or guidance. Her parents take scant interest in her or each other, so she roams freely, visiting a deserted sheepfold where she's told the monster lives. When a man appears there one day, a young soldier fleeing from the government, she brings him food and clothing. Strictly speaking, *Spirit of the Beehive* is not a horror film. Nor is *Cria!* (*Cria cuervos*), directed three years later by Carlos Saura. *Cria!* tells the story of another girl named Ana (played by the same actor) who grows up seeing little love between her military father and adoring mother. As in Erice's film, the realities of Spanish politics (figured as distant, Fascist father figures) and social institutions (represented by dysfunctional families) appear on the periphery of a child's fantasy life, which takes the forms of horror cinema.

In Spanish-language movies of the 2000s, well after Franco's death in 1975, children's fantasies assume more frightening shapes and the politics become more pointed. In *The Devil's Backbone* (*El espinazo del diablo*, 2001), by Mexican director Guillermo del Toro, the ghost of a dead boy haunts a shelter for civil war orphans

FIGURE 3.16   In *Pan's Labyrinth* (*El laberinto del fauno*, 2006), Mexican director Guillermo del Toro draws on a tradition of ghost stories set during the Spanish Civil War.

(see Close-up: *The Devil's Backbone*). In *Pan's Labyrinth*, also by del Toro, the daughter of a Fascist officer in an isolated Spanish town takes refuge in a fantasy world of monsters that includes a giant toad, a satyr, and a cannibalistic blind man who seems to have stepped out from one of Francisco Goya's grisly paintings (Figure 3.16). The motifs of motherhood and phantom orphans are skillfully reworked and given a new twist in *The Orphanage* (*El orfanato*), directed by J.A. Bayona and produced by del Toro in 2007. In each of these films, the repressed specters of national traumas rise up from a pool, a well, a cellar, or some other subterranean source in the form of demons or phantom ghosts.

Since Franju's *Eyes Without a Face* had appeared in 1960, few horror films of note were made in France until the new millennium, when a wave of edgy, intensely shocking films broke on the international scene. While some films, like Michael Haneke's *Hidden* (*Caché*, 2005), were nuanced studies in suspense and psychological intrigue, many more were high-octane blood-fests: Grand Guignol spectacles of extreme horror. Leading the pack was Christophe Gans's *Brotherhood of the Wolf* (*Le pacte des loups*, 2001), which blended moments of horror with romance, fantasy, erotica, martial arts, and costume drama. Based on historical events, its story centers on a legendary beast that terrorized the countryside in eighteenth-century France. A figure of rebellious defiance and supernatural ferocity, the Beast seems to embody the worst impulses of the French Revolution. Gans's film became one of France's highest-grossing exports in two decades, encouraging French directors to mix their genres, heighten the horror, and give fans something new. Gaspar Noé appalled some audiences and fascinated others with *Irreversible* (*Irréversible*, 2002), a film that reverses the chronological sequence of events leading to scenes of relentless rape and maniacal revenge. In *High Tension* (*Haute tension*, 2005),

Alexandre Aja spiced up the familiar story of a serial killer with elaborately choreographed death scenes and an unexpected ending. Even Claire Denis, director of art films like *Chocolate* (*Chocolat*, 1988) and *Good Work* (*Beau travail*, 1999), disturbed many of her followers with *Trouble Every Day* (2001) a film that begins as a conventional romance but steers the honeymoon to a harrowing end. With death becoming ever more gruesome and sex more pornographic, it's no wonder that this trend has been dubbed the New French Extremity.

The hunger for extreme experiences was duly noted by Metro-Tartan, a London-based distributor of East Asian genre films. The president of Tartan spotted a niche market in the West for the kind of gory, eroticized fare that Hollywood was reluctant to produce but Hong Kong and Seoul were all too eager to supply. One executive described the style as "slick and glossy, with fast, MTV-style editing … and sensibility, typified by over-the-top grotesque[ness] to the point of being surreal."[27] Tartan also recognized the distributing potential of new DVD technologies for exporting foreign-language films en masse overseas. So the high-profile label "Asian Extreme" was born. It was under this brand name that such acclaimed films as *Audition* and *Battle Royale* (*Batoru rowaiaru*, 2000) from Japan, *Oldboy* (*Oldeuboi*, 2003) and *A Tale of Two Sisters* (*Janghwa, Hongryeon*, 2003) from Korea, *Hard-Boiled* (*Lat sau san taam*, 1992) and *Infernal Affairs* (*Mou gaan dou*, 2002) from Hong Kong, and *The Eye* (*Gin gwai*, 2002) and *Bangkok Dangerous* (2008) from Thailand, came to Western audiences.

The deluge of Asian horror films in the 2000s, -and their subsequent Hollywood remakes, began with *Ring* (*Ringu*, 1998), a Tartan release of the Japanese film directed by Hideo Nakata (see Close-up: *Ring*). *Ring* was not as extreme in its imagery or emotional range as *Audition* or *Battle Royale*. Rather, it introduced a new aesthetic, based on mystery and measured pacing, as well as a new breed of monster, the techno-ghost. In *Ring*, the avenging spirit strikes through the medium of videotape, anticipating future ghosts that use computers, the Internet, and mobile phones to reach their victims. Young cult followers around the world, especially in the United States, began to speak of J-Horror (J for Japanese) as a very cool phenomenon (see Deep Focus on Japanese Cinemas for a more complete account of J-Horror and its cultural roots).

At nearly the same time, global horror fans were turning to South Korea, where a surge of well-made genre films were transforming a historically local industry into an international powerhouse. For centuries, the Korean Peninsula had been under the domination of foreign powers, including China, Japan, and the United States. After the Korean War (1950–1953), when it was split from the communist north (officially, the Democratic People's Republic of Korea), South Korea (the Republic of Korea) was ruled by a succession of military dictatorships from 1961 to 1992, a period of political suppression and rapid economic development. Within a few decades, South Korea became a fully modern, industrialized nation, competing with Japan and China for the lion's share of trade in East Asia.

Korea's film industry, originally modeled on Hollywood's studio system, reached a highpoint during the late 1950s and 1960s, its "Golden Age," when production soared from 20 to over 200 films a year. Most of these were commercial features that mixed popular genres and cultural styles for domestic audiences. Production plummeted again in the 1970s and early 1980s under tight government control, but several factors contributed to a resurgence of creativity in the late 1980s, known as the "Korean New Wave." Many of the young directors in this movement had learned their craft in the old studios but sought to redefine Korean cinema free of government censorship and Hollywood influence. They focused on contemporary social issues and experimented with new forms, capturing the world's attention at art film festivals. By the next decade, filmmaking had undergone yet another change. The Asian fiscal crisis of 1997 turned out to be a good thing for the South Korean movie industry, which shifted from big family-controlled conglomerates (*chaebôl*) to independent companies financed by venture capital. By 2001, South Korea had one of the strongest commercial industries in the world and a robust local market to support it. By 2006, the market share for local films had reached an unprecedented 60%, the number of theatre screens was increasing exponentially, and the average attendance per screen was nearly triple that of US theatres.[28] The "new Korean cinema" that emerged from this eruption of activity, with its high production values, eclectic styles, and focus on popular taste, is a particularly rich vein for students of horror.

The trend began much earlier. Kim Ki-young's *The Housemaid* (*Hanyo*, 1960), for example, one of the most popular movies of the Golden Age, combined moments of horror with family melodrama. The head of the household is a respectable music teacher who works overtime to pay for his wife's dream house. The housemaid comes from a lower class but is as ambitious, and more rapacious, than the wife. She seduces the husband and threatens to cry rape, eventually taking over the house and everybody in it. Kim introduces many of the themes that still preoccupy Korean horror films today: the corrosive power of material greed, class conflict, the threat of powerful women, and the fragility of social institutions that can crack under the pressures of an all too hasty effort to modernize. Im Sang-soo's 2010 remake of *The Housemaid* confirms that the effort and its anxieties continue to plague Korean households. In 1998, Kim Ji-woon focused his lens on another family in *The Quiet Family* (*Joyonghan Gajok*), a dark comedy in which a series of bizarre misunderstandings and deaths besets a mountain guest lodge. While the bodies pile up, references to contemporary Korean events – North Korean spies, the 1980 Kwangju Massacre, the 1997 financial crisis – play in the background on the television news. As these references suggest, there is a strong correlation between Korean horror, Korean history, and Korean institutions.

One of the most persistently haunted institutions is South Korea's school system. *Whispering Corridors* (*Yeogo goedam*, 1998) is set in a girls' high school where an authoritarian teacher is mysteriously murdered before the first day of classes. Rumors circulate through the corridors that the ghost of a dead student has returned in the body of a student. In *Memento Mori* (*Yeogo goedam*, 1999), two students struggle to maintain their special friendship in a college preparatory girls' school that offers little room for privacy or individuality. In the film's harrowing finale, the spirit

FIGURE 3.17   Kim Ji-woon's *A Tale of Two Sisters* (*Janghwa, Hongryeon*, 2003) dramatizes the horrors of adolescence for a young Korean audience and its global counterparts. Remade in the United States as *The Uninvited* (Dir. Charles Guard, 2009).

of a suicidal student returns to wreak havoc on the school and those who made her life so miserable. In Bong Joon-ho's *Memories of Murder* (*Salinui chueok*, 2003), the institutional targets are South Korea's police system and its government. Based on a real incident, Korea's first reported serial killings, Bong's film follows two detectives as they try to track down the evasive rapist/murderer. One detective is methodic and urbane, a great admirer of the FBI. The other is a likeable bungler who works by instinct. Viewed allegorically, they represent two aspects of Korean society: the modern, scientific city dweller and the superstitious rural man still living in the past. While the investigation goes on and on, police chiefs change as frequently as heads of state, and the case is never solved, as in fact it never was in real life. *Memories of Murder* mixes horror, crime, and comedy, but it is cleverly, carefully composed.

So is Kim Ji-woon's *A Tale of Two Sisters* (*Janghwa, Hongryeon*, 2003), although Kim's precise timing and meticulous attention to *mise-en-scène* are sometimes overlooked by audiences trying to make sense of its confusing plotline and deliberately puzzling point of view (Figure 3.17). Like *The Housemaid* and *The Quiet Family*, it centers on a dysfunctional household; like *Whispering Corridors* and *Memento Mori*, it focuses on the anxieties of teenage girls. The characters include a weak and distant father, an abusive step-mother, and two young girls bound by a fierce, sisterly affection – figures that appear again and again in Korean films. Like instances of Korean horror, *A Tale of Two Sisters* can be read as a supernatural story or a psychological study, but what makes it new is Kim's refusal to provide a clear narrative or a conclusive ending. The Hollywood remake of this film (*The Uninvited*, 2009) supplies more clarity and closure for American audiences, making it an instructive example of comparative cultural expectations.

While each of these Korean films includes some degree of sexuality and violence, none compares to the work of Park Chan-wook for sheer emotional extremity. Park shocked many viewers of *Oldboy* with scenes in which a man devours a live octopus and slices off his own tongue. But these scenes are not necessarily gratuitous. *Oldboy* won the Grand Prix at Cannes because it had something to say and said it with unflinching skill. Together with *Sympathy for Mr. Vengeance* (*Boksuneun naui geot*, 2002) and *Sympathy for Lady Vengeance* (*Chinjeolhan geumjassi*, 2005), Park's "Vengeance Trilogy" mounts a brutal attack on a society in which emotions run rampant and the state offers neither justice nor protection. His work, like many instances of K-Horror, raises a persistent question about genres and motives. To what degree do the popular formulas of horror, martial arts, or romance serve as convenient vehicles for social messages and to what extent are the messages themselves pretexts for indulging in the sexuality and violence of the genres?

Again and again, across the world's filmmaking traditions, we find similar patterns of innovation and appropriation, assimilation and bids for cultural identity. Filmmakers from Africa to Asia and Australia reach into their local heritage of scary stories and combine them with transposable parts from a store of global iconography. They use these hybrid horrors to explore the present-day anxieties of their people in a cinematic language that is increasingly transnational. In sub-Saharan countries like Mali and Nigeria, for example, where masks are portals to the spirit world, masks and spirits appear regularly in films about contemporary issues. In 1997, Adama Drabo jolted and amused Malian audiences with *Skirt Power* (*Taafe Fanga*), a film in which an abused wife dons an ancient Alberga mask to scare the men in her village into doing the cooking, housekeeping, and childcare. After they have traded places for a while, the men and women agree to restore the gender balance in their community. More recently, an entire industry has emerged in Nigeria, a form of filmmaking that mixes shaman rituals and *juju* magic with Hollywood chase scenes and special effects to dramatize the country's uneasy transition to modernity. Popularly known as Nollywood, this proliferation of inexpensively made videos nearly rivals Bollywood in output and income, with more than 2,000 new titles a year sold on DVDs to local markets and diaspora communities. In Thailand, another part of the world where a belief in spirits is part of everyday life, ghost movies have been popular since the silent era. Deeply rooted in Thai folklore, these films are populated with shape-shifting animals (snakes, crocodiles) and pre-Buddhist spirits (*pii*) like the nasty *pii bporp* (an evil demon with a special appetite for human livers) and the *pii dtai tang krom* (the ghost of a woman who has died in childbirth). *Nang Nak* (1999) is based on the oft-told story of a warrior who returns from battle to his beloved wife and child, not knowing they are dead. The wife's spirit clings to him tenaciously until a Buddhist priest tries to free him in an elaborate exorcism. *Phobia 2* (2009) tells five stories of contemporary Thailand; in each case, the protagonists are grotesquely punished by ghosts for violating traditional Thai values.

Looking back at the long history of horror and its many incarnations, it is possible to see how much of the genre developed through a process of global exchange.

The Universal classics of the 1930s borrowed freely from European movements like German Expressionism and French Surrealism, from British Gothic and Parisian Grand Guignol. Hollywood's monsters were in turn imitated by filmmakers throughout the world, who made local adjustments and often added innovations of their own. As each new generation of zombies, psychos, slashers, cannibals, or techno-ghosts arose, embodying the particular terrors of their place and time, the web of transnational indebtedness grew ever more complex. From simple borrowing to outright theft, from postmodern homage to intertextual pastiche, from cycles and franchises to sequels and remakes, the course of modern filmmaking has left a zigzag trail of give and take that crisscrosses national divides. All this activity invites us to question previous notions of Hollywood and national cinema. It demonstrates, for example, how Hollywood, for all its economic might and cultural authority, has never been a simple, monolithic force. Hollywood is always evolving, as it did from the vertically integrated studio system of the 1940s and 1950s to the transnational conglomerates and packaging services of more recent times. Further, Hollywood reflects popular tastes as much as it creates them. Equally, what constitutes a "national culture" is no longer as distinctive as it once seemed. While the people of France or of Korea are certainly bound to each other by common languages, histories, and values, the boundaries that define them as nations now appear to be more porous. What we may call French or Korean culture is really a composite of many influences, a fusion of internal and external currents. As the world becomes increasingly interconnected, we may well ask whether the monsters on our movie screens are becoming more or less alike.

Filmography

Country	English Language Title	Original Title	Director	Date
Germany	The Cabinet of Dr. Caligari	Das Cabinet des Dr. Caligari	Robert Wiene	1920
Germany	Nosferatu	Nosferatu, eine Symphonie des Grauens	F.W. Murnau	1922
USA	The Phantom of the Opera		Rupert Julian	1925
USA	Dr. Jekyll and Mr. Hyde		Rouben Mamoulian	1931
USA	Dracula		Tod Browning	1931
USA	Frankenstein		James Whale	1931
USA	Freaks		Tod Browning	1932
Germany	Vampyr	Der Traum des Allan Grey	Carl Theodor Dreyer	1932
USA	The Mummy		Karl Freund	1932

(Continued)

Filmography (*Continued*)

Country	English Language Title	Original Title	Director	Date
USA	The Bride of Frankenstein		James Whale	1935
USA	The Wolf Man		George Waggner	1941
USA	Cat People		Jacques Tourneur	1942
USA	I Walked with a Zombie		Jacques Tourneur	1943
Japan	Ugetsu	Ugetsu monogatari	Kenji Mizoguchi	1953
Japan	Godzilla	Gojira	Ishiro Honda	1954
USA	Invasion of the Body Snatchers		Don Siegel	1956
USA	I Was a Teenage Werewolf		Gene Fowler	1957
UK	The Tingler		William Castle	1959
Japan	The Ghost Story of Yotsuya	Tokaido Yotsuya kaidan	Nobuo Nakagawa	1959
France	Eyes Without a Face	Les yeux sans visage	Georges Franju	1960
USA	Psycho		Alfred Hitchcock	1960
UK	Circus of Horrors		Sidney Hayers	1960
UK	Peeping Tom		Michael Powell	1960
USA	The Fall of the House of Usher		Roger Corman	1960
UK/USA	The Innocents		Jack Clayton	1961
USA	Tales of Terror		Roger Corman	1962
Japan	Onibaba	Onibaba	Kaneto Shindo	1964
Japan	Kwaidan	Kaidan	Masaki Koboyashi	1964
USA	Night of the Living Dead		George Romero	1968
USA	Rosemary's Baby		Roman Polanski	1968
UK	Dracula Has Risen from the Grave		Freddie Francis	1968
UK	The Abominable Dr. Phibes		Robert Fuest	1971
USA	Blacula		William Crain	1972
USA	The Exorcist		William Friedkin	1973
Spain	The Spirit of the Beehive	El espíritu de la colmena	Victor Erice	1973
USA	The Texas Chain Saw Massacre		Tobe Hooper	1974
USA	Jaws		Steven Spielberg	1975

Country	English Language Title	Original Title	Director	Date
USA	Carrie		Brian De Palma	1976
Italy	Suspiria	Suspiria	Dario Argento	1977
USA	The Hills Have Eyes		Wes Craven	1977
USA	Dawn of the Dead		George Romero	1978
USA	Halloween		John Carpenter	1978
USA	Dracula		John Badham	1979
UK/ USA	Alien		Ridley Scott	1979
UK/ USA	The Shining		Stanley Kubrick	1980
USA	Friday the 13th		Sean Cunningham	1980
Canada	The Changeling		Peter Medak	1980
Hong Kong	Spooky Encounters	Gui da gui	Sammo Kam-bo Hung	1980
USA	The Howling		Joe Dante	1981
UK/ USA	An American Werewolf in London		John Landis	1981
USA	Poltergeist		Tobe Hooper	1982
Colombia	Pure Blood	Pura sangre	Luis Ospina	1982
Canada	Videodrome		David Cronenberg	1983
USA	A Nightmare on Elm Street		Wes Craven	1984
USA	Re-Animator		Stuart Gordon	1985
Hong Kong	A Chinese Ghost Story	Ch'ien-nü Yu-hun / Sien nui yau wan	Siu-tung Ching	1987
India	The Old Mansion	Purani Haveli	Tylsi and Shyam Ramsay	1989
USA	Silence of the Lambs		Jonathan Demme	1991
USA	Bram Stoker's Dracula (aka Dracula)		Francis Ford Coppola	1992
Mexico	Cronos	Cronos	Guillermo del Toro	1993
USA	Mary Shelley's Frankenstein (aka Frankenstein)		Kenneth Branagh	1994
Japan	Ring	Ringu	Hideo Nakata	1998

(Continued)

Filmography (*Continued*)

Country	English Language Title	Original Title	Director	Date
South Korea	Whispering Corridors	Yeogo goedam	Ki-hyeong Park	1998
USA	The Blair Witch Project		Daniel Myrick and Sanchez Eduardo	1999
USA	The Sixth Sense		M. Night Shyamalan	1999
USA	Sleepy Hollow		Tim Burton	1999
Japan	Audition	Odishon	Takashi Miike	1999
USA	What Lies Beneath		Robert Zemeckis	2000
USA/ Spain	The Others	Los otros	Alejandro Amenábar	2001
Mexico	The Devil's Backbone	El espinazo del diablo	Guillermo del Toro	2001
France	Brotherhood of the Wolf	Le pacte des loups	Christophe Gans	2001
USA	The Ring*		Gore Verbinski	2002
UK	28 Days Later		Danny Boyle	2002
Japan	Ju-on: The Grudge	Ju-on	Takashi Shimizu	2002
South Korea	A Tale of Two Sisters	Janghwa, Hongryeon	Jee-woon Kim	2003
Japan	One Missed Call	Chakushin ari	Takashi Miike	2003
USA	The Grudge*		Takashi Shimizu	2004
Russia	Night Watch	Nochnoy dozor	Timur Bekmambetov	2004
Japan	Marebito		Takeshi Shimizu	2004
Australia	Wolf Creek		Greg McLean	2005
Mexico	Pan's Labyrinth	El laberinto del fauno	Guillermo del Toro	2006
Spain/ Mexico	The Orphanage	El orfanato	Juan Antonio Bayona	2007
USA	Paranormal Activity		Oren Peli	2007
Sweden	Let the Right One In	Låt den rätte komma in	Tomas Alfredson	2008
USA	One Missed Call*		Eric Valette	2008
USA	Twilight		Catherine Hardwicke	2008

Country	English Language Title	Original Title	Director	Date
USA	The Uninvited*		Charles and Thomas Guard	2009
Hong Kong	Dream Home	Wai dor lei ah yut ho	Ho-cheung Pang	2009
USA	Let Me In*		Matt Reeves	2010
UK	The Woman in Black		James Watkins	2012
Spain	Mama	Mama	Andrés Muschietti	2013

*indicates Hollywood remakes

Notes

1. H.P. Lovecraft, "Supernatural Horror in Literature," in Collected Essays, Vol. 2, ed. S.T. Joshi (Hippocampus Press, 2006).

2. Stephen King, "Why We Crave Horror Movies," Playboy, January 1981, 150–154 and 237–246.

3. Carl Jung, The Archetypes and the Collective Unconscious (Princeton University Press, 1980), 43.

4. Joanne Cantor and Mary Beth Oliver, "Developmental Differences in Responses to Horror," in James Weaver and Ron Tamborini, ed., Horror Films: Current Research on Audience Preference and Reactions (Lawrence Erlbaum Associates, 1996), 230.

5. Bruce Kawin, "Children of the Light," in Barry Keith Grant, ed. Film Genre Reader II (University of Texas Press, 1995), 322. See also Kawin's more recent and comprehensive study of the genre, Horror and the Horror Film (Anthem Press, 2012).

6. Rick Worland, The Horror Film: An Introduction (Wiley-Blackwell, 2007).

7. Ludwig Wittgenstein, Philosophical Investigations, trans. G.E.M. Anscombe (Basil Blackwell, 1953), §66.

8. Rick Altman, Film/Genre (Macmillan, 1999).

9. Thomas Schatz, Hollywood Genres: Formals, Filmmaking, and the Studio System (Random House, 1981), 37–38.

10. Dracula, DVD, Spanish version directed by George Melford for Universal Studios, 1931 (75th Anniversary Edition, Universal Studios Home Entertainment, 2006).

11. Karl Marx, Capital: A Critique of Political Economy, Vol. 1, trans. Ben Fowkes (Penguin, 1976), 364.

12. Ann Radcliffe, "On the Supernatural in Poetry," The New Monthly Magazine and Literary Journal 16(1): 1826.

13. Paul Wells, The Horror Genre: From Beelzebub to Blair Witch (Wallflower Press, 2000), 3.

14. Adam Lowenstein, Shocking Representation: Historical Trauma, National Cinema, and the Modern Horror Film (Columbia University Press, 2005), 1.

15. Siegfried Kracauer, From Caligari to Hitler: A Psychological History of the German Film (Princeton University Press, 1947).

16. Thomas Elsaesser, Weimar Cinema and After: Germany's Historical Imaginary (Routledge, 2000).

17. David Skal, The Monster Show: A Cultural History of Horror (Norton, 1993), 63–80.

18. Skal, 114.

19. See Reynold Humphries, The American Horror Film: An Introduction (Edinburgh University Press, 2002), Chapter 3.

20. Skal, 255.

21. Andrew Syde and Dolores Tierney, "Importation/Mexploitation, or, How a Crime-Fighting, Vampire-Slaying Mexican Wrestler Almost Found Himself in an Italian Sword-and-Sandals Epic," in Steven Schneider and Tony Williams, eds., Horror International (Wayne State University Press, 2005), 33–55.

22. Lowenstein, 44.

23. Tony Williams, *Hearths of Darkness: The Family in the American Horror Film* (Fairleigh Dickinson University Press, 1996), 185.

24. See Barbara Creed, "Horror and the Monstrous-Feminine: An Imaginary Abjection?" in Sue Thornham, ed., *Feminist Film Theory: A Reader* (New York University Press, 1999), 251–266 and Isabel Cristina Pinedo, *Recreational Terror: Women and the Pleasures of Horror Film Viewing* (State University of New York Press, 1997).

25. See John McCarty, *Splatter Movies: Breaking the Last Taboo of the Screen* (St. Martin's Press, 1984); Carol Clover, *Men, Women, and Chain Saws: Gender in the Modern Horror Film* (Princeton University Press,

1992); Robin Wood, "Returning the Look: *Eyes of a Stranger*," and Vera Dika, "The Stalker Film: 1978–81." The latter two essays appear in Gregory Waller, ed., *American Horrors: Essays on the Modern American Horror Film* (University of Illinois Press, 1987).

26. Quoted in Stephen Prince, *The Horror Film* (Rutgers University Press, 2004), 143.

27. Quoted in Jinhee Choi and Mitsuyo Wada-Marciano, eds., *Horror to the Extreme: Changing Boundaries in Asian Cinema* (Hong Kong University Press, 2008), Introduction, n. 8.

28. Frances Gateword, ed., *Seoul Searching: Culture and Identity in Contemporary Korean Cinema* (State University of New York Press, 2007), 3.

Further Reading

Beck, Jay and Vicente Rodríguez Ortega, eds. *Contemporary Spanish Cinema and Genre*. Manchester University Press, 2009.

Blake, Linnie. *The Wounds of Nations: Horror Cinema, Historical Trauma and National Identity*. Manchester University Press, 2008.

Clover, Carol. *Men, Women, and Chain Saws: Gender in the Modern Horror Film*. Princeton University Press, 1992.

Creed, Barbara. "Horror and the Monstrous-Feminine: An Imaginary Abjection?" In Sue Thornham, ed., *Feminist Film Theory: A Reader*, 251–266. New York University Press, 1999.

De Ville, Donna. "Menopausal Monsters and Sexual Transgression in Argento's Art Horror." In Robert Weiner and John Cline, eds., *Cinema Inferno: Celluloid Explosions from the Cultural Margins*, 53–75. Scarecrow Press, 2010.

Dixon, Wheeler. *A History of Horror*. Rutgers University Press, 2000.

Eisner, Lotte. *The Haunted Screen: Expressionism in the German Cinema and the Influence of Max Reinhardt*. University of California Press, 1973.

Fischer, Dennis. *Horror Film Directors, 1931–1990*. McFarland & Company, 1991.

Humphries, Reynold. *The American Horror Film: An Introduction*. Edinburgh University Press, 2002.

Huss, Roy and Theodore Ross, eds. *Focus on The Horror Film*. Prentice Hall, 1972.

Iaccino, James. *Psychological Reflections on Cinematic Terror: Jungian Archetypes in Horror Films*. Praeger, 1994.

Lowenstein, Adam. *Shocking Representation: Historical Trauma, National Cinema, and the Modern Horror Film*. Columbia University Press, 2005.

Kawin, Bruce. "Children of the Light." In Barry Keith Grant, ed., *Film Genre Reader*, 308–329. University of Texas Press, 1995.

Kawin, Bruce. *Horror and the Horror Film*. Anthem Press, 2012.

Marriott, James and Kim Newman. *Horror: The Definitive Guide to the Cinema of Fear*. André Deutsch, 2006.

Marriott, James. *Horror Films*. Virgin Books, 2004.

Murphy, Robert, ed. *The British Cinema Book*, 3rd edition. Palgrave Macmillan (BFI), 2009.

Paul, Louis. *Italian Horror Film Directors*. McFarland & Company, 2005.

Pinedo, Isabel Cristina. *Recreational Terror: Women and the Pleasures of Horror Film Viewing*. State University of New York Press, 1997.

Pirie, David. *A New Heritage of Horror: The English Gothic Cinema*. I.B. Tauris, 2008.

Prince, Stephen, ed. *The Horror Film*. Rutgers University Press, 2004.

Schneider, Steven and Tony Williams, eds. *Horror International*. Wayne State University Press, 2005.

Skal, David. *The Monster Show: A Cultural History of Horror*. Norton, 1993.

Thompson, Kirsten Moana. *Apocalyptic Dread: American Film at the Turn of the Millennium*. State University of New York Press, 2007.

Waller, Gregory, ed. *American Horrors: Essays on the Modern American Horror Film*. University of Illinois Press, 1987.

Weaver, James and Ron Tamborini. *Horror Films: Current Research on Audience Preference and Reactions*. Lawrence Erlbaum Associates, 1996.

Wells, Paul. *The Horror Genre from Beelzebub to Blair Witch*. Wallflower, 2000.

Williams, Linda. "Film Bodies: Ge Excess." In Sue Thornham, e *Theory: A Reader*, 251–266. New Press, 1999.

Williams, Tony. *Hearths of Darkness: The Family in the American Horror Film*. Farleigh Dickinson University Press, 1996.

Worland, Rick. *The Horror Film: An Introduction*. Wiley-Blackwell, 2007.

DEEP FOCUS ON JAPANESE CINEMAS

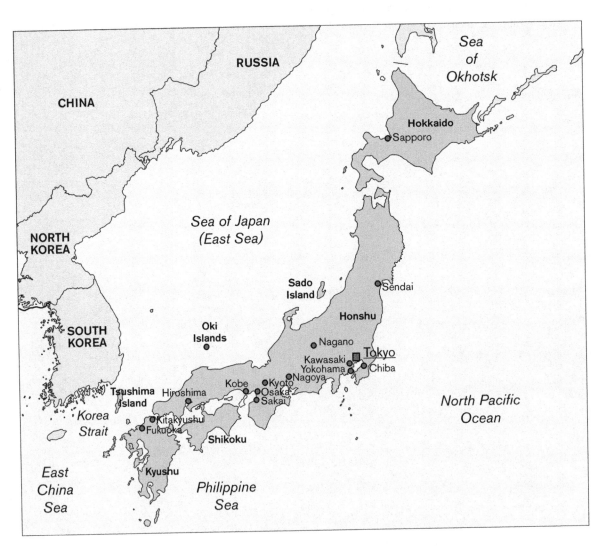

FIGURE 3.18   Map of Japan and neighboring countries.

World Cinema through Global Genres, First Edition. William V. Costanzo.
© 2014 John Wiley & Sons, Inc. Published 2014 by John Wiley & Sons, Inc.

There is a telling story about the opening of Japan to Western commerce. During Commodore Perry's first expedition to the isolated islands in 1853, the American naval officer sought to make the *shogun* sign a trade agreement, trying to intimidate the Japanese leader with his ships' big iron cannons. When Perry returned in 1854, the Japanese had cannons of their own, copied from the American arsenal but made from hollowed tree trunks. However true the story may be to historical details, it illustrates a certain dynamic between Japan and the West. Since 1853, Japan has been quick to borrow foreign technology, mastering the basics, adapting foreign tools and trends to local conditions, transforming them through the sieve of native culture, and giving back something in return. Sometimes the Japanese aim can seem unilaterally aggressive, sometimes a matter of mutual exchange. Today, some 160 years after Perry's visit, it's the Americans who are likely to be doing the copying, particularly those in the movie industry.

In Unit I, we saw patterns of cross-influence surrounding the Warrior Hero. Kurosawa's *Seven Samurai* (1954) inspired Sturges's *The Magnificent Seven* (1960), while Kurosawa in turn acknowledged the debt of his samurai movies to American Westerns. The interplay of swords and guns has become even more rapid and reciprocal in contemporary hybrid films like Tarantino's *Kill Bill* duet (2003, 2004) and Miike's *Sukiyaki Western Django* (2007). In Unit III, we see similar patterns within the horror genre. After World War II, for example, *Godzilla* (*Gojira*, 1954) borrowed freely from *King Kong* (1933), and more recently, Hollywood revived its stock of horror films with remakes of Japanese hits like *Ring* (1998) and *Ju-on: The Grudge* (2002). The big guns of the media industry keep shifting between East and West.

Early History and Culture

The group of islands that we call Japan covers a land area slightly smaller than France but with more than twice the population, about 130 million. People have been living on these volcanic islands for some 10,000 years, although their consolidation as a culture or a nation is relatively recent. The Japanese people did not even have their own written language until the eighth or ninth century. Much of Japan's unique historical development has been attributed to its isolation from the Asian continent, 115 miles across the Sea of Japan, which reduced the opportunities for influence and invasion by older, larger cultures like China.

Japan's prehistory is a progression of successive cultures, one layer building on another, eventually blending diverse groups together into a homogeneous society. By the third century, a complex political arrangement of autonomous tribal units, called *uji*, was beginning to evolve, eventually led by the Yamato clan, which traced its origin back to a mythical sun goddess. By the sixth century, the islands were linked by a feudal system of military leaders and vassals that would persist for more than 700 years. The leadership would change, controlled by powerful families like the Fujiwaras and Tokugawas, but the system would continue to follow a strict *Bushido* code, the "way of the warrior," by which the courage and loyalty of *samurai* fighters were rewarded by their commanders with wealth and social status. The most powerful leaders became known as *shoguns*, the hereditary rulers of Japan from 1192 to 1867 with one notable exception. In 1467, a conflict known as the Onin War began, leading to a century of political and social chaos. Dubbed the age of "Warring States," this is the period setting for many action films, including Kurosawa's *Seven Samurai*. It's when the formerly prestigious samurai became masterless *ronin*, vying with peasants for survival. The country was united again under a powerful shogun from the Tokugawa clan, which ruled over an alliance of local lords (*daimyos*) from 1600 to 1868. Although the Tokugawa shoguns were essentially feudal monarchs, they presided over a flowering of modern, urban culture centered in the city of Edo, now known as Tokyo.

The Edo period, as the Tokugawa era is also called, was a rich epoch for the arts. A new form of theatre emerged, called *Kabuki*, combining stylized drama, dance, elaborate make-up, and stunning costumes into a popular form of entertainment. Kabuki appealed to general audiences just as the traditional *Noh* drama had amused the upper classes for two centuries. *Bunraku*, a form of life-size puppet theatre for adults, also became fashionable, along with *haiku* poetry and woodblock prints of the "floating world," or *ukiyo-e*. This era of prosperity and extraordinary creativity flourished in a climate of self-imposed isolation. One Tokugawa shogun, Ieyasu, was especially suspicious of foreigners. He courted commerce with European traders but repulsed their efforts to introduce Christianity into Japan, expelling missionaries, executing converts, closing ports, and encouraging a backlash of nationalist fervor. Buddhism and Confucianism, influential imports from China, were abandoned in favor of Shinto, the indigenous religion of Japan, with its animist beliefs in local deities (*kami*), its emphasis on rituals and shrines, its celebration of the bounty and beauty of nature. In Shinto, the inside (*uchi*) is associated with safety, the outside (*soto*) with danger. It is this environment of national resistance to foreigners that Perry encountered in 1853.

Japan would later return to the task of preserving its traditions and defining itself as a national culture free from external impurities, but a new era of open trade and social reform began in 1868. Assuming the name of Meiji ("enlightened rule"), a new government dismantled the old feudal system, establishing the emperor as the nominal head of a Shinto state. It initiated land reforms, legalized Christianity, encouraged commerce with the West, and introduced elements of democracy. Japan was now on the high road to modernity – and imperial ambition. When the Meiji emperor died in 1912, Japan had modernized its armed forces, scoring military victories against China and Russia. By 1919, when World War I ended in the peace treaty of Versailles, Japan had signed on as one of the Big Five powers of the new world order.

Modern Japan and the Film Industry

Timeline (Figure 3.19)

Dates	National History	Film History
1467–1477	Onin War sets off social chaos of "Warring States Period"	
1600–1868	Edo Period (Tokugawa Shogun unites the country in 1615)	
1853	Japan opens trade to Admiral Perry and the West	
1868–1912	Meiji Restoration spurs nation building	
1895	Japan takes over Taiwan from China	
1897		French cinematograph introduced to Japan
1899		First Japanese film screened in Tokyo
1910	Japan annexes Korea	
1912		Nikkatsu Studio founded
1919	Japan becomes one of the Big Five powers at the end of World War I	
1920		Shochiku Studio founded
1923	Great Kanto earthquake devastates Tokyo	
1936		Toho Studio founded
1937	Japan invades China	
1941	Japan attacks Pearl Harbor, pulling the United States into World War II	
1942		Daiei Studio opens
1945	United States drops atom bombs on Hiroshima and Nagasaki, ending World War II	
1945–1952	US occupation of Japan	
1950		Kurosawa's *Rashomon*

(*Continued*)

Timeline (*Continued*)

Dates	National History	Film History
1953		Ozu's *Tokyo Story* (*Tokyo monogatari*) Mizoguchi's *Ugetsu* (*Ugetsu monogatari*)
1950s–1970s	Economic miracle	
1952	United States explodes first H-bomb in Pacific	Honda's *Godzilla* (*Gojira*)
1964		Tashigahara's *Woman in the Dunes* (*Suna no onna*) Kobayashi's *Kwaidan* (*Kaidan*)
1985		Itami's *Tampopo*
1986		Miyazaki's *Castle in the Sky* (*Tenku no shiro Rapyuta*)
1988		Otomo's *Akira*
1991	Recession ("Lost Decade") begins	
1995	Sarin gas attack on Tokyo subway by Aum Shinrikyo cult Great Hanshin earthquake kills 6,000 in Kobe	Oshii's *Ghost in the Shell* (*Kokaku kidotai*)
1997	Asian Financial Crisis	
1998		Nakata's *Ring* (*Ringu*)
2003		Miike's *One Missed Call* (*Chakushin ari*)
2004		Shimizu's *Marebito*
2011	Earthquake and tsunami damage Fukushima nuclear plant	

While the technology of motion pictures was still young at this time, these cultural conditions and subsequent historical events help to explain the course of Japan's film industry. Soon after the French cinematograph was introduced in 1897, Japan quickly embraced the new technology. In 1899, the first Japanese film was screened in Tokyo at a Kabuki theatre, establishing a link between motion pictures and traditional drama that would persist for decades. Japan adopted the Hollywood studio system, establishing major independent production companies in 1912 (Nikkatsu), 1920 (Shochiku), and 1936 (Toho), each with its own distinctive style and genre specialties. Nikkatsu divided its productions into traditional period dramas (*jidaigeki*), filmed in Kyoto, and contemporary dramas (*gendaigeki*), filmed in Tokyo. Shochiku pioneered a form of social realism called "New Drama" (*shingeki*), based on Western models. Toho favored popular genres like comedy and musicals.

The 1930s was a golden age of great classical directors like Yasujiro Ozu, Kenji Mizoguchi, and Sadao Yamanaka. During World War II, when Japan's military elite took over most things in the country, the government founded its own studio, Daiei, which promoted nationalist themes and made pictures from 1942 to 1971. The late 1930s and early 1940s was a period of propaganda, censorship, and nostalgia for military glory (with a special focus on the Tokugawa period), although Kurosawa managed to make several promising films during this time. After the Japanese defeat in 1945, the Allied Occupation introduced another form of censorship. Under a directive of the Supreme Commander of the Allied Powers (SCAP), "anything infused with militarism, revenge, nationalism, or anti-foreignism ... or approving feudal loyalty or treating life lightly" was prohibited.[1] This effectively eliminated all samurai movies as well as much Kabuki and Bunraku drama until 1952.

The 1950s marked another golden era, a period of vigorous postwar growth when Japanese film studios returned to national genres and audiences returned to local theatres en masse. Ozu continued to focus his meticulous lens on contemporary family life with *Tokyo Story* (*Tokyo monogatari*, 1953) and *Good Morning* (*Ohayo*, 1959). Mizoguchi explored the sorrows of women's lives in historical dramas like *The Life of Oharu* (*Saikaku ichidai onna*, 1952), *Ugetsu* (*Ugetsu monogatari*, 1953) and *Sansho the Bailiff* (*Sansho dayu*, 1954). Japanese films began to circulate abroad, especially those of Kurosawa, who won international festival awards for *Rashomon* (1950) and *Seven Samurai*. Less artistic, perhaps, but no less influential, was Ishiro Honda's *Gojira* (1954), which unleashed the nuclear monster known as Godzilla in the West.

In the 1960s and 1970s, like their Hollywood counterparts, Japanese studios met the challenges of television by appealing to the youth market with films that challenged old taboos. Just as a "New Hollywood" of brash, young filmmakers emerged in the United States, Japan saw a "new wave" (*nubero bagu*) of assistant directors experiment with graphic violence (Masahiro Shinoda's *Double Suicide/Shinju: Ten no amijima*, 1969) and eroticism Nagisa Oshima (*In the Realm of the Senses/Ai no korida*, 1976). Hiroshi Tashigahara's surrealist fantasy, *Woman in the Dunes* (*Suna no onna*, 1964), was a big hit at festivals. But the initiative with most potential for international appeal was probably Japan's unique form of animated movies, known globally as *anime*. The country's early experiments with children's cartoons on television in the 1960s (*Astro Boy*, 1963–1966; *Speed Racer*, 1967) blossomed into a profusion of original, full-length features for adults by the 1980s (*Barefoot Gen/Hadashi no Gen*, 1983; *Castle in the Sky/Tenku no shiro Rapyuta*, 1986; *Grave of the Fireflies/Hotaru no haka*, 1988) to the point where anime now accounts for some 60% of Japan's film production.

The 1980s, a time of vigorous economic growth for Japan, bred a few fresh talents like Juzo Itami (*Tampopo*, 1985), but the big flood of independents broke free only after the bubble burst in 1991. The deluge of internationally recognized directors includes Takeshi Kitano (*Fireworks/Hana-bi*, 1997), Shohei Imamura (*The Eel/Unagi*, 1997), Hayao Miyazaki (*Princess Mononoke/Mononoke-hime*, 1997), Takashi Miike (*Audition/Odishon*, 1999), Hirokazu Kore-eda (*After Life/Wandafuru raifu*, 1999), Mamoru Oshii (*Ghost in the Shell 2: Innocence/Innocence*, 2004), Satoshi Kon (*Paprika/Papurika*, 2006), and of course the classics of modern J-Horror.

Genres and Aesthetics

Such lists of filmmakers and selected works say little about their contribution to the art of cinema or the cultural traditions of Japan. For that we need a closer look at Japanese aesthetics and popular genres. A defining feature of early Japanese cinema is its close connection to the stage traditions that preceded it. As we've seen, the first Japanese movie was screened in a Kabuki theatre. Film audiences in Tokyo regarded the new art form as an outgrowth of Kabuki, Noh, and Bunraku drama. Directors planted their camera in front of the performers, as if the film frame marked the fixed boundaries of a stage. They preferred long takes, uninterrupted by close-ups, cutaways, point of view shots, or other editing techniques. During the silent era, professional storytellers, called *benshi*, would narrate the story, perform the dialogue, and comment on the action while musicians played traditional instruments. These roles were a natural extension of the Bunraku narrator, the Kabuki chorus, and the drums and flute that accompanied Noh plays. The benshi formed a powerful group, commanding high salaries and resisting the conversion to sound movies. As a result, silent movies continued to dominate the Japanese industry long after they had disappeared elsewhere in the world.

The theatrical legacy persisted even longer in the form of a stylized aesthetic. While English documentary, French realism, and classical Hollywood depended on photography's facility for capturing the visible world, Japanese cinema generally preferred to stage reality. It favored presentation over representation, telling over showing. We see this, for example, in Ozu's work, where the camera typically is fixed just below the height of someone kneeling on a *tatami* mat while a family converses over dinner (Figure 3.20). Every shot is carefully arranged to reveal the relationships of each figure to the others and their setting. There is little movement of the camera, little action from the characters; what counts most is the social interaction, the play of emotions beneath an apparently simple, placid surface. Kurosawa, by contrast, keeps his camera and characters in continual motion in films like *Rashomon* (Figure 3.21) and *Seven Samurai* (Figure 1.26, see Close-up: *Seven Samurai*). Each frame is meticulously composed, but the actions speak louder than words. This is one reason why, in own his time, Kurosawa was

FIGURES 3.20 and 3.21   Two approaches to Japanese filmmaking.

FIGURE 3.20 Yasujiro Ozu prefers static shots that reveal character through gestures and dialogue rather than through action, in films like *Tokyo Story* (*Tokyo monogatari*, 1953).

FIGURE 3.21 Akira Kurosawa keeps his actors and his camera moving in films like *Rashomon* (1950).

often criticized as the least Japanese director by his fellow countrymen and why he was most readily embraced by Western audiences.

Three Japanese genres in particular appealed to Americans in the 1950s and 1960s. One was the samurai film, with its exotic feudal settings and elaborately choreographed swordfights. Some US servicemen back from the war, with recent memories of combat behind them and the rough and tumble culture of the Old West behind that, found it easy to relate to movies like Kurosawa's *Bodyguard* (*Yojimbo*, 1961) and Kenji Misumi's *The Tale of Zatoichi* (*Zatoichi monogatari*, 1962). Yet while samurai movies found a cult following in the United States, they never gained the popularity of frontier heroes. The Bushido code of loyalties that tied samurai warriors to their military masters and the Confucian principles of benevolent paternalism by which they formed a kind of family were far removed from the rugged individualism of the cowboy. Whereas the Japanese actor Toshiro Mifune is often torn by the competing claims of *ninjo* (personal feelings) and *giri* (social obligations), John Wayne's struggles are mostly private, a matter of his personal code of honor. And while Kurosawa's *jidaigeki* often conclude with the gentle sadness of *mono no aware*, a deep sense of the transience of things, John Ford's Westerns usually end with the hero riding into the wilderness after a tough job well done.

A genre that proved more popular abroad was the prehistoric monster film, known as *kaiju eiga* in Japan. The huge success of *Godzilla* in 1954 inspired 16 sequels and a dozen other prehistoric monster movies, including *Rodan* (*Radon*, 1956), *Mothra* (*Mosura*, 1961), and *Ghidorah, the Three-Headed Monster* (*San Daikaiju: Chikyu saidai no kessen*, 1965). In contrast to most of their American counterparts, these creatures have names and personalities. They seem more human, more like the sympathetic King Kong than the impersonal insects in *Tarantula* (1955) or *Them!* (1954). One of the best ways to see the differences between Japan's and Hollywood's approach to the genre is to compare the American releases to the Japanese originals. After *Gojira*, for example, when Embassy Pictures released *Godzilla, King of the Monsters!* in the United States, the studio reedited the film, cutting 30 minutes of footage and inserting new scenes. It also added a voice-over narration by Raymond Burr, who plays an American reporter. Burr is also spliced into the story as a central character. The references to nuclear disaster are more overt in the American release, with footage of a mushroom cloud and a devastated Tokyo added to the opening as well as the explicit warning that the same force "at this very moment still prevails and could at any time lash out with its terrible destruction anywhere else in the world." This preoccupation with nuclear power and its role in Cold War politics occurs again and again in American and British sci-fi movies like *The Thing from Another World* (1951) and *X: The Unknown* (1955). In Japan, a country plagued by natural disasters, the monster is more often associated with volcanoes (*Rodan*), dust devils (*Mothra*), or the ocean (*Godzilla*).

A third genre, especially important in the evolution of horror cinema, is the Japanese ghost narrative, or *kaidan*. In Chapter 3, we saw how movies like *Ugetsu* and *Onibaba* drew on a long tradition of stories about restless spirits, or *yurei*, dramatized in countless Noh and Kabuki plays. We learned how tales about wronged women, victims of arrogant men and their vainglorious wars, became vehicles for questioning Japan's military past. Masaki Kobayashi's *Kwaidan* (*Kaidan*, 1964) is a collection of four stories based indirectly on these folk tales. Interestingly, Kobayashi based his film on a retelling by Lafcadio Hearn, a Greek-born writer who lived in Ireland, the United States, and Japan. It was in Japan that Hearn (also known as Yakumo Koizumi) became fascinated with the country's legends, putting many of them in his own 1904 publication, *Kwaidan: Stories and Studies of Strange Things*. Here was another example of international borrowing, in this case a Japanese director reclaiming a piece of his own heritage from a Western source. In the film's first story, "The Black Hair," a poor samurai deserts his first wife to remarry for money and social status, but the second marriage turns out badly. When he tries to make amends and return to his true love, he finds his old house as quiet as a cemetery. The floorboards are broken and grass has sprouted through the *tatami* mats, but he sees a light glimmering from one room. There, seated at her spinning wheel, is his faithful wife, her black hair uncut since his departure (Figure 3.22). He embraces the lovely features he has missed all these years, murmuring words of sorrow and regret before he lies down by her side. But when he awakens the next day, all he sees is a skull, some ragged clothes, and a shock of dark black hair. Kobayashi's slow buildup, his exquisite cinematography and spare use of sound, make the scene a haunting instant of pure horror.

"The Black Hair" reads like a morality tale in which the ghost is not an evil force but the spirit of a human being who died without a peaceful resolution to her life. The plot and theme reflect Japan's religious traditions. According to Shinto beliefs, ghosts can move freely between the permeable boundaries of the living world (*kono-yo*, or simply "here") and the world of the dead (*ano-yo*, "there"). A spirit

FIGURE 3.22 Masaki Koboyashi's *Kwaidan* (*Kaidan*, 1964) draws on the Japanese tradition of restless spirits, usually female ghosts that haunt their male tormentors.

deprived of love or justice may haunt the living until the balance is restored. In Buddhist thought, desire is the root of suffering. Life is not a battle between good and evil but a journey toward a state of inner peace, an emptying of self. The wife's ghost is dreadful not because she's evil but because her decay embodies the painful illusion of desire. Not only do these ideas permeate early films like *Kwaidan*, *Onibaba*, and *Ugetsu*; they also pervade later horror movies like *Ring* (*Ringu*, 1998) and *One Missed Call* (*Chakushin ari*, 2003), in which the ghost works largely through technology.

Anime

Japanese spirits may also operate through the technology of anime, as in Mamoru Oshii's *Ghost in the Shell* (*Kokaku kidotai*, 1995). In Oshii's film, the spirit inhabits a mechanical body, a cyborg or robot animated by a human will. The cybernetic body and its transformations embody modern anxieties about identity. Are we free agents or machines? Do we act fully on our own or more like puppets in a Bunraku play? The animated robot may also be a metaphor for motion pictures, the art of giving life to inanimate objects, a cinematic counterpart to the animist arts of Shinto.

The point is often made that anime comes out of a strong visual tradition, that Japan's pictorial arts are among the richest of the world. Susan Napier describes this culture as "pictocentric,"[2] pointing to the colorful costumes of Kabuki and *ukiyo-e* woodblock prints of the Edo period as examples. The Japanese appreciation of design is everywhere, in their carefully groomed gardens, in the refinements of their tea ceremony, even in their penmanship, which has evolved into the elevated art form of *calligraphy*. More recent is the phenomenon of *manga* literature, a form of visual storytelling that resembles comic books but with a much wider range of themes and readers. Manga has found a following among young readers in the United States, but in Japan, everyone reads manga, from children to adults.

At first glance, anime may look like manga set in motion. In fact, most anime productions are based on manga sources. But the art and technology of anime are more complex than that, as a brief historical account makes clear. While Japanese filmmakers have been making animated films since the days of silent motion pictures, anime really came of age as a global force in the 1960s with *Astro Boy*, Japan's first animated television series. The boy in the title (known in Japan as *Tetsuwan atomu*, "The Almighty Atom") is created by a scientist to replace the man's dead son. This father figure gives the boy laser fingers, a computer brain, and atomic fuel for food, but he abandons his creation when he realizes that it will never grow up like a human boy. Though its animation was relatively crude, *Astro Boy* anticipated many of the visual and thematic elements of later works: a cybernetic body with spiked hair, round eyes, and a pug nose; the promises and risks of modern science; a troubled relationship between father and son. The series was quickly exported and adapted for American children, anticipating a trend repeated for such television anime as *Speed Racer* (1967) and *Robotech* (1985).

Budget limitations forced Japanese animators to cut corners, using fewer drawings per minute than Disney did in its "full animation" films. As a result, the action seemed relatively static, backgrounds lacked detail, and characters appeared to jump from pose to pose instead of going through the fluid alterations of emotion, not unlike the masks of Noh theatre or the stylized gestures of Kabuki. While Disney used a sophisticated system of multi-plane cameras, adding depth and realism to productions like *Bambi* (1942) or *Snow White and the Seven Dwarfs* (1937), Japanese studios confined motion to a two-dimensional plane, much like the flat perspective of Edo era paintings. All this gave anime a distinctive quality that is consistent with Japan's aesthetic traditions. In other words, financial constraints were turned into cultural capital. Anime and its distinctive style became national assets for competing in the global marketplace.

A good case can be made that the true essence of anime lies in the magic of transformation, one shape morphing into another, a quality shared with *origami*, the Japanese art of paper folding, and transformer toys. As Japan's animation artists developed their craft, these transformations grew more stylish and elaborate. In the extraordinary final scene of Katsuhiro Otomo's *Akira* (1988), a boy with psychic powers undergoes a physical metamorphosis. The film is set in a futuristic world, after World War III, when Tokyo is a wasteland roamed by police squads and biker gangs. The government wants to use the boy, Tetsuo, for his special abilities, but these powers prove to be beyond even his control. In the film's cathartic conclusion, Tetsuo is cornered by the army at the old Tokyo Olympics site. There he finds the remains of Akira, not the messianic figure he expected but a pile of encapsulated organs left by research scientists. Flushed with anger and a strange new feeling of omnipotence, his body begins to change (Figure 3.23). A fleshy lip sprouts from his right arm, expanding into a gigantic pink protrusion of

FIGURE 3.23   The magic of anime movies may be linked to Japanese traditions like origami paper folding, Noh drama masks, Shinto animism, and transformer toys. In Katsuhiro Otomo's *Akira* (1988), a troubled boy is transformed into the embodiment of adolescent fears about life's changes.

fingers, tentacles, and cusps, both phallic and womb-like. His torso heaves and swells like a mass of mutating cancerous cells, engulfing everything and everyone around. He is a victim of its hideous, organic growth. There is much to notice in this scene. On one level, Tetsuo's physical transformation reflects normal adolescent fears about the body and its changes. Growing up is an awkward, messy process, when physical signs of sexual maturity begin to take shape, inspiring both fascination and revulsion. It is a time when individual needs conflict with pressures to belong, when feelings of helplessness mix with fantasies of grandeur. Without a proper family, poised between authority figures (an eccentric scientist, a patriarchal general) and competing peers (the free-spirited bikers, three fellow psychics, a government spy, and a girlfriend named Kaori), he must decide who he wants to be. On another level, Tetsuo represents the body of historical Japan. Surrounded by mementos of the past – a tank named "samurai spirit," the mushroom cloud of Hiroshima, the Olympic stadium symbolizing Japan's resurgence in 1964 – he faces either an apocalyptic ending or a cataclysmic rebirth. On the level of myth, these options recall the Carnivalesque anarchy of ancient festivals or the figure of the monstrous feminine, whose life-giving powers and all-consuming drive to swallow and contain are visible in Tetsuo's oozing pink fluids, the ingesting advances of his flesh, and the chaos of it all.

As anime evolved, it took on many genres and subgenres, including melodrama (*Grave of the Fireflies/Hotaru no haka*, 1988), science fiction (*Ghost in the Shell*), antiwar critique (*Neon Genesis Evangelion/Shin seiki evangerion*, 1995–1996,TV), teen romance (*Oh My Goddess!/A Megami-sama* 2005–2006, TV), neo-noir (*Animatrix/Animatorikkusu*, 2003), martial arts (*Samurai Champloo/Samurai chanpuru*, 2004, TV), and a few forms special to anime: cyberpunk (*Battle Angel Alita/Gunnm*, 1993) and *mecha* (short for mechanical devices piloted by humans, like the war machines in *The Sky Crawlers/Sukai kurora*, 2008). Many of these films featured spectacular scenes of horror. Tetsuo's transformation in *Akira*, for example, is a terrifying vision of body horror. In *Blood: The Last Vampire* (2000), a sword-wielding female, the last remaining vampire, is hired to hunt down a throng of blood-sucking bat-like creatures who are terrorizing an American army base. Set in 1966, *Blood* reflects the uneasy partnership between Japan and the United States as they entered the war in Vietnam.

The alternate worlds of anime offer rich fields of study for film theorists. The theme park in *Spirited Away* (*Sen to Chihiro no kamikakushi*, 2001), where greedy adults turn into pigs, may be interpreted as a cartoon critique of consumerism. The adolescent *shojos*, young girls looking both innocent and enticing in their school uniforms, is a favorite subject of feminist studies, which see shojos sometimes as cute objects of male desire (*Serial Experiments Lain*, 1998, TV), sometimes as assertions of female power (*Revolutionary Girl Utena/Shojo kakumei Utena*, 1999). In her "Cyborg Manifesto," Donna Haraway views the cyborg as the metaphor for a new, transgressive form of feminine identity, free of the rigid dualities of human/machine, body/soul, culture/nature, male/female that have long restricted women in the West.[3] Indeed, the generally fluid identities of Japanese anime – cosmopolitan cities detached from their local roots, characters that belong to no particular ethnic group, stories removed from history and culture – make these films seem quintessentially global and postmodern.

J-Horror

By the start of the new millennium, the canons of Japanese cinema were reaching new global targets in the form of J-Horror. Earlier expressions of the genre had mixed Japanese and Western elements with mixed results. The haunted habitats in *House* (*Hausu*, 1977) and *Sweet Home* (*Suito homu*, 1989), for example, reflected anxieties about family not unlike those explored in *Amityville Horror* (1979) and *The Shining* (1980), but with Japanese furnishings and ghosts. The grotesque deformations of the human body in *Horror of a Deformed Man* (*Kyofu kikei ningen: Edogawa Rampo zenshū*, 1969) and *Tetsuo: The Iron Man* (*Tetsuo*, 1989) have parallels in *Videodrome* (1983) and *Re-Animator* (1985), but some of their imagery is drawn from medieval scrolls depicting sinners suffering Buddhist hells. In any case, none of these earlier horror films circulated much outside of Japan.

The world-wide popularity of films like *Ring, Ju-on: The Grudge*, and *Pulse* (*Kairo*, 2001) is bound up with new technologies of the 1990s and 2000s. This is a matter of content and style as well as marketing and exhibition. First, these films are *about* technology. Their ghosts often attack people through the media of videotape, cell phones, surveillance cameras, and the Internet. Much of their emotional force comes from a general uneasiness about technology taking over our lives. Second, they borrow the aesthetics of new media to create an effective visual style. The digital look and feel of early J-Horror films reflect the fact that many were made cheaply on videotape, giving familiar images an uncanny appearance. This quality lingers in the grainy images of *Pulse*, lending an eerie, spectral radiance to its Internet phantoms. Digital media also influence the way these stories are told. The fragmentary narrative structure of *Ju-on*, for example, has been compared to the modularity of television series or the "chapter format" of the DVD.[4] Viewers can watch their favorite scenes repeatedly and out of sequence, inventing new forms of spectatorship. Third, in terms of distribution, the same permeable boundaries that enable ghosts to move between technologies and human realms have allowed filmmakers to spread their stories through different media. J-Horror arrived at a time when distinctions between cinema, video, television, and computers were beginning to blur. The *Ju-on* franchise thrives in multiple formats: as theatrical film releases, through television broadcasts, and on DVDs. No longer dependent on big companies that control the world's print labs and theatres, Japanese filmmakers can distribute their work directly, anywhere across the globe where viewers have access to a DVD player or the Internet.

A good example of a film that crosses all these boundaries and more is Takeshi Shimizu's *Marebito* (2004). Shot, edited, and distributed on digital media, its story follows the labyrinthine twists and turns of non-linear narration. Masuoka is a freelance video journalist obsessed with the look of terror he sees on a man's face just before the man commits suicide. His explorations lead to an underground passage, where he discovers a vast network of subterranean tunnels and the elusive creatures that live there. One of these creatures, a naked young woman, is chained to a wall. He frees her, takes her home, and eventually learns that she is not quite human. She crawls on all fours like an animal, cannot speak, and feeds on blood. To keep her alive, he becomes a murderer, first killing a demented woman who has been following him, then slaying a would-be actress, collecting their blood in water bottles to bring home. During his shopping trips, Masuoka sets up surveillance cameras in his apartment so he can track the girl remotely on his cell phone (Figure 3.24). His suspicions are aroused when a 12-second video segment mysteriously disappears. *Marebito* is a reflexive work, highly conscious of its cinematic debts and themes. Masuoka photographs his victims like the protagonist of *Peeping Tom* (1960), his captive acts like a cat woman or a vampire, and he is haunted by the suicide's restless ghost. The subterranean tunnels beneath Tokyo turn out to be a legacy of the last war, perhaps of other buried histories, like those beneath other cities of the world. It is also a subconscious realm of repressed personal demons, a fantasy land contrasting with the "real world" above ground. As Masuoka alternates between these two mental states, we come to realize that the demented woman, the naked girl, and everything else may have alternate identities too frightening for Masuoka to confront, until he is willing to look into the face of fear itself.

These dual planes of existence in *Marebito* highlight one of the most fascinating and troubling contradictions of Japan. Here is a country renowned for its attentiveness to social etiquette. It is a place where people bow respectfully to one another, wear face masks in the subway, and remove their shoes before entering a home. A complex system of honorifics is built into its very language, regulating the politics

FIGURE 3.24   A frame from Takeshi Shimizu's *Marebito* (2004). New digital aesthetics and fear of modern technology contribute to the global popularity of J-Horror.

of polite communication between men and women, children and adults, employers and employees. Yet, beneath these elaborate civilities lies a realm of primitive urges and raw desire. Perhaps this paradox is not unique to Japan, only more pronounced. Perhaps it's what gives Japanese art such power and resonance abroad, placing Japanese films and J-Horror in particular among the most engaging topics of global cinema today.

Notes

1. Quoted in Colette Balmain, *Introduction to Japanese Horror Film* (Edinburgh University Press, 2008), 23.
2. Susan Napier, *Anime from Akira to Howl's Moving Castle: Experiencing Contemporary Japanese Animation* (Palgrave, 2005), 21.
3. Donna Haraway, "A Cyborg Manifesto: Science, Technology, and Socialist-Feminism in the Late Twentieth Century," in *Simians, Cyborgs and Women: The Reinvention of Nature* (Routledge, 1991), 149–181.
4. See Jinhee Choi and Mitsuyo Wada-Marciano, *Horror to the Extreme: Changing Boundaries in Asian Cinema* (Hong Kong University Press, 2009), 28–33.

Further Reading

Balmain, Colette. *Introduction to Japanese Horror Film.* Edinburgh University Press, 2008.

Blake, Linnie. *The Wounds of Nations: Horror Cinema, Historical Trauma and National Identity.* Manchester University Press, 2008.

Brown, Seven. *Cinema Anime: Critical Engagements with Japanese Animation.* Palgrave, 2006.

Choi, Jinhee and Mitsuyo Wada-Marciano, *Horror to the Extreme: Changing Boundaries in Asian Cinema.* Hong Kong University Press, 2009.

Davis, Darrell William. *Picturing Japaneseness: Monumental Style, National Identity, Japanese Film.* Columbia University Press, 1996.

Haraway, Donna. "A Cyborg Manifesto: Science, Technology, and Socialist-Feminism in the Late Twentieth Century." In *Simians, Cyborgs and Women: The Reinvention of Nature,* 149–181. Routledge, 1991.

Kawai, Hayao. *The Japanese Psyche: Major Motifs in the Fairy Tales of Japan.* Woodstock, 1996.

Lowenstein, Adam. *Shocking Representation: Historical Trauma, National Cinema, and the Modern Horror Film.* Columbia University Press, 2005.

MacWilliams, Mark, ed. *Ja Explorations in the World of * Sharpe, 2008.

McDonald, Keio. *Reading a Context.* University of Hawa

McRoy, Jay. *Nightmare Japan: Contempora Horror.* Rodopi, 2008.

Napier, Susan. *Anime from Akira to Howl's Moving Castle: Experiencing Contemporary Japanese Animation.* Palgrave, 2005.

Richie, Donald. *A Hundred Years of Japanese Film.* Kodansha International, 2001.

CLOSE-UP

HALLOWEEN

FIGURE 3.25   John Carpenter's *Halloween* (1978).

Directed by John Carpenter.
Script by John Carpenter and Debra Hill.
Cinematography by Dean Cundey.
Edited by Tommy Lee Wallace and Charles Bornstein.
Music by John Carpenter.
Art Direction and Production Design by Tommy
    Lee Wallace.
Produced by Falcon International Productions
    and Compass International Pictures in 1978.
Running Time: 91 minutes.

Dr. Sam Loomis	Donald Pleasence
Laurie Strode	Jamie Lee Curtis
Annie Brackett	Nancy Kyes
Lynda van der Klok	P.J. Soles
Sheriff Leigh Brackett	Charles Cyphers
Lindsey Wallace	Kyle Richards
Tommy Doyle	Brian Andrews
The Shape	Nick Castle

World Cinema through Global Genres, First Edition. William V. Costanzo.
© 2014 John Wiley & Sons, Inc. Published 2014 by John Wiley & Sons, Inc.

Halloween is a good occasion for a scary movie. It's the time when children play with fear, masquerading as monsters, ghosts, and goblins, shouting "trick or treat" at their neighbor's door. There is nothing playful, though, about the holiday's historic origins, which have been linked to All Hallows Eve, or All Souls' Day, the Catholic feast of prayer for the dead, and before that to the Celtic festival of Samhain, a pagan celebration in which the bones of slaughtered livestock were tossed into a roaring bonfire. John Carpenter's 1978 movie uses Halloween and its spooky legacy to link the innocence of children with a supernatural evil force, to mix juvenile amusements with the menace of death in a horror film that set new cinematic standards for the genre.

Carpenter sets the film in middle-class America, in the quiet Midwestern town of Haddonfield, Illinois, where a six-year old boy named Michael Myers stabs his 17-year-old sister with a kitchen knife on Halloween. Fifteen years later, on October 30, 1978, Michael breaks out of the asylum where he has spent all this time under the care of Dr. Samuel Loomis (played by Donald Pleasence), his psychiatrist. Dr. Loomis makes his way to Haddonfield to warn the residents that Michael is at large and dangerous. Among those most at risk are three teenage girls, Annie, Lynda, and Laurie. Annie is the sheriff's daughter, a high-spirited teen who smokes marijuana and takes her babysitting responsibilities lightly. Instead of watching Lindsey, the neighbors' little girl, Annie drops her off with her friend Laurie so she can spend the evening with her boyfriend Paul. Lynda, a flighty girl who talks nonstop, makes similar plans with her boyfriend Bob. So Laurie, who is either more mature or less popular with boys, ends up babysitting for the two children: Lindsey and a little boy named Tommy Doyle.

Laurie becomes the "Final Girl," the last in a series of chosen victims. Left alone with the children in Tommy's house, she must face the murderer with her fear and whatever resources she can muster. Why she has survived this long is worth considering. She is more intelligent than her friends, a better student, more conscientious about her caretaking responsibilities. The fact that she has no date and no boyfriend also suggests that she is sexually inactive, perhaps a virgin. Do these qualities give her a special immunity from Michael Myers's murderous vengeance? Is there a moral message here? He attacks her several times, but twice she fights back, first stabbing him in the neck with a sewing needle and later lunging at his torso with his own knife after thrusting a bent hangar into his eye. But these wounds, which would kill any normal man, do not stop Myers. His strength seems supernatural. Even after Dr. Loomis arrives and shoots him in the chest six times, sending him off the balcony to the ground two stories below, he doesn't die. When Loomis looks down a second time, Myers has disappeared.

Carpenter plays with the idea that Michael is inhuman. Tommy, who reads comic books like *Tarantula Man* and watches scary movies like *Forbidden Planet* (1956) and *The Thing from Another World* (1951) on television, is fascinated with monsters. He's both curious and terrified. The big kids at school delight in frightening him with stories of the "bogey man," which is what he imagines when he sees Michael's shadow cross the street. Michael's identity is kept deliberately obscure. For most of the film, he wears a nondescript white mask. We catch brief glimpses of him in a window, behind the shrubbery, as a dark silhouette in the back seat of a car or at the top of the stairs. Sometimes, we only hear his breathing, muffled by the mask. Dr. Loomis, who should know, describes him as pure evil. "When I met him, 15 years ago," he explains to Sheriff Brackett, "I was told there was nothing left. No reason, no conscience, no understanding, not even the most rudimentary sense of life or death, good or evil, right or wrong. I met this six-year-old child, with this blank, pale, emotionless face and, the blackest eyes … the devil's eyes." Carpenter himself encourages this supernatural interpretation by referring to his monster in the credits simply as "The Shape." At the same time, the Shape acts much like a troubled child who never grew up. He wears the white mask as if he were playing trick or treat, like the neighborhood kids who are running from door to door. At one point, he puts on a white sheet to scare Lynda, who thinks it's her boyfriend pretending to be a ghost. Throughout the film, he acts like a voyeur, peeping into windows to watch teenage girls in various states of undress as he once watched his sister make out on the sofa. It's as if Michael's psychological development were arrested at age six, when sexual curiosity and repressed rage first erupted in violence.

Some critics find a conservative agenda in the film, pointing out that the main victims are promiscuous, pot-smoking teens. Tony Williams, for example, sees Michael as a "patriarchal avenger" who "slaughtered the youthful children of the 1960s generation, especially when they engaged in illicit activities involving sex and drugs."[1] Gregory Albert Waller also notes this shift from the old Universal monsters, "creatures of the id" who represented repressed urges, to a new "super-ego figure" who punishes the young for their uninhibited indulgences.[2] Others find classic illustrations of Freudian, Lacanian, or Jungian psychology. Reynold Humphries identifies an Oedipal moment in the scene when Michael kills his sister, noting that it takes place in his mother's bedroom (the camera glances quickly at the sheets before the murder) and that the girl is seated naked at the vanity mirror: he has not progressed beyond the narcissistic mirror stage of psychological development.[3] James Iaccino sees Dr. Loomis as a primordial father figure, an archetype of the wise old man whose function is to protect Laurie, an archetype of the self-sacrificing woman.[4] While some gender-conscious critics condemn the film for offering yet more images of violence against women, feminists like Carol Clover point out that Myers's victims include men as well as women and that Laurie can be regarded as a positive image of femininity: smart, resilient, and capable of fighting back.[5] Carpenter himself disclaims any ethical or political intentions, depicting *Halloween* as a horror movie plain and simple. According to Carpenter, his choices were all motivated by practical reasons of craft. "The one girl who is the most sexually uptight just keeps stabbing this guy with a long knife. She's the most sexually frustrated. She's the one that's killed him. Not because she's a virgin but because all that sexually repressed energy starts coming out. She uses all those phallic symbols on the guy."[6]

John Carpenter came of age during the "Hollywood renaissance" of the 1960s and 1970s, when filmmakers like Arthur Penn and Sam Peckinpah were breaking away from the classical conventions of the old studio system with youth oriented movies like *Bonnie and Clyde* (1967) and *The Wild Bunch* (1969). Born in Kentucky in 1948, he began making home movies with an 8mm camera at the age of eight, experimenting with his interest in fantasy, action, and special effects. Like George Lucas, another member of the film school generation, he studied cinema at the University of Southern California, writing scripts, directing an Oscar winning short, and making his first features: a sci-fi film (*Dark Star*, 1974) and a contemporary Western, *Assault on Precinct 13* (1976). But while many of the energetic "movie brats" went on to make independent art films, Carpenter preferred to work within established commercial genres, considering himself more of an artisan than an artist. Yet despite his adherence to B-movie aesthetics, which tend to feed the expectations of his audience, his work articulates a consistent personal vision, like the work of Howard Hawks, his Hollywood hero. Perhaps that's why Laurie and Tommy watch *The Thing from Another World*, a film directed by Hawks that Carpenter would later remake as *The Thing* in 1982.

The production history of *Halloween* offers some insight into how low-budget genre films were made in the United States after the decline of Hollywood's big studios. Irwin Yablans, an independent producer from Brooklyn, had an idea for a film about a serial killer who stalked and murdered babysitters. After seeing Carpenter's previous film, *Assault on Precinct 13*, at an international festival, Yablans invited the young man to direct another feature. The budget would be limited to $320,000, provided by a Syrian American financier. This meant that shooting would be quick (21 days), local (most of it was shot in Pasadena, California), and with no expensive sets or costumes (Tommy Lee Wallace, the film's set designer, art director, location scout, and co-editor, reportedly purchased a William Shatner mask for $1.98 and turned it into something eerily featureless). Carpenter co-wrote the script in three weeks with Debra Hill, who had worked with him on *Assault*. Some decisions, like the Halloween setting, were deliberate. Others, though, were improvised from their personal lives or favorite films, like many of the names of characters and settings. The place name of Haddonfield, Illinois was taken from Hill's home town of Haddonfield, New Jersey. Some of its street names came from Bowling Green, Kentucky, where Carpenter grew up. Sheriff Leigh Brackett was named after a screenwriter who worked with Howard Hawks. Dr. Loomis took his name from Janet Leigh's boyfriend in Hitchcock's *Psycho*. And Michael Myers was the name of a British film producer who had helped to promote Carpenter's previous film.

With so little money for the cast, the team could afford only one big star. Both Peter Cushing and Christopher Lee turned down the part of Dr. Loomis, but British actor Donald Pleasence was intrigued enough to sign on, spending a total of five days on the set. Jamie Lee Curtis, who plays the female lead, had never acted in a film before, although as the daughter of Janet Leigh, she made the role an ideal successor to her mother's Marion in *Psycho* (1960). For the role of Michael Myers, Carpenter chose a college friend, Nick Castle. When Castle asked for the psychological motivation of his character, Carpenter said, "Just walk." Their work in *Halloween* became the launching pad for life-long film careers: Castle as actor and director, Curtis as the screaming victim in a long run of horror films before branching into comedy, drama, and television work.

On the set and on the screen, Carpenter made good use of new technologies. The recently invented Panaglide gyroscopic camera, a precursor of the Steadicam, gave his cinematographer Dean Cundey the means for stalking Michael Myers's victims from the killer's point of view, floating through the air like a phantom. Carpenter also used widescreen formats to advantage. The elongated dimensions of Panavision gave him ample space to focus on his central protagonist while the monster lurks in the background. The Shape's first appearance to Laurie is in the right corner of the frame; his first attack on Tommy comes from the extreme left. This stresses Myers's marginal position in society while keeping audiences on edge. Among the film's most influential innovations is its moody musical score, composed by Carpenter himself. Instead of an expensive symphonic track, he synthesized odd sounds from simple sources. As the camera slowly zooms into the grinning face of a jack-o'-lantern in the opening credit sequence, we hear three sounds reverberate on the keyboard, rising or descending in semitones while a brief, high-pitched piano motif continues nervously in 5/4 time, an insistent and unsettling technique borrowed from Italian Horror-master Dario Argento's *Suspiria* (1977). Later on, we hear shrill metallic sounds as piercing as the thrust of knife blades and as chilling as a woman's scream.

Halloween's huge box office success inspired a franchise that includes ten slasher films, novels, and comic books. It has also influenced innumerable horror movies and directors. Carpenter's use of ordinary settings, his prowling camera, the free-spirited teenage victims, and chaste Final Girl have become staples of the slasher film, most notably *Friday the 13th* (1980) and *A Nightmare on Elm Street* (1984). The Shape became a prototype for a long line of remorseless and relentless serial killers. And Carpenter achieves all this with very little bloodshed. Most important, as in all his films, Carpenter never loses touch with the pleasures that his fans derive from watching movies. With more than 17 features behind him, he still retains the sense of sheer delight in cinema that he once enjoyed while editing horror fanzines in his early days.

Questions

1. On a scale from 1 to 10, how scary would you rate Carpenter's film? What makes it frightening for you? What doesn't work, and why?

2. Compile a list of Do's and Don't's for slasher films like *Halloween*. Here are some starters: Don't hide in the closet. Don't turn out the lights. Do think of household items as weapons. Never fool around when your parents are away.

3. Trace the influence of *Halloween* on other slasher films. What new codes and conventions did it help to establish, and where do you see these influences appear?

4. Try watching a scene from the movie with the sound turned off. Then watch it again with sound. What does the sound track add? Alternatively, try listening to a scene with the

screen turned black. What feelings to you get from just the audio? How do the visuals and audio complement each other in your chosen scene?

5. What was happening in the United States when *Halloween* was made? In what ways does the film reflect its time? Consider its characters, plot, set-

ting, themes, and visual style. How well does the original *Halloween* hold up today?

6. At least nine sequels of *Halloween* have appeared since 1978. How do you explain the popularity of this franchise? Watch one of the later versions and compare it to Carpenter's original. Explain why you prefer one over the other.

Notes

1. Tony Williams, "Trying to Survive on the Darker Side: 1980s Family Horror," in Barry Keith Grant, ed., *The Dread of Difference: Gender and the Horror Film* (University of Texas Press, 1996), 164–165.

2. Gregory Waller, ed., *American Horrors: Essays on the Modern American Horror Film* (University of Illinois Press, 1987), 80.

3. Reynold Humphries, *The American Horror Film: An Introduction* (Edinburgh University Press, 2002), 140.

4. James Iaccino, *Psychological Reflections on Cinematic Terror: Jungian Archetypes in Horror Films* (Praeger, 1994).

5. Carol Clover, *Men, Women, and Chain Saws: Gender in the Modern Horror Film* (Princeton University Press, 1992), 37.

6. *Halloween: A Cut Above the Rest*, documentary bonus feature film, DVD, Divimax 25th Anniversary Edition of *Halloween* (Anchor Bay, 2003).

Further Reading

Boulenger, Gilles. *John Carpenter: The Prince of Darkness*. Silman-James Press, 2003.

Conrich, Ian. *The Cinema of John Carpenter: The Technique of Terror*. Wallflower Press, 2004.

Cumbow, Robert C. *Order in the Universe: The Films of John Carpenter*. Scarecrow Filmmakers Series, 1990.

Fischer, Dennis. *Horror Film Directors, 1931–1990*. McFarland & Company, 1991.

Jones, Kent. "American Movie Classic: John Carpenter." *Film Comment* 35(1) (January 1999): 26–31.

Muir, John Kenneth. *The Films of John Carpenter*. McFarland & Company, 2005.

CLOSE-UP
SUSPIRIA

FIGURE 3.26 Dario Argento's *Suspiria* (1977).

Directed by Dario Argento.
Script by Dario Argento and Daria Nicolodi.
Cinematography by Luciano Tovoli.
Edited by Francesco Fraticelli.
Music by Goblin.
Production Design by Giuseppe Bassan.
Special Effects by Germano Natali.
Produced by Seda Spettacoli.
Distributed in the United States by International
    Classics in 1977 (dubbed).
In Italian, English, German, Russian, and Latin
    with English subtitles; also dubbed into English.
Running Time: 98 minutes.

Suzy Bannion	Jessica Harper
Sara	Stefania Casini
Daniel	Flavio Bucci
Mark	Miguel Bosé
Olga	Barbara Magnolfi
Sonia	Susanna Javicoli
Pat Hingle	Eva Axén
Prof. Milius	Rudolf Schündler
Miss Tanner	Alida Valli
Madame Blanc	Joan Bennett

World Cinema through Global Genres, First Edition. William V. Costanzo.
© 2014 John Wiley & Sons, Inc. Published 2014 by John Wiley & Sons, Inc.

Given Italy's reputation for emotional flamboyance, its violent political history, and the extravagant imagination of its artists, it's not surprising that the land of Verdi, Dante, Machiavelli, and Michelangelo would spawn some of the most powerful works of horror cinema. Italy became a nation only in the nineteenth century, but the collective consciousness of its people was shaped for centuries by the grotesque imagery of Michelangelo's *Last Judgment*, terrifying moments from Dante's *Inferno*, and thunderous choruses from Verdi's operas. Machiavelli's advice in *The Prince* for using methodical brute force, assassination, and deceit in the interest of political gain fed stereotyped notions that appear in Shakespeare's tragedies and Jacobean dramas of revenge. It is from this tradition of visceral art that the subgenre known as *giallo* arose in the 1960s. Named after the lurid color of cheap paperbacks (*giallo* means yellow in Italian), the earliest *giallo* films were murder mysteries and thrillers. Mario Bava defined the trend by staging elaborate scenes of creative cruelty and stylish bloodletting, putting mood ahead of plausibility, provoking fear and paranoia in his audience. Bava's most talented successor is Dario Argento, and *Suspiria* is arguably Argento's most important work, becoming a cult classic and a major influence on directors around the world.

Suspiria is set in Freiburg, Germany, where a young American named Suzy Bannion (Jessica Harper) has come to study ballet at the Tanzakademie, a prestigious dance academy. She arrives on a dark and stormy night, hailing a taxi to take her in the pouring rain through a gloomy forest to the school's forbidding red facade. There she sees another student run off in terror, never to return. When Suzy finds the door locked, she spends the night in town, returning the next day to be greeted by the school's directors, the stern Miss Tanner (Alida Valli) and a sweetly duplicitous Madame Blanc (Joan Bennett). The other girls treat her as an unwelcome outsider, but she makes friends with Sarah, another social outcast. Together, the two girls uncover the school's secrets: a maze of disappearing students, strange after-class activities, winding corridors, and hidden doors, all leading to a final confrontation between Suzy and the academy's ancient founder, Helena Markos. The film has the feel of a fairy tale, an Italian *Alice in Wonderland* – or *Through the Looking-Glass* – with Suzy's curiosity propelling her journey into a surrealistic environment of frightening events and supernatural beings.

According to Argento's own account, the story originated with his travels through the "magic triangle" bordering Switzerland, France, and Germany, an area associated with mysticism and satanic rites.[1] Rudolf Steiner had established a Waldorf school there in 1919 to promote the spiritual teachings of his Anthroposophical Society. He was accused of encouraging paganism, and the school burned down under mysterious circumstances. Argento's co-writer and long-time collaborator, Daria Nicolodi, suggests other sources, including the true story of her grandmother, a pianist who enrolled in a music academy that turned out to be a haven for black magic. Frightened by her teachers' demonic designs, Daria's grandma ran away. The film's title comes from *Suspiria de Profundis* (Latin for "Sighs from the Depths"), a collection of essays by the nineteenth-century English writer Thomas De Quincey, whose visionary prose reflects his addiction to opium. Argento took De Quincey's notions about three maternal figures – *Mater Suspiriorum* ("Our Lady of Sighs"), *Mater Lacrymarum* ("Our Lady of Tears"), and *Mater Tenebrarum* ("Our Lady of Darkness") – to organize a trilogy of matriarchal monsters: *Suspiria*, *Inferno* (1980), and *Mother of Tears* (2007) respectively. Viewed from feminist perspectives, these three films, and Argento's female characters in general, have been interpreted as signs of the director's personal views of women and as symptoms of Italian society.

Born in Rome in 1940, Dario was the son of Salvatore Argento, a film producer/executive, and Elda Luxardo, a Brazilian-born photographer. As a child, he spent hours in his mother's studio, acquiring her fascination with the human face and exploring the many hallways and staircases that would figure in his films. He cultivated solitude, reading a lot, going to the movies, indulging in imaginative visions, exploring the dark side of human nature. His actors describe him as a nervous man, "always studying you, peering into your soul."[2] Argento began his film career as a critic and screen writer. He worked with Bernardo Bertolucci on the script for Sergio Leone's *Once Upon a Time in the West* (1968), discovering an affinity for the director of spaghetti Westerns who was more interested in the look and feel of his movies than in the logic of their plots. Argento's directorial debut, *The Bird with the Crystal Plumage* (*L'ucello dalle piume di cristallo*, 1970), was a *giallo* mystery. A big hit in Italy, it led quickly to two other thrillers in his "animal trilogy": *The Cat o' Nine Tails* (*Il gatto a nove code*, 1971) and *Four Flies on Grey Velvet* (*4 mosce di velluto grigio*, 1971). After a brief detour in television drama, he made *Deep Red* (*Profondo rosso*, 1975), developing a meticulous attention to the suspenseful pacing and ingenious mechanics of murder that he cultivated in all his later films. Still working in Italy and occasionally abroad, he had directed more than 20 films and TV episodes by 2013.

For those who look for narrative coherence and realistic acting, Argento's reputation as a director's director may seem a bit mysterious at first. *Suspiria* is more like a series of elaborately staged, artificial spectacles rather than a well-plotted story. The dialogue sounds corny, hollow, especially since it was dubbed during post-production, divorced from its live dramatic moment on the set. But this disjunction between the actors' voices and their actions gives their words an eerie, disembodied quality that contributes to the mood. As for the episodic plot, random acts of pointless aggression from an unknown source can be more frightening than the motivated violence of a serial killer.

Argento disorients his viewers with a repertoire of bizarre camera angles, dizzying tracking shots, sudden close-ups, and disruptive shifts in pacing. In the film's first terrifying scene, when Pat, the fleeing student, finds refuge in her friend's apartment, a quick sequence of reverse angle shots shows a window being thrust open from Pat's point of view, cuts to her friend bursting through the door, then tracks back out through the window as she closes it. "It was just the wind," she says, but the camera's hesitation on the other side tells us otherwise. Moments later, an extreme exterior long shot of Pat framed in the tiny dormer window is followed by a series of medium shots and close-ups from inside, accompanied on the soundtrack by a cacophony of chimes and strings, as she anxiously paces the room, then squints through the plate glass into the darkness (See Figure 3.26). The anticipation is excruciating. Suddenly, we see a pair of disembodied eyes, and a hairy arm breaks through, driving her face against the window pane. What follows is even scarier and more bizarre: a rapid-fire montage of shattering glass, violated bodies, and dripping blood. All this takes place in an incongruous Art Deco setting, with wallpaper inspired by Escher's visual illusions, illuminated by garishly colored lights.

The color scheme in *Suspiria* was influenced by Disney's use of Technicolor in *Snow White and the Seven Dwarfs* (1937). The Technicolor process was already passé in 1977, but Argento managed to get one of the last remaining machines and used it with filters to intensify the contrast between primary colors. The less realistic, the better. Although this method slowed down production, Argento and his crew were willing to craft each scene painstakingly, constructing and adjusting every set by hand with the pride of artisans. The scene in which a blind man and his seeing-eye wolfhound confront an invisible threat in the vast, empty square of Koenigsplatz was shot on a set that took weeks to build and light. Greek columns surround the square at odd angles as in a surrealist painting by De Chirico. When the dog starts barking, the camera accentuates the man's distress by jumping between low angle and extreme high angle shots. Now it's below him, now it's lurking behind the columns, now fixed on a stone eagle, then hovering above him like a demon in flight. The question is not if he'll be attacked, but when and from where.

No less important than these visual effects is the movie's distinctive soundtrack. Argento hired the Italian rock music band Goblin to compose most of the score, which they created with an assortment of African percussion instruments, bells, gongs, chimes, plastic cups, and hammers. For the opening sequence in the taxi, they set a melody from Verdi to 5/4 time, achieving an eerie syncopated beat that was later imitated in *Halloween* and other horror films throughout the world.

At times, *Suspiria* seems like a fairy tale for adults. If Suzy is another Alice exploring an enchanted world, her Alice is properly paranoiac, for this world is a sinister place. The authorities cannot be trusted, especially the women, who use the school as a cover for their evil practices. Their indulgence in supernatural phenomena is explained in rational terms by two men in the film. Sarah's psychiatrist believes that witchcraft is a form of madness spreading through the world. "Bad luck isn't wrought by broken mirrors," he says, "but by broken minds." A German professor of occult studies explains that witchcraft gives women power, power to do harm. The coven's wealth comes from doing injury to others. These accounts suggest an ongoing conflict between male and female forces that is reflected in the gendered spaces of the film. Women are associated with interiors richly decorated and softened with curved lines. Men are linked to the outdoors; their architectural markers are monochromatic columns and skyscrapers, like the white Greek façades of Koenigsplatz and the towering office building where the psychiatrists meet.

Argento has been criticized for perpetuating stereotypes. Most of his victims are girls, and the older women in this film are wicked. But some men are also victims, and some are part of the evil. It is even possible to regard witchcraft as a subversive bid for wealth and power in a world dominated by male rationality, a patriarchal order that brands strong women as heretics. Ultimately, *Suspiria* reflects the historical gender relationships in a country where the Catholic Church is still run by men and the popular media regularly display women as sexual objects. Argento borrows another page from history in the blind man episode, for Koenigsplatz was the site of Nazi rallies under Hitler, and the wolfhound was Hitler's favorite pet. This vicious night attack on a defenseless citizen hauntingly evokes the horrors of World War II.

Suspiria and its kindred *giallo* films are not for everyone. The spectacular violence of Argento's grisly imagery, his privileging of emotion and atmosphere over character and story, his allegiance to the hallucinatory experience of dreams: these are what his dedicated fans admire. In addition to this worldwide following, the circle of Argentophiles includes some of cinema's most respected directors. John Carpenter considers *Suspiria* "one of the greatest horror movies ever made … an incredible work of art, simple and profound."[3] George Romero invited Argento to produce his *Dawn of the Dead* (1978) and continued to work with him on other projects. Martin Scorsese and Joe Dante count his work among their favorites, a taste to be sampled, cultivated, or acquired.

Questions

1. What do you find most compelling, original, or troubling in *Suspiria*? In other words, what stands out as distinctive in Argento's filmmaking?

2. Consider the moments of exposition in the film, the scenes when someone (like the psychologist or the German professor) offers background information to explain what happens at the dance academy. How do they account for the supernatural events? How seriously are we meant to take such explanations?

3. George Romero has compared Argento to artists like Paul Gauguin and Vincent Van Gogh, more concerned with their subjective vision than with objective portraits of the world. To what extent does *Suspiria* seem like a work of impressionism, expressionism, or surrealism?

4. The dance academy is a feminized space, managed, decorated, and inhabited chiefly by women. Pay close attention to its layout and furnishings, its wallpaper and color schemes. What do these things say about the women in this film?

5. Notice how certain visual details (like water, glass, doors, hallways, and the color red) are repeated as motifs. What functions does this repetition serve? What links these motifs to each other and to the film's broader themes?

6. Select one scene for a close shot-by-shot analysis. Log the director's decisions about shot duration, set design, camera work, lighting, color, sound, dialogue, and action. What reasons can you give for these decisions? What do they contribute to the scene's overall effect?

7. In *Broken Mirrors/Broken Minds*, Maitland McDonagh offers a formalist analysis of *Suspiria* based on the work of Vladimir Propp, the scholar of Russian folk tales.[4] McDonagh compares Suzy's journey to traditional narratives: the hero leaves home, is given warnings, gets tricked by the villain, witnesses the injury of a family member, and so on. To what extent does the film's plot follow Propp's taxonomy or correspond to other fairy tales you know?

Notes

1. "Interview with Co-Writer/Director Dario Argento," bonus feature on DVD with *Suspiria* 2-Disc Special Edition (Blue Underground, 2009).
2. "Interview."
3. *Dario Argento: An Eye for Horror*, TV film, directed by Leon Ferguson (Produced by CreaTVty, 2002 / Distributed by Independent Film Channel, 2004).
4. Maitland McDonagh, *Broken Mirrors/Broken Minds: The Dark Dreams of Dario Argento* (Sun Tavern Fields, 1991), 134–135.

Further Reading

De Ville, Donna. "Menopausal Monsters and Sexual Transgression in Argento's Art Horror." In Robert Weiner and John Cline, eds., *Cinema Inferno: Celluloid Explosions from the Cultural Margins*, 53–75. Scarecrow Press, 2010.

Fischer, Dennis. *Horror Film Directors, 1931–1990*. McFarland & Company, 1991.

McDonagh, Maitland. *Broken Mirrors/Broken Minds: The Dark Dreams of Dario Argento*. Sun Tavern Fields, 1991.

CLOSE-UP

THE DEVIL'S BACKBONE

FIGURE 3.27   Guillermo del Toro's *The Devil's Backbone* (*El espinazo del diablo*, 2001).

Directed by Guillermo del Toro.
Produced by Guillermo del Toro and Pedro
   Almodóvar.
Script by Guillermo del Toro, Antonio Tra-
   shorras, and David Muñoz.
Cinematography by Guillermo Navarro.
Edited by Luis de la Madrid. Music by Javier
   Navarrete.
Art Direction by César Macarrón.
Narrated by Federico Luppi.
Released in the United States by Sony Pictures in 2001.
In Spanish with English subtitles.
Running Time: 106 minutes.

Dr. Casares	Federico Luppi
Carmen	Marisa Paredes
Jacinto	Eduardo Noriega
Carlos	Fernando Tielve
Jaime	Iñigo Garcés
Santi	Junio Valverde
Conchita	Irene Visedo

World Cinema through Global Genres, First Edition. William V. Costanzo.
© 2014 John Wiley & Sons, Inc. Published 2014 by John Wiley & Sons, Inc.

"What is a ghost? A tragedy doomed to repeat again and again? An instant of pain, perhaps. Something dead which still seems to be alive. An emotion suspended in time. Like a blurred photograph. Like an insect trapped in amber." The question is posed by an unseen narrator during the opening credit sequence of *The Devil's Backbone*, a Spanish-language film by Mexican director Guillermo del Toro. What we do see is a montage of unsettling images: the arched entrance to a dark cellar; a bomb falling on a battle-scarred landscape; a young boy lying on a brick floor, shuddering, his head in a puddle of his own blood. Then bubbles rise from his mouth as the boy sinks into a pool of polluted, amber water, his limbs now tied with rope. Finally, in a liquid potion of the same amber color we make out the limbs and face of a human embryo, soft and vulnerable, but with a spinal column bristling with pointed spikes. In the next 100 minutes of the film, del Toro weaves these pictures into one of the most haunting narratives in cinema: a story about phantoms that won't die, about the supernatural power of repressed wrongs, about personal pain and historical trauma, entrapment and escape.

Although made in 2001, *The Devil's Backbone* acquires much of its cultural weight and resonance from a tradition of national cinema that links horror to the Spanish Civil War. Like its predecessors – Victor Erice's *The Spirit of the Beehive* (*El espíritu de la colmena*, 1973), Carlos Saura's *Cria!* (*Cria cuervos*, 1976), and Alejandro Almenábar's *The Others* (*Los otros*, 2001) – as well as del Toro's own more recent *Pan's Labyrinth* (*El laberinto del fauno*, 2006), *The Devil's Backbone* is set during a three-year period, from 1936 to 1939, when Spaniards and their sympathizers fought each other with ferocious hatred. The two opposing groups polarized around the Nationalists on one side and the Republicans on the other. General Franco led the right-wing Nationalist army, supported by Mussolini's Fascists. The left-wing government, elected by popular vote, was supported by Stalin's Communist forces and an International Brigade of sympathizers from some 55 different countries. It was a bloody preview of World War II, with atrocities committed by both sides.

Del Toro sets his movie in an orphanage, miles from the nearest town. In this isolated cluster of old buildings, a kind of fortress in the desert, Carmen and Dr. Casares run a boarding school for boys who have lost their parents in the war. When a new boy named Carlos arrives, he thinks he'll be there for a short time. He doesn't realize that he too is an orphan. At first he's bullied by a group of older boys, led by their ringleader, Jaime, but through a series of tests and trials, he proves his courage and gains their respect. Carlos and Jaime become close friends, sharing toys and secrets as boys do everywhere. But this is more than a coming of age story. Jaime's secret involves a murder and a ghost. The orphanage, it seems, is haunted.

The ghost manifests itself to Carlos in the dormitory as a disembodied sigh, then as an unseen presence in the kitchen, a shadow, footprints, a pale face with deep-set eyes and a smoking head wound. This, he learns, is Santi, a young orphan who died under circumstances known only to Jaime and the murderer. Carlos forms a special bond with Santi, who warns that many in the orphanage will die.

Meanwhile, we learn about the social dynamics of the place. Dr. Casares is a polished, older gentleman, an Argentine by birth who memorizes poetry and calls himself a man of science. He is in love with Carmen, the middle-age matriarch with a wooden leg who has feelings for him but knows that he cannot satisfy her physical needs. For that purpose, she relies on Jacinto, a handsome hulk of a young man who harbors a seething resentment of her, of Dr. Casares, and of everyone else in the orphanage. If Santi is the movie's phantom, Jacinto is its all too human monster. These characters form a kind of dysfunctional family. They are a microcosm of the Spanish nation at odds with itself. The war within the walls reflects the larger war without.

Del Toro provides several reminders of the historical conflict. In one scene, when Dr. Casares goes to town, he sees nine Republican soldiers being lined against a wall for execution. There are two Spaniards, six Canadians, and one man from China. Casares recognizes one of the Spaniards, his friend Ayala, and pretends not to know the man, although his reaction to the gunshots says otherwise. As James Rose notes in his study guide, the scene recalls Francisco Goya's famous painting, *The Third of May 1808*, commemorating Spanish resistance to Napoleon in 1814.[1] Another reference to war is the huge bombshell in the orphanage's courtyard. Dropped by enemy aircraft (an allusion to the bombing of Guernica in 1937?), it never exploded, making it an ominously silent portent. When the explosion does come, it's from within.

Although Casares tells Carlos that the orphanage is not a prison, everyone seems to be confined. Carmen is restricted by her wooden leg, Casares by cowardice and impotence, the boys by their dependence on adults. Jacinto, who wants to escape more than anyone else, is a captive of his poverty and self-inflicted emotional isolation. He will not leave without the gold ingots locked in Carmen's safe. These people are like insects trapped in amber. Their personal tragedies, like the blunders of history, are condemned to recur. In this respect, Santi's ghost stands for everybody's inner burden, the buried load that will not remain repressed.

Del Toro's sophisticated style works largely through the tonal and visual vocabulary of cinema, through recurring motifs that link individual moments to each other and to the film's broad themes. There are the amber, oval shapes of the cellar door, the insect caught in time, the embryos suspended in glass cylinders like artificial wombs. There are the sounds and sights of water: dripping from a tap, brimming in a glass pitcher, tainted in the cistern and the cylinders with the flotsam and jetsam of decay. There are images of heavy weights (Carmen's leg, gold ingots, boys carrying a wooden statue of Christ on the cross), of weapons (wooden poles used as spears, a rifle used as a prod), of entrapment (a comic book version of *The Count of Monte Cristo*, the cistern, the orphanage itself). In one of the few scenes where these motifs are put into words, Casares talks about the fetuses with Carlos. They are in the doctor's study when the boy asks, "Do you believe in ghosts?" Pointing to the chemicals and wall charts that surround them, Dr. Casares replies, "As you can see, I'm a man of science." "But Spain," he adds, "is full of superstition. Europe is sick with fear now, and fear sickens the soul. And that makes us see things." Casares walks over to a cylinder where the spinal column of a fetus stands out in the liquid. The townsfolk call this "the devil's backbone," believing that it happens to children who should never have been born, but he attributes the condition to poverty and disease. Nevertheless, Casares sells this "limbo water" in town to those who drink it as a cure for ailments like blindness and impotence. "Rubbish," he concludes, but that does not prevent him from taking a sip himself after the boy goes running from the room.

In his many interviews, del Toro offers autobiographical accounts of many details in the film. Born in Mexico in 1964, he was raised by his "grandmother" (actually, his grandmother's sister) in a strict Catholic household. As a child, he made short Super 8 movies, casting his mother and friends in various roles. A close uncle introduced him to horror literature and film. When the man died at an early age, Guillermo inherited his books and moved into his room, where he says he heard his dead uncle sigh for 20 minutes. Guillermo left the room, never to return, certain that he had heard a ghost. In another incident, he wandered into the morgue of a hospital and saw a pile of discarded fetuses. The moment shocked him into atheism, a condition that he clung to despite efforts by his devout grandmother to exorcize him. The fetuses, the phantom sigh, and Catholic iconography all appear in *The Devil's Backbone*, together with the Jesuit classroom where he went to school and the secret, illustrated diary that he still keeps today.

Del Toro studied screenwriting at the University of Guadalajara and spent eight years designing special effects and make-up, forming his own effects company, Necropia. After some professional work in film and television, he directed his first feature, *Cronos*, in 1993. *Cronos* is a kind of vampire story. An aging antiques dealer, played by Federico Luppi (later cast as Dr. Casares), finds the secret of eternal life in a strange device created by a medieval alchemist. Trapped in the device, enmeshed with the mechanical clockwork, is a living insect that injects a rejuvenating fluid into the owner's flesh. Del Toro's macabre imagination and cinematic skills were applauded by critics and won the young director a trip to Hollywood, where he was given a $30 million budget to make *Mimic* (1997), a science fiction horror film. Although del Toro disliked relinquishing creative control, what he learned about American equipment and techniques served him well in later projects, including *Pan's Labyrinth* as director, *The Orphanage* (*El orfanato*, 2007) as producer, and five contributions to the *Hellboy* franchise (as director or producer, 2004–2008).

In the director's audio commentary for *The Devil's Backbone*, del Toro gives an unusually articulate description of the movie's artistic and cultural sources.[2] He traces the origin of Gothic romance to *The Castle of Otranto*, Horace Walpole's 1764 novel, noting how the tradition mixes genres in a contemporary way but still follows certain conventions: a haunted place that harbors a dark secret, simmering sexuality and violence, a pure-hearted protagonist who solves the mystery. Del Toro links Gothic ghost stories to children's fairy tales, with their own symbolic codes (step-parents, deceitful strangers, ovens, keys) intended as cautionary narratives. He sees these scary lessons as precursors to the modern horror tale. Horror goes beyond conventional morality; it celebrates the darkness, the ugly, the bizarre in all of us. If horror has a lesson to teach, it is about understanding the Other. It teaches that a rational man of science, a man who refuses to believe in ghosts, can become a ghost himself.

Questions

1. There is only one mention of "the devil's backbone" in the film, when Dr. Casares explains the "limbo water" to Carlos in his office. Why do you think del Toro chose this phrase for the movie's title? What associations does the term stir up beyond its literal meaning?

2. The names of four main characters begin with the letter C and two begin with the letter J. What connects these characters besides their first initial? Is there a clear division between protagonists and antagonists in this story, or are there changes in the characters or in our perceptions of them?

3. In his audio commentary, the director says that every character lacks something. Make a list of the main figures and explain what's missing in their lives.

4. In the schoolroom scene, the children hear a story about mammoths and the prehistoric men who hunted them with primitive weapons. What lesson do the boys learn from this, and how do they apply it to their own survival needs?

5. Del Toro pays close attention to the color palette of this film. Notice which scenes are lit in pink and amber, which scenes in blues and grays. What moods are evoked by these tones? How does the film use color to organize the themes and pacing of the story?

6. Explore the role of warfare in this movie. To what extent is it about the historical Spanish Civil War, about the mentality of Fascists and Socialists, about Us vs. Them?

Notes

1. James Rose, *Studying the Devil's Backbone* (Auteur, 2010), 31–32.

2. Guillermo del Toro, Audio commentary, *The Devil's Backbone*, Special Edition DVD (Sony Pictures Home Entertainment, 2004).

Further Reading

Derry, Charles. "Guillermo del Toro." In *Dark Dreams 2.0: A Psychological History of the Modern Horror Film from the 1950s to the 21st Century*, 315–329. McFarland & Company, 2009.

Earles, Steve. *The Golden Labyrinth: The Unique Films of Guillermo del Toro*. Noir Publishing, 2009.

Rose, James. *Studying the Devil's Backbone*. Auteur, 2010.

CLOSE-UP
RING

FIGURE 3.28   Hideo Nakata's *Ring* (*Ringu*, 1998).

Directed by Hideo Nakata.
Script by Hiroshi Takahashi.
Based on the novel by Koji Suzuki.
Cinematography by Junichiro Hayashi.
Edited by Nobuyuki Takahashi.
Music by Kenji Kawai.
Production Design by Iwao Saito.
Produced by Toho Company in 1998.
In Japanese with English titles.
Running Time: 96 minutes.

Reiko Asakawa (newspaper reporter)	Nanako Matsushima
Ryuji Takayama (ex-husband, teacher)	Hiroyuki Sanada
Yoichi Asakawa (their son)	Rikiya Otaka
Mai Takano	Miki Nakatani
Tomoko Oishi	Yuko Takeuchi
Masami	Hitomi Sato
Takashi Yamamura	Yoichi Numata
Yoshino	Yutaka Matsushige
Koichi Asakawa	Katsumi Muramatsu
Shizuko Yamamura	Masako
Sadako Yamamura	Rie Ino

World Cinema through Global Genres, First Edition. William V. Costanzo.
© 2014 John Wiley & Sons, Inc. Published 2014 by John Wiley & Sons, Inc.

When *Ring* (*Ringu*, 1998) was first released in the United States, Americans who saw it were both fascinated and bewildered. Here was something new and strange, yet uncannily familiar: a contemporary horror film that mixes ghosts and video cassettes in a style that seems both cosmopolitan and distinctly Japanese. The film and its story struck a chord that reverberated worldwide. In Japan, it set a record for gross box office receipts and launched a whole franchise of sequels, prequels, and *manga* books. In the United States, it was remade as *The Ring* (2002), reaping even higher sales figures and stimulating an enormous global appetite for Asian horror. Looking closely at Nakata's work – its structure and aesthetics, its motifs and themes, its origins and influence on other films – gives us another opportunity to understand how an international genre like horror can cross national boundaries, carrying some of its cultural baggage along with it.

The immediate source for *Ring* is a 1991 novel by Koji Suzuki, which is loosely based on the Japanese folk tale of *Bancho Sarayashiki*. In the novel, the protagonist is a man, and the avenging spirit's gender is ambiguous, the result of a rare genetic disease. Restless spirits that haunt the living are regular features of Japanese ghost stories like *Bancho Sarayashiki*, in which a man takes advantage of a young woman from a lower class. When the woman dies, her ghost returns to avenge her mistreatment. She becomes a *yurei*, a paranormal force driven by unresolved emotions. Before motion pictures began to tell her tales of woe, the *yurei* was a popular figure in classical ghost narratives, or *kaidan*, dating back to the Edo Period (circa 1601–1868) and continuing to haunt the audiences of *no* and *kabuki* theatre. *Kaidan* movies of the 1950s and 1960s, like *Ugetsu* (*Ugetsu monogatari*, 1953) and *Onibaba* (1964), perpetuated much of the literary genre's iconography and aesthetic style. Typically, the *yurei* has clawed fingers and long, unkempt, black hair that falls over her pale face, obscuring her penetrating eyes. She may dwell in a haunted house, the site of some past trauma, or emerge from the watery depths, from a lake or well. In contrast to classical Hollywood's forward driving, trimly plotted movies, which typically follow the logic of cause and effect, these Japanese films work by indirection and ellipsis. Meanings are suggested rather than spelled out; portions of the narrative are skipped. While these departures from realism and rationality are hallmarks of Japanese aesthetics, they are also found in Western art: in French Surrealism, for example, or German Expressionism. They are particularly well suited for the kind of horror that makes *Ring* so effective.

In the opening scene, two teenage girls are troubled by rumors of a mysterious videotape. Masami tells Tomoko that a boy in the village of Izu died seven days after watching it. At first, Tomoko pretends to be skeptical but then admits that she and three close friends watched such a video before receiving a puzzling phone call. Meanwhile, Tomoko's aunt Reiko has been investigating the video curse for her job. Reiko is a single mother and a professional journalist. When she learns that her niece and the three friends are dead, Reiko becomes obsessed with the case. She learns that the four teens spent the weekend in a rental cabin on the Izu peninsula, where she goes looking for the videotape, taking her son along and later enlisting the help of her ex-husband, Ryuji. What they discover pulls them deep into the local history of Izu and exposes them all to harm.

Some thrillers that track the progress of an investigation – *Psycho* (1960), *The Changeling* (1980), *The Orphanage* (2007) – depend on a combination of suspense, surprise, shock, and psychological insight for their emotional impact. *Ring* is more interested in mystery and tension than in pop psychology or body gore. It slowly builds a sense of apprehension that is hard to shake off even after the final scene. There is no comforting resolution since solving the mystery doesn't end the threat, which continues like a virus. The virus metaphor works in several ways. The curse spreads through technological means, like a computer virus, moving through the medium of video or the telephone, but with biological consequences. Every victim who sees the tape and gets a phone call dies with his or her face frozen in a mortifying stare. Like an organic virus or a chain letter, the curse invades its host (the tape, the phone, the human victim) and uses it to multiply. It's a struggle for survival between the virus and its carrier.

Reiko traces the curse to two women with psychic powers, Shizuko and her daughter Sadako, both long dead. Shizuko's life on a volcanic island and her reputation for predicting natural disasters suggest one interpretation of the curse, linking her to a long series of geologically generated monsters from Godzilla to Rodan. But both women are also victims of male derision and aggression, linking them to the female ghosts in *Ugetsu* and *Onibaba*. They suffer because they transgress man-made boundaries. A patriarchal panel dismisses Shizuko's telepathic talents as witchcraft. Sadako's father abuses her and tries to stifle her voice forever in a well. There is a kind of justice, then, in her refusal to be silenced, in crossing the line between technology and humankind, in projecting her pain through a television screen into the world of the living. The water imagery associated with Sadako's death, a symbol of repressed trauma in so many horror films, suggests a deeper historical significance to critics like Linnie Blake. Blake points out that Sadako (which means "chaste" in Japanese) was the name of a sick child of Hiroshima who believed she would be cured if she could fold 644 origami paper cranes. When she died in 1955, she came to represent "all that was destroyed by Japan's territorial ambitions and the concomitant decision of the United States to unleash the nuclear menace upon the civilians of Japan."[1]

But why would an innocent girl like Sadako target other teenagers or a single mother like Reiko? One answer is that forces of nature and supernatural powers are not bound by logic or morality. *Ring* gains much of its force by avoiding explanations. The dead do with us as they please, much to our horror. Another answer is that the film evokes cultural anxieties about unsupervised young adults who rent cottages on weekends and about working parents who focus more on work than on parenting. In this regard, Nakata may be following the lead of American films like *Halloween* (1978) and *Friday the 13th* (1980), with their sexually active teenage victims. He certainly owes something to other Western directors when he shows Sadako crawling through a television screen (a stunt borrowed from David Cronenberg's *Videodrome*, made in 1983) or whenever an eerie blend of synthesized metallic noises haunts his sound track (as in Dario Argento's *Suspiria*, 1977).

We hear this ominously grating sound just before Reiko watches the video. Then the white noise of the television set gives way to a low rumbling as a strange sequence of images appears on the screen. We see a moon at night, a woman combing her hair in an oval mirror, a page filled with Japanese words, human figures struggling uphill, a man pointing to his right, a close-up of a human eye with the word "Sada" printed on the pupil, and an abandoned well. None of these images is clear or stable. The moon is obscured by clouds, the woman's reflection seems to jump on the wall, the words wriggle on the page (one, larger than the others, means "Eruption"), the man's face is hidden by a towel, and the well is too grainy to make out in detail. How are these things related? What do they mean? Reiko just stares at the screen, barely noticing the figure that stands beside her for a moment before vanishing. Then the phone rings.

The soundtrack bristles and rumbles once again when Reiko and Ryuji find the well beneath Cabin B4. Reiko has a brief vision of the murder, rendered in a black and white flashback, as if she's reading Sadako's mind. The laborious process of draining the well begins. There are close-ups of ropes and buckets, of Sadako's scratch marks on the inside of the well, of the couple's individual faces as they work in desperate silence. A repetitive progression of high notes on the soundtrack reminds us that time is running out.

Hideo Nakata was born in Okayama, Japan in 1961. His debut feature, *Don't Look Up* (*Joyu-rei*, 1996), was far from a triumph, but it enabled him to make *Ring* with a budget of $1.2 million, shooting it in five weeks. Some effects, like the grainy look of the cursed video and the scene in which Sadako climbs through the television screen, were achieved in post-production. The finished film broke box office records in Japan, encouraging Nakata to rush out a sequel, *Ring 2* (1999), before filming another story by Koji Suzuki, *Dark Water* (*Honogurai mizu no soko kara*) in 2002. In 2005, Hollywood invited him to direct *The Ring Two*, the American remake of his sequel. His growing body of work now includes *Chaos* (*Kaosu*, 2000), *Kaidan* (2007), and *The Incite Mill* (*Inshite miru: 7-kakan no desu gemu*, 2010).

In addition to Nakata's *Ring 2*, *Ring* inspired another sequel (*Spiral/Rasen*, 1998) and a prequel (*Ring 0: Birthday/Ringu 0: Basudei*, 2000) in Japan, a remake in South Korea (*The Ring Virus/Ring*, 1999), and an American video game known as *The Ring: Terror's Realm* (2000). The Hollywood remake of Nakata's *Ring* was directed by Gore Verbinski, who went on to direct three films in the *Pirates of the Caribbean* franchise (2003–2007). Verbinski stays close to the original for much of his movie, even following some of Nakata's camerawork, although he moves the setting to Seattle and gives American names to the main characters. Reiko and Ryuji become Rachel (played by Naomi Watts) and Noah (Martin Henderson), with slight alterations in their roles. Sadako becomes Samara, who has a different personal history: before her murder she is institutionalized by her adoptive parents, Richard and Anna Morgan. Once the tape is found, Verbinski's alterations become more pronounced. In a detailed comparison of the two versions, Valerie Wee explains the differences in cultural terms, arguing that *Ring* follows the "presentational aesthetic" of Japanese art, privileging ambiguity and stylized form over narrative logic, while *The Ring* reflects a Western preference for clarity, closure, and realistic storytelling.[2] All these variations of *Ring* contributed to a resurgence of the genre that includes Higuchinsky's *Spiral* (*Uzumaki*, 2000), Kiyoshi Kurosawa's *Pulse* (*Kairo*, 2001), Takashi Shimizu's *Ju-on: The Grudge* (*Ju-on*, 2002), and a host of global followers.

Questions

1. An urban legend is a story that circulates among contemporary individuals who believe it to be true, much as folktales did in earlier times. Like a chain letter or a pyramid scheme, it may gain credibility and strength with each retelling. In what respects is the video curse in *Ring* an urban legend? How did it start, how is it perpetuated, and when do you think it will end?

2. *Ring* belongs to a subgenre known as techno-horror, which includes Canada's *Videodrome* and Japan's *One Missed Call* (*Chakushin ari*, 2003) among others. What do such movies reveal about our fears of and fascination with technology today?

3. How well do we get to know the characters in *Ring*? To what extent are we interested in their relationships apart from their connection to the video curse?

4. Whom do you consider to be the monster in this film? How do the victims and aggressor(s) compare to those in other horror films you know?

5. Compare *Ring* to its American remake, *The Ring*. What makes Nakata's film distinctly Japanese? What cultural difference do you find in Verbinski's version? What seems to be universal in these films?

6. *Ring* began as a novel and was adapted for television, movies, *manga*, and video games. Explore the aesthetic or commercial side of these adaptations. How does each medium alter the experience? What business interests are at work behind each variation?

7. Valerie Wee examines the videotape sequence in *Ring* and *The Ring*, finding influences from surrealist cinema and music videos in the latter that reach beyond its Japanese counterpart. Make your own comparative study before reading Wee's essay in *Cinema Journal*.

Notes

1. Linnie Blake, *The Wounds of Nations: Horror Cinema, Historical Trauma and National Identity* (Manchester University Press, 2008), 53.

2. Valerie Wee, "Visual Aesthetics and Ways of Seeing: Comparing *Ringu* and *The Ring*," *Cinema Journal* 50(2) (Winter 2011): 41–60.

Further Reading

Blake, Linnie. "*Nihonjinron*, Women, Horror: Post-War National Identity and the Spirit of Subaltern Vengeances in *Ringu* and *The Ring*." In *The Wounds of Nations: Horror Cinema, Historical Trauma, and National Identity*, 44–68. Manchester University Press, 2008.

Kalat, David. *J-Horror: The Definitive Guide to "The Ring," "The Grudge," and Beyond*. Vertical, 2007.

Meikle, Denis. *The Ring Companion.* Titan Books, 2005.

Suzuki, Koji. *Ring* [original Japanese novel]. Translated by R.B. Rohmer and Glynne Walley. Random House, 2003.

Takahashi, Hiroshi and Misao Inagaki. *The Ring* [manga adaptation of the movie *Ringu*]. Dark Horse Comics, 2003.

Wee, Valerie. "Visual Aesthetics and Ways of Seeing: Comparing *Ringu* and *The Ring.*" *Cinema Journal* 50(2) (Winter 2011): 41–60.

UNIT IV
THE ROAD MOVIE

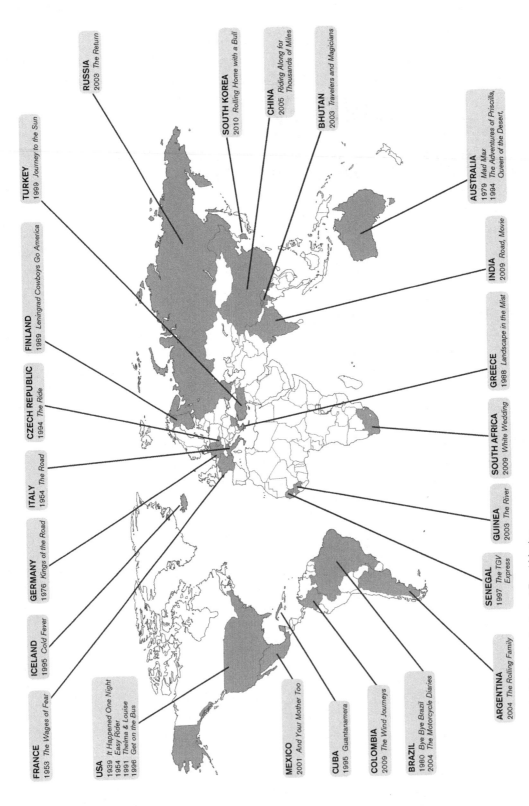

FIGURE 4.1   A global map of selected Road Movies.

CHAPTER 4
THE ROAD MOVIE

Some seven minutes into *Easy Rider* (1969), when the opening credits begin, the film's two young heroes set off across the desert landscape on a pair of customized motorcycles (Figure 4.2). Billy (Dennis Hopper) wears a bushman's hat and the buckskin outfit of a Western frontiersman. Wyatt (Peter Fonda) wears a black leather jacket and matching pants. Blazoned across Wyatt's helmet and his gas tank are the stars and stripes. After tossing aside his wristwatch in a symbolic gesture, he and Billy race up the trail toward the horizon, disappearing in a cloud of dust. The camera catches them in tight close-ups, in lyrical long shots, and from every angle as the dirt road turns to asphalt and they speed off into the wind. Riding side by side, these biker buddies and their bikes are one, all gleaming metal and raucous roar. When they cross the Colorado River, the sound track bursts into song. Steppenwolf's lyrics about looking for adventure out on the highway seem to speak for the two youths and their high expectations. "Like a true nature's child," they were "born to be wild." But moments later, as night falls and the travelers pull up at a motel, they are greeted by the first sign of trouble. The owner takes one look, walks back through the doorway, and turns on the neon "no" over the "vacancy" sign.

With its promise of freedom and adventure on the open road, evoking the thrill of mobility as well as the devastating comedown of a trip gone wrong, *Easy Rider* is widely considered to be an exemplar of the 1960s and a milestone in the evolution of the road movie. Barbara Klinger describes it as "an instant emblem of its generation."[1] Lee Hill calls it "the landmark independent film that almost single-handedly created the road movie as a vital post-60s genre."[2] Shari Roberts agrees that "the road film did not exist as a recognizable genre until, roughly, the release of *Easy Rider* in 1969."[3]

In this chapter, we'll be returning to *Easy Rider* again and again as we explore the many roles of travel in our culture and our cinemas. What does the trail, the road,

World Cinema through Global Genres, First Edition. William V. Costanzo.
© 2014 John Wiley & Sons, Inc. Published 2014 by John Wiley & Sons, Inc.

FIGURE 4.2   Peter Fonda and Dennis Hopper on customized motorcycles blaze a trail for the American road movie in *Easy Rider* (Dir. Dennis Hopper, 1969).

the highway mean for Americans and other people of the world? What defines the road movie as a genre: its characters, stories, look, and themes? Why does the genre appear at particular times in history? What influences paved the way for *Easy Rider* and its followers? Where has the road taken us, and where is it likely to lead?

Questions of Genre: *Easy Rider* as Exemplar of the Road Movie

For centuries, roads have served a range of purposes both physically and symbolically. The roads built by early Romans unified an empire, bearing military troops and Latin culture over three continents and returning wealth and power back to Rome. Before that, commanding horse-drawn chariots had criss-crossed the vast imperial roadways of ancient Persia. During medieval times in Europe, when central authority withered and the old roads fell into disrepair, they became avenues for pillage, rape, and highway robbery. An open road may signify liberty and independence, but roads also have their ruts and forking paths, their detours and dead ends. These and other variations of the roadway are all reflected in the movies, from the murky, convoluted alleys of film noir in the 1940s to the light-hearted cross-country road race comedies of the 1970s. But what makes these cinematic thoroughfares worth looking at together, as a group? At what point do they constitute a genre, like the Western or the horror film? Is *The Wizard of Oz* (1939) a road movie because Dorothy follows the yellow brick road? Is a post-apocalyptic film like *Mad Max Beyond Thunderdome*, aka *Mad Max 3* (1985) a road film if it is set in a world without roads? And why do these questions matter?

Taking *Easy Rider* as a standard of the genre, we see how much of the movie's iconography depicts the essential ingredients of life on the road. First, there are the vehicles: those sleek motorcycles, of course, but also the drug dealer's Rolls Royce near the beginning of the film and the Southerners' pickup truck that passes them near the end. The bikes embody the spirit of autonomy, mobility pared down to an engine and a seat, without the baggage – or protection – of a framework and a trunk. In this counterculture film, conventional cars and trucks represent commercial encumbrances and threats to freedom. Next, there is the land through which the movie's heroes travel: the open country of the American Southwest, romanticized in gorgeous panorama shots, and the more populated areas of the American South, depicted as squalid and confining. Third, there is the road itself, a visual motif represented in countless shots of dirt trails, dotted highways, and crowded city streets. As the journey continues, the landscape loses its glamor, and the original promise of the open road darkens. Along the way, Billy and Wyatt make camp in the open and stop at different sites. They share an outdoor dinner with a rancher's family, stay at a hippie commune, get arrested for joining a small-town parade without a permit, face hostility in a rural diner, visit a brothel in New Orleans, drop acid in a cemetery, and head toward Florida, where they plan to live in style with the money they made by selling Mexican cocaine. The journey reveals a cross-section of America, each stop an opportunity to explore its people and their values.

But the protagonists in this movie are decidedly deficient in self-awareness or self-expression. Wyatt seems to like the idea of settling down and living off the land, but Billy's restless irritability keeps tugging them back to the road. Neither one can articulate his dreams or frustrations beyond the clipped clichés of counterculture slang. Instead, the role of spokesman is given to the unnamed hitchhiker whom they bring to the commune and, more pointedly, to George Hanson, the young ACLU lawyer (played by Jack Nicholson) whom they meet in jail. George's disheveled suit and tie contrast sharply with the travelers' self-conscious costumes, just as his chatty good nature sets off their sullen silence. George may not know how to roll a joint, but he understands the nature of freedom and its risks. "Freedom: talking about it and being it, that's two different things," he says, adding "It's real hard to be free when you're bought and sold in the marketplace." George knows that the local townspeople fear what Billy and Wyatt represent, which makes the townies dangerous.

Easy Rider, like most road pictures, is populated with a range of characters from different social groups, including the townies, commune hippies, and brothel girls. But its central figures are the two young men who undertake the trip together. Film scholars note how many of the protagonists in road-centered films are male buddies: Bob Hope and Bing Crosby in *Road to Morocco* (1942), for example; George Raft and Humphrey Bogart in *They Drive by Night* (1940); and later Jon Voight and Dustin Hoffman in *Midnight Cowboy* (1969) or Robert De Niro and Charles Grodin in *Midnight Run* (1988). But it is equally true that the central traveling companions may be male and female, like Clark Gable and Claudette Colbert in *It Happened*

One Night (1939), Desi Arnaz and Lucille Ball in *The Long, Long Trailer* (1953), or Warren Beatty and Faye Dunaway in *Bonnie and Clyde* (1967). It was not until *Thelma & Louise* (1991), however, that two women (Geena Davis and Susan Sarandon) got to ride in the front seat, a moment in film history that opened the road to all sorts of couples, bringing issues of gender, race, and sexual orientation to the fore.

Scholars point out certain cinematic features of *Easy Rider* that typify the genre's visual and tonal style. The fluid camerawork by cinematographer Laszlo Kovacs captures the cyclists in motion, two figures speeding against the awe-inspiring backdrop of the American southwest. With sweeping panoramas and dynamic point-of-view shots, Kovacs captures the experience, putting us in the saddle, out on the road. At one point, the hitchhiker on the back of Wyatt's bike stretches out one hand and the frame expands in that direction, opening our vision to include the rolling landscape and the windy feel of freedom. Working in the late 1970s, Kovacs experimented with the new technology of mobile cameras, borrowing techniques from French new wave directors, such as jump cuts (disrupting the flow of action to create disorienting effects), lens flares (light beams radiating from the desert sun), and rapid zooms and dolly shots (jerking the viewer's field of vision in or out). These deliberate departures from the Hollywood studio style draw attention to themselves, reminding us that movies are a form of artifice and helping to set stylistic precedents for a generation of "new Hollywood" directors.

Dennis Hopper, who directed *Easy Rider*, was among the young, independent-minded filmmakers who pointed Hollywood in a new direction at a time when the old studio system needed young blood and fresh ideas. His vision of the 1960s counterculture is reflected in the movie's fragmented – some would say deliberately inarticulate – aesthetics. The incoherence of the acid trip montage sequence, for example, with its grainy 16 mm texture, its disjointed editing, and rambling sound track, seems to hold up a distorted mirror to a generation that has lost its way. Mirrors and montages have become staples of the road film, part of its grammar, as we'll see. By combining several brief shots in quick succession, a montage can show us different angles of a journey, summarize its history, or characterize a stretch of road as squalid or spectacular. Similarly, a windscreen or rear view mirror can help to shift our perspective or it can function symbolically, affording glimpses of the future or a receding past. But one of Hopper's most enduring innovations was *Easy Rider*'s rock score. By adding lyrics by musicians like Steppenwolf, Jimi Hendrix, Bob Dylan, and The Byrds to the sound track, Hopper captured the spirit of the 1960s and gave voice to his characters, however inarticulate they might be.

The original poster for *Easy Rider* announced, "A man went looking for America. And couldn't find it anywhere …" In this version of the film's plot, the story is a quest for national identity, a search that ends in disappointment and disaster. Other movies of the road follow the trajectory of quest narratives. The film director in *Sullivan's Travels* (1941) is looking for the soul of Great Depression America. He wants to understand the true nature of poverty in order to make a socially conscious film.

In *The Wizard of Oz*, Dorothy yearns to follow the rainbow to make her dreams come true. The truckers in *They Drive by Night* risk their lives for money, the means to a better life. The newlywed couple in *The Long, Long Trailer* hope to find marital bliss by yoking the husband's road job to a mobile home. Tellingly, the narrative structure in all these films is circular. Sullivan and Dorothy end up where they began. The truckers and trailer owners discover what they were searching for right under their noses. These well-travelled roads all lead home. But for Billy and Wyatt, as for many other nomadic protagonists, the highway to adventure, freedom, or identity is a one-way street to tragedy. Will the hitchhiker in *Detour* reach the woman he loves? Can the outlaw couple in *Bonnie and Clyde* escape the law? Fate conspires with the rules of the road movie to reveal the human flaws that condemn their journeys to bad ends. These are archetypal narratives, journeys of the hero through paths of self-discovery or self-destruction. As with horror films or wedding movies, we can find the archetypal characters (mentors, tricksters, doubles) and stages (the call to adventure, crossing the threshold, trials and ordeals) described by Joseph Campbell and made familiar in countless tales in every culture of the globe.

European Precedents

Hopper and other American directors who took their cameras on the road were deeply influenced by trends in European cinema, particularly Italian Neorealism (*neorealismo*) and the French New Wave (*La Nouvelle Vague*). From the Italians (Roberto Rossellini, Luchino Visconti, Vittorio De Sica, Federico Fellini), they learned the value of shooting on location, using non-professional actors and long takes to capture the gritty realities of life in the streets. From the French filmmakers (Jean-Luc Godard, François Truffaut, Alain Resnais), they learned to use hand-held cameras, jump cuts, and long tracking shots to disrupt the continuity of classical film narration, drawing attention instead to the artifice of cinema and the existential anguish of their characters. Rossellini's *Voyage to Italy* (*Viaggio in Italia*, 1954) follows a wealthy English couple on their meandering tour of Italy, the first time they have been alone in eight years of marriage. Their trip together becomes an opportunity to face each other and the rifts in their souring relationship. Strictly speaking, with its glossy photography and focus on the upper class, *Voyage to Italy* belongs to Rossellini's post-neorealist period, but Fellini's *La Strada* (1954) follows a very different kind of couple on a different kind of road. Gelsomina (played by Giulietta Masina, the director's wife), is a gentle, innocent young woman who is sold by her mother to a traveling performer, a brutish strongman called Zampanò (Anthony Quinn) who takes her as his spouse and domestic slave. Their mobile home is a makeshift canvas-covered wagon on two wheels lashed to a sputtering motorcycle. Fellini tracks their plodding progress through the rural countryside of southern Italy, capturing with his sympathetic, moving camera the force of poverty, ignorance, and unarticulated love on aimless lives. This journey through the lower depths, filmed in grainy black and white using actual outdoor locations and non-professionals in supporting roles, bears many of the hallmarks of neorealist aesthetics, though its poetic moments and strong focus on character anticipate the director's move to a more personal, imaginative style (see Close-up: *La Strada*).

Another influential auteur from Europe, Swedish director Ingmar Bergman, put some of his best actors on the road in *Wild Strawberries* (*Smultronstället*, 1957). Victor Sjöström plays an aging professor on his way to receive a prestigious life achievement award. Driving with his son's wife (Ingrid Thulin), he makes a detour to his childhood summer home, visits his 94-year-old mother, picks up three young hitchhikers, and nearly hits a Volkswagen approaching in the wrong lane. While Bergman gives us memorable glimpses of the Swedish landscape and upper-middle-class society, he is more interested in the professor's inner life, depicted in surrealistic dream sequences and through conversations in the car. As in *Voyage to Italy*, the enforced intimacy of the automobile's front seat leads to unexpected revelations and self-examination. Bergman's camera locks us in this space for much of the film, setting off the central relationship between a cynical old man and his distressed daughter-in-law with visions of a terminally bitter couple (from the Volkswagen) in the middle seat and the young hitchhikers, still unmarried, in the back. The professor gets to see these reflections of his own early love and loveless marriage in the rearview mirror.

In sharp contrast to Bergman's introspective vision of the road, one man's personal journey through the past, is Henri-Georges Clouzot's 1953 thriller, *The Wages of Fear/Le salaire de la peur*. The film's first half introduces the four men who will volunteer to transport a truckload of explosives through 300 miles of rough terrain to a burning oilfield. As foreigners in a small South American village, these men are stuck in listless, restless, uneventful lives, but the film's second half makes up for this inactivity. Clouzot's nerve-ratcheting scenes of trucks rumbling through the darkness with their deadly load (Figure 4.3) make the suspense in *They Drive by Night* seem sluggish by comparison. The camera fixes on the drivers' sweaty faces as gears grind, the corrugated road groans underneath, and the speed gauge inches toward the danger zone. Strictly speaking, Clouzot was too early for the *Nouvelle Vague*, but the insistent way his camera probes beneath the facades of his characters and scrapes down to the bare nub of their existence anticipates the way directors like Godard keep highlighting the absurdities of life.

It is in *Breathless* (*À bout de souffle*, 1960), Godard's early masterpiece, that film historians find the existential link between European and American road movies. Devin Orgeron devotes a whole chapter to the film in his study of the genre, referring to the cinematic cross-talk between Godard, Hopper, and Wim Wenders as "one of the twentieth century's most enduring international cinematic conversations."[4] At the beginning of *Breathless*, Michel (played by Jean-Paul Belmondo) steals an Oldsmobile from an American serviceman, reenacting a scene that he has seen in countless gangster pictures. Like Michel, Godard is fascinated with America, but while Michel mindlessly embraces American pop culture, Godard appropriates it for a pointed critique. As Dudley Andrew puts it, when Michel breaks into the Olds, Godard is "carjacking a Hollywood genre and putting it into drive."[5] At the

FIGURE 4.3   *The Wages of Fear* (*Le salaire de la peur*). Henri-Georges Clouzot's 1953 thriller is one of many European precedents for the global road movie.

same time, Godard flouts the rules of Hollywood editing, deliberately disrupting narrative continuity with jump cuts and out-of-sync dialogue. The effect is to push us away from the characters and their story, contributing to a sense of alienation that distinguishes the French New Wave and its American imitators from classical Hollywood. *Breathless* heralds some of the genre's most persistent themes. When Michel and his girlfriend steal a Cadillac from a Paris garage, they take to the road with the abandon of mobile criminals, anticipating later outlaw couples like Bonnie and Clyde. Michel's rambling speech, the outpouring of banalities that match his random actions, prefigures other inarticulate travelers like Billy and Wyatt. Godard himself would return to these themes and to the road, most notably in *Weekend* (1967), his savage satire of consumer culture, with its notorious ten-minute tracking shot of a single traffic jam (see Close-up: *Breathless*).

The Literary Path to *Easy Rider*

Although film critics have been writing about road movies for only about 20 years, literary scholars and historians have long been studying journey narratives from nearly every part of the world, from the *Bible* and *The Odyssey* to *The Canterbury Tales* and *Journey to the West*. Many of the motivations and motifs of the road movie can be found in these earlier texts. The long journey of the Israelites from Egypt to the land of Canaan in *Exodus* is both an escape (from bondage) and a quest (for the Holy Land). Homer's epic (dating from around the eighth century BC) traces the sea voyage of Odysseus through extraordinary trials and adventures until the Greek hero finally arrives home. Chaucer's *Canterbury Tales* (from fourteenth-century England) recounts the stories told by a band of pilgrims from a cross-section of medieval society on their way to a holy shrine. *Journey to the West* (published around 1590) follows another pilgrimage, from China to India, a lively expedition of adventure, social critique, and spiritual insight. The episodic structure of these narratives, known as *picaresque*, follows the meandering trajectory of their displaced characters from place to place, an opportunity to view the land, its people, and their institutions with an outsider's eye.

The literary work closest to *Easy Rider* in spirit and in time undoubtedly is Jack Kerouac's autobiographical novel, *On the Road*. When it was published in 1957, Kerouac's account of his cross-country road trips caught the restless energy, reckless spontaneity, and buoyant optimism of postwar youth. One day, Sal Paradise, Kerouac's fictional double, looks at a map and decides to "follow one great red line across America." He soon discovers that the real way to see the country is to zigzag between the highway and the back roads, hitching rides and catching buses, "reading the American landscape" as he goes along. His encounters with people and places en route offer a sampling of the nation in motion: "Wild Negroes with bop caps and goatees came laughing by; then longhaired brokendown hipsters straight off Route 66 from New York; then old desert rats, carrying packs and heading for a park bench at the Plaza; then Methodist ministers with raveled sleeves, and an occasional Nature Boy saint in beard and sandals. I wanted to meet them all, talk to everybody."[6]

Eleven years later, Tom Wolfe caught the attention of another generation in *The Electric Kool-Aid Acid Test*. Wolfe's book recounted the rollicking adventures of Ken Kesey and his "Merry Pranksters" as they crossed America from west to east in a bus splashed with psychedelic paint. Kesey, already famous as the author of *One Flew Over the Cuckoo's Nest* (1962), tried to make a movie of this trip, a "cinema novel" as he called it, but he never succeeded in synching the images and sounds. It was not until 2011 that the movie-going public got to see the footage in *Magic Trip*, a documentary edited by Alex Gibney and Alison Ellwood. *Magic Trip* shows how Kesey fused the road trip with the drug-induced acid trip, accomplishing for the hippie generation what Kerouac had done for the Beats – and anticipating the cemetery scene in *Easy Rider* when Billy and Wyatt swallow LSD.

While literature and cinema had taken audiences on these and other journeys long before, *Easy Rider* was a kind of culmination, the pivotal point of a new film form. In the 1930s, socially conscious movies like *Sullivan's Travels* and *The Grapes of Wrath* (1940) had spoken to their generation about economic hard times, class barriers, and social injustice. In the 1940s, *Road to Morocco* and *Detour* (1945) had addressed another generation as it went to war, projecting both its lighter moments and shadowy fears onto the screen. During the postwar period, the nation sought to realize the American dream, to settle down amid the peace and secure comforts that our boys had fought for in Europe and the Pacific. But the restlessness of yet another generation erupted into violence, mirrored in dozens of nostalgic Westerns and a new subgenre of cowboys on motorbikes. John Wayne, as the obsessive Indian hunter in *The Searchers* (1956), hardly understood the meaning of his journeys through the frontier landscape any more than Marlon Brando, as the sullen biker in *The Wild One* (1953), understood the motives of his wandering from town to town, from bar to bar, from fight to fight. Their goal was the journey, their only home the trail or the highway, which is why they always ended the movie headed toward the setting sun. *Easy Rider* borrowed pieces from all these earlier genre films, patching them together in an independent production whose story about two tongue-tied drifters spoke for the next generation just as it was coming of age.

Automated Pictures and the Automobile

The 1890s produced two technical innovations that would change the way people viewed the world: motion pictures and the motorcar. From their seat in a moving automobile, passengers could now watch the landscape roll by at the breathtaking speed of 14 m.p.h. Or, from their stationary seats in a movie theatre, they could look at scenes of simulated motion on the screen. In her study of the multimedia road story, Katie Mills uses the word "automobility" to highlight this historical and perceptual connection between cinema and cars.[7] The key concepts here are autonomy and mobility. Automobiles enabled riders to navigate the nation's roadways independently, linking the American ideal of individual freedom to mechanized movement. Motion pictures replicated this sense of mobile freedom through the machinery of cameras and projectors. It was only a matter of time before the road movie emerged as a vehicle for exploring individual identity and liberty in a "culture of rampant motion."[8]

The silent movies of this early period explored the new freedoms of automated motion. The Lumière brothers in France and Cecil Hepworth in England broke through the rectangular limits of traditional theatre, transcending the proscenium arch with shots of oncoming trains (*The Arrival of a Train at La Ciotat Station/L'arrivée d'un train en gare de La Ciotat*, 1895, Figure 4.4) and headlong rushing motorcars (*How It Feels to be Run Over*, 1900). These early movies celebrated speed but also cautioned about the risks of traveling on machines. In his transnational history of the road film, Devin Orgeron describes early subgenres that focused on the new hazards of the street (as in *The Automobile Accident/Accident d'automobile*, 1901) and new options for escaping from home (*The Elopement*, 1907).[9]

By the 1920s, both cars and cinema were being mass-produced. The studios of Hollywood were turning out movies using methods modeled on the assembly lines of Detroit. A network of spreading roadways was unified by the Federal Aid Highway Act of 1925, which standardized the names of interstate highways with a system of numerical designations and iconic signs. Americans now could travel clear across the country on paved roads like Highway 66 on their own set of wheels. Meanwhile, a vast system of movie theatres was stretching from coast to

FIGURE 4.4   The moving picture's romance with mechanized motion can be traced back to the earliest films, like *The Arrival of a Train at La Ciotat* (*L'arrivée d'un train en gare de La Ciotat*), screened in France by the Lumière Brothers in 1895.

coast, part of the film industry's integrated system of production, distribution, and exhibition. No longer a mere novelty, the principle of automobility had become big business. It was also becoming part of the American psyche.

American Precursors of the Road Movie

Movies of the Great Depression of the 1930s repeatedly depict Americans on the move. In *The Grapes of Wrath*, the Joads pile their possessions on a truck and head west from Oklahoma in search of work, displaced from their family farm by drought and callous bankers. A montage sequence shows them passing signs for Oklahoma City, Sallisaw, and Checotah on Highway 66, lumbering through the southwestern landscape as they're joined by a caravan of other refugees. Their only home is the dilapidated truck and the roadside migrant camps in California where they find temporary rest. Members of the family are buried by the roadside or forced to flee on foot, but as Ma Joad explains in the film's last scene, crammed in the front seat with her remaining family, "We'll go on forever, Pa, 'cause we're the people." *It Happened One Night* offers more images of the people in transit. While an ambitious reporter (played by Clark Gable) pursues a spoiled socialite (Claudette Colbert) down the east coast, they encounter a full spectrum of social classes riding buses, trains, planes, motorcycles, and an autogyro, stopping at diners, motels, and motor camps en route. One of the film's comic highlights occurs when Gable, proud of his macho, working-class know-how, tries to teach Colbert how to hitch a ride. After several failed efforts with his thumb, he watches open-mouthed as she steps into the road, lifts her skirt above one knee, and stops the next car in its tracks (Figure 4.5).

FIGURE 4.5 Socialite Claudette Colbert teaches reporter Clarke Gable how to hitch a ride in *It Happened One Night* (Dir. Frank Capra, 1934), proving that the open road is fair game for any class of Americans.

Hollywood continued to supply light entertainment during the next decade. Bob Hope and Bing Crosby made six travel comedies between 1940 and 1953, taking them on the road to exotic lands like Singapore, Zanzibar, Morocco, Rio, the Klondike, and Bali. *Road to Morocco* typifies the whacky, self-reflexive humor in this popular series, two zany Americans abroad making fun of international stereotypes and themselves. The "road to" series also plays on the history of vaudeville, when so many entertainers toured the country. During World War II, American performers took their shows on the roads of Europe and the Pacific to entertain the troops. Hope's first combat show was for the USO in Morocco. Hollywood followed their lead with patriotic showbiz movies like *This Is the Army* (1943), which Steven Cohan calls the "quintessential military road show."[10]

The war itself, of course, was nothing like show business. By the time the men came marching home, they had acquired a heavy load of cynicism and distrust. This darker outlook was reflected in the stories and visual style of film noir, a genre that emerged during the 1940s and 1950s. The heroes of movies like Raoul Walsh's *They Drive by Night* and Edgar Ulmer's *Detour* are typically anxious men, obsessed and even paranoiac. As a rule, the leading woman is a femme fatale, sexy and mysterious, not to be trusted. The film noir plots are as convoluted as the streets that lead their heroes deep into a shadowy web of danger and intrigue, in contrast to the well-lit spaces of the open highway. Theirs is a nocturnal world of grainy visuals and low-key lighting, where it's almost always raining or about to rain. We see this repeatedly in Walsh's film, where exhausted truckers desperate for cash drive all night through all kinds of weather. In one tense nighttime scene, George Raft spots another truck weaving on and off the road ahead and speeds up in a dodgy effort to wake the driver. Just as he and Bogart pull alongside the wobbly rig, they see a pair of headlights coming at them in their lane – the eyes of death in every trucker's nightmare. *Detour* opens with the credits superimposed over the moving image of a deserted highway, the dotted white line falling into the distance mile after mile. Then the screen goes black and a man emerges from the darkness, shambling along the road, his face without expression. Hitching from New York to Los Angeles to be with his girl, Al (Tom Neal) assumes the identity of a man who picks him up on the road; later Al is blackmailed by Vera (Ann Savage), a hard-bitten woman who sees through his pretense. In addition to the distinctive qualities of film noir, *Detour* exhibits many of the stylistic features of the classic road movie. A hitchhiking montage shows him walking west and thumbing rides superimposed over a street map while his voice rambles on about the evils of money and the risks of life on the road. Later, when he gets behind the wheel with Vera, the camera explores the interaction from every angle, their faces reflected in the side and rear view mirrors as if each viewpoint offers new psychological insights.

Of all the film forms that predate and prefigure the classic road movie, none is more important than the Western, the genre that shaped the grand myth of America's frontier. *Easy Rider* pays homage to its Western origins in many ways. Wyatt's name and dress hark back to the days of Wyatt Earp, while Billy's name evokes the romantic legend of Billy the Kid. Hopper's film begins in a Mexican border town, and an early scene contrasts the art of horseshoeing with motorcycle maintenance. Hopper, like many Americans, had grown up on stories about cowboys and Indians, particularly John Ford's popular screen versions of the myth. Ford's *Stagecoach* (1939) traces the perilous journey of a horse-drawn coach through hostile Apache territory. As the stage travels from a settled town in Arizona to an outpost in New Mexico, we get to know its passengers, a microcosm of frontier society. In addition to the driver and his shotgun guard, there is a self-important banker, a high-toned Christian woman, a courtly southern gentleman, a meek whisky salesman, an alcoholic doctor, a kind-hearted prostitute, and the pregnant wife of a cavalry officer. A band of cavalry escorts them part way, and on the road they meet an outlaw, John Wayne in his breakthrough role as The Ringo Kid. The deeper they travel into the wilderness, the more layers of civilization are stripped away, revealing what each individual is truly made of. Ford gives these characters social significance and some psychological depth, but he treats the Indians as part of the exotic background, as moving targets viewed against the majestic mesas of the desert. In *The Searchers* (1956), Ford gives Native Americans a more important role in the drama, although his reverence for the landscape remains fixed. In this later film, Wayne plays the part of an ex-Civil War veteran in search of Debbie, his abducted niece, and revenge for the massacre of her family. Most of *The Searchers* takes place on the trail. Wayne's character, Ethan, is as nomadic as the Comanche tribe that he pursues. Although an objective of his quest is to bring Debbie home, it leaves him ultimately homeless and alone. Such Westerns gave Ford and other directors a chance to develop allegorical interpretations of the journey motif while perfecting cinematic methods that proved well suited to the road film: how to shoot a moving vehicle against a landscape that is always changing shape.

In due time, the vehicles were mechanized and the landscape grew more thickly settled. By the 1950s, war veterans and their families were building new communities all across America and celebrating the pleasures of domestic life. But this national focus on homemaking did not mean that Americans had abandoned the road. By 1953, the United States had 6% of the world's population and 60% of its cars.[11] Travel and television were beginning to compete with movies for middle-class consumer dollars. Hollywood responded to the challenge with films like *The Long, Long Trailer*, in which two television stars – Lucille Ball and Desi Arnaz – take their own home with them on the highway. The couple's 40-foot mobile home is the brainchild of newlywed Tacy (Ball), who wants to be together with her husband Nick (Arnaz) while he travels for his job. Trying to play the perfect housewife in a moving kitchen is a comic recipe for disaster. The scene in which Tacy attempts to make a Caesar salad while the trailer bounces over rocky roads is vintage Lucille Ball. Abounding in hilarious mishaps and images of social status (Tacy packs the high-price trailer with gleaming kitchenware and fancy clothes), *The Long, Long Trailer* is a lighthearted celebration of the consumerism and family ideals that counterculture road films soon would take to task. The heroes of this emerging subgenre preferred motorbikes to mobile homes. Their affinity with the wild frontier is dramatized in *The Wild One*, a film that helped make Marlon Brando famous and put bikers on the movie map. An open road appears behind the film's opening credits while, in the distance, we just make out a band of vehicles coming toward us. Slowly, in an exceedingly long take, the bikes grow larger, then suddenly speed up in a howl of angry engines, skidding past us on the blacktop along both sides of the painted line. At their head is Brando, looking confident and cool in his black leather jacket, sideburns, sunshades, and slanted cap. Soon, Johnny (Brando) is leading the Black Rebels Motorcycle Club into town and into trouble. These bikers are rebels without a cause, inarticulate about their motives or their feelings. When someone asks Johnny what he's rebelling against, he fires back a curt response. "Whaddaya got?" His engine's roar seems to speak for him and his cohorts. In this coupling of tongue-tied rebel road heroes and their defiant machines, *The Wild One* anticipates a whole line of motorcycle movies leading up to *Easy Rider* and beyond.

Compared with their later brethren, like the Australian motorcycle thugs in *Mad Max* (1979), Johnny and the Black Rebels seem relatively harmless, more rowdy than dangerous. So does the Hell's Angel gang in Roger Corman's exploitation film, *The Wild Angels* (1966). Corman, a master of producing cheaply made genre movies for the youth market, added drugs, sex, and rock and roll to the formula of juvenile delinquents on Harley choppers. Peter Fonda stars as Heavenly Blues, another inarticulate biker, with Nancy Sinatra as his girlfriend. The film's first scene contrasts Blues and his carefree lifestyle with the domestic confinements of suburbia. A housewife runs after her toddler, who is peddling his tricycle beyond the safety of their picket fence, catching the boy just in time before he runs into the front end of a motorcycle. She shakes him, crying "No, no, no," then glances up as the camera pans to Blues, mounted in the saddle of his Harley, a cigarette dangling from his mouth. Blues snuffs out the cigarette (or is it a joint?), kick starts his engine, and rides out onto the open road while the toddler returns to his gated prison. It turns out that Blues is headed for a party of young rebels, male and female, who dance and splash half-naked in a river. The scene is meant to be an image of unbridled hedonism. In 1967, Corman directed *The Trip*, in which Peter Fonda takes his first dose of LSD. With its hallucinatory drug sequence, a screenplay by Jack Nicholson, and a secondary role played by Dennis Hopper, *The Trip* takes one step further down to road toward *Easy Rider*.

The year 1967 produced another film even more important to the genre's evolution. Some would say that *Bonnie and Clyde* is as pivotal as *Easy Rider*. Many would claim that it's a better movie. In any case, Arthur Penn's treatment of Clyde Barrow and Bonnie Parker, the legendary outlaw couple of the 1930s, put road movies on a new course. Penn romanticized the legend by casting Warren Beatty and Faye Dunaway in the leading roles. He infused their story with the social consciousness of the Great Depression, aligning their actions with the sentiments of common folk against the big banks and the law. Most significantly, he popularized a certain image of the outlaw couple on the road.

Bonnie and Clyde was not the screen's first pair of gun-toting, mobile lovers. Nearly 20 years earlier, John H. Lewis had created a minor cult sensation with *Gun Crazy* (1950), a noir thriller that transcended its B-movie budget with fierce sexual energy and striking imagery. When Bart and Annie meet at a shooting competition, their mutual attraction, feel for firearms, and hunger for the good (material) things in life set them on the path of crime, a search for the American dream gone awry. *Gun Crazy* was a daring achievement in its time, but its reception could not compare to the impact of *Bonnie and Clyde*. Penn's film was a popular sensation, generating fierce critical debate and substantial box office revenues. It captured the spirit of the 1960s counterculture and set precedents for a long line of outlaw road films from *Badlands* (1973) to *Natural Born Killers* (1994).

Penn opens the movie with an extreme close-up of Bonnie's cherry-colored lips. His mobile camera follows her restless movements as she fidgets in the confines of her bedroom. Alternating between quick cuts and languid long takes, we catch her staring at the slanted ceiling, scanning her naked image in the mirror, and banging on the prison bars of her bed, her pent up sensuality ready to explode. Moments later, soon after she spies Clyde through the window (he's preparing to steal her mother's car), Bonnie is out by his side, sipping cokes from long-necked bottles, daring him to prove that he's really served time for armed robbery. On impulse, Clyde pulls out his gun, holding it suggestively against his thigh as he looks away, flicking a wooden matchstick with his teeth. Bonnie is enchanted. She reaches out her hand, challenging him to use it. "All right," he whispers. "You just wait right here and keep your eyes open." The holdup is shown in an extreme long shot of the deserted, dusty street. Before the scene is over, they're pulling away together in the getaway car, leaving behind a row of F.D. Roosevelt posters on the fence (Figure 4.6). What begins as an impulse becomes a career and a cause. The couple moves from petty heists to bank robberies, egged on by a press that glorifies them

FIGURE 4.6   *Bonnie and Clyde* (Dir. Arthur Penn, 1967) combines elements from Depression movies, gangster pictures, film noir, and the French New Wave, setting a new course for the road film: gun-toting lovers on the run.

as modern Robin Hoods helping the poor stand up against the Establishment. Along the way, they pick up an auto mechanic, Clyde's brother and his wife, and another couple, forming the Barrows Gang. But the joyride cannot last. Relationships deteriorate, actions grow more violent, and the journey ends in one of the most famous ambush scenes in movie history. In a balletic montage of rapid-fire cuts and slow motion photography, Bonnie and Clyde are riddled with bullets, their bodies twitching with each shot. Their car, too, is full of bullet holes, reminding us of its role in the fatal love triangle.

Thematically and stylistically, it's easy to see what Penn borrows from Hollywood by way of the French New Wave. *Bonnie and Clyde* pieces together elements from Depression movies, gangster films, and film noir, buoying the story with high-key lighting, fast-paced editing, and upbeat banjo music, adding stylish jump cuts and hand-held camerawork taken from Godard. He leaves us with a vision of the road as a great escape route to adventure, glamor, and celebrity but also as a vehicle for cultural critique and cinematic virtuosity.

The 1970s: Existential Journeys

By the early 1970s, it was clear that a new generation of directors had taken the wheel. These brash young talents knew how to reach the new audiences that Hollywood sought. Some had learned their craft by working in the studios. Others had graduated from the nation's film schools and gained practical experience on Roger Corman's sets. Dennis Hopper belonged to this second group. So did Terrence Malick, Francis Ford Coppola, and Steven Spielberg. Taking their cue from the success of *Bonnie and Clyde* and *Easy Rider*, nearly all of them tried their hand at road movies. In Malick's *Badlands* (1973), an outlaw couple (Martin Sheen and Sissy Spacek) drive from state to state on a wild killing spree. In Coppola's *The Rain People* (1969), a pregnant woman (Shirley Knight) leaves her husband and drives across the country. In Spielberg's *The Sugarland Express* (1974), another woman (Goldie Hawn) helps to break her husband out of jail and outrun the law hoping they can rescue their son from a foster home.

David Laderman classifies these and other road films of the period as variations on two motifs: the quest for freedom and the outlaw couple. Using Thomas Schatz's terminology for generic evolution, Laderman regards *Easy Rider* and *Bonnie and Clyde* as defining moments in the genre's "experimental stage," when its heroes, stories, themes, and film conventions begin to coalesce into a distinctive form.[12] According to Laderman, the genre's "classical stage" begins in the early 1970s, when the road movie comes into its own. As the idealism of the 1960s sours in the 1970s and American movies adopt postwar European styles and sensibilities, the genre takes a more cynical turn, veering away from optimistic social criticism toward darker visions of existential angst. It begins to resemble the psychological journeys of Bergman, Clouzot, and Fellini through allegorical landscapes in search of meaning.

Few directors travel the road between Europe and America more intently than Wim Wenders, the German filmmaker who explores the genre from both sides of the Atlantic. Like Godard, Wenders is interested in American culture and uses the automobile to criticize what he sees as a dangerous global trend toward mobility and speed. His own films are unhurried, subtle, introspective meditations. In *Kings of the Road* (*Im Lauf der Zeit*, 1976), two men meet when one tries to drown himself by driving his VW Beetle headlong into a lake. Robert (Hanns Zischler), the would-be suicide, joins Bruno (Rüdiger Vogler), a traveling mechanic who repairs movie projectors, and the two set off together through the border towns of East and West Germany. Although they come from very different backgrounds, Robert and Bruno share a fondness for pop music and much else. Both are emotionally scarred and lonely drifters, estranged from women and the stability of home. They speak more in gestures than in words; doing things and traveling are substitutes for conversation. Their lack of clear direction and uncertainty about the future were familiar problems for young Germans of the time. Wenders himself drifted from medicine to philosophy and art before making film his métier. As they wander through the bleak landscape of postwar Europe, we feel their weariness and wariness. In the languishing movie theatres that they visit, the great tradition of German cinema has been replaced by Hollywood fare. Fragments of Americana are everywhere. "The Yanks have colonized our subconscious," someone says. *Kings of the Road* is the last and best of his German road trilogy, which includes *Alice in the Cities* (1973) and *Wrong Move* (1974), but Wenders would later pursue the genre in the United States itself, most notably in *Paris, Texas* (1984). His poetic sensibility and the inspired imagery of his cinematographer, Robby Müller, would help to usher in the New German Cinema and leave their mark on a generation of directors in America and throughout the world.

FIGURE 4.7 Two outcasts wander through the desolate landscape of America's heartland in Terrence Malick's *Badlands* (1973), importing the existential tone of European road films to the United States.

In *Badlands*, the landscape is the open plains stretching from South Dakota to Montana. Most of the action takes place off main roads, in the secluded woods and featureless prairielands where fugitives can hide. Close-ups of plant and animal life alternate with spectacular panorama shots that capture the beauty of this land as well as its unsettling desolation (Figure 4.7). Malick's camera probes a dreadful emptiness at the core of America's heartland that is both physical and moral, something hinted at in the film's title. This vacuity is reflected in the story's two main characters, Kit (Sheen) and Holly (Spacek). Kit's journey begins on a garbage truck and ends in a high-speed chase by the police. As a human being, Kit is a cipher, as feebly self-aware as he is self absorbed. Impulsive and inarticulate, Kit can be awkwardly courteous one moment and deadly violent the next. Holly calls him "trigger happy," but he seems strangely detached from his own actions and emotions. Holly, too, seems disconnected from her feelings. Yet in contrast to Kit's fumbling with words, she keeps a journal filled with lyrical sentiments from the romantic books she's read. The passages she reads aloud as the film's voiceover narration are expressive, often lyrical, though her voice is listless and dispassionate.

Malick based his film loosely on the true story of a 19-year-old boy who murdered the family of his 14-year-old lover in 1958 and took her on a killing spree. Their flight as a fugitive couple is partly modeled on *Bonnie and Clyde*, as is their preoccupation with celebrity. Kit is compared twice to James Dean, and like Clyde, he clearly enjoys what he believes to be his legendary status, building his own stone monument when he is captured and tossing out souvenirs when interviewed. So Sheen's Kit deliberately takes his place in a long line of narcissistic males (Brando, Dean, Hopper, Beatty) struggling to find a self and a home. Malick also includes self-conscious references to Westerns, juvenile delinquent movies of the 1950s, and even screwball comedy, but his strongest affinities are with European auteurs. His alienated characters seek relief from a kind of existential malaise, but like Michel in *Breathless*, Kit's vision turns out to be more manic than romantic. And like Billy in *Easy Rider*, he is too restless for a real home. The idyllic tree house that he builds for Holly in the woods is a fantasy from children's books, a temporary rest stop. Other images of home – his friend's isolated prairie lodge, a wealthy man's mansion, and the house of Holly's father that he burns to ashes – all give way to the coercions of an insistent and aimless mobility.

If *Badlands* seems more allegorical and aesthetically motivated than previous American road films, it's worth remembering that Malick studied philosophy at Harvard and Oxford before enrolling in the American Film Institute. In scene after scene, tone and metaphor trump plot, character, or social critique. When Kit sets fire to Holly's house, florid flames envelop her piano, her dolls, her bed, and her father's body in a sepia montage of transcendent beauty. When they build their tree house in a willow grove, the hues and textures of the forest are exquisitely detailed. And before Kit's capture, the couple dances slowly in the soft glow of their headlights to the tune of Nat King Cole's "A Blossom Fell." In the words of the song, "the dream has ended, for true love dies." For each moment, the mood is inevitably shattered, broken by a call to the road. Although Malick wrote, directed, and produced *Badlands* independently on a small budget, it was picked up and successfully distributed by Warner Bros. Malick's subsequent films have been few and far between, but his originality and influence have proved long-lasting.

The 1980s – Racing Comedies and Postmodern Pastiche

Even before the box office success of *Cannonball Run* (1981) and *Cannonball Run II* (1984), Hollywood had been tinkering with a formula for cross-country racing comedies to attract crowds to the theatres. Back in 1963, MGM had hired Stanley Kramer, a director of serious "message movies," to make *It's a Mad, Mad, Mad, Mad World*. The project's whacky plot involves a group of strangers who meet by chance and race each other through southern California and Nevada to find a stash of stolen cash. The studio gambled on a big budget, an all-star cast, and the super-size screen dimensions of Cinerama to pull audiences away from their TV sets. Many of MGM's endearingly mindless ingredients – slapstick humor, car wrecks, high speed, and an anarchic drive bent on outwitting the law – show up again in Charles Bail's *Gumball Rally* (1976), a much cheaper collaboration between First Artists and Warner Bros. The ten competing teams in *Gumball Rally* set out from New York City on an illegal road race to Long Beach, California, chased by a fanatic police lieutenant of the LAPD. There are no speed limits, no catalytic converters, and no rules, except for "the first rule of Italian driving," memorably enunciated by Raúl Juliá as he throws away his rear-view mirror: "What's a-behind me is not important."

Films like *Gumball Rally*, *Cannonball Run*, and *National Lampoon's Vacation*, aka *Vacation* (1983) exploit the lighter side of driving, steering the genre toward the high road of entertainment. But the 1980s also had their darker patches. *Planes,*

Trains, & Automobiles appeared in 1987, the year the stock market crashed. Directed by John Hughes, the film stars Steve Martin as Neal Page, a high-powered business-man who misses his flight and ends up traveling in coach class with an accident-prone shower-ring salesman named Del Griffith (played by John Candy). At first, Del seems to be a loser, but Neal eventually learns that he's a skilled traveler with many friends, and the two men end up sharing a Thanksgiving family dinner. A similar theme runs through *Rain Man* (1988), in which a self-centered yuppie named Charlie Babbit (Tom Cruise) is forced to take his autistic younger brother Raymond (Dustin Hoffman) on a cross-country journey in a Buick Roadmaster. Raymond's antics and extraordinary memory are a constant source of frustration and bewilderment for Charlie, but the trip becomes a chance for them to bond. By the time the brothers arrive at their destination, they have rediscovered their lost family in each other. This preoccupation with family, in recovering the values of home, reflects a campaign issue of Ronald Reagan, whose presidency spanned most of the decade. It is especially prominent in *Back to the Future* (1985), where the automobile journey is through time rather than space, a nostalgic return to the past in the interest of family togetherness. As the title of this conservative film suggests, the best vision for the road ahead may be in the rear-view mirror.

Raising Arizona (1987) combines many of these elements and, being a creation of the Coen brothers (directed by Joel, produced by Ethan), swerves manically between dark comedy and lightheaded parody. The plot involves another outlaw couple, Herbert I. and Edwina, whose crime reflects the era's fixation on family. They steal a baby. HI (Nicolas Cage) is a hapless soul stuck in the penal system's revolving door. Ed (Holly Hunter) is the cop who takes his mug shots. In a send-up montage of romantic wedding films, they fall in love, get married, and move into a trailer "starter home," but when Ed realizes she cannot conceive, she pressures HI to kidnap one of Nathan Arizona's quintuplets, which she has read about in the papers. If ironic film allusions are an index of postmodernism, the Coens are mas-ters of the trend. *Raising Arizona* brims with sly references to horror films, Road Runner cartoons, melodrama, and of course the road movie. HI's nightmare vision of the Lone Biker of the Apocalypse comes straight out of a Mad Max film. Perhaps the Coens' most original contribution to the genre is the image of a baby sitting in the middle of the highway as a vehicle speeds toward it. Laderman sees this as "an apt visual metaphor for the road movie's infantilized treatment in late 1980s."[13] Perhaps so, but this movie's cartoonish treatment of American culture appeals to our inner infant even as it spoofs our national embrace of violence and consumerism. Consider the chase scene in which HI is chased through a super-market by trigger-happy store clerks while he hugs a stolen box of diapers. An abundance of products scatters through the aisles, and everybody seems to have a gun. Or consider the ostentatious home of Nathan Arizona, a self-made million-aire who has more babies than he can handle and more money than he needs. Do we deplore these images of excess, or do we cheer for more violence and mayhem?

In 1984, the American independent filmmaker Jim Jarmusch made *Stranger Than Paradise*, a self-consciously postmodern take on the road movie that he described sarcastically as "a semi-neorealist black comedy in the style of an imaginary Eastern European film director obsessed with Ozu and familiar with the 1950s American television show *The Honeymooners*."[14] In the same year, Wenders released *Paris, Texas*, which he filmed in the American Southwest. A few years later, Finnish director Aki Kaurismäki brought a fictional rock band from Eastern Europe to the United States in *Leningrad Cowboys Go America* (1989). Each film, in its own way, explored the crossroads between Europe and America traveled earlier by Godard, Wenders, and Hellman. The genre was becoming increasingly and more deliberately global.

Paris, Texas opens with an aerial shot of the Texan desert, its colorful mesas evoking John Ford's Westerns. Far below, a man is walking alone. This is Travis (Harry Dean Stanton), wearing a heavy beard, a red cap, and a yellow tie. When his brother Walt (Dean Stockton) is summoned from L.A. to pick him up, we learn that Travis has been missing for four years. Since Travis refuses to fly ("I don't want to leave the ground"), the two men drive by car, an opportunity to bond that is frustrated by Travis's gloomy silence. Like the brothers in *Rain Man*, one is a successful businessman, the other a social dropout. And like many road partners before them, they are poor conversationalists. Transportation seems to be a substitute for communication. Travis begins to emerge from his shell only after Walt projects a reel of Super-8 film of their life from earlier days. Significantly, the vacation footage depicts a united, joyful family on the road. The simple images of these home movies are freighted with Reaganite nostalgia, a deep longing for the idealized happy home before its rupture. While *Paris, Texas* continues Wenders's focus on family estrangement, it feels more optimistic than *Kings of the Road*. Robby Muller's photography brings out the rich, primary colors of the landscape, which works in tandem with Ry Cooder's soulful musical score to comment on Travis's long journey toward redemption.

Bagdad Café (1987), filmed in the Mojave Desert by another German director, is even more upbeat. Percy Adlon's film brings a middle-class German tourist, a heavyset woman named Jasmin, to a truck stop run by an angry African American woman named Brenda. Both women have separated from their husbands, each in her own way. More of a road stop movie than a road film, *Bagdad Café* is about alternatives to the traditional nuclear family. The café hosts a kaleidoscope of characters – black and white, Latino and Native American, dropouts and yuppies, young and old – who all manage to live together. As a European, Jasmin initially is treated as an alien intruder, but gradually she becomes part of the family, transforming the run-down diner into a thriving cabaret with the aid of magic from a box. Adlon plays lightheartedly with stereotypes. The first time Jasmin eyes Brenda, she imagines herself boiled in an African pot. Uncomfortable with Brenda's untidiness, she attacks the task of housekeeping with Germanic willpower. But Adlon also gives us moments of transatlantic understanding. Brenda's son loves Bach, and the resident tattoo artist reads Thomas Mann. In its broad inclusiveness, *Bagdad Café* anticipates the multicultural road films of the 1990s.

In contrast to Adlon's colorful characters and cinematography, Jarmusch chose to shoot *Stranger Than Paradise* in black and white. Tom DiCillo's photography gives the film a flat, documentary realism, accentuating the crumbling walls and broken pavement of the urban landscape. The film's soundtrack combines an edgy score of string instruments (reminiscent of Hungarian composer Béla Bartók) and the grungy lyrics of downtown club culture. The overall effect is decidedly downbeat. Jarmusch's plot is minimal. A young Hungarian woman named Eva (Eszter Balint) visits her cousin Willie (musician John Lurie) in Manhattan en route to Cleveland, Ohio. Together with Willie's goofy friend Eddie (another musician, Richard Edson), they travel first to Ohio, then to Florida. The film mocks these characters and their lifestyle with deadpan humor. At one point, Eva watches as Willie peels the tinfoil from his evening meal. "Why is it called a TV dinner?" she asks. "You're supposed to eat it while you watch TV," he says. "This is how we eat in America." His efforts to explain football are equally unhelpful, revealing his mindless acceptance of a national culture that makes little sense to an outsider. In addition to such critical asides, Jarmusch seems more interested in trying out new film techniques than in telling a story. The whole film consists of 67 single-take vignettes separated by black leaders, like snapshots in a photo album, the director once observed. The performances feel raw and improvised, as if we're watching unrehearsed reality. As a road film, *Stranger Than Paradise* brings European alienation closer to America, using an immigrant's outsider status to chart the aimless drift of American life. For all her shuttling between Hungary and the States, Eva wonders if it's worth the journey. As Eddie puts it, "You know, it's funny. You come to someplace new, and everything looks the same."

Kaurismäki's style has much in common with Jarmusch's minimalist aesthetic and dry wit, but its premise could have been invented by the Coen brothers (or the Marx brothers). When the Leningrad Cowboys fail to get a gig "somewhere in the tundra," they are advised to take their music to America because the people there "are happy with anything." The band arrives in New York wearing fur coats, sunshades, pointed shoes, and bushy haircuts that resemble foxtails blown over their brows. It turns out that the New World doesn't look much better than the Old World. The only jobs to be had are in cheap bars and seedy clubs. Even the beach is cold and empty. What makes *Leningrad Cowboys Go America* a road movie is their rock-and-road tour from Manhattan to Mexico, which they finish in a used Cadillac with two men seated in the trunk and a coffin on the roof. For the most part, their journey is a rambling run of sight gags and one-liners, but their music improves as they go along. In Langtry, Texas, they make a big hit with the biker crowd by playing "Born to Be Wild" from *Easy Rider*. Kaurismäki's film was so successful that the Leningrad Cowboys became a real band, doing concert tours and making two more movies in the 1990s.

The 1990s – Multicultural Highways and New Visions of Home

If road movies in America were to follow Schatz's evolutionary scheme, they might have passed from the *experimental* stage preceding *Easy Rider* to the *classic* models of the early 1970s and continue through an era of stylistic *refinement* in the 1980s to a self-reflexive *baroque* period, in which style and content merge. As we've seen, the genre does begin to turn in on itself during the 1980s with films that play with and even mock its own conventions. And in the hands of postmodern directors like Oliver Stone and David Lynch, film technique often seems to overwhelm meaning. But the genre's course does not follow a consistently straight line. Instead, it takes side trips, faces detours, doubles back and reinvents itself, or leaps ahead of schedule. In the 1990s, Ridley Scott revisits the buddy road film with *Thelma & Louise*, sparking a feminist debate by putting women behind the wheel. Other movies of the decade bring previously marginalized groups from the roadside to the center of consciousness, training the headlights on gay men in *My Own Private Idaho* (1991), on African Americans in *Get on the Bus* (1996), on Native Americans in *Smoke Signals* (1998), and on an aging generation in *The Straight Story* (1999). In other words, the American road becomes a multicultural highway, reflecting a new national awareness of diversity – and Hollywood's search for new niche audiences. Road movies of the period also offer changing visions of the family. As the conservative Reagan/Bush era (1981–1993) gives way to the liberal presidency of Bill Clinton (1993–2001), sociologists like Stephanie Coontz and Shere Hite focus attention on the emergence of new family forms. The "traditional" nuclear unit envisioned in *Back to the Future* yields to more flexible arrangements like those in *Bagdad Café*. The family itself comes under attack in Oliver Stone's *Natural Born Killers* (1993), which presents a savage indictment of family dysfunction in his "I Love Mallory" parody, a dark family sitcom, complete with laugh tracks, that mocks idealized television shows like *Father Knows Best*. Mickey and Mallory, the outlaw couple in Stone's movie, are psychopathic products of child abuse who can never go home again but who create their own ironic version of family on the road. But in *The Straight Story*, David Lynch tells a different story, suggesting that it's possible to rebuild a broken family even late in life, although the highway home may be extremely slow. Meanwhile, as cinema becomes increasingly global, the road movie is appropriated in other countries, where increased mobility both solves and creates problems for immigrant populations, nomadic groups, and tourism, as we'll see in films from Europe, Africa, Asia, Latin America, and places between.

Thelma & Louise is widely credited with reviving the genre in the United States by adding a new twist, paving the way for a parade of revisionist road movies bearing serious social and political messages. The two women named in the title recall the male buddies of *Easy Rider* and the outlaw couple of *Bonnie and Clyde*, combining the themes of quest and escape (see Close-up: *Thelma & Louise*). Thelma is escaping from the prison of her suburban household, Louise from a dead end waitress job. When they stop at a roadside bar en route to a weekend getaway vacation, an unexpected incident turns them into hunted fugitives. Their cross-country flight in a 1966 T-Bird convertible becomes a quest for freedom and a meaningful relationship. Some see *Thelma & Louise* as a turning point in feminist filmmaking, a moment when strong, assertive women finally replace the traditionally male rebels of the road. Others argue that any feminist critique is compromised by the concluding scene or complicated by the way the film's protagonists simply mimic male models without offering new alternatives, a road movie ideology and aesthetic of their own. Still, although directed by a man, *Thelma & Louise* was written by Callie Khouri, who won an Oscar for Best Original Screenplay, one of the few women ever to receive that award. The film itself, a critical and box office sensation in its day, continues to be one of the most often watched and discussed road films of all times.

Recognizing the popular interest in women on the road, Hollywood director Herbert Ross followed up his earlier melodrama, *Steel Magnolias* (1989), with *Boys on the Side* (1995), a comedy about three women who bond during a cross-country journey to the West. The film capitalizes on contemporary sexual politics by making one of the three main characters a lesbian (Whoopi Goldberg), one a fussy realtor infected with HIV (Mary-Louise Parker), and the third a pregnant woman habituated to abusive men (Drew Barrymore). In keeping with the genre's conventional motifs, the trio's journey is partly an escape from the law, partly the search for an alternative to home: sisterhood as family. While *Boys on the Side* was traveling the well-worn path of mass market entertainment, independent filmmakers like Gus Van Sant were blazing new trails. Van Sant's *My Own Private Idaho* is a bolder, more original approach to gay relationships. Its rambling plot centers on two male hustlers, Mike (River Phoenix) and Scott (Keanu Reeves), whose search for Mike's mother takes them through the Pacific Northwest, with a side trip to Italy. While earlier buddy films may have played with images of masculinity, the homoeroticism here is not the closeted kind. The two men are outlaws by virtue of their openly sexual orientation. Van Sant reinvests the genre's familiar themes and iconography with fresh significance, combining an edgy realism with surrealistic cinematography. One moment, he gives us evocative night scenes of deserted highways and abandoned cityscapes; another, he shows us dreamy views of clouds or symbolic salmon leaping against the current towards home. Together with Gregg Araki's *The Living End* (1992), another gay road film, *My Own Private Idaho* helped to usher in the New Queer Cinema of the 1990s, a movement that soon spread across the seas.

The Adventures of Priscilla, Queen of the Desert (1994) brings drag queens to the Australian outback. As three transvestite performers take their campy cabaret show on the road, their outlandish costumes and flamboyant antics contrast comically with the surroundings. We see a plume of peacock feathers floating through the desert. We watch the trio lip-synch Gloria Gaynor's "I Will Survive" in full drag accompanied by Aborigine musicians. We wonder what will happen when they dance before an audience of locals wearing gabardine. Although director Stephen Elliott plays with sexist and racist stereotypes, he respects his protagonists as complex individuals, regarding them with empathy, even affection. He also demonstrates a wily awareness of road movie conventions. The film's title refers not to a person, but to the school bus in which the trio travels, a character in its own right (Figure 4.8). One of them keeps repainting it, not unlike Ken Kesey's magic bus. "It's not purple," he prissily insists. "It's lavender." A hit at festivals, with cult fans, and even popular audiences, *Priscilla* helped to widen the reception of gay-themed films and gave a big boost to the Australian film industry abroad.

Like Australian Aborigines, Native Americans have appeared in road films as part of the landscape and occasionally as individuals, but not until *Powwow Highway* (1989)

FIGURE 4.8   Traveling through the Australian outback in high style. An aerial shot from *The Adventures of Priscilla, Queen of the Desert* (Dir. Stephan Elliott, 1994) reflects a new global acceptance of diversity in the 1990s.

did they get to steer the story, and not until Chris Eyre's *Smoke Signals* were they directed by another Native American. *Powwow Highway* follows a pair of mismatched travelers. Buddy Red Bow, the younger man, is an activist fighting for the rights of his displaced people on a Cheyenne reservation in Montana. Philbert Bono, the older man, regards the voyage as a spiritual journey, talking to his old Buick as if it were a pony. Since Philbert is the driver, Buddy is forced to take the highway and its byways at a slower pace, a life lesson in higher consciousness. Gary Farmer, the actor who plays Philbert, was later cast as Arnold, the father who saves a baby from a burning house in *Smoke Signals*. Though hailed as a hero by his people on the Coeur d'Alene reservation, Arnold harbors a dark secret and vanishes one day, leaving behind his wife and a son named Victor. Years later, when Victor learns that Arnold has died in Phoenix, the young man begins a journey from Idaho to retrieve his father's remains. The journey, intercut with frequent flashbacks, becomes an expedition to recover the past: to learn his father's secret, to face issues of abandonment and anger. Reluctantly, Victor is accompanied by his tagalong acquaintance Thomas, the baby Arnold saved 22 years earlier who has grown up as an orphan under his grandmother's care. Once off the reservation, Victor and Thomas learn to face who they are as individuals and as Indians. Their first lesson in ethnic identity comes on the bus to Phoenix. "Indians ain't supposed to smile," Victor tells his buddy. "Get Stoic. You gotta look like a warrior … like you just came back from hunting a buffalo." Moments later, a couple of hostile white men take their seats and intimidate them to the back of the bus. "The cowboys always win," Thomas observes aloud. But they retaliate by chanting a made-up song about Tom Mix, Charles Bronson, and John Wayne's teeth. Significantly, their journey is a round trip. With the help of Thomas, Victor comes to terms with his father and his anger. The two travelers return as buddies to the reservation, to a renewed sense of home, and to their native roots. In the film's final montage, while Thomas's voice utters a redemptive poem about fathers and sons, the camera follows a long tracking shot up river, like a salmon returning to its place of origin.

Victor and Thomas take the bus to Phoenix because they can't afford to drive. The travelers in Spike Lee's *Get on the Bus* have a different motive. They have chartered the bus to take them to the Million Man March in Washington, DC, a historical event organized by Louis Farrakhan in the name of black unity in 1995. Most of the film follows the journey of a dozen or so black men who board as strangers and interact with each other along the way, becoming a mobile community. The group includes the level-headed bus driver (Charles Dutton), a truck driver handcuffed to his son by court order, a mixed-race cop who considers himself black, a self-centered actor, a gay couple, a young Muslim trying to atone for his former life as a gang-banger, a film student, and "Pop" (Ossie Davis), an old-timer who recalls the civil rights movement of the 1960s. The bus is a microcosm of African American men, their points of conflict and solidarity dramatically enacted on the road. There is a break-down in the desert, a challenge by Southern state troopers, and plenty of roadside stops and traveling highway shots. Lee also employs postmodern film techniques (canted angles, hand-held camerawork, colored filters) that draw attention to themselves. But much of this cinematic formalism is attributed to the film student, viewed through his camcorder, so that it seems to be in quotes. Spike Lee's central focus is the ongoing dialogues among black men – on attitudes toward women, gay blacks, light-skin blacks, white people, crime, the law, work, and politics, attitudes that threaten to disrupt the group's common goal. As always, Lee's film is primarily by, about, and for African Americans. There are occasional swipes at the mainstream media's representation. "Hollywood thinks they got us all figured out," says one of the passengers. "And the evening news. They sum us up with the 4 R's: rap, rape, rob, and riot." Later, a black cop accuses a Black Muslim of having an unrealistic view of ghetto life. "All you know about South Central is what you see in the movies, brought to you by folks who don't even go south of the Santa Monica Freeway." *Get on the Bus* clearly offers different views than this.

While films like *Thelma & Louise*, *My Own Private Idaho*, *Smoke Signals*, and *Get on the Bus* re-envisioned the road movie of the 1990s in terms of sexual and racial politics, bringing marginalized groups front and center, directors like Oliver Stone and David Lynch used the genre to examine the breakdown of family values in the heartland of America. The characters and plot trajectory of *Natural Born Killers* are hardly new. Mickey (Woody Harrelson) and Mallory (Juliette Lewis) form an outlaw couple who share a passion for aggression and each other, murdering their way to stardom on a cross-country contest with the law. What makes Stone's film stand out from *Gun Crazy*, *Badlands* or *Thelma & Louise* is its relentless, random violence and frenetic visual style. It's like *Bonnie and Clyde* on speed. There is nothing subtle about Stone's over-the-top film technique, which keeps shifting between documentary black and white photography and gaudy psychedelic colors, between undercranked fast footage and slow motion, an MTV aesthetic spiked with moments of rock music, oblique angles, and animation. The opening title montage presents their road trip as a hallucinatory joy ride, an adrenaline rush through the fun house of a demented imagination fed by the mass media. Are Mickey and Mallory on a quest for freedom, a hedonistic pleasure binge, or a flight from childhood nightmares? The script leaves little doubt that they both come from broken homes. The sitcom parody of Mallory's dysfunctional household mocks the image of 1950s families idealized by conservatives in the 1970s. Flashbacks of Mickey's childhood show him and his mother at the mercy of an abusive patriarch. But their twisted attitudes are also ascribed to the American media. As if to document this influence, Stone splices in hundreds of violent images from movies, television, comic books, and newspapers throughout the film. The media industry's exploitation of violence is summed up in "American Maniacs," a sensational television program written, directed, and produced by Wayne Gale (Robert Downey, Jr.), who wants to interview the couple for his show. Gayle has turned Mickey and Mallory into celebrities to boost his ratings. "With a vengeance straight out of the Bible," he reports, "they have turned Highway 666 into a candy land of murder and mayhem." Off camera, though, he refers to his show as "junk food for the brain" and his audiences as "those nitwits in zombie-land." Stone's cynicism toward the media underscores a contradiction that has raised objections from viewers and reviewers alike. By ramping up the level of its sexuality and violence in hyper-stylized imagery, does *Natural Born Killers* contribute to the very culture it professes to critique? How can it condemn the merchandise in which it trades? The opening scene in which Mallory flirts with a man in a diner and then assaults him seems like a metaphor for the film's own mode of operation. It tries to seduce its spectators with sex and violence, then attacks them for taking the bait.

Coming at the end of the decade, *The Straight Story* seems like an antidote to Stone's ironic excesses and to Lynch's own postmodern parody in *Wild at Heart* (1990). While Lynch's earlier film is nearly as manic and cartoonish as *Natural Born Killers* and *Raising Arizona*, *The Straight Story*, as its title slyly hints, is as straightforward and slow as growing grass. In fact, the vehicle of choice for the movie's aging hero, Alvin Straight (Richard Farnsworth), is a lawnmower, a John Deere 110 riding tractor, which he hitches to a trailer one day and sets out on a six-week journey across Iowa to Wisconsin. Lynch recycles some of the road film's best-known actors (Sissy Spacek as Alvin's daughter, Harry Dean Stanton as Lyle) and familiar motifs (images of burning homes, campfires, a car accident, miles and miles of straight roads). But he also reinvests the genre with conservative mid-western values, adding the fresh perspective of a generation rarely allowed behind the wheel. One of the film's most poignant scenes shows Alvin sharing drinks and war stories with another veteran. Farnsworth plays his part with deep conviction, perhaps because he knew that he was dying of cancer while *The Straight Story* was being made and that he would take his own life soon after its release.

European Crossroads: Nomads, Immigrants, and Tourists

Across the Atlantic from America, the 1990s witnessed seismic waves of geopolitical transformation. With the collapse of the Soviet Union in 1991 and the creation of the European Union in 1993, the Eurasian map was changing rapidly. To the west, the EU was erasing old borders, reducing trade barriers, and encouraging transnational flow of goods and people. To the east, new boundaries were being drawn around territories that had been forcibly united under the USSR. These shifts in power and allegiances set a flood of refugees, immigrants, and exiles in motion. As Ewa Mazierska and Laura Rascaroli observe in their study of postmodern travel and the European road movie, "Mobility has ceased to be the exception to the rule, and has itself become the rule."[15]

Generally, the grand myth of the open road celebrated in American films like *Easy Rider* has less relevance in Europe, where national borders, languages, and histories traditionally have impeded easy passage. The European landscape is more densely populated, travel is often made by public transportation, and characters are less likely to be rebels or outlaws than ordinary citizens on the move. We have already seen how European road movies of the 1950s (*Voyage to Italy*, *La Strada*, *Wild Strawberries*) differ in spirit from their Hollywood counterparts, assuming allegorical significance, leaning more toward social and psychological analysis than toward any celebration of freedom in an open land. We have also noticed how some European auteurs (Godard, Wenders, Kaurismäki) engage in two-way conversations with American versions of the genre, sometimes finding traces of Americana in France, Germany, or Finland, sometimes transplanting European characters on US soil. These trends continue through the 1970s and 1980s. The celebrated Greek director Theo Angelopoulos uses the trope of travel to explore issues of local politics and social malaise in *The Travelling Players* (*O Thiassos*, 1975) and *Landscape in the Mist* (*Topio stin omichli*, 1988). The first film follows a troupe of performers through decades of warfare and dictatorship, betrayal and jealousy, re-enacting age-old dramas on historical and personal scales. The second film follows two young siblings on a quest to find their father in Germany (Figure 4.9). Although both stories are journey narratives, Angelopoulos invests them with motionless moments of symbolic weight and spiritual grace. *The Vagabond* (*Sans toit ni loi*, 1985), by French director Agnès Varda, is no less enigmatic. Mona, the film's young protagonist (Sandrine Bonnaire), comes from a good home and possesses employable skills but has chosen to drift through life. Varda uses a deft documentary style to trace Mona's journey, exposing the conditions that led this alienated individual to end her life frozen in a ditch.

Angelopoulos and Varda give us figures that float through bleak landscapes devoid of substance or an affirming core. Although these characters may have some vague destination as their goal, they seem more like nomads in a desert. Postmodern theorists like Gilles Deleuze and Félix Guattari use the word *nomadism* to represent alternative lifestyles that may appear as rootless wandering to some but may also be seen in more positive terms, as a form of resistance or freedom from the mainstream culture's ideological constraints. A good place to look at the phenomenon of modern nomadism is *Gadjo Dilo* (1997), Tony Gatlif's film about Romanian Gypsies. The title means "crazy stranger" in Romani, the Indic language spoken by Gypsies in Romania and elsewhere. It is the name given to Stéphane, the film's young protagonist, a musicologist from Paris who wanders into a Gypsy village near Bucharest in search of the voice beloved by his late father.

FIGURE 4.9   Two Greek children in search of their father face the risks of crossing borders in Theo Angelopoulos's *Landscape in the Mist* (*Topio stin omichli*, 1988).

His condition at the beginning of the film – ragged and hungry, a nomad who doesn't speak the native language of the region – reverses the roles that Gypsies usually play in movies and in European culture. Here the outsider is the Frenchman. Gatlif was himself an outsider when he moved with his Gypsy family from Algeria to France in 1948. His portrait of the Romani community pulsates with the animated spirit of its subject, made all the more vital by the threat of ethnic cleansing hovering over the scene.

While the nomads in *Gadjo Dilo* spend little time on the road, the director of *Dear Diary* (*Caro diario*, 1993) does a good deal of wandering through his native Italy. Nanni Moretti's title alludes to the film's structure, which links writing with traveling, journaling with journeys. Part One, "On My Vespa," follows Moretti on his motorbike through Rome. He takes a carefree pleasure in riding through familiar streets, noting the city's history in its architecture, randomly interviewing people on the street. Mazierska and Rascaroli call this "urban nomadism," a condition of being perpetually "in transit," moving from the present to the present.[16] In Part Two, "The Islands," Moretti hops from island to island off the coast of Sicily, looking for the ideal retreat but finding only inhabitants possessed by various obsessions. In the final section, "Doctors," he searches for the right cure to alleviate his ceaseless itch. Perhaps Moretti's constant mobility is itself an obsession, a symptomatic itch, but it also gives him – and us – a chance to see a slice of the modern Italy that is replacing the old country. Gianni Amelio gives us an even wider swath in *The Stolen Children* (*Il ladro di bambini*, 1992). Based on the true story of a young girl placed in prostitution by her own mother, Amelio's film traces the girl's journey with her brother and the policeman assigned to escort them to an orphanage. When the assignment doesn't go as planned, Antonio, the 25-year-old *carabiniere*, ends up taking them nearly the length of Italy, from Milan and Bologna to Rome,

Calabria, and Sicily. Along the way, they stop at police stations and orphanages, visit fast food restaurants and resorts, travel on trains and the national *autostrada*: those homogenized spaces of modern life that are erasing the unique character of local places. Amelio reminds us that each path threaded through the country is part of a larger fabric of insensitivity and institutional indifference that impoverishes all. *The Stolen Children* (its title recalls Vittorio De Sica's 1948 classic, *Bicycle Thieves, Ladri di biciclette*) revives the neorealist spirit of postwar Italy, when directors like De Sica and Rossellini trained their cameras on the streets and filmed the stories of ordinary people struggling day to day. Like De Sica, Amelio makes use of non-professional actors, unpicturesque locations, straightforward chronology, and documentary-style camera work. His respect for authenticity, the antithesis of Hollywood, shows up in his photography as well. The grainy images, for example, or the harsh sunlight that occasionally washes out a scene, evoke emotional truths about the texture of people's lives and the fragility of their identity. Amelio is never sentimental or sensational. His hallmarks are simplicity and objectivity, yet he views his subject with deep understanding, with a clear eye for the telling moment, the revelatory detail.

Travelers in European journey films take to the road for a variety of reasons. In Jan Svěrák's *The Ride* (*Jízda*, 1994), two 30-year old buddies feel lost between the old Czechoslovakia of the communist era and the new post-communist Czech Republic. Franta and Radek decide to buy a dilapidated car and pretend they're in a road movie. But confined to a country that lacks the open spaces of America, and without the proper documents, they watch their plans go awry in the absurdist style of 1960s Czech comedies. Their crazy ride is a chance to explore issues of national identity at a particular moment in Czech history. Further south, in Bulgaria, Stephan Komandarev dramatizes generational conflicts of mobility and identity in *The World Is Big and Salvation Lurks Around the Corner* (*Svetat e golyam i spasenie debne otvsyakade*, 2008). When a young Bulgarian named Sashko loses his parents and his memory in an accident on a German autobahn, his grandfather travels from the old country to rescue him. Their journey home on a tandem bicycle binds them physically and metaphorically; Sashko provides the muscle while the old man steers. Although the film is advertised on the DVD jacket as "one of the major crowd-pleasers of the year," its clever script and cinematic style add layers to the story. Komandarev cuts back and forth between two journeys: a family's perilous escape to the West from Soviet Bulgaria and Sashko's return home with his grandfather in a new Europe without border guards. Sashko's amnesia represents the confusion of a generation that has lost its way on the fluid map of political and cultural values.

While the characters in these films often seem like displaced persons in their own lands, an increasing number of European movies focus on the plight of immigrants and refugees. Manuel Poirier's *Western* (1997) follows two outsiders, a Spanish salesman and a Russian hitchhiker, as they traverse a cross-section of Brittany in western France. Emmanuel Finkiel's *Voyages* (1999) covers wider ground. It begins with a transport of Jews from Warsaw to Auschwitz, but these Jews are not being shipped to the Nazi extermination camps in cattle cars. They are on a tour bus sometime in the present, and though most are elderly and some are Holocaust survivors, there is none of the solemnity we might expect. Their talk is full of petty arguments and medical complaints. *Voyages* is a triptych of fragmentary stories about disconnected, yet interwoven lives. The three narrative threads take us to post-communist Poland, to the middle-class neighborhoods of Paris, and into the noisy streets of Tel Aviv, subtly dramatizing the long-term effects of prejudice and genocide.

Voyages updates one of the world's oldest and saddest journey narratives, the story of the wandering Jew. But many road trips start on a lighter note. Tourists on vacation, for example, set out for the sheer pleasure of sampling someplace new, away from the tedium of home. In *Italian for Beginners* (*Italiensk for begyndere*, 2000), three men and three women, all lonely hearts in need of companionship under the gray skies of Denmark, take an adult class in Italian. The language's romantic appeal, with its promise of milder climes, becomes the bright spot in their dull routines and a catalyst for new relationships. As they become involved in one another's lives, they make plans to realize a common dream: a class field trip to Venice. *Italian for Beginners* is the first romantic comedy to come from the otherwise rigorous Dogme film group and the first Dogme film to be directed by a woman. The Dogme manifesto, created by Danish filmmakers in 1995, proposed a set of rigorous aesthetic principles designed to "purify" the medium. According to these rules, all shooting must be on location with a hand-held camera. There can be no external props, special lighting effects, optical filters, or music tracks. By the end of the 1990s, the self-imposed discipline of Dogme aesthetics had resulted in a small number of influential films, including Thomas Vinterberg's bitterly satirical *Celebration* (*Festen*, 1998), Lars von Trier's *The Idiots* (*Idioterne*, 1998), and Søren Kragh-Jacobsen's *Mifune's Last Song* (*Mifunes sidste sang*, 1999). By applying the same stylistic codes to a holiday movie, director Lone Scherfig gave the movement a new direction and a more forgiving lease on life. Eric Rohmer took the principles of another cinematic movement on vacation. One of the original directors of the French New Wave, Rohmer explored the holiday mentality in film after film. The characters in *Claire's Knee* (*Le genou de Claire*, 1970), *Pauline at the Beach* (*Pauline à la plage*, 1982), *A Winter's Tale* (*Conte d'hiver*, 1992), and *A Summer's Tale* (*Conte d'été*, 1996) seek personal fulfillment in new surroundings, though always in France, working out personal issues while free from the emotional constraints of work and home. While these films may not fit some conceptions of the road movie, Mazierska and Rascaroli devote an entire chapter to Rohmer's interest in the "social geography" of holiday travel.[17]

Journeys through Africa, Asia, Latin America, and Places Between

As cinema advances into the third millennium, what we have been calling the road movie twists and turns into new configurations while it travels around the globe, taking in the local landscapes, people, and their stories as new material for its ever changing vision of mobility. With so many nations and films to choose from, we can make only a selective tour.

The continent of Africa is vast: large enough to fit China, India, Europe, the United States, Argentina, and New Zealand within the compass of its 11.7 million square miles. Africa's 1 billion people speak more than 1,000 languages and span a great diversity of social systems, customs, and religions. Yet the inhabitants of this broad region have much in common, reflecting the unique values, institutions, and historical realities in this part of the world. Among other things, Africans share a long tradition of journey narratives passed down from generation to generation by oral storytellers, known as *griots* in French. The griot may give a fresh spin to a well-known tale with each retelling, meandering from the main path, adapting the details to a given audience, adding bits of local history and landmarks along the way. The journeys in these tales are often allegorical, expeditions of personal growth about young people coming to terms with issues of identity and community. As motion pictures have taken on the traditional task of storytelling, African directors have become cinematic griots. In *Yeelen* (*Brightness*, 1987), for example, Malian filmmaker Souleymane Cissé brings a thirteenth-century legend of the Bambara people to the screen. Niankoro, a young man with magical powers, leaves home on a quest for spiritual enlightenment, furtively pursued by his father, a malevolent sorcerer who abandoned him at birth. A timeless story of initiation and generational conflict, powerfully evoking primal moments with its resonant imagery, *Yeelen* approaches the condition of myth, demonstrating the paradox that stories have more global appeal when they are rooted in local soil. *Keita! Voice of the Griot* (*Keita! L'héritage du griot*, 1996) uses a story from the African epic *Sundjata* to measure the distance between past and future. In the film, an aging griot travels to the home of a 13-year-old boy in Ouagadougou, the capital of Burkina Faso. The boy's parents want him to learn French and grow up in the modern way, but the griot tells him that he's descended from an ancient line of storytellers with an obligation to tradition. The fact that Dani Kouyaté, the film's director, is from an ancient family of griots and that his father plays the part of the old man in the movie strengthens the connections between traditional storytelling and contemporary filmmaking, casting Keita's journey as a parable of Africa's future. As Kouyaté put it in a 1995 interview, "Sometimes when you don't know where you're heading, you have to return to where you came from ... before continuing your journey. Today, with all the things happening to her, Africa has trouble finding which direction to take – modernity, tradition, or some other road."[18] African directors continue to explore such roads in films like Raymond Rajaonarivelo's *When the Stars Meet the Sea* (*Quand les étoiles rencontrent la mer*, 1996), from Madagascar; Gaston Kaboré's *Buud Yam* (1997), from Burkina Faso; Moussa Touré's *The TGV Express* (*TGV*, 1998), from Senegal; Mama Keita's *The River* (*Le fleuve*, 2003), from Guinea; and Jann Turner's *White Wedding* (2009), from South Africa.

Across the Mediterranean Sea from North Africa, traveling toward the Middle East, we pass through Turkey on the way to Iran, both predominantly Islamic countries. *Journey to the Sun* (*Güneşe yolculuk*, 1999), directed by Yesim Ustaoglu, follows Mehmet, a young man who has migrated from western Turkey to Istanbul, where he befriends an ethnic Kurd named Berzan from the remote southeast. When Berzan is killed by the police and he himself is mistaken for a Kurdish terrorist, Mehmet undertakes a journey to return his friend's body to his birth village. His arduous passage through a countryside that is both stunning and austere dramatizes the plight of immigrants amid the ethnic strife of modern Turkey. *Ten* (2002) is one of several road movies by Iranian director Abbas Kiarostami. The film consists of ten scenes, all filmed by digital cameras fixed on the interior of a single car, each scene capturing a personal conversation between the female driver and her various passengers as she drives around the capital city of Tehran. *Ten* is a highly original take on the relationship of language to mobility, giving us an intimate view of social issues in Iran without external commentary.

Further east, past the mountainous terrain of Pakistan and Afghanistan, lies the vast subcontinent of India, home of the world's largest movie industry. Dev Benegal, the director of *Road, Movie* (2009), added a comma in his title perhaps to emphasize the parallel that he draws between vehicles in motion and motion pictures. The film's hero is Vishnu, a restless young man who sees no future in his father's hair oil business. Instead, he gets behind the wheel of a 1942 Chevy truck and agrees to drive it across the desert to the sea. No ordinary truck, the Chevy turns out to be a mobile theatre, still equipped with 35 mm projectors and cans of old film. With the help of a few passengers picked up along the way, Vishnu discovers the magic of movies, their power to entertain, enchant, and liberate. Like Scheherazade, the fabled Persian queen who saved her skin by telling stories to her would-be executor, Vishnu and his companions use their store of films to mollify menacing forces in a hostile land (Figure 4.10). *Road,*

FIGURE 4.10 Dev Benegal's *Road, Movie* (2009) gives the genre a Bollywood twist. Here, the protagonist projects a Hindi film onto the façade of a police station to entertain his jailors, much like Scheherazade.

FIGURE 4.11 A restless traveler from the Himalayan country of Bhutan takes the high road to enlightenment in *Travelers and Magicians* (*Dzongkha*, Dir. Khyentse Norbu, 2003).

Movie adapts many of the genre's traditional themes and visual motifs, including traveling montages and hallucinatory scenes, giving a Bollywood twist to a familiar truism: sometimes you need to travel miles away to find your own way home. A similar idea is illustrated in *Travelers and Magicians* (2003), the first feature film from Bhutan, the landlocked kingdom high in the Himalayas between India and China. Written and directed by Khyentse Norbu, a reincarnate lama (a reborn high priest of Tibetan Buddhism), the film takes the form of a parable. Dondup, a young government official bored with the slow pace of his isolated village, hankers for a better life in the United States. When he misses the bus out, he's forced to travel by foot along the narrow Lateral Road, where he meets a monk, an apple seller, and other travelers (Figure 4.11). To pass the time, the monk tells a story about a restless farm boy, shown in flashbacks that parallel Norbu's personal progress. Norbu is so focused on his vision of America that he fails to see the beauty surrounding him. Gradually, he becomes more mindful of the here and now, realizing the Buddhist teaching that what matters most is not the destination but how you make the journey. Combining striking views of the local landscape with a figurative form of storytelling native to the region, *Travelers and Magicians* is a good example of how the road film can conform to its host culture. There is another spiritual message in *Rolling Home with a Bull* (*So-wa hamque yeohang-ha-neun beob*, 2010) a South Korean film directed by Im Soon-rye. The bull in the title is a real animal, stolen by an aspiring poet from his family farm and taken on the road. While the protagonist searches for a buyer and a better life, he is pursued by his ex-lover, who has just lost her husband. The bull has a literal life of its own, but it is also a Buddhist symbol of enlightenment. The poet's journey becomes both a comic romp through the Korean countryside and a spiritual pilgrimage of self realization.

Further east from Korea, across the Sea of Japan, Japanese filmmakers have produced their own versions of the road film. Ryuichi Hiroki's *Vibrator* (2003) is about a 31-year-old woman who meets a 28-year-old truck driver in a roadside convenience store. Soon they are in the cab of his truck making love. She is bulimic and uses alcohol to silence the demons in her head. He tells tales about his early life of crime. Most of the film follows their journey through the wintry landscape of Japan as they talk and take halting steps toward real intimacy: a pair of lonely hearts from Japan's lost generation. At one point, the trucker relinquishes his place behind the wheel and lets her drive the rig. Despite its title and the director's earlier training in the "pink film" (softcore pornography) industry, *Vibrator* is less about sex than an exploration of the way companionship with strangers on the road can build compassion and exorcize inner demons. Japan's large and fervent film audience makes Japan an attractive market, which is one reason Japanese actors appear as heroes in movies made in other countries. *Riding Alone for Thousands of Miles* (*Qian li zou dan qi*, 2005) is a Chinese-Japanese co-production directed by mainland China's Zhang Yimou. One of the small-scale movies that Zhang made between his epic blockbusters (*Hero*, 2002; *House of Flying Daggers*, 2004; *Curse of the Golden Flower*, 2006), it features a strong performance by Japan's veteran actor, Ken Takakura, as an aged Japanese father estranged from his only son. While the younger man lies dying of cancer in a hospital, Gou-ichi Takata, the father, learns that his son has a passion for Chinese folk opera and was making a video in China's rural Yunnan Province. Without knowing anything about video, traditional music, or a word of Mandarin, Takata sets out on a single-minded mission that takes him far beyond anything he had in mind. *Riding Alone* is about repairing two sets of relationships: between two generations and between two peoples. It is also a chance to showcase the most culturally diverse of China's 23 provinces. Zhang's camera captures the majesty of Yunnan's snow-capped mountains, its haunting labyrinthine caverns, its lush tropical forests, and most of all, the emotional generosity of its people. *Cold Fever* (*Á köldum klaka*, 1995) is another co-production, with dialogue in four languages (English, Japanese, German, and Icelandic) that reflect its financing. This time the Japanese protagonist, a successful businessman named Hirata, travels in an easterly direction, to the tiny island nation of Iceland in the Atlantic Ocean. Like Takata, Hirata is out to resolve a generational rift. He needs to perform a sacred ritual at the spot where his parents died seven years earlier. Director Fridrik Fridriksson plays with the conventions of the road movie. Hirata travels by air, bus, taxi, truck, jeep, horseback, and an old French Citroën sedan, making the obligatory roadside stops, listening to pop music, taking unexpected detours, and encountering an odd array of characters along the way, including a psychic, a funeral photographer, and an outlaw couple named Jack and Jill. What makes the film truly unique, however, is the Icelandic landscape in midwinter, a mystical synthesis of fire and ice that inspires visions of terrifying spirits and awesome natural events.

Clearly, in addition to exploring certain themes and cinematic styles, the road movie also has become a convenient vehicle for exporting cultural values, promoting tourism, and reaching global markets. Nowhere is this more apparent than in Latin America, which has produced dozens of films about journeys, most of them within the last 20 years. Following the international success of films like *Central Station* (*Centro do Brasil*, 1998), *Y tu mamá también*, 2001), and *The Motorcycle Diaries* (*Diarios de motocicleta*, 2004), filmmakers from Mexico and Colombia to Argentina and Brazil have found a genre that plays well in the festival circuit and often even in commercial theatres. They also have found that local governments are willing to fund such projects for the sake of fostering positive images of their country's population and natural beauty. This is not to say that Latin American road films are mainly motivated by money. Far from it. Cinema south of Hollywood has a rich, extensive, varied, independent history, featuring some of the most talented and innovative filmmakers in the world, as we'll see when we explore the subject further in Deep Focus on Latin American Cinemas.

Meanwhile, back in the United States, Hollywood and independent film practitioners have continued to push the genre in old and new directions. There have been whacky cross-country comedies like *Rat Race* (2001), eccentric character studies like *Sideways* (2001), satirical mockumentaries like *Borat* (2006), and grim, post-apocalyptic fables like *The Road* (2009). The paths that these films take may seem far removed, at times, from the original course of *Easy Rider* and its predecessors, but they show how a genre like the road film can persist, adapt, and reinvent itself. Like the ancient oral and literary traditions of travel tales to which it is related, the road film speaks to the human predilection for travel, to our fascination with vehicles of locomotion, our visions of freedom, the pleasures of adventure, the promise of self-realization, the experience of life as a journey. More pointedly, road films remind us of that special kinship between movies and mobility: the projector as an engine of our dreams, the screen as a wide windshield, the world framed and fading fast, like the landscape in a rear-view mirror. Seated in a theatre or our living room, we get to ride the road vicariously, taking every curve and detour without the risks, knowing we need only click our heels and we'll be safe at home in Kansas.

Filmography

Country	English Language Title	Original Title	Director	Date
USA	*Wild Boys of the Road*		William Wellman	1933
USA	*It Happened One Night*		Frank Capra	1934
UK	*The 39 Steps*		Alfred Hitchcock	1935
USA	*You Only Live Once*		Fritz Lang	1937
USA	*The Wizard of Oz*		Victor Fleming	1939
USA	*Stagecoach*		John Ford	1939
USA	*The Grapes of Wrath*		John Ford	1940

(Continued)

Filmography (*Continued*)

Country	English Language Title	Original Title	Director	Date
USA	*They Drive by Night*		Raoul Walsh	1940
USA	*Sullivan's Travels*		Preston Sturges	1941
USA	*Road to Morocco*		Dan Butler	1942
USA	*Detour*		Edgar Ulmer	1945
USA	*They Live by Night*		Nicholas Ray	1948
USA	*Gun Crazy* (aka *Deadly is the Female*)		Joseph H. Lewis	1950
USA	*The Wild One*		Laslo Benedek	1953
France	*The Wages of Fear*	*Le salaire de la peur*	Henri-Georges Clouzot	1953
USA	*The Long, Long Trailer*		Vincente Minnelli	1953
Italy	*Journey to Italy* (aka *Voyage to Italy*)	*Viaggio in Italia*	Roberto Rossellini	1954
Italy	*The Road*	*La Strada*	Federico Fellini	1954
India	*Song of the Little Road*	*Pather Panchali*	Satyajit Ray	1955
Sweden	*Wild Strawberries*	*Smultronstället*	Ingmar Bergman	1957
USA	*North by Northwest*		Alfred Hitchcock	1959
France	*Breathless*	*À bout de souffle*	Jean-Luc Godard	1960
USA	*It's a Mad, Mad, Mad, Mad World*		Stanley Kramer	1963
Italy	*The Easy Life*	*Il sorpasso*	Dino Risi	1964
USA	*The Wild Angels*		Roger Corman	1966
France	*Weekend*	*Week End*	Jean-Luc Godard	1967
USA	*Bonnie and Clyde*		Arthur Penn	1967
USA	*Easy Rider*		Dennis Hopper	1969
USA	*Midnight Cowboy*		John Schlesinger	1969
USA	*Five Easy Pieces*		Bob Rafelson	1970
USA	*Two-Lane Blacktop*		Monte Hellman	1971
USA	*Badlands*		Terrence Malick	1973
Germany	*Kings of the Road*	*Im Lauf der Zeit*	Wim Wenders	1976
France	*The Truck*	*Le camion*	Marguerite Duras	1977

Country	English Language Title	Original Title	Director	Date
Australia	*Mad Max*		George Miller	1979
Brazil	*Bye Bye Brazil*	*Bye Bye Brasil*	Carlos Diegues	1980
USA	*Cannonball Run*		Hal Needham	1981
USA/ Germany	*Paris, Texas*		Wim Wenders	1984
USA	*Stranger Than Paradise*		Jim Jarmusch	1984
USA	*Back to the Future*		Robert Zemeckis	1985
France	*Vagabond*	*Sans toit ni loi*	Agnès Varda	1985
USA/ Germany	*Bagdad Café* (aka *Out of Rosenheim*)		Percy Adlon	1987
USA	*Planes, Trains & Automobiles*		John Hughes	1987
USA	*Raising Arizona*		Joel Coen	1987
Mali	*Brightness*	*Yeelen*	Souleymane Cissé	1987
USA	*Midnight Run*		Martin Brest	1988
USA	*Rain Man*		Barry Levinson	1988
Greece	*Landscape in the Mist*	*Topio stin omichli*	Theodoros Angelopoulos	1988
UK	*Powwow Highway*		Jonathan Wacks	1989
Finland	*Leningrad Cowboys Go America*		Aki Kaurismäki	1989
USA	*My Own Private Idaho*		Gus Van Sant	1991
USA	*Thelma & Louise*		Ridley Scott	1991
Slovenia	*Grandma Goes South*	*Babica gre na jug*	Vinci Vogue Anzlovar	1991
Argentina	*The Voyage*	*El viaje*	Fernando E. Solanas	1992
Italy	*The Stolen Children*	*Il ladro di bambini*	Gianni Amelio	1992
Italy	*Dear Diary*	*Caro diario*	Nanni Moretti	1993
Australia	*The Adventures of Priscilla, Queen of the Desert*		Stephan Elliott	1994
Czech Republic	*The Ride*	*Jizda*	Jan Sverák	1994
USA	*Natural Born Killers*		Oliver Stone	1994

(*Continued*)

Filmography (*Continued*)

Country	English Language Title	Original Title	Director	Date
Cuba	*Guantanamera*	*Guantanamera*	Tomás Gutiérrez Alea	1995
Iceland	*Cold Fever*	*Á köldum klaka*	Fridrik Thor Fridriksson	1995
USA	*Boys on the Side*		Herbert Ross	1995
USA	*Get on the Bus*		Spike Lee	1996
Burkina Faso	*Keita! Voice of the Griot*	*Keita! L'héritage du griot*	Dani Kouyaté	1996
France	*Western*		Manuel Poirier	1997
Senegal	*The TGV Express*	*TGV*	Moussa Touré	1997
Burkina Faso	*Buud Yam*	*Buud Yam*	Gaston Kaboré	1997
USA	*Smoke Signals*		Chris Eyre	1998
Brazil	*Central Station*	*Central do Brasil*	Walter Salles	1998
Turkey	*Journey to the Sun*	*Günese yolculuk*	Yesim Ustaoglu	1999
France	*Voyages*	*Voyages*	Emmanuel Finkiel	1999
USA	*The Straight Story*		David Lynch	1999
Mexico	*Without a Trace* (aka *Leaving No Trace*)	*Sin dejar huella*	María Novaro	2000
USA	*Rat Race*		Jerry Zucker	2001
Mexico	*And Your Mother Too*	*Y tu mamá también*	Alfonso Cuarón	2001
Morocco	*The Wind Horse*	*Aoud rih / Le cheval de vent*	Aoulad-Syad Daoud	2002
Mauritania	*Waiting for Happiness*	*Heremakono / En attendant le bonheur*	Abderrahmane Sissako	2002
Argentina	*Minimal Stories* (aka *Intimate Stories*)		Carlos Sorín	2002
UK	*Heartlands*		Damien O'Donnell	2002
Japan	*Vibrator*		Ryuichi Hiroki	2003
Guinea	*The River*	*Le fleuve*	Mama Keita	2003
Bhutan	*Travelers and Magicians*	*Dzongkha*	Khyentse Norbu	2003
Russia	*The Return*	*Vozvrashchenie*	Andrey Zvyagintsev	2003
Argentina	*The Rolling Family*	*Familia rodante*	Pablo Trapero	2004

Country	English Language Title	Original Title	Director	Date
Brazil	*The Motorcycle Diaries*	*Diarios de motocicleta*	Walter Salles	2004
China	*Riding Alone for Thousands of Miles*	*Qian li zou dan qi*	Yimou Zhang	2005
Ecuador	*How Much Further*	*Que tan lejos*	Tania Hermida	2006
Bulgaria	*The World is Big and Salvation Lurks Around the Corner*	*Svetat e golyam i spasenie debne otvsyakade*	Stefan Komandarev	2008
South Africa	*White Wedding*		Jann Turner	2009
USA	*The Road*		John Hillcoat	2009
Colombia	*The Wind Journeys*	*Los viajes del viento*	Ciro Guerra	2009
India	*Road, Movie*	*Road, Movie*	Dev Benegal	2009
Uruguay	*Beyond the Road*	*Por el camino*	Charly Braun	2010
South Korea	*Rolling Home with a Bull*	*So-wa hamque yeohang-ha-neun beob*	Im Soon-Rye	2010
USA	*Magic Trip*		Alex Gibney and Alison Ellwood	2011
Brazil/ France/ USA	*On the Road*		Walter Salles	2012
USA	*Identity Thief*		Seth Gordon	2013

Notes

1. Barbara Klinger, "The Road to Dystopia : Landscaping the Nation in *Easy Rider*," in Steven Cohan and Ina Rae Hark, ed., *The Road Movie Book* (Routledge, 1997), 179.
2. Quoted in David Laderman, *Driving Visions: Exploring the Road Movie* (University of Texas Press, 2002), 43.
3. Shari Roberts, "Western Meets Eastwood: Genre and Gender on the Road," in Steven Cohan and Ina Rae Hark, eds., *The Road Movie Book* (Routledge, 1997), 51.
4. Devin Orgeron, *Road Movies: From Muybridge and Méliès to Lynch and Kiarostami* (Palgrave Macmillan, 2008), 76.
5. Dudley Andrew, "*Breathless* Then and Now," booklet accompanying *À bout de souffle* DVD (Criterion Collection, 2007).
6. Jack Kerouac, *On the Road* (1957, reissued Penguin, 1976), 87.
7. Katie Mills, *The Road Story and the Rebel: Moving Through Film, Fiction, and Television* (Southern Illinois University Press, 2006), 3.
8. Mills, 17.
9. Orgeron, 27–45.
10. Steven Cohan, "Almost Like Being at Home: Showbiz Culture and Hollywood Road Trips in the 1940s and 1950s," in Steven Cohan and Ina Rae Hark, eds., *The Road Movie Book* (Routledge, 1997), 115.

11. Laderman, 147.

12. Laderman, 82.

13. Laderman, 164.

14. Jim Jarmusch, quoted in "Some Notes on *Stranger Than Paradise*," Press Book, *Stranger Than Paradise* Special DVD Edition (Criterion Collection, 1984), 8.

15. Ewa Mazierska and Laura Rascaroli, *Crossing New Europe: Postmodern Travel and the European Road Movie* (Wallflower Press, 2006), 1.

16. Mazierska and Rascaroli, 131–132.

17. Mazierska and Rascaroli, 33–56.

18. Maria Eriksson Baaz and Mai Palmberg, *Same and Other: Negotiating African Identity in Cultural Production* (Nordiska Afrikainstitutet, 2001), 99.

Further Reading

Cohan, Steven and Ina Rae Hark, eds. *The Road Movie Book*. Routledge, 1997.

Corrigan, Timothy. *A Cinema Without Walls: Movies and Culture After Vietnam*. Rutgers University Press, 1991.

Lackey, Kris. *Road Frames: The American Highway Narrative*. University of Nebraska Press, 1997.

Laderman, David. *Driving Visions: Exploring the Road Movie*. University of Texas Press, 2002.

Mazierska, Ewa and Laura Rascaroli. *Crossing New Europe: Postmodern Travel and the European Road Movie*. Wallflower Press, 2006.

Mills, Katie. *The Road Story and the Rebel: Moving Through Film, Fiction, and Television*. Southern Illinois University Press, 2006.

Orgeron, Devin. *Road Movies: From Muybridge and Méliès to Lynch and Kiarostami*. Palgrave Macmillan, 2008.

Paes de Barros, Deborah. *Fast Cars and Bad Girls: Nomadic Subjects and Women's Road Stories*. Peter Lang, 2004.

Sargeant, Jack and Stephanie Watson, eds. *Lost Highways: An Illustrated Guide to the Road Movie*. Creation Books, 1999.

Sherrill, Rowland. *Road-Book America: Contemporary Culture and the New Picaresque*. University of Illinois Press, 2000.

Sturken, Marita. *Thelma & Louise*. British Film Institute, 2000.

Williams, Mark. *Road Movies: The Complete Guide to Cinema on Wheels*. Proteus, 1982.

Wood, Jason. *100 Road Movies*. British Film Institute. 2007.

DEEP FOCUS ON LATIN AMERICAN CINEMAS

FIGURE 4.12   Map of Latin America.

World Cinema through Global Genres, First Edition. William V. Costanzo.
© 2014 John Wiley & Sons, Inc. Published 2014 by John Wiley & Sons, Inc.

Our focus on the road movie as a global genre gives us a chance to look more closely at filmmaking in a part of the world that is close to us in many ways. You may have already noticed that many of the movies from Latin America that have crossed the border in recent years are journey films. Think of *Guantanamera* (1995), *Central Station* (*Central do Brasil*, 1997), *Y tu mamá también* (2001), or *The Motorcycle Diaries* (*Diarios de motocicleta*, 2004). The reasons for this trend are partly economic. Film financing tends to follow the proven pathways of success. But there are also important cultural dimensions to the genre. The trope of travel offers close-up views of lands and peoples for those of us who might otherwise know little about life in the Andes Mountains, the rain forests of the Amazon, or the plateaus of Patagonia. The varied cinematic traditions of Latin America, road movies in particular, afford glimpses of the nearly 600 million descendants of the Mayas, Incas, Aztecs, Spanish conquistadores, African slaves, and others who inhabit its 7,880,000 square miles. From these films, we learn more about their histories, their cultures, and the lifestyles they have carved out for themselves in a landscape that includes the world's largest river, highest waterfall, and longest mountain range.

We'll use the term Latin America because the word "Latin" captures affinities of language and culture that are missing in the strictly geographical meaning of Central or South America. Those regions of the Americas in which the Latin-based languages of Spanish and Portuguese predominate include the North American nation of Mexico, the Caribbean islands, the great land mass of South America, and the isthmus of Central America that connects the northern and southern subcontinents. This area is significantly larger in size and population than Anglo-America, a region that includes Canada, the United States, and a few other territories (like Bermuda and Belize) connected by the English language and a common British heritage. As the proportion of Spanish speakers in the US population grows – more than 16% by 2010 – even this distinction between Anglos and Latinos is being blurred.

Much of the linguistic and religious make-up of Latin America is a legacy of European colonialism. Those fifteenth-century explorers who claimed most of the New World for Spain and Portugal left strong imprints in the form of Romance languages and Roman Catholicism. Today, Spanish is the mother tongue of some 20 Latin American countries, while Portuguese is the official language of Brazil, the largest and most populated country in the region. Mexico alone has more than twice as many Spanish speakers as Spain itself. Brazil has 16 times as many Portuguese speakers as Portugal. Some 70% of the people in Latin America consider themselves Catholic, a higher proportion of the population than in Europe, Africa, or Asia. But these figures obscure the region's rich diversity, its multilayered pyramid of cultures and influences, including Jews and a growing Protestant community. At its base are the indigenous peoples who inhabited the continent before Columbus: descendants of the Mayas, Aztecs, and other Native Americans who established advanced civilizations, each with its own language, belief system, social hierarchy, technologies, and arts. Added to these pre-Columbian traditions, often replacing them by force, are the influences of European nations, chiefly Spain, Portugal, and France – particularly strong during the colonial period from the sixteenth through nineteenth centuries. In addition to their Western ways, the colonial powers imported African slaves, whose descendants also helped to shape the cultural landscape. In the twentieth century, the United States became a major player, exporting its own brand of popular culture as it sought to direct the region's political and economic future.

These multi-stranded threads run through all the arts: through the Constructivist drawings of Manuel Rendón, the populist murals of Diego Rivera, the folk-inspired paintings of Frida Kahlo, the volumetric sculptures of Fernando Botero, the labyrinthine stories of Jorge Luis Borges, the magical realism of Gabriel García Márquez's novels, the passionate cadences of Pablo Neruda's poetry. Their echoes can be heard in the *merengue* of the Caribbean, the *bossa nova* of Brazil, the Argentinean and Uruguayan *tangos*. What makes these art forms so unique, so distinct from their counterparts elsewhere in the world, is the way they have combined with indigenous or African traditions, forming a hybrid culture of old and new. There is probably no better place to see this cultural synthesis in action than in the cinema.

Anyone who reads about the history of cinema in Latin America will encounter certain words that are charged with conflicting meanings and undertones. A good introduction to these terms and the ideologies behind them is the groundbreaking book by Ella Shohat and Robert Stam, *Unthinking Eurocentrism: Multiculturalism and the Media*. Shohat and Stam seek to shift their readers from an ethnocentric to a multicultural way of thinking, broadening their view of other cultures beyond their own inherited assumptions and biases in ways that respect the viewpoints and beliefs of those other cultures. In their words, multiculturalism means "seeing world history and contemporary social life from the perspective of the radical equality of peoples in status, potential, and rights."[1] Shohat and Stam trace the history of terms used to describe regions like Latin America – expressions such as "Colonial," "Underdeveloped," and "Third World" – analyzing the ethnocentric attitudes embedded in these terms. They point out, for example, that referring to a nation as a "Third World" country may suggest something third rate, but that the term was given a positive spin by Latin American filmmakers in the 1960s when they announced the notion of a "Third Cinema" distinct from movies of the capitalist "First World" and the socialist "Second World." Shohat and Stam argue that the long period during which Third World countries were held as colonies of Europe has left a damaging legacy in our thought and discourse. They contend that "colonialism is ethnocentrism armed, institutionalized, gone global," that a form of "neo-colonialism" has replaced direct political and military control with indirect, economic forms of control, that "post-colonial" theory represents an effort "to transcend the (presumed) binarisms of Third Worldist militancy,"[2] that is, to move beyond oppositional distinctions between "them" and "us." Another widely used term is New Latin American Cinema (NLAC). Zuzana Pick traces the NLAC movement back to events like the Viña del Mar international festival of 1967, when filmmakers from several nations united in their common struggles for "political autonomy, freedom of expression, and social change,"[3] ideals that were closely allied to the goals of Third Cinema.

Timeline (Figure 4.13)

Date	Country	National or Regional History	Film History
1492	Latin America	Columbus claims land in Cuba and Hispaniola for the Spanish crown	
1494	Latin America	Treaty of Tordesillas divides Portuguese and Spanish territories in the New World	
1804	Haiti	Haiti breaks away from France	
1825	Latin America	Most Spanish-speaking nations achieve independence from Spain	
1846–1848	Mexico	Mexican-American War	
1898	Cuba	Spanish-American War	
1899–1902	Colombia	Thousand Days War	
1910–1921	Mexico	Mexican Revolution	
1919	Mexico		Enrique Rosas's *The Grey Automobile* (*El automóvil gris*)
1931	Mexico		Russia's Sergei Eisenstein arrives in Mexico
1933	Argentina		John Reinhart's *Tango Bar* whets national appetite for tango comedies
1933	USA	FDR initiates the Good Neighbor Policy	
1935	Brazil		João de Barro and Wallace Downey introduce the *chanchada* musical with *Alô, Alô Brasil!*
1936	Mexico		Fernando de Fuentes launches ranch comedy craze with *Out on the Big Ranch* (*Allá en el Rancho Grande*)
1936–1939	Spain	Spanish Civil War	
1943	Mexico		Emilio Fernández's *María Candelaria* (*Xochimilco*)
1948–1958	Colombia	Period of "La Violencia"	
1950	Mexico		Luis Buñuel's *The Young and the Damned* (*Los olvidados*)

Date	Country	National or Regional History	Film History
1951–1964	Brazil	Democratically elected presidents govern Brazil until a military coup in 1964	Lima Barreto's *Cangaceiro* (*O Cangaceiro*)
1959	Cuba	Fidel Castro comes to power after Cuban Revolution	Castro establishes the ICAIC film school
1962	Cuba	Cuban Missile Crisis	
1963	Brazil		Carlos Diegues's *Ganga Zumba* and Nelson Pereira dos Santos's *Barren Lives* (*Vidas Secas*) set the Cinema Novo movement in motion
1966–1969	Brazil	Military presidency of Artur Costa e Silva	
1966–1973	Argentina	Class conflicts erupt in an "Argentine Revolution"	
1967	Bolivia	Ernesto "Che" Guevara executed in Bolivia	
1968	Mexico	Tlatelolco massacre: army shoots student demonstrators	
1968	Cuba		Tomás Gutiérrez Alea's *Memories of Underdevelopment* (*Memorias del subdesarrollo*)
1968–1973	Brazil	Guerrilla warfare against Brazil's dictatorship	
1969	Argentina		"Toward a Third Cinema" published by Fernando Solanas and Octavio Getino
1969	Bolivia		Jorge Sanjinés's *Blood of the Condor* (*Yawar Mallku*)
1970	Argentina		Solanas and Getino's *Hour of the Furnaces* (*La hora de los hornos*)
1970	Brazil		Dos Santos's *How Tasty Was My Little Frenchman* (*Como era gostoso meu francês*)
1970–1973	Chile	Salvador Allende's leftist presidency	
1971	Bolivia	Military dictator Hugo Banzer replaces leftist General Juan José Torres	

(Continued)

Timeline (*Continued*)

Date	Country	National or Regional History	Film History
1973	Chile	Pinochet's military coup replaces Allende with rightist regime	
1975	Spain	Franco dies	
1976–1983	Argentina	"Dirty war" period of political repression	
1977–1990	Chile		Patricio Guzmán's *The Battle of Chile* (*La batalla de Chile*)
1979	Latin America		First International Festival of New Latin American Cinema in Cuba
1980	Brazil		Diegues's *Bye Bye Brazil* (*Bye Bye Brasil*)
1982	Spain	PSOE introduces democracy and economic growth	
1983	Argentina	Raúl Alfonsin restores democracy to Argentina	
1984	Argentina		María Luisa Bemberg's *Camila*
1985	Argentina		Luis Puenzo's *The Official Story* (*La historia official*)
1986	Mexico		Paul Leduc's *Frida* (*Frida, naturaleza viva*)
1990	Colombia		Victor Gaviria's *Rodrigo D: No future* (*Rodrigo D: No futuro*)
1992	Mexico		Alfonso Arau's *Like Water for Chocolate* (*Como agua para chocolate*)
1995	Argentina		"Ley de Cinema" (cinema law) provides state support for filmmaking
1999–2002	Argentina	Financial crisis	
2000	Argentina		Fabián Bielinsky's *Nine Queens* (*Nueve Reinas*)
2000	Mexico		Alejandro González Iñárritu's *Amores Perros*

Date	Country	National or Regional History	Film History
2001	Mexico		Alfonso Cuarón's *Y tu mamá también*
2002	Brazil		Fernando Meirelles's *City of God* (*Cidade de Deus*)
2003	Colombia		Cinema Law revives filmmaking in Colombia
2004	Argentina		Pablo Trapero's *Rolling Family* (*Familia rodante*)

A brief historical outline will help to identify some of the larger forces at work in these movements and ideas. Before Columbus, the Americas were inhabited for millennia, perhaps as long as 30,000 years, by people who settled throughout the Western Hemisphere. Many developed complex agricultural societies and large cities, building the monumental architecture that still stands in what is now called Mexico, Central America, and the Andes. During the Colonial Period, beginning in 1492, Spain, Portugal, and later France sent explorers, missionaries, soldiers, and adventurers to extend their growing empires. For more than 300 years, European rulers used the sword, the cross, and other means to dominate the region. In 1804, Haiti became the first colony to break its bonds. By 1825, most colonies had gained independence. It was in this postcolonial period of revolution, warfare, and nation building that the borders of most Latin American countries were fixed. Through much of the nineteenth century, however, and well into the next, these new nations were economically dependent on outside powers like France, Great Britain, and the United States. US interests were promoted through a series of policies and treaties. The Monroe Doctrine of 1825 shifted Washington's focus from Europe to the Western Hemisphere, where it assumed the role of "Big Brother" with the help of military muscle and financial clout. Theodore Roosevelt gained control of the Panama Canal in 1904. Franklin Roosevelt strengthened US influence in 1933 through the Good Neighbor Policy, which was later leveraged to create a united front during World War II. During the Cold War against Russia and its allies, the US government pursued a policy of containment and selective support, seeking to isolate its enemies and prop up friendly regimes. The 1960s and 1970s were ripe for revolution and dictatorships. In Brazil, a military coup overthrew leftist president João Goulart in 1964. In Bolivia, Hugo Banzer muscled out leftist General Juan José Torres in 1971. In Chile, Augusto Pinochet ousted democratically elected Salvador Allende in 1973. Similar events took place in Uruguay and Argentina while military forces battled leftist groups in Nicaragua, Guatemala, and San Salvador. With the rise of globalization in the 1980s and 1990s, Washington maintained ties to countries in economic crisis through trade agreements and financial institutions like the World Bank and the International Monetary Fund. All of these movements and events figure in Latin American cinema, sometimes as a central focal point, sometimes hovering in the background or just off screen.

The Early Years

Modernity and motion pictures arrived in Latin America at about the same time, as Ana López and other scholars note. When the agents of Edison and the Lumière Brothers came to Rio de Janeiro, Buenos Aires, Mexico City, Montevideo, or Santiago, they introduced cinema as one of the technological marvels of the modern world. Their movies highlighted the novelties and thrills of the big city, often taking as their subjects those other foreign imports of the day that featured movement: automobiles, trolley cars, and trains. Not long after watching the arrival of a French train on Brazilian screens, cameramen were training their lenses on local trains and streetcars, making short travel films like *Trip from the Mountains to the Sea* (*Viagem à serra do mar*, 1910). So right at the beginning, Latin American filmmakers took their cameras on the tracks or on the road. They also took projectors, traveling from town to town with mobile cinemas, reels on wheels. López emphasizes that "the cinema experienced by Latin Americans was – and still is – predominantly foreign." They became "voyeurs of, rather than participants in, modernity."[4] Argentineans in particular looked across the Atlantic Ocean toward Europe for their models. In 1910, three quarters of the adults in Buenos Aires were European immigrants who aspired to make their nation's capital the "Paris of the Southern hemisphere."[5]

Elsewhere, though, Latin Americans wanted to make movies about local issues for local audiences using local talent. They wanted to create a national cinema. In Mexico, where a national rebellion was raging, *La Revolutión Mexicana* became a favorite subject between 1910 and 1918. It was celebrated in feature films like *Mexican Insurrection* (*Insurrección en México*, 1911) and in documentaries like *Complete History of the Revolution* (*Historia completa de la Revolución de 1910–1915*, 1915). The revolutionary general Pancho Villa himself became a movie star, staging battles in broad daylight so they could be filmed. Between 1917 and 1921, Mexico produced some 75 feature-length films, a record for the silent period. The most significant of these, according to López, is Enrique Rosas's *The Grey Automobile* (*El automóvil gris*, 1919) – a road movie. Based on the real-life story of a band of house thieves, it follows their daring exploits and flight from the police to their capture and condemnation, incorporating actual footage of the execution into the narrative. Rosas borrows elements of Italian melodrama and Hollywood technique (close-ups, iris shots), adapting them to Mexican subjects and shooting on location in Mexico City. This hybrid blend of foreign methods and domestic content continued well into the sound years.

The shift from silent films to synchronized sound was a setback for the fledgling Latin American film industry. The new technology of sound was bulky and expensive. It became easier and cheaper to import Hollywood movies than to make them at home. Studios like Paramount began turning out "Hispanic" films in the 1930s, deliberately targeting Spanish-speaking audiences. This marketing decision coincided with Franklin Roosevelt's Good Neighbor Policy and World War II. Since the war made it difficult to export movies to Europe, Hollywood turned south. Here was an opportunity to develop lucrative new markets while building cultural ties between the two adjoining continents. Cultural icons flowed in both directions. Carmen Miranda, originally a Portuguese immigrant in Brazil, moved to Hollywood where she embodied a certain image of South America by dancing the samba in her tutti-frutti hat. Disney contributed to this iconography with *Three Caballeros* (1944), an animated film in which Donald Duck opens three educational gifts from his Latin American friends. Several Spanish-speaking stars made live cameo appearances, including Dora Luz and Aurora Miranda, Carmen's sister. Meanwhile, as part of this neighborly gift exchange, the American director Orson Welles was sent to Brazil in 1942 to film the carnival in Rio. But Welles seemed more interested in filming the poverty that he found in the *favelas*, Rio's hillside slums. He was soon recalled, and his project, *It's All True*, was never finished. Another world renowned director, Russia's Sergei Eisenstein, met a similar fate. Eisenstein arrived in Mexico in 1931 to make a film about the local culture. After meeting Diego Rivera, he described his film project as a "moving fresco" of the people and their history from before the Conquest to the Revolution. While Eisenstein never got to fulfill his original conception, several films were made from his footage (*Thunder Over Mexico*, 1933; *¡Qué viva México!*, 1979) and his influence on Mexican directors resonated long after his departure.

Despite Hollywood's strong hand in local exhibition, Latin American filmmakers were experimenting with their own distinctive genres. In 1936, Mexico's Fernando de Fuentes directed *Out on the Big Ranch* (*Allá en el Rancho Grande*), a kind of cowboy musical that includes elements of comedy, melodrama, popular music, and folkloric themes. This formula's immense success launched one of Mexico's most popular genres, the *comedia ranchera* (ranch comedy), featuring a line of colorful *charros* (Mexican horsemen) as stars. Brazil introduced its own unique genre, the *chanchada*, with *Alô, Alô Brasil!* (1935), entertaining audiences with music, comedy, and plenty of samba dancing. The dance of choice in Argentina was the tango, celebrated in *comedias tangueras* (tango comedies) like John Reinhart's *Tango Bar* (1933). These and other home-grown film forms drew freely from North American models but tailored them to local Latin tastes and talents within the international marketplace. They ushered in a Golden Age of Latin American cinema and paved the way for national film narratives.

There are times when it makes sense to speak of Latin American cinema collectively: during the early silent years, for instance, or during the 1960s and 1970s when filmmakers began speaking of a cross-continental New Latin American Cinema movement or a transnational Third Cinema, or during the globalism of the 1990s and beyond. In general, however, the unique history of each nation's film industry requires individual attention. Here we have space only for those film traditions that have been the most consistent, influential, and robust. What follows, then, are short sketches of filmmaking in Mexico, Brazil, Argentina, Cuba, and more briefly, a few selected countries with emerging industries.

Mexico

By the 1940s, the Golden Age of Mexican Cinema was in full bloom. Comic actors like Mario Cantinflas, dubbed the "Mexican Charlie Chaplin," and later Germán Valdés, better known as "Tin-Tan," were household names throughout the Spanish-speaking world. So were Dolores del Rio, the soulful beauty in *María Candelaria* (*Xochimilco*, 1943) and María Félix, the imperious star of *Doña Bárbara* (1943). By 1943, Mexico was turning out 75 films a year, more than any other Spanish-speaking country. By 1947, cinema had become the nation's third largest industry. Much of the industry's success in Mexico stems from its ability to produce appealing stars and entertaining genres for a general audience. But Mexico also benefited by its favored nation status in the United States, a position it enjoyed until the Mexican government supported the Cuban Revolution in 1959. And there is more to many of these genre films than easy laughs and tears. *Doña Bárbara* is based on a classic Venezuelan novel, a regionalist work that dramatizes a perennial Latin American theme: the conflict between civilization and the barbarism inflicted on humanity by a savage land. *María Candelaria* is set in the Indian community of Xochimilco on the eve of revolution. The lyrical cinematography of Gabriel Figueroa pays homage to the natural landscape and its people, in keeping with director Emilio "Indio" Fernández's goal of forging a national consciousness grounded in indigenous culture (Figure 4.14). His work enlists the popular appeal of melodrama in the service of nation building.

This idealistic project of the 1940s was subverted in the 1950s by Luis Buñuel. Born in Spain, Buñuel had become a naturalized citizen of Mexico after living in France and the United States. He found work in the commercial industry of his adopted country making genre films but soon set his own agenda. *The Young and the Damned* (*Los olvidados*, 1950) is a turning point in Mexican cinema. Set in the slums of Mexico City, it follows the lives of street kids as they struggle to survive under bleak conditions. Buñuel hired Figueroa as his cinematographer, but in contrast to the romanticized imagery of *María Candelaria*, he focuses the camera on the seamy side of urban reality. Life here is nasty, brutish, and short. People live in wooden shacks with corrugated roofs. A blind beggar beats off thieves with a wooden stick. A motley gang of children amuse themselves by rolling a legless man downhill. Stylistically, *Los olvidados* follows the episodic structure of a picaresque novella and employs familiar neorealist techniques – outdoor shooting, gritty photography, non-professional actors – but its unsentimental heart is far from the traditionally sanctioned values of "God, nation, and home." Initially regarded as an insult to Mexico, Buñuel's work was ahead of its time, setting a new

FIGURE 4.14 Director Emilio Fernández and cinematographer Gabriel Figueroa foreground the natural landscape of Mexico and its people in *María Candelaria* (*Xochimilco*, 1943).

course with its unflinching social critique and violent, often surreal imagery that others soon would follow.

Some directors continued to make genre films throughout the 1960s and 1970s, branching into horror, action films, and a uniquely Mexican hybrid involving masked professional wrestlers like El Santo: the *lucha libre* (free wrestling) film. Others experimented with serious themes and character studies. In *Hell Without Limits* (*El lugar sin límites*, 1977), Arturo Ripstein deploys the conventions of *cabarateras* (brothel melodramas), a particularly popular genre in Mexico, to explore issues of machismo, homophobia, and political power. So much in this film depends on a red truck and a red flamenco dress. Alejandro Jodorowsky pushed even further beyond the limits of genre. Jodorowsky had left his native Chile to study in Paris, where he absorbed the impulses of surrealism and anarchism that he would bring to Mexico. *The Mole* (*El Topo*, 1970), his film about a violent gunslinger in search of spiritual enlightenment, defies classification. It became an instant cult hit among counterculture figures like John Lennon. These were heady times for film enthusiasts in Mexico, who formed cine clubs, published journals, and built Latin America's first national film school, the CUEC, with government support. By 1976, however, state sponsorship had ended with a new president who favored independent production. A new generation of directors came of age in the 1980s, some turning out international hits like Paul Leduc's *Frida, Still Life* (*Frida, naturaleza viva*, 1986) and Jaime Humberto Hermosillo's *Doña Herlinda and Her Son* (*Doña Herlinda y su hijo*, 1985). By the next decade, Mexican filmmakers like Alejandro González Iñárritu, Alfonso Cuarón, and Guillermo del Toro would be global phenomena.

Brazil

In their invaluable compendium on Brazilian cinema, Robert Stam and Randal Johnson identify some striking similarities between Brazil and the United States. Both nations were forged as European colonies, expanding through the conquest of vast territories, the displacement of indigenous peoples, the importation of African slaves, and settlement by a variety of immigrant groups. But while the United States soon achieved economic independence along with its political freedom, Brazil remained heavily reliant on other nations. Although Brazilians have exported gold, sugar, rubber, coffee, and other natural resources during times of plenty, the flow of goods has mostly been *to* rather than *from* the Brazilian heartland. This lopsided trade balance includes cultural products like movies.[6]

A typically Brazilian response to the barrage of foreign films and influence is parody. If local filmmakers lacked Hollywood's financial resources, they could still make fun of Hollywood's polished style and conventions with spoofs of exotic melodramas in the 1930s or Westerns in the 1950s, a tradition of deft mockery that still continues. Another response is to assimilate film movements overseas and apply them to local subjects, as Mário Peixoto did in his avant-garde masterpiece *Limits* (*Limite*, 1931) and Humberto Mauro did in *Brutal Gang* (*Ganga Bruta*, 1933), adapting German expressionism and Soviet montage to life in the *favelas* of Rio and Brazil's rugged interior. Yet another strategy is aggressive imitation. Beginning in the 1940s, Brazilian production companies like Atlântida Studio in Rio churned out comedies, *chanchada* musicals, and Hollywood-style commercial products. But one company, Vera Cruz, wanted to displace imports with "100% Brazilian" films. Modeled on the studio system of MGM, but with auteurist aspirations, the company hired world-famous documentary director Alberto Cavalcanti to direct production. During its short lifespan, Vera Cruz made period dramas like *The Landowner's Daughter* (*Sinhá Moça*, 1953), favourably compared to *Gone with the Wind*, and award-winning classics like *Cangaceiro* (*O Cangaceiro*, 1953) a "Northeastern" Western set in the *sertão* (backcountry) of northeastern Brazil.

As in Mexico, the postwar period was relatively prosperous for Brazil. Under democratically elected presidents (Vargas from 1951 to 1954, Kubitschek from 1956 to 1961), the country enjoyed a period of stability and progress, a decade of enthusiastic nation building culminating in the construction of a modern new capital city, Brasilia, in 1960. But the euphoria was not to last. The economy began to falter under the next president, João Goulart (1961–1964), whose social programs and foreign policies created enemies at home. In 1964, a military coup toppled Goulart, replacing him with a series of dictators who became increasingly suppressive. Hundreds, then thousands of suspected opponents were deported, imprisoned, tortured, or killed. A bitter guerrilla war raged from 1968 to 1973. Yet, as often happens in times of stress, the 1960s and 1970s comprised one of the most artistically productive eras in the history of Brazil.

The cinematic innovations during these turbulent times are generally known as *Cinema Novo*. While nearly every film-producing country seems to have its "New

Cinema," some more than one, this movement stands out in the history of Latin American moviemaking for sheer raw energy and political purpose. Its champions defined themselves initially through opposition. In the bold language of manifestos, they declared war on Hollywood imitations, commercialism, the "exoticizing" impulses of co-productions, and the "picturesque" pretensions of Vera Cruz. Instead, they sought to create a "populist art," taking "the people" as their theme, the *favela* and *sertão* as their settings, honestly embracing conflict, violence, and perplexity.[7] Johnson and Stam divide the movement into three phases. In the first phase, roughly corresponding to Goulart's regime, directors like Carlos Diegues, Glauber Rocha, and Nelson Pereira dos Santos sought to make independent, politically committed films, drawing on the low-budget techniques, though not necessarily the themes, of Italian neorealism and the French New Wave. Bold works like Diegues's *Ganga Zumba* (1963), dos Santos's *Barren Lives* (*Vidas Secas*, 1963), and Rocha's *Black God, White Devil* (*Deus e o Diabo na Terra do Sol*, 1964) made good on their claims to use the camera as a gun, aiming it at colonialism, dictatorship, and middle-class complacency. In phase two, from the coup of 1964 to 1968, when an even more reactionary group took power, the earlier optimism of these directors turned to disillusionment as the leftist front collapsed, a self-reflective angst summed up in the title of Rocha's *Land in Anguish* (*Terra en Transe*, 1967). Having failed to engage the public, the movement launched a third phase, adopting a new strategy, more allegorical than dogmatic. Joaquim Pedro de Andrade's *Macunaíma* (1969) follows the misadventures of a black man born fully grown to an old Indian woman in the Amazon Jungle. When a spring miraculously turns him white, he heads for Rio in search of a magical stone. A parody of Brazil's foundation myth – three races united as one – and a comic reflection of the social chaos after the coup, it was a big hit with Brazilian audiences, opening a new direction for Cinema Novo, known as *Tropicalismo*. Tropicalism deliberately courted bad taste, stressing grotesque characters and unsavory situations. Some of its practitioners turned the "low production values" of bad lighting and dim screens into virtues, announcing an "aesthetics of garbage" to parallel an "aesthetics of poverty." Some explored the comic side of cannibalism, like dos Santos in *How Tasty Was My Little Frenchman* (*Como era gostoso meu francês*, 1970), literalizing the metaphor of consumerism, an indigenous culture turning the tables on its voracious colonial oppressors (Figure 4.15). In one of the era's most powerful films, *Antônio das Mortes* (*O Dragão da Maldade contra o Santo Guerreiro*, 1969), Rocha wove the motifs of hunger, violence, and murder into a complex work that is at once lyrical, starkly realistic, mythic, and bizarre.

By 1971, Cinema Novo had run its course, but it was not an isolated phenomenon. Like-minded directors in Argentina, Cuba, and Bolivia were writing their own manifestos and making films of liberation. They were all part of the so-called Third Cinema movement that rolled across the Third World from Vietnam to Angola, inspiring revolutionary leaders like Che Guevara and Ho Chi Minh. Brazil itself survived the crisis of the early 1970s, gradually freeing itself from dictatorship and military rule. In 1989, Fernando Collor de Mello became its first democratically

FIGURE 4.15   Nelson Pereira dos Santos offers a comic critique of consumerism in *How Tasty Was My Litte Frenchman* (*Como era gostoso meu francês*, 1970).

elected president in 29 years. Meanwhile, important movies continued to be made, like Bruno Barreto's *Dona Flor and Her Two Husbands* (*Dona Flor e seus dois maridos*, 1976), Carlos Diegues's *Xica da Silva* (1977), and his *Bye Bye Brazil* (*Bye Bye Brasil*, 1980). The production and distribution for many of these films were supported by a central government agency, Embrafilme. When Collor dismantled the agency in 1990, he opened Brazil to a new era of globalization.

Argentina

The second largest country in South America after Brazil, with one of the subcontinent's most robust cultures and economies, Argentina has produced some of the region's most important movies. Its filmmakers have used their cameras to dramatize the nation's turbulent history, explore its cultural traditions, and traverse its distinctive geography, from the Andes Mountains in the West to its eastern Atlantic shoreline and the sparsely vegetated, steppe-like plains of Patagonia stretching southward toward Antarctica.

By 1929, Argentina had the world's fourth largest per capita GDP, an index of its high standard of living. But the stock market crash of that year sent the country spiraling into the Great Depression as well as an era of corruption and political persecution known as the "Infamous Decade." Argentineans suffered through years of social unrest and military coups well into the 1980s. Among the best known leaders of this time were General Juan Perón and his wife Eva ("Evita"), whose strong-handed version of populism attracted fervent support and fierce opposition during three disrupted presidencies in the 1940s, 1950s, and 1970s.

From 1966 to 1973, while protest movements were challenging the *status quo* around the world, Argentina was a battleground of class warfare known as "the Argentine Revolution." From 1976 to 1983, the country was plunged into an internal "dirty war." Thousands who opposed the self-appointed military regime were rounded up and imprisoned or executed. More than 30,000 people are estimated to have "disappeared." After deepening economic problems and a failed effort to seize the Falkland Islands from Great Britain, the military junta restored political freedom in 1983, returning Argentina to its first democratic elections in ten years.

Against this historical backdrop, filmmaking in Argentina followed the paths of commercial production and political activism that we have seen elsewhere in Latin America. With the arrival of sound in the 1930s, Argentineans flocked to theatres where they could watch their favorite dance, the tango, performed to synchronized music by their favorite stars. José Ferreyra was the era's most popular director, making 24 features in 20 years. During the late 1930s and early 1940s, the industry as a whole averaged some 40 films per year. Increasingly, though, these films were influenced by Hollywood genres, especially comedy and romance. During World War II and in its aftermath, the United States managed to dominate local exhibition despite Perón's protectionist policies. It was not until the 1960s that the Third Cinema movement inspired a new generation of directors with new energy and purpose. Fernando Solanas and Octavio Getino proclaimed their cause in a bold manifesto, "Toward a Third Cinema," urging a cinematic revolt against the "foreign army of occupation," calling for a "decolonization of culture," choosing as their weapon the projector, "a gun that can shoot 24 frames per second."[8] Matching their words with action, Solanas and Getino constructed *Hour of the Furnaces* (*La hora de los hornos*, 1970), a four-hour documentary secretly made during the dirty war deploying a radically confrontational style as its call to arms. Forced into exile by death threats, Solanas did not return until 1983. His French-Argentine co-production *Tangos* (*El exilio de Gardel*, 1985) strikes a milder, less didactic tone. Set among his fellow expatriates in Paris, it uses the tango to express their longing for life in Buenos Aires, their homeland.

By then, the dirty war was over and the new, democratically elected Alfonsín government (1983–1989) was trying to restore a wounded nation to social stability and economic health. Raúl Alfonsín ended censorship and offered state support for exportable films that would recoup their costs abroad and promote a new image of the nation. He appointed Manuel Antín to head the National Cinema Institute (INC). Antín was a veteran filmmaker who favored art house films for intellectuals and middle-class audiences. A number of well-made films were made on his watch, including María Luisa Bemberg's *Camila* (1984), Luis Puenzo's *The Official Story* (*La historia oficial*, 1985), and Héctor Olivera's *Night of the Pencils* (*La noche de los lápices*, 1986). Each of these three films deals one way or another with state-sponsored terror. Although *Camila* is a melodrama set in the mid-1800s, its true story about a young lover executed by a brutal dictator reminded viewers of the recent military regime. Puenzo's film is less oblique, approaching the trauma of the 1970s through the eyes of a wealthy woman who adopts a child only to learn that it may have

FIGURE 4.16   Luis Puenzo's *The Official Story* (*La historia oficial*, 1985) introduced the outside world to Argentina's "Dirty War" of 1976–1983.

been one of the *desaparecidos*, those who "disappeared" during the dirty war (see Figure 4.16). Olivera's film is even more direct. It recreates in graphic terms the capture and torture of real students who were victims of the military junta. *Night of the Pencils* won several festival awards and *The Official Story* was Argentina's first Oscar winner, but only *Camila* was popular with local audiences. These and other movies of the 1980s helped the nation heal its wounds, serving as a kind of community catharsis, clearing the way for a new Argentine cinema in the 1990s.

Cuba

The Republic of Cuba is the largest and most populated island nation in the Caribbean. Under Spanish rule from Columbus's arrival in 1492 to the end of the Spanish-American War in 1898, its people endured a wobbly succession of governments for another 60 years in the long shadow of its nearest neighbor, the United States. Then the Cuban Revolution ended Batista's dictatorship in 1959, replacing him with Fidel Castro, who ruled for more than 50 years as the head of a communist state modeled on the Soviet Union. Castro's contentious relationship with the United States was marked by a series of alarming events, including the ill-fated Bay of Pigs invasion in 1961, the Missile Crisis in 1962, and the mass migration of Cubans from Mariel to Florida in the 1980s. Castro's firm control during these years had a profound effect on all aspects of Cuban life, including the movies. For years, the island had enjoyed a mixture of Spanish, African, indigenous, and North American influences. In his comprehensive book on Cuban cinema, Michael Chanan notes how Cuba's "highly syncretistic culture celebrated rumba and surrealism, Yoruba gods and Catholic transcendentalism, in equal measure."[9] Castro's single-minded conception of society and art was very clear: "Within the Revolution, everything; against it, nothing." Since there was relatively little innovation in Cuban filmmaking before 1959, it offers an instructive example of how a politically defined agenda can both open and constrain the art of cinema.

During the first 60 years of motion pictures, Cuba produced few notable features, mostly musical comedies and melodramas for the commercial market, but its lush landscape and vibrant music regularly served as an exotic setting for Hollywood and Mexican productions. Despite this imbalance, Cubans were enthusiastic filmgoers. Castro understood the screen's immense popular appeal and sought to harness its power for his political program. Within months, he had created ICAIC, the Cuban Institute of Cinematographic Art and Industry, to lead the effort, putting his friend Alfredo Guevara in charge. Sympathetic international filmmakers of stature like France's Chris Marker, Holland's Joris Ivens, and the USSR's Mikhail Kalatozov came to help. A new generation of young Cuban directors was trained in the new spirit of revolutionary cinema. By 1965, ICAIC controlled all production, distribution, and exhibition on the island. In those early years, most of the energy and funding went into documentaries, didactic pictures meant to educate the people and rally them behind the cause. A few were feature films that transcended the single-minded methods and goals of *agitprop*, agitation and propaganda. In *Lucía* (1968), Humberto Solás deftly wove elements of melodrama and politics to reconstruct 60 years of national history, ending with a clever critique of machismo. In *Death of a Bureaucrat* (*Muerte de un burócrata*, 1966), Tomás Gutiérrez Alea used comedy to poke fun at bureaucratic tunnel vision. Alea's next film, *Memories of Underdevelopment* (*Memorias del subdesarrollo*, 1968), followed the inner struggles of a Cuban intellectual caught in the aftermath of revolution . The depths of his character and moral alienation were probed with a complexity more typical of European art films, which is why it won several international awards and continues to be one of the most studied and widely discussed of all Cuban films.[10]

Castro's revolutionary vision stretched well beyond national borders. In 1979, ICAIC created the International Festival of New Latin American Cinema, held every year in Havana to showcase ideologically committed films and strengthen regional solidarity. In the 1980s, Cuba's Third World Film School opened its doors to train new filmmakers from around the world. By then, ICAIC was being run by Julio García Espinosa, who replaced Guevara after a controversy surrounding *Cecilia* (1982), Solas's expensive historical drama set during a nineteenth-century slave rebellion. Espinosa, a veteran director, called for an "imperfect cinema," one which favored content over form. The goal, he emphasized, was to represent the people's struggles and the reasons for their problems, not to highlight artistic originality or technical quality. Yet filmmakers continued to make popular, innovative films like Juan Carlos Tabío's *House for Swap* (*Se permuta*, 1985), a kind of urban romance comedy, and Juan Padrón's *Vampires in Havana* (*¡Vampiros en La Habana!*, 1985), an animated horror film. In 1991, Espinosa himself was retired after the stormy reception of another controversial film, Daniel Díaz Torres's *Alice in Wondertown* (*Alicia en el pueblo de Maravillas*, 1991).

The drive for an ideologically committed political cinema lasted longer in Cuba than in Argentina or Brazil, but the forces that were nudging all film industries toward a commercially oriented globalism in the 1990s caught up with Cuba after the fall of the Soviet Union. Without the financial backing of their most powerful communist ally, Cuban filmmakers were forced to rely increasingly on capitalist funding. *Cecilia* was co-produced with Spain's Ibermedia company. *Strawberry and Chocolate* (*Fresa y chocolate*, 1993), Alea and Tabío's witty comedy about a lovelorn macho party member and his new gay acquaintance, was a co-production of Cuba, Spain, Mexico, and the United States. Alea and Tabío would go on to make *Guantanamera* (1995), a satirical road movie about transporting a corpse across the country. Two years later, Castro publicly attacked the film, apparently without having seen it or remembering that its celebrated director was someone he respected.[11] This lapse of memory and Castro's subsequent apology were further signs of the changing times.

Elsewhere in Latin America

The Republic of Colombia, occupying the northwestern corner of South America, is the only nation on the subcontinent to border both the Pacific and the Atlantic oceans. With the fourth largest population in Latin America (after Brazil, Mexico, and Argentina) and the region's third largest cinema audience, Colombia might be expected to have a comparable cinematic history, but its film production has only been sporadic until recently. One reason is the specter of recurring violence. In 1899, a struggle between the nation's two main political parties erupted in the brutal Thousand Days War. In 1948, an even longer civil conflict broke out, ravaging the nation for some ten years. But the longest period of armed aggression began in the 1960s when government forces, left-wing rebels, and right-wing paramilitary units attacked each other in the streets and countryside, opening wounds that were later aggravated by the activities of powerful drug cartels during the 1980s and 1990s. Yet, throughout these trying times, resourceful directors found ways to make important films. In 1927, P.P. Jambrina made *Garras de oro* (*The Dawn of Justice – Alborada de justicia*), a satirical denunciation of the sale of Panama to the United States. After only two public screenings, it was reportedly withdrawn from theatres under pressure from Washington, although prints of the original film have since resurfaced.[12] In 1954, a group of young directors made *The Blue Lobster* (*La langosta azul*), a short experimental film in the European tradition of surrealism. Among the group was Gabriel García Márquez, who had studied film in Rome and later became Colombia's most celebrated writer. In 1978, the government sought to jump start the nation's film industry through a state-funded company, FOCINE. Among the movies that emerged from this effort were Luis Ospina's *Pure Blood* (*Pura sangre*, 1982), a vampire thriller with political overtones, and Víctor Gaviria's *Rodrigo D: No future* (*Rodrigo D: No futuro*, 1990), a searching story of slum kids in Medellín, filmed on location in the uncompromising style of

Buñuel. Production was difficult through much of the 1990s, but conditions improved with the Cinema Law of 2003, and the Colombian government found other ways of encouraging directors to make strong films and enter the global market. Meanwhile, Colombian issues and talents were gaining greater visibility around the world through international productions like *Real Women Have Curves* (2002), *Our Lady of the Assassins* (*La virgin de los sicarios*, 2000), and *Maria Full of Grace* (*María llena eres de gracia*, 2004). The first was directed for HBO by Colombian-born Patricia Cordoso. The second was based on a story by Colombian novelist Fernando Vallejo. The third featured Colombian actress Catalina Sandino as the pregnant woman who becomes a drug mule, carrying packets of "grace" (cocaine) in her body. All three films were marketed globally.

South of Colombia and west of Brazil, the Republic of Peru includes stretches of the Andes Mountains, Amazon forests, and Pacific coast. Like many of its neighbors, the nation's multiethnic population shares a rich pre-Columbian heritage, a long period of Spanish domination, and a recent history marked by political violence and fiscal crises. Despite some earlier, occasional efforts, it was not until the 1970s that filmmaking in Peru really took off. Within a few years, over 150 companies sprang up under the government's supportive policies. While few of these survived, several talented, productive directors emerged, most notably Francisco Lombardi. His *Death at Dawn* (*Muerte al amanecer*, 1977) was the first feature to pay for itself through local screenings. Based on the true story of a child murderer, it used this well-known event to raise political issues of power and imprisonment. In *The Mouth of the Wolf* (*La boca del lobo*, 1988), Lombardi focused his lens on Peru's guerrilla group, "The Shining Path," again mixing political subjects with popular film conventions.

Perched high in the Andes southeast of Peru, the land-locked nation of Bolivia is one of the poorest in Latin America. Once part of the proud Inca Empire and still home to one of the continent's largest indigenous populations, Bolivia has struggled through long periods of revolution, dictatorship, and warfare with neighboring countries. In 1952, a broad-based revolutionary force (the MNR) came to power, initiating land reforms and nationalizing the country's tin mines. In 1964, a military junta staged a coup. Che Guevara was killed there in 1967, reportedly by order of the CIA, while leading rebel forces against this military government. Under such precarious conditions, determined filmmakers like Jorge Sanjinés still managed to make important movies. He was the first to use non-professional actors from indigenous communities to tell their stories from their point of view. His *And So It Is* (*Ukamau*, 1966) dramatizes the unequal social standing of native "Indians," *mestizos* (citizens of mixed European and native heritage), and white Bolivians. *Blood of the Condor* (*Yawar Mallku*, 1969), ostensibly about a sterilization program run by the Peace Corps – an actual event – is a damning parable of foreign interference. It is also beautifully filmed in black and white. When its screening was banned in the capital city of La Paz, spectators marched in the streets. Within two years, the Peace Corps was expelled from the country.

Stretching southwards from Bolivia along a narrow strip between the Andes Mountains and the Pacific coastline lies the Republic of Chile. Chile proclaimed its independence in 1817, but its people, like their neighbors, have long struggled with civil unrest, economic instability, and a stratified society. In 1970, Salvador Allende of Chile's Socialist Party came to power, but his "Popular Unity" coalition government was overthrown in 1972 by General Augusto Pinochet, whose repressive military regime ruled for 18 years. During that time, Chile's best filmmakers, most of whom had come of age during the 1960s, were sent to prison or into exile. Patricio Guzmán was arrested during the coup while shooting *The Battle of Chile* (*La batalla de Chile*, 1975–1980). After a brief imprisonment, he fled to Europe and then Cuba, where he managed to complete his monumental three-part documentary. Miguel Littin remained in Latin America, making *The Widow of Montiel* (*La viuda de Montiel*, 1979) in Mexico and *Alsino and the Condor* (*Alsino y el cóndor*, 1982) in Nicaragua. Raúl Ruiz settled in Europe, where year after year he produced a remarkable body of work, leaving a legacy of over 100 movies after his death in 2011.

Before the 1990s, the rest of South America – Uruguay, Venezuela, and even Paraguay – made modest contributions to the art and industry of cinema. So did Caribbean countries like Puerto Rico and the Dominican Republic. Central America produced far fewer films, mostly shorts and documentaries. The best known feature films to focus on contemporary issues in these areas were made by foreign companies, like *El Norte* (1983), a British-American co-production partly set in Guatemala, *Under Fire* (1983), set in Nicaragua, and *Salvador* (1986) set in El Salvador. Directors from these countries would have to wait for the new infrastructures of globalism to make films of their own.

Globalism and the Road Movie

Globalism views the world as a complex network of interconnected elements – economies, information, peoples, cultures – a network that transcends national barriers and spans entire continents. At a time when money, talent, ideas, and cultural artifacts flow so freely across borders, it becomes harder to speak of Latin America in terms of national cinemas, as we have been doing from the early sound era through the 1980s. While funds, people, and films have always crossed boundaries from the earliest days of motion pictures, the sheer speed and volume of exchange reached a critical mass in the 1990s. To take just two examples, consider the cases of Alfonso Cuarón and Alejandro González Iñárritu. Born in Mexico City in 1961, Cuarón came to international prominence in 2001 with *Y tu mamá también* (roughly translated as *"and your mother, too"*), his lighthearted film about two teenage boys who take a road trip through Mexico. *Y tu mamá también* is a Mexican production, shot in Mexico with Spanish-speaking actors, but Cuarón's next film was *Harry Potter and the Prisoner of Azkaban* (2004), a US-British co-production with a bigger budget and English-speaking actors. In 2006, he directed a segment of the

French film *Paris, Je t'aime* and the sci-fi drama *Children of Men*, set in London with an international cast that speaks six languages. Should someone like Cuarón, who crosses national boundaries so easily, be considered a Mexican director? What about Alejandro González Iñárritu, another child of Mexico City, whose films include *Amores Perros* (2000), filmed in Spanish, *21 Grams* in English (2003), and *Babel* (2006), a multilingual drama that shifts between Mexico, Morocco, Tokyo, and the United States. The very point of *Babel's* interlocking stories, as the title suggests, is that its globetrotting characters are all connected.

This shift to global filmmaking is not just a matter of actors, languages, and plotlines. A few countries began to rebuild more flexible infrastructures in the 1990s. In 1995, Argentina created INCAA, a new government agency, enacting pro-cinema legislation, opening film schools, and encouraging co-productions. Similar initiatives were taken by Mexico's IMCINE. But the general trend was toward privatization. When Brazil's state agency, Embrafilme, was abolished, new laws offered incentives to private investors. After the failure of Colombia's FOCINE, a new "Cine Law" sought to boost filmmaking by decentralizing production and redirecting attention beyond national boundaries. Money began to flow in through co-productions, and Colombia's international prestige started to rise through festival awards. The Mar del Plata International Film Festival in Argentina, defunct for 26 years, was revived in 1996. Argentina, Brazil, and others worked jointly through Mercosur, a kind of Common Market of the South, to facilitate transnational production, distribution, and exhibition throughout the region. One major consequence was a surge in film activity. Critics began writing about a Brazilian *retomada* (return), an Argentine *nueva onda* (new wave), a "Latin renaissance," and even a "New Latin American cinema."

Another outcome of this shift was in the kinds of movies being made. More films began to take on a global flavor. *Amores Perros* may be set in the streets of Mexican city and feature a largely Mexican cast, but its aggressive close-ups, rapid fire cutting, and oscillating narrative seem closer to the frenzied, visceral style popularized north of the border by the likes of *Pulp Fiction* (1994) and MTV. The same trend is visible in feature films like Fabián Bielinsky's *Nine Queens* (*Nueve Reinas*, 2000) from Argentina and Fernando Meirelles's *City of God* (*Cidade de Deus*, 2002) from Brazil. The success of such films abroad, both in mainstream theatres and at festivals, helped to give wider currency to what amounted to a new global aesthetic. *Amores Perros* and *City of God*, set in the slums of Rio, may also be considered genre films, part of a global interest in street gangs that includes Johannesburg, South Africa (*Tsotsi*, 2005), Jakarta, Indonesia (*Merantau*, 2009), and Kochi, India (another *City of God / Malayalam*, 2011). *Nine Queens*, ostensibly about con-men, belongs to a related subgenre of crime films, setting its clever story during Argentina's financial crisis. Because Bielinsky combined both artistic and commercial aspirations, he has been called an "industrial auteur," a term that may be applied equally to Cuarón, Iñárritu, or Meirelles.

This is not to say that all Latin American directors after 1990 followed the same road. Many of the best filmmakers chose the path of national identity, seeking to capture images and explore styles that express the uniqueness of *Mexicanidad* or *Colombianidad*. Mexico's Arturo Ripstein (*Deep Crimson/Profundo carmesí*, 1996) and Carlos Reygadas (*Silent Light/Stellet licht*, 2007) have become respected artisans, each creating a body of work with a markedly personal style. More mainstream but still distinctly Mexican are María Novaro, whose *Danzón* (1991) celebrates the local popularity of a Cuban dance; Alfonso Arau, whose *Like Water for Chocolate/Como agua para chocolate* (1992) leans on the tradition of magical realism to tell a story about oppressed women; and Carlos Carrera, whose *The Crime of Father Amaro/El crimen del Padre Amaro* (2002) was vigorously opposed by Roman Catholic groups. In Argentina, independent-minded directors like Israel Adrián Caetano, Bruno Stagnaro, Lucrecia Martel, and Pablo Trapero have broken away from earlier conventions, avoiding allegory or didactic politics, using the camera to explore marginal characters in ordinary places. *Pizza, Beer, and Cigarettes* (*Pizza, birra, faso*, 1998), co-directed by Caetano and Stagnaro, is about a group of teenage misfits squatting in the same house. Martel's *The Swamp* (*La ciénaga*, 2001), set in the high northwestern plains, focuses on two families trapped in a claustrophobic world of suffocating heat and social oppression. Trapero's *Rolling Family* (*Familia rodante*, 2004), although a road movie, refuses to exoticize the Argentinean landscape, concentrating instead on the van's interior and family relationships that are always on the verge of exploding.

Elsewhere, in Chile and Colombia for example, directors still struggled with the past or strove to move beyond it. After the fall of Pinochet's regime, Ricardo Larraín returned from exile and made *The Frontier* (*La frontera*, 1991), about the experience of being exiled in one's own country. Sebastián Lelio's intense family drama, *The Sacred Family* (*La sagrada familia*, 2005), takes a different turn, exploring the liberating and threatening sides of female sexuality. Meanwhile, the former and future faces of Colombia continue to inspire cross-national collaborations. Some projects still bear the heavy yoke of *La Violencia*, including *Our Lady of the Assassins, Maria Full of Grace, Real Women Have Curves*, Ciro Guerra's *The Wanderer's Shadow* (*La sombra del caminante*, 2004), and Felipe Aljure's *El colombian dream* (2005), although they may veer toward comedy, drama, or dance. Surveying the region's recent cinematic landscape in 2003, Walter Salles noted that these multiple directions make it difficult to speak of a single movement. "There is not just one Latin American cinema," he wrote. "There are *cinemas*; made of contradictory currents that often collide, yet come together in a desire to portray our realities in an urgent and visceral manner. We make films that are, like the melting-pot that characterizes our cultures, impure, imperfect and plural."[13]

Salles, who has made several Brazilian road films, suggests why the genre has become particularly important for Latin American directors. As in the United States, road films "show national identities in transformation." Observing how globalization fosters new kinds of movement, migrations driven by economic motives, he finds that "the most interesting road movies are those in which the identity crisis of the protagonist mirrors the identity crisis of the culture itself." Following this lead, we'll look more closely at a number of Latin examples, from Argentina to Uruguay.

Fernando Solanas's *The Voyage* (*El viaje*, 1992) follows one individual's journey through five countries in search of his Latin American identity. Martín, the film's 17-year-old protagonist, covers some 30,000 miles, traveling by any means of transportation he can find from the southern tip of Argentina to Mexico in the far north. In contrast to the realistic, semi-documentary style of the director's earlier films, *The Voyage* is a work of absurdist fantasy, populated by characters inspired by a comic strip left by the young man's absent father. This is a film in which snow falls indoors, floodwaters from Chile invade the streets of Buenos Aires, and the entire continent is tilted – unnatural events that take on allegorical import. Significantly, the film begins in a school, where cataclysmic rumblings knock presidential portraits off the walls and release the stone horse from a statue of San Martín, Argentina's celebrated liberator. Set free from these symbols of South American history, Martín (his name is no accident) leaves school and begins a journey that becomes an alternative lesson in the history, geography, and culture of his people. Ostensibly, Martín wants to find his real father, another symbolic figure. The road leads him past the sea-swept Straits of Magellan, the high plains of Patagonia, the Inca ruins at Machu Picchu, Amazon forests, and deserts as well as a sinister coal mine in Rio Turbio, a gold mine in Sierra Pelada, and miles of penned-up sheep – in other words, across a range of emblematic landscapes that evoke the grandeur and disfigurement of Latin American topography. Along the way, he meets a mad *mestizo* taxi driver from the Caribbean named Américo, listens to a speech by President Frog, and makes love to a multiplicity of women. This is a film about alternatives. In contrast to the Hollywood conventions of credible characters and continuity editing, Solanas offers caricature and montage construction. His episodic structure breaks the rules of a tightly plotted script. His vision of cultural diversity – a mosaic of languages, ethnicity, and race – differs sharply from the grand narratives of national unity, a homogeneous Latino culture, or global convergence. By the time Martín arrives in Mexico, his view of the continent and his place within it have been transformed.

Minimal Stories (*Historias mínimas*, 2002), an Argentinean film directed by Carlos Sorín, is more modest in scope and intention, as its title suggests. Its three interwoven stories focus on three people bound for the town of San Julián in southern Patagonia. Don Justo, a lonely old man, has heard that his runaway dog was spotted there. Roberto, a fastidious traveling salesman, wants to impress a pretty widow by bringing a cake for her son's birthday. María, a poor young mother, has a chance to win a game show prize if she can get to the television studio in time. Roberto keeps making changes to the cake, converting it from a soccer ball to a unisex turtle before finally smashing it in a fit of jealousy. With the help of a kindly policeman, Don Justo has a chance at reconciliation with the only one who truly cares for him. Working mostly with non-professional actors, a rudimentary script, and a small crew, Sorín manages to convey a lot with his minimal resources. The daily preoccupations of his characters and intense close-ups of their faces are set against the windswept grandeur of the landscape. Their humane reception by local Argentineans along the road contrasts pointedly with the chilly, consumer-laden television broadcasts running in

FIGURES 4.17 and 4.18   The Latin American Family on Wheels: *Bye Bye Brazil and Rolling Family.*

FIGURE 4.17   Carlos Diegues's *Bye Bye Brazil* (*Bye Bye Brasil*, 1980).

FIGURE 4.18   Pablo Trapero's *Rolling Family* (*Familia rodante*, 2004).

the background. While *Minimal Stories* is an instructive example of the South American road film, its various trailers tell another interesting story – about marketing. One of the trailers focuses on the comic escapades of Roberto and his cake. Another concentrates on the old man's sentimental journey to his pet. Both end with a reference to the film's festival award in San Sebastian, Spain. In contrast, the US trailer features rapid cuts between all three stories, adding English subtitles and a comparison to David Lynch's *The Straight Story*, with no mention of San Sebastian.[14]

Like Sorín's film, Trapero's *Rolling Family* uses the intimacy of road travel to engage his viewers in other people's lives, this time with a large extended Argentinean family (Figure 4.18). When 84-year-old Emilia is invited to be matron of honor at a wedding in her home town, she decides to take 12 of her relatives along. The whole group piles into a home-made motor home and sets off from Buenos Aires to Misiones, 600 miles away near the northern border with Brazil. What happens on the way – the petty intrigues, minor triumphs, emotional breakdowns, and family feuds – offers enough comedy and drama for a whole *telenovela*, the kind of fare so popular in Latin American television. But in Trapero's hands, the two-day trek is much more than a traveling soap opera. His hand-held camera work, tight framing, and non-professional actors (Emilia is played by the director's grandmother) give the film an authentic feel, as if we were in the van witnessing each moment while it happens. At the same time, we're very much aware that the film's title is metaphoric. This family embodies all the chaos and charm of Argentinean society at large.

Beyond that northern border, in Brazil, road movies had been exploring the vast landscape and its multiethnic inhabitants for years. One of the most popular of these films is *Bye Bye Brazil* (*Bye Bye Brasil*, 1980), directed by Carlos Diegues, one of the pioneers of Cinema Novo. Outwardly more conventional than his earlier work, *Bye Bye Brazil* centers on a ragtag circus traveling from one small town to another (see Figure 4.17). Calling itself the Caravana Rolidei, the troupe includes Gypsy Lord (its charismatic impresario who doubles as magician and clairvoyant), his dark-eyed lover (a rumba dancer who goes by the name of Salomé), and a black strongman named Swallow. Along the way, they're joined by a young accordion player, Ciço, who falls for Salomé to the dismay of his pregnant wife. The show itself is an amusingly tawdry affair, a jumble of conventional circus tricks patched together with bravado and imagination. In one number, fake snow falls inside the tent while Bing Crosby croons "White Christmas" on a phonograph, proof, boasts Gypsy Lord, that the Brazilian backlands are now part of the civilized world. The caravan's journey is both naturalistic and metaphorical, a chance to explore the country from its arid northeastern *sertão* through the lush Amazon forest to the Central Plateau. Back roads and highways take them through sleepy villages and bustling cities, past bulldozers and palm groves. In one town, a religious procession prays for rain while a traveling projectionist packs his bags, for there is no future here. So the caravan heads for Altamira, "land of plenty," where they find plenty of cinemas, music shops, Coca-Cola, traffic jams, and "fishbone" television antennas, but not much for their circus. They have arrived too late, for the Trans-Amazonian Highway has already created this consumer paradise. The only way for the players to survive is to prostitute themselves. Salomé does this literally, returning with money that will transform the show into a glitzy, Hollywood version of its former self. True to its title, Diegues's film is a farewell to the old Brazil, rendered obsolete like the old caravan, superseded by industrialization, new forms of entertainment, and a voraciously consuming new world order. His filmmaking aesthetics, like the Caravana Rolidei and Brazilian cinema itself, has adapted to the changing times, fulfilling Embrafilme's state mandate to "create a national identity through the preservation of regional diversity,"[15] producing a road movie that is also a spirited, darkly comic critique of that identity.

Walter Salles, who certainly understands how genres can evolve with the times, offered a more optimistic view of the future with *Central Station (Central do Brasil)*. His female protagonist is Dora, a retired teacher who makes a living by writing letters for illiterate Brazilians but never mailing them. At 67, Dora has lost her own ability to communicate. She leads a cynical, confined existence until a 9-year-old boy named Josué leads her to the possibility of a more fulfilling life. When Josué loses his mother, Dora reluctantly agrees to find his father (Figure 4.19), who is somewhere in the heartland of Brazil. Their long journey takes them from the cold streets of Rio to a new settlement in the *sertão*. When they reach the Catholic shrine at Bom Jesus, part way, Dora learns that letters are like prayers, messages of hope that deserve to be delivered. After a striking scene in the shrine when she becomes delirious, Dora finally puts her literacy skills to good use. This scene, reminiscent of the hallucinatory drug montage in *Easy Rider* and certain surrealistic moments in Cinema Novo, is all the more startling in a feature distinguished by the realistic touches of a former documentary filmmaker. *Central do Brasil*, the film's title, may refer to the central train station in Rio de Janeiro or the heart of the nation. Josué's search for his lost father and Dora's search for her lost feelings can be seen as a modern Odyssey about the voyage home that teaches us who we are. They can also be understood in broader terms: the old Brazil of the 1980s, with its culture of cynicism and indifference, meeting the new Brazil, with its unwillingness to accept its given lot, choosing instead a bold, new future.

FIGURES 4.19 and 4.20   Coming of Age on the Latin American Road. Two journeys of self-discovery and historical change.

FIGURE 4.19 "Is it far, my father's house?" A scene from *Central Station* (*Central do Brasil*, Dir. Walter Salles, 1998).

FIGURE 4.20 "Tell me, have you ever had sex with girls beside your girlfriends?" A casual moment in *Y tu mamá también* (Dir. Alfonso Cuarón, 2001).

As if to confirm this hopeful vision, Vicente Amorim's *The Middle of the World* (*O Caminho das Nuvens*, 2003) opens and closes with a view of clouds. The camera moves down to a married couple who have stopped their bicycles at a sign that reads "Middle of the Road Square." They are Romão and Rose, beleaguered parents who are taking their five children on a grueling pilgrimage because he believes that Father Cicero will give him a job to support his family. It turns out that Cicero has been dead for generations, but the priest's shrine is celebrated as a site of miracles by millions of believers. Romão's faith is strong, but it is partly driven by machismo pride, a stubborn insistence on his patriarchal control of the family. While his children peddle their bikes for hundreds of miles, learn to sing for food, go hungry, and are tempted to go astray, his single-minded project threatens the welfare of those he feels obligated to protect. Their 2,000-mile trip from northeastern Brazil to Rio de Janeiro ends at Corcovado Peak, overlooking the city from behind the outstretched arms of an iconic 125-foot statue of Jesus. Amorim's film is filled with such national imagery and self-conscious references to the road film, which by 2001 had become a highly popular genre in Brazil and almost a national sport. Ten years later, *The New York Times* ran an article about a Brazilian couple that was completing a 23,000 mile trip from Tierra del Fuego to Alaska – on a motorcycle.[16]

Mexicans were also leaping into the driver's seat. Nine years after the success of *Danzón*, María Novaro directed *Without a Trace* (*Sin dejar huella*, 2000), a female buddy movie that takes two women from the Texas border to Cancún. Ana and Aruelia are both on the run when they meet on the road. Ana, a well-educated art student from Spain, is wanted by the police for dealing in fake Mayan relics. Aruelia, a street-smart single mother, has stolen money from her drug-dealing boyfriend. As they travel together in an old jeep, their differences fall away. They begin to look and act more like each other. Novaro's script stresses the ill-treatment of women and the Mayan community, which strengthens their bonds. But unfortunately for Novaro, the critics compared her film unfavorably to *Thelma & Louise*, an example of how a transcultural genre can sometimes work against its local application.

More successful with both critics and audiences, both locally and globally, was Alfonso Cuarón's *Y tu mamá también*, which was nominated for an Oscar and won three awards in Venice. In Mexico, the film took in a record $2.2 million in its opening weekend. Besides breaking box office records, Cuarón's film broke a number of taboos about depicting sexuality on screen. Many critics agreed, however, that its frank dialogue and explicit scenes are far from gratuitous. This road trip starts with a proposition. Two teenage boys invite a 27-year-old woman to the beach. Julio and Tenoch are best friends, carefree adolescents preoccupied with sex, drugs, and sex. Ana, a Mexican who grew up in Spain, is an attractive married woman whose husband has been unfaithful. Their drive together from Mexico City to the "Mouth of Heaven" beach is a chance for the boys to act out male fantasies and for us to analyze Freud's sex drive in action (Figure 4.20). The boys flaunt their bodies narcissistically, a state of mind symbolically suggested in the pool scenes. Sex is not just about pleasure; it is a power game that uses women to stake out territory and establish alpha-male supremacy. Julio and Tenoch continually compete with each other, using their sexual conquests to keep score. But as they drive further from home, the game takes a surprising turn. Is sharing the same woman another move in the game or a way to be closer to each other, a mask for homoerotic feelings? This possibility leaves both boys stunned. If this road trip is a voyage of self-discovery, as many are, it is also in some ways a voyage of self-destruction, Freud's death drive. The many references to death along the way – the traffic jam caused by a migrant worker's demise, a cross marking a fatal accident, a herd of pigs destined for slaughter – prefigure personal tragedy at the journey's end. If these psychological dimensions are suggested rather than insisted on, so are its political dimensions. Tenoch is a child of the rich and privileged. His parents host an ostentatious wedding at which the Mexican president is an honored guest. Julio, as his buddy, gets to enjoy the free ride. Money never seems to be a problem. They roll through police road blocks when others are stopped at gunpoint. But as their journey ends, the ruling party is defeated for the first time in 70 years. Their lives and their country are on the brink of a new era. So their coming of age story is also a story about Mexico, poised to reinvent itself. Cuarón's films are part of that invention. Financed entirely with private funds, featuring two stars from Mexican soap operas (Diego Luna and Gael Garcia Bernal, childhood friends in real life), *Y tu mamá también* together with *Amores Perros* helped to redefine Mexican cinema, and Mexico itself, for a global audience.

As the road movie gained momentum in Argentina, Brazil, and Mexico, it was also catching on in smaller countries like Cuba, Colombia, Ecuador, and Uruguay. Cuba's best known road film, not surprisingly, is by Tomás Gutiérrez Alea and Juan Carlos Tabío, the co-directors of *Strawberry and Chocolate. Guantanamera* is Gutiérrez's final work, a life-affirming elegy that celebrates the buoyant spirit of Cuba's people while laughing at the limitations of its politics. At the center of the story is a corpse that must be carried from one end of Cuba to the other. The hearse becomes a vehicle for taking us on a cross-country expedition through a cross-section of the Cuban public. We meet a truck driver named Mariano, a model of machismo with a lady friend at every truck stop. We encounter a number of Mariano's assertive women and some of his male friends, who trade robustly in dollars and black market goods. We get to know Georgina, a schoolteacher whose suffocating marriage to a posturing bureaucrat is sapping her vitality. At the same time, we catch glimpses of a beleaguered national economy. The highways in this road movie are nearly always empty. Crowds huddle on the back of passing trucks that act as public transportation. While the official stores offer a spare, unappetizing choice of goods, colorful markets in meats and vegetables thrive behind closed gates. Meanwhile, the radio blares out official statistics about record-breaking harvests. As far-fetched as the story's premise might seem, it is based on actual events that were reported in the Cuban press during the 1980s, when gasoline shortages led Cuban officials to devise a plan by which coffins were required to be transferred from one vehicle to another across internal boundaries so that no province would exceed its fuel quota. The movie's star, Mirtha Ibarra, underscored the movie's real-life origins when she observed, "It's not a comedy of the absurd, but a comedy drawn from reality, an X-ray of the island of Cuba."[17]

Ciro Guerra turned the X-ray camera on his native Colombia in *The Wind Journeys* (*Los viajes del viento*, 2009). Filmed in some 80 locations in the country's north, where people still speak indigenous languages like Palenquero, Wayuunaiki, and Ikn in addition to Spanish, *The Wind Journeys* is the story of a local folk singer and the boy who idolizes him. After his wife's sudden death, Ignacio Carrillo decides to end his career as a *vallenato* minstrel because he believes the accordion that brought him fame is cursed. He mounts his donkey and begins a 500-mile trek through grasslands, forests, mountains, and a clay-baked desert to return the instrument to its maker. Fermín, the boy, keeps badgering the old man to take him along as an apprentice, initiating a contentious relationship that slowly deepens as they make their way together across the region. In one town, Carrillo competes against a boastful singer who uses sorcery against opponents. The two men engage in a ritual form of musical combat that ends in violence. In another town, two local men are dueling with machetes on a bridge. One insists that Carrillo play during the duel while they fight to the last breath. This is still the country of *La Violencia*, which seems to be inextricably linked to its music. When the accordion is stolen, Fermín must fight a man twice his size to win it back. At each stage of the journey, Carrillo and Fermín encounter another segment of the Colombian population and another test. In a grove, the boy finds a clan of African drummers. Desperate to prove himself and join the brotherhood, he finds the inner strength and rhythm to beat his drum until the woods resound. This scene, too, ends with spilled blood. Later, high in the Sierras, Carrillo is rescued by a community of Indians. This time, his music is accompanied by the purifying melody of a *gaita*, an indigenous flute. The journey thus becomes a kind of musical Odyssey tracing the components of Colombian music to their various multicultural roots. During the movie's final credits, while the accordion (a wind instrument) plays a final tune, the camera pulls back from a hovel in a barren land, showing snapshots of the landscape: a sparkling ocean, purple mountains, scraggy desert brush. As a tiny figure crosses the sands, a shadow falls, and the only music is the wind itself. *The Wind Journeys* is a film of striking landscapes and arresting faces, many beautifully photographed, as if Guerra wanted to balance a legacy of aggression with more positive images of the nation.

The Wind Journeys has been both praised and pummeled for its picturesque photography: praised as a showcase of Colombia's ethnic and geological diversity, pummeled as a travelogue for foreign export. But it is also a richly plotted, carefully constructed film. The machete duel on the bridge, for example, is shot with a minimum of dialogue. After a few shots that set up the situation (a man with a machete has hired Ignacio to play music while he engages another man in mortal combat on the village bridge), the fight scene begins with a long shot of the machete man walking resolutely toward us across the wooden bridge with a group of supporters and onlookers behind (Figure 4.21). In the next shot, he continues walking, but now the camera emphasizes his isolation in an extreme long shot from the river (Figure 4.22); he crosses alone, nearly to the midpoint, then stops, waiting for his adversary. Figure 4.23 shows this other man from the first man's point of view. This second man, too, strides toward us with a machete, shrugging off a woman who tries desperately to stop him. Now the camera shifts back to the river view, an extreme long shot of two men face to face with weapons on a bridge (Figure 4.24). This striking image may remind us of similar face-offs in Westerns or samurai movies (Guerra was fond of Westerns in his youth), but here the setting is Colombia, the men are fishermen with machetes, and the musical accompaniment comes not from an off-screen orchestra but from the protagonist's accordion, whose playing signals the commencement of combat. In the following shots, the camera shifts between Ignacio (Figure 4.25), the duelists, and the onlookers, who watch like soundless statues. Their silence and Ignacio's mournful tune accentuates the spectacle's absurdity. Instead of engaging in the struggle, as a typical Western might, the camera observes their hesitant, hacking strokes from a distance, catching their motions as shadows on the bridge or reflections in the river. Back and forth they struggle, hugging and disentangling each other. A splash of blood sprays across the wooden slats; one man falls backwards through the wooden railing into the water some eight feet below (Figure 4.26). The crowd never flinches. Meanwhile, the first man drops his weapon, falls to his knees, and crumbles on the bridge. Ignacio, still playing, caught in long shot from below, slowly approaches the broken railing and looks down (Figure 4.27). The last shot is a close-up of the fallen fighter from the waterline, some tawdry shacks behind, as he releases his last breath and the camera sinks into the murky depths (Figure 4.28). As incredibly grotesque as the scene may seem, Guerra says he based it on an historical incident in Nueva Venecia reported in 2005.[18]

Similar points may be made about *How Much Further* (*Qué tan lejos*, 2006), a road film by Ecuador's Tania Hermida. As if to highlight the appeal to tourists, one of the film's two female protagonists is a travel agent from Spain. The other is a local student activist. The two women meet on a bus headed south from the capital of

FIGURES 4.21–4.28   A machete duel in Ciro Guerra's *The Wind Journeys* (*Los viajes del viento*, 2009) captures a moment from Colombia's violent history.

FIGURE 4.21

FIGURE 4.25

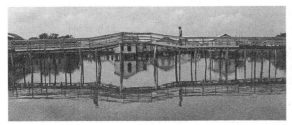

FIGURE 4.22

FIGURE 4.26

FIGURE 4.23

FIGURE 4.27

FIGURE 4.24

FIGURE 4.28

Quito. When the bus is stopped by a workers' strike, they decide to hitchhike. Their journey takes them through some of the country's most scenic regions offering spectacular vistas of the mountains and the ocean, but it also reveals a land of political turmoil, economic hardship, and social injustice. This divided view of Ecuador leaves contradictory impressions for both tourists and Ecuadorians to reconcile.

Beyond the Road (*Por el camino*, 2010) also pairs a foreigner and a Latino. This time the country is Uruguay and the fellow travelers are a young Belgian woman in search of romance and a wealthy Argentinean who has left a banking job in New York to reclaim his family inheritance on the Uruguayan coast. Their encounter with dramatic landscapes and personal drama is another journey of inner and outer exploration. Road films like these – and there are dozens more – continue to win festival awards and secure distribution abroad.

As we've seen, the road movie can be a formula for success for many Latin American directors. With its promise of a ready-made audience come funding opportunities by governments eager to export attractive national images and by co-production companies ready to exploit cultural affinities and the genre's touristic appeal. Road movies also offer filmmakers a chance to take their own measure of the themes explored through the genre by Dennis Hopper, Wim Wenders, Ridley Scott, Theo Angelopoulos, and David Lynch. They can set out on their own search for adventure, intimacy, national identity, freedom, justice, escape, and a way back home. By adapting the road film to local landscapes and indigenous cultures, by tailoring it to native cinematic styles, by connecting it to important regional issues, they extend the road into new territory. Thanks to films like *The Voyage*, *Guantanamera*, or *Motorcycle Diaries*, the people of Argentina, Cuba, or Brazil are no longer merely voyeurs of modernity. They get to sit behind the wheel and drive.

To be sure, as the trajectory of Latin American cinemas shows, its filmmakers have been pursuing their own course for a long time. From the Golden Age of humanistic genre films in the 1940s and 1950s, through the militantly political phase of the 1960s and the complexly pluralistic and reflexive movies of the 1970s and 1980s, they have continuously reshaped the languages of film to address the most pressing topics of concern to Latin Americans. Even in their road films, in an age of globalization, their vehicles remain distinctively Latin. Some scholars and critics are concerned about this new direction. Speculating on the future of New Latin American Cinema, Paul Schroeder Rodriguez worries that "a new generation of filmmakers has succeeded in reinserting Latin American cinema into the global cinematic marketplace by appropriating some of the very conventions that the NLAC rejected out of principle."[19] Expressing similar concerns, Juana Suárez, a leading scholar of Colombian cinema, offers advice that might apply across the new face of Latin America. "To become a solid industry and part of the transnational order," she writes, Colombian cinema needs to venture "more into the realm of imagination, relying less on facile formulae as a passport into the transnational sphere."[20] Whatever position one may take, it is important to understand why a genre like the road film (or horror, or the wedding film) becomes popular and how it travels across borders, carrying cultural baggage along with it and merging with other visions of the road. The paths taken by contemporary filmmakers need not merge into one homogeneous highway or yield autonomy to the machinery of autopilot. The long history of cinemas in Latin America is a mosaic of diversity, commitment, and imagination, and it is still in the making. What may be different today is a deeper understanding of how all roads are connected.

Notes

1. Ella Shohat and Robert Stam, *Unthinking Eurocentrism: Multiculturalism and the Media* (Routledge, 1994), 5.

2. Shohat and Stam, 16–36.

3. Zuzana M. Pick, *The New Latin American Cinema: A Continental Project* (University of Texas Press, 1983), 13.

4. Ana López, "Early Cinema and Modernity in Latin America," *Cinema Journal* 40(1) (Fall 2000): 53–54.

5. John King, *Magical Reels: A History of Cinema in Latin America* (Verso, 1990), 11.

6. Randal Johnson and Robert Stam, eds., *Brazilian Cinema*, expanded edition (Columbia University Press, 1995), 17–19.

7. Carlos Diegues, "Cinema Novo," in Johnson and Stam, *Brazilian Cinema*, 64–67, and "History of Cinema Novo," *Framework* 12 (1979): 19–27.

8. Fernando Solanas and Octavio Getino, "Towards a Third Cinema," *Tricontinental* 14 (October 1969 [Havana]): 107–132, reprinted in Michael Chanan, ed., *Twenty-Five Years of New Latin American Cinema* (BFI, 1983), 17–23. Available at: http://documentaryisneverneutral.com/words/ camasgun.html (accessed June 16, 2013).

9. Michael Chanan, *Cuban Cinema* (University of Minnesota Press, 2004), 5.

10. King, 155.

11. Chanan, 2.

12. See Juana Suárez, Ramiro Arbeláez, and Laura Chesak, "*Garras de oro* (*The Dawn of Justice – Alborada de justicia*): The Intriguing Orphan of Colombian Silent Films," *The Moving Image* 9(1) (Spring 2009): 54–82.

13. Walter Salles, "Preface," in Alberto Elena and Marina Díaz López, eds., *The Cinema of Latin America* (Wallflower, 2003), iv.

14. See trailers for *Minimal Stories* (*Historias mínimas*, dir. Carlos Sorín, 2002), DVD (Optimum Releasing, 2003).

15. Quoted in Timothy Barnard and Peter Fist, eds., *South American Cinema: A Critical Filmography 1915–1994* (University of Texas Press, 1996), 189.

16. Jim Dwyer, "The Point is That You Don't Have to Spend a Lot of Money to Do What You Love," *The New York Times*, September 13, 2013. Available at: http://www.nytimes.com/2011/09/16/ nyregion/brazilian-couple-traverses-the-americas-on-motorcycle.html?_r=0 (accessed June 16, 2013).

17. Larry Rother, "A Final Journey into the Heart of Cuba," *The New York Times*, July 20, 1997. Available at: http://www.nytimes.com/1997/07/20/movies/ a-final-journey-into-the-heart-of-cuba. html?pagewanted=all&src=pm (accessed June 16, 2013).

18. Letter from Ciro Guerra, November 19, 2012. See Inter-American Commission on Human Rights, Report No. 88/06, Petition 1306-05, "Admissibility, Nueva Venecia Massacre, Colombia, October 21, 2006." Available at: http://www.cidh.oas.org/ annualrep/2006eng/COLOMBIA.1306.05eng. htm (accessed June 16, 2013).

19. Paul Schroeder Rodriguez, "After New Latin American Cinema," *Cinema Journal* 51(2) (Winter 2012): 87–112.

20. Juana Suárez, "At the Transnational Crossroads: Colombian Cinema and Its Search for a Film Industry," in Nayibe Bermúdez Barrios, ed., *Latin American Cinemas: Local Views and Transnational Connections* (University of Calgary Press, 2011), 277–310 at 299.

Further Reading

Aguilar, Gonzalo. *Other Worlds: New Argentine Film.* Translated by Sarah Ann Wells. Palgrave, 2008.

Amaya, Hector. *Screening Cuba: Film Criticism as Political Performance during the Cold War.* University of Illinois Press, 2010.

Barnard, Timothy and Peter Fist, eds. *South American Cinema: A Critical Filmography: 1915–1994.* University of Texas Press, 1996.

Barrios, Nayibe Bermúdez, ed. *Latin American Cinemas: Local Views and Transnational Connections.* University of Calgary Press, 2011.

Berg, Charles Ramírez. *Cinema of Solitude: A Critical Study of Mexican Film, 1967–1983.* University of Texas Press, 1992.

Chanan, Michael. *Cuban Cinema.* University of Minnesota Press, 2004.

Dennison, Stephanie and Lisa Shaw. *Popular Cinema in Brazil, 1930–2001*. Manchester University Press, 2004.

Elena, Alberto and Marina Díaz López. *The Cinema of Latin America*. Wallflower Press, 2003.

Falicov, Tamara Leah. *The Cinematic Tango: Contemporary Argentine Film*. Wallflower Press, 2007.

Hart, Stephen M. *A Companion to Latin American Film*. Tamesis, 2004.

Hernandez-Rodriguez, R. *Splendors of Latin Cinema*. Praeger, 2010.

Johnson, Randal and Robert Stam, eds. *Brazilian Cinema*. Columbia University Press, 1995.

King, John. *Magical Reels: A History of Cinema in Latin America*. Verso, 1990.

Konstantarakos, Myrto. "New Argentine Cinema." In Linda Badley, R. Barton Palmer, and Steven Jay Schneider, eds., *Traditions in World Cinema*, 130–140. Rutgers, 2006.

Levine, Robert and John Crocitti, ed. *The Brazil Reader: History, Culture, Politics*. Duke University Press, 1999.

López, Ana. "Early Cinema and Modernity in Latin America." *Cinema Journal* 40(1) (Fall 2000): 53–54.

Martin, Michael, ed. *New Latin American Cinema*, 2 Vols. Wayne State University Press, 1997.

Nagib, Lúcia. *The New Brazilian Cinema*. I.B. Tauris. 2003.

Noble, Andrea. *Mexican National Cinema*. Routledge, 2005.

Page, Joanna. *Crisis and Capitalism in Contemporary Argentine Cinema*. Duke University Press, 2003.

Pick, Zuzana M. *The New Latin American Cinema: A Continental Project*. University of Texas Press, 1983.

Régo, Cacilda and Carolina Rocha, eds. *New Trends in Argentine and Brazilian Cinema*. Intellect, 2011.

Shaw, Deborah, ed. *Contemporary Latin American Cinema: Breaking Into the Global Market*. Rowan & Littlefield, 2007.

Shohat, Ella and Robert Stam. *Unthinking Eurocentrism: Multiculturalism and the Media*. Routledge, 1994.

Stam, Robert. *Tropical Multiculturalism: A Contemporary History of Race in Brazilian Cinema and Culture*. Duke University Press, 1997.

Suárez, Juana. *Critical Essays on Colombian Cinema and Culture: Cinembargo Colombia*. Translated by Laura Chesak. Palgrave, 2012.

William, David Foster. *Contemporary Argentine Cinema*. University of Missouri Press, 1992.

CLOSE-UP
THELMA & LOUISE

FIGURE 4.29   Ridley Scott's *Thelma & Louise* (1991).

Directed by Ridley Scott.
Script by Callie Khouri.
Cinematography by Adrian Biddle.
Edited by Thom Noble.
Music by Hans Zimmer.
Production design by Norris Spencer.
Produced by Ridley Scott and Mimi Polk.
Produced and distributed in the United States by
    MGM in 1991.
Running Time: 130 minutes.

Louise Sawyer	Susan Sarandon
Thelma Dickinson	Geena Davis
Hal Slocombe	Harvey Keitel
Jimmy Lennox	Michael Madsen
Darryl Dickinson	Christopher McDonald
J.D.	Brad Pitt
Max	Stephen Tobolowsky

World Cinema through Global Genres, First Edition. William V. Costanzo.
© 2014 John Wiley & Sons, Inc. Published 2014 by John Wiley & Sons, Inc.

When *Thelma & Louise* arrived on American movie screens in 1991, it stirred up ripples of response that spread across the country and became a tidal wave. The film received six Oscar nominations and was featured on the cover of *Time*, *Newsweek*, and *U.S. News and World Report*. Professional critics were highly positive, praising its "thrilling, life-affirming energy" (Janet Maslin in *The New York Times*), and "dazzling visuals" (*Variety*), calling it "wincingly funny, pertinent and heart-breaking" (Richard Schickel in *Time*), "a zeitgeist picture with a potent cultural impact" (Peter Canavese). But some reviewers and many ordinary viewers, especially men, saw the film as a sadistic revenge story, a case of rampant male-bashing that promoted female violence.[1] Women viewers, on the other hand, generally liked the way *Thelma & Louise* hijacked a male genre and put women at its center. This time, the road buddies flaunting the law and having all the fun were female. Taking up the debate in academic terms, film scholars focused on feminist issues. Some maintained that the film exposed gender inequalities and offered new, liberating roles for modern women; others argued that it misrepresented feminism, simply reversing gender roles associated with violence, pleasure, and revenge.[2] Clearly, the film had struck a national nerve.

A lesser film might have provoked less controversy. But *Thelma & Louise* had a big-name director, major stars, and a reported budget of $17.5 million. Ridley Scott was well known as the director of *Alien* (1979), *Blade Runner* (1982), *Legend* (1985), and *Black Rain* (1989). Born in England in 1937, he had studied at the Royal College of Art before working as a set designer for the British Broadcasting Company. So he was already a mature, experienced filmmaker when he began directing his first feature, *The Duellists*, in 1977. As he later noted in his DVD commentary, it was the "feminist aspects" of *Thelma & Louise* that appealed to him when he first read the script.[3] Most of his earlier protagonists had been male, with the notable exception of Sigourney Weaver's role in *Alien*, which was originally written for a man. Now he had a chance to learn more about women's perspectives through Callie Khouri's script. In 1990, Khouri was relatively unknown in Hollywood. She had begun writing her screenplay in 1988, mostly in private, while producing music videos for a living. Working out the characters' biographies and other details over a period of months, she drew on her personal experience, film knowledge, and imagination to create her female "hero's journey."[4] To bring these heroes to life, Scott cast Geena Davis as Thelma and Susan Sarandon as Louise, both accomplished film actors with rising reputations.

At the beginning of the story, Louise finds herself in a dead end job and a moribund relationship. She waits on tables in a diner and has been waiting years for her boyfriend, a lazy lounge musician, to marry her. Thelma is a suburban housewife. Married to an abusive, self-important businessman and surrounded by a kitchen full of expensive, lifeless gadgets, she lives in a gilded cage. When the two friends take off for a getaway weekend in Louise's 1966 Thunderbird, their light-hearted talk is filled with the spirit of adventure, like two mischievous schoolgirls playing hooky. But a chance encounter at a local bar changes everything. Suddenly, the carefree tone turns dark, the outing turns into an urgent flight, and the screwball comedy becomes an outlaw road movie. The women's relationship changes too. At the start, Louise is the older, wise-cracking, level-headed foil to Thelma's blithe, sometimes negligent impetuosity. Their characters are on comic display as they prepare for the big trip. Louise packs her shoes and dresses in neat plastic bags while Thelma dumps a drawer full of assorted clothing into her suitcase. Later, these roles will shift as Thelma learns to take control, exchanging her makeup and frilly wardrobe for a T-shirt, jeans, and a sense of responsibility.

As Thelma and Louise leave the cramped interiors of small town Arkansas, heading for the open spaces of the American Southwest, their friendship opens too. Their casual acquaintance deepens into something more, a special bond that they have never had with men. Most of the men they flee from or meet along the way offer scant promise of companionship or mutual respect. Thelma's husband Darryl (Christopher McDonald) is arrogant and controlling; Louise's boyfriend Jimmy (Michael Madsen) is fearful of commitment. A man in a bar becomes sexually abusive, a truck driver makes obscene gestures from his cab, and a cocky state trooper wields his badge as an icon of entitlement. The women cut each of these male caricatures down to size, turning that supreme symbol of masculine power – the pistol – against them. Even those men who seem to offer sexual satisfaction or protection – a handsome drifter named J.D. (Brad Pitt) and a sympathetic detective (Harvey Keitel) – are no substitute for the sisterhood that Thelma and Louise discover on the road. We feel this bond develop gradually in the film's many traveling montages, but nowhere more poignantly than when they drive through the Canyonlands at night. Louise is at the wheel. Thelma leans back cozily bedside her, musing dreamily, "I always wanted to travel. I just never got the opportunity." Louise takes a quick glance toward her, saying, "Ya' got it now." The camera dissolves back and forth between them, catching their pensive looks head on, then pulls back for a poetic panorama of the moonlit cliffs. While we watch their silent faces glowing in the magic light, we hear "The Ballad of Lucy Jordan" on the soundtrack. A plaintive voice on the soundtrack sings about a woman who realizes at the age of 37 that she'll never ride through Paris in a sports car with the warm wind in her hair. Shel Silverstein's poetic lyrics, soulfully sung by Marianne Faithfull, seem to echo their silent sentiments, thoughts that prepare us for the film's finale at the edge of the Grand Canyon.

Ridley Scott shot most of the film in California, substituting Bakersfield for Arkansas and the deserts east of Los Angeles for much of the Southwest, but some scenes were filmed near Moab, Utah and the Grand Canyon in Arizona. Scott's cinematographer shot the Canyonlands scene using a "day for night" technique, running the camera in daylight with extra lights and later adjusting the exposure to make it seem like night time. Notice how he illuminates their faces, the cliffs, and even the trailing dust in a phosphorescent glow. Scott went out of his way to capture the road film's iconography, those long stretches of highway, the telephone poles, smooth tracking shots that follow the T-bird on its journey, cross-cutting between the road and home. Only this time, it's the women who are moving while the men are mostly stationary. To be sure, Detective Slocombe and the FBI are on the trail, but their pursuit doesn't become fully mobile until the big final scene, when a fleet of patrol cars, a helicopter, and dozens of armed lawmen confront the fugitives at the canyon's edge. Scott shot two versions of this ending before deciding to conclude with the film's celebrated freeze frame of Thelma and Louise rather than with a close-up of Slocombe's face. From start to finish, women are the heart of this story, with men nudged to the margins.

The film's complex relationship to gender and genre is particularly instructive if we compare it to earlier road movies. The classical blueprint exemplified by *Easy Rider* focuses on two male buddies searching for adventure and identity on the open highway. Billy and Wyatt discover the best and worst of America and themselves as they ride from the frontierland of the Old West to the redneck country of the American South. *Thelma & Louise* reverses this trajectory in geographic terms, but more importantly it subverts the story formula by putting women behind the wheel. In Khouri's words, "They [women in earlier pictures] were never driving the story because they were never driving the car."[5] Even in films that feature mobile women running from the law, the women are often innocent companions of men (like the faithful wife in *You Only Live Once*, 1937) or film noir *femmes fatales* (like the blackmailing hitchhiker in *Detour*, 1945). In contrast, Thelma and Louise are neither peripheral nor wicked. Nor are they, like the trigger-happy women in *Gun Crazy* (1950) and *Bonnie and Clyde* (1967), hell bent on violent action. Although they do use firearms to hold up stores and deflate male egos, they tend to temper these moments with a feminine civility that's usually played for laughs. After Thelma robs a convenience store at gunpoint, Louise reminds her not to litter. And like good citizens, they apologize politely to a policeman before locking him in the trunk of his own car.

In scene after scene, *Thelma & Louise*'s careful visual composition rewards close attention. Consider how Scott introduces tonal and thematic values even before the story starts. The opening credits first appear in white lettering on a black background that fades into a desert landscape, shown in black and white. The camera pans right to a dirt road leading toward the mountains, then cranes up slightly above the road as the image slowly takes on color, deepens, and finally fades to black as the last titles are displayed. Is this changing view of the open road meant to announce the genre or anticipate the future? Do the transitions between black and white photography and color reflect swings between everyday experience and imagination, grim reality and hope? Does the dimming screen imply a fatalistic view, a glimpse of possibility fading into darkness? Scott fills the frame with mirrors, windows, and photographs that raise questions of perspective. In one poignant, silent scene, Louise sits alone in her car smoking a cigarette when she spots an older woman in a diner looking at her through a window. Quickly, she begins to fix her lipstick in the rear-view mirror, then stops, shrugs, and tosses the lipstick away. The next moment, she hears Thelma's voice screaming, "Drive, Louise! Drive! Drive the car!" Thelma jumps in and Louise takes off, listening while her companion proudly tells her how she's just robbed a convenience store at gunpoint. While Thelma talks, we see a flashback of the robbery, not as expected from her point of view but in a black and white surveillance video. A room full of men is watching the video in a police station. These shifts in perspective – two women staring at each other across the barrier of time, the law's patriarchal view of Thelma's adventure as a crime – illustrate the film's layered complexity. Another moment, much discussed by feminists, is the motel scene when Thelma looks at J.D.'s ripped body. The camera slowly tilts up along his torso, his abs accentuated by lamplight, before the couple plunges into wild lovemaking. Here, in contrast to so many films in which women are the erotic object of "the male gaze," the camera identifies with Thelma's look. We are invited to watch the scene through the lens of female desire.

Whether or not we accept this invitation is a topic worth exploring. In one study of how university students responded to the film, a communications researcher found that reactions depended on which factors were considered relevant. Most men in the study did not like the film. They minimized issues of sexism and the marginalization of women, ignored issues like attempted rape and suicide, and arrived at an overwhelmingly negative assessment of the film. For many of these male students, this was a story about women taking revenge against men, a story in which the male figures are all unrealistic caricatures. Most of the female students, on the other hand, focused on issues of sexism, friendship, and the reversal of traditional roles. These women were particularly sensitive to the experience of rape. They appreciated the film as an empowering story of two women who take a stand and form a strong, fulfilling relationship with each other.[6] In the BFI study of *Thelma & Louise*, Marita Sturken argues that the film is not a revenge narrative but "a story of bad luck, impulsive action and the consequences of violence" since the protagonists ultimately pay for their behavior. She believes that the final kiss "symbolizes a union of two heterosexual women as friends."[7] How spectators of both genders respond depends partly on what perspective they assume, with whom they identify, what issue they count as relevant or dismiss. In this respect, *Thelma & Louise* is a perfect test case for exploring the fascinating topic of audience response to any film.

Questions

1. Thelma and Louise seem to switch roles somewhere on the road. Describe the two women at the beginning of their journey and at the end. What accounts for the change? Where does it seem to happen?
2. After discussing the film with male and female viewers, do you find any patterns of response along gender lines? How differently do the men and women see the story and its characters? Try to explain any differences you find.
3. *Thelma & Louise* is often said to reverse traditional gender roles in movies that feature violence. Take a scene in the film that links gender and violence.

How does the scene subvert or affirm conventional expectations?

4. What other films does *Thelma & Louise* remind you of? What points of comparison can you make? Based on your comparison, what can you say about *Thelma & Louise* as a road movie or an exemplar of another genre?
5. Investigate the controversy over *Thelma & Louise*. Read what critics said about the film during its original release and find out what scholars and other viewers have thought since then. What seems to be at the root of the negative and positive comments? Which of the arguments seem most convincing to you?

Notes

1. See Brenda Cooper, "The Relevancy of Gender Identity in Spectators' Interpretation of *Thelma & Louise*," *Cultural Studies in Mass Communication* 16 (1999): 20–41.

2. See Jessica Enevold, "The Daughters of Thelma and Louise: New? Aesthetics of the Road," in Kristi Siegel, ed., *Gender, Genre, and Identity in Women's Travel Writing* (Peter Lang, 2004), 73–95, and Sharon Willis, "Hardware and Hard Bodies, What Do Women Want? A Reading of *Thelma and Louise*," in Jim Collins, Hilary Radner, and Ava Preacher Collins, eds., *Film Theory Goes to the Movies* (Routledge, 1993), 120–128.

3. *Thelma & Louise*, Director's commentary, DVD (MGM, 1992).

4. *Thelma & Louise*, Audio commentary by Callie Khouri, Susan Sarandon, and Geena Davis, DVD (MGM, 1992).

5. Katie Mills, *The Road Story and the Rebel: Moving Through Film, Fiction, and Television* (Southern Illinois University Press, 2006), 193.

6. Cooper, 20–41.

7. Marita Sturken, *Thelma & Louise* (British Film Institute, 2000), 65 and 77.

Further Reading and Other Media

Cooper, Brenda. "The Relevancy of Gender Identity in Spectators' Interpretation of *Thelma & Louise*." *Cultural Studies in Mass Communication* 16 (1999): 20–41.

Enevold, Jessica. "The Daughters of Thelma and Louise: New? Aesthetics of the Road." In Kristi Siegel, ed., *Gender, Genre, and Identity in Women's Travel Writing*, 73–95. Peter Lang, 2004.

Griggers, Cathy. "*Thelma and Louise* and the Cultural Generation of the New Butch-Femme." In Jim Collins, Hilary Radner, and Ava Preacher Collins, eds., *Film Theory Goes to the Movies*, 129–141. Routledge, 1993.

Laderman, David. *Driving Visions: Exploring the Road Movie*, 184–194. University of Texas Press, 2002.

Mills, Katie. *The Road Story and the Rebel: Moving Through Film, Fiction, and Television*, 192–198. Southern Illinois University Press, 2006.

Sturken, Marita. *Thelma & Louise*. British Film Institute, 2000.

Thelma & Louise. DVD. MGM, 1992. (DVD includes alternate ending and two audio commentaries: by director Ridley Scott and by Susan Sarandon, Geena Davis, and writer Callie Khouri.)

CLOSE-UP
LA STRADA

FIGURE 4.30   Federico Fellini's *The Road* (*La Strada*, 1954).

Directed by Federico Fellini.
Script by Federico Fellini, Tullio Pinelli, and Ennio
   Flaiano.
Produced by Dino De Laurentiis and Carlo Ponti.
Cinematography by Otello Martelli.
Edited by Leo Catozzo. Music by Nino Rota.
Italian release (Dino de Laurentiis Distribuzione)
   in 1954.
US release (Trans Lux) in 1956.
In Italian with English subtitles.
Running Time: 107 minutes.

Zampanò	Anthony Quinn
Gelsomina	Giulietta Masina
Matto (The Fool)	Richard Basehart
Giraffa	Aldo Silvani
Widow	Marcella Rovere
Nun	Livia Venturini

World Cinema through Global Genres, First Edition. William V. Costanzo.
© 2014 John Wiley & Sons, Inc. Published 2014 by John Wiley & Sons, Inc.

Federico Fellini's film about two unlikely traveling companions is a milestone in the evolution of road movies and Italian neorealism. It is also a chance to study a classic, an enduring work of cinema by one of its most important artists. The story and its characters seem simple enough. A circus strong man named Zampanò (Anthony Quinn) chooses a country girl, Gelsomina (Giulietta Masina), as a companion for his traveling show. Gelsomina is as naïve and trusting as a child, perhaps a little "strange," as her mother says when the beleaguered woman sells her off so she can feed her other children. Zampanò, gruff and self-absorbed, treats her as a servant, expecting her to cook his meals and beat a drum while he breaks an iron chain across his chest, a stunt that he repeats in town after town along the dusty roads of postwar Italy. On the outskirts of Rome, they meet *Il Matto*, the Fool (Richard Basehart), who performs daring aerial feats on a high wire above astonished crowds. We might be tempted to see their journey as a parable of human imbalance or a failure of communication. Zampanò, a creature of excessive brawn and brutish force, never speaks his mind or feelings. The Fool is sensitive, intelligent, but aloof. Gelsomina, with her tiny body and underdeveloped brain, seems to be all heart. But such reductive readings miss the qualities that make *La Strada* stand out from hundreds of contemporary films. Fellini was not the kind of director who uses film to send messages or illustrate ideas. He worked intuitively with images and feelings, coaxing characters to life beyond the limits of the screen, creating moments that are magical, even mystical, reverberating long after the film is over. Among Fellini's abundant and celebrated accomplishments, *La Strada* holds a special place, which is why even 12 years after its release, he called it "the complete catalog of my entire mythological world."[1]

Fellini's real world began in 1920, when he was born to middle-class parents in the seaside town of Rimini in northeastern Italy. From his earliest days, he was captivated by all forms of entertainment, including comics, radio, theatre, motion pictures, and the circus. In interviews, he liked to tell how he once skipped school and ran off with a small traveling music show. Later, he found employment as a cub reporter, began writing sketches for the radio, and worked his way into the movies, first as a rewrite man, adding gags to scripts, then as a screenwriter of comedies. During World War II, he fell in love with Giulietta Masina, who would become his wife and the leading actress in *La Strada*. It was after the war that he met Rossellini and worked with the celebrated neorealist director on *Rome, Open City* (*Roma, città aperta*, 1945), *Paisan* (*Paisà*, 1946), and a segment of *L'amore* ("The Miracle"/"Il miracolo," 1948), in which he appeared as an actor. With *Variety Lights* (*Luci del varietà*, 1950) he became a director, completing the so-called "character trilogy" with *The White Sheik* (*Lo sceicco bianco*, 1952) and *I Vitelloni* (1953). Speaking with another filmmaker, Gideon Bachmann, in the 1950s, Fellini said, "all my films to date are concerned with people looking for themselves." Likening his creative process to a voyage, he explained that "the most important part is what you discover on the way."[2]

It seems fitting that the production of Fellini's great road movie (*la strada* means "the road" in Italian) itself followed the trajectory of a journey. According to the director, it began not with a concept but with a feeling, "an undefined sense of melancholy, a sense of guilt as pervasive as a shadow, vague and consuming, composed of memories and forebodings."[3] Fellini imagined "two creatures who remain together because of fate," drawing on his artistic skills to transform the mental pictures into sketches and designs: the bowler hat and shawl of Gelsomina, the actress-clown; the dark figure of Zampanò; the road; the circus; the countryside and villages of the Apennine Mountains between Rome and Tuscany. This method of relying on visual renderings continued throughout Fellini's film career. He used shooting scripts chiefly to get funding, to organize his imagery for other eyes. Much of his creativity happened on the set. Since all dialogue was later dubbed, he could improvise and shout directions while the cameras rolled.

But La Strada is not the work of a single individual. For four months, Fellini worked on the script and dialogue with his collaborator Tullio Pinelli. He also worked with Nino Rota, who composed the movie's score, including the haunting melody associated with Gelsomina. The first time we hear it, the Fool introduces the tune to her on his toy violin. Later, she learns to play it on her trumpet. Near the film's end, a young woman sings it while hanging out the wash. The melody's transmission from one person to another seems to trace a spiritual journey from initiation to grace and fulfillment. Masina's Gelsomina is not just naïve. Her slow-wittedness borders on saintliness. She reveals a special affinity for children, religious imagery, and the natural world. One moment, she mimics the branches of a tree; another, she instinctively imitates the nuns. In one of the film's most mysterious and poignant scenes, some children lead her from a wedding party up a flight of stairs to a dark room where a sick child sits in bed. At first she tries to entertain him with her clown act, but when Osvaldo's pale face fails to respond, she steps closer, peering into his eyes as if they mirror hers, or perhaps they offer a brief glimpse of something otherworldly. Ultimately, she becomes the means by which Zampanò finds a measure of redemption. It's the Fool who plants the seed of self-conscious intentionality, who suggests that her rambling life may have a purpose, like the tiny stone he holds up before her in his famous "parable of the pebble" speech. Basehart keeps the scene from being heavy or pedantic with a mixture of casual humor, compassion, and wonderment. Despite his cardboard wings, he is not just the allegorical figure of an angel but a flawed and fully human being. Quinn's Zampanò also moves beyond mere symbolism. Despite his inarticulately bestial behavior throughout the film, in the final beach scene he is capable of looking up at the stars not through the eyes of a wild beast but with the expressive gaze of suffering humanity.

The oceans at the beginning and ending of La Strada are connected by a long and winding road. As in Hollywood's Great Depression road films of the 1930s, the motives for travel are largely economic. Gelsomina's mother, a widow, cannot afford to feed her struggling family. Zampanò survives by hitching an old motorcycle to a canvas-covered wagon because no single town can supply the spectators that he depends on for his livelihood. He and the other itinerant showmen that he meets lead nomadic lives, striking tents after each show, taking their belongings with them, never growing roots. Like the nuns who rotate among convents every two years, they never get to form attachments. It is by leaving home, abandoning the familiar comforts and forging ahead into the unknown that we learn who we are and what we're meant for. This sense of life as a journey of discovery links *La Strada* to the great tradition of road narratives. And as Fellini liked to say, "All my films are about journeys, real or imaginary."[4]

La Strada's relationship to neorealism is more complex. The Italian directors traditionally associated with the movement – Roberto Rossellini, Luchino Visconti, Vittorio De Sica, Pietro Germi – sought a new aesthetic during and after World War II. In contrast to the slick, sanitized propaganda movies made under Mussolini's fascist regime, they wanted to show life as it really was, to focus on ordinary people coping day by day. From 1942 to 1952, this meant training the camera on the political struggles, poverty, and unemployment faced by the working class. Rossellini's *Rome, Open City* is based on real events that occurred when the Italian Resistance fought against German control. De Sica's *Bicycle Thieves* (*Ladri di biciclette*, 1948) follows a boy and his father whose desperate search for a job leads to a disastrous theft. At a time when film stock was scarce, studios were unavailable, and budgets were minuscule, these filmmakers relied on grainy footage, outdoor locations, and non-professional actors, which not only saved money but also gave their films a realistic, almost documentary feel. Although the movement had generally run its course in Italy by the late 1950s, it continued to have a strong and widespread impact elsewhere in the world, on the French New Wave, for example, in Latin America, Africa, India, Japan, Iran, and in other places where directors with limited means have confronted social issues with a camera and commitment.

Fellini's early work, especially the scripts he wrote for other directors, was rooted in neorealism, and he continued to align himself with the movement for years. As late as 1956, he said to Bachmann, "All my work is definitely in the neorealist style,"[5] by which he meant "a way of seeing reality without prejudice, without any preconceived ideas … looking at reality with an honest eye." But as his work became more personal, more poetic, he was accused of betraying neorealist ideals. Marxist critics raised a furor in the press, pointing to a "Crisis of Neo-Realism," claiming he had abandoned true social responsibility for sentimental, self-indulgent projects. Yet for those who most value Fellini's films, their strength, vitality, and lasting value lie in his imaginative vision. *La Strada* won the Academy Award for Best Foreign Language film in 1956. The next year, his *Nights of Cabiria* (*Le notti di Cabiria*) won an Oscar for Masina's performance in the title role. Fellini's reputation grew even stronger with *La Dolce Vita* (1960), *8½* (1963), and *Juliette of the Spirits* (*Giulietta degli spiriti*, 1965), continuing through films like *Satyricon* (1969), *Amarcord* (1973), and *Intervista* (1987). Long after his death in 1993, he continues to be appreciated as an original creative artist, sensitive and full of life, a man of rare sincerity who never compromised, remaining faithful and responsible to no school but his own.

Questions

1. Describe the three main characters in *La Strada*: Gelsomina, Zampanò, and The Fool. To what extent do they act like real people, to what extent like figures in a parable? Did your view of these individuals change in the course of the film? If so, what accounts for the shift in your perception?

2. Fellini uses visual motifs like water, religious imagery, and the road itself throughout the film. Find examples of these recurring images and explain how they work to tie the narrative together and suggest deeper meanings in the story.

3. Read about Fellini's personal life. What talents and interests from his childhood did he develop later as a filmmaker? Pay particular attention to his drawing skills, his knack for telling tales, and his interest in the circus. Where do these show up in *La Strada*?

4. In addition to its title, what makes *La Strada* a road movie? What does it have in common with other examples of the genre that you know? To what extent does it depart from your expectations of what a road movie should be?

5. Find a moment in the film that you believe best exemplifies the principles of neorealism and identify those principles. Look for scenes that seem to stray from these principles. Do agree with those critics who accused Fellini of betraying the neorealist style?

Notes

1. Quoted in Peter Bondanella and Manuela Gieri, eds., *La Strada* (Rutgers University Press, 1987), 9–10.

2. Federico Fellini, "The Road Beyond Neo-Realism," in Bondanella and Gieri, 215–220.

3. Federico Fellini, "The Genesis of *La Strada*," in Bondanella and Gieri, 181–184.

4. *Federico Fellini's Autobiography: Clips from His Life*, documentary film on Disc 2 of *La Strada* (The Criterion Collection, 2003).

5. Fellini, "The Road Beyond Neo-Realism."

Further Reading and Other Media

Bondanella, Peter. *The Cinema of Federico Fellini.* Princeton University Press, 1992.

Bondanella, Peter and Manuela Gieri, eds. *La Strada.* Rutgers University Press, 1987.

Cardullo, Bert, ed. *Federico Fellini: Interviews.* University Press of Mississippi, 2006.

Kezich, Tullio. *Federico Fellini: His Life and Work.* Faber and Faber, 2002.

La Strada. DVD, 2 Discs. The Criterion Collection, 2003.

CLOSE-UP
BREATHLESS

FIGURE 4.31   Jean-Luc Godard's *Breathless* (*À bout de souffle*, 1960).

Directed by Jean-Luc Godard.
Screenplay by Godard, based on an original treatment by François Truffaut.
Produced by Georges de Beauregard.
Cinematography by Raoul Coutard.
Edited by Cécile Decugis.
Music by Martial Solal.
French release in 1960.
US release in 1961.
In French with English subtitles.
Running Time: 89 minutes.

Patricia Franchini	Jean Seberg
Michel Poiccard	Jean-Paul Belmondo
Liliane	Liliane Dreyfus
Inspector Vital	Daniel Boulanger
Parvulesco	Jean-Pierre Melville
Antonio Berruti	Henri-Jacques Huet
Used Car Dealer	Claude Mansard
Carl Zumbach	Roger Hanin
Editor	Van Doude
The Snitch	Jean-Luc Godard

World Cinema through Global Genres, First Edition. William V. Costanzo.
© 2014 John Wiley & Sons, Inc. Published 2014 by John Wiley & Sons, Inc.

Jean-Luc Godard's *Breathless* (*À bout de souffle*) is one of the landmarks of world cinema. A sensation when it first appeared in 1960, it continues to be studied in film classes everywhere. The initial reviews were mixed. Described as "wildly cruel and pitilessly anarchic" in Britain's *Sight and Sound*, it was hailed in the French press as "a masterstroke of extraordinary power" (*Le Monde*) that promised "a new future to the art of the screen" (*Le Figaro littéraire*). American reviewers found it "sordid" (*The New York Times*), "daringly cubistic" (*Time*), "a film of flawless consistency and uncompromised truth" (*The New Republic*).[1] While it may not be everyone's idea of great art or riveting entertainment, critics and scholars generally agree that *Breathless* marks a defining moment in the history of film.

Groundbreaking movies often emerge when the ground is ready. In 1960, the time was ripe for a film like *À bout de souffle*, whose French title may be more accurately translated as "Out of Breath" or "Last Gasp." The high-toned "cinema of quality" long admired in France was losing its grip, and mainstream Hollywood itself was running out of steam. A new generation of hip, free-spirited youth was ready for a fresh breath. Godard's first feature film swept into theatres on the rising crest of a French New Wave, *La nouvelle vague*, in the wake of Claude Chabrol's *The Handsome Serge* (*Le beau Serge*, 1958) and François Truffaut's *The 400 Blows* (*Les quatre cents coups*, 1959).

At that moment, Chabrol, Truffaut, and a band of other young directors (among them Jacques Rivette, Eric Rohmer, and Alain Resnais) were busy making waves. Rejecting the classical styles and subjects of "Papa's cinema," they set out with portable equipment and light budgets to reinvigorate the language of film. Like the Italian neorealists of the 1940s and 1950s, they favored non-professional actors and outdoor locations to lower costs and give their work a documentary flavor. They delivered slices of life instead of well-made stories, ordinary people instead of stars, focusing on the here and now instead of the nation's epic past or literary heritage. They also experimented with innovative film techniques, shooting in low lighting on sensitive film stock, running the camera in long takes, and breaking the rules of continuity editing. Many became committed to contemporary social issues, caught up in the liberation politics and existential anguish of the time. Yet they borrowed freely from commercial genre films and incorporated a variety of art forms, high and low. The resulting films, though never a formal school or movement, were vigorous, inventive, and "authentic."

While most of the old guard had come up through the studio system and was trained in its industrial methods, the core of this new generation began as film enthusiasts and critics. They had joined the cinema clubs of Paris and watched thousands of old movies from the Cinémathèque's archives. They had written hundreds of reviews for newer films in the influential film journal *Cahiers du Cinéma*, calling for a cinema of *auteurs* (authored by individual directors) distinguished by their *mise-en-scène* (how shots are staged, framed, and photographed). Godard saw little difference between criticism and filmmaking. "While I was a critic," he wrote in 1962, "I considered myself already a *cinéaste*. Today ... instead of writing a critique I direct a film. I consider myself an essayist. I do essays, but ... I film them instead of writing them."[2] Later, he would insist that "Cinema is not a craft. It is an art. One is always alone on the set as before the blank page."[3]

As a director and a personality, Jean-Luc Godard is hard to pin down. An intellectual who works from instinct, accused of being exasperatingly lazy yet stubbornly resolute, arrogant yet shy, he appeals to a variety of audiences with a unique mixture of formula and spontaneity, of pop culture and high art. Even his national identity straddles borders. Born in Paris in 1930, Godard was the second of four children in a bourgeois Franco-Swiss family. His father was a doctor and his mother came from a family of wealthy bankers. During World War II, he became a naturalized Swiss citizen, studying first in Switzerland, then in France. It was during the first phase of his adult life, from 1949 to 1960, that Godard developed his enthusiasm for motion pictures. Although officially enrolled in a program of ethnology at the Sorbonne, he spent much of this time at the ciné-clubs and Cinémathèque. Family problems pulled him back to Switzerland, interrupting his ambitions for three years, but he returned to Paris and began writing for *Cahiers*, taking on odd film jobs and making a few short movies of his own. One of these shorts was "Charlotte et son Jules" (1960), in which Jean-Paul Belmondo chatters non-stop about women while an ex-girlfriend primps and pouts silently around his bedroom. Belmondo's free-wheeling dialogue and gestures feel like a dress rehearsal for Godard's debut feature.

Based initially on a seven-page treatment by Truffaut,[4] *Breathless* represents a few days in the lives of a petty thief, Michel Poiccard (played by Belmondo), and his American girlfriend, Patricia Franchini (Jean Seberg). Godard once reportedly described *Breathless* as "a documentary about Belmondo and Seberg."[5] His comment speaks to a natural affinity between the camera and the actors, as if they were playing themselves while we follow the course of their relationship. Seberg, an American from Iowa, was "discovered" by Otto Preminger, who selected her from thousands of contestants to play the title role in *Saint Joan* (1957). It was a tortuous experience for the aspiring young actress, only 17 during the screen test. After the film flopped, she would claim that Otto Preminger, the producer and director, terrorized her on and off the set, although she made a second film for him, *Bonjour Tristesse* (1958), another disappointment, before seeking solitary refuge on the French Riviera. If Hollywood had given up on her, the French saw something promising in her performances. It was Truffaut who suggested to Godard that Seberg's mid-Western charm had a dark side that would work well in *Breathless*. To get her, Godard's producer, Georges de Beauregard, reportedly paid Preminger $15,000, a sixth of the film's entire budget. Belmondo was another matter. Born in 1933, a Frenchman through and through, he was an easygoing, athletic young man who had trained to be a boxer before turning to acting as a career. His screen models included Pierre Brasseur and Humphrey Bogart. Godard used Belmondo's natural grace and his affinity for Bogart, getting him to play a petty thief and lady's man who imagines himself to be the hero in a crime film.

Poiccard's character is based on the true story of Michel Portail, a small-time hood deported from the United States for petty crimes. Portail fell in love with an

American journalist and lived a fast life in Paris until he got in trouble with the French police. One day in 1952, he stole a car, drove it to his sick mother in western France, and wound up killing a motorcycle cop on the highway. After hiding out in Paris for two weeks, he was turned in by his girlfriend. Truffaut read about Portail in the tabloids and wrote his treatment in 1956, later giving it to his friend Godard, who used it and Truffaut's name to secure funding for his film. For the crew, de Beauregard recruited talent from earlier productions. Raoul Coutard, a former war photographer, became Godard's cameraman. Cécile Decugis, who had also worked with Truffaut, became his editor. Pierre Rissient signed on as assistant director.

Both cast and crew later attested to Godard's unorthodox production methods.[6] Working from private notebooks, he revised Truffaut's conception of the story, making various changes, altering characters, enlarging a bedroom scene, and adding his own ending. Much of the dialogue seems to have been improvised day by day. Godard would write lines at the last moment and shout them to his actors during the shoot. On some days, he'd film continuously for hours. On others, he'd stop after a few takes, announcing that he'd run out of ideas. Since the inexpensive Caméflex camera ran too erratically to sync with sound, all dialogue was dubbed in later, giving it a disconnected quality. This proved well suited to the film's theme of alienation. In fact, many of Godard's innovations, some of which became hallmarks of the French New Wave, were motivated by necessity. Without money for standard equipment, Godard used a mail cart or a wheelchair for his tracking shots, which turned out to be more versatile than tracks. When Michel enters a travel agency looking for his contact Mr. Tolmachoff, the camera moves with him, circling to his left in one continuous motion as a woman at the counter points in that direction. When he walks left, the camera backtracks smoothly in front of him, keeping pace with his determined gait, then sweeping around him once again when he changes course. The lengthy, uninterrupted tracking shot conveys his nervous energy and relentless determination.

Without expensive studio lights, Coutard experimented with high-sensitive film stock that made his indoor shooting, like the 25-minute scene in Patricia's hotel room, seem more natural. This improvisational approach extended to the editing room. To save time, Godard shortened scenes by cutting pieces from within individual shots, resulting in the famous jump cuts that disrupt normal expectations of continuity. We see this in the restaurant when Patricia dines with her publisher. Or again, just before she telephones the police, we see her walking with a newspaper from left to right. The camera pans with her in long shot, then abruptly cuts to a medium shot of her walking in the opposite direction. Do these cuts suggest anxiety or a change of heart? Perhaps no practice is as characteristic, or as irksome to some, as Godard's fondness for allusions. The film is crammed with literary quotes, postmodern references, and private jokes. Take the scene when Michel and Patricia share a long kiss in the Napoléon movie theatre. The movie on the screen is *Westbound* (1959) by Budd Boetticher, a director much appreciated by the *Cahiers* critics, but what sounds like the movie's dialogue is really two French poems dubbed in Godard's voice. This sly conflation of American and French culture is pure Godard.

Godard's fascination with American culture and Hollywood film genres is on display throughout the film, alternating between homage and critique. *Breathless* is dedicated to Monogram Pictures, the low-budget studio that produced commercial pictures from 1931 to 1953. At times, Godard seems to enjoy playing with conventions of film noir and other forms of crime movies, saluting many of the directors he admired at the Cinémathèque. There are allusions to Nicholas Ray, John Huston, and Jean-Pierre Melville, who has a cameo role as the celebrated novelist Parvulesco. At other times, Godard seems to mock his main character for buying into American ideals and iconography. Michel steals American cars and swipes gestures from Hollywood actors, swaggering like James Cagney, hiding behind a newspaper and a cloud of cigarette smoke, and wiping that thumb across his lips like Humphrey Bogart. When he passes a poster advertising Robert Aldrich's *Ten Seconds to Hell*, we realize that the movie's tag line, "live dangerously to the end," could well be the code by which this wannabe gangster lives and dies. In contrast, it's the American girl Patricia who is more attached to European high culture, associated in the film with Renoir and Picasso, Mozart and Chopin. This dichotomy is echoed in the film's two musical motifs, a jazzy tune for Michel, a romantic score for Patricia. It also figures in the way *Breathless* anticipates road movie themes and aesthetics, bridging European prototypes like Roberto Rossellini's *Voyage to Italy* (1953) and American successors like Arthur Penn's *Bonnie and Clyde* (1967).

Today, *Breathless* is widely studied as a manifesto of French New Wave style. Godard's hand-held camera seems to be as restive as Michel, constantly in motion as it follows him. But the director doesn't want us to identify with his protagonist. He reminds us repeatedly that what we're watching is a movie, a construction of reality, not reality itself. Sometimes, Michel's voice and lips are out of sync. At other times, when we expect the camera to cut back and forth between two speakers in a typical shot/reverse angle shot pattern, Godard defies the convention, making us uncomfortably aware that he is breaking the rules. The jump cuts that interrupt Patricia's conversation with her publisher deliberately break the flow of speech and action, shattering the spell of verisimilitude. These departures from the classical Hollywood style keep us at a distance. Instead of being absorbed into the story, we are nudged into viewing Michel and the mentality he represents from a position of critical detachment. Many of these stylistic features turn up later in American road films by independent directors who felt a kinship with European existentialism.

What audiences responded to most in the 1960s, however, was not so much the film's technique as its raw energy, its authenticity, the sense of "real life coming at you full speed without explanation," as D.A. Pennebaker put it.[7] After *Breathless*, Godard's restless energy found new directions. Dudley Andrew divides his subsequent career into phases.[8] In the second phase, from 1961 to 1968, Godard became a "professional" filmmaker, breaking with the *Cahiers* group and producing 14 features that included musical comedy, science fiction, crime, and anti-war films marked with his personal and increasingly political stamp. A third phase began with the radical political protests of 1968 and ended in 1972, a period of intense reappraisal during which he made more than a dozen experimental, militant, and self-critical films. Since then, Godard has continued to reinvent himself, adding video and hybrid new forms to his repertoire, fascinating some, vexing others, but always following his own path.

Questions

1. *Breathless* was considered groundbreaking when it was first shown in 1960. What made it so innovative then? What new ground did it break? How original does it seem today? What changes in filmmaking and audience expectations since 1960 might account for the way this film is viewed in our own time?

2. What drives a man like Michel Poiccard? Describe his appearance, his mannerisms, and speculate on what makes him act the way he does. Do the same for Patricia Franchini. Why do you think they are drawn to each other, and how do you explain their failure to connect? To what extent do these two characters and their relationship seem dated, symptoms of a particular place and time? To what degree can we relate to them today?

3. Analyze a scene that seems typical of Godard's direction. What choices about framing, camera work, lighting, sound, or editing make the scene "Godardian"? Consider how a classical Hollywood director might have handled the scene. What is the overall effect of Godard's choices on you as a viewer?

4. Jean-Luc Godard is known as one of the most original and influential figures in modern cinema. Learn more about his life, his thinking, and his films. Sample some of his work from different stages of his varied career. What conclusions do you draw about the value of Godard's contributions?

5. Investigate the origins and influence of the French New Wave. Who were its strongest proponents? What were they trying to achieve? How did they influence the course of cinema in France and elsewhere in the world?

6. Watch some other examples of French New Wave films and compare them to *Breathless*. Consider their subjects, stories, themes, and cinematic styles. Based on your observations, do these movies seem to form a unified movement, like German Expressionism or Italian Neorealism, or a group of loosely related films?

Notes

1. Dudley Andrew, ed., *Breathless* (Rutgers University Press, 1987), 189–194.

2. Quoted in *Cahiers du Cinéma* (December 1962), in Toby Mussman, ed., *Jean-Luc Godard*, trans. Rose Kaplan (Dutton, 1968), 101.

3. Jean-Luc Godard, in Tom Milne, ed., *Godard on Godard* (Viking, 1972), 76.

4. Truffaut's treatment is reproduced in Andrew, *Breathless*, 154–160.

5. Quoted in D.A. Pennebaker, "Pennebaker on *Breathless*," video interview (Criterion Collection DVD, 2007), Disc 2.

6. Interviews on Criterion DVD.

7. Interview on Criterion DVD.

8. Andrew, *Breathless*, 22–24.

Further Reading and Other Media

Andrew, Dudley, ed. *Breathless*. Rutgers University Press, 1987.

Breathless. DVD, 2 Discs. The Criterion Collection, 2007. (Includes *À bout de souffle*, a booklet containing interviews, the Truffaut treatment, Godard's scenario, and an essay by Dudley Andrew, "*Breathless* Then and Now.")

Milne, Tom, ed. *Godard on Godard*. Viking, 1972.

Mussman, Toby, ed. *Jean-Luc Godard*. Translated by Rose Kaplan. Dutton, 1968.

CLOSE-UP

THE MOTORCYCLE DIARIES

FIGURE 4.32   Walter Salles's *The Motorcycle Diaries* (*Diarios de motocicleta*, 2004).

Directed by Walter Salles.
Script by José Rivera.
Based on *The Motorcycle Diaries* by Ernesto "Che"
  Guevara and *With Che Through Latin America* by
  Alberto Granado.
Cinematography by Eric Gautier.
Edited by Daniel Rezende.
Music by Gustavo Santaolalla.
Production design by Carlos Conti.
Produced by Michael Nozik, Edgard Tenenbaum,
  and Karen Tenkhoff.
Distributed in the United States by Focus Features
  in 2004.
In Spanish, with English subtitles.
Running time: 126 minutes.

Ernesto "Fuser" *Guevara*	Gael García Bernal
Alberto "Mial" *Granado*	Rodrigo de la Serna
Celia de la Serna	Mercedes Morán
Chichina Ferreyra	Mía Maestro
Ernesto Guevara *Lynch*	Jean Pierre Noher
Roberto Guevara	Lucas Oro
Celita Guevara	Marina Glezer
Ana María Guevara	Sofia Bertolotto
Juan Martín Guevara	Franco Solazzi
Uncle Jorge	Ricardo Díaz Mourelle
Doctor Hugo Pesce	Gustavo Bueno

World Cinema through Global Genres, First Edition. William V. Costanzo.
© 2014 John Wiley & Sons, Inc. Published 2014 by John Wiley & Sons, Inc.

Ernesto Guevara de la Serna, commonly called "Che," is one of the great legends of our time. Even those who only know his face from the many coffee mugs and T-shirts bearing his image – those earnest eyes framed by his iconic beard and the black beret captured in Alberto Korda's 1960 photograph – recognize him as a figure of rebellious youth. Long after his death in 1967, admirers still revere him as a counterculture hero: the Argentinean-born champion of the Cuban Revolution, a brilliant Marxist intellectual and tactical genius of guerilla warfare. For others, he represents something dangerous and distinctly unheroic: the risks of dogmatic thinking and a ruthless drive for bloody violence.

The Motorcycle Diaries (*Diarios de motocicleta*) is about Guevara before the man became the myth. Set in 1952, it follows him and his companion Alberto Granado on an eight-month road trip through South America. Guevara was 23, a medical student near the end of his studies, and Granado was a 29-year-old biochemist. Director Walter Salles based the film partly on Guevara's diary (*Notes on a Latin American Journey*). The lines from Guevara's book that open the movie focus on the young men's journey rather than their roles in history or legend: "This isn't a tale of heroic feats. It's about two lives running parallel for a while, with common aspirations and similar dreams." There is no mention of Che's later escape from Guatemala during the military coup of 1954, his first meeting with Fidel Castro in 1955, or his transformation into "El Comandante," a leader of revolutionary forces in Cuba, the Congo, and Bolivia.

The two travelers' common aspirations are spelled out clearly even before the trip begins. Their goal is to explore a continent they have only known from books. Their plan is to journey more than 5,000 miles: first from Buenos Aires, Argentina westward to Patagonia and into Chile, then north through Peru and Colombia to Venezuela, stopping to work at the San Pablo Leper Colony along the way. Their vehicle of choice is "The Mighty One" (*La Poderosa II* in Spanish), a gasping 1939 Norton 500cc motorcycle that leaks oil and belches smoke. Their method is improvisation. Despite their parallel paths, it's clear from the start that "Fuser" (as Alberto calls Ernesto) and "Mial" (Alberto's nickname) have very different personalities. Mial is energetic and outgoing, an enthusiastic dancer and irascible con-artist whose personal objective is to bed as many women as he can. Fuser is more idealistic, introspective, and honest to a fault. When a farmer asks him to inspect a growth on his neck, Fuser tells him flatly it's a tumor without sparing the man's feelings or Mial's hopes for a free meal. Fuser has also been asthmatic since childhood. These flaws and their rascally behavior make the protagonists more likeable, more human than heroic, but also set the stage for their gradual maturation.

Like the motorcycle buddies in *Easy Rider*, Fuser and Mial are in search of adventure. They're on a romantic expedition to explore a continent that becomes a journey of self-discovery. Like Billy and Wyatt, they travel through iconic national landscapes: through the flatlands of Patagonia, along the rocky coast of Chile, up into the snow-blanketed Andes, to the mystical ruins of Machu Picchu in Peru and the Amazon rainforest bordering Brazil. Here and there, like the protagonists of *Easy Rider*, they make stops that offer visions of possible futures. When they visit

Fuser's girlfriend, she is vacationing in Miramar. The luxury resort and its snooty residents represent the kind of privileged life they might have as middle-class professionals. The leper colony in the Amazon represents another option, a career as dedicated medical workers among the suffering poor. At one point, high in the Andes, Alberto muses that he'll marry an Incan descendant and start an Indo-American revolution. It's when their bike breaks down and they are forced to travel on foot or hitch rides on passing trucks that they begin to rub shoulders with poor farmers and unemployed workers. But as sympathetic as they are to the lower classes, as much as they have to scrounge for food and shelter, we know that their poverty is temporary. They have only to click their heels to be back in their comfortable, middle-class homes.

Salles infuses the film with references to familiar journey narratives. At times, Alberto seems to be playing an earthy Sancho Panza to Ernesto's idealistic Don Quixote. At other times, he's more like Dean Moriarty, Sal Paradise's wacky companion in Kerouac's *On the Road*. But the imagery of *Easy Rider* is always close at hand. Early in *The Motorcycle Diaries*, when the bikers first set out, the camera tracks down a long stretch of open highway before their motorcycle rides into the frame and speeds ahead, leaving us behind. We travel with them for a while, glimpsing them in close-ups from this side and the other. Even the sun flares remind us of Dennis Hopper's photography. In their imagination, they're outlaws, leaving civilization, getting closer to the land. They pass a herd of cattle and try to race two men on horseback, but The Mighty One sputters and fails. Now it's the camera that moves ahead, leaving them behind.

Like a journal, the film is divided into dated sections, giving the place name and elevation at key points in the journey. It shifts between narrative and dramatic modes, between telling and showing, supplementing the voice of Guevara's diary with dialogue and action. It also swings back and forth between mobility and stasis, from light to dark and back again. But while the diaries are loosely episodic, Salles gives more structure to the film. As the journey progresses, the tone grows darker. Mid-way through the film, Albert and Ernesto meet a married couple forced off their land and hunted by the police because of their communist affiliation. Sitting at a makeshift campfire at night, their gaunt faces made hauntingly tragic by Eric Gautier's chiaroscuro lighting, these Chilean migrant workers don't understand why anyone would travel just for the sake of traveling. Ernesto's observations, taken from the diaries, mark this as a pivotal point in his budding social consciousness. Huddling together with this struggling couple, sharing *mate*, bread, and cheese around a fire in the cold desert air, he feels closer to the proletariat. The diary entry is even more politically explicit: "It's a great pity that they repress people like this. ... the communism gnawing at [their] entrails was no more than a natural longing for something better."[1] Later, when they reach the Chilean copper mines at Chuquicamata, Ernesto bristles at the boss's mistreatment of the workers. Here, the film is more overt than the book about his anger when we see him cursing the Anaconda Mining Company and throwing a rock at the company truck. His voice-over comment identifies this moment as another landmark in his social education. "As we left Chuquicamata we could feel the world changing," he says, "or was it us?" The film offers other glimpses into Ernesto's evolving thoughts. At Machu Picchu, sacred home of the ancient Incas, the camera lingers on his face before it cuts to what he sees, a massive stony tower rising high above the clouds. Ernesto writes visibly in his note book, "The Incas knew astronomy, brain surgery, mathematics ... but the Spanish invaders had gunpowder." This is when Alberto offers his half-baked idea for a Tupac revolution. Ernesto's response is telling: "without guns there is no revolution."

When asked about the relationship between *The Motorcycle Diaries* and Che's later life, Walter Salles once cited the Argentine writer Jorge Luis Borges: "In every moment of our lives, we not only carry our past but our future."[2] The scenes at Chuquicamata and Machu Picchu seem to bear this out. But the motives behind the film are even broader. When executive producer Robert Redford invited Salles to direct the project, the Brazilian filmmaker had already made several documentaries and two award-winning feature films about journeys: *Central Station* (*Central do Brasil*, 1998) and *Behind the Sun* (*Abril Despedaçado*, 2001). Salles did three years of research, retracing Guevara's journey and meeting with Alberto Granado, who was still living in Havana. To write the script, he hired Puerto Rican playwright José Rivera, who drew not only from Guevara's diaries, but also from Granado's account (*Traveling with Che Guevara*) and several biographical works, most notably *Ernesto Guevara también conocido como el Che*, by Mexico's Paco Ignacio Taibo II. For the role of Ernesto, Salles cast Gael García Bernal, the Mexican actor who had won acclaim for his performances in *Amores Perros* (2000) and *Y tu mamá también* (2001). At the time, Bernal was exactly the same age as Guevara when he made the trip. To help him prepare, he read the same books that Guevara had read up until then. For the part of Alberto, Salles chose Argentinean actor Rodrigo de la Serna, who happens to be related to the Guevara family.

Shooting proceeded chronologically over an 84-day period, with cast and crew following the original itinerary, making personal connections to the landscape and its people. At the San Pablo Leper Colony, they met patients who had been treated by Guevara and Granado 50 years earlier. Many of the locals, like "Don" Nestor and the Quechua women in Chile, were ordinary people encountered in the streets, giving a realistic flavor to those scenes. When we see these people later in flashbacks, static but alive in black and white, we're reminded of the fine line between documentary and fiction. Cinematographer Eric Gautier, an admirer of the French New Wave and its fondness for *cinéma vérité*, did most of the filming with a lightweight Super-16 camera and natural light, seeking to follow the actors instead of fixing them within the frame. When they ride on wheels, he tracks them with traveling shots; when they're on foot, so is he. At the same time, his lens captures the mysterious mists of Machu Picchu, the ancient architecture of Cuzco, or the faded splendor of colonial Lima – not merely as picturesque backdrops, but as integral parts of the drama. The landscape of South America is as much a character as the two protagonists who travel through it. Much of the music on the soundtrack was played by Gustavo Santaolalla, an Argentinean musician who used mambos and tangos, panpipes and a *charango* guitar to strengthen the regional identity of each scene.

Near the end of the San Pablo sequence, Guevara swims across the Amazon River at night, risking an attack by asthma or alligators in the cold, dark waters. The scene not only emphasizes his courage, but it makes a symbolic point. By leaving the hospital staff on one bank and fighting his way to the patients on the other side, he bridges a long-standing class division, allying with the poor, ailing, unprivileged class. In the diaries, this moment is less heroic. It happens in broad daylight, takes two hours, and represents little more an annoying delay. Guevara gives it only two sentences. However, the scene before this swim, when Guevara gives his farewell toast, follows the book almost word for word. The speech's ending enunciates one of the film's important themes. "We believe, and this journey has only confirmed this belief, that the division of America into unstable and illusory nations is a complete fiction. We are one single *mestizo* race from Mexico to the Magellan Straits." These words could also speak for the film itself. Made with the collaborative talents of a Brazilian director, a Puerto Rican writer, lead actors from Mexico and Argentina, and non-professional actors from Chile and Peru, *The Motorcycle Diaries* is a truly Pan-Latin American production, a road movie that bridges borders and embodies an important regional trend. Further, as a co-production made with funding from Argentina, Chile, Peru, France, the United States, and Great Britain, it illustrates a form of globalization that still drives the industry today. This may be one reason why the film has won so many international festival awards and continues to be so popular with audiences around the world.

Questions

1. Compare the characters of Ernesto and Alberto as represented in this film. Describe their appearance, personalities, social status, and personal goals. What motivates each one to undertake the journey? Note any changes that you observe during the course of their trip.

2. In his departing speech at the San Pablo leper colony, Ernesto asserts that the borders dividing Latin America into separate states are fictions. What evidence can you find in the film to support his belief in "one single *mestizo* race from Mexico to the Magellan Straits"?

3. What did you learn about South America from *The Motorcycle Diaries*? What confirmed your previous views, and what surprised you? Do you think the film was intended primarily for Latino audiences or for outsiders?

4. Notice how the film integrates views of the people and the landscape. Where is the main focus on character or on place? What does Salles seem to be saying about Latin Americans in relation to their geography, history, and culture?

5. Read the diary on which Salles based his film. How faithful is the movie to the letter and spirit of Guevara's original writing? How do you explain the differences?

6. Do some research on "Che" Guevara, the historical individual and legendary figure. Then watch the film again. What new light does your research cast on your experience of the movie?

7. Compare *Motorcycle Diaries* to *Easy Rider*. What features of the classic road movie do they share? What differences in geography, history, and culture between North and South America are highlighted by your comparison?

Notes

1. Ernesto Guevara, *The Motorcycle Diaries: Notes on a Latin American Journey* (Ocean Press, 2004), 78.
2. Quoted in Richard Porton, "Road to Revolution," *Film Journal International* (October 1, 2004). Available at: http://www.filmjournal.com/filmjournal/esearch/article_display.jsp?vnu_content_id=1000720831 (accessed June 17, 2013).

Further Reading and Other Media

Bueno, Ferndada. "*Motorcycle Diaries*: The Myth of Che Guevara in the Twenty-First Century." *Confluencia* 23(1) (Fall 2007): 107–114.

Carte, Rebecca, "Trickster, Traveler, Cultural Hero: Ernesto 'Che' Guevara." *Studies in Latin American Popular Culture* 27 (2008): 167–183.

Granado, Alberto. *Traveling with Che Guevara: The Making of a Revolutionary*. Pimlico, 2003.

Guevara, Ernesto. *The Motorcycle Diaries: Notes on a Latin American Journey*. Ocean Press, 2004.

Porton, Richard. "Road to Revolution." *Film Journal International* (October 1, 2004). Available at: http://www.filmjournal.com/filmjournal/esearch/article_display.jsp?vnu_content_id=1000720831 (accessed June 17, 2013).

The Motorcycle Diaries. DVD. Focus Features, 2004. (Widescreen Edition. Special features include *The Making of* publicity short plus brief interviews with actor Gael García Bernal, composer Gustavo Santaolalla, and Guevara's real-life traveling companion, Alberto Granado.)

Williams, Claire. "*Los diarios de motocicleta* as Pan American Travelogue." In Deborah Shaw, ed., *Contemporary Latin American Cinema: Breaking into the Global Market*, 11–27. Rowman & Littlefield, 2007.

GLOSSARY

180 degree rule. A principle of cinematography that keeps the camera on one side of an imaginary line drawn through the action so that the actors remain in consistent relation to each other. Watching a sequence filmed according to this "rule" is considered less confusing because characters on the left or right of the screen (like the opposing armies in a battle sequence) remain in that position from shot to shot.

Academy ratio. The original standard dimensions of the projected image on a movie screen, fixed by the Academy of Motion Pictures as three units high by four units wide: an aspect ratio of 1.33:1.

Adaptation. A movie based on a book, usually a novel.

Aerial shot. A shot in which the action is filmed from above, with the camera typically mounted on a crane or in a helicopter.

Allegory. A form of storytelling in which people, things, and events represent abstract ideas, like youth, greed, good, or evil.

Ambient sound. Local background noises usually recorded before or after the shoot to lend authenticity to the sound track.

Anamorphic lens. A special lens for compressing a wide image onto standard 35mm film in the camera or for unsqueezing the image in a projector to create a widescreen image.

Animation. An effect created when a drawing or object is changed slightly every time the camera stops. When the film is projected, the objects appear to move of their own accord.

Anime. Japanese animated feature films.

Archetypes. Impersonal and universal forms of human experience shared by people around the world, often spanning stories and myths from different cultures. Carl Jung posited the existence of a collective unconscious, a shared system of archetypes that includes a range of important moments (initiation,

World Cinema through Global Genres, First Edition. William V. Costanzo.
© 2014 John Wiley & Sons, Inc. Published 2014 by John Wiley & Sons, Inc.

courtship, marriage, death), individuals (the great mother, father, devil), and motifs (the creation, the deluge).

Aspect ratio. The relationship between the horizontal and vertical dimensions of the screen.

Assembly cut (Editor's cut). An edited version of the film in which the best shots are trimmed and joined end to end into a tentative order.

Assistant director. Handles delegated tasks like planning the day's shooting, managing the extras, or keeping intruders off the set.

Auteur theory (Auteurism). Holds that film directors are the authors of their films, like the writers of novels who bear responsibility for the artistic vision and integrity of their work.

Automated dialogue replacement (ADR). The process of synchronizing an actor's voice with the actor's image on the screen during post-production. This is done when there is too much noise on the set, or when a movie filmed in one language is recorded into another, or when the script is altered after shooting.

Avant-garde. An artistic movement of experimental films that deliberately violate the conventions of mainstream movies.

Backlighting. A strong light from behind separates the subject from the background. Backlighting creates a silhouette effect when the subject is not illuminated from the front.

Best boy. A key assistant who may be responsible for day-to-day operation of lighting, costumes, or equipment on or off the set.

Blaxploitation films. Cheaply made Hollywood movies of the 1970s that exploited the box office value of black performers for black audiences.

Blocking. The term for walking the actors through each movement before shooting.

Boom shot (Crane shot). A shot in which the camera moves vertically through space, sometimes lifted by a boom or crane.

Bushido code. Samurai warriors of feudal Japan followed this set of moral principles, "the way of the warrior," involving honor, loyalty, thrift, and mastery of martial skills.

Camera obscura. Literally "dark room" in Latin, the term from which the word camera is derived.

Camera operator. Runs the camera under the cinematographer's supervision.

Carnivalesque. A mode of storytelling, in literature or film, that uses broad humor and grotesque exaggeration to subvert the status quo. Russian critic Mikhail Bakhtin related the term to the concept of carnival, a moment of liberation that turns the normal order upside down.

Celluloid. Film coated with light-sensitive chemicals. When exposed to light through the aperture of a motion picture camera, a celluloid strip becomes a series of still photographs that can be developed and projected as a movie.

Cinema novo ("New cinema"). Film movement of the 1960s led by Brazilian director Glauber Rocha, characterized by native folklore traditions and a Marxist view of poverty.

Cinéma vérité.   The use of hand-held cameras, natural lighting, shooting on location, improvised plots, and deliberately disruptive editing techniques, which make films look more like real life than artificial constructs.

CinemaScope.   A widescreen process developed in 1952 using an anamorphic lens to squeeze a panoramic view onto standard 35mm film and later project the image onto a screen with an aspect ratio of 2.35:1.

Cinématographe.   An invention by Louis and August Lumière used to record and project motion pictures for a theater audience in 1895.

Cinematographer, or **Director of photography (DP).**   Responsible for the camera work and related operations.

Cinerama.   A widescreen process introduced in 1952 that used three interlocked cameras to produce movies that were projected onto a curved screen with an aspect ratio of 2.77:1.

Classical Hollywood cinema (Hollywood style).   A distinctively American mode of making movies that favors efficient, plot-driven, character-centered, seamlessly-edited stories.

Close-up (CU).   A shot in which the camera is relatively near the subject. For example, a close-up might show an actor's head or hand.

Cognitive studies.   An interdisciplinary movement concerned with the nature of perception and thought. Cognitive film studies draw on empirical tests and computer simulations to understand how movies work in terms of mental representations and processes.

Colonialism.   A policy or system by which one power (the colonizer) exploits another (the colony) for economic gain.

Computer-generated imagery (CGI).   Visual elements of a movie created on a computer using digital technology.

Continuity editing.   A set of film editing conventions that creates a sense of uninterrupted flow. Developed to keep audiences focused on the characters and story rather than on film technique, this approach became a hallmark of the classical Hollywood style.

Co-productions.   Films that combine the resources of several film companies, often from different countries, thereby increasing the opportunities for funding, talent, and audience appeal.

Crane shot (Boom shot).   A shot in which the camera moves vertically through space, sometimes lifted by a boom or crane.

Cross cutting (Parallel montage).   An editing technique that shows two simultaneous actions in alternating shots, the camera shifting from one action to the other.

Cuer.   A film technician who helps to keep track of dialogue during a shoot.

Cultural studies.   A critical movement concerned with the cultural contexts of films and other forms of popular culture. Critical studies often focus on the ideological messages of films, who creates them, how they are encoded, and how they are perceived by various audiences.

Cutaway.   A shot of something off screen, like an airplane flying overhead, that is inserted (cut) into a scene.

Cut-in. A shot inserted into a scene revealing details of the scene, such as a close-up of a gun in the murderer's hand.

Cycle. A succession of films with similar subjects, themes, or tone. The cycle of American movies released in the 1940s and early 1950s that featured hard-boiled male characters, dangerous women, dark themes, and low-key lighting was later regarded by some critics as a genre, called film noir.

Daguerreotype. A process for reproducing sharp, permanent images on treated metal plates, developed by the French chemist Louis Daguerre in 1837, the forerunner of modern photography.

Dailies (Rushes). The film from a day's shooting, usually printed overnight and viewed the next day by the director and the editor.

Das Neue Kino ("The new cinema"). Film movement originating in West Germany during the 1960s.

Deconstruction. An approach to cinema opposed to structuralism, holding that any effort to categorize films by genre, history, or any other category is inadequate. Practitioners seek to deconstruct the text by exposing its internal contradictions.

Depth of field. The area within a photograph or movie frame that remains in sharp focus.

Development. The first stage of filmmaking starts with an idea and ends with a proposal.

Dialogue. Words on the sound track spoken aloud by actors in the film.

Diaspora. A dispersal of people with a common origin or culture, such as the scattering of Jews after their exile in Babylon or the African diaspora to the New World through the slave trade.

Diegetic sound. Sound emanating from within the world of the story, like a song playing on a car radio as distinct from non-diegetic sound, like orchestral music added afterwards to augment a scene's emotional effect.

Digital compositing. The process of combining digital images on a computer.

Digital non-linear editing. The process of assembling electronic images, stored as computer files, into a sequence. This process allows editors to choose selected scenes or individual frames at will and recombine them automatically.

Digital photography. A process for recording images in electronic form that can be manipulated on a computer.

Director. Has the responsibility of directing the actors, supervising the technicians, and managing all action on the set.

Director's cut. A tighter version of the edited film than the assembly cut. It may include some sound and is often screened for the studio executives.

Discourse. The manner of narrating the story (how it is told) in a film as distinct from the story's content (what is told).

Dissolve. A visual effect in which one image seems to blend into the next. A dissolve is made by superimposing a fade-out over a fade-in.

Distributor. A company responsible for releasing a film. Distributors arrange for the circulation of films to theatres and for home viewing. A film may have different distributors for different parts of the word.

Dogme.   A Danish movement begun in the 1990s advocating a policy of artistic self-discipline. The Dogme Manifesto outlined this policy as a reaction to a film culture considered to be too unrestrained and superficial.

Dolly shot (Tracking shot).   A shot in which the camera moves horizontally through space with, towards, or away from the subject. The heavy cameras of earlier years required wheels (on dollies) or tracks for smooth movement on the ground.

Dubbing.   A process by which dialogue is recorded after the shooting and synchronized with the lip movement of actors in the scene.

DVD (Digital video disk).   A high-density medium for storing large amounts of data on a compact disk in digital form, especially high-resolution audio-visual material like a full-length movie.

Editing (Cutting).   The process of compiling a film from its constituent parts. Shots filmed separately are spliced together (cut, edited) into a continuous sequence.

Editor.   A film specialist, often working in consultation with the director, who selects the best takes from a day's shoot, trims each shot, and assembles the shots into scenes (shots related in time and space) and sequences (segments of film composed of scenes from different times or locations but unified by a common idea).

Essentialism.   A belief that the identity of a group, such as a nation or an ethnic community, is characterized by certain attributes or traits. An essentialist view of Chinese people, for example, might emphasize their common heritage, language, and physical features instead of their diversity.

Establishing shot.   The opening of a movie intended to orient the viewer.

Ethnography.   A branch of anthropology that studies the cultures of various people. Ethnographic films tend to focus on the cultural differences of societies, often in exotic, non-Western locations.

Exhibition.   A branch of the movie industry that deals with public screenings. Exhibitors are those who own, manage, and operate movie theatres.

Exoticism.   In film studies, the term usually refers to a misplaced emphasis on the strange and foreign aspects of a land and its people. Robert Flaherty, for instance, is sometimes charged with exploiting the exoticism of Eskimo life in his "ethnographic" film, *Nanook of the North* (1922).

Expressionism.   An artistic movement that seeks to render subjective emotional and mental states on film, especially popular in Germany during the 1920s.

Eye-level shot.   A shot that duplicates how most of us face each other in everyday life, from the height of a person's eyes.

Eyelight.   A small spotlight placed near the camera to add sparkle to the subject's eyes.

Eyeline match.   A cutaway showing what an actor sees.

Fade.   A visual effect created by darkening or lightening each successive frame. In a fade-out, the image gradually grows black. In a fade-in, the image emerges from a black screen.

Feminism.   In film study, Feminist theory focuses on the way women are represented in movies and the ideological forces that shape their representation.

Fifth generation.   A name given to Chinese filmmakers who emerged from Beijing's film school after Mao's Cultural Revolution of the 1960s and 1970s.

Fill light.   Provides a weaker, broader glow than the key light and is used to fill in shadows.

Film noir.   A genre originating in the 1940s characterized by dark lighting, seedy characters, sudden violence, unsentimental dialogue, intricate plots, disorienting camera angles, and a hard-boiled outlook on life.

Film stock.   Undeveloped celluloid, or film stock, may vary in sensitivity to light, fast film stock being more sensitive than slow film stock.

Fine cut.   The final version of the edited film forwarded to the sound mixers and photographic laboratory for final processing.

First-run theatres.   Theatres that are granted exclusive rights to exhibit a new movie during its initial release within a prescribed zone.

Floodlight.   A light that washes the scene with a diffuse form of illumination.

Focal length.   The distance from the plane of the film to the optical center of the lens when the lens is set to infinity. A short focal length produces a wider image, making objects seem farther away. A long focal length produces the opposite effect.

Foley editing.   A process by which live sound effects are replaced with synchronized substitutes. For example, the sound of hollow coconut shells being thumped in a studio might be used to simulate the sound of horses on the screen.

Frame.   (1) An individual photograph on a strip of film. (2) The rectangular area in which the image appears on screen.

Framing.   Refers to the way shots are composed (the elements of each shot arranged within the rectangle of the camera's viewfinder).

Freeze frame.   A special effect created by reprinting the same frame many times in succession so that the action seems to stop suddenly.

French *nouvelle vague* (French new wave).   A group of young creative directors who began their careers as critics for *Cahiers du cinéma* and revitalized French filmmaking in the late 1950s and early 1960s. The term may also refer to the cinematic style of these directors.

Freudianism.   Based on the work of Sigmund Freud, Freudian film theory explores the sexual dimensions of movies and the role of unconscious drives.

Front lighting.   A form of illumination that may soften a face, flattening the features and sometimes hiding facial marks.

Full shot.   Shows an entire human figure and much of the set.

Gaffer.   The chief electrician, responsible for lighting the set as directed by the cinematographer.

Genre.   A classification of films into categories like Westerns, gangster movies, or romantic comedies.

Globalism. Can be understood as a view of the whole world as a complex network of interconnected elements (economies, information, peoples, cultures) that transcends national barriers and spans entire continents.

Globalization. The process by which worldwide integration accelerates over time.

Gofers. Run errands for everybody else, who order them to "go for this" and "go for that."

Grips. Take care of equipment, sets, and props during a shoot.

HDTV (High-definition television). The use of special cameras and recording equipment to produce high-quality pictures. High-definition digital images have a higher resolution than analog television images (1080 lines versus 480) and use a wider screen format (16:9 width to height ratio versus 4:3).

High-angle shot. A segment of film photographed from above the subject.

High-key lighting. A method of flooding a scene with bright illumination, giving it a cheerful, buoyant tone.

Hybridity. Refers to the way things are mixed. For example, *Cowboys and Aliens* (2011) is a hybrid genre film, a mixture of science fiction and the Western.

Impressionism. An approach to cinema that intensifies psychological experience through techniques like superimposition, slow motion, and out-of-focus photography.

Insert (Cut-in). A shot of some detail, like the close-up of a gun in the actor's pocket, inserted into a scene or sequence.

Intertextuality. Refers to the way texts are shaped by other texts. The meanings we attach to a given film may be influenced by our intertextual knowledge of similar films.

Iris. A circular mask surrounding the screen image, sometimes used to draw attention to a detail or to close a scene.

Jump cut. Discontinuity created when the action in two consecutive shots does not match up.

Key light. The chief light illuminating the subject to be filmed.

Kinetograph. A precursor of the modern camera, William Dickson's Kinetograph (patented by Thomas Edison) used a roll of celluloid film to record sequential photographs that were then viewed through a peephole in his **Kinetoscope**. Perforations in the film allowed it to be moved behind a shutter frame by frame creating the illusion of motion pictures.

Letterboxing (also called **Widescreen**). A method of adapting widescreen movies to the boxy dimensions of a television screen by placing blank bars above and below the full frame so that its orginal aspect ratio is preserved.

Long shot (LS). A shot in which the camera is relatively far from the subject. A long shot might show the actor's entire figure running through a field.

Low-angle shot. A segment of film taken from below the subject.

Low-key lighting. A method of lighting in which the illumination is low and soaked with shadows, creating an ominous or melancholy mood.

Marxism. Based on the work of German philosopher Karl Marx, Marxist film theory is concerned with social class and the economic forces that account for poverty and wealth.

Master shot. A continuous long shot covering the entire action. Portions of the action may be filmed again, from different distances and angles. Later, the best shots will be selected and edited for continuity, using the master shot as a general guide.

Matching action. An editing convention that joins two shots (with a **match cut**) so that the action in one shot seems to continue in the following shot.

Matte shot. A special effect that uses an opaque screen or matte to obscure certain portions of the frame. The film is exposed twice, first with one matte, then with a second matte that reveals the area obscured by the first. When projected, the two separately filmed sections of the frame appear as a single image.

Medium shot (MS). A shot in which the camera is at a medium distance from the subject. A medium shot might show an actor's body from the ankles, knees, or waist up.

Melodrama. A form of storytelling that stresses strong emotional content and often makes sharp distinctions between good and evil.

Method acting. A school of performers based on the teachings of Constantine Stanislavski. Method actors try to get in character by identifying personally with the role, making emotional connections between their character's plight and events in their own lives, drawing on genuine feeling rather than relying on external acting techniques.

Mise-en-scène. Refers to what happens within a movie frame (literally, what is put into the scene), including staging, lighting, camera work, costume, and set design.

Mixing. The process of blending separate sound tracks (dialogue, sound effects, music, voice over narration) into a single channel, or **composite master**, which is then synchronized with the edited print of the film.

Monomyth. In *The Hero with a Thousand Faces*, Joseph Campbell compared the culture heroes in myths from around the world. He found common elements in their stories that form the basis of a foundational narrative, the journey of the hero, which he calls the monomyth.

Montage. (1) A term for the dynamic editing of film, a concept developed by the Soviet director Sergei Eisenstein. In contrast to Hollywood's practice of continuity editing, Eisenstein's jagged editing technique is sometimes called **dialectical montage** (emphasizing conflict), **intellectual montage** (emphasizing ideas), or simply **Soviet montage**. (2) An editing technique that combines related shots in quick succession, usually to show the passage of time or to illustrate an idea, such as the process of falling in love.

Multiculturalism. A view of human diversity that advocates appreciation of and respect for differences in culture, religion, or sexual identity. Moving beyond mere tolerance, multiculturalism involves an active commitment to previously marginalized people, changing the way they are represented in the media, and empowering them through various other means.

Negative cost. All expenses incurred to produce the first negative of a film, from pre-production to post-production.

Negative. When undeveloped celluloid film is exposed to light, the portions of the chemical coating that receive the most light turn darkest, forming a negative image of the visual event. This makes it possible to reproduce the image, for when light is directed through the negative onto another piece of film, a **positive print** is the result.

Neorealism. An artistic movement originating in Italy after World War II, characterized by the use of nonprofessional actors, location shooting, gritty photography, and a focus on common people struggling with their daily lives.

Nickelodeons. Beginning in 1905, the earliest movie theatres in America charged customers a nickel a week for a program of vaudeville acts and silent movies, often with a live piano accompaniment.

Offshoring. The relocation of part or all of a film's production to another country. Although sometimes used synonymously with outsourcing, the latter term refers more specifically to the practice of contracting selected services to an outside organization.

Outsourcing. The process of contracting an existing business process which an organization previously performed internally to an independent organization, where the process is purchased as a service.

Optical effects. The name for fades, dissolves, superimposition, and other visual tricks, commonly produced by the photographic lab after the film is shot.

Orientalism. Originally used by art historians to describe the imitation of East Asian or Middle Eastern art forms by Western artists, the term acquired negative force with Edward Said, who used it to criticize false Western assumptions about the Middle East.

Pan and scan. A method of adapting widescreen movies to the boxy dimensions of a television screen by masking parts of the original image.

Panning shot (or **pan**). A length of film taken by a camera while it pivots horizontally left or right.

Parallel montage (Cross cutting). Two simultaneous actions are shown in alternating shots, the camera shifting from one to the other.

Pastiche. A form of imitation by which a film or other work of art incorporates bits and pieces of earlier works, often for comic effect.

Patriarchy. A social structure in which men are the primary authority figures, implying privilege as well as power.

Poetic realism. An artistic movement popular in France during the 1930s that derives from literary naturalism and blends lyrical photography with realistic characters.

Point-of-view editing. A form of film editing designed to engage us in the world of the characters by emphasizing their perspective. A **point-of-view (POV) shot** shows what the character sees.

Postcolonialism (or **Postcolonial theory**).   Examines the consequences of colonial history on attitudes, identity, and power. **Postcolonial studies** may explore how colonized cultures have been subjugated or have resisted domination, and how certain views held by colonizing nations have persisted or taken new forms.

Postmodernism.   A trend of self-conscious borrowing that began to influence filmmaking in the latter part of the twentieth century. Postmodern thinking is skeptical of modern science, abandoning the notion of absolute truth in favor of a pluralistic view: what we call reality is largely a cultural construction, a matter of diverse interpretations of experience. Postmodern films tend to subvert the unifying master narratives of modernism (comprehensive stories, or explanations of events that transcend history and culture) by mixing styles and genres, incorporating elements from other films (through **intertextual** references or makeshift **pastiche**), and calling attention to their own artificiality.

Post-production.   A stage of filmmaking that begins with filmed footage and ends with a completed movie. It includes the process of editing, adding sound, and applying certain special effects like **computer-generated imagery (CGI)**.

Pre-production.   A stage of filmmaking that precedes the actual shooting. In pre-production, the approved concept for a movie may be developed into a full screenplay and steps are taken to prepare for the shoot, such as scouting locations, casting actors, and selecting a crew.

Producer.   The person who bears the ultimate responsibility for the final film.

Production.   (1) The process of making a movie that precedes distribution and exhibition. (2) A stage of the production process between pre-production and post-production. It is during this production phase that the actual shooting takes place: the set is lighted, the actors perform their roles, and the camera rolls.

Production Code.   The Motion Picture Production Code listed what was or was not permitted in Hollywood films. Created in 1930 with the approval of the Hays Office, the Code was a way for the industry to avoid outside censorship by regulating itself.

Production mixer.   Decides how to set up the sound equipment for the best sound.

Psychoanalytic spectatorship theory.   Based on the works of Sigmund Freud and Jacques Lacan, this view of film seeks to connect the spectator's film experience with key moments in the development of the human psyche, identifying the source of visual pleasure with terms like **scopophilia** (the pleasure of looking), **narcissism** (a form of self-love or unhealthy self-absorption), and **voyeurism** (an erotic interest in spying on people at intimate moments).

Reaction shot.   Shows a character's response to something important.

Rear projection.   A special effect created when the action is filmed in front of a screen while another action is projected on the screen from behind.

Reception theory.   A form of film study concerned with the roles played by viewers in determining what a movie means.

Release print.   The final version of a film, produced from the **negative** and approved for distribution in theatres.

Reverse angle shot. A shot that reverses the point of view, created when the camera turns 180 degrees in the opposite direction. The **shot/reverse angle shot sequence** is a standard method for shooting dialogue between two individuals, alternating between the perspectives of each speaker.

Runaway productions. Movies that are produced overseas, relying on foreign labor and facilities.

Rushes (Dailies). The film from a day's shooting, usually printed overnight and viewed the next day by the director and the editor.

Samurai. The military nobility of feudal Japan, similar to European knights in armor, were skilled swordsmen and archers who followed a strict **Bushido code.**

Scene. A segment of film usually composed of several shots of the same general action, time, and location.

Scoring session. A rehearsal of the studio orchestra during which it plays music specially composed or arranged for a film. The recorded music is then added to the film's sound track.

Screenplay. A full version of the film narrative that fleshes out the action, dialogue, and perhaps some directions for the camera. Although sometimes used synonymously with **scenario** or **script**, a scenario generally is more of an outline.

Screwball comedy. A variation of romantic comedy originating in the 1930s and featuring the zany antics of the male and female leads, who typically begin at odds and end up happily married.

Scrim. A translucent shade placed between the subject and a light source to soften the illumination.

Script supervisor. Keeps track of the script, noting which shots are filmed, ever on the lookout for variant readings and visual discontinuities, like a change in lighting or the length of a lit cigarette. On some sets, these latter discrepancies are sometimes the responsibility of a **continuity person.**

Segue. A gradual transition between sounds, the auditory equivalent of a **dissolve.**

Semiotics. The study of signs, symbols, and how they work in language or another sign system, like body movement, cinema, or even clothing.

Sequence. A segment of film often composed of scenes from different times and locations but unified by a common idea or thematic concern.

Setup. The position of the camera (angle, location) before shooting begins.

Shooting schedule. Lists the dates, locations, and personnel for each shot in the script.

Shooting script. A version of the screenplay that provides a shot-by-shot blueprint of the film. Shots are usually numbered for reference on the set and during editing.

Shot. A single length of film produced by a continuous running of the camera.

Shutter. A mechanical device, usually a revolving plate, between the lens and the film to stop the light just long enough so that the image frozen on a single frame of film can be moved out of position and a new frame moved in its place. Without a shutter, a movie camera would produce an undifferentiated blur on the moving film and a projector would project a blurred image on the screen.

Sidelight. Adds solidity and depth to the subject by accentuating prominent features.

Slapstick. A form of comedy based on rowdy physical situations, like a Keystone Kops chase or a pie in the face.

Slow motion. When the camera is speeded up, or **overcranked**, the action appears slower during projection.

Sound cut. A sharp shift from one sound to another.

Sound effects (SFX). Noises on the sound track that appear to emanate from things on the set, such as a roaring brook, the whistling wind, or gunfire. Some sound effects may be recorded live; others are taken from a pre-recorded sound library or created during post-production by a **Foley artist**, who simulates the sound creatively.

Sound track. A magnetic or optical stripe of recorded sound commonly placed alongside the picture on a strip of film.

Special effects (SPFX). Tricks used to replicate imagined events, like simulated explosions and flying superheroes.

Spectatorship. How do spectators interpret what they see and hear? What cultural and private filters color their perceptions? What makes them accept a film's illusions as reality or resist its ideological messages? Such questions inform the study of spectatorship. The term **spectator** may refer to viewers as "typical" individuals while the term **audience** refers to actual viewers whose behaviors and attitudes may be studied in historical contexts.

Spotlight. A light that projects a concentrated beam on the subject.

Star system. A method of exploiting the popularity of individual actors to ensure success at the box office. The image of each star (the star's **persona**) is carefully crafted and promoted by a studio, an agent, or the individual performer.

Steadicam. A stabilization device that gives flexibility to the camera operator by combining the fluidity of a dolly with the freedom of handheld filming. A counterbalance weight helps to keep the camera level during any movement.

Stop-motion photography. A special effect created by interrupting the shooting at intervals. As a result, objects seem to move at a rapid rate. If the scene is rearranged during intervals, objects can appear to move of their own volition.

Structuralism. An interpretive method of film study that examines relationships between elements of a film. A structuralist reading emphasizes the formal codes and conventions (the "languages of film") by which viewers ascribe meanings to a film.

Studio system. An arrangement for controlling all phases of film production, distribution, and exhibition that flourished in the 1930s and 1940s. A typical film studio contained everything it needed to produce a film from start to finish, organized hierarchically and run like an assembly plant.

Subsidiary rights. Marketing options beyond a film's theatrical release in the United States. These rights may include foreign sales, cable and network television, video and DVD, books, television series, clothing, and toys.

Subtitles. Textual versions of film dialogue that appear at the bottom of the screen. These are usually translations of words spoken in a foreign language. Subtitles are distinct from **intertitles**, which refer to printed text (also known as **title cards**) spliced into silent movies to represent dialogue, narration, or commentary.

Superimposition. A double exposure in which one image appears over another.

Surrealism. An artistic movement beginning in the 1920s that sought to liberate imagination from the control of reason. Surrealist filmmakers like Luis Buñuel and Salvador Dalí sought to reproduce the unconscious, associative patterns of dreams on screen.

Synopsis. A brief description of a movie's plot.

Take. (1) An unedited shot. (2) An attempt to film a shot with a movie camera. Each repetition of the same shot is a new take.

Technicolor. A process in which the primary colors of an image are recorded on separate strips of film and recombined in the lab.

Technique acting. A traditional method of stage and screen performance. Technique actors try to convey character by imitating visible behavior, in contrast to **method actors**, who make personal connections to their roles. For traditional actors like Laurence Olivier, each gesture is a technique, a sign deliberately adopted to represent a given mood.

Telephoto lens. Also called a **long-focus lens** because it is relatively longer than a normal lens, a telephoto lens takes in a narrow field of view and a shallower depth of field, typically resulting in close-up views that slow down motion toward the camera.

Third cinema. A Latin American film movement originating in the 1960s opposed to Hollywood, colonialism, and the capitalist system. Coined in the 1960s by Argentine directors Fernando Solanas and Octavio Getino, the term inspired other film movements in emerging ("Third World") countries, from Iran to sub-Saharan Black Africa.

Three-dimensional (3-D) photography. Uses two lenses spaced 2.5 inches apart to record a scene as if it were being viewed by a pair of human eyes.

Tilt shot. A shot taken by a camera while it pivots up or down along a vertical axis.

Todd-AO. A wide-film process introduced in 1955 to give viewers a greater sense of presence through a combination of special cameras, 70mm film, and special sound technology.

Tracking shot (Dolly shot). A shot in which the camera moves horizontally through space with, towards, or away from the subject.

Transition. A term for the visual effects that join two shots, such as **fades** (an image disappears into black or emerges from the darkness), **wipes** (one image appears to push another off the screen), or **dissolves** (one image blends into another).

Transnational cinema.   Refers to a tendency of film production and distribution to cross national boundaries. As more films are classified as transnational, more attention among film scholars has shifted from national cinemas to topics like co-productions, postcolonialism, and globalization.

Treatment.   A more complete version of the story than a synopsis. A treatment may contain scenes, character development, and some dialogue, much like a short story, but without detailed descriptions of the set or camera setups.

Undercranking.   When the camera is slowed down, or undercranked, during shooting, motion appears faster during projection.

VCR (Video cassette recorder).   An electronic device for recording and playing back video images and sound on a videocassette. The sound and images on a videocassette are stored in analog form on magnetic tape.

Vertical integration.   A business practice enabling film studios to control the three sectors of production, distribution, and exhibition.

VHS (Video home system).   The standard video system for home use, which plays half-inch videocassettes on a VCR.

Voice-over (V-O).   Words on a sound track that are not spoken aloud or in sync with the picture, such as the silent thoughts of a character or the narration in a documentary film.

Wide-angle lens.   Also called a **short-focus lens**, because it's shorter than a normal lens, a wide-angle lens takes in a larger field of view so that objects seem smaller and farther away. Since this lens also produces a greater depth of field, more objects along the line of sight appear within focus than with a normal or a telephoto lens.

Widescreen.   A movie image with more width than the Academy ratio was introduced in the early 1950s, standardized in Europe as 1.66:1 and in the United States as 1.85:1.

Wipe.   A visual effect in which one image seems to wipe another off the screen.

Wuxia.   A Chinese term, sometimes translated as "martial hero," designating a popular genre in which male or female warriors fight with swords, magic, and acrobatic skill for the greater good.

Zoom lens.   A lens that combines the features of normal, long, and wide-angle lenses, enabling the filmmaker to change the focal length during shooting. A **zoom shot** may move smoothly from a close-up to a long shot or vice versa. Twisting the lens toward the wide angle position **zooms out**; twisting toward the telephoto position **zooms in**.

INDEX

Note: Page numbers in italics refer to illustrations.

World Cinema through Global Genres, First Edition. William V. Costanzo.
© 2014 John Wiley & Sons, Inc. Published 2014 by John Wiley & Sons, Inc.

Anderson, J.L. 76n(7)
Andes Mountains 336, 341, 348, 353, 354, 387, 388
Andrade, Joaquim Pedro de 347
Andrew, Dudley 300, 333n(5), 383, 384nn(1, 4)
Andrews, Naveen 177
Angelopoulos, Theo 321, *322*, 331, 365
Anglo-America *see* Bermuda; Canada; United States
animation 4, 263, 319, 343, 351, 392
   altered craft of 11
   relatively crude 264
   unique form of 259
Animatrix (2003) 265
anime 259, 263–6, 392
Annaprasan 169
Anthroposophical Society 277
Antín, Manuel 349
anti-trust legislation 3, 4
Antônio das Mortes (1969) 347
Aparajito (1956) 164
Apennine Mountains 376
Appadurai, Arjun 26, 41n(12)
Appiah, Kwame Anthony 28, 41nn(15–16)
Apu trilogy (1950s) 164
Apur Sansar (1959) 164
Arab films 152
Araki, Gregg 317
Arau, Alfonso 356
Arbeláez, Ramiro 366n(12)
archetypes 40, 105n, 215, 272, 392
   pre-existing 207
Argentina 344, 348
   co-production 390
   dance of choice in 343
   Dirty War (1976–83) *340*, 349, *350*
   drive for ideologically committed political cinema 352
   DVD distributors 4
   films of liberation 347
   independent-minded directors 356
   road movies *294*, 329, 333, 332, *341*, 357, 358, 361, 365
   Third Cinema 18
   see also Alfonsín; Borges; Buenos Aires; Getino; INCAA; Mar del Plata; Patagonia; Santaolalla; Solanas; tangos
Argento, Dario 229, 249, 274, *276*, 277–81, 289
Argento, Salvatore 278
Aristotle 168
Arizona 306, 370
Arnaz, Desi 298, 307
Arrival of a Train at La Ciotat Station, The (1896) 15, 303, *304*

art cinema 28, 38, 241, 273
Art Deco 279
Arya, Sameer *187*, 189
Asani Sanket (1973) 164
Ashanti (Shequoiya Douglas) 177, 178
Ashoka 165
Asia 4, 6, 246, 316
   establishing colonies in 27
   genre films 38
   Soviet influence in 23
   see also Central Asia; East Asia; South Asia; Southeast Asia
Asian fiscal crisis 68
Asoka (2001) 177
aspect ratio 17, 393, 394, 398
Asrani *113*, 115
Assault on Precinct 13 (1976) 273
assembly cut 393, 395
   rough 8
assistant directors 7, 259, 382, 393
Astro Boy (1963–6) 259, 264
Atlântida Studio 346
Attack of the Crab Monsters (1957) 223
audiences
   adolescent 239
   aggressive images to shock 210
   appeals to 169, 220, 239, 256, 381, 394
   art house 89
   attention focused on 225
   black 393
   bolder steps to shock 218
   brash young talents and the new 309
   broader outlines of character and story recognizable to 36
   change in setting brings the story closer to 184
   common denominator that speaks to all 90
   courting 89
   cult 68
   diaspora 176
   distinction between spectators and 19, 403
   encouraged to make connections to current events 229
   expectations of 273, 384(Q1)
   fact-based ethnographic research about 20
   female 154
   foreign 33, 34, 87
   general 256, 344
   genre that aims to horrify 37
   global *151*, 361
   impact of subgenre on 57
   international *178*, 195(Q4)
   lower-class 163

   mainstream 90, 176
   mass 56, 160, 259
   meanings unfamiliar to 117(Q1)
   middle-class 20, 163, 349
   multicultural 194
   national 227
   native 170; *see also* local audiences
   niche 185, 186(Q5), 316
   one culture appropriates another and adapts for 50
   popular 28, 64, 228, 317
   questions about 129
   rapport with 132
   reactions of 137, 209
   regional 225, 352
   response of 372, 383
   Spanish-speaking, deliberately targeting 343
   struggling between tradition and modernity 173
   sympathetic characters for 214, 237
   tastes of, response to 68
   theme with special resonance for 116
   youthful/young 234, 241, *245*
   see also local audiences; Western audiences
Audition (1999) 234, 243, 250, 260
Auschwitz 323
Austen, Jane 176, 177, *178*
Australia 2, 4, 65
   horror films *204*, 206, 234, 240, 246, 250
   road movies *294*, 307, 317, *318*, 333
   wedding films 127, 139–40, 155, 189
Austrians 49, 209
auteurs 82, 103, 164, 312, 321, 346, 380, 393
   artistic aspirations of 38
   independent-minded 3, 28
   industrial 355
   influential 300
Automobile Accident, The (1901) 303
avant-garde film 18, 211, 218, 346, 393
Avenging Conscience, The (1914) 218
Awaara (1951) 115, *161*, 163, 166, 167, 191
Aztecs 336

B-movie aesthetics 273
Baaz, Maria Eriksson 334n(18)
Babel (2006) 355
Bachchan, Amitabh *113*, 114, 165, 167, 169, 175
Bachmann, Gideon 375, 377
Back to the Future (1985) 233, 313, 316, 331
Bad Day at Black Rock (1955) 103
Badham, John 213, 249
Badlands (1973) 308, 310, *311*, 312, 319, 330
Bagdad Café (1987) 314, 316, 331

emotional development 122
Enevold, Jessica 373n(2)
England 4, 205, 213, 225, 303, 369
  Anglo-Saxon 39
  class conflict 177
  eighteenth-century 88
  fourteenth-century 301
  nuptial rites 127
English language connections 336
Enter the Dragon (1973) 57, 64–5, 73, 77n(15), 122–3
Epstein, Jean 18
Eraserhead (1977) 231
Erice, Victor 241, 248, 283
Escher, M.C. 279
essentialism 19, 396
establishing shots 16, 396
  broad 69
ethnography 19, 150, 198, 396
  fact-based research about audiences 20
ethnoscapes 26
Eurocentric bias 26
Euro-horror 227
Europe 6, 342, 354
  genre films 38
European Union *22*
exhibition 2, 37, 63, 129, 266, 304, 351, 396, 397, 403, 405
  first city to host new films from other countries 5
  local 343, 349
  process of making a movie that precedes 401
  special efforts to appeal to women 20
  studios became involved in 3
  tent theatres and playhouses 160–3
  transnational 355
  turning TVs into hubs for movies 11
Exorcist, The (1973) 208, 228, 232, 248
exoticism 191n(4), 396
expressionism 18, 217–18, 229, 280(Q3)
  realism abandoned for 164
  see also German Expressionism
Eye, The (2002) 243
eye-level shots 13, 396
eyeline matches 16, 396
Eyes Without a Face (1960) *204*, 218, 226, *227*, 242, 248
Eyre, Chris 318, 332

400 Blows, The (1959) 380
fade effects 8, 371, 396, 400, 404
  superimposing 395
Fairbanks, Douglas 169, 173
Faithfull, Marianne 370
Falkland Islands *335*, 349

Fall of the House of Usher, The (1928) 18, 248
Famous Monsters of Filmland (magazine) 229
Fan Xuepeng 57
Fantastic Factory, The (production unit) 241
Farmer, Gary 318
Farnsworth, Richard 320
Farrakhan, Louis 319
Fate of Lee Khan, The (1973) 59, 76
Father Knows Best (TV show) 316
Father of the Bride (1950/1991) *126*, 127, 128, 131, *132*, 133, 146, 155
Faust: Love of the Damned (2001) 241
Fearless Vampire Killers, The (1967) 213
Federal Aid Highway Act (US 1925) 303
Félix, María 344
Fellini, Federico 299, 310, 330, *374*, *375–8*
Female Knight-Errant, The (1925) 57
Female Pirate, The (1929) 57
feminism 98(Q9), 129, 144, 229, 233, 266, 272, 278, 372
  misrepresented 369
  theorists 19, 397
  third-wave 20
  turning point in filmmaking 316
  see also postfeminism
femmes fatales 211, 371
Ferguson, Leon 281n(3)
Fernández, Emilio 344, *345*
Ferreyra, José 349
Fertile Memory (1980) 200
FESPACO (Pan-African Film Festival) 24
Fiddler on the Roof (1971) *151*, 152, *155*
Fifth Generation (China) 81, *85*, 86, 397
fight scenes 57, 58, 69, 95, 238, 363
  rock 'n' roll music added to 226
Figueroa, Gabriel 344
Fiji 175
film festivals 25, 244
  international *164*
  see also Cannes; FESPACO; Mar del Plata; Tours
film noir *221*, 222, 296, 305, *309*, 395, 397
  distinctive qualities of 306
  femmes fatales 371
  playing with conventions of 383
film text 1, 29–30, 37, 129
final scenes 201(Q7), 289
  narrative subplots resolved in 190
fine cut 8, 397
Finkiel, Emmanuel 323
Finland *294*, 333
  see also Kaurismäki
Fireworks (1997) 260
First Artists 312
First Blood (1982) 57

Fischer, Terence 225
Fist, Peter 366n(15)
Fistful of Dollars, A (1964) 45, 49, 74, 107
Fists of Fury (1972) 64, 66, 76–7n(15), 120
Five Vengeful Girls (1928) 57
flashbacks 12, 30, 60, 114, 132, 182, 184, 221, 327
  black and white 290, 371–2, 389
  childhood 320
  events typically presented in 222
  journey intercut with 318
Fleming, Victor 329
Fletcher, Anne 156
Florida 297, 315, 350
focal length 12, 405
  long/short 397
Focillon, Henri 210, 211, 213
FOCINE (Colombian state-funded company) 352, 355
Foley editing 8, 397
Fonda, Henry 115
Fonda, Jane 137
Fonda, Peter 295, *296*, 307, 308
For a Few Dollars More (1965) 49
Forbidden Planet (1956) 271
Ford, John 51, 54, 74, 107, 165, 261, 306, 314, 329
foreign films 33–6, 80
  Brazilian response to barrage of 346
Forest Gump (1994) 83
formal analysis 30
Foshan 70
Foster, Jody 239
Four Flies on Grey Velvet (1971) 278
Four Weddings and a Funeral (1994) *126*, 127, 135, 149–50, 155
Fowkes, Ben 251n(11)
Fowler, Gene 248
Fox, James 4
Fox, Vivica A. 54
Fox Talbot, William Henry 10
frames 13, 30, 51, 96, 102, 132, *268*, 274, 278, 349, 380, 388, 389, 395, 398, 399
  darkening or lightening 396
  expanding 298
  meticulously composed 260
  moved out of position 402–3
  see also freeze frames
France 3, 33, 51, 189, 227, 336, *338*, 344, 351, 390
  box office revenue for US films 5
  budget for an art film 4
  Colonial Period 341
  complex flows of Chinese talent, funding, imagery and themes 87
  co-productions 4, 89
  horror films *204*, 211, 218, 226, 234, 241, 242, 248, 250, 277

Gowariker, Ashutosh *162*
Goya, Francisco 242, 284
Gramsci, Antonio 28
Granado, Alberto 387, 388, 389, 390(Q1)
Grand Canyon 370
Grand Guignol 206, 229, 238, 242, 247
 see also Théâtre du Grand Guignol
Grand Illusion (1937)
Grant, Barry Keith 251n(5), 275n(1)
Grant, Hugh 135
Grapes of Wrath (1940) 302, 304, 329
Grave of the Fireflies (1988) 259
Grease (1978) 178
Great Depression (1930s) 220, 298, 304, 308,
 309, 348, 376
Great Dictator, The (1940) 115
Great Escape, The (1963) 103
Great Kanto earthquake (Japan 1923) *257*
Great Train Robbery, The (1903) 15, 47, 74
Great Woman, The (1929) 57
Greek Orthodox Church 183
 see also My Big Fat Greek Wedding
Green Hornet, The (ABC TV show) 119
Grey Automobile, The (1919) 342
Griffith, D.W. 15–16, 218
Grimes, Ronald 150–1, 157n(10)
grips 7, 398
Grodin, Charles 297
Guangzhou *79, 89*
Guantanamera (1995) *294*, 332, 336, 352,
 361–2, 365
Guard, Charles *245*
Guatemala 183, *335*, 341, 354, 387
Guattari, Félix 321
Guernica 284
Guerra, Ciro 356, 362, 363, *364*, 366n(18)
Gueuns, Jean-Pierre 41n(8)
Guevara, Alfredo 351
Guevara de la Serna, Ernesto (Che) *339*, 347,
 353, *386*, 387–91
Guinea 325
Gumball Rally (1976) 312
Gun Crazy (1950) 308, 319, 371
Gunfight at the O.K. Corral (1957) 103, 104
Guns of the Magnificent Seven (1969) 104
Gutiérrez Alea, Tomás 24, 332, *339*, 351,
 352, 361
Guyana 175, *335*
Guzmán, Patricio *340*, 354

HAHK (Hum Aapke Hain Koun...! 1994) *126*,
 151, 153, 155, *162*, 171–2, *173*, 174–5,
 176, 179, 188
Haiti 23, 240, *335*, *338*, 341

Hall, Stuart 19
Halloween (1978) *204*, 231–2, 233, 234, 249,
 270, 271–5, 279, 289
Hammer Studios 26, 213, 214, 225, 227, 228,
 229, 231, 237
Han Dynasty 68
hand-held cameras 188, 190, 309, 319, 358,
 383, 394
 shaky, tracking shot 232
 shooting on location with 324
hand-held devices 28, 29
Handsome Serge, The (1958) 380
Haneke, Michael 242
Hanks, Tom *181*, 184
Hara Kiri: Death of a Samurai (2011) 76
Harakiri (1962) *44*, 53, 74
Haraway, Donna 266, 268n(3)
Hard-Boiled (1992) 243
Hardwicke, Catherine *212*, 250
Hare Rama Hare Krishna (1971) 165
Hark, Ina Rae 333n(1, 3, 10)
Harper, Jessica *276*, 277
Harrelson, Woody 319
Harry Potter movies 11, 25, 39, 354
Hart, William S. 50
Harvard 188
Hathaway, Anne 136, 139
Havana 351, 389
Hawks, Howard 273
Hawn, Goldie 310
HBO (Home Box Office) 184, 185, 186n(1), 353
HDTV (high-definition television) 398
Hearn, Lafcadio 262
Heaton, Louis 105n(2)
Heigl, Katherine 147–9
Hell Without Limits (1977) 345
Hellboy franchise 285
Hellman, Monte 314, 330
Henderson, Martin 177, 290
Hendrix, Jimi 298
Hepworth, Cecil 303
Hermida, Tania 363
Hermosillo, Jaime Humberto 345
Hero (2002) 33, 59–61, *62*, 86–7, 328
Hidden (2005) 242
Hidden Fortress, The (1958) 107
high-angle shots 13, *14*, 121, 398
 extreme 279
high-key lighting 14, 309, 398
High Noon (1952) *44*, 48, 58, 74
High Tension (2003) 234, 242–3
Higuchinsky 291
Hill, Lee 295
hillbilly horror 208, 209, 230

cannibalism a popular motif in 238
Hills Have Eyes, The (1977) 210, 230, 231, 235,
 238, 249
Himalayas 327
Hinds, Anthony 225
Hinds, William 225
Hindustani(s) 160, 175
Hiroki, Ryuichi 328
Hiroshima 216, 223, 224, *257*, 265, 289
Hispanics 65, 177, 343
historical development 255
Hitchcock, Alfred 218, 226, 228, 230, 231,
 240, 248, 273, 329, 330
Hite, Shere 316
Hitler, Adolf 115, 280
Ho, Leonard 67
Ho Chi Minh 347
Hoffman, Dustin 297, 313
Hogan, P.J. *138*, 139, 155
Holi festival *169*
Holland 351
Hollywood 23, 26, 37, 66, 72, 89, 93, 97, 119,
 122, 139, 160, 166, 182, 184, 186, 188,
 211, 285, 319, 359, 369, 381, 384n(3)
 antithesis of 323
 artists who emigrated to (1930s/1940s)
 218–19
 assembly-line methods 303
 big studios as parts of conglomerates 5–6
 Bollywood and 177
 borrowings from 309, 342
 challenges of television 259
 chase scenes and special effects 246
 cinema free of influence of 244
 continuity editing 16, 357, 394, 399
 co-production with Hong Kong 64, 67
 cost of average feature 4
 created 2
 credible characters 357
 critics of 28
 cutting 69
 decline of big studios 273
 easier and cheaper to import movies
 from 343
 emphasis on stars and genres 3
 enormous budgets 5
 exotic setting for productions 351
 film movement opposed to 404
 financial resources 346
 German cinema replaced by 310
 historical dominance of 206
 Indians' marked preference for 170
 lost audience 229
 mainstream running out of steam 380

imperialism 27, 72, 81, 235, 238
    cultural 28, 50
impressionism 18, 280(Q3), 398
In Blood: The Last Vampire (2000) 266
In the Realm of the Senses (1976) 259
Inagaki, Hiroshi 52, *53*, 74
INCAA (Argentinian Instituto Nacional de
    Cine y Artes Audiovisuales) 349, 355
Incas 336, 357, 388, 389
Incite Mill, The (2010) 290
India 3, 168–80, *294*, 326, *330*, 333, 377
    bustling movie halls 20
    classical cinema 160–5
    history, politics, and film 165–7
    horror films 216, 235, *236*, 237, 238, 240, 249
    pilgrimage from China to 302
    wedding films 39
    see also Bengal; Bollywood; Calcutta;
        Delhi; East India Company; Gandhi;
        Hyderabad; IPTA; Kapoor; Kashmir;
        Kochi; Madras; Mumbai; Nehru;
        Punjab
India Cabaret (1985) 188
Indian Communist party 166
Indiana Jones (1981/1984/1989) 233
indigenous languages 362
Indonesia 68, 355
    see also Bali
Infernal Affairs (2002) 243
Innocents, The (1961) 228, 232, 248
INSAS (Belgian Institut National Supérieur
    des Arts du Spectacle) 200
inserts 117(Q5), 169, 262
    see also cut-ins; cutaways
Inside Track 177
International Brigade 283
international cinema 25
International Festival of New Latin
    American Cinema 351
International Monetary Fund 342
Internationale, The (left-wing anthem) 238
Internet 20, 176, 243, 266, 267
intertextuality 37, 128, 247, 398, 401
    rich connections 89
    self-conscious 191
intertitles 33, 404
Intervista (1987) 377
Intifada 200
Invasion of the Body Snatchers (1956) *204*,
    223, 248
Iowa 320, 381
IPTA (Indian People's Theatre Association) 166
Iran 3, 5, 18, 325, 326, 377, 404
    Islamic revolution (1979) 25
Ireland 262

iris shots 342, 398
Iron Curtain 20–3
Irreversible (2002) 242
Islam 325
    fundamentalism 25
    poetry/imagery 168
Israel *126*, 142–3, 152, 154–6, 198, 199, 200, 301
    see also Palestine
Istanbul 326
It Came from Beneath the Sea (1955) 223
It Happened One Night (1939) 146, *294*, 297–8,
    304, *305*, 329
Italian for Beginners (2000) 324
Italian Neorealism 18, 27, 299, 323, 347, 375,
    380, 384(Q6), 400
Italian Resistance 377
Italy 3, 4, 28, 74, 122, 189
    horror films *204*, 206, 213, 227, 229,
        235–6, 241, 249, 274, 277–80
    road movies *294*, 317, 322–3, 342,
        377, 383
    wedding films 127, 141, 150, 156
    see also Amelio; Bologna; Calabria; De
        Sica; Fellini; Germi; Leone; Milan;
        Rimini; Rome; Rossellini; Sicily;
        Tuscany; Venice; Visconti
Itami, Juzo *258*, 260
Itami, Mansaku 52, 73
It's a Mad, Mad, Mad, Mad World (1963) 312, 330
It's Alive (1974) 231
Ivens, Joris 351

Jaa, Tony 123(Q4–Q5)
Jackson, Peter 239
Jacobean dramas 277
Jain, P.C. 179n(7)
Jakarta 355
Jambrina, P.P. 352
James, Henry 228
Jameson, Fredric 208
Japan 2, 3, 51, 62, 240, 328, 332, 377
    Allied Occupation (1945–1952)
        52, 107
    budget for an art film 4
    co-productions 89
    feudal 101, 103, 224
    horror films 28, 39, 179, *204*, 205, 206,
        216, 223, *224*, 226, 229, 234, 241, 243,
        248–50, *254*, 255–69, 287, 288–92
    invasions by 24, *84*, 87, 119
    Kanto Plain 51
    karate experts 120, 122
    new waves 18, 233
    pact that made Cold War ally of US 53
    prosperity 230, 232

Sengoku (Warring States) period 108
signs of social stress 239
    see also anime; Kabuki; Kurosawa; *manga*;
        Meiji; *Noh*; samurai; Shinto;
        Sino-Japanese War; Sony; Toho;
        Tokugawa; Tokyo
Jarmusch, Jim 313–15, 331, 334n(14)
Jaws (1975) 231, 248
Jazz Singer, The (1927) 10
Jeet Kune Do 63, 64, 119
Jewish Americans 139
Jewison, Norman *151*, 155
jidai-geki 52
Jinnah, Mohammed Ali 165
Jodorowsky, Alejandro 345
Johannesburg 355
Johar, Karan 155, *162*, 175
Johnson, Randal 346, 347, 366nn(6–7)
Joshi, S.T. 251n(1)
Journey to the Sun (1999) 325–6
Journey to the West (attr. Wu Cheng'en)
    301, 302
Joy Luck Club, The (1993) 83
Ju Dou (1990) 60
Jukti Takko Aar Gappo (1974) 165
Juliá, Raúl 312
Julian, Rupert 247
Juliette of the Spirits (1965) 377
jump cuts 12, 298, 299, 301, 383, 398
    famous 382
    stylish 309
Jung, Carl Gustav 40, 62, 207–8, 215,
    251n(3), 272, 392–3
Ju-on: The Grudge (2002) *204*, 250, 255, 266,
    267, 291

Kaagaz Ke Phool (1959) 183
Kaboré, Gaston 32
Kabuki theatre 51, 52, 224, 256, 258, 259,
    260, 262, 263, 254, 288
    samurai women 54
Kahlo, Frida 337
Kaidan (2007) 290
Kairen, Xian 56
Kalatozov, Mikhail 351
Kama Sutra: A Tale of Love (1996) 188, 189,
    191(Q1)
Kaplan, Rose 384n(2)
Kapoor, Raj 115, *161*, 163, 165, 166, 167, 169,
    170, *171*, *187*, 191
Kapoor, Shammi 165
Karachi 116
Karloff, Boris 205, 219, 220, 229
Kashmir *159*, *161*, 166, 175
Kaur, Raminder 179n(9)

scenes (cont'd)
  conflict 112(Q5)
  cultural information underlying 36
  death 243
  dynamic rhythm between 15
  elaborate 277
  emotions of 12, 15, 60, 185(Q4)
  explicit 361
  famous 228, 309
  favorite 267
  fierce combat 64
  graphic 216, 226–7
  grotesque 363
  hallucinatory 327
  intimate 91
  key 128, 131
  lighting of 12, 14
  memorable 128, 190, 223
  motel 371
  mysterious 376
  nerve-ratcheting 300
  party 14, 178
  poignant 320, 371, 376
  pool 361
  predictable 210
  proposal 146, 149, 154
  psychological dimensions of 139
  rape 242
  rearranged during intervals 403
  recycled 102
  rescue 136
  revenge 115, 242
  schoolroom 286(Q4)
  shortened 382
  shots assembled into 7
  shower 228
  silent 371
  sophisticated transitions between 15
  spectacular 266
  stock 48
  strengthening the regional identity of 390
  transformation 235
  understanding of 33
  visceral 69
  wordless 211
  see also action scenes; battle scenes; fight
    scenes; final scenes; mise-en-scène; night
    scenes; opening scenes; wedding scenes
Schamus, James 89, 90, 97, 98nn(5, 7–8), 192
Schatz, Thomas 37–8, 47, 76n(1), 154,
  157n(1), 210, 251n(9), 310, 315
Scheider, Roy 4
Schepisi, Fred 4
Scherfig, Lone 324
Schickel, Richard 369

Schneider, Steven 251n(21)
Schreck, Max 211
Schroeder Rodriguez, Paul 366n(19)
scopophilia 19, 401
Scorsese, Martin 107, 225, 280
Scotland 4
Scott, Ridley 231, 249, 316, 331, 365, 368,
  369–73
Scream (1996) 239
screenplays 6, 184, 187, 308, 317, 369, 379, 402
  approved concept for movie may be
    developed into 401
  see also scripts
screenwriters 11, 63, 65, 97, 220, 273, 285, 375
  handbook widely used by 41
  see also scriptwriters
script development 6, 89
script supervisors 7, 402
scripts 4, 7, 87, 96, 113, 173, 189, 221, 278,
  402, 319–20, 360, 369
  adding gags to 375
  aficionados fond of quoting lines from
    104(Q6)
  allegorical 25
  altered after shooting 393
  bilingual 88, 90
  changed in deference 103
  collaborative 89, 108, 111, 273, 276, 282,
    374, 376
  comparing to original novel 94
  designed to evoke nostalgia 131
  guidebook for 41
  hybrid 90
  memorable lines in 105(Q6)
  shooting 6, 376, 402
scriptwriters 29, 107, 129, 162, 166, 177, 181,
  184, 189, 192, 193, 195(Q4), 270, 273,
  287, 368, 377, 386, 389
  structure for 37
Searchers, The (1956) 41, 48–9, 74, 302–3, 306
Seattle 119, 290
Seberg, Jean 381
Seeta and Geeta (1972) 116
Selig Polyscope Company 218
Selznick, David O. 103
Sembene, Ousmane 23, 24, 152, 155
semi-neorealism 314
Sen, Hiralal 163
Senegal 126, 274, 325, 331
  see also Dakar; Sembene; Xala
Sengupta, Shombit 179n(4)
Sense and Sensibility (1995) 88, 195
sequences 61, 65, 121, 135–7, 147, 291(Q7), 390
  carefully composed shot 115
  continuous 10, 15, 396

credit 173, 274, 283
dream 163, 169, 300
electronic images as computer files
  assembled into 395
fantasy 178
filmed according to the 180-degree rule 392
hallucinatory drug 308
lifted, repackaged and sold separately 153
montage 7–8, 298, 304
opening 274, 279, 283
reversed chronological 242
shot inserted into 398
shot/reverse-angle shot 16, 278, 402
surrealistic 300
Serial Experiments Lain (1998) 266
setups 7, 402, 405
Seven Samurai (1954) 45, 46, 47, 50, 52, 101,
  103, 106–12, 114, 214, 255, 256, 260
  idea of remaking 104
  Magnificent Seven and 105(Q7), 117(Q7), 255
Sex and the City (2008) 19, 126, 135, 146, 147,
  149, 154, 156, 184–5
Shah, Naseeruddin 189
Shahane, Renuka 171
Shakespeare, William 134, 188, 277
Shanghai 24, 56, 63, 64, 79, 82, 84, 88, 120
Shankman, Adam 130, 147, 156
Shaolin Soccer (2001) 68
Shatner, William 273
Shaw Brothers Studio 56, 58, 67, 68, 82, 120, 214
Sheen, Martin 310, 311
Shek, Dean 67
Shelley, Mary Wollstonecraft 216, 218,
  239, 249
Sheriff of Fractured Jaw, The (1958) 44,
  49, 74
Shimizu, Takashi 250, 258, 267, 268, 291
Shimura, Takashi 47, 106, 108, 109
Shindo, Kaneto 224, 248
Shining, The (1980) 210, 235, 249, 266
Shinkokugeki 51
Shinoda, Masahiro 259
Shinto 256, 262–3, 265
Shirmer Encyclopedia of Film 154
Shivers (1975) 231
Shochiku (production company) 259
Shohat, Ella 337, 366nn(1–2)
Shohei Imamura (1997) 260
Sholay (1975) 44, 50, 75, 113, 114–17, 162,
  165, 167
Shome, Tilotama 187, 189–90
shooting schedule 7, 402
Shootist, The (1976) 49, 75
shots
  assembled into scenes 7

carefully composed 115
dynamic point-of-view 298
inserted 398
zoom 405
see also aerial shots; crane shots;
establishing shots; eye-level shots; full
shots; high-angle shots; iris shots; long
shots; low-angle shots; medium shots;
panning shots; reaction shots;
reverse-angle shots; tilt shots; tracking
shots
Shower (1999) 153
Shree 420 (1955) 163, 166, 167, 170, 171
Shumway, David 157n(12)
shutters 398, 402–3
moveable 10
timed 10
Shyamalan, M. Night 239, 240, 250
Shyer, Charles 132, 146, 155
Sicily 141, 322, 323
Sideways (2001) 329
Siegel, Don 54, 75, 223, 248
Siegel, Kristi 373n(2)
Sierra Pelada 357
Sight and Sound (magazine) 380
Sikh extremists 166
Silence of the Lambs, The (1991) 239
silent films 15, 23, 57, 161, 211, 218
action intelligible without intertitle
cards 33
American comedians of 66
early deaths in 210
narrators for 82
shift to synchronized sound 342
useful skill for acting in 219
wuxia movies date back to early days
of 56
Silent Light (2007) 356
Silverstein, Shel 370
Singapore 63, 68, 87, 122, 175, 305
Singin' in the Rain (1952) 70
Sinha, Ajay 179n(9)
Sino-Japanese War
First (1894–5) 83
Second (1937–45) 80, 82, 84
Sioux language 48
Sippy, G.P. 113, 114, 116, 117(Q7)
Sippy, Ramesh 50, 75, 113, 114, 116, 162, 165
Sirk, Douglas 173
Sivan, Santosh 177
Sixth Sense, The (1999) 239–40, 250
Sjöström, Victor 300
Skal, David 219, 220, 251nn(17–18, 20)
Skirt Power (1997) 246
Sky Crawlers, The (2008) 266

slapstick 183, 403
slasher films 209, 226, 230, 231, 234, 247
American, prototype for 228
staples of 274
teenage 233, 239
Slotkin, Richard 103, 105n(1)
Slovak Republic 23
slow motion 18, 96, 115, 309, 319, 398, 403
Slumdog Millionaire (2008) 162, 170
Smarzowski, Wojciech 133, 141, 142,
150, 156
Smoke Signals (1998) 316, 318, 319, 332
Snake in the Eagle's Shadow (1978) 66, 89
Snow White and the Seven Dwarfs (1937)
264, 279
So Far From India (1983) 188
socialist realism 81, 85
Solanas, Fernando 24, 339, 349, 366n(8), 404
Solás, Humberto 24, 351
Sometimes Things Do Happen see KKHH
Son of Dracula (1943) 213
Son of Frankenstein (1939) 219
Sony Pictures 6, 26, 282, 286n(2)
Sophocles 188
Sorín, Carlos 357, 366n(14)
sound effects 15, 112(Q5), 123(Q7), 399, 403
breakthroughs in 68
exaggerated 69
replaced with synchronized substitutes
8, 397
soundtracks 8, 15, 112(Q5), 121, 123(Q1),
190, 191, 274(Q4), 289, 295, 403
advantages of preserving the original 33
blending 399
lending authenticity to 392
optical 10
recorded music added to 402
words spoken/not spoken aloud 395, 405
South Africa 126, 139, 156, 175, 294, 325, 333
see also Cape Town; Johannesburg
South America 336, 343
see also Argentina; Bolivia; Brazil; Chile;
Colombia; Ecuador; Guyana;
Paraguay; Peru; Uruguay
South Asia 22
diaspora from 175
Sholay a massive hit in 114
see also Afghanistan; Bangladesh; India;
Pakistan; Sri Lanka
South Dakota 311
South Korea 44, 48, 50, 68, 75, 79, 232, 290
chaebôl 244
horror films 204, 206, 233, 239, 241,
243–4, 245, 246, 250, 254
road movies 294, 327, 333

Southeast Asia 63, 65, 240
see also Indonesia; Malaysia; Myanmar;
Singapore; Thailand; Vietnam
Southern California 2
Soviet montage 16–18, 399
adapting 346
Soviet Union 21, 23, 141, 167
atomic weapons 223
collapse/demise of Communism 20, 232,
238, 320, 352
communist state modeled on 350
new moderating leadership 230
Spacek, Sissy 310, 311, 320
spaghetti Westerns 72, 74–5, 165, 278
most famous 49–50
Spain 27, 45, 49, 72, 358, 360, 361, 363
Colonial Period 338, 341, 350, 353, 389
co-production 241, 352
horror films 205–6, 213, 216, 227, 241–2,
248, 250, 251, 282, 283–6
Latin American nations achieve
independence from 338
resistance to Napoleon (1814) 284
see also Buñuel; Dalí; Franco; Goya;
Guernica
Spanish-American War (1898) 350
Spanish Civil War (1936–1939) 216, 241, 242,
283, 286(Q6), 338
Spanish conquistadores 336
Spanish language 33, 213, 241, 282, 283, 336,
344, 354, 355, 362, 386, 387
audiences deliberately targeted 343
special effects 8, 67, 246, 273, 276, 285, 397,
399, 401, 403
advances in 235
spectators 29, 51, 69, 127, 195, 210, 228, 353, 376
distinction between audiences and 19, 403
female 19, 234
identification with character 19, 168, 233
stand-in 137–8
spectatorship 403
important issues about reception and 182
inventing new forms of 267
see also psychoanalytic spectatorship
theory
Speed Racer (1967) 259, 264
Spielberg, Steven 107, 309, 248, 309, 310
Spiral (1998) 290, 291
Spirit of the Beehive, The (1973) 241, 248, 283
Spirited Away (2001) 266
Spooky Encounters (1980) 204, 212, 214, 249
spotlights 396, 403
Spring in a Small Town (1948) 81, 84
Squyres, Tim 95
Sri Lanka 159, 166, 175

Made in the USA
Monee, IL
11 February 2020

21650310R00247